IMAGINATIVE  LITERATURE

ALTON C. MORRIS
BIRON WALKER
PHILIP BRADSHAW
*University of Florida*

# IMAGINATIVE LITERATURE

## Fiction, Drama, Poetry

SECOND EDITION

**HARCOURT BRACE JOVANOVICH, INC.**

*New York / Chicago / San Francisco / Atlanta*

© 1973 by Harcourt Brace Jovanovich, Inc.

ISBN: 0-15-540727-9

Library of Congress Catalog Card Number: 72-91858

Printed in the United States of America

ACKNOWLEDGMENTS

Paintings by Ms. Petie Brigham, Roanoke, Virginia
Cover: "Round Is for Sad" (Collection of Laurie Feinberg, New York City)
Page 1: "Hello" (Collection of the artist)
Page 113: "Death Row" (Collection of Laurie Feinberg, New York City)
Page 251: "Memory" (Collection of the artist)

# Preface

The welcome accorded the first edition of *Imaginative Literature* has prompted the editors to offer a revised volume. In addition to those selections found most teachable in the first edition, the revision includes many new selections that we believe will be of special interest and concern to students today. The Camus play provides a drama with an existentialist theme; short stories by McPherson, Barthelme, Borges, Hughes, Babel, and Mishima represent modern American and international literature; new poems by Auden, Hopkins, Cullen, and Thomas, and new poets—Fandel, Still, Symons, Sissman, Updike, Holbrook, Brooks, Hughes, Clifton, Hayden, Stafford, Walker, Dickey, Cabral, Creeley, Sexton, and Plath—round out the poetry collection.

*Imaginative Literature* meets the need for an anthology that can be used easily and effectively in a great variety of freshman and sophomore English courses. It includes enough readings for a term or for an entire year, depending on the intensiveness of the course or the amount of time that can be devoted to the reading and criticism of literature. The arrangement of selections should give the instructor maximum freedom in adapting selections to his own program.

Our choice of selections throughout the book was determined by literary merit and by the interest and needs of students in introductory courses. But in our final choices from the great body of stories, plays, and poems available, we were guided by principles derived from long experience as teachers—principles we believe a majority of college instructors will endorse.

First, if the literary experience does not give pleasure, the reader will devote little of himself to it now and perhaps none of himself later. Most of these selections have been tried in the classroom and found appealing to students. Second, we believe selections should challenge the college student. Most students are eager to involve themselves in the feelings and ideas that constitute sensitive adult life, and many are aware of and desire to bridge the chasm between popular and informed taste. We have, therefore, included a wide variety of short stories, plays, and poems with the complex and mature ideas that students will need as they learn to face complex experience.

The students' previous reading may not have contained much contemporary literature. We believe that, since twentieth-century literature speaks directly to twentieth-century man, the introductory course should include many selections concerned with the ideas and with the use of the idiom that students encounter in contemporary books and periodicals. Though the traditional is generously represented here, this collection also includes much of what may be considered the best of modern works.

We have attempted to make the editorial materials—introductions, headnotes, glossary of poetic terms, and notes on the poets—helpful without making them intrusive. An Instructor's Manual, available to instructors who are using the anthology, provides a prefatory statement for each section, questions for most of the selections, and suggested projects for discussion or writing about comparisons and relationships between and among selections.

We wish to express our sincere appreciation to users of the first edition for their helpful suggestions for revision, and to our colleagues at the University of Florida for their encouragement and support.

Alton C. Morris
Biron Walker
Philip Bradshaw

# Contents

## THE SHORT STORY

# DRAMA

# POETRY

## The Poet as Storyteller

## The Poet as Singer

## The Poet as Wit and Humorist

## The Poet as Portrayer of Character

## The Poet as Elegist

## The Poet as Critic and Philosopher

# IMAGINATIVE LITERATURE

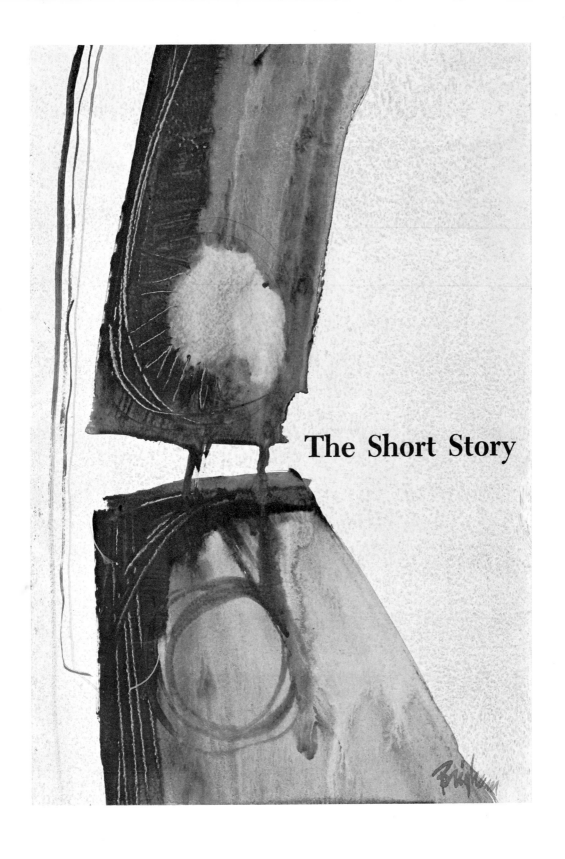

# The Short Story

T he art of story-telling is doubtless older than the records of civilization. Even the so-called modern short story, which was the latest of the major literary types to evolve, has an ancient lineage. Perhaps the oldest and most direct ancestor of the short story is the *anecdote*—an illustrative story, straight to the point. The ancient *parable* and *fable*, starkly brief narratives used to enforce some moral or spiritual truth, anticipate the severe brevity and unity of some short stories written today. With the Middle Ages came such types as the *exemplum*, a brief story used to support the text of a sermon, and the *ballad*, folk verse centered about a dramatic episode. During the sixteenth, seventeenth, and eighteenth centuries numerous forerunners of the short story appeared, such as the *sketch* and the *tale*—loosely constructed prose narratives, not so compact, intense, and comprehensive as the short story. Though these early narratives sometimes bear close resemblance to the modern short story, few, if any, of them exemplify its specialized artistry.

THE DEVELOPMENT OF THE SHORT STORY. The short story as it is known today began with Nathaniel Hawthorne and Edgar Allan Poe. The first typical story of each of these writers was published in 1835—Poe's "Berenice" and Hawthorne's "The Ambitious Guest." Though it now seems naïve, Poe's horror story demonstrated the author's mastery of a new type of narrative. His characters may be strange, the action of his plots far removed from ordinary experience, and his scenes fantastic, but everything in his stories is subordinate to narrative suspense and emotional effect.

Hawthorne's stories are as closely knit and unified as Poe's. But Hawthorne, unlike Poe, is primarily a moralist, and his constant focus on a moral problem—selfishness, pride, ambition—is usually the unifying factor of his story. It was this quality in his work that caused Poe, when reviewing the *Twice-Told Tales* in 1842, to observe:

A skillful literary artist has constructed a tale. If wise, he has not fashioned his thoughts to accommodate his incidents; but having conceived, with deliberate care, a certain unique or single effect to be wrought out, he then invents such incidents—he then combines such events as may best aid him in establishing this preconceived effect. If his very initial sentence tend not to the outbringing of this effect, then he has failed in his first step. In the whole composition there should be no word written, of which the tendency, direct or indirect, is not to the one pre-established design.

This celebrated passage is now generally considered the first significant definition of the type. And, along with an earlier stricture in the same essay—a story must not be so long that it "cannot be read at one sitting"—Poe's phrase "a certain unique or single effect" remains, with remarkable accuracy, the hallmark of the short story even today. By 1842, then, Hawthorne and Poe had isolated and defined the essential characteristics of the short story—brevity, unity, intensity. Forty years later an American critic, Brander Matthews, rephrased Poe's definition and supplied a label: the short story, called the "Short-story" (spelled with a hyphen) "to emphasize the distinction between the Short-story and the story which is merely short." In the meantime, two other American writers had made significant contributions to this literary form: Bret Harte, with his stories of early life in California, started a vogue of local-color stories, and Henry James produced the first of his long series of peculiarly modern psychological investigations of the human mind and heart.

Later developments of the short story remain for the most part within the limits set by these writers and critics. One must not, however, overlook the far-reaching effect on the American short story of two foreign writers, Guy de Maupassant and Anton Chekhov. Maupassant showed remarkable ingenuity in inventing means to gain dramatic compression and considerable boldness in relentlessly subordinating everything to a central effect. The structural neatness of countless "plotted" stories owes, ultimately, something to Maupassant's technique. Chekhov's practice of presenting a segment of life, objective and seemingly plotless yet highly suggestive and penetrating, has been another influence on the short story—perhaps second to none in recent years. Many writers agree with Chekhov that life poses questions but has no answers for them. The artist, they believe, is therefore obliged only to give a unified impression of some part of life. The major development in the short story in recent decades has, in fact, been the work of a group of writers who seek to create an "impression." The great masters who influenced this group are, in addition to Chekhov and James, Gustave Flaubert, Stephen Crane, James Joyce, and D. H. Lawrence. Some of the best known of the group are Seán O'Faoláin, Franz Kafka, Frank O'Connor, Albert Camus, Marcel Aymé, and Friedrich Dürrenmatt in Great Britain and Europe, and Ernest Hemingway, William Faulkner, John Steinbeck, and Eudora Welty in the United States.

The flowering of the short story was one of the principal literary events of the first half of the twentieth century, especially in the United States, where the rapid growth of periodicals and the tempo and pressure of American life provided special inducements. Scores of writers discovered dynamic materials in the isolated communities and forgotten backwoods, the humdrum towns, the congested cities; they presented the lost generation, the gangster, the neglected artist, the immigrant, the lingering pioneer; they wrote about Harlem, Chicago, Winesburg, the Prairies, the Appalachian Mountains, the Deep South.

THE ART OF THE SHORT STORY.   An awareness of the essential characteristics already pointed out—brevity, unity, intensity—increases the reader's understanding and enjoyment of a short story. In addition, some knowledge of the specialized techniques by which these qualities are produced makes communication between writer and reader more satisfying.

*Scene.*   In all forms of fiction, from the longest novel to the shortest short story, the basic elements are the same: scene, character, and action. The least important is scene, which in most instances merely "sets the stage" and, because of the premium on space in the short story, is handled as quickly as possible. Yet in some stories the scene is of basic importance—in "The Open Boat," for example, where the sea becomes the central force in the men's existence. And many of the most eminent authors (including Conrad and Faulkner) make scene contribute to the intensity of the story. Notice, for instance, how thoroughly Conrad treats scene in "The Lagoon" and how central that element is to the whole story.

*Character.*   The primary concern of most authors is character: "Take care of character," Galsworthy said; "action and dialogue will take care of themselves." Theme and meaning evolve from the interrelation between a character and the circumstances of his life. Yet there is in the short story neither time nor space to show development or disintegration; this is the province of the novel. Furthermore, the focus is usually on one character; other characters are portrayed only in complementary detail. In Faulkner's "Spotted Horses," for instance, the main character is Flem Snopes. The other characters serve only to emphasize his personality and predicament. In most stories the main character is easily discovered. If the reader identifies the main character early in the story, he will more accurately understand the intricate relationships among the characters and consequently gain a fuller appreciation of what they do and say.

*Action.*   For many readers action is the most important element of fiction. In fact, the success of some stories—those of Saki, for example—rests mainly on an ingenious plot. Yet many of the best short-story writers today often minimize action, lest it destroy that delicate balance of all the elements on which their total achievement depends. Still, everyone agrees that some plot is indispensable. But the action by which plot is developed must, in the short story, be limited to a critical moment in the life of the chief character. His whole life history cannot be told; that again is the province of the novel. The essential of plot is conflict; it alone causes tension and creates suspense. The conflict may be of various kinds: it may be an inner conflict (as in "The Chrysanthemums"), a conflict among people (as in "The Three Strangers"), a conflict between the characters and their surroundings (as in "The Open Boat"). Ordinarily the action follows a definite pattern. It begins with the *incentive moment* (first point of conflict), develops through a series of entanglements (*complication*), reaches a peak of intensity (*climax*), and becomes disentangled in the *resolution*. Though it would hardly be wise to graph the action of a story, fixing precisely the incentive moment, the climax, and the last moment of suspense, it is helpful, even in casual reading, to note the beginning of the conflict, to follow the increasing tension to the highest point of interest, and to watch the suspense subside and come to rest.

Scene, character, and plot are combined into a continuum of existence, an illusion of reality, so that the reader willingly suspends disbelief and enters into the experience of the story. In working the elements into a pattern of continuous experience, the writer makes use chiefly of two techniques—summary and drama (sometimes referred to as the "long view" and the "short view"). If he decides to hurry over a certain part of the story, he simply describes or summarizes what happens. But those parts which are crucial he presents in vivid detail. In such parts the characters usually break into dialogue. Thus by using the long view the author can economize, and by using the short view, he can gain the intensity that marks the short story.

The elements of scene, character, and plot may be discovered by analyzing a story, but they are in reality inseparable; and the art of the short story in no small degree depends on the skill of the writer in making all of them illuminate the theme of the story. Furthermore, the action of the story itself must be related to the life that existed before the story began and will continue to exist after the story ends. It is the relation between the specific action of the story and this enveloping action that affords the shock of discovery in the resolution and gives the story meaning.

Though the major devices which constitute the art of the short story concern the handling of the basic elements of scene, character, and action, there are a few special techniques that are of particular importance to the reader.

*Enveloping Action.*   Since the short story presents only a fragment of experience, the writer employs special techniques in order to give the reader a feeling that the fragment is a part of a continuous experience. Sometimes he begins and ends his story with a sentence or phrase that refers to the larger experience. More often, however, he interweaves the momentary events of the story with the routine action of the characters' lives in order to create this impression. For instance, in "The Three Strangers" the curious conduct and dialogue of the first two strangers is interrupted time and again by details that keep the reader aware that this confrontation is only a brief episode in the long flow of the lives of the Fennels and their guests. Through cumulative references the author develops in the reader an impression of the continuous experience from which the specific experience was extracted.

*Point of View.*   For both the writer and reader of the short story, an important consideration is point of view, that is, through whose eyes the story is seen and by whose consciousness the material is interpreted. All stories are told from one of two broad points of view or from some variation of the two. In one of these, the *first person*, the author tells the story as if he knew only what one character—the narrator, speaking as the "I" in the story—knows about the story's events and characters. This one character to whose knowledge and understanding the author intentionally limits himself may be a main or a minor character or even an outside observer. "Guests of the Nation" and "An Old Manuscript" are told from the first-person main-character point of view, and "Spotted Horses" from the first-person outside-observer point of view.

The second of the two broad points of view—generally called the *omniscient*—is used in various special ways, and the accepted terminology for these is unrevealing. In the first place, the word "omniscient" signifies that the author knows everything—not merely the externalities some spectator might see but also the inner workings of the minds of the characters. Second, all omniscient stories are necessarily third-person stories. With these two matters clearly in mind, the reader can distinguish the three main specializations of the omniscient story. First, *third person* is the designation given to the omniscient story in which the author freely moves inside and outside the minds of any and all characters; he knows all and may do as he chooses. "The Lagoon" is a typical third-person story. The second prominent type of the omniscient story, known as the *central intelligence,* limits the author to moving inside and outside the consciousness of only one character, either a major or minor one. In "The Open Boat" the journalist is the central intelligence, the one character whose mind Crane enters or withdraws from at will. The third most prominent variety is the *scenic.* Although the scenic is in reality an omniscient and third-person point of view, these features are subtly obscured. They are present, however; to deny them is equivalent to saying that a story can be told without a teller. It is enough to say that the scenic story does not invade the consciousness of any character; by being presented almost entirely through dialogue, it calls no attention to the identity of the teller. In effect, the teller is effaced almost to the point of non-existence. This is the technique used in "Porcupines at the University," a technique much the same as that used in Strindberg's play "The Stronger."

These narrative methods vary chiefly in two respects—the amount of freedom they allow and the degree of directness they permit. For the writer, fixing on a point of view is of utmost importance, since, if he is to realize the full value of his material, he must choose a convenient position from which to tell the story. For the reader, an awareness of point of view is also highly important, for once he has discovered through whose eyes he is to see what happens, the story unfolds more logically and can be more readily interpreted.

*Language.*    In the modern short story, language is a critical component—hardly less decisive than in poetry. Since a story is built around a particular isolated experience, the language in which it is set down must suggest the quality of that experience: the language must be incisive, suggestive, and alert. In a well-written story, one need not read beyond the first few sentences to find words that reveal its unique quality. Since so much of a short story is often presented dramatically, the language of dialogue is of particular importance. Perhaps no modern writer excels William Faulkner in writing dialogue full of meaningful cadence and rhythm. In "Spotted Horses," for example, when Mrs. Armstid sees that her husband is about to buy a worthless horse from the Texas stranger and the swindler Flem Snopes, she says, "He hain't no more despair than to buy one of them things. And us not five dollars ahead of the pore house, he hain't no more despair." In context, which includes some vivid descriptive detail, this remark reveals, with poetic accuracy, the character and role of Mrs. Armstid, which are a significant part of the story.

*Ethical Insight.*    To many readers the highest test of fiction is ethical insight into the world of universal and ideal truth. Modern short stories may still depend on adventure, but not necessarily on the adventure of action in strange and dangerous places. They may be concerned with adventure in understanding human nature—complex and contradictory, amusing and surprising, comic and tragic. As we have said, theme is developed by showing how the limited action of the story is related to the enveloping action of its background in life. It is the struggle between these two forces that constitutes the main tension, the resolution of which makes the point of the story.

For a writer to attain the unity required of a successful short story, his feeling toward scene, character, action, and theme must be consistent. Since a short story is usually read at one sitting, and since the focus is so narrow, a writer must be extraordinarily skillful in utilizing all the potential of his materials. It was, indeed, this central point of the art of the short story with which Poe was concerned when he observed that a "skillful literary artist" conceives "with deliberate care, a certain unique or single effect to be wrought out."

## W. SOMERSET MAUGHAM

# Appointment in Samarra

William Somerset Maugham (1874–1966), British author, was born in Paris and attended Heidelberg University. He was educated to be a doctor, achieved financial success through his dramas and popular success as a novelist. His greatest novel, *Of Human Bondage*, 1915, like most of his writing, treats the unpredictability of human conduct and the thralldom of man by his passions. His first published novel was *Liza of Lambeth*, 1897. His writings include more than forty novels, several collections of short stories, books of literary criticism, and other nonfiction—*The Gentleman in the Parlour*, 1930; an autobiography, *The Summing Up*, 1938; and *A Writer's Notebook*, 1949, excerpts from his journals. *Points of View*, 1958, reflected his interest in appraising fiction and its practitioners. His twenty-odd plays are chiefly drawing-room comedies.

"Appointment in Samarra" fulfills the essential requirements of a short story: it has strict unity, intensity, and, of course, brevity. Mr. Maugham's restraint gives the story a gem-like quality. Perhaps no story has ever made better use of dramatic irony.

There was a merchant in Bagdad who sent his servant to market to buy provisions, and in a

APPOINTMENT IN SAMARRA   From *Sheppey* by W. Somerset Maugham. Copyright 1933 by the Literary Executor of W. Somerset Maugham. Reprinted by permission of A. P. Watt and Son.

little while the servant came back, white and trembling, and said, "Master, just now when I was in the market-place I was jostled by a woman in the crowd and when I turned I saw it was Death that jostled me. She looked at me and made a threatening gesture; now, lend me your horse, and I will ride away from this city and avoid my fate. I will go to Samarra and there Death will not find me." The merchant lent him his horse, and the servant mounted it, and he dug his spurs in its flanks and as fast as the horse could gallop he went. Then the merchant went down to the market-place and he saw Death standing in the crowd and he came to Death and said, "Why did you make a threatening gesture to my servant when you saw him this morning?" "That was not a threatening gesture," Death said. "It was only a start of surprise. I was astonished to see him in Bagdad, for I had an appointment with him tonight in Samarra."

# JAMES THURBER

# The Rabbits Who Caused All the Trouble

James Thurber (1894–1961), born in Columbus, Ohio, and educated at Ohio State University, began his literary career in journalism. From 1927 to 1933, he was on the staff of the *New Yorker,* to which he frequently contributed drawings and stories. Some of his best-known books are *Is Sex Necessary?* (in collaboration with E. B. White), 1929, a parody of books on sex education; *My Life and Hard Times,* 1933, an autobiography; *The Thurber Carnival,* 1945, a collection of his best work to that date; *The Beast in Me, and Other Animals,* 1948; *Thurber Country,* 1953; and *Lanterns and Lances,* 1961. In 1940 he collaborated with Elliott Nugent, who had been a fellow student at Ohio State, on a play, *The Male Animal,* a comedy about university life. Thurber also wrote a number of fairy tales and fables for children and adults which contain acute comments on present-day life.

From Aesop's time to the present, many writers have chosen to disguise the human character in animal fables. "The Rabbits Who Caused All the Trouble" illustrates Thurber's whimsy as well as the deftness of the fable form.

Within the memory of the youngest child there was a family of rabbits who lived near a pack of wolves. The wolves announced that they did not like the way the rabbits were living. (The wolves were crazy about the way they themselves were living, because it was the only way to live.) One night several wolves were killed in an earthquake and this was blamed on the rabbits, for it is well known that rabbits pound on the ground with their hind legs and cause earthquakes. On another night one of the wolves was

killed by a bolt of lightning and this was also blamed on the rabbits, for it is well known that lettuce-eaters cause lightning. The wolves threatened to civilize the rabbits if they didn't behave, and the rabbits decided to run away to a desert island. But the other animals, who lived at a great distance, shamed them, saying, "You must stay where you are and be brave. This is no world for escapists. If the wolves attack you, we will come to your aid, in all probability." So the rabbits continued to live near the wolves and one day there was a terrible flood which drowned a great many wolves. This was blamed on the rabbits, for it is well known that carrot-nibblers with long ears cause floods. The wolves descended on the rabbits, for their own good, and imprisoned them in a dark cave, for their own protection.

When nothing was heard about the rabbits for some weeks, the other animals demanded to know what had happened to them. The wolves replied that the rabbits had been eaten and since they had been eaten the affair was a purely internal matter. But the other animals warned that they might possibly unite against the wolves unless some reason was given for the destruction of the rabbits. So the wolves gave them one. "They were trying to escape," said the wolves, "and, as you know, this is no world for escapists."

*Moral: Run, don't walk, to the nearest desert island.*

FRANZ KAFKA

# An Old Manuscript

Franz Kafka (1883–1924) was born in Prague of Czechoslovakian Jewish ancestry. He received a doctorate in jurisprudence from Karls-Ferdinand, a German university in Prague. A high-strung, sensitive individual, he continually sought new outlets for his intellectual interests and came under various influences—the Zionist Max Brod, Franz Werfel, Kierkegaard, and Pascal. With the encouragement of Brod, Kafka published his first books, *Observations* and *The Judgment*, in 1913. Thereafter he wrote steadily despite his ever declining health. *Metamorphosis* was published in 1915; *The Trial* in 1925; *The Castle* in 1926—the last two posthumously. In the summer of 1923 he married and enjoyed a few months of contentment, during which he wrote *A Little Woman*. By Christmas of 1923, however, he was again very ill and in June 1924 he died of tuberculosis.

Kafka was a part of a movement known as existentialism, which views the world essentially as cosmic chaos, absurd and hostile to man. His writings are rich in symbols that communicate his despairing attitude toward civilization. Typical of this aspect of Kafka's art, "An Old Manuscript" involves more than the literal meaning conveys.

It looks as if much has been neglected in our country's system of defense. We have not concerned ourselves with it until now and have gone about our daily work; but things that have been happening recently begin to trouble us.

I have a cobbler's workshop in the square that lies before the Emperor's palace. Scarcely have I taken my shutters down, at the first glimpse of dawn, when I see armed soldiers already posted in the mouth of every street opening on the square. But these soldiers are not ours, they are obviously nomads from the North. In some way that is incomprehensible to me they have pushed right into the capital, although it is a long way from the frontier. At any rate, here they are; it seems that every morning there are more of them.

As is their nature, they camp under the open sky, for they abominate dwelling houses. They

AN OLD MANUSCRIPT  Reprinted by permission of Schocken Books Inc. from *The Penal Colony* by Franz Kafka. Copyright © 1948 by Schocken Books Inc.

busy themselves sharpening swords, whittling arrows and practicing horsemanship. This peaceful square, which was always kept scrupulously clean, they have made literally into a stable. We do try every now and then to run out of our shops and clear away at least the worst of the filth, but this happens less and less often, for the labor is in vain and brings us besides into danger of falling under the hoofs of the wild horses or of being crippled with lashes from the whips.

Speech with the nomads is impossible. They do not know our language, indeed they hardly have a language of their own. They communicate with each other much as jackdaws do. A screeching of jackdaws is always in our ears. Our way of living and our institutions they neither understand nor care to understand. And so they are unwilling to make sense even out of our sign language. You can gesture at them till you dislocate your jaws and your wrists and still they will not have understood you and will never understand. They often make grimaces; then the whites of their eyes turn up and foam gathers on their lips, but they do not mean anything by that, not even a threat; they do it because it is their nature to do it. Whatever they need, they take. You cannot call it taking by force. They grab at something and you simply stand aside and leave them to it.

From my stock, too, they have taken many good articles. But I cannot complain when I see how the butcher, for instance, suffers across the street. As soon as he brings in any meat the nomads snatch it all from him and gobble it up. Even their horses devour flesh; often enough a horseman and his horse are lying side by side, both of them gnawing at the same joint, one at either end. The butcher is nervous and does not dare to stop his deliveries of meat. We understand that, however, and subscribe money to keep him going. If the nomads got no meat, who knows what they might think of doing; who knows anyhow what they may think of, even though they get meat every day.

Not long ago the butcher thought he might at least spare himself the trouble of slaughtering, and so one morning he brought along a live ox. But he will never dare to do that again. I lay for a whole hour flat on the floor at the back of my workshop with my head muffled in all the clothes and rugs and pillows I had, simply to keep from hearing the bellowing of that ox, which the nomads were leaping on from all sides, tearing morsels out of its living flesh with their teeth. It had been quiet for a long time before I risked coming out; they were lying overcome round the remains of the carcass like drunkards round a wine cask.

This was the occasion when I fancied I actually saw the Emperor himself at a window of the palace; usually he never enters these outer rooms but spends all of his time in the innermost garden; yet on this occasion he was standing, or so at least it seemed to me, at one of the windows, watching with bent head the ongoings before his residence.

"What is going to happen?" we all ask ourselves. "How long can we endure this burden and torment? The Emperor's palace has drawn the nomads here but does not know how to drive them away again. The gate stays shut; the guards, who used to be always marching out and in with ceremony, keep close behind barred windows. It is left to us artisans and tradesmen to save our country; but we are not equal to such a task; nor have we ever claimed to be capable of it. This is a misunderstanding of some kind; and it will be the ruin of us."

JOHN COLLIER

# The Chaser

John Collier (1901–     ) is a widely read British short-story writer, currently residing in Hollywood, California. His stories have been especially popular with movie and television producers. Among his books are *His Monkey Wife, or Married to a Chimp*, 1930; *Full Circle*, 1933; *Defy the Foul Fiend*, 1934; *Presenting Moonshine*, 1941; *The Touch of Nutmeg*, 1943; and *Fancies and Goodnights*, 1951.

Mr. Collier is a master of the ironic and fantastic tale, but in his best stories, such as "The Chaser," the underlying commentary is on real people and real motives no matter how unreal the surface situation. Often compared to Saki, he is a consummate artist of the short short story.

Alan Austen, as nervous as a kitten, went up certain dark and creaky stairs in the neighborhood of Pell Street, and peered about for a long time on the dim landing before he found the name he wanted written obscurely on one of the doors.

He pushed open this door, as he had been told to do, and found himself in a tiny room, which contained no furniture but a plain kitchen table, a rocking-chair, and an ordinary chair. On one of the dirty buff-colored walls were a couple of shelves, containing in all perhaps a dozen bottles and jars.

An old man sat in the rocking-chair, reading a newspaper. Alan, without a word, handed him the card he had been given. "Sit down, Mr. Austen," said the old man very politely. "I am glad to make your acquaintance."

"Is it true," asked Alan, "that you have a certain mixture that has—er—quite extraordinary effects?"

"My dear sir," replied the old man, "my stock in trade is not very large—I don't deal in laxatives and teething mixtures—but such as it is, it

is varied. I think nothing I sell has effects which could be precisely described as ordinary."

"Well, the fact is—" began Alan.

"Here, for example," interrupted the old man, reaching for a bottle from the shelf. "Here is a liquid as colorless as water, almost tasteless, quite imperceptible in coffee, milk, wine, or any other beverage. It is also quite imperceptible to any known method of autopsy."

"Do you mean it is a poison?" cried Alan, very much horrified.

"Call it a glove-cleaner if you like," said the old man indifferently. "Maybe it will clean gloves. I have never tried. One might call it a life-cleaner. Lives need cleaning sometimes."

"I want nothing of that sort," said Alan.

"Probably it is just as well," said the old man. "Do you know the price of this? For one teaspoonful, which is sufficient, I ask five thousand dollars. Never less. Not a penny less."

"I hope all your mixtures are not as expensive," said Alan apprehensively.

"Oh dear, no," said the old man. "It would be no good charging that sort of price for a love potion, for example. Young people who need a love potion very seldom have five thousand dollars. Otherwise they would not need a love potion."

"I am glad to hear that," said Alan.

"I look at it like this," said the old man. "Please a customer with one article, and he will come back when he needs another. Even if it *is* more costly. He will save up for it, if necessary."

"So," said Alan, "you really do sell love potions?"

"If I did not sell love potions," said the old man, reaching for another bottle, "I should not have mentioned the other matter to you. It is only when one is in a position to oblige that one can afford to be so confidential."

"And these potions," said Alan. "They are not just—just—er—"

"Oh, no," said the old man. "Their effects are permanent, and extend far beyond casual impulse. But they include it. Bountifully, insistently. Everlastingly."

"Dear me!" said Alan, attempting a look of scientific detachment. "How very interesting!"

"But consider the spiritual side," said the old man.

"I do, indeed," said Alan.

"For indifference," said the old man, "they substitute devotion. For scorn, adoration. Give one tiny measure of this to the young lady—its flavor is imperceptible in orange juice, soup, or cocktails—and however gay and giddy she is, she will change altogether. She will want nothing but solitude, and you."

"I can hardly believe it," said Alan. "She is so fond of parties."

"She will not like them any more," said the old man. "She will be afraid of the pretty girls you may meet."

"She will actually be jealous?" cried Alan in a rapture. "Of me?"

"Yes, she will want to be everything to you."

"She is, already. Only she doesn't care about it."

"She will, when she has taken this. She will care intensely. You will be her sole interest in life."

"Wonderful!" cried Alan.

"She will want to know all you do," said the old man. "All that has happened to you during the day. Every word of it. She will want to know what you are thinking about, why you smile suddenly, why you are looking sad."

"That is love!" cried Alan.

"Yes," said the old man. "How carefully she will look after you! She will never allow you to be tired, to sit in a draught, to neglect your food. If you are an hour late, she will be terrified. She will think you are killed, or that some siren has caught you."

"I can hardly imagine Diana like that!" cried Alan, overwhelmed with joy.

"You will not have to use your imagination," said the old man. "And, by the way, since there are always sirens, if by any chance you *should,* later on, slip a little, you need not worry. She will forgive you, in the end. She will be terribly hurt, of course, but she will forgive you—in the end."

"That will not happen," said Alan fervently.

"Of course not," said the old man. "But, if it did, you need not worry. She would never divorce you. Oh, no! And, of course, she herself will never give you the least, the very least, grounds for—uneasiness."

"And how much," said Alan, "is this wonderful mixture?"

"It is not as dear," said the old man, "as the glove-cleaner, or life-cleaner, as I sometimes call it. No. That is five thousand dollars, never a penny less. One has to be older than you are, to indulge in that sort of thing. One has to save up for it."

"But the love potion?" said Alan.

"Oh, that," said the old man, opening the drawer in the kitchen table, and taking out a tiny, rather dirty-looking phial. "That is just a dollar."

"I can't tell you how grateful I am," said Alan, watching him fill it.

"I like to oblige," said the old man. "Then customers come back, later in life, when they are rather better off, and want more expensive things. Here you are. You will find it very effective."

"Thank you again," said Alan. "Good-by."

"*Au revoir,*" said the old man.

# DONALD BARTHELME

# Porcupines at the University

Donald Barthelme (1931–    ) is widely acclaimed as a leader in experimental fiction techniques in the United States. He has published novels—such as *Snow White*, 1967—as well as his perhaps better known short stories, many of which appeared originally in the *New Yorker*. His two recent collections of stories are *Unspeakable Practices, Unnatural Acts*, 1964, and *City Life*, 1970.

"Porcupines at the University" is an amusing but trenchant commentary on some thorny contemporary issues—and on people, both those among us who pose the problems and those whom we rely on to deal with them.

"'And now the purple dusk of twilight time/ steals across the meadows of my heart,'" the Dean said.

His pretty wife, Paula, extended her long graceful hands full of Negronis.

A scout burst into the room, through the door. "Porcupines!" he shouted.

"Porcupines what?" the Dean asked.

"Thousands and thousands of them. Three miles down the road and comin' fast!"

"Maybe they won't enroll," the Dean said. "Maybe they're just passing through."

"You can't be sure," his wife said.

"How do they look?" he asked the scout, who was pulling porcupine quills out of his ankles.

"Well, you know. Like porcupines."

"Are you going to bust them?" Paula asked.

"I'm tired of busting people," the Dean said.

"They're not people," Paula pointed out.

"*De bustibus non est disputandum*," the scout said.

"I suppose I'll have to do something," the Dean said.

Meanwhile the porcupine wrangler was wrangling the porcupines across the dusty and overbuilt West.

Dust clouds. Yips. The lowing of porcupines. "Git along theah li'l porcupines."

And when I reach the great porcupine canneries of the East, I will be rich, the wrangler reflected. I will sit on the front porch of the Muehlebach Hotel in New York City and smoke me a big seegar. Then, the fancy women.

"All right you porcupines step up to that yellow line."

There was no yellow line. This was just an expression the wrangler used to keep the porcupines moving. He had heard it in the Army. The damn-fool porcupines didn't know the difference.

The wrangler ambled along reading the ads in a copy of *Song Hits* magazine. "Play Harmonica in 5 Mins.!," and so forth.

The porcupines scuffled along making their little hops. There were four-five thousand in the herd. Nobody had counted exactly.

An assistant wrangler rode in from the outskirts of the herd. He too had a copy of *Song Hits* magazine, in his hip pocket. He looked at the head wrangler's arm, which had a lot of little holes in it.

"Hey Griswold."

"Yeah?"

"How'd you get all them little holes in your arm?"

"You ever try to slap a brand on a porkypine?"

Probably the fancy women will be covered with low-cut dresses and cheap perfume, the wrangler thought. Probably there will be hundreds of them, hundreds and hundreds. All after my medicine bundle containing my gold and my lucky drill bit. But if they try to rush me I will pull my guitar. And sing them a song of prairie virility.

"Porcupines at the university," the Dean's wife said. "Well, why not?"

"We don't have *facilities* for four or five thousand porcupines," the Dean said. "I can't get a dial tone."

"They could take Alternate Life Styles," Paula said.

"We've already got too many people in Alternate Life Styles," the Dean said, putting down the telephone. "The hell with it. I'll bust them myself. Singlehanded. Lye."

"You'll get hurt."

"Nonsense, they're only porcupines. I'd better wear my old clothes."

"Bag of dirty shirts in the closet," Paula said.

The Dean went into the closet.

Bags and bags of dirty shirts.

"Why doesn't she ever take these shirts to the laundry?"

Griswold, the wrangler, wrote a new song in the saddle:

> Fancy woman fancy woman
> How come you don't do right
> I oughta rap you in the mouth
>     for the way you acted
> In the porte-cochere of the Trinity
>     River Consolidated
>     General High last Friday
> Nite.

I will sit back and watch it climbing the charts, he said to himself. As recorded by Merle Travis.

First, it will be a Bell Ringer. Then, the Top Forty. Finally a Golden Oldie.

"All right you porcupines. Git along."

The herd was moving down a twelve-lane trail of silky-smooth concrete. Signs along the trail said things like "NEXT EXIT 5 MI." and "RADAR IN USE."

"Griswold, some of them motorists behind us is gettin' awful edgy."

"I'm runnin' this here porky-pine drive," Griswold said, "and I say we better gettum off the road."

The herd was turned onto a broad field of green grass. Green grass with white lime lines on it at ten-yard intervals.

The Ed Sullivan show, the wrangler thought. Well, Ed, how I come to write this song, I was on a porky-pine drive. The last of the great porky-pine drives you might say. We had four-five thousand head we'd fatted up along the Tuscalora and we was headin' for New York City.

The Dean loaded a gleaming Gatling gun capable of delivering three hundred and sixty rounds a minute. The Gatling gun sat in a mule-drawn wagon and was covered with an old piece of canvas. Formerly it had sat on a concrete slab in front of the R.O.T.C. Building.

First, the Dean said to himself, all they see is this funky old wagon pulled by this busted-up old mule. Then, I whip off the canvas. There stands the gleaming Gatling gun capable of delivering three hundred and sixty rounds a minute. My hand resting lightly, confidently on the crank. They shall not pass, I say. *Ils ne passeront pas.* Then, the porcupine hide begins to fly.

I wonder if these rounds are still good?

The gigantic Gatling gun loomed over the herd like an immense piece of bad news.

"Hey Griswold."

"What?"

"He's got a gun."

"I *see* it," Griswold said. "You think I'm blind?"

"What we gonna do?"

"How about vamoosing?"

"But the herd—"

"Them li'l porcupines can take care of their own selves," Griswold said. "God damn it. I guess we better parley." He got up off the grass, where he had been stretched full length, and walked toward the wagon.

"What say potner?"

"Look," the Dean said. "You can't enroll those porcupines. It's out of the question."

"That so?"

"It's out of the question," the Dean repeated. "We've had a lot of trouble around here. The cops won't even speak to me. We can't *take* any more trouble." The Dean glanced at the herd. "That's a mighty handsome herd you have there."

"Kind of you," Griswold said. "That's a mighty handsome mule *you* got."

They both gazed at the Dean's terrible-looking mule.

Griswold wiped his neck with a red bandanna. "You don't want no porky-pines over to your place, is that it?"

"That's it."

"Well we don't *go* where we ain't wanted," the wrangler said. "No call to throw down on us with that . . . *machine* there."

The Dean looked embarrassed.

"You don't know Mr. Ed Sullivan, do you?" Griswold asked. "He lives around here somewheres, don't he?"

"I haven't had the pleasure," the Dean said. He thought for a moment. "I know a booker in Vegas, though. He was one of our people. He was a grad student in comparative religion."

"Maybe we can do a deal," the wrangler said. "Whichaway is New York City?"

"Well?" the Dean's wife asked. "What were their demands?"

"I'll tell you in a minute," the Dean said. "My mule is double-parked."

The herd turned onto the Cross-Bronx Expressway. People looking out of their cars saw thousands and thousands of porcupines. The porcupines looked like badly engineered vacuum-cleaner attachments.

Vegas, the wrangler was thinking. Ten weeks at Caesars Palace at a sock 15 Gs a week. "The Ballad of the Last Drive." Leroy Griswold singing his smash single, "The Ballad of the Last Drive."

"Git along theah li'l porcupines."

The citizens in their cars looked at the porcupines, thinking: What is wonderful? Are these porcupines wonderful? Are they significant? Are they what I need?—

## SHIRLEY JACKSON

# After You, My Dear Alphonse

Shirley Jackson (1919–1966) was an essayist, novelist, and short-story writer, much of whose work originally appeared in the *New Yorker*. Her books include *The Road Through the Wall*, 1948; *The Lottery, or The Adventures of James Harris*, 1949; *Life Among the Savages*, 1953; *Raising Demons*, 1957; *The Haunting of Hill House*, 1959; and *We Have Always Lived in the Castle*, 1962.

Children not infrequently put their elders to shame. In this story, the innocent eye is at work with all its resultant irony.

AFTER YOU, MY DEAR ALPHONSE    Reprinted from *The Lottery* by Shirley Jackson, by permission of Farrar, Straus & Giroux, Inc. Copyright 1943, 1949 by Shirley Jackson. First published in *The New Yorker*.

Mrs. Wilson was just taking the gingerbread out of the oven when she heard Johnny outside talking to someone.

"Johnny," she called, "you're late. Come in and get your lunch."

"Just a minute, Mother," Johnny said. "After you, my dear Alphonse."

"After *you*, my dear Alphonse," another voice said.

"No, after *you*, my dear Alphonse," Johnny said.

Mrs. Wilson opened the door. "Johnny," she said, "you come in this minute and get your lunch. You can play after you've eaten."

Johnny came in after her, slowly. "Mother," he said, "I brought Boyd home for lunch with me."

"Boyd?" Mrs. Wilson thought for a moment. "I don't believe I've met Boyd. Bring him in, dear, since you've invited him. Lunch is ready."

"Boyd!" Johnny yelled. "Hey, Boyd, come on in!"

"I'm coming. Just got to unload this stuff."

"Well, hurry, or my mother'll be sore."

"Johnny, that's not very polite to either your friend or your mother," Mrs. Wilson said. "Come sit down, Boyd."

As she turned to show Boyd where to sit, she saw he was a Negro boy, smaller than Johnny but about the same age. His arms were loaded with split kindling wood. "Where'll I put this stuff, Johnny?" he asked.

Mrs. Wilson turned to Johnny. "Johnny," she said, "what is that wood?"

"Dead Japanese," Johnny said mildly. "We stand them in the ground and run over them with tanks."

"How do you do, Mrs. Wilson?" Boyd said.

"How do you do, Boyd? You shouldn't let Johnny make you carry all that wood. Sit down now and eat lunch, both of you."

"Why shouldn't he carry the wood, Mother? It's his wood. We got it at his place."

"Johnny," Mrs. Wilson said, "go on and eat your lunch."

"Sure," Johnny said. He held out the dish of scrambled eggs to Boyd. "After you, my dear Alphonse."

"After *you*, my dear Alphonse," Boyd said.

"After *you*, my dear Alphonse," Johnny said. They began to giggle.

"Are you hungry, Boyd?" Mrs. Wilson asked.

"Yes, Mrs. Wilson."

"Well, don't you let Johnny stop you. He always fusses about eating, so you just see that you get a good lunch. There's plenty of food here for you to have all you want."

"Thank you, Mrs. Wilson."

"Come on, Alphonse," Johnny said. He pushed half the scrambled eggs on to Boyd's plate. Boyd watched while Mrs. Wilson put a dish of stewed tomatoes beside his plate.

"Boyd don't eat tomatoes, do you, Boyd?" Johnny said.

"*Doesn't* eat tomatoes, Johnny. And just because you don't like them, don't say that about Boyd. Boyd will eat *anything*."

"Bet he won't," Johnny said, attacking his scrambled eggs.

"Boyd wants to grow up and be a big strong man so he can work hard," Mrs. Wilson said. "I'll bet Boyd's father eats stewed tomatoes."

"My father eats anything he wants to," Boyd said.

"So does mine," Johnny said. "Sometimes he doesn't eat hardly anything. He's a little guy, though. Wouldn't hurt a flea."

"Mine's a little guy, too," Boyd said.

"I'll bet he's strong, though," Mrs. Wilson said. She hesitated. "Does he . . . work?"

"Sure," Johnny said. "Boyd's father works in a factory."

"There, you see?" Mrs. Wilson said. "And he certainly has to be strong to do that—all that lifting and carrying at a factory."

"Boyd's father doesn't have to," Johnny said. "He's a foreman."

Mrs. Wilson felt defeated. "What does your mother do, Boyd?"

"My mother?" Boyd was surprised. "She takes care of us kids."

"Oh. She doesn't work, then?"

"Why should she?" Johnny said through a mouthful of eggs. "You don't work."

"You really don't want any stewed tomatoes, Boyd?"

"No, thank you, Mrs. Wilson," Boyd said.

"No, thank you, Mrs. Wilson, no, thank you, Mrs. Wilson, no, thank you, Mrs. Wilson," Johnny said. "Boyd's sister's going to work, though. She's going to be a teacher."

"That's a very fine attitude for her to have, Boyd." Mrs. Wilson restrained an impulse to pat

Boyd on the head. "I imagine you're all very proud of her?"

"I guess so," Boyd said.

"What about all your other brothers and sisters? I guess all of you want to make just as much of yourselves as you can."

"There's only me and Jean," Boyd said. "I don't know yet what I want to be when I grow up."

"We're going to be tank drivers, Boyd and me," Johnny said. "Zoom." Mrs. Wilson caught Boyd's glass of milk as Johnny's napkin ring, suddenly transformed into a tank, plowed heavily across the table.

"Look, Johnny," Boyd said. "Here's a foxhole. I'm shooting at you."

Mrs. Wilson, with the speed born of long experience, took the gingerbread off the shelf and placed it carefully between the tank and the foxhole.

"Now eat as much as you want to, Boyd," she said. "I want to see you get filled up."

"Boyd eats a lot, but not as much as I do," Johnny said. "I'm bigger than he is."

"You're not much bigger," Boyd said. "I can beat you running."

Mrs. Wilson took a deep breath. "Boyd," she said. Both boys turned to her. "Boyd, Johnny has some suits that are a little too small for him, and a winter coat. It's not new, of course, but there's lots of wear in it still. And I have a few dresses that your mother or sister could probably use. Your mother can make them over into lots of things for all of you, and I'd be very happy to give them to you. Suppose before you leave I make up a big bundle and then you and Johnny can take it over to your mother right away . . ." Her voice trailed off as she saw Boyd's puzzled expression.

"But I have plenty of clothes, thank you," he said. "And I don't think my mother knows how to sew very well, and anyway I guess we buy about everything we need. Thank you very much though."

"We don't have time to carry that old stuff around, Mother," Johnny said. "We got to play tanks with the kids today."

Mrs. Wilson lifted the plate of gingerbread off the table as Boyd was about to take another piece. "There are many little boys like you, Boyd, who would be grateful for the clothes someone was kind enough to give them."

"Boyd will take them if you want him to, Mother," Johnny said.

"I didn't mean to make you mad, Mrs. Wilson," Boyd said.

"Don't think I'm angry, Boyd. I'm just disappointed in you, that's all. Now let's not say anything more about it."

She began clearing the plates off the table, and Johnny took Boyd's hand and pulled him to the door. "'Bye, Mother," Johnny said. Boyd stood for a minute, staring at Mrs. Wilson's back.

"After you, my dear Alphonse," Johnny said, holding the door open.

"Is your mother still mad?" Mrs. Wilson heard Boyd ask in a low voice.

"I don't know," Johnny said. "She's screwy sometimes."

"So's mine," Boyd said. He hesitated. "After *you*, my dear Alphonse."

# JORGE LUIS BORGES

# The Man on the Threshold

Jorge Luis Borges (1899–     ), a versatile Argentine essayist, poet, and fiction writer as well as a translator, has an international reputation based particularly upon his short stories. *Ficciones*, which appeared in 1945 and was reissued in 1956, and *Labyrinths*, 1962, are collections of some of his better known stories and essays translated into English.

A curious and suspicious parallel exists between the immediate characters and events of the major story here and those of the tale within the tale, which is, reportedly, of the distant past.

Bioy Casares brought back with him from London to Buenos Aires a strange dagger with a triangular blade and a hilt in the shape of an H; a friend of ours, Christopher Dewey of the British Council, told us that such weapons were commonly used in India. This statement prompted him to mention that he had held a job in that country between the two wars. (*"Ultra Auroram et Gangen,"* I recall his saying in Latin, misquoting a line from Juvenal.) Of the stories he entertained us with that night, I venture to set down the one that follows. My account will be faithful; may Allah deliver me from the temptation of adding any circumstantial details or of weighing down with interpolations from Kipling the tale's Oriental character. It should be remarked that the story has a certain ancient simplicity that it would be a pity to lose—something perhaps straight out of the Arabian Nights.

The precise geography [Dewey said] of the events I am going to relate is of little importance.

THE MAN ON THE THRESHOLD From the book *The Aleph And Other Stories, 1933–1969* by Jorge Luis Borges. Edited and translated by Norman Thomas di Giovanni in collaboration with the author. English translation © 1968, 1969, 1970 by Emecé Editores, S.A., and Norman Thomas di Giovanni; © 1970 by Jorge Luis Borges, Adolfo Bioy-Casares and Norman Thomas di Giovanni. Published by E. P. Dutton and Co., and used with their permission.

Besides, what would the names of Amritsar or Oudh mean in Buenos Aires? Let me only say, then, that in those years there were disturbances in a Muslim city and that the central government sent out one of their best people to restore order. He was a Scotsman from an illustrious clan of warriors, and in his blood he bore a tradition of violence. Only once did I lay eyes on him, but I shall not forget his deep black hair, the prominent cheekbones, the somehow avid nose and mouth, the broad shoulders, the powerful set of a Viking. David Alexander Glencairn is what he'll be called in my story tonight; the names are fitting, since they belonged to kings who ruled with an iron sceptre. David Alexander Glencairn (as I shall have to get used to calling him) was, I suspect, a man who was feared; the mere news of his coming was enough to quell the city. This did not deter him from putting into effect a number of forceful measures. A few years passed. The city and the outlying district were at peace; Sikhs and Muslims had laid aside their ancient enmities, and suddenly Glencairn disappeared. Naturally enough, there was no lack of rumors that he had been kidnapped or murdered.

These things I learned from my superior, for the censorship was strict and the newspapers made no comment on (nor did they even record, for all I recall) Glencairn's disappearance. There's a saying that India is larger than the world; Glencairn, who may have been all-powerful in the city to which he was destined by a signature scrawled across the bottom of some document, was no more than a cog in the administration of Empire. The inquiries of the local police turned up nothing; my superior felt that a civilian might rouse less suspicion and achieve greater results. Three or four days later (distances in India are generous), I was appointed to my mission and was working my way without hope of success through the streets of the commonplace city that had somehow whisked away a man.

I felt, almost at once, the invisible presence of a conspiracy to keep Glencairn's fate hidden. *There's not a soul in this city* (I suspected) *who is not in on the secret and who is not sworn to keep it.* Most people upon questioning professed an unbounded ignorance; they did not know who Glencairn was, had never seen him, had never heard anyone speak of him. Others, instead, had caught a glimpse of him only a quarter of an hour before talking to So-and-So, and they even accompanied me to the house the two had entered and in which nothing was known of them, or which they had just that moment left. Some of those meticulous liars I went so far as to knock down. Witnesses approved my outbursts, and made up other lies. I did not believe them, but neither did I dare ignore them. One afternoon, I was handed an envelope containing a slip of paper on which there was an address.

The sun had gone down when I got there. The quarter was poor but not rowdy; the house was quite low; from the street I caught a glimpse of a succession of unpaved inner courtyards, and somewhere at the far end an opening. There, some kind of Muslim ceremony was being held; a blind man entered with a lute made of a reddish wood.

At my feet, motionless as an object, an old, old man squatted on the threshold. I'll tell what he was like, for he is an essential part of the story. His many years had worn him down and polished him as smooth as water polishes a stone, or as the generations of men polish a sentence. Long rags covered him, or so it seemed to me, and the cloth he wore wound around his head was one rag more. In the dusk, he lifted a dark face and a white beard. I began speaking to him without preamble, for by now I had given up all hope of ever finding David Alexander Glencairn. The old man did not understand me (perhaps he did not hear me), and I had to explain that Glencairn was a judge and that I was looking for him. I felt, on speaking these words, the pointlessness of questioning this old man for whom the present was hardly more than a dim rumor. *This man might give me news of the Mutiny or of Akbar* (I thought) *but not of Glencairn.* What he told me confirmed this suspicion.

"A judge!" he cried with weak surprise. "A judge who has got himself lost and is being searched for. That happened when I was a boy. I have no memory for dates, but Nikal Seyn (Nicholson) had not yet been killed before the wall of Delhi. Time that has passed stays on in memory; I may be able to summon back what happened then. God, in his wrath, had allowed people to fall into corruption; the mouths of men were full of blasphemy and of deceit and of fraud. Yet not all were evil, and when it was known that the queen was about to send a man who would carry out in this land the law of England, those who were less evil were cheered, for they felt that law is better than disorder. The Christian came to us but it was not long before he too began deceiving and oppressing us, in concealing abominable crimes, and in selling decisions. We did not blame him in the beginning; the English justice he administered was not familiar to anyone, and the apparent excesses of the new judge may have obeyed certain valid arcane reasoning. Everything must have a justification in his book, we wished to think, but his kinship with all evil judges the world over was too obvious to be overlooked, and at last we were forced to admit that he was simply a wicked man. He turned out to be a tyrant, and the unfortunate people (in order to avenge themselves for the false hopes they had once placed in him) began to toy with the idea of kidnapping him and submitting him to judgment. To talk was not enough; from plans they had to move to action. Nobody, perhaps, save the very foolish or the very young, believed that that rash scheme could be carried out, but thousands of Sikhs and Muslims kept their word and one day they executed—incredulous—what to each of them had seemed impossible. They sequestered the judge and held him prisoner in a farmhouse beyond the outskirts of the town. Then they called together all those who had been wronged by him, or, in some cases, orphans and widows, for during those years the executioner's sword had not rested. In the end—this was perhaps the most difficult—they sought and named a judge to judge the judge."

At this point, the old man was interrupted by some women who were entering the house. Then he went on, slowly.

"It is well known that there is no generation that does not include in it four upright men who are the secret pillars of the world and who justify it before the Lord: one of these men would have made the perfect judge. But where are they to be found if they themselves wander the world lost and nameless, and do not know each other when they meet, and are unaware of the high destiny that is theirs? Someone then reasoned that if fate forbade us wise men we should seek out the witless. This opinion prevailed. Students of the Koran, doctors of law, Sikhs who bear the name of lions and who worship one God, Hindus who worship a multitude of gods, Mahavira monks who teach that the shape of the universe is that of a man with his legs spread apart, worshippers of fire, and black Jews made up the court, but the final ruling was entrusted to a madman."

Here he was interrupted by people who were leaving the ceremony.

"To a madman," he repeated, "so that God's wisdom might speak through his mouth and shame human pride. His name has been forgotten, or was never known, but he went naked through the streets, or was clothed in rags, counting his fingers with a thumb and mocking at the trees."

My common sense rebelled. I said that to hand over the verdict to a madman was to nullify the trial.

"The defendant accepted the judge," was his answer, "seeing, perhaps, that because of the risk the conspirators would run if they set him free, only from a man who was mad might he not expect a sentence of death. I heard that he laughed when he was told who the judge was. The trial lasted many days and nights, drawn out by the swelling of the number of witnesses."

The old man stopped. Something was troubling him. In order to bridge the lapse, I asked him how many days.

"At least nineteen," he replied.

People who were leaving the ceremony interrupted him again; wine is forbidden to Muslims, but the faces and voices were those of drunkards. One, on passing, shouted something to the old man.

"Nineteen days—exactly," he said, setting matters straight. "The faithless dog heard sentence passed, and the knife feasted on his throat."

He had spoken fiercely, joyfully. With a different voice now he brought the story to an end. "He died without fear; in the most vile of men there is some virtue."

"Where did all this happen?" I asked him. "In a farmhouse?"

For the first time, he looked into my eyes. Then he made things clear, slowly, measuring his words. "I said that he had been confined in a farmhouse, not that he was tried there. He was tried in this city, in a house like any other, like this one. One house differs little from another; what is important to know is whether the house is built in Hell or in Heaven."

I asked him about the fate of the conspirators.

"I don't know," he told me patiently. "These things took place and were forgotten many years ago now. Maybe what they did was condemned by men, but not by the Lord."

Having said this, he got up. I felt his words as a dismissal, and from that moment I no longer existed for him. Men and women from all the corners of the Punjab swarmed over us, praying and intoning, and nearly swept us away. I wondered how, from courtyards so narrow they were little more than long passageways, so many persons could be pouring out. Others were coming from the neighboring houses; it seems they had leaped over the walls. By shoving and cursing, I forced my way inside. At the heart of the innermost courtyard, I came upon a naked man, crowned with yellow flowers, whom everyone kissed and caressed, with a sword in his hand. The sword was stained, for it had dealt Glencairn his death. I found his mutilated body in the stables out back.

## E. B. WHITE

# The Door

Elwyn Brooks White (1899–      ) is well-known for his writings in the *New Yorker* and his "One Man's Meat" column in *Harper's*, 1938–1943. A characteristic volume is *The Second Tree from the Corner*, 1953, a collection of familiar essays. In 1959 White revised William Strunk's *Elements of Style*, a composition textbook he had used as a student. Among the moderns, he is unsurpassed as a writer of children's stories. *Charlotte's Web*, 1952, continues to be a best-seller; his more recent work, *The Trumpet of the Swan*, 1970, is another.

In "The Door" the effects of the ersatz and gimmicky world that technology has created are shown in the growing disorientation of the main character's personality.

Everything (he kept saying) is something it isn't. And everybody is always somewhere else. Maybe it was the city, being in the city, that made him feel how queer everything was and that it was something else. Maybe (he kept thinking) it was the names of the things. The names were tex and frequently koid. Or they were flex and oid or they were duroid (sani) or flexsan (duro), but everything was glass (but not quite glass) and the thing that you touched (the surface, washable, crease-resistant) was rubber, only it wasn't quite rubber and you didn't quite touch it but almost. The wall, which was glass but thrutex, turned out on being approached not to be a wall, it was something else, it was an opening or doorway— and the doorway (through which he saw himself approaching) turned out to be something else, it was a wall. And what he had eaten not having agreed with him.

He was in a washable house, but he wasn't sure. Now about those rats, he kept saying to himself. He meant the rats that the Professor had driven crazy by forcing them to deal with problems which were beyond the scope of rats, the

insoluble problems. He meant the rats that had been trained to jump at the square card with the circle in the middle, and the card (because it was something it wasn't) would give way and let the rat into a place where the food was, but then one day it would be a trick played on the rat, and the card would be changed, and the rat would jump but the card wouldn't give way, and it was an impossible situation (for a rat) and the rat would go insane and into its eyes would come the unspeakably bright imploring look of the frustrated, and after the convulsions were over and the frantic racing around, then the passive stage would set in and the willingness to let anything be done to it, even if it was something else.

He didn't know which door (or wall) or opening in the house to jump at, to get through, because one was an opening that wasn't a door (it was a void, or koid) and the other was a wall that wasn't an opening, it was a sanitary cupboard of the same color. He caught a glimpse of his eyes staring into his eyes, in the thrutex, and in them was the expression he had seen in the picture of the rats—weary after convulsions and the frantic racing around, when they were willing and did not mind having anything done to them. More and more (he kept saying) I am confronted by a problem which is incapable of solution (for this time even if he chose the right door, there would be no food behind it) and that is what madness is, and things seeming different from what they are. He heard, in the house where he was, in the city to which he had gone (as toward a door which might, or might not, give way), a noise—not a loud noise but more of a low prefabricated humming. It came from a place in the base of the wall (or stat) where the flue carrying the filterable air was, and not far from the Minipiano, which was made of the same material nailbrushes are made of, and which was under the stairs. "This, too, has been tested," she said, pointing, but not at it, "and found viable." It wasn't a loud noise, he kept thinking, sorry that he had seen his eyes, even though it was through his own eyes that he had seen them.

First will come the convulsions (he said), then the exhaustion, then the willingness to let anything be done. "And you better believe it *will* be."

All his life he had been confronted by situations which were incapable of being solved, and there was a deliberateness behind all this, behind this changing of the card (or door), because they would always wait till you had learned to jump at the certain card (or door)—the one with the circle—and then they would change it on you. There have been so many doors changed on me, he said, in the last twenty years, but it is now becoming clear that it is an impossible situation, and the question is whether to jump again, even though they ruffle you in the rump with a blast of air—to make you jump. He wished he wasn't standing by the Minipiano. First they would teach you the prayers and the Psalms, and that would be the right door (the one with the circle) and the long sweet words with the holy sound, and that would be the one to jump at to get where the food was. Then one day you jumped and it didn't give way, so that all you got was the bump on the nose, and the first bewilderment, the first young bewilderment.

I don't know whether to tell her about the door they substituted or not, he said, the one with the equation on it and the picture of the amoeba reproducing itself by division. Or the one with the photostatic copy of the check for thirty-two dollars and fifty cents. But the jumping was so long ago, although the bump is . . . how those old wounds hurt! Being crazy this way wouldn't be so bad if only, if only. If only when you put your foot forward to take a step, the ground wouldn't come up to meet your foot the way it does. And the same way in the street (only I may never get back to the street unless I jump at the right door), the curb coming up to meet your foot, anticipating ever so delicately the weight of the body, which is somewhere else. "We could take your name," she said, "and send it to you." And it wouldn't be so bad if only you could read a sentence all the way through without jumping (your eye) to something else on the same page; and then (he kept thinking) here was that man out in Jersey, the one who started to chop his trees down, one by one, the man who began talking about how he would take his house to pieces, brick by brick, because he faced a problem incapable of solution, probably, so he began to hack at the trees in the yard, began to pluck with trembling fingers at the bricks in the house. Even if a house is not washable, it is worth taking down. It is not till later that the exhaustion sets in.

But it is inevitable that they will keep changing the doors on you, he said, because that is what they are for; and the thing is to get used to it and not let it unsettle the mind. But that would mean not jumping, and you can't. Nobody can not jump. There will be no not-jumping. Among rats, perhaps, but among people never. Everybody has to keep jumping at a door (the one with the circle on it) because that is the way everybody is, specially some people. You wouldn't want me, standing here, to tell you, would you, about my friend the poet (deceased) who said, "My heart has followed all my days something I cannot name"? (It had the circle on it.) And like many poets, although few so beloved, he is gone. It killed him, the jumping. First, of course, there were the preliminary bouts, the convulsions, and the calm and the willingness.

I remember the door with the picture of the girl on it (only it was spring), her arms outstretched in loveliness, her dress (it was the one with the circle on it) uncaught, beginning the slow, clear, blinding cascade—and I guess we would all like to try that door again, for it seemed like the way and for a while it was the way, the door would open and you would go through winged and exalted (like any rat) and the food would be there, the way the Professor had it arranged, everything O.K., and you had chosen the right door for the world was young. The time they changed that door on me, my nose bled for a hundred hours—how do you like that, Madam? Or would you prefer to show me further through this so strange house, or you could take my name and send it to me, for although my heart has followed all my days something I cannot name, I am tired of the jumping and I do not know which way to go, Madam, and I am not even sure that I am not tired beyond the endurance of man (rat, if you will) and have taken leave of sanity. What are you following these days, old friend, after your recovery from the last bump? What is the name, or is it something you cannot name? The rats have a name for it by this time, perhaps, but I don't know what they call it. I call it plexikoid and it comes in sheets, something like insulating board, unattainable and ugli-proof.

And there was the man out in Jersey, because I keep thinking about his terrible necessity and the passion and trouble he had gone to all those years in the indescribable abundance of a householder's detail, building the estate and the planting of the trees and in spring the lawn-dressing and in fall the bulbs for the spring burgeoning, and the watering of the grass on the long light evenings in summer and the gravel for the driveway (all had to be thought out, planned) and the decorative borders, probably, the perennials and the bug spray, and the building of the house from plans of the architect, first the sills, then the studs, then the full corn in the ear, the floors laid on the floor timbers, smoothed, and then the carpets upon the smooth floors and the curtains and the rods therefor. And then, almost without warning, he would be jumping at the same old door and it wouldn't give: they had changed it on him, making life no longer supportable under the elms in the elm shade, under the maples in the maple shade.

"Here you have the maximum of openness in a small room."

It was impossible to say (maybe it was the city) what made him feel the way he did, and I am not the only one either, he kept thinking—ask any doctor if I am. The doctors, they know how many there are, they even know where the trouble is only they don't like to tell you about the prefrontal lobe because that means making a hole in your skull and removing the work of centuries. It took so long coming, this lobe, so many, many years. (Is it something you read in the paper, perhaps?) And now, the strain being so great, the door having been changed by the Professor once too often . . . but it only means a whiff of ether, a few deft strokes, and the higher animal becomes a little easier in his mind and more like the lower one. From now on, you see, that's the way it will be, the ones with the small prefrontal lobes will win because the other ones are hurt too much by this incessant bumping. They can stand just so much, eh, Doctor? (And what is that, pray, that you have in your hand?) Still, you never can tell, eh, Madam?

He crossed (carefully) the room, the thick carpet under him softly, and went toward the door carefully, which was glass and he could see himself in it, and which, at his approach, opened to allow him to pass through; and beyond he half expected to find one of the old doors that he had known, perhaps the one with the circle, the one with the girl her arms outstretched in loveliness and beauty before him. But he saw instead a moving stairway, and descended in light (he kept thinking) to the street below and to the other people. As he stepped off, the ground came up slightly, to meet his foot.

# YUKIO MISHIMA

# Swaddling Clothes

*Kamikuzu*
TRANSLATED BY IVAN MORRIS

Yukio Mishima (1925–1970), by birth and name Kimitake Hiraoka, was born to an honored samurai family. After establishing himself as Japan's greatest literary figure with some seventeen novels, thirty-three plays, and eighty short stories, he committed *seppuku*—a spectacular, grisly ritual suicide. As well as being a writer, he was a gifted actor and an unusually well-conditioned athlete and sportsman. A recent collection of his short stories, translated into English by Edward G. Seidensticker, is *Death in Midsummer and Other Stories*, 1966.

In Japanese the title of this story is "Kamikuzu," *wastepaper*. In it the sensitive main character tries to understand her implication in and reaction to an incident that poses questions about human worth and dignity.

He was always busy, Toshiko's husband. Even tonight he had to dash off to an appointment, leaving her to go home alone by taxi. But what else could a woman expect when she married an actor—an attractive one? No doubt she had been foolish to hope that he would spend the evening with her. And yet he must have known how she dreaded going back to their house, unhomely with its Western-style furniture and with the bloodstains still showing on the floor.

Toshiko had been oversensitive since girlhood: that was her nature. As the result of constant worrying she never put on weight, and now, an adult woman, she looked more like a transparent picture than a creature of flesh and blood. Her delicacy of spirit was evident to her most casual acquaintance.

Earlier that evening, when she had joined her husband at a night club, she had been shocked to find him entertaining friends with an account

of "the incident." Sitting there in his American-style suit, puffing at a cigarette he had seemed to her almost a stranger.

"It's a fantastic story," he was saying, gesturing flamboyantly as if in an attempt to outweigh the attractions of the dance band. "Here this new nurse for our baby arrives from the employment agency, and the very first thing I notice about her is her stomach. It's enormous—as if she had a pillow stuck under her kimono! No wonder, I thought, for I soon saw that she could eat more than the rest of us put together. She polished off the contents of our rice bin like that. . . ." He snapped his fingers. "'Gastric dilation'—that's how she explained her girth and her appetite. Well, the day before yesterday we heard groans and moans coming from the nursery. We rushed in and found her squatting on the floor, holding her stomach in her two hands, and moaning like a cow. Next to her our baby lay in his cot, scared out of his wits and crying at the top of his lungs. A pretty scene, I can tell you!"

"So the cat was out of the bag?" suggested one of their friends, a film actor like Toshiko's husband.

"Indeed it was! And it gave me the shock of my life. You see, I'd completely swallowed that story about 'gastric dilation.' Well, I didn't waste any time. I rescued our good rug from the floor and spread a blanket for her to lie on. The whole time the girl was yelling like a stuck pig. By the time the doctor from the maternity clinic arrived, the baby had already been born. But our sitting room was a pretty shambles!"

"Oh, that I'm sure of!" said another of their friends, and the whole company burst into laughter.

Toshiko was dumbfounded to hear her husband discussing the horrifying happening as though it were no more than an amusing incident which they chanced to have witnessed. She shut her eyes for a moment and all at once she saw the newborn baby lying before her: on the parquet floor the infant lay, and his frail body was wrapped in bloodstained newspapers.

Toshiko was sure that the doctor had done the whole thing out of spite. As if to emphasize his scorn for this mother who had given birth to a bastard under such sordid conditions, he had told his assistant to wrap the baby in some loose newspapers, rather than proper swaddling. This callous treatment of the newborn child had offended Toshiko. Overcoming her disgust at the entire scene, she had fetched a brand-new piece of flannel from her cupboard and, having swaddled the baby in it, had laid him carefully in an armchair.

This all had taken place in the evening after her husband had left the house. Toshiko had told him nothing of it, fearing that he would think her oversoft, oversentimental; yet the scene had engraved itself deeply in her mind. Tonight she sat silently thinking back on it, while the jazz orchestra brayed and her husband chatted cheerfully with his friends. She knew that she would never forget the sight of the baby, wrapped in stained newspapers and lying on the floor—it was a scene fit for a butchershop. Toshiko, whose own life had been spent in solid comfort, poignantly felt the wretchedness of the illegitimate baby.

I am the only person to have witnessed its shame, the thought occurred to her. The mother never saw her child lying there in its newspaper wrappings, and the baby itself of course didn't know. I alone shall have to preserve that terrible scene in my memory. When the baby grows up and wants to find out about his birth, there will

be no one to tell him, so long as I preserve silence. How strange that I should have this feeling of guilt! After all, it was I who took him up from the floor, swathed him properly in flannel, and laid him down to sleep in the armchair.

They left the night club and Toshiko stepped into the taxi that her husband had called for her. "Take this lady to Ushigomé," he told the driver and shut the door from the outside. Toshiko gazed through the window at her husband's smiling face and noticed his strong, white teeth. Then she leaned back in the seat, oppressed by the knowledge that their life together was in some way too easy, too painless. It would have been difficult for her to put her thoughts into words. Through the rear window of the taxi she took a last look at her husband. He was striding along the street toward his Nash car, and soon the back of his rather garish tweed coat had blended with the figures of the passers-by.

The taxi drove off, passed down a street dotted with bars and then by a theatre, in front of which the throngs of people jostled each other on the pavement. Although the performance had only just ended, the lights had already been turned out and in the half dark outside it was depressingly obvious that the cherry blossoms decorating the front of the theatre were merely scraps of white paper.

Even if that baby should grow up in ignorance of the secret of his birth, he can never become a respectable citizen, reflected Toshiko, pursuing the same train of thoughts. Those soiled newspaper swaddling clothes will be the symbol of his entire life. But why should I keep worrying about him so much? Is it because I feel uneasy about the future of my own child? Say twenty years from now, when our boy will have grown up into a fine, carefully educated young man, one day by a quirk of fate he meets that other boy, who then will also have turned twenty. And say that the other boy, who has been sinned against, savagely stabs him with a knife. . . .

It was a warm, overcast April night, but thoughts of the future made Toshiko feel cold and miserable. She shivered on the back seat of the car.

No, when the time comes I shall take my son's place, she told herself suddenly. Twenty years from now I shall be forty-three. I shall go to that young man and tell him straight out about everything—about his newspaper swaddling clothes, and about how I went and wrapped him in flannel.

The taxi ran along the dark wide road that was bordered by the park and by the Imperial Palace moat. In the distance Toshiko noticed the pinpricks of light which came from the blocks of tall office buildings.

Twenty years from now that wretched child will be in utter misery. He will be living a desolate, hopeless, poverty-stricken existence—a lonely rat. What else could happen to a baby who has had such a birth? He'll be wandering through the streets by himself, cursing his father, loathing his mother.

No doubt Toshiko derived a certain satisfaction from her somber thoughts: she tortured herself with them without cease. The taxi approached Hanzomon and drove past the compound of the British Embassy. At that point the famous rows of cherry trees were spread out before Toshiko in all their purity. On the spur of the moment she decided to go and view the blossoms by herself in the dark night. It was a strange decision for a timid and unadventurous young woman, but then she was in a strange state of mind and she dreaded the return home. That evening all sorts of unsettling fancies had burst open in her mind.

She crossed the wide street—a slim, solitary figure in the darkness. As a rule when she walked in the traffic Toshiko used to cling fearfully to her companion, but tonight she darted alone between the cars and a moment later had reached the long narrow park that borders the Palace moat. Chidorigafuchi, it is called—the Abyss of the Thousand Birds.

Tonight the whole park had become a grove of blossoming cherry trees. Under the calm cloudy sky the blossoms formed a mass of solid whiteness. The paper lanterns that hung from wires between the trees had been put out; in their place electric light bulbs, red, yellow, and green, shone dully beneath the blossoms. It was well past ten o'clock and most of the flower-viewers had gone home. As the occasional passers-by strolled through the park, they would automatically kick aside the empty bottles or crush the waste paper beneath their feet.

Newspapers, thought Toshiko, her mind going back once again to those happenings. Blood-stained newspapers. If a man were ever to hear of that piteous birth and know that it was he who had lain there, it would ruin his entire life. To think that I, a perfect stranger, should from now on have to keep such a secret—the secret of a man's whole existence. . . .

Lost in these thoughts, Toshiko walked on through the park. Most of the people still remaining there were quiet couples; no one paid her any attention. She noticed two people sitting on a stone bench beside the moat, not looking at the blossoms, but gazing silently at the water. Pitch black it was, and swathed in heavy shadows. Beyond the moat the somber forest of the Imperial Palace blocked her view. The trees reached up, to form a solid dark mass against the night sky. Toshiko walked slowly along the path beneath the blossoms hanging heavily overhead.

On a stone bench, slightly apart from the others, she noticed a pale object—not, as she had at first imagined, a pile of cherry blossoms, nor a garment forgotten by one of the visitors to the park. Only when she came closer did she see that it was a human form lying on the bench. Was it, she wondered, one of those miserable drunks often to be seen sleeping in public places? Obviously not, for the body had been systematically covered with newspapers, and it was the whiteness of those papers that had attracted Toshiko's attention. Standing by the bench, she gazed down at the sleeping figure.

It was a man in a brown jersey who lay there, curled up on layers of newspapers, other newspapers covering him. No doubt this had become his normal night residence now that spring had arrived. Toshiko gazed down at the man's dirty, unkempt hair, which in places had become hopelessly matted. As she observed the sleeping figure wrapped in its newspapers, she was inevitably reminded of the baby who had lain on the floor in its wretched swaddling clothes. The shoulder of the man's jersey rose and fell in the darkness in time with his heavy breathing.

It seemed to Toshiko that all her fears and premonitions had suddenly taken concrete form. In the darkness the man's pale forehead stood out, and it was a young forehead, though carved with the wrinkles of long poverty and hardship. His khaki trousers had been slightly pulled up; on his sockless feet he wore a pair of battered gym shoes. She could not see his face and suddenly had an overmastering desire to get one glimpse of it.

She walked to the head of the bench and looked down. The man's head was half buried in his arms, but Toshiko could see that he was surprisingly young. She noticed the thick eyebrows and the fine bridge of his nose. His slightly open mouth was alive with youth.

But Toshiko had approached too close. In the silent night the newspaper bedding rustled, and abruptly the man opened his eyes. Seeing the young woman standing directly beside him, he raised himself with a jerk, and his eyes lit up. A second later a powerful hand reached out and seized Toshiko by her slender wrist.

She did not feel in the least afraid and made no effort to free herself. In a flash the thought had struck her, Ah, so the twenty years have already gone by! The forest of the Imperial Palace was pitch dark and utterly silent.

## JAMES ALAN MC PHERSON

# On Trains

James Alan Mc Pherson (1943–    ), a teacher of English at Iowa State University, graduated from the Harvard Law School in 1968. In addition to articles and stories in national magazines, he has published a collection of short stories, *Hue and Cry*, 1969.

This noncommittal, scenic story presents for the reader's contemplation some of the ironies involved in race relations—and human relations.

The waiters say she got on the train in Chicago, after transferring from Dearborn Station. She was plump and matronly and her glasses were tinted so that she might have been a tourist seeking protection from the sun; but there was neither sun nor fresh air on the train and she was very pale and a little wrinkled, the way clerks or indoor people grow after many years of their protected, colorless kind of life. She was, indeed, that nondescript type of person one might be aware of but never really see in a supermarket or at a bargain basement sale, carefully and methodically fingering each item; or on a busy street corner waiting for the light to change while others, with less conscious respect for the letter of the law, flowed around her. She rode

ON TRAINS  From *Hue and Cry*. Copyright © 1968, 1969 by James Alan Mc Pherson. Reprinted by permission of Atlantic-Little, Brown and Co.

for a whole day before coming into the dining car for a meal: then she had the $1.95 Special. She asked for buttermilk and wanted "light-bread" instead of rolls. The black waiters all grinned at each other in their secret way.

When she finished her meal she sat reading a book and looking out at the yellow and green flatlands of North Dakota until the steward had to ask her to leave so that the waiters could clean up the table for the next setting. She did not protest, but left with an indignant flourish of her dress. The automatic door to the car leading to the Pullman section hissed angrily behind her. The steward called her a bitch between his teeth and the waiter who had served her, standing next to the steward with his tray under his arm, grinned broadly, showing his own smoke-stained teeth. But when he saw that she had left no tip he called her a cheap bitch aloud and the steward scowled at him.

After the last setting the waiters sat down to eat their dinner. Two Pullman porters came in with their coffee cans, begging for handouts. They were very greedy and, if given one can of free coffee, would continue to come back for more during the length of the trip, as if the first can had entitled them to all that they could drink. They sat down at the waiters' table and watched the waiters eat. The waiters were very greedy too. They ate ravenously. The porters watched the waiters for a while, then one of them closed his eyes and began to doze. The other one, an old fellow with aged and tired eyes like an owl's, looked out at the floating gold of the sunset across the passing wheatfields. He watched until the fields became patterns of black and fading gold. Then he turned to the waiters.

"We got a old Southern gal back there," he said.

"We had her up here," one of the waiters said between huge mouthfuls of beef. "She got good service but she didn't leave no tip."

"She had me polishin' her shoes," the porter said, "but I don't reckon she'll pay off when she gets off. I didn't put much work out on it anyway." He stretched his thin legs under the table. They cracked with the sound of dead autumn branches underfoot.

A woman in pants passed through the car. Her hair was cut somewhat like a little girl's Dutch Boy and a ringlet of it curled against her cheek. She blew at it out of the corner of her mouth and smiled knowingly at the men seated around the table. "Which way to the club car?" she asked. Her lipstick was above the line of her mouth so that it looked like a red moustache. She was not at all pretty and not at all young.

"Two cars ahead," one waiter said.

She turned to go, took a few steps and then looked back at the men. The two waiters were looking her over, one porter was still dozing, and the other, the tired one, was seemingly not aware of her.

"How late does it stay open?"

"Till twelve," the same waiter said.

"Chicago time," the other waiter added.

They watched her move through the door.

"She'll tip big tomorrow," one of them said.

"Yeah."

"That old biddy knows where the club car is. She been in there all day. I seen her battin' them greasy eyes at John Perry on the bar."

"Maybe he'll take care of business for her tonight," the tired Pullman porter said. But there was no humor in it, and all of their laughs were only polite.

"If he does she'll tip big tomorrow," one of the waiters said again.

The porter with the owl eyes pushed the dozing porter. "Time to get the beds down, Tim," he said. Tim got up slowly and they took their coffee cans and trudged down the aisle toward the Pullman section. As they reached the door it opened and the lady who had transferred from Dearborn came into the car. The two porters stood on either side of the aisle and let her pass between them. They wore white jackets with silver buttons which were embossed: "Pullman Company." Together with their caps with silver plates, which also read "Pullman Porter," and black pants, they looked like two painted black statues before the entrance to some fine suburban home. She did not notice them, but passed directly through the car, leaving behind her a scent of something sweet and strong.

When she entered the club car the woman with the Dutch bob was sitting at the bar talking to John Perry, the bartender, who stood behind the bar leaning with his arms on its waxed red surface. They were very close and the Dutch woman was smiling mysteriously. There was no one else in the car. The Dearborn lady seated herself at a deuce near the far end of the car and began to stare at John Perry as he said something low and soft and smile-provoking to the painted thing on the stool across from him. The Dearborn lady cleared her throat. John Perry placed his dark, thick hand closer to the other, softer hand on the bar and did not look up. The painted woman made a throaty chuckle, like the confusing sound one might hear near a car parked by a frog pond on a summer night.

"I want some service," the lady at the end of the car finally said. "I've been here for ten minutes now and I want some service."

The bartender looked annoyed as he went over to her table. "What'll it be lady?" he said. His voice was deep and smooth and almost as greasy as the painted woman's lips; and it had that familiar ring of professional servitude, which is peculiar to small, serving people who like their work.

"I want a Benedictine and brandy."

"No Benedictine. This is a train, lady."

She paused. "I'll have a crème de menthe then."

"We don't have that neither."

"Try bourbon and water, honey," the woman at the bar said, and she lifted her glass for the woman to see. "He makes it very good. I'm going to have another one myself." She looked at the bartender as she pushed a five-dollar bill across the bar. "Make yourself one too," she told him.

The lady at the deuce looked at her fiercely.

She finally ordered a rosé, paid for it, and settled back, taking turns watching the immediate reflections of the two at the bar in the window next to her face and the darkness of the passing countryside beyond their reflections. The train lumbered on and it made the only noise, save for an occasional giggle and a deep-throated chuckle from the bar. Finally the woman got up from the stool and said, "See you later on" to the bartender. She said it with a contrived, unnatural seductivity and took her time moving out of the car. The Dearborn lady, still seated at the table and facing the window, saw it all through her tinted glasses.

The bartender began to whistle as he washed the glasses. He was a robust fellow but he moved very gracefully behind the bar, like a dancer. Still, he splashed a great deal of water on the floor. He glanced over at the lady once or twice as she, in turn, looked alternately at the darkness beyond the thick window glass and at him. But only her eyes moved. Then the man moved out from behind the bar and came toward her. She stiffened and gathered her purse and got up, all very quickly. He was wiping the tables and whistling as she hurried out of the car.

## II

In the Pullman car, the porter was still making the beds. He shuffled from one roomette to the next, not wasting a single step. The occupants came out of their rooms and stood in the hall while he swished and tucked their sheets. Then he knocked on the Dearborn lady's door. "Porter!" he barked, the way a street-corner concessionaire would say "Hot Dogs!" There was no answer, so he went in and began turning down the bed. She came up behind him and watched his back as he moved about the small compartment. She was breathing very hard.

"What time do you lock the doors to the car?" she asked.

"The doors ain't never locked," he said, not turning to face her.

"How do you keep people out?" She paused, and then said: "My luggage is in the hall. It's very expensive."

"I'll watch out for it. I sit up all night."

"Inside the car?"

"Yes ma'am."

"But I . . . we have to sleep. We have to sleep in here," she said. She was very excited now.

"Yes ma'am." He did not stop his work; nor did he look at her, but answered her questions and made the bed with the proficiency and cool detachment of one used to confronting stupidity in the intelligent. It was bargained and paid for in the price of her ticket and his was a patient and polite endurance of her right to be stupid. "I'm a Pullman porter," he said. "I been a Pullman porter for forty-three years." He had finished the bed and he smoothed down a light ripple in the red blanket. His hands were rough and wrinkled and the backs of his fingers were very black. "Forty-three years," he repeated reminiscently, half to himself. She could not see his eyes.

"Well, you can't stay in here tonight," she said, and moved into the small compartment as if to possess it entirely with her presence.

The porter backed out. "It's my job," he said.

She was extremely nervous now and ran her hands lightly over the sides of her dress. Her hands stuck to the thin silk. "You go get the Pullman Conductor," she said. "I can talk to him." She began to pace up and down the little length of the roomette.

The porter returned in a few minutes with the Pullman Conductor. The blue-suited conductor entered the compartment while the porter stood outside the door and watched them, his dark old eyes flashing from one face to the other.

"He sits up in the car, lady," the conductor said. "It's his job. He has to be here if anyone rings for him at night." The conductor was very irritated. He had already started to undress for bed and his tie hung loosely about his neck. The lady was perspiring now and the little beads of sweat glistened on her temples in the glare of the white light overhead.

"I can't and I won't sleep in the same car with that . . . that gentleman!"

"That's your business if you don't sleep, lady," the conductor said. "He stays in the car." The conductor was very mad now. The lines in his forehead grew very red and his nose, which was small, grew larger and redder with his controlled breathing.

"We have a *right* to sleep here without these people coming in *doing* things."

"What's he done to you, lady?"

"He's black! He's black!" And she said it with the exasperation and utter defeat of an inexperienced teacher whose patience has been exhausted and who can only stamp the right answer into the mind of a stupid child.

"He's a porter," the conductor said.

The porter, who stood all the while like a child waiting for punishment, seemed to droop and wither and grow smaller; and his eyes, which had only minutes before flashed brightly from the face of the conductor to the enraged face of the lady, now seemed to dull and turn inward as only those who have learned to suffer silently can turn their eyes inward. He was a very old man and he grew older, even older than his occupation or the oldest and most obsequious Pullman porter.

People were looking out of their compartments and the Dearborn lady, hearing them, raised her voice in a plea. "He sleeps in here. He sleeps in here with us!" she shouted to them. Down the hall, the painted woman opened the door to Compartment G and listened and smiled and shook her head, and then closed the door again. And the rest listened and weighed the thought, which was a new one deserving some consideration. But the conductor said that it was necessary for comfort and they agreed and returned to their rooms. Only the porter stood outside the door looking guilty.

It was finally decided that the Dearborn lady would take a seat in the coaches for the night. She wanted it that way. The porter would sleep as he had always slept: sitting up in the back of the car with his eyes closed and his mind awake and his coffee can by his side and the small bright night-light over his bowed head, and his ear next to the buzzer in case someone should ring. Everyone agreed that it was the way things should be; it was necessary for comfort, and besides, it was his job.

And later that night, when John Perry, the bartender, who danced and splashed a great deal of water when he washed glasses, stole into the dark sleeping car, he paused for a minute before the bent old man on the porter's seat. The coffee can had fallen over on the seat and John Perry picked it up and placed it on the floor next to the old man's feet. Then he knocked very softly on the door to Compartment G. And after a while it was opened and quickly closed behind him.

# LANGSTON HUGHES

# On the Road

Langston Hughes (1902–1967) attended Columbia and Lincoln universities. He was a literary contributor to the Harlem Renaissance, a black cultural movement; an editor and anthologizer of the works of his people; and a prolific writer—especially of short stories and poems. His autobiography, *The Big Sea*, was issued in 1940; *Selected Poems* appeared in 1965. In 1966 *The Langston Hughes Reader* supplied a representative selection of his many writings. In the year of his death, 1967, a further work, *The Panther and the Lash*, appeared.

"On the Road" is a symbolic story about racism and charity.

He was not interested in the snow. When he got off the freight, one early evening during the depression, Sargeant never even noticed the snow. But he must have felt it seeping down his neck, cold, wet, sopping in his shoes. But if you had asked him, he wouldn't have known it was snowing. Sargeant didn't see the snow, not even under the bright lights of the main street, falling white and flaky against the night. He was too hungry, too sleepy, too tired.

The Reverend Mr. Dorset, however, saw the snow when he switched on his porch light, opened the front door of his parsonage, and found standing there before him a big black man with snow on his face, a human piece of night with snow on his face—obviously unemployed.

Said the Reverend Mr. Dorset before Sargeant even realized he'd opened his mouth: "I'm sorry. No! Go right on down this street four blocks and turn to your left, walk up seven and you'll see the Relief Shelter. I'm sorry. No!" He shut the door.

Sargeant wanted to tell the holy man that he had already been to the Relief Shelter, been to hundreds of relief shelters during the depression

years, the beds were always gone and supper was over, the place was full, and they drew the color line anyhow. But the minister said, "No," and shut the door. Evidently he didn't want to hear about it. And he *had* a door to shut.

The big black man turned away. And even yet he didn't see the snow, walking right into it. Maybe he sensed it, cold, wet, sticking to his jaws, wet on his black hands, sopping in his shoes. He stopped and stood on the sidewalk hunched over—hungry, sleepy, cold—looking up and down. Then he looked right where he was—in front of a church. Of course! A church! Sure, right next to a parsonage, certainly a church.

It had *two* doors.

Broad white steps in the night all snowy white. Two high arched doors with slender stone pillars on either side. And way up, a round lacy window with a stone crucifix in the middle and Christ on the crucifix in stone. All this was pale in the street lights, solid and stony pale in the snow.

Sargeant blinked. When he looked up, the snow fell into his eyes. For the first time that night he *saw* the snow. He shook his head. He shook the snow from his coat sleeves, felt hungry, felt lost, felt not lost, felt cold. He walked up the steps of the church. He knocked at the door. No answer. He tried the handle. Locked. He put his shoulder against the door and his long black body slanted like a ramrod. He pushed. With loud rhythmic grunts, like the grunts in a chain-gang song, he pushed against the door.

"I'm tired . . . Huh! . . . Hongry . . . Uh! . . . I'm sleepy . . . Huh! I'm cold . . . I got to sleep somewheres," Sargeant said. "This here is a church, ain't it? Well, uh!"

He pushed against the door.

Suddenly, with an undue cracking and screaking the door began to give way to the tall black Negro who pushed ferociously against it.

By now two or three white people had stopped in the street, and Sargeant was vaguely aware of some of them yelling at him concerning the door. Three or four more came running, yelling at him.

"Hey!" they said. "Hey!"

"Uh-huh," answered the big tall Negro, "I know it's a white folks' church, but I got to sleep somewhere." He gave another lunge at the door. "Huh!"

And the door broke open.

But just when the door gave way, two white cops arrived in a car, ran up the steps with their clubs, and grabbed Sargeant. But Sargeant for once had no intention of being pulled or pushed away from the door.

Sargeant grabbed, but not for anything so weak as a broken door. He grabbed for one of the tall stone pillars beside the door, grabbed at it and caught it. And held it. The cops pulled and Sargeant pulled. Most of the people in the street got behind the cops and helped them pull.

"A big black unemployed Negro holding onto our church!" thought the people. "The idea!"

The cops began to beat Sargeant over the head, and nobody protested. But he held on.

And then the church fell down.

Gradually, the big stone front of the church fell down, the walls and the rafters, the crucifix and the Christ. Then the whole thing fell down, covering the cops and the people with bricks and stones and debris. The whole church fell down in the snow.

Sargeant got out from under the church and went walking on up the street with the stone pillar on his shoulder. He was under the impression that he had buried the parsonage and the Reverend Mr. Dorset who said, "No!" So he laughed, and threw the pillar six blocks up the street and went on.

Sargeant thought he was alone, but listening

to the *crunch, crunch, crunch* on the snow of his own footsteps, he heard other footsteps, too, doubling his own. He looked around, and there was Christ walking along beside him, the same Christ that had been on the cross on the church—still stone with a rough stone surface, walking along beside him just like he was broken off the cross when the church fell down.

"Well, I'll be dogged," said Sargeant. "This here's the first time I ever seed you off the cross."

"Yes," said Christ, crunching his feet in the snow. "You had to pull the church down to get me off the cross."

"You glad?" said Sargeant.

"I sure am," said Christ.

They both laughed.

"I'm a hell of a fellow, ain't I?" said Sargeant. "Done pulled the church down!"

"You did a good job," said Christ. "They have kept me nailed on a cross for nearly two thousand years."

"Whee-ee-e!" said Sargeant. "I know you are glad to get off."

"I sure am," said Christ.

They walked on in the snow. Sargeant looked at the man of stone.

"And you have been up there two thousand years?"

"I sure have," Christ said.

"Well, if I had a little cash," said Sargeant, "I'd show you around a bit."

"I been around," said Christ.

"Yeah, but that was a long time ago."

"All the same," said Christ, "I've been around."

They walked on in the snow until they came to the railroad yards. Sargeant was tired, sweating and tired.

"Where you goin'?" Sargeant said, stopping by the tracks. He looked at Christ. Sargeant said, "I'm just a bum on the road. How about you? Where you goin'?"

"God knows," Christ said, "but I'm leavin' here."

They saw the red and green lights of the railroad yard half veiled by the snow that fell out of the night. Away down the track they saw a fire in a hobo jungle.

"I can go there and sleep," Sargeant said.

"You can?"

"Sure," said Sargeant. "That place ain't got no doors."

Outside the town, along the tracks, there were barren trees and bushes below the embankment, snow-gray in the dark. And down among the trees and bushes there were makeshift houses made out of boxes and tin and old pieces of wood and canvas. You couldn't see them in the dark, but you knew they were there if you'd ever been on the road, if you had ever lived with the homeless and hungry in a depression.

"I'm side-tracking," Sargeant said. "I'm tired."

"I'm gonna make it on to Kansas City," said Christ.

"O.K.," Sargeant said. "So long!"

He went down into the hobo jungle and found himself a place to sleep. He never did see Christ no more. About 6:00 A.M. a freight came by. Sargeant scrambled out of the jungle with a dozen or so more hobos and ran along the track, grabbing at the freight. It was dawn, early dawn, cold and gray.

"Wonder where Christ is by now?" Sargeant thought. "He musta gone on way on down the road. He didn't sleep in this jungle."

Sargeant grabbed the train and started to pull himself up into a moving coal car, over the edge of a wheeling coal car. But strangely enough, the car was full of cops. The nearest cop rapped Sargeant soundly across the knuckles with his night stick. Wham! Rapped his big black hands for clinging to the top of the car. Wham! But Sargeant did not turn loose. He clung on and tried to pull himself into the car. He hollered at the top of his voice, "Damn it, lemme in this car!"

"Shut up," barked the cop. "You crazy coon!" He rapped Sargeant across the knuckles and punched him in the stomach. "You ain't out in no jungle now. This ain't no train. You in jail."

Wham! across his bare black fingers clinging to the bars of his cell. Wham! between the steel bars low down against his shins.

Suddenly Sargeant realized that he really was in jail. He wasn't on no train. The blood of the night before had dried on his face, his head hurt terribly, and a cop outside in the corridor was hitting him across the knuckles for holding onto the door, yelling and shaking the cell door.

"They musta took me to jail for breaking down the door last night," Sargeant thought, "that church door."

Sargeant went over and sat on a wooden bench against the cold stone wall. He was emptier than ever. His clothes were wet, clammy cold wet, and shoes sloppy with snow water. It was just about dawn. There he was, locked up behind a cell door, nursing his bruised fingers.

The bruised fingers were his, but not the *door*. Not the *club*, but the fingers.

"You wait," mumbled Sargeant, black against the jail wall. "I'm gonna break down this door, too."

"Shut up—or I'll paste you one," said the cop.

"I'm gonna break down this door," yelled Sargeant as he stood up in his cell.

Then he must have been talking to himself because he said, "I wonder where Christ's gone? I wonder if he's gone to Kansas City?"

# ISAAC BABEL

# Shabos Nahamu

Isaak Emmanuilovich Babel (1894–1941), born in Odessa, was of Jewish middle-class origin. Stalinist censorship limited his productivity, often deterring him from attempting to publish or rejecting most of what he did submit. Consequently, his reputation—now international in scope—is based chiefly upon some fifty short stories, although he also published one play, *Marya*, 1935, and a few miscellaneous works. His service in the Red Army figures prominently as background in the one collection of his stories published in his lifetime, *Red Cavalry*, 1926. He was arrested in 1939, his manuscripts seized and doubtless destroyed. From that time until 1957 his works were suppressed in Russia, but since then, a gradual attempt has been made to do them justice both at home and abroad. His *Collected Stories*, edited and translated into English by Walter Morison, appeared in 1955. *You Must Know Everything Stories, 1915–1937*, a later presentation of his fiction and the source of the following story, was published in 1966.

In this Decameron-like folk story the opportunist Hershele softens his harsh lot by fleecing a pair of fools who invite and deserve the treatment he gives them.

The morning goes by, the evening comes—and it's the fifth day of the week. Another morning goes by, the evening comes—and it's the sixth day. On the sixth day, on Friday, you have to pray. When you've prayed, you take a stroll through the *shtetl* in your best hat and then come back home for supper. When he gets home, a good Jew has a glass of vodka—neither God nor the Talmud says he can't have two—and eats his gefilte fish and his currant cake. After supper he feels good. He tells stories to his wife; then he goes to sleep with one eye closed and his mouth open. He sleeps, but his wife in the kitchen hears music, as though the blind fiddler had come from the *shtetl* and was standing under the window playing.

That's how it is with every Jew. But Hershele was different from other Jews. No wonder he was famous in all of Ostropole, in all of Berdichev,

and in all of Vilyuisk. Hershele celebrated only one Friday in six. On the others he sat with his family in the darkness and cold. His children cried, and his wife gave him hell. Each reproach was as heavy as a cobblestone. Hershele used to answer back in verse.

Once, so the story goes, Hershele thought he would look ahead a little. He went off to the fair on Wednesday to earn some money for Friday. Where there's a fair you'll find a *pan*, and where there's a *pan* you'll find ten Jews. But you'd be lucky to earn three pennies from ten Jews. They all listened to Hershele's funny stories, but when it was time to pay, they weren't around any more. Hershele went back home with a belly as empty as a wind instrument.

"What did you earn?" his wife asked.

"I earned life everlasting," he said, "Both the rich and the poor promised it to me."

Hershele's wife had only ten fingers. She bent them back one by one. Her voice was like thunder in the mountains. "Every other wife has a husband like everybody else's. But I have a husband who feeds his wife on funny stories. May God take away the use of his tongue, and his hands, and his feet in the New Year."

"Amen," Hershele said.

"In everybody else's windows the candles burn as if they'd set fire to oak trees in the house, but I have candles as thin as matches, and there's so much smoke from them it shoots up to heaven. Everybody else has white bread, but all my husband brings me is firewood as wet as newly washed hair—"

Hershele said not a single word in reply. Why add fuel to the flames when they're burning so brightly as it is? That's point number one. And then, point number two, what can you say to a cantankerous wife when she's right? When she got tired of shouting, Hershele went and lay down on his bed and thought, "Maybe I should go and see Rabbi Boruhl?" (Everybody knew that Rabbi Boruhl suffered from black melancholia and that only Hershele with his talk could make him feel better.) "Maybe I should go to Rabbi Boruhl? It's true the *tsadik's* servants give me only bones and keep the meat for themselves. Meat is better than bones, but bones are better than air. I'll go to Rabbi Boruhl."

Hershele got up and went out to harness his mare. She gave him a stern and sad look.

"It's all very well, Hershele," her eyes said, "you didn't give me any oats yesterday, you didn't give me any oats the day before yesterday, and I didn't get anything today either. If you don't give me any oats tomorrow, I'll have to start thinking about whether I'm going to live."

Hershele flinched before her searching look, lowered his eyes, and stroked her soft lips. Then he sighed so loud that the mare understood everything, and he said: "I'll go to Rabbi Boruhl on foot."

When Hershele set off, the sun was high in the sky. The sweltering road ran on ahead. Carts drawn by white oxen and piled with sweet-smelling hay lumbered slowly along. Peasants sat on these high carts, dangling their legs and swishing their long whips. The sky was dark blue, and the whips were black. When he'd gone about five miles, Hershele reached a forest. The sun was already leaving its place in the sky, which was ablaze with gentle fires. Barefoot girls were bringing the cows in from the fields. The cows' pink udders, heavy with milk, swayed to and fro.

The forest met Hershele with cool shade and soft twilight. Green leaves bent over and stroked each other with their flat hands, whispered together faintly up there in the treetops, and then fell back, rustling and quivering, into their places. Hershele did not hear their whispering. The orchestra playing in his belly was as big as anything hired by Count Potocki for a gala evening. He still had a long way to go. Dusk was hurrying in from the edges of the earth, closing in over Hershele's head, and spreading out across the world. Unblinking lamps lit in the sky, and the earth fell silent.

It was night when Hershele arrived at an inn. A light was burning in a small window. Zelda, the landlady, was sitting in her warm room by this window, sewing baby clothes. Her belly was so big it looked as if she were going to have triplets. Hershele looked at her small red face with its light-blue eyes and wished her good evening. "Can I stop here and rest for a while, ma'am?"

"Sure you can."

Hershele sat down. His nostrils heaved like a pair of blacksmith's bellows. There was a red-hot fire blazing in the stove. Water was boiling in a large caldron and frothing over snow-white dumplings. A fat chicken was bobbing up and down in a golden broth. There was a smell of currant cake from the oven. Hershele sat on a bench writhing like a woman in labor. More plans were hatching in his head at that moment than King Solomon ever had wives. It was quiet in the room, the water was boiling, and the chicken tossed and pitched on its golden waves.

"Where is your husband, ma'am?" Hershele asked.

"My husband has gone to the *pan* to pay his rent," she said, and paused. Her childlike eyes grew round and large. Suddenly she went on: "And I am sitting here at the window thinking. I would like to ask you a question. I suppose you travel up and down the world, and you've studied with the rabbi, and you know about our Jewish ways. But nobody ever taught me anything. Tell me: will *shabos nahamu* be coming soon?"

"Oho," thought Hershele, "a very good question indeed. All kinds of potatoes grow in God's garden."

"I'm asking because my husband promised me

that when *shabos nahamu* comes, we'll go and visit my mother. And I'll buy you a dress, he says, and a new wig, and we'll go to Rabbi Motalemi to ask him for a son to be born to us instead of a daughter. But that will only be when *shabos nahamu* comes. I suppose he's a man from the other world, this *shabos nahamu*?"

"You are quite right, ma'am," Hershele replied. "God himself put those words into your mouth. You will have both a son and a daughter. I am *shabos nahamu*, ma'am."

The baby clothes slipped from Zelda's knees. She got up and bumped her head on a rafter, because she was tall, Zelda was, and plump and red and young. Her high breasts looked like two bags tightly packed with grain. Her light-blue eyes opened wide like a child's.

"I am *shabos nahamu*," Hershele repeated. "For two months now I've been doing my rounds, helping people. It's a long journey from heaven down to earth. My shoes are all worn out. I bring you greetings from all your people up there."

"From Aunt Pesya?" Zelda shouted, "and from Father, and from Aunt Golda? You know them?"

"Who doesn't know them?" Hershele said. "I often talk with them just like I'm talking with you now."

"How are they getting on up there?" Zelda asked, clasping her trembling hands on her belly.

"Not too well," Hershele replied sadly. "What sort of life do you think it is for a dead person? There isn't much fun up there."

Zelda's eyes filled with tears.

"They're cold," Hershele went on, "and hungry. They eat the same as angels, you see. They're not supposed to eat more than the angels. And how much do angels eat? They're quite happy with a drink of water. You wouldn't get a glass of vodka up there once in a hundred years."

"Poor Father," Zelda whispered, quite shaken.

"At Passover you get a *latke*, and one blintze has to last you twenty-four hours."

"Poor Aunt Pesya," Zelda shuddered.

"I have to go hungry myself," Hershele continued, and turned his face away as a tear rolled down his nose and fell into his beard. "There's nothing I can do about it, you see: up there I'm treated like everybody else—"

Hershele didn't manage to get any further.

With a patter of her large feet, Zelda bore down on him with plates, bowls, glasses, and bottles. When Hershele began to eat, she saw that he really was a man from the other world.

To start off with, Hershele had chicken liver garnished with fat and chopped onion. He drank it down with a glass of high-class vodka flavored with orange peel. Then he had fish, mashing soft boiled potatoes into the savory sauce that went with it and putting half a jarful of red horseradish on the side of his plate—a horseradish at the mere sight of which five *pans* in all their finery would have wept tears of envy.

After the fish Hershele did his duty by the chicken and the broth with blobs of fat swimming in it. The dumplings, bathed in molten butter, jumped into Hershele's mouth like hares fleeing from a hunter. We don't have to say anything about what happened to the currant cake. What do you think happened to it, if you consider that Hershele sometimes never saw a currant cake from one end of the year to the other?

When he had finished, Zelda got together all the things that she had decided to ask Hershele to take to the other world for Father, Aunt Pesya, and Aunt Golda. For her father she put out a new prayer shawl, a bottle of cherry brandy, a jar of raspberry jam, and a pouch full of tobacco. For Aunt Pesya she got out some warm gray socks, and for Aunt Golda an old wig, a large comb, and a prayer book. Lastly, she gave Hershele a pair of boots, some goose cracklings, and a silver coin.

"Give them our regards, Mister Shabos Nahamu, give them all our kind regards" were her parting words to Hershele as he set off with the heavy bundle. "Or would you like to wait a little until my husband comes back?"

"No," said Hershele. "I must be on my way. You don't think you're the only one I have to look after, do you?"

When he had gone about a mile, Hershele stopped to draw breath, threw the bundle down, sat on it, and took stock of the situation. "As you well know, Hershele," he said to himself, "the world is full of fools. The landlady in that inn was a fool. But perhaps her husband is not a fool, perhaps he has large fists, fat cheeks, and a long whip. If he comes home and chases after you in the forest, what then?"

Hershele wasted no time seeking an answer to this question. He immediately buried the bundle in the ground and marked the spot so that he would be able to find it again.

Then he ran back the way he had come, stripped naked, put his arms around a tree, and began to wait. He did not have to wait long. At dawn Hershele heard the crack of a whip, the smacking lips of a horse and the thud of its hooves. This was the innkeeper in hot pursuit of Mister Shabos Nahamu.

When he reached the naked Hershele with his arms around a tree, the innkeeper stopped his horse and looked as silly as a monk on meeting the devil.

"What are you doing here?" he asked.

"I am a man from the other world," Hershele replied gloomily. "I have been robbed of important papers which I was taking to Rabbi Boruhl."

"I know who robbed you," shouted the innkeeper. "I have a bone to pick with him too. Which way did he go?"

"I cannot tell you which way he went," Hershele whispered bitterly. "If you will lend me your horse I will soon catch up with him, while you wait for me here. Undress and stand by this tree. Hold it up and do not leave it until I return. It is a holy tree, and many things in our world depend on it."

Hershele only had to take one look at a man to see what he was made of. He had seen right away that the innkeeper was not much brighter than his wife. And sure enough, the innkeeper got undressed and stood by the tree. Hershele climbed onto the cart and drove back to where he had left the bundle. He dug it up and went on to the edge of the forest.

Here Hershele shouldered the bundle again, left the horse, and took the road which led to the house of the holy Rabbi Boruhl. It was morning already. The roosters were crowing with their eyes shut. The innkeeper's horse wearily plodded back with the empty cart to the place where she had left her master.

He was waiting for her, huddled against the tree, naked under the rays of the rising sun. He was cold, and he kept shifting from foot to foot.

## EUDORA WELTY

# A Worn Path

Eudora Welty (1909–      ) lives in Jackson, Mississippi, where she was born. She was educated at Mississippi State College for Women, the University of Wisconsin, where she took her A.B. degree, and Columbia University. After the publication of her first few short stories, mainly in the *Southern Review,* her stories began to appear in almost every reputable anthology. Her books include *A Curtain of Green,* 1941; *The Wide Net,* 1943; *Delta Wedding,* 1946; *The Golden Apples,* 1949; *The Ponder Heart,* 1954; *The Bride of the Innisfallen,* 1955; *The Shoe Bird,* 1964, a children's story; *Losing Battles,* 1970; *One Time, One Place,* 1971; and *The Optimist's Daughter,* 1972.

"A Worn Path," typically Welty in its Southern setting and its familiar-grotesque main character, is among her best short stories. The odyssey of Phoenix Jackson is a warm and moving story, because the difficulties of this frail old woman's life are transformed by her innocence and dignity into something close to joy.

It was December—a bright frozen day in the early morning. Far out in the country there was an old Negro woman with her head tied in a red rag, coming along a path through the pinewoods. Her name was Phoenix Jackson. She was very old and small and she walked slowly in the dark pine shadows, moving a little from side to side in her steps, with the balanced heaviness and lightness of a pendulum in a grandfather clock. She carried a thin, small cane made from an umbrella, and with this she kept tapping the frozen earth in front of her. This made a grave and persistent noise in the still air, that seemed meditative like the chirping of a solitary little bird.

She wore a dark striped dress reaching down to her shoe tops, and an equally long apron of bleached sugar sacks, with a full pocket: all neat and tidy, but every time she took a step she might have fallen over her shoelaces, which dragged from her unlaced shoes. She looked straight ahead. Her eyes were blue with age. Her skin had a pattern all its own of numberless branching wrinkles and as though a whole little tree stood in the middle of her forehead, but a golden color ran underneath, and the two knobs of her cheeks were illumined by a yellow burning under the dark. Under the red rag her hair came down on her neck in the frailest of ringlets, still black, and with an odor like copper.

Now and then there was a quivering in the thicket. Old Phoenix said, "Out of my way, all you foxes, owls, beetles, jack rabbits, coons and wild animals! . . . Keep out from under these feet, little bob-whites. . . . Keep the big wild hogs out of my path. Don't let none of those come running my direction. I got a long way." Under her small black-freckled hand her cane, limber as a buggy whip, would switch at the brush as if to rouse up any hiding things.

On she went. The woods were deep and still. The sun made the pine needles almost too bright to look at, up where the wind rocked. The cones dropped as light as feathers. Down in the hollow was the mourning dove—it was not too late for him.

The path ran up a hill. "Seem like there is chains about my feet, time I get this far," she said, in the voice of argument old people keep to use with themselves. "Something always take a hold of me on this hill—pleads I should stay."

After she got to the top she turned and gave a full, severe look behind her where she had come. "Up through pines," she said at length. "Now down through oaks."

Her eyes opened their widest, and she started down gently. But before she got to the bottom of the hill a bush caught her dress.

Her fingers were busy and intent, but her skirts were full and long, so that before she could pull them free in one place they were caught in another. It was not possible to allow the dress to tear. "I in the thorny bush," she said. "Thorns, you doing your appointed work. Never want to let folks pass, no sir. Old eyes thought you was a pretty little *green* bush."

Finally, trembling all over, she stood free, and after a moment dared to stoop for her cane.

"Sun so high!" she cried, leaning back and looking, while the thick tears went over her eyes. "The time getting all gone here."

At the foot of this hill was a place where a log was laid across the creek.

"Now comes the trial," said Phoenix.

Putting her right foot out, she mounted the log and shut her eyes. Lifting her skirt, leveling her cane fiercely before her, like a festival figure in some parade, she began to march across. Then she opened her eyes and she was safe on the other side.

"I wasn't as old as I thought," she said.

But she sat down to rest. She spread her skirts on the bank around her and folded her hands over her knees. Up above her was a tree in a pearly cloud of mistletoe. She did not dare to close her eyes, and when a little boy brought her a plate with a slice of marble-cake on it she spoke to him. "That would be acceptable," she said. But when she went to take it there was just her own hand in the air.

So she left that tree, and had to go through a barbed-wire fence. There she had to creep and crawl, spreading her knees and stretching her fingers like a baby trying to climb the steps. But she talked loudly to herself: she could not let her dress be torn now, so late in the day, and she could not pay for having her arm or her leg sawed off if she got caught fast where she was.

At last she was safe through the fence and risen up out in the clearing. Big dead trees, like black men with one arm, were standing in the purple stalks of the withered cotton field. There sat a buzzard.

"Who you watching?"

In the furrow she made her way along.

"Glad this not the season for bulls," she said, looking sideways, "and the good Lord made his snakes to curl up and sleep in the winter. A pleasure I don't see no two-headed snake coming around that tree, where it come once. It took a while to get by him, back in the summer."

She passed through the old cotton and went into a field of dead corn. It whispered and shook and was taller than her head. "Through the maze now," she said, for there was no path.

Then there was something tall, black, and skinny there, moving before her.

At first she took it for a man. It could have been a man dancing in the field. But she stood still and listened, and it did not make a sound. It was as silent as a ghost.

"Ghost," she said sharply, "who be you the ghost of? For I have heard of nary death close by."

But there was no answer—only the ragged dancing in the wind.

She shut her eyes, reached out her hand, and touched a sleeve. She found a coat and inside that an emptiness, cold as ice.

"You scarecrow," she said. Her face lighted. "I ought to be shut up for good," she said with laughter. "My senses is gone. I too old. I the oldest people I ever know. Dance, old scarecrow," she said, "while I dancing with you."

She kicked her foot over the furrow and, with mouth drawn down, shook her head once or twice in a little strutting way. Some husks blew down and whirled in streamers about her skirts.

Then she went on, parting her way from side to side with the cane, through the whispering field. At last she came to the end, to a wagon track where the silver grass blew between the red ruts. The quail were walking around like pullets, seeming all dainty and unseen.

"Walk pretty," she said. "This the easy place. This the easy going."

She followed the track, swaying through the quiet bare fields, through the little strings of trees silver in their dead leaves, past cabins silver from weather, with the doors and windows boarded shut, all like old women under a spell sitting there. "I walking in their sleep," she said, nodding her head vigorously.

In a ravine she went where a spring was silently flowing through a hollow log. Old Phoenix bent and drank. "Sweet-gum makes the water sweet," she said, and drank more. "Nobody know who made this well, for it was here when I was born."

The track crossed a swampy part where the moss hung as white as lace from every limb. "Sleep on, alligators, and blow your bubbles." Then the track went into the road.

Deep, deep the road went down between the high green-colored banks. Overhead the live-oaks met, and it was as dark as a cave.

A black dog with a lolling tongue came up out of the weeds by the ditch. She was meditating, and not ready, and when he came at her she only hit him a little with her cane. Over she went in the ditch, like a little puff of milkweed.

Down there, her senses drifted away. A dream visited her, and she reached her hand up, but nothing reached down and gave her a pull. So she lay there and presently went to talking. "Old woman," she said to herself, "that black dog come up out of the weeds to stall you off, and now there he sitting on his fine tail, smiling at you."

A white man finally came along and found her—a hunter, a young man, with his dog on a chain.

"Well, Granny!" he laughed. "What are you doing there?"

"Lying on my back like a June-bug waiting to be turned over, mister," she said, reaching up her hand.

He lifted her up, gave her a swing in the air, and set her down. "Anything broken, Granny?"

"No sir, them old dead weeds is springy enough," said Phoenix, when she had got her breath. "I thank you for your trouble."

"Where do you live, Granny?" he asked, while the two dogs were growling at each other.

"Away back yonder, sir, behind the ridge. You can't even see it from here."

"On your way home?"

"No sir, I going to town."

"Why, that's too far! That's as far as I walk when I come out myself, and I get something for my trouble." He patted the stuffed bag he carried, and there hung down a little closed claw. It was one of the bob-whites, with its beak hooked bitterly to show it was dead. "Now you go on home, Granny!"

"I bound to go to town, mister," said Phoenix. "The time come around."

He gave another laugh, filling the whole landscape. "I know you old colored people! Wouldn't miss going to town to see Santa Claus!"

But something held old Phoenix very still. The deep lines in her face went into a fierce and different radiation. Without warning, she had seen with her own eyes a flashing nickel fall out of the man's pocket onto the ground.

"How old are you, Granny?" he was saying.

"There is no telling, mister," she said, "no telling."

Then she gave a little cry and clapped her hands and said, "Git on away from here, dog! Look! Look at that dog!" She laughed as if in admiration. "He ain't scared of nobody. He a big black dog." She whispered, "Sic him!"

"Watch me get rid of that cur," said the man. "Sic him, Pete! Sic him!"

Phoenix heard the dogs fighting, and heard the man running and throwing sticks. She even heard a gunshot. But she was slowly bending forward by that time, further and further forward, the lids stretched down over her eyes, as if she were doing this in her sleep. Her chin was lowered almost to her knees. The yellow palm of her hand came out from the fold of her apron. Her fingers slid down and along the ground under the piece of money with the grace and care they would have in lifting an egg from under a setting hen. Then she slowly straightened up, she stood erect, and the nickel was in her apron pocket. A bird flew by. Her lips moved. "God watching me the whole time. I come to stealing."

The man came back, and his own dog panted about them. "Well, I scared him off that time," he said, and then he laughed and lifted his gun and pointed it at Phoenix.

She stood straight and faced him.

"Doesn't the gun scare you?" he said, still pointing it.

"No, sir, I seen plenty go off closer by, in my day, and for less than what I done," she said, holding utterly still.

He smiled, and shouldered the gun. "Well, Granny," he said, "you must be a hundred years old, and scared of nothing. I'd give you a dime if I had any money with me. But you take my advice and stay home, and nothing will happen to you."

"I bound to go on my way, mister," said Phoenix. She inclined her head in the red rag. Then they went in different directions, but she could hear the gun shooting again and again over the hill.

She walked on. The shadows hung from the oak trees to the road like curtains. Then she smelled wood-smoke, and smelled the river, and she saw a steeple and the cabins on their steep steps. Dozens of little black children whirled around her. There ahead was Natchez shining. Bells were ringing. She walked on.

In the paved city it was Christmas time. There were red and green electric lights strung and criss-crossed everywhere, and all turned on in the daytime. Old Phoenix would have been lost if she had not distrusted her eyesight and depended on her feet to know where to take her.

She paused quietly on the sidewalk where people were passing by. A lady came along in the crowd, carrying an armful of red-, green- and silver-wrapped presents; she gave off perfume like the red roses in hot summer, and Phoenix stopped her.

"Please, missy, will you lace up my shoe?" She held up her foot.

"What do you want, Grandma?"

"See my shoe," said Phoenix. "Do all right for out in the country, but wouldn't look right to go in a big building."

"Stand still then, Grandma," said the lady. She put her packages down on the sidewalk beside her and laced and tied both shoes tightly.

"Can't lace 'em with a cane," said Phoenix. "Thank you, missy, I doesn't mind asking a nice lady to tie up my shoe, when I gets out on the street."

Moving slowly and from side to side, she went into the big building, and into a tower of steps, where she walked up and around and around until her feet knew to stop.

She entered a door, and there she saw nailed up on the wall the document that had been stamped with the gold seal and framed in the gold frame, which matched the dream that was hung up in her head.

"Here I be," she said. There was a fixed and ceremonial stiffness over her body.

"A charity case, I suppose," said an attendant who sat at the desk before her.

But Phoenix only looked above her head. There was sweat on her face, the wrinkles in her skin shone like a bright net.

"Speak up, Grandma," the woman said. "What's your name? We must have your history, you know. Have you been here before? What seems to be the trouble with you?"

Old Phoenix only gave a twitch to her face as if a fly were bothering her.

"Are you deaf?" cried the attendant.

But then the nurse came in.

"Oh, that's just old Aunt Phoenix," she said. "She doesn't come for herself—she has a little grandson. She makes these trips just as regular as clockwork. She lives away back off the Old Natchez Trace." She bent down. "Well, Aunt Phoenix, why don't you just take a seat? We won't keep you standing after your long trip." She pointed.

The old woman sat down, bolt upright in the chair.

"Now, how is the boy?" asked the nurse.

Old Phoenix did not speak.

"I said, how is the boy?"

But Phoenix only waited and stared straight ahead, her face very solemn and withdrawn into rigidity.

"Is his throat any better?" asked the nurse. "Aunt Phoenix, don't you hear me? Is your grandson's throat any better since the last time you came for the medicine?"

With her hands on her knees, the old woman waited, silent, erect and motionless, just as if she were in armor.

"You musn't take up our time this way, Aunt Phoenix," the nurse said. "Tell us quickly about your grandson, and get it over. He isn't dead, is he?"

At last there came a flicker and then a flame of comprehension across her face, and she spoke.

"My grandson. It was my memory had left me. There I sat and forgot why I made my long trip."

"Forgot?" The nurse frowned. "After you came so far?"

Then Phoenix was like an old woman begging a dignified forgiveness for waking up frightened in the night. "I never did go to school, I was too old at the Surrender," she said in a soft voice. "I'm an old woman without an education. It was my memory fail me. My little grandson, he is just the same, and I forgot it in the coming."

"Throat never heals, does it?" said the nurse, speaking in a loud, sure voice to old Phoenix. By now she had a card with something written on it, a little list. "Yes. Swallowed lye. When was it?—January—two-three years ago—"

Phoenix spoke unasked now. "No, missy, he not dead, he just the same. Every little while his throat begin to close up again, and he not able to swallow. He not get his breath. He not able to help himself. So the time come around, and I go on another trip for the soothing medicine."

"All right. The doctor said as long as you came to get it, you could have it," said the nurse. "But it's an obstinate case."

"My little grandson, he sit up there in the house all wrapped up, waiting by himself," Phoenix went on. "We is the only two left in the world. He suffer and it don't seem to put him back at all. He got a sweet look. He going to last. He wear a little patch quilt and peep out holding his mouth open like a little bird. I remembers so plain now. I not going to forget him again, no, the whole enduring time. I could tell him from all the others in creation."

"All right." The nurse was trying to hush her now. She brought her a bottle of medicine. "Charity," she said, making a checkmark in a book.

Old Phoenix held the bottle close to her eyes, and then carefully put it into her pocket.

"I thank you," she said.

"It's Christmas time, Grandma," said the attendant. "Could I give you a few pennies out of my purse?"

"Five pennies is a nickel," said Phoenix stiffly.

"Here's a nickel," said the attendant.

Phoenix rose carefully and held out her hand. She received the nickel and then fished the other nickel out of her pocket and laid it beside the new one. She stared at her palm closely, with her head on one side.

Then she gave a tap with her cane on the floor.

"This is what come to me to do," she said. "I going to the store and buy my child a little windmill they sells, made out of paper. He going to find it hard to believe there such a thing in the world. I'll march myself back where he waiting, holding it straight up in this hand."

She lifted her free hand, gave a little nod, turned around, and walked out of the doctor's office. Then her slow step began on the stairs, going down.

# CARSON MC CULLERS

# A Tree. A Rock. A Cloud.

Carson McCullers (1917–1968), was born in Columbus, Georgia, and began writing at an early age. Her first novel, *The Heart Is a Lonely Hunter*, 1940, was well received. Since then many other books have appeared: *Reflections in a Golden Eye*, 1941; *A Member of the Wedding*, a novel that was also produced as a play and a movie, 1946; *The Ballad of the Sad Cafe*, 1951; *Seven*, a volume of short stories, 1954; and *Clock Without Hands*, 1961.

This story presents, in a simple, direct, but moving way, the requirements for the growth of the emotion we call love.

It was raining that morning, and still very dark. When the boy reached the streetcar café he had almost finished his route and he went in for a cup of coffee. The place was an all-night café owned by a bitter and stingy man called Leo. After the raw, empty street the café seemed friendly and bright: along the counter there were a couple of soldiers, three spinners from the cotton mill, and in a corner a man who sat hunched over with his nose and half his face down in a beer mug. The boy wore a helmet such as aviators wear. When he went into the café he unbuckled the chin strap and raised the right flap up over his pink little ear; often as he drank his coffee someone would speak to him in a friendly way. But this morning Leo did not look into his face and none of the men were talking. He paid and was leaving the café when a voice called out to him:

"Son!" Hey Son!"

He turned back and the man in the corner was crooking his finger and nodding to him. He had brought his face out of the beer mug and he seemed suddenly very happy. The man was long and pale, with a big nose and faded orange hair.

"Hey Son!"

A TREE. A ROCK. A CLOUD. From *The Ballad of the Sad Cafe* by Carson McCullers. Reprinted by permission of the publisher, Houghton Mifflin Company.

The boy went toward him. He was an under-sized boy of about twelve, with one shoulder drawn higher than the other because of the weight of the paper sack. His face was shallow, freckled, and his eyes were round child eyes.

"Yeah Mister?"

The man laid one hand on the paper boy's shoulders, then grasped the boy's chin and turned his face slowly from one side to the other. The boy shrank back uneasily.

"Say! What's the big idea?"

The boy's voice was shrill; inside the café it was suddenly very quiet.

The man said slowly: "I love you."

All along the counter the men laughed. The boy, who had scowled and sidled away, did not know what to do. He looked over the counter at Leo, and Leo watched him with a weary, brittle jeer. The boy tried to laugh also. But the man was serious and sad.

"I did not mean to tease you, Son," he said. "Sit down and have a beer with me. There is something I have to explain."

Cautiously, out of the corner of his eye, the paper boy questioned the men along the counter to see what he should do. But they had gone back to their beer or their breakfast and did not notice him. Leo put a cup of coffee on the counter and a little jug of cream.

"He is a minor," Leo said.

The paper boy slid himself up onto the stool. His ear beneath the upturned flap of the helmet was very small and red. The man was nodding at him soberly. "It is important," he said. Then he reached in his hip pocket and brought out something which he held up in the palm of his hand for the boy to see.

"Look very carefully," he said.

The boy stared, but there was nothing to look at very carefully. The man held in his big, grimy palm a photograph. It was the face of a woman, but blurred, so that only the hat and the dress she was wearing stood out clearly.

"See?" the man asked.

The boy nodded and the man placed another picture in his palm. The woman was standing on a beach in a bathing suit. The suit made her stomach very big, and that was the main thing you noticed.

"Got a good look?" He leaned over closer and finally asked: "You ever seen her before?"

The boy sat motionless, staring slantwise at the man. "Not so I know of."

"Very well." The man blew on the photographs and put them back into his pocket. "That was my wife."

"Dead?" the boy asked.

Slowly the man shook his head. He pursed his lips as though about to whistle and answered in a long-drawn way: "Nuuu—" he said. "I will explain."

The beer on the counter before the man was in a large brown mug. He did not pick it up to drink. Instead he bent down and, putting his face over the rim, he rested there for a moment. Then with both hands he tilted the mug and sipped.

"Some night you'll go to sleep with your big nose in a mug and drown," said Leo. "Prominent transient drowns in beer. That would be a cute death."

The paper boy tried to signal to Leo. While the man was not looking he screwed up his face and worked his mouth to question soundlessly: "Drunk?" But Leo only raised his eyebrows and turned away to put some pink strips of bacon on the grill. The man pushed the mug away from him, straightened himself, and folded his loose crooked hands on the counter. His face was sad as he looked at the paper boy. He did not blink, but from time to time the lids closed down with delicate gravity over his pale green eyes. It was nearing dawn and the boy shifted the weight of the paper sack.

"I am talking about love," the man said. "With me it is a science."

The boy half slid down from the stool. But the man raised his forefinger, and there was something about him that held the boy and would not let him go away.

"Twelve years ago I married the woman in the photograph. She was my wife for one year, nine months, three days, and two nights. I loved her. Yes. . . ." He tightened his blurred, rambling voice and said again: "I loved her. I thought also that she loved me. I was a railroad engineer. She had all home comforts and luxuries. It never crept into my brain that she was not satisfied. But do you know what happened?"

"Mgneeow!" said Leo.

The man did not take his eyes from the boy's face. "She left me. I came in one night and the house was empty and she was gone. She left me."

"With a fellow?" the boy asked.

Gently the man placed his palm down on the counter. "Why naturally, Son. A woman does not run off like that alone."

The café was quiet, the soft rain black and endless in the street outside. Leo pressed down the frying bacon with the prongs of his long fork. "So you have been chasing the floozie for eleven years. You frazzled old rascal!"

For the first time the man glanced at Leo. "Please don't be vulgar. Besides, I was not speaking to you." He turned back to the boy and said in a trusting and secretive undertone: "Let's not pay any attention to him. O.K.?"

The paper boy nodded doubtfully.

"It was like this," the man continued. "I am a person who feels many things. All my life one thing after another has impressed me. Moonlight. The leg of a pretty girl. One thing after another. But the point is that when I had enjoyed anything there was a peculiar sensation as though it was laying around loose in me. Nothing seemed to finish itself up or fit in with the other things. Women? I had my portion of them. The same. Afterwards laying around loose in me. I was a man who had never loved."

Very slowly he closed his eyelids, and the gesture was like a curtain drawn at the end of a scene in a play. When he spoke again his voice was excited and the words came fast—the lobes of his large, loose ears seemed to tremble.

"Then I met this woman. I was fifty-one years old and she always said she was thirty. I met her at a filling station and we were married within three days. And do you know what it was like? I just can't tell you. All I had ever felt was gathered together around this woman. Nothing lay around loose in me any more but was finished up by her."

The man stopped suddenly and stroked his long nose. His voice sank down to a steady and reproachful undertone: "I'm not explaining this right. What happened was this. There were these beautiful feelings and loose little pleasures inside me. And this woman was something like an assembly line for my soul. I run these little pieces of myself through her and I come out complete. Now do you follow me?"

"What was her name?" the boy asked.

"Oh," he said. "I called her Dodo. But that is immaterial."

"Did you try to make her come back?"

The man did not seem to hear. "Under the circumstances you can imagine how I felt when she left me."

Leo took the bacon from the grill and folded two strips of it between a bun. He had a gray face, with slitted eyes, and a pinched nose saddled by faint blue shadows. One of the mill workers signaled for more coffee and Leo poured it. He did not give refills on coffee free. The spinner ate breakfast there every morning, but the better Leo knew his customers the stingier he treated them. He nibbled his own bun as though he grudged it to himself.

"And you never got hold of her again?"

The boy did not know what to think of the man, and his child's face was uncertain with mingled curiosity and doubt. He was new on the paper route; it was still strange to him to be out in the town in the black, queer early morning.

"Yes," the man said. "I took a number of steps to get her back. I went around trying to locate her. I went to Tulsa where she had folks. And to Mobile. I went to every town she had ever mentioned to me, and I hunted down every man she had formerly been connected with. Tulsa, Atlanta, Chicago, Cheehaw, Memphis. . . . For the better part of two years I chased around the country trying to lay hold of her."

"But the pair of them had vanished from the face of the earth!" said Leo.

"Don't listen to him," the man said confidentially. "And also just forget those two years. They are not important. What matters is that around the third year a curious thing begun to happen to me."

"What?" the boy asked.

The man leaned down and tilted his mug to take a sip of beer. But as he hovered over the mug his nostrils fluttered slightly; he sniffed the staleness of the beer and did not drink. "Love is a curious thing to begin with. At first I thought only of getting her back. It was a kind of mania. But then as time went on I tried to remember her. But do you know what happened?"

"No," the boy said.

"When I laid myself down on a bed and tried to think about her my mind became a blank. I couldn't see her. I would take out her pictures and look. No good. Nothing doing. A blank. Can you imagine it?"

"Say Mac!" Leo called down the counter. "Can you imagine this bozo's mind a blank!"

Slowly, as though fanning away flies, the man waved his hand. His green eyes were concentrated and fixed on the shallow little face of the paper boy.

"But a sudden piece of glass on a sidewalk. Or a nickel tune in a music box. A shadow on a wall at night. And I would remember. It might happen in a street and I would cry or bang my head against a lamppost. You follow me?"

"A piece of glass . . ." the boy said.

"Anything. I would walk around and I had no power of how and when to remember her. You think you can put up a kind of shield. But remembering don't come to a man face forward— it corners around sideways. I was at the mercy of everything I saw and heard. Suddenly instead of me combing the countryside to find her she begun to chase me around in my very soul. *She chasing me*, mind you! And in my soul."

The boy asked finally: "What part of the country were you in then?"

"Ooh," the man groaned. "I was a sick mortal. It was like smallpox. I confess, Son, that I boozed. I fornicated. I committed any sin that suddenly appealed to me. I am loath to confess it but I will do so. When I recall that period it is all curdled in my mind, it was so terrible."

The man leaned his head down and tapped his forehead on the counter. For a few seconds he stayed bowed over in this position, the back of his stringy neck covered with orange furze, his hands with their long warped fingers held palm to palm in an attitude of prayer. Then the man straightened himself; he was smiling and suddenly his face was bright and tremulous and old.

"It was in the fifth year that it happened," he said. "And with it I started my science."

Leo's mouth jerked with a pale, quick grin. "Well none of we boys are getting any younger," he said. Then with sudden anger he balled up a dishcloth he was holding and threw it down hard on the floor. "You draggletailed old Romeo!"

"What happened?" the boy asked.

The old man's voice was high and clear: "Peace," he answered.

"Huh?"

"It is hard to explain scientifically, Son," he said. "I guess the logical explanation is that she and I had fleed around from each other for so long that finally we just got tangled up together and lay down and quit. Peace. A queer and beautiful blankness. It was spring in Portland and the rain came every afternoon. All evening I just stayed there on my bed in the dark. And that is how the science come to me."

The windows in the streetcar were pale blue with light. The two soldiers paid for their beers and opened the door—one of the soldiers combed his hair and wiped off his muddy puttees before they went outside. The three mill workers bent silently over their breakfasts. Leo's clock was ticking on the wall.

"It is this. And listen carefully. I meditated on love and reasoned it out. I realized what is wrong with us. Men fall in love for the first time. And what do they fall in love with?"

The boy's soft mouth was partly open and he did not answer.

"A woman," the old man said. "Without science, with nothing to go by, they undertake the most dangerous and sacred experience in God's earth. They fall in love with a woman. Is that correct, Son?"

"Yeah," the boy said faintly.

"They start at the wrong end of love. They begin at the climax. Can you wonder it is so miserable? Do you know how men should love?"

The old man reached over and grasped the boy by the collar of his leather jacket. He gave him a gentle little shake and his green eyes gazed down unblinking and grave.

"Son, do you know how love should be begun?"

The boy sat small and listening and still. Slowly he shook his head. The old man leaned closer and whispered:

"A tree. A rock. A cloud."

It was still raining outside in the street: a mild, gray, endless rain. The mill whistle blew for the six o'clock shift and the three spinners paid and went away. There was no one in the café but Leo, the old man, and the little paper boy.

"The weather was like this in Portland," he said. "At the time my science was begun. I meditated and I started very cautious. I would pick up something from the street and take it home with me. I bought a goldfish and I concentrated on the goldfish and I loved it. I graduated from one thing to another. Day by day I was getting this technique. On the road from Portland to San Diego—"

"Aw shut up!" screamed Leo suddenly. "Shut up! Shut up!"

The old man still held the collar of the boy's jacket; he was trembling and his face was earnest and bright and wild. "For six years now I have gone around by myself and built up my science. And now I am a master. Son. I can love anything. No longer do I have to think about it even. I see a street full of people and a beautiful light comes in me. I watch a bird in the sky. Or I meet a traveler on the road. Everything, Son. And anybody. All stranger and all loved! Do you realize what a science like mine can mean?"

The boy held himself stiffly, his hands curled tight around the counter edge. Finally he asked: "Did you ever really find that lady?"

"What? What say, Son?"

"I mean," the boy asked timidly. "Have you fallen in love with a woman again?"

The old man loosened his grasp on the boy's collar. He turned away and for the first time his green eyes had a vague and scattered look. He lifted the mug from the counter, drank down the yellow beer. His head was shaking slowly from side to side. Then finally he answered: "No, Son. You see that is the last step in my science. I go cautious. And I am not quite ready yet."

"Well!" said Leo. "Well well well!"

The old man stood in the open doorway. "Remember," he said. Framed there in the gray damp light of the early morning he looked shrunken and seedy and frail. But his smile was bright. "Remember I love you," he said with a last nod. And the door closed quietly behind him.

The boy did not speak for a long time. He pulled down the bangs on his forehead and slid his grimy little forefinger around the rim of his

My scissors are all sharp."

...ight, then. Take a pot," he continued ..., "a bent pot, or a pot with a hole. I ...e it like new so you don't have to buy ...ones. That's a saving for you."

...she said shortly. "I tell you I have noth-...that for you to do."

...ce fell to an exaggerated sadness. His ...k on a whining undertone. "I ain't had ...to do today. Maybe I won't have no ...night. You see I'm off my regular road. ...olks on the highway clear from Seattle ...Diego. They save their things for me to ...up because they know I do it so good ...them money."

...orry," Elisa said irritably. "I haven't ...for you to do."

...es left her face and fell to searching the ...They roamed about until they came to ...santhemum bed where she had been ..."What's them plants, ma'am?"

...ritation and resistance melted from ...ce. "Oh, those are chrysanthemums, ...tes and yellows. I raise them every year, ...an anybody around here."

...of a long-stemmed flower? Looks like ...uff of colored smoke?" he asked.

...it. What a nice way to describe them." ...smell kind of nasty till you get used to ...e said.

...good bitter smell," she retorted, "not ...ll."

...nged his tone quickly. "I like the smell

...ten-inch blooms this year," she said. ...n leaned farther over the fence. "Look. ...lady down the road a piece, has got ...garden you ever seen. Got nearly every ...wer but no chrysanthemums. Last time ...ding a copper-bottom washtub for her ...ard job but I do it good), she said to ...u ever run acrost some nice chrys-...s I wish you'd try to get me a few ...at's what she told me."

...yes grew alert and eager. "She couldn't ...vn much about chrysanthemums. You ...them from seed, but it's much easier ...e little sprouts you see there."

...e said. "I s'pose I can't take none to

...es you can," Elisa cried. "I can put ...mp sand, and you can carry them right

along with you. They'll take root in the pot... you keep them damp. And then she can tra... plant them."

"She'd sure like to have some, ma'am. You s... they're nice ones?"

"Beautiful," she said. "Oh, beautiful." Her ey... shone. She tore off the battered hat and sho... out her dark pretty hair. "I'll put them in... flower pot, and you can take them right wi... you. Come into the yard."

While the man came through the picket fenc... Elisa ran excitedly along the geranium-bordere... path to the back of the house. And she returne... carrying a big red flower pot. The gloves wer... forgotten now. She kneeled on the ground by th... starting bed and dug up the sandy soil with he... fingers and scooped it into the bright new flowe... pot. Then she picked up the little pile of shoot... she had prepared. With her strong fingers she... pressed them into the sand and tamped around... them with her knuckles. The man stood over her... "I'll tell you what to do," she said. "You remem-ber so you can tell the lady."

"Yes, I'll try to remember."

"Well, look. These will take root in about a... month. Then she must set them out, about a foot... apart in good rich earth like this, see?" She lifted... a handful of dark soil for him to look at. "They'll... grow fast and tall. Now remember this. In July... tell her to cut them down, about eight inches... from the ground."

"Before they bloom?" he asked.

"Yes, before they bloom." Her face was tight... with eagerness. "They'll grow right up again.... About the last of September the buds will start."

She stopped and seemed perplexed. "It's the... budding that takes the most care," she said hesi-tantly. "I don't know how to tell you." She... looked deep into his eyes, searchingly. Her... mouth opened a little, and she seemed to be... listening. "I'll try to tell you," she said. "Did you... ever hear of planting hands?"

"Can't say I have, ma'am."

"Well, I can only tell you what it feels like.... It's when you're picking off the buds you don't... want. Everything goes right down into your fin-ger-tips. You watch your fingers work. They do... it themselves. You can feel how it is. They pick... and pick the buds. They never make a mistake.... They're with the plant. Do you see? Your fingers... and the plant. You can feel that, right up your... arm. They know. They never make a mistake."

empty cup. Then without looking at Leo he finally asked:

"Was he drunk?"

"No," said Leo shortly.

The boy raised his clear voice higher. "Then was he a dope fiend?"

"No."

The boy looked up at Leo, and his flat little face was desperate, his voice urgent and shrill. "Was he crazy? Do you think he was a lunatic?" The paper boy's voice dropped suddenly with doubt. "Leo? Or not?"

But Leo would not answer him. Leo had run

a night café for fourteen years, and he held him-self to be a critic of craziness. There were the town characters and also the transients who roamed in from the night. He knew the manias of all of them. But he did not want to satisfy the questions of the waiting child. He tightened his pale face and was silent.

So the boy pulled down the right flap of his helmet and as he turned to leave he made the only comment that seemed safe to him, the only remark that could not be laughed down and despised:

"He sure has done a lot of traveling."

## JOHN STEINBECK

# The Chrysanthemums

John Steinbeck (1902–1968) was born in Salinas, California, and attended Stanford University. *Pastures of Heaven*, 1932, a collection of short stories about a rural community in the Salinas Valley, foreshadowed his later style. *Tortilla Flat*, 1935, first brought him attention as a writer, and this success was followed by *In Dubious Battle*, 1936; *Of Mice and Men*, 1937; and *The Grapes of Wrath*, 1939, for which he received the Pulitzer Prize. During World War II he was a war reporter for the New York *Herald Tribune*. In 1941, with Edward F. Ricketts, he wrote *Sea of Cortez*, a report of their explorations in the Gulf of California. *East of Eden*, 1952, was his first major novel after the war. This was followed by *The Winter of Our Discontent*, 1961; and *Travels with Charley*, 1962, an account of his journey across America. *America and Americans* appeared in 1966. In 1962 he was awarded the Nobel Prize for Literature and in 1964 he received the Presidential Medal of Freedom.

Mr. Steinbeck's short stories and novels tend to begin realistically and conclude symbolically. This tendency is vividly displayed in *The Grapes of Wrath*. It is also shown in "The Chrys-anthemums," where the reader senses a strong conflict but, because of indirection in the telling of the story, must draw his own inference.

The high grey-flannel fog of winter closed off the Salinas Valley from the sky and from all the rest of the world. On every side it sat like a lid on the mountains and made of the great valley a

THE CHRYSANTHEMUMS   From *The Long Valley* by John Steinbeck. Copyright 1937, © renewed 1965 by John Stein-beck. Reprinted by permission of The Viking Press, Inc.

closed pot. On the broad, level land floor the gang plows bit deep and left the black earth shining like metal where the shares had cut. On the foothill ranches across the Salinas River, the yellow stubble fields seemed to be bathed in pale cold sunshine, but there was no sunshine in the valley now in December. The thick willow scrub along the river flamed with sharp and positive yellow leaves.

It was a time of quiet and of waiting. The air was cold and tender. A light wind blew up from the southwest so that the farmers were mildly hopeful of a good rain before long; but fog and rain did not go together.

Across the river, on Henry Allen's foothill ranch there was little work to be done, for the hay was cut and stored and the orchards were plowed up to receive the rain deeply when it should come. The cattle on the higher slopes were becoming shaggy and rough-coated.

Elisa Allen, working in her flower garden, looked down across the yard and saw Henry, her husband, talking to two men in business suits. The three of them stood by the tractor shed, each man with one foot on the side of the little Fordson. They smoked cigarettes and studied the machine as they talked.

Elisa watched them for a moment and then went back to her work. She was thirty-five. Her face was lean and strong and her eyes were as clear as water. Her figure looked blocked and heavy in her gardening costume, a man's black hat pulled low down over her eyes, clod-hopper shoes, a figured print dress almost completely covered by a big corduroy apron with four big pockets to hold the snips, the trowel and scratcher, the seeds and the knife she worked with. She wore heavy leather gloves to protect her hands while she worked.

She was cutting down the old year's chrysanthemum stalks with a pair of short and powerful scissors. She looked down toward the men by the tractor shed now and then. Her face was eager and mature and handsome; even her work with the scissors was over-eager, over-powerful. The chrysanthemum stems seemed too small and easy for her energy.

She brushed a cloud of hair out of her eyes with the back of her glove, and left a smudge of earth on her cheek in doing it. Behind her stood the neat white farm house with red geraniums close-banked around it as high as the windows. It was a hard-swept looking little house, with hard-polished windows, and a clean mud-mat on the front steps.

Elisa cast another glance toward the tractor shed. The strangers were getting into their Ford coupe. She took off a glove and put her strong fingers down into the forest of new green chrys-

anthemum sprouts that were growing around the old roots. She spread the leaves and looked down among the close-growing stems. No aphids were there, no sowbugs or snails or cutworms. Her terrier fingers destroyed such pests before they could get started.

Elisa started at the sound of her husband's voice. He had come near quietly, and he leaned over the wire fence that protected her flower garden from cattle and dogs and chickens.

"At it again," he said. "You've got a strong new crop coming."

Elisa straightened her back and pulled on the gardening glove again. "Yes. They'll be strong this coming year." In her tone and on her face there was a little smugness.

"You've got a gift with things," Henry observed. "Some of those yellow chrysanthemums you had this year were ten inches across. I wish you'd work out in the orchard and raise some apples that big."

Her eyes sharpened. "Maybe I could do it, too. I've a gift with things, all right. My mother had it. She could stick anything in the ground and make it grow. She said it was having planters' hands that knew how to do it."

"Well, it sure works with flowers," he said.

"Henry, who were those men you were talking to?"

"Why, sure, that's what I came to tell you. They were from the Western Meat Company. I sold those thirty head of three-year-old steers. Got nearly my own price, too."

"Good," she said. "Good for you."

"And I thought," he continued, "I thought how it's Saturday afternoon, and we might go into Salinas for dinner at a restaurant, and then to a picture show—to celebrate, you see."

"Good," she repeated. "Oh, yes. That will be good."

Henry put on his joking tone. "There's fights tonight. How'd you like to go to the fights?"

"Oh, no," she said breathlessly. "No, I wouldn't like fights."

"Just fooling, Elisa. We'll go to a movie. Let's see. It's two now. I'm going to take Scotty and bring down those steers from the hill. It'll take us maybe two hours. We'll go in town about five and have dinner at the Cominos Hotel. Like that?"

"Of course I'll like it. It's good to eat away from home."

"All right, then. I'll go get up a couple of horses."

She said, "I'll have plenty of time to transplant some of these sets, I guess."

She heard her husband calling Scotty down by the barn. And a little later she saw the two men ride up the pale yellow hillside in search of the steers.

There was a little square sandy bed kept for rooting the chrysanthemums. With her trowel she turned the soil over and over, and smoothed it and patted it firm. Then she dug ten parallel trenches to receive the sets. Back at the chrysanthemum bed she pulled out the little crisp shoots, trimmed off the leaves of each one with her scissors and laid it on a small orderly pile.

A squeak of wheels and plod of hoofs came from the road. Elisa looked up. The country road ran along the dense bank of willows and cottonwoods that bordered the river, and up this road came a curious vehicle, curiously drawn. It was an old spring-wagon, with a round canvas top on it like the cover of a prairie schooner. It was drawn by an old bay horse and a little grey-and-white burro. A big stubble-bearded man sat between the cover flaps and drove the crawling team. Underneath the wagon, between the hind wheels, a lean and rangy mongrel dog walked sedately. Words were painted on the canvas in clumsy, crooked letters. "Pots, pans, knives, sisors, lawn mores, Fixed." Two rows of articles, and the triumphantly definitive "Fixed" below. The black paint had run down in little sharp points beneath each letter.

Elisa, squatting on the ground, watched to see the crazy, loose-jointed wagon pass by. But it didn't pass. It turned into the farm road in front of her house, crooked old wheels skirling and squeaking. The rangy dog darted from between the wheels and ran ahead. Instantly the two ranch shepherds flew out at him. Then all three stopped, and with stiff and quivering tails, with taut straight legs, with ambassadorial dignity, they slowly circled, sniffing daintily. The caravan pulled up to Elisa's wire fence and stopped. Now the newcomer dog, feeling outnumbered, lowered his tail and retired under the wagon with raised hackles and bared teeth.

The man on the wagon seat called out, "That's a bad dog in a fight when he gets started."

Elisa laughed. "I see he is. How soon does he generally get started?"

The man caught it heartily. "Some weeks," he said. H the wheel. The hor like unwatered flow

Elisa saw that he his hair and beard old. His worn bl spotted with grea peared from his fa laughing voice cea they were full of eyes of teamsters hands he rested on and every crack v his battered hat.

"I'm off my ge "Does this dirt roa the Los Angeles h

Elisa stood up in her apron pock winds around and think your team

He replied with prise you what th

"When they ge

He smiled for a started."

"Well," said E if you go back to the highway ther

He drew a big and made it sing. I go from Seattle year. Takes all m way. I aim to fol

Elisa took off the apron pocket the under edge fugitive hairs. "I a way to live," s

He leaned c "Maybe you not I mend pots and got any of them

"Oh, no," sh that." Her eyes

"Scissors is th "Most people ju 'em, but I know a little bobbit k it sure does the

"No.

"All earnestly can mak no new

"No," ing like

His fa voice to a thing supper t I know to San I sharpen and save

"I'm anything

His ey ground. the chry working.

The i Elisa's fa giant whi bigger th

"Kind a quick

"That'

"They them," h

"It's a nasty at

He cha myself."

"I had

The ma I know the nices kind of fl I was me (that's a me, 'If y anthemur seeds.' Th

Elisa's have kno can raise to root th

"Oh," her, then

"Why some in d

You can feel it. When you're like that you can't do anything wrong. Do you see that? Can you understand that?"

She was kneeling on the ground looking up at him. Her breast swelled passionately.

The man's eyes narrowed. He looked away self-consciously. "Maybe I know," he said. "Sometimes in the night in the wagon there—"

Elisa's voice grew husky. She broke in on him. "I've never lived as you do, but I know what you mean. When the night is dark—why, the stars are sharp-pointed, and there's quiet. Why, you rise up and up! Every pointed star gets driven into your body. It's like that. Hot and sharp and—lovely."

Kneeling there, her hand went out toward his legs in the greasy black trousers. Her hesitant fingers almost touched the cloth. Then her hand dropped to the ground. She crouched low like a fawning dog.

He said, "It's nice, just like you say. Only when you don't have no dinner, it ain't."

She stood up then, very straight, and her face was ashamed. She held the flower pot out to him and placed it gently in his arms. "Here. Put it in your wagon, on the seat, where you can watch it. Maybe I can find something for you to do."

At the back of the house she dug in the can pile and found two old and battered aluminum saucepans. She carried them back and gave them to him. "Here, maybe you can fix these."

His manner changed. He became professional. "Good as new I can fix them." At the back of his wagon he set a little anvil, and out of an oily tool box dug a small machine hammer. Elisa came through the gate to watch him while he pounded out the dents in the kettles. His mouth grew sure and knowing. At a difficult part of the work he sucked his under-lip.

"You sleep right in the wagon?" Elisa asked.

"Right in the wagon, ma'am. Rain or shine I'm dry as a cow in there."

"It must be nice," she said. "It must be very nice. I wish women could do such things."

"It ain't the right kind of a life for a woman."

Her upper lip raised a little, showing her teeth. "How do you know? How can you tell?" she said.

"I don't know, ma'am," he protested. "Of course I don't know. Now here's your kettles, done. You don't have to buy no new ones."

"How much?"

"Oh, fifty cents'll do. I keep my prices down and my work good. That's why I have all them satisfied customers up and down the highway."

Elisa brought him a fifty-cent piece from the house and dropped it in his hand. "You might be surprised to have a rival some time. I can sharpen scissors, too. And I can beat the dents out of little pots. I could show you what a woman might do."

He put his hammer back in the oily box and shoved the little anvil out of sight. "It would be a lonely life for a woman, ma'am, and a scarey life, too, with animals creeping under the wagon all night." He climbed over the singletree, steadying himself with a hand on the burro's white rump. He settled himself in the seat, picked up the lines. "Thank you kindly, ma'am," he said. "I'll do like you told me; I'll go back and catch the Salinas road."

"Mind," she called, "if you're long in getting there, keep the sand damp."

"Sand, ma'am? . . . Sand? Oh, sure. You mean around the chrysanthemums. Sure I will." He clucked his tongue. The beasts leaned luxuriously into their collars. The mongrel dog took his place between the back wheels. The wagon turned and crawled out the entrance road and back the way it had come, along the river.

Elisa stood in front of her wire fence watching the slow progress of the caravan. Her shoulders were straight, her head thrown back, her eyes half-closed, so that the scene came vaguely into them. Her lips moved silently, forming the words "Good-bye—good-bye." Then she whispered, "That's a bright direction. There's a glowing there." The sound of her whisper startled her. She shook herself free and looked about to see whether anyone had been listening. Only the dogs had heard. They lifted their heads toward her from their sleeping in the dust, and then stretched out their chins and settled asleep again. Elisa turned and ran hurriedly into the house.

In the kitchen she reached behind the stove and felt the water tank. It was full of hot water from the noonday cooking. In the bathroom she tore off her soiled clothes and flung them into the corner. And then she scrubbed herself with a little block of pumice, legs and thighs, loins and chest and arms, until her skin was scratched and red. When she had dried herself she stood in front of a mirror in her bedroom and looked at her body. She tightened her stomach and threw out her chest. She turned and looked over her shoulder at her back.

After a while she began to dress, slowly. She put on her newest underclothing and her nicest stockings and the dress which was the symbol of her prettiness. She worked carefully on her hair, pencilled her eyebrows and rouged her lips.

Before she was finished she heard the little thunder of hoofs and the shouts of Henry and his helper as they drove the red steers into the corral. She heard the gate bang shut and set herself for Henry's arrival.

His step sounded on the porch. He entered the house calling, "Elisa, where are you?"

"In my room, dressing. I'm not ready. There's hot water for your bath. Hurry up. It's getting late."

When she heard him splashing in the tub, Elisa laid his dark suit on the bed, and shirt and socks and tie beside it. She stood his polished shoes on the floor beside the bed. Then she went to the porch and sat primly and stiffly down. She looked toward the river road where the willow-line was still yellow with frosted leaves so that under the high grey fog they seemed a thin band of sunshine. This was the only color in the grey afternoon. She sat unmoving for a long time. Her eyes blinked rarely.

Henry came banging out of the door, shoving his tie inside his vest as he came. Elisa stiffened and her face grew tight. Henry stopped short and looked at her. "Why—why, Elisa. You look so nice!"

"Nice? You think I look nice? What do you mean by 'nice'?"

Henry blundered on. "I don't know. I mean you look different, strong and happy."

"I am strong? Yes, strong. What do you mean 'strong'?"

He looked bewildered. "You're playing some kind of a game," he said helplessly. "It's a kind of a play. You look strong enough to break a calf over your knee, happy enough to eat it like a watermelon."

For a second she lost her rigidity. "Henry! Don't talk like that. You didn't know what you said." She grew complete again. "I'm strong," she boasted. "I never knew before how strong."

Henry looked down toward the tractor shed, and when he brought his eyes back to her, they were his own again. "I'll get out the car. You can put on your coat while I'm starting."

Elisa went into the house. She heard him drive to the gate and idle down his motor, and then she took a long time to put on her hat. She pulled it here and pressed it there. When Henry turned the motor off she slipped into her coat and went out.

The little roadster bounced along on the dirt road by the river, raising the birds and driving the rabbits into the brush. Two cranes flapped heavily over the willow-line and dropped into the river-bed.

Far ahead on the road Elisa saw a dark speck. She knew.

She tried not to look as they passed it, but her eyes would not obey. She whispered to herself sadly, "He might have thrown them off the road. That wouldn't have been much trouble, not very much. But he kept the pot," she explained. "He had to keep the pot. That's why he couldn't get them off the road."

The roadster turned a bend and she saw the caravan ahead. She swung full around toward her husband so she could not see the little covered wagon and the mismatched team as the car passed them.

In a moment it was over. The thing was done. She did not look back. She said loudly, to be heard above the motor, "It will be good, tonight, a good dinner."

"Now you're changed again," Henry complained. He took one hand from the wheel and patted her knee. "I ought to take you in to dinner oftener. It would be good for both of us. We get so heavy out on the ranch."

"Henry," she asked, "could we have wine at dinner?"

"Sure we could. Say! That will be fine."

She was silent for a while; then she said, "Henry, at those prize fights, do the men hurt each other very much?"

"Sometimes a little, not often. Why?"

"Well, I've read how they break noses, and blood runs down their chests. I've read how the fighting gloves get heavy and soggy with blood."

He looked around at her. "What's the matter, Elisa? I didn't know you read things like that." He brought the car to a stop, then turned to the right over the Salinas River bridge.

"Do any women ever go to the fights?" she asked.

"Oh, sure, some. What's the matter, Elisa? Do you want to go? I don't think you'd like it, but I'll take you if you really want to go."

She relaxed limply in the seat. "Oh, no. No. I don't want to go. I'm sure I don't." Her face was turned away from him. "It will be enough if we can have wine. It will be plenty." She turned up her coat collar so he could not see that she was crying weakly—like an old woman.

# FLANNERY O'CONNOR

# A Late Encounter with the Enemy

Flannery O'Connor (1925–1964) was born in Georgia and educated at Georgia State College for Women and the State University of Iowa, where she received a master's degree in fine arts in 1947. Her first novel, *Wise Blood*, appeared in 1952. After publishing stories in the *Partisan Review, Harper's Bazaar, Mademoiselle,* and other magazines, she published a collection of ten stories, *A Good Man Is Hard to Find and Other Stories,* 1955. For her story "Greenleaf" she won first prize in the 1957 O. Henry Memorial Awards. Her last works are a novel, *The Violent Bear It Away,* 1960, and a collection of stories, *Everything That Rises Must Converge,* 1965. A volume of her essays, edited by Sally and Robert Fitzgerald, appeared in 1969. *The Complete Stories of Flannery O'Connor,* 1971, won the National Book Award in fiction for that year.

"A Late Encounter with the Enemy" is typical of Miss O'Connor's work. In it, the reader finds bizarre, brutal, and often mindless characters who tend to be almost, but not quite, beyond the realm of one's experience.

General Sash was a hundred and four years old. He lived with his granddaughter, Sally Poker Sash, who was sixty-two years old and who prayed every night on her knees that he would live until her graduation from college. The General didn't give two slaps for her graduation but he never doubted he would live for it. Living had got to be such a habit with him that he couldn't conceive of any other condition. A graduation exercise was not exactly his idea of a good time, even if, as she said, he would be expected to sit on the stage in his uniform. She said there would be a long procession of teachers and students in their robes but that there wouldn't be anything to equal *him* in his uniform.

A LATE ENCOUNTER WITH THE ENEMY  Copyright, 1953, by Flannery O'Connor. Reprinted from her volume *A Good Man Is Hard to Find and Other Stories* by permission of Harcourt Brace Jovanovich, Inc.

He knew this well enough without her telling him, and as for the damn procession, it could march to hell and back and not cause him a quiver. He liked parades with floats full of Miss Americas and Miss Daytona Beaches and Miss Queen Cotton Products. He didn't have any use for processions and a procession full of schoolteachers was about as deadly as the River Styx to his way of thinking. However, he was willing to sit on the stage in his uniform so that they could see him.

Sally Poker was not as sure as he was that he would live until her graduation. There had not been any perceptible change in him for the last five years, but she had the sense that she might be cheated out of her triumph because she so often was. She had been going to summer school every year for the past twenty because when she started teaching, there were no such things as degrees. In those times, she said, everything was normal but nothing had been normal since she was sixteen, and for the past twenty summers, when she should have been resting, she had had to take a trunk in the burning heat to the state teacher's college; and though when she returned in the fall, she always taught in the exact way she had been taught not to teach, this was a mild revenge that didn't satisfy her sense of justice. She wanted the General at her graduation because she wanted to show what she stood for, or, as she said, "what all was behind her," and was not behind them. This *them* was not anybody in particular. It was just all the upstarts who had turned the world on its head and unsettled the ways of decent living.

She meant to stand on that platform in August with the General sitting in his wheel chair on the stage behind her and she meant to hold her head very high as if she were saying, "See him! See him! My kin, all you upstarts! Glorious upright old man standing for the old traditions! Dignity! Honor! Courage! See him!" One night in her sleep she screamed, "See him! See him!" and turned her head and found him sitting in his wheel chair behind her with a terrible expression on his face and with all his clothes off except the general's hat and she had waked up and had not dared to go back to sleep again that night.

For his part, the General would not have consented even to attend her graduation if she had not promised to see to it that he sit on the stage. He liked to sit on any stage. He considered that he was still a very handsome man. When he had been able to stand up, he had measured five feet four inches of pure game cock. He had white hair that reached to his shoulders behind and he would not wear teeth because he thought his profile was more striking without them. When he put on his full-dress general's uniform, he knew well enough that there was nothing to match him anywhere.

This was not the same uniform he had worn in the War between the States. He had not actually been a general in that war. He had probably been a foot soldier; he didn't remember what he had been; in fact, he didn't remember that war at all. It was like his feet, which hung down now shriveled at the very end of him, without feeling, covered with a blue-gray afghan that Sally Poker had crocheted when she was a little girl. He didn't remember the Spanish-American War in which he had lost a son; he didn't even remember the son. He didn't have any use for history because he never expected to meet it again. To his mind, history was connected with processions and life with parades and he liked parades. People were always asking him if he remembered this or that—a dreary black procession of questions about the past. There was only one event in the past that had any significance for him and that he cared to talk about: that was twelve years ago when he had received the general's uniform and had been in the premiere.

"I was in that preemy they had in Atlanta," he would tell visitors sitting on his front porch. "Surrounded by beautiful guls. It wasn't a thing local about it. It was nothing local about it. Listen here. It was a nashnul event and they had me in it—up onto the stage. There was no bobtails at it. Every person at it had paid ten dollars to get in and had to wear his tuxseder. I was in this uniform. A beautiful gul presented me with it that afternoon in a hotel room."

"It was in a suite in the hotel and I was in it too, Papa," Sally Poker would say, winking at the visitors. "You weren't alone with any young lady in a hotel room."

"Was, I'd a known what to do," the old General would say with a sharp look and the visitors would scream with laughter. "This was a Hollywood, California, gul," he'd continue. "She was from Hollywood, California, and didn't have any part in the pitcher. Out there they have so many beautiful guls that they don't need that they call them a extra and they don't use them for nothing but presenting people with things and having their pitchers taken. They took my pitcher with her. No, it was two of them. One on either side and me in the middle with my arms around each of them's waist and their waist ain't any bigger than a half a dollar."

Sally Poker would interrupt again. "It was Mr. Govisky that gave you the uniform, Papa, and he gave me the most exquisite corsage. Really, I wish you could have seen it. It was made with gladiola petals taken off and painted gold and put back together to look like a rose. It was exquisite. I wish you could have seen it, it was. . . ."

"It was as big as her head," the General would snarl. "I was tellin it. They gimme this uniform and they gimme this soward and they say, 'Now General, we don't want you to start a war on us. All we want you to do is march right up on that stage when you're innerduced tonight and answer a few questions. Think you can do that?' 'Think I can do it!' I say. 'Listen here. I was doing things before you were born,' and they hollered."

"He was the hit of the show," Sally Poker would say, but she didn't much like to remember the premiere on account of what had happened to her feet at it. She had bought a new dress for the occasion—a long black crepe dinner dress with a rhinestone buckle and a bolero—and a pair of silver slippers to wear with it, because she was supposed to go up on the stage with him to keep him from falling. Everything was arranged for them. A real limousine came at ten minutes to eight and took them to the theater. It drew up under the marquee at exactly the right time, after the big stars and the director and the author and the governor and the mayor and some less important stars. The police kept traffic from jamming and there were ropes to keep the people off who couldn't go. All the people who couldn't go watched them step out of the limousine into the lights. Then they walked down the red and gold foyer and an usherette in a Confederate cap and little short skirt conducted them to their special seats. The audience was already there and a group of UDC members began to clap when they saw the General in his uniform and that started everybody to clap. A few more celebrities came after them and then the doors closed and the lights went down.

A young man with blond wavy hair who said he represented the motion-picture industry came out and began to introduce everybody and each one who was introduced walked up on the stage and said how really happy he was to be here for this great event. The General and his granddaughter were introduced sixteenth on the program. He was introduced as General Tennessee Flintrock Sash of the Confederacy, though Sally Poker had told Mr. Govisky that his name was George Poker Sash and that he had only been a major. She helped him up from his seat but her heart was beating so fast she didn't know whether she'd make it herself.

The old man walked up the aisle slowly with his fierce white head high and his hat held over his heart. The orchestra began to play the Confederate Battle Hymn very softly and the UDC members rose as a group and did not sit down

again until the General was on the stage. When he reached the center of the stage with Sally Poker just behind him guiding his elbow, the orchestra burst out in a loud rendition of the Battle Hymn and the old man, with real stage presence, gave a vigorous trembling salute and stood at attention until the last blast had died away. Two of the usherettes in Confederate caps and short skirts held a Confederate and a Union flag crossed behind them.

The General stood in the exact center of the spotlight and it caught a weird moon-shaped slice of Sally Poker—the corsage, the rhinestone buckle and one hand clenched around a white glove and handkerchief. The young man with the blond wavy hair inserted himself into the circle of light and said he was *really* happy to have here tonight for this great event, one, he said, who had fought and bled in the battles they would soon see daringly re-acted on the screen, and "Tell me, General," he asked, "how old are you?"

"Niiiiiinnttty-two!" the General screamed.

The young man looked as if this were just about the most impressive thing that had been said all evening. "Ladies and gentlemen," he said, "let's give the General the biggest hand we've got!" and there was applause immediately and the young man indicated to Sally Poker with a motion of his thumb that she could take the old man back to his seat now so that the next person could be introduced; but the General had not finished. He stood immovable in the exact center of the spotlight, his neck thrust forward, his mouth slightly open, and his voracious gray eyes drinking in the glare and the applause. He elbowed his granddaughter roughly away. "How I keep so young," he screeched, "I kiss all the pretty guls!"

This was met with a great din of spontaneous applause and it was at just that instant that Sally Poker looked down at her feet and discovered that in the excitement of getting ready she had forgotten to change her shoes: two brown Girl Scout oxfords protruded from the bottom of her dress. She gave the General a yank and almost ran with him off the stage. He was very angry that he had not got to say how glad he was to be here for this event and on the way back to his seat, he kept saying as loud as he could, "I'm glad to be here at this preemy with all these beautiful guls!" but there was another celebrity going up the other aisle and nobody paid any attention to him. He slept through the picture, muttering fiercely every now and then in his sleep.

Since then, his life had not been very interesting. His feet were completely dead now, his knees worked like old hinges, his kidneys functioned when they would, but his heart persisted doggedly to beat. The past and the future were the same thing to him, one forgotten and the other not remembered; he had no more notion of dying than a cat. Every year on Confederate Memorial Day, he was bundled up and lent to the Capitol City Museum where he was displayed from one to four in a musty room full of old photographs, old uniforms, old artillery, and historic documents. All these were carefully preserved in glass cases so that children would not put their hands on them. He wore his general's uniform from the premiere and sat, with a fixed scowl, inside a small roped area. There was nothing about him to indicate that he was alive except an occasional movement in his milky gray eyes, but once when a bold child touched his sword, his arm shot forward and slapped the hand off in an instant. In the spring when the old homes were opened for pilgrimages, he was invited to wear his uniform and sit in some conspicuous spot and lend atmosphere to the scene. Some of these times he only snarled at the visitors but sometimes he told about the premiere and the beautiful girls.

If he had died before Sally Poker's graduation, she thought she would have died herself. At the beginning of the summer term, even before she knew if she would pass, she told the Dean that her grandfather, General Tennessee Flintrock Sash of the Confederacy, would attend her graduation and that he was a hundred and four years old and that his mind was still clear as a bell. Distinguished visitors were always welcome and could sit on the stage and be introduced. She made arrangements with her nephew, John Wesley Poker Sash, a Boy Scout, to come wheel the General's chair. She thought how sweet it would be to see the old man in his courageous gray and the young boy in his clean khaki—the old and the new, she thought appropriately—they would be behind her on the stage when she received her degree.

Everything went almost exactly as she had planned. In the summer while she was away at school, the General stayed with other relatives and they brought him and John Wesley, the Boy Scout, down to the graduation. A reporter came to the hotel where they stayed and took the General's picture with Sally Poker on one side of him and John Wesley on the other. The General, who had had his picture taken with beautiful girls, didn't think much of this. He had forgotten precisely what kind of event this was he was going to attend but he remembered that he was to wear his uniform and carry the sword.

On the morning of the graduation, Sally Poker had to line up in the academic procession with the B.S.'s in Elementary Education and she couldn't see to getting him on the stage herself—but John Wesley, a fat blond boy of ten with an executive expression, guaranteed to take care of everything. She came in her academic gown to the hotel and dressed the old man in his uniform. He was as frail as a dried spider. "Aren't you just thrilled, Papa?" she asked. "I'm just thrilled to death!"

"Put the soward acrost my lap, damm you," the old man said, "where it'll shine."

She put it there and then stood back looking at him. "You look just grand," she said.

"God damm it," the old man said in a slow monotonous certain tone as if he were saying it to the beating of his heart. "God damm every goddam thing to hell."

"Now, now," she said and left happily to join the procession.

The graduates were lined up behind the Science building and she found her place just as the line started to move. She had not slept much the night before and when she had, she had dreamed of the exercises, murmuring, "See him, see him?" in her sleep but waking up every time just before she turned her head to look at him behind her. The graduates had to walk three blocks in the hot sun in their black wool robes and as she plodded stolidly along she thought that if anyone considered this academic procession something impressive to behold, they need only wait until they saw that old General in his courageous gray and that clean young Boy Scout stoutly wheeling his chair across the stage with the sunlight catching the sword. She imagined that John Wesley had the old man ready now behind the stage.

The black procession wound its way up the two blocks and started on the main walk leading to the auditorium. The visitors stood on the grass, picking out their graduates. Men were pushing back their hats and wiping their foreheads and women were lifting their dresses slightly from the shoulders to keep them from sticking to their backs. The graduates in their heavy robes looked as if the last beads of ignorance were being sweated out of them. The sun blazed off the fenders of automobiles and beat from the columns of the buildings and pulled the eye from one spot of glare to another. It pulled Sally Poker's toward the big red Coca-Cola machine that had been set up by the side of the auditorium. Here she saw the General parked, scowling and hatless in his chair in the blazing sun while John Wesley, his blouse loose behind, his hip and cheek pressed to the red machine, was drinking a Coca-Cola. She broke from the line and galloped to them and snatched the bottle away. She shook the boy and thrust in his blouse and put the hat on the old man's head. "Now get him in there!" she said, pointing one rigid finger to the side door of the building.

For his part the General felt as if there were a little hole beginning to widen in the top of his head. The boy wheeled him rapidly down a walk and up a ramp and into a building and bumped him over the stage entrance and into position where he had been told and the General glared in front of him at heads that all seemed to flow together and eyes that moved from one face to another. Several figures in black robes came and picked up his hand and shook it. A black procession was flowing up each aisle and forming to stately music in a pool in front of him. The music seemed to be entering his head through the little hole and he thought for a second that the procession would try to enter it too.

He didn't know what procession this was but there was something familiar about it. It must be familiar to him since it had come to meet him, but he didn't like a black procession. Any procession that came to meet him, he thought irritably, ought to have floats with beautiful guls on them like the floats before the preemy. It must be something connected with history like they were always having. He had no use for any of it. What happened then wasn't anything to a man living now and he was living now.

When all the procession had flowed into the black pool, a black figure began orating in front of it. The figure was telling something about history and the General made up his mind he wouldn't listen, but the words kept seeping in through the little hole in his head. He heard his own name mentioned and his chair was shuttled forward roughly and the Boy Scout took a big bow. They called his name and the fat brat bowed. Goddam you, the old man tried to say, get out of my way, I can stand up!—but he was jerked back again before he could get up and take the bow. He supposed the noise they made was for him. If he was over, he didn't intend to listen to any more of it. If it hadn't been for the little hole in the top of his head, none of the words would have got to him. He thought of putting his finger up there into the hole to block them but the hole was a little wider than his finger and it felt as if it were getting deeper.

Another black robe had taken the place of the first one and was talking now and he heard his name mentioned again but they were not talking about him, they were still talking about history. "If we forget our past," the speaker was saying, "we won't remember our future and it will be as well for we won't have one." The General heard some of these words gradually. He had forgotten history and he didn't intend to remember it again. He had forgotten the name and face of his wife and the names and faces of his children or even if he had a wife and children, and he had forgotten the names of places and the places themselves and what had happened at them.

He was considerably irked by the hole in his head. He had not expected to have a hole in his head at this event. It was the slow black music that had put it there and though most of the music had stopped outside, there was still a little of it in the hole, going deeper and moving around in his thoughts, letting the words he heard into the dark places of his brain. He heard the words, Chickamauga, Shiloh, Johnston, Lee, and he knew he was inspiring all these words that meant nothing to him. He wondered if he had been a general at Chickamauga or at Lee. Then he tried to see himself and the horse mounted in the middle of a float full of beautiful girls, being driven slowly through downtown Atlanta. Instead, the old words began to stir in his head as if they were trying to wrench themselves out of place and come to life.

The speaker was through with that war and had gone on to the next one and now he was approaching another and all his words, like the black procession, were vaguely familiar and irritating. There was a long finger of music in the General's head, probing various spots that were words, letting in a little light on the words and helping them to live. The words began to come toward him and he said, Dammit! I ain't going to have it! and he started edging backwards to get out of the way. Then he saw the figure in the black robe sit down and there was a noise and the black pool in front of him began to rumble and to flow toward him from either side to the black slow music, and he said, Stop dammit! I can't do but one thing at a time! He couldn't protect himself from the words and attend to the procession too and the words were coming at him fast. He felt that he was running backwards and the words were coming at him like musket fire, just escaping him but getting nearer and nearer. He turned around and began to run as fast as he could but he found himself running toward the words. He was running into a regular volley of them and meeting them with quick curses. As the music swelled toward him, the entire past opened up on him out of nowhere and he felt his body riddled in a hundred places with sharp stabs of pain and he fell down, returning a curse for every hit. He saw his wife's narrow face looking at him critically through her round gold-rimmed glasses; he saw one of his squinting baldheaded sons; and his mother ran toward him with an anxious look; then a succession of places—Chickamauga, Shiloh, Marthasville—rushed at him as if the past were the only future now and he had to endure it. Then suddenly he saw that the black procession was almost on him. He recognized it, for it had been dogging all his days. He made such a desperate effort to see over it and find out what comes after the past that his hand clenched the sword until the blade touched bone.

The graduates were crossing the stage in a long file to receive their scrolls and shake the president's hand. As Sally Poker, who was near the end, crossed, she glanced at the General and saw him sitting fixed and fierce, his eyes wide open, and she turned her head forward again and held it a perceptible degree higher and received her scroll. Once it was all over and she was out of the auditorium in the sun again, she located her kin and they waited together on a bench in the shade for John Wesley to wheel the old man out. That crafty scout had bumped him out the back way and rolled him at high speed down a flagstone path and was waiting now, with the corpse, in the long line at the Coca-Cola machine.

FRANK O'CONNOR

# Guests of the Nation

Frank O'Connor (1903–1966), whose real name was Michael O'Donovan, was born in Cork, Ireland, and attended the Christian Brothers School there. He was financially unable to pursue a university education, but he educated himself and developed his ability as a writer while he worked as a librarian. In 1931 his first book of short stories, *Guests of the Nation*, was published; it was followed by many volumes of short stories and verse, by plays, criticism, a history of Michael Collins and the Irish Revolution, and his autobiography, *An Only Child*, 1961.

GUESTS OF THE NATION    From *More Stories* by Frank O'Connor. Published 1954 by Alfred A. Knopf, Inc. Reprinted by permission of the publisher.

"Guests of the Nation," like all Mr. O'Connor's short stories, is noted for its technical skill. "Storytelling," he says, "is the nearest thing one can get to the quality of the pure lyric poem. It doesn't deal with problems; it doesn't have any solutions to offer; it just states the human condition."

At dusk the big Englishman, Belcher, would shift his long legs out of the ashes and say "Well, chums, what about it?" and Noble or me would say "All right, chum" (for we had picked up some of their curious expressions), and the little Englishman, Hawkins, would light the lamp and bring out the cards. Sometimes Jeremiah Donovan would come up and supervise the game and get excited over Hawkins's cards, which he always played badly, and shout at him as if he was one of our own "Ah, you divil, you, why didn't you play the trey?"

But ordinarily Jeremiah was a sober and contented poor devil like the big Englishman, Belcher, and was looked up to only because he was a fair hand at documents, though he was slow enough even with them. He wore a small cloth hat and big gaiters over his long pants, and you seldom saw him with his hands out of his pockets. He reddened when you talked to him, tilting from toe to heel and back, and looking down all the time at his big farmer's feet. Noble and me used to make fun of his broad accent, because we were from the town.

I couldn't at the time see the point of me and Noble guarding Belcher and Hawkins at all, for it was my belief that you could have planted that pair down anywhere from this to Claregalway and they'd have taken root there like a native weed. I never in my short experience seen two men to take to the country as they did.

They were handed on to us by the Second Battalion when the search for them became too hot, and Noble and myself, being young, took over with a natural feeling of responsibility, but Hawkins made us look like fools when he showed that he knew the country better than we did.

"You're the bloke they calls Bonaparte," he says to me. "Mary Brigid O'Connell told me to ask you what you done with the pair of her brother's socks you borrowed."

For it seemed, as they explained it, that the Second used to have little evenings, and some of the girls of the neighbourhood turned in, and, seeing they were such decent chaps, our fellows couldn't leave the two Englishmen out of them.

Hawkins learned to dance "The Walls of Limerick," "The Siege of Ennis," and "The Waves of Tory" as well as any of them, though, naturally, we couldn't return the compliment, because our lads at that time did not dance foreign dances on principle.

So whatever privileges Belcher and Hawkins had with the Second they just naturally took with us, and after the first day or two we gave up all pretence of keeping a close eye on them. Not that they could have got far, for they had accents you could cut with a knife and wore khaki tunics and overcoats with civilian pants and boots. But it's my belief that they never had any idea of escaping and were quite content to be where they were.

It was a treat to see how Belcher got off with the old woman of the house where we were staying. She was a great warrant to scold, and cranky even with us, but before ever she had a chance of giving our guests, as I may call them, a lick of her tongue, Belcher had made her his friend for life. She was breaking sticks, and Belcher, who hadn't been more than ten minutes in the house, jumped up from his seat and went over to her.

"Allow me, madam," he says, smiling his queer little smile, "please allow me"; and he takes the bloody hatchet. She was struck too paralytic to speak, and after that, Belcher would be at her heels, carrying a bucket, a basket, or a load of turf, as the case might be. As Noble said, he got into looking before she leapt, and hot water, or any little thing she wanted, Belcher would have it ready for her. For such a huge man (and though I am five foot ten myself I had to look up at him) he had an uncommon shortness—or should I say lack?—of speech. It took us some time to get used to him, walking in and out, like a ghost, without a word. Especially because Hawkins talked enough for a platoon, it was strange to hear big Belcher with his toes in the ashes come out with a solitary "Excuse me, chum," or "That's right, chum." His one and only passion was cards, and I will say for him that he was a good card-player. He could have fleeced myself and Noble, but whatever we lost to him Hawkins lost to us, and Hawkins played with the money Belcher gave him.

Hawkins lost to us because he had too much old gab, and we probably lost to Belcher for the same reason. Hawkins and Noble would spit at one another about religion into the early hours of the morning, and Hawkins worried the soul out of Noble, whose brother was a priest, with a string of questions that would puzzle a cardinal. To make it worse, even in treating of holy subjects, Hawkins had a deplorable tongue. I never in all my career met a man who could mix such a variety of cursing and bad language into an argument. He was a terrible man, and a fright to argue. He never did a stroke of work, and when he had no one else to talk to, he got stuck in the old woman.

He met his match in her, for one day when he tried to get her to complain profanely of the drought, she gave him a great comedown by blaming it entirely on Jupiter Pluvius (a deity neither Hawkins nor I had ever heard of, though Noble said that among the pagans it was believed that he had something to do with the rain). Another day he was swearing at the capitalists for starting the German war when the old lady laid down her iron, puckered up her little crab's mouth, and said: "Mr. Hawkins, you can say what you like about the war, and think you'll deceive me because I'm only a simple poor countrywoman, but I know what started the war. It was the Italian Count that stole the heathen divinity out of the temple in Japan. Believe me, Mr. Hawkins, nothing but sorrow and want can follow the people that disturb the hidden powers."

A queer old girl, all right.

## II

We had our tea one evening, and Hawkins lit the lamp and we all sat into cards. Jeremiah Donovan came in too, and sat down and watched us for a while, and it suddenly struck me that he had no great love for the two Englishmen. It came as a great surprise to me, because I hadn't noticed anything about him before.

Late in the evening a really terrible argument blew up between Hawkins and Noble, about capitalists and priests and love of your country.

"The capitalists," says Hawkins with an angry gulp, "pays the priests to tell you about the next world so as you won't notice what the bastards are up to in this."

"Nonsense, man!" says Noble, losing his temper. "Before ever a capitalist was thought of, people believed in the next world."

Hawkins stood up as though he was preaching a sermon.

"Oh, they did, did they?" he says with a sneer. "They believed all the things you believe, isn't that what you mean? And you believe that God created Adam, and Adam created Shem, and Shem created Jehoshophat. You believe all that silly old fairytale about Eve and Eden and the apple. Well, listen to me, chum. If you're entitled to hold a silly belief like that, I'm entitled to hold a silly belief—which is that the first thing your God created was a bleeding capitalist, with morality and Rolls-Royce complete. Am I right, chum?" he says to Belcher.

"You're right, chum," says Belcher with his amused smile, and got up from the table to stretch his long legs into the fire and stroke his moustache. So, seeing that Jeremiah Donovan was going, and that there was no knowing when the argument about religion would be over, I went out with him. We strolled down to the village together, and then he stopped and started blushing and mumbling and saying I ought to be behind, keeping guard on the prisoners. I didn't like the tone he took with me, and anyway I was bored with life in the cottage, so I replied by asking him what the hell we wanted guarding them at all for. I told him I'd talked it over with Noble, and that we'd both rather be out with a fighting column.

"What use are those fellows to us?" says I.

He looked at me in surprise and said: "I thought you knew we were keeping them as hostages."

"Hostages?" I said.

"The enemy have prisoners belonging to us," he says, "and now they're talking of shooting them. If they shoot our prisoners, we'll shoot theirs."

"Shoot them?" I said.

"What else did you think we were keeping them for?" he says.

"Wasn't it very unforeseen of you not to warn Noble and myself of that in the beginning?" I said.

"How was it?" says he. "You might have known it."

"We couldn't know it, Jeremiah Donovan," says I. "How could we when they were on our hands so long?"

"The enemy have our prisoners as long and longer," says he.

"That's not the same thing at all," says I.

"What difference is there?" says he.

I couldn't tell him, because I knew he wouldn't understand. If it was only an old dog that was going to the vet's, you'd try and not get too fond of him, but Jeremiah Donovan wasn't a man that would ever be in danger of that.

"And when is this thing going to be decided?" says I.

"We might hear tonight," he says. "Or tomorrow or the next day at latest. So if it's only hanging round here that's a trouble to you, you'll be free soon enough."

It wasn't the hanging round that was a trouble to me at all by this time. I had worse things to worry about. When I got back to the cottage the argument was still on. Hawkins was holding forth in his best style, maintaining that there was no next world, and Noble was maintaining that there was; but I could see that Hawkins had had the best of it.

"Do you know what, chum?" he was saying with a saucy smile. "I think you're just as big a bleeding unbeliever as I am. You say you believe in the next world, and you know just as much about the next world as I do, which is sweet damn-all. What's heaven? You don't know. Where's heaven? You don't know. You know sweet damn-all! I ask you again, do they wear wings?"

"Very well, then," says Noble, "they do. Is that enough for you? They do wear wings."

"Where do they get them, then? Who makes them? Have they a factory for wings? Have they a sort of store where you hands in your chit and takes your bleeding wings?"

"You're an impossible man to argue with," says Noble. "Now, listen to—" And they were off again.

It was long after midnight when we locked up and went to bed. As I blew out the candle I told Noble what Jeremiah Donovan was after telling me. Noble took it very quietly. When we'd been in bed about an hour he asked me did I think we ought to tell the Englishmen. I didn't think we should, because it was more than likely that the English wouldn't shoot our men, and even if they did, the brigade officers, who were always up and down with the Second Battalion and knew the Englishmen well, wouldn't be likely to want them plugged. "I think so too," says Noble. "It would be great cruelty to put the wind up them now."

"It was very unforeseen of Jeremiah Donovan anyhow," says I.

It was next morning that we found it so hard to face Belcher and Hawkins. We went about the house all day scarcely saying a word. Belcher didn't seem to notice; he was stretched into the ashes as usual, with his usual look of waiting in quietness for something unforeseen to happen, but Hawkins noticed and put it down to Noble's being beaten in the argument of the night before.

"Why can't you take a discussion in the proper spirit?" he says severely. "You and your Adam and Eve! I'm a Communist, that's what I am. Communist or anarchist, it all comes to much the same thing." And for hours he went round the house, muttering when the fit took him. "Adam and Eve! Adam and Eve! Nothing better to do with their time than picking bleeding apples!"

### III

I don't know how we got through that day, but I was very glad when it was over, the tea things were cleared away, and Belcher said in his peaceable way: "Well, chums, what about it?" We sat round the table and Hawkins took out the cards, and just then I heard Jeremiah Donovan's footstep on the path and a dark presentiment crossed my mind. I rose from the table and caught him before he reached the door.

"What do you want?" I asked.

"I want those two soldier friends of yours," he says, getting red.

"Is that the way, Jeremiah Donovan?" I asked.

"That's the way. There were four of our lads shot this morning, one of them a boy of sixteen."

"That's bad," I said.

At that moment Noble followed me out, and the three of us walked down the path together, talking in whispers. Feeney, the local intelligence officer, was standing by the gate.

"What are you going to do about it?" I asked Jeremiah Donovan.

"I want you and Noble to get them out; tell them they're being shifted again; that'll be the quietest way."

"Leave me out of that," says Noble under his breath.

Jeremiah Donovan looks at him hard.

"All right," he says. "You and Feeney get a few tools from the shed and dig a hole by the far end of the bog. Bonaparte and myself will be after you. Don't let anyone see you with the tools. I wouldn't like it to go beyond ourselves."

We saw Feeney and Noble go round to the shed and went in ourselves. I left Jeremiah Donovan to do the explanations. He told them that he had orders to send them back to the Second Battalion. Hawkins let out a mouthful of curses, and you could see that though Belcher didn't say anything, he was a bit upset too. The old woman was for having them stay in spite of us, and she didn't stop advising them until Jeremiah Donovan lost his temper and turned on her. He had a nasty temper, I noticed. It was pitch-dark in the cottage by this time, but no one thought of lighting the lamp, and in the darkness the two Englishmen fetched their top-coats and said good-bye to the old woman.

"Just as a man makes a home of a bleeding place, some bastard at headquarters thinks you're too cushy and shunts you off," says Hawkins, shaking her hand.

"A thousand thanks, madam," says Belcher. "A thousand thanks for everything"—as though he'd made it up.

We went round to the back of the house and down towards the bog. It was only then that Jeremiah Donovan told them. He was shaking with excitement.

"There were four of our fellows shot in Cork this morning and now you're to be shot as a reprisal."

"What are you talking about?" snaps Hawkins. "It's bad enough being mucked about as we are without having to put up with your funny jokes."

"It isn't a joke," says Donovan. "I'm sorry, Hawkins, but it's true," and begins on the usual rigmarole about duty and how unpleasant it is.

I never noticed that people who talk a lot about duty find it much of a trouble to them.

"Oh, cut it out!" says Hawkins.

"Ask Bonaparte," says Donovan, seeing that Hawkins isn't taking him seriously. "Isn't it true, Bonaparte?"

"It is," I say, and Hawkins stops.

"Ah, for Christ's sake, chum!"

"I mean it, chum," I say.

"You don't sound as if you meant it."

"If he doesn't mean it, I do," says Donovan, working himself up.

"What have you against me, Jeremiah Donovan?"

"I never said I had anything against you. But why did your people take out four of our prisoners and shoot them in cold blood?"

He took Hawkins by the arm and dragged him on, but it was impossible to make him understand that we were in earnest. I had the Smith and Wesson in my pocket and I kept fingering it and wondering what I'd do if they put up a fight for it or ran, and wishing to God they'd do one or the other. I knew if they did run for it, that I'd never fire on them. Hawkins wanted to know was Noble in it, and when we said yes, he asked us why Noble wanted to plug him. Why did any of us want to plug him? What had he done to us? Weren't we all chums? Didn't we understand him and didn't he understand us? Did we imagine for an instant that he'd shoot us for all the so-and-so officers in the so-and-so British Army?

By this time we'd reached the bog, and I was so sick I couldn't even answer him. We walked along the edge of it in the darkness, and every now and then Hawkins would call a halt and begin all over again, as if he was wound up, about our being chums, and I knew that nothing but the sight of the grave would convince him that we had to do it. And all the time I was hoping that something would happen; that they'd run for it or that Noble would take over the responsibility from me. I had the feeling that it was worse on Noble than on me.

IV

At last we saw the lantern in the distance and made towards it. Noble was carrying it, and Feeney was standing somewhere in the darkness behind him, and the picture of them so still and silent in the bogland brought it home to me that we were in earnest, and banished the last bit of hope I had.

Belcher, on recognizing Noble, said: "Hallo, chum," in his quiet way, but Hawkins flew at him at once, and the argument began all over again, only this time Noble had nothing to say for himself and stood with his head down, holding the lantern between his legs.

It was Jeremiah Donovan who did the answering. For the twentieth time, as though it was haunting his mind, Hawkins asked if anybody thought he'd shoot Noble.

"Yes, you would," says Jeremiah Donovan.

"No, I wouldn't, damn you!"

"You would, because you'd know you'd be shot for not doing it."

"I wouldn't, not if I was to be shot twenty times over. I wouldn't shoot a pal. And Belcher wouldn't—isn't that right, Belcher?"

"That's right, chum," Belcher said, but more by way of answering the question than of joining in the argument. Belcher sounded as though whatever unforeseen thing he'd always been waiting for had come at last.

"Anyway, who says Noble would be shot if I wasn't? What do you think I'd do if I was in his place, out in the middle of a blasted bog?"

"What would you do?" asks Donovan.

"I'd go with him wherever he was going, of course. Share my last bob with him and stick by him through thick and thin. No one can ever say of me that I let down a pal."

"We had enough of this," says Jeremiah Donovan, cocking his revolver. "Is there any message you want to send?"

"No, there isn't."

"Do you want to say your prayers?"

Hawkins came out with a cold-blooded remark that even shocked me and turned on Noble again.

"Listen to me, Noble," he says. "You and me are chums. You can't come over to my side, so I'll come over to your side. That show you I mean what I say? Give me a rifle and I'll go along with you and the other lads."

Nobody answered him. We knew that was no way out.

"Hear what I'm saying?" he says. "I'm through with it. I'm a deserter or anything else you like. I don't believe in your stuff, but it's no worse than mine. That satisfy you?"

Noble raised his head, but Donovan began to speak and he lowered it again without replying.

"For the last time, have you any messages to send?" says Donovan in a cold, excited sort of voice.

"Shut up, Donovan! You don't understand me, but these lads do. They're not the sort to make a pal and kill a pal. They're not the tools of any capitalist."

I alone of the crowd saw Donovan raise his Webley to the back of Hawkins's neck, and as he did so I shut my eyes and tried to pray. Hawkins had begun to say something else when Donovan fired, and as I opened my eyes at the bang, I saw Hawkins stagger at the knees and lie out flat at Noble's feet, slowly and as quiet as a kid falling asleep, with the lantern-light on his lean legs and bright farmer's boots. We all stood very still, watching him settle out in the last agony.

Then Belcher took out a handkerchief and began to tie it about his own eyes (in our excitement we'd forgotten to do the same for Hawkins), and, seeing it wasn't big enough, turned and asked for the loan of mine. I gave it to him and he knotted the two together and pointed with his foot at Hawkins.

"He's not quite dead," he says. "Better give him another."

Sure enough, Hawkins's left knee is beginning to rise. I bend down and put my gun to his head; then, recollecting myself, I get up again. Belcher understands what's in my mind.

"Give him his first," he says. "I don't mind. Poor bastard, we don't know what's happening to him now."

I knelt and fired. By this time I didn't seem to know what I was doing. Belcher, who was fumbling a bit awkwardly with the handkerchiefs, came out with a laugh as he heard the shot. It was the first time I heard him laugh and it sent a shudder down my back; it sounded so unnatural.

"Poor bugger!" he said quietly. "And last night he was so curious about it all. It's very queer, chums, I always think. Now he knows as much about it as they'll ever let him know, and last night he was all in the dark."

Donovan helped him to tie the handkerchiefs about his eyes. "Thanks, chum," he said. Donovan asked if there were any messages he wanted sent.

"No, chum," he says. "Not for me. If any of you would like to write to Hawkins's mother, you'll find a letter from her in his pocket. He and his mother were great chums. But my missus left me eight years ago. Went away with another fellow and took the kid with her. I like the feeling of a home, as you may have noticed, but I couldn't start again after that."

It was an extraordinary thing, but in those few minutes Belcher said more than in all the weeks before. It was just as if the sound of the shot had started a flood of talk in him and he could go on the whole night like that, quite happily, talking about himself. We stood round like fools now that he couldn't see us any longer. Donovan looked at Noble, and Noble shook his head. Then Donovan raised his Webley, and at that moment Belcher gives his queer laugh again. He may have thought we were talking about him, or perhaps he noticed the same thing I'd noticed and couldn't understand it.

"Excuse me, chums," he says. "I feel I'm talking the hell of a lot, and so silly, about my being so handy about a house and things like that. But this thing came on me suddenly. You'll forgive me, I'm sure."

"You don't want to say a prayer?" asks Donovan.

"No, chum," he says. "I don't think it would help. I'm ready, and you boys want to get it over."

"You understand that we're only doing our duty?" says Donovan.

Belcher's head was raised like a blind man's, so that you could only see his chin and the tip of his nose in the lantern-light.

"I never could make out what duty was myself," he said. "I think you're all good lads, if that's what you mean. I'm not complaining."

Noble, just as if he couldn't bear any more of it, raised his fist at Donovan, and in a flash Donovan raised his gun and fired. The big man went over like a sack of meal, and this time there was no need of a second shot.

I don't remember much about the burying, but that it was worse than all the rest because we had to carry them to the grave. It was all mad lonely with nothing but a patch of lantern-light between ourselves and the dark, and birds hooting and screeching all round, disturbed by the guns. Noble went through Hawkins's belongings to find the letter from his mother, and then joined his hands together. He did the same with Belcher. Then, when we'd filled in the grave, we separated from Jeremiah Donovan and Feeney and took our tools back to the shed. All the way we didn't speak a word. The kitchen was dark and cold as we'd left it, and the old woman was sitting over the hearth, saying her beads. We walked past her into the room, and Noble struck a match to light the lamp. She rose quietly and came to the doorway with all her cantankerousness gone.

"What did ye do with them?" she asked in a whisper, and Noble started so that the match went out in his hand.

"What's that?" he asked without turning round.

"I heard ye," she said.

"What did you hear?" asked Noble.

"I heard ye. Do ye think I didn't hear ye, putting the spade back in the houseen?"

Noble struck another match and this time the lamp lit for him.

"Was that what ye did to them?" she asked.

Then, by God, in the very doorway, she fell on her knees and began praying, and after looking at her for a minute or two Noble did the same by the fireplace. I pushed my way out past her and left them at it. I stood at the door, watching the stars and listening to the shrieking of the birds dying out over the bogs. It is so strange what you feel at times like that that you can't describe it. Noble says he saw everything ten times the size, as though there were nothing in the whole world but that little patch of bog with the two Englishmen stiffening into it, but with me it was as if the patch of bog where the Englishmen were was a million miles away, and even Noble and the old woman, mumbling behind me, and the birds and the bloody stars were all far away, and I was somehow very small and very lost and lonely like a child astray in the snow. And anything that happened to me afterwards, I never felt the same about again.

# JOHN CHEEVER

# The Swimmer

John Cheever (1912–     ) is an outstanding figure in contemporary American fiction. He has published both novels and short stories: *The Way Some People Live*, 1942; *The Enormous Radio*, 1954; *The Wapshot Chronicle*, 1957; *The Housebreaker of Shady Hill*, 1959; *Some People, Places and Things That Will Not Appear in My Next Novel*, 1961; *The Wapshot Scandal*, 1964; *The Brigadier and the Golf Widow*, 1964; and *Bullet Park*, 1969.

"The Swimmer," like many of Cheever's short stories, presents his concern with well-to-do suburbanites. Neddy Merrill, as *Time* put it, "turns an unsuspected corner and falls off the edge of things into outer darkness."

It was one of those midsummer Sundays when everyone sits around saying: "I *drank* too much last night." You might have heard it whispered by the parishioners leaving church, heard it from the lips of the priest himself, struggling with his cassock in the *vestiarium*, heard it from the golf links and the tennis courts, heard it from the wildlife preserve where the leader of the Audubon group was suffering from a terrible hangover. "I *drank* too much," said Donald Westerhazy. "We all *drank* too much," said Lucinda Merrill. "It must have been the wine," said Helen Westerhazy. "I *drank* too much of that claret."

This was at the edge of the Westerhazys' pool. The pool, fed by an artesian well with a high iron content, was a pale shade of green. It was a fine day. In the west there was a massive stand of cumulus cloud so like a city seen from a distance—from the bow of an approaching ship—that it might have had a name. Lisbon. Hackensack. The sun was hot. Neddy Merrill sat by the green water, one hand in it, one around a glass of gin. He was a slender man—he seemed to have the especial slenderness of youth—and while he

was far from young he had slid down his banister that morning and given the bronze backside of Aphrodite on the hall table a smack, as he jogged toward the smell of coffee in his dining room. He might have been compared to a summer's day, particularly the last hours of one, and while he lacked a tennis racket or a sail bag the impression was definitely one of youth, sport, and clement weather. He had been swimming and now he was breathing deeply, stertorously as if he could gulp into his lungs the components of that moment, the heat of the sun, the intenseness of his pleasure. It all seemed to flow into his chest. His own house stood in Bullet Park, eight miles to the south, where his four beautiful daughters would have had their lunch and might be playing tennis. Then it occurred to him that by taking a dogleg to the south-west he could reach his home by water.

His life was not confining and the delight he took in this observation could not be explained by its suggestion of escape. He seemed to see, with a cartographer's eye, that string of swimming pools, that quasi-subterranean stream that curved across the county. He had made a discovery, a contribution to modern geography; he would name the stream Lucinda after his wife. He was not a practical joker nor was he a fool but he was determinedly original and had a vague and modest idea of himself as a legendary figure. The day was beautiful and it seemed to him that a long swim might enlarge and celebrate its beauty.

He took off a sweater that was hung over his shoulders and dove in. He had an inexplicable contempt for men who did not hurl themselves into pools. He swam a choppy crawl, breathing either with every stroke or every fourth stroke and counting somewhere well in the back of his mind the one-two one-two of a flutter kick. It was not a serviceable stroke for long distances but the domestication of swimming had saddled the sport with some customs and in his part of the world a crawl was customary. To be embraced and sustained by the light green water was less a pleasure, it seemed, than the resumption of a natural condition, and he would have liked to swim without trunks, but this was not possible, considering his project. He hoisted himself up on the far curb—he never used the ladder—and started across the lawn. When Lucinda asked where he was going he said he was going to swim home.

The only maps and charts he had to go by were remembered or imaginary but these were clear enough. First there were the Grahams, the Hammers, the Lears, the Howlands, and the Crosscups. He would cross Ditmar Street to the Bunkers and come, after a short portage, to the Levys, the Welchers, and the public pool in Lancaster. Then there were the Hallorans, the Sachses, the Biswangers, Shirley Adams, the Gilmartins, and the Clydes. The day was lovely, and that he lived in a world so generously supplied with water seemed like a clemency, a beneficence. His heart was high and he ran across the grass. Making his way home by an uncommon route gave him the feeling that he was a pilgrim, an explorer, a man with a destiny, and he knew that he would find friends all along the way; friends would line the banks of the Lucinda River.

He went through a hedge that separated the Westerhazys' land from the Grahams', walked under some flowering apple trees, passed the shed that housed their pump and filter, and came out at the Grahams' pool. "Why, Neddy," Mrs. Graham said, "what a marvelous surprise. I've been trying to get you on the phone all morning. Here, let me get you a drink." He saw then, like any explorer, that the hospitable customs and

traditions of the natives would have to be handled with diplomacy if he was ever going to reach his destination. He did not want to mystify or seem rude to the Grahams nor did he have the time to linger there. He swam the length of their pool and joined them in the sun and was rescued, a few minutes later, by the arrival of two carloads of friends from Connecticut. During the uproarious reunions he was able to slip away. He went down by the front of the Grahams' house, stepped over a thorny hedge, and crossed a vacant lot to the Hammers'. Mrs. Hammer, looking up from her roses, saw him swim by although she wasn't quite sure who it was. The Lears heard him splashing past the open windows of their living room. The Howlands and the Crosscups were away. After leaving the Howlands' he crossed Ditmar Street and started for the Bunkers', where he could hear, even at that distance, the noise of a party.

The water refracted the sound of voices and laughter and seemed to suspend it in midair. The Bunkers' pool was on a rise and he climbed some stairs to a terrace where twenty-five or thirty men and women were drinking. The only person in the water was Rusty Towers, who floated there on a rubber raft. Oh how bonny and lush were the banks of the Lucinda River! Prosperous men and women gathered by the sapphire-colored waters while caterer's men in white coats passed them cold gin. Overhead a red de Haviland trainer was circling around and around and around in the sky with something like the glee of a child in a swing. Ned felt a passing affection for the scene, a tenderness for the gathering, as if it was something he might touch. In the distance he heard thunder. As soon as Enid Bunker saw him she began to scream: "Oh look who's here! What a marvelous surprise! When Lucinda said that you couldn't come I thought I'd *die*." She made her way to him through the crowd, and when they had finished kissing she led him to the bar, a progress that was slowed by the fact that he stopped to kiss eight or ten other women and shake the hands of as many men. A smiling bartender he had seen at a hundred parties gave him a gin and tonic and he stood by the bar for a moment, anxious not to get stuck in any conversation that would delay his voyage. When he seemed about to be surrounded he dove in and swam close to the side to avoid colliding with Rusty's raft. At the far end of the pool he bypassed the Tomlinsons with a broad smile and jogged up the garden path. The gravel cut his feet but this was the only unpleasantness. The party was confined to the pool, and as he went toward the house he heard the brilliant, watery sound of voices fade, heard the noise of a radio from the Bunkers' kitchen, where someone was listening to a ballgame. Sunday afternoon. He made his way through the parked cars and down the grassy border of their driveway to Alewives' Lane. He did not want to be seen on the road in his bathing trunks but there was no traffic and he made the short distance to the Levys' driveway, marked with a private property sign and a green tube for the *New York Times*. All the doors and windows of the big house were open but there were no signs of life; not even a dog barked. He went around the side of the house to the pool and saw that the Levys had only recently left. Glasses and bottles and dishes of nuts were on a table at the deep end, where there was a bathhouse or gazebo, hung with Japanese lanterns. After swimming the pool he got himself a glass and poured a drink. It was his fourth or fifth drink and he had swum nearly half the length of the Lucinda River. He felt tired, clean, and pleased at that moment to be alone; pleased with everything.

It would storm. The stand of cumulus cloud—that city—had risen and darkened, and while he sat there he heard the percussiveness of thunder again. The de Haviland trainer was still circling overhead and it seemed to Ned that he could almost hear the pilot laugh with pleasure in the afternoon; but when there was another peal of thunder he took off for home. A train whistle blew and he wondered what time it had gotten to be. Four? Five? He thought of the provincial station at that hour, where a waiter, his tuxedo concealed by a raincoat, a dwarf with some flowers wrapped in newspaper, and a woman who had been crying would be waiting for the local. It was suddenly growing dark; it was that moment when the pin-headed birds seem to organize their song into some acute and knowledgeable recognition of the storm's approach. Then there was a fine noise of rushing water from the crown of an oak at his back, as if a spigot there had been turned. Then the noise of fountains came from the crowns of all the tall trees. Why did he love storms, what was the meaning of his excitement when the door sprang open and

the rain wind fled rudely up the stairs, why had the simple task of shutting the windows of an old house seemed fitting and urgent, why did the first watery notes of a storm wind have for him the unmistakable sound of good news, cheer, glad tidings? Then there was an explosion, a smell of cordite, and rain lashed the Japanese lanterns that Mrs. Levy had bought in Kyoto the year before last, or was it the year before that?

He stayed in the Levys' gazebo until the storm had passed. The rain had cooled the air and he shivered. The force of the wind had stripped a maple of its red and yellow leaves and scattered them over the grass and the water. Since it was midsummer the tree must be blighted, and yet he felt a peculiar sadness at this sign of autumn. He braced his shoulders, emptied his glass, and started for the Welchers' pool. This meant crossing the Lindleys' riding ring and he was surprised to find it overgrown with grass and all the jumps dismantled. He wondered if the Lindleys had sold their horses or gone away for the summer and put them out to board. He seemed to remember having heard something about the Lindleys and their horses but the memory was unclear. On he went, barefoot through the wet grass, to the Welchers', where he found their pool was dry.

This breach in his chain of water disappointed him absurdly, and he felt like some explorer who seeks a torrential headwater and finds a dead stream. He was disappointed and mystified. It was common enough to go away for the summer but no one ever drained his pool. The Welchers had definitely gone away. The pool furniture was folded, stacked, and covered with a tarpaulin. The bathhouse was locked. All the windows of the house were shut, and when he went around to the driveway in front he saw a for-sale sign nailed to a tree. When had he last heard from the Welchers—when, that is, had he and Lucinda last regretted an invitation to dine with them? It seemed only a week or so ago. Was his memory failing or had he so disciplined it in the repression of unpleasant facts that he had damaged his sense of the truth? Then in the distance he heard the sound of a tennis game. This cheered him, cleared away all his apprehensions and let him regard the overcast sky and the cold air with indifference. This was the day that Neddy Merrill swam across the county. That was the day! He started off then for his most difficult portage.

Had you gone for a Sunday afternoon ride that day you might have seen him, close to naked, standing on the shoulders of route 424, waiting for a chance to cross. You might have wondered if he was the victim of foul play, had his car broken down, or was he merely a fool. Standing barefoot in the deposits of the highway—beer cans, rags, and blowout patches—exposed to all kinds of ridicule, he seemed pitiful. He had known when he started that this was a part of his journey—it had been on his maps—but confronted with the lines of traffic, worming through the summery light, he found himself unprepared. He was laughed at, jeered at, a beer can was thrown at him, and he had no dignity or humor to bring to the situation. He could have gone back, back to the Westerhazys', where Lucinda would still be sitting in the sun. He had signed nothing, vowed nothing, pledged nothing not even to himself. Why, believing as he did, that all human obduracy was susceptible to common sense, was he unable to turn back? Why was he determined to complete his journey even if it meant putting his life in danger? At what point had this prank, this joke, this piece of horseplay become serious? He could not go back, he could not even recall with any clearness the green water at the Westerhazys', the sense of inhaling the day's components, the friendly and relaxed voices saying that they had *drunk* too much. In the space of an hour, more or less, he had covered a distance that made his return impossible.

An old man, tooling down the highway at fifteen miles an hour, let him get to the middle of the road, where there was a grass divider. Here he was exposed to the ridicule of the northbound traffic, but after ten or fifteen minutes he was able to cross. From here he had only a short walk to the Recreation Center at the edge of the Village of Lancaster, where there were some handball courts and a public pool.

The effect of the water on voices, the illusion of brilliance and suspense, was the same here as it had been at the Bunkers' but the sounds here were louder, harsher, and more shrill, and as soon as he entered the crowded enclosure he was confronted with regimentation. "ALL SWIMMERS MUST TAKE A SHOWER BEFORE USING THE POOL. ALL SWIMMERS MUST USE THE FOOTBATH. ALL SWIMMERS MUST WEAR THEIR IDENTIFICATION DISKS." He took a shower, washed his feet in a cloudy and bitter solution and made his way to the edge of the water. It stank of chlorine and looked to him like a sink. A pair of lifeguards in a pair of towers blew police whistles at what seemed to be regular intervals and abused the swimmers through a public address system. Neddy remembered the sapphire water at the Bunkers' with longing and thought that he might contaminate himself—damage his own prosperousness and charm—by swimming in this murk, but he reminded himself that he was an explorer, a pilgrim, and that this was merely a stagnant bend in the Lucinda River. He dove, scowling with distaste, into the chlorine and had to swim with his head above water to avoid collisions, but even so he was bumped into, splashed and jostled. When he got to the shallow end both lifeguards were shouting at him: "Hey, you, you without the identification disk, get outa the water." He did, but they had no way of pursuing him and he went through the reek of suntan oil and chlorine out through the hurricane fence and passed the handball courts. By crossing the road he entered the wooded part of the Halloran estate. The woods were not cleared and the footing was treacherous and difficult until he reached the lawn and the clipped beech hedge that encircled their pool.

The Hallorans were friends, an elderly couple of enormous wealth who seemed to bask in the suspicion that they might be Communists. They were zealous reformers but they were not Communists, and yet when they were accused, as they sometimes were, of subversion, it seemed to gratify and excite them. Their beech hedge was yellow and he guessed this had been blighted like the Levys' maple. He called hullo, hullo, to warn the Hallorans of his approach, to palliate his invasion of their privacy. The Hallorans, for reasons that had never been explained to him, did not wear bathing suits. No explanations were in order, really. Their nakedness was a detail in their uncompromising zeal for reform and he stepped politely out of his trunks before he went through the opening in the hedge.

Mrs. Halloran, a stout woman with white hair and a serene face, was reading the *Times*. Mr. Halloran was taking beech leaves out of the water with a scoop. They seemed not surprised or displeased to see him. Their pool was perhaps the oldest in the county, a fieldstone rectangle, fed by a brook. It had no filter or pump and its waters were the opaque gold of the stream.

"I'm swimming across the county," Ned said.

"Why, I didn't know one could," exclaimed Mrs. Halloran.

"Well, I've made it from the Westerhazys'," Ned said. "That must be about four miles."

He left his trunks at the deep end, walked to the shallow end, and swam this stretch. As he was pulling himself out of the water he heard Mrs. Halloran say: "We've been *terribly* sorry to hear about all your misfortunes, Neddy."

"My misfortunes?" Ned asked. "I don't know what you mean."

"Why, we heard that you'd sold the house and that your poor children . . ."

"I don't recall having sold the house," Ned said, "and the girls are at home."

"Yes," Mrs. Halloran sighed. "Yes . . ." Her voice filled the air with an unseasonable melancholy and Ned spoke briskly. "Thank you for the swim."

"Well, have a nice trip," said Mrs. Halloran.

Beyond the hedge he pulled on his trunks and fastened them. They were loose and he wondered if, during the space of an afternoon, he could have lost some weight. He was cold and he was tired and the naked Hallorans and their dark water had depressed him. The swim was too much for his strength but how could he have guessed this, sliding down the banister that morning and sitting in the Westerhazys' sun? His arms were lame. His legs felt rubbery and ached at the joints. The worst of it was the cold in his bones and the feeling that he might never be warm again. Leaves were falling down around him and he smelled woodsmoke on the wind. Who would be burning wood at this time of year?

He needed a drink. Whiskey would warm him, pick him up, carry him through the last of his journey, refresh his feeling that it was original and valorous to swim across the county. Channel swimmers took brandy. He needed a stimulant. He crossed the lawn in front of the Hallorans' house and went down a little path to where they had built a house for their only daughter Helen and her husband Eric Sachs. The Sachses' pool was small and he found Helen and her husband there.

"Oh, *Neddy*," Helen said. "Did you lunch at Mother's?"

"Not *really*," Ned said. "I *did* stop to see your parents." This seemed to be explanation enough. "I'm terribly sorry to break in on you like this but I've taken a chill and I wonder if you'd give me a drink."

"Why, I'd *love* to," Helen said, "but there hasn't been anything in this house to drink since Eric's operation. That was three years ago."

Was he losing his memory, had his gift for concealing painful facts let him forget that he had sold his house, that his children were in trouble, and that his friend had been ill? His eyes slipped from Eric's face to his abdomen, where he saw three pale, sutured scars, two of them at least a foot long. Gone was his navel, and what, Neddy thought, would the roving hand, bed-checking one's gifts at 3 A.M. make of a belly with no navel, no link to birth, this breach in the succession?

"I'm sure you can get a drink at the Biswangers'," Helen said. "They're having an enormous do. You can hear it from here. Listen!"

She raised her head and from across the road, the lawns, the gardens, the woods, the fields, he heard again the brilliant noise of voices over water. "Well, I'll get wet," he said, still feeling that he had no freedom of choice about his means of travel. He dove into the Sachses' cold water and, gasping, close to drowning, made his way from one end of the pool to the other. "Lucinda and I want *terribly* to see you," he said over his shoulder, his face set toward the Biswangers'. "We're sorry it's been so long and we'll call you *very* soon."

He crossed some fields to the Biswangers' and the sounds of revelry there. They would be honored to give him a drink, they would be happy to give him a drink, they would in fact be lucky to give him a drink. The Biswangers invited him and Lucinda for dinner four times a year, six weeks in advance. They were always rebuffed and yet they continued to send out their invitations, unwilling to comprehend the rigid and undemocratic realities of their society. They were the sort of people who discussed the price of things at cocktails, exchanged market tips during dinner, and after dinner told dirty stories to mixed company. They did not belong to Neddy's set—they were not even on Lucinda's

Christmas card list. He went toward their pool with feelings of indifference, charity, and some unease, since it seemed to be getting dark and these were the longest days of the year. The party when he joined it was noisy and large. Grace Biswanger was the kind of hostess who asked the optometrist, the veterinarian, the real-estate dealer and the dentist. No one was swimming and the twilight, reflected on the water of the pool, had a wintry gleam. There was a bar and he started for this. When Grace Biswanger saw him she came toward him, not affectionately as he had every right to expect, but bellicosely.

"Why, this party has everything." she said loudly, "including a gate crasher."

She could not deal him a social blow—there was no question about this and he did not flinch. "As a gate crasher," he asked politely, "do I rate a drink?"

"Suit yourself," she said. "You don't seem to pay much attention to invitations."

She turned her back on him and joined some guests, and he went to the bar and ordered a whiskey. The bartender served him but he served him rudely. His was a world in which the caterer's men kept the social score, and to be rebuffed by a part-time barkeep meant that he had suffered some loss of social esteem. Or perhaps the man was new and uninformed. Then he heard Grace at his back say: "They went for broke overnight—nothing but income—and he showed up drunk one Sunday and asked us to loan him five thousand dollars. . . ." She was always talking about money. It was worse than eating your peas off a knife. He dove into the pool, swam its length and went away.

The next pool on his list, the last but two, belonged to his old mistress, Shirley Adams. If he had suffered any injuries at the Biswangers' they would be cured here. Love—sexual rough-house in fact—was the supreme elixir, the pain-killer, the brightly colored pill that would put the spring back into his step, the joy of life in his heart. They had had an affair last week, last month, last year. He couldn't remember. It was he who had broken it off, his was the upper hand, and he stepped through the gate of the wall that surrounded her pool with nothing so considered as self-confidence. It seemed in a way to be his pool as the lover, particularly the illicit lover, enjoys the possessions of his mistress with an authority unknown to holy matrimony. She was

there, her hair the color of brass, but her figure, at the edge of the lighted, cerulean water, excited in him no profound memories. It had been, he thought, a lighthearted affair, although she had wept when he broke it off. She seemed confused to see him and he wondered if she was still wounded. Would she, God forbid, weep again?

"What do you want?" she asked.

"I'm swimming across the county."

"Good Christ. Will you ever grow up?"

"What's the matter?"

"If you've come here for money," she said, "I won't give you another cent."

"You could give me a drink."

"I could but I won't. I'm not alone."

"Well, I'm on my way."

He dove in and swam the pool, but when he tried to haul himself up onto the curb he found that the strength in his arms and his shoulders had gone, and he paddled to the ladder and climbed out. Looking over his shoulder he saw, in the lighted bathhouse, a young man. Going out onto the dark lawn he smelled chrysanthemums or marigolds—some stubborn autumnal fragrance—on the night air, strong as gas. Looking overhead he saw that the stars had come out, but why should he seem to see Andromeda, Cepheus, and Cassiopeia? What had become of the constellations of midsummer? He began to cry.

It was probably the first time in his adult life that he had ever cried, certainly the first time in his life that he had ever felt so miserable, cold, tired, and bewildered. He could not understand the rudeness of the caterer's barkeep or the rudeness of a mistress who had come to him on her knees and showered his trousers with tears. He had swum too long, he had been immersed too long, and his nose and his throat were sore from the water. What he needed then was a drink, some company, and some clean dry clothes, and while he could have cut directly across the road to his home he went on to the Gilmartins' pool. Here, for the first time in his life, he did not dive but went down the steps into the icy water and swam a hobbled side stroke that he might have learned as a youth. He staggered with fatigue on his way to the Clydes' and paddled the length of their pool, stopping again and again with his hand on the curb to rest. He climbed up the ladder and wondered if he had the strength to get home. He had done what he wanted, he had swum the county, but he was so stupefied with exhaustion that his triumph seemed vague. Stooped, holding onto the gateposts for support, he turned up the driveway of his own house.

The place was dark. Was it so late that they had all gone to bed? Had Lucinda stayed at the Westerhazys' for supper? Had the girls joined her there or gone someplace else? Hadn't they agreed, as they usually did on Sunday, to regret all their invitations and stay at home? He tried the garage doors to see what cars were in but the doors were locked and rust came off the handles onto his hands. Going toward the house, he saw that the force of the thunderstorm had knocked one of the rain gutters loose. It hung down over the front door like an umbrella rib, but it could be fixed in the morning. The house was locked, and he thought that the stupid cook or the stupid maid must have locked the place up until he remembered that it had been some time since they had employed a maid or a cook. He shouted, pounded on the door, tried to force it with his shoulder, and then, looking in at the windows, saw that the place was empty.

# JOSEPH CONRAD

# The Lagoon

Joseph Conrad (1857–1924) was born of Polish parents in the Ukraine and was named Jozef Teodor Konrad Nalecz Korzeniowski. He spent his childhood and early youth in Russia as an exile with his parents, who left him an orphan at the age of twelve to be brought up by his uncle in Cracow, Poland. As a boy, Conrad was fascinated by romantic tales of adventure at sea, and at seventeen he went to sea in the French merchant service. In 1878 he changed over to the British service; by 1884 he had become a ship's master, a British citizen, and had acquired an extraordinary command of English—the language in which he did all his writing. His first novel, *Almayer's Folly*, was begun in 1889 but not published until 1895. It was followed by *An Outcast of the Islands*, 1896; *The Nigger of the Narcissus*, 1897; *Lord Jim*, 1900; and many other novels, several collections of short stories, reminiscences, and literary essays.

In "The Lagoon," as in all of his writings, Conrad is preoccupied with man's need for fidelity, honor, and courage. Here, as elsewhere, he is a master both at creating an atmosphere through richly realistic settings and at probing deep into the moral and psychological motives of his characters.

The white man, leaning with both arms over the roof of the little house in the stern of the boat, said to the steersman—

"We will pass the night in Arsat's clearing. It is late."

THE LAGOON  From *Tales of Unrest* by Joseph Conrad. Reprinted by permission of J. M. Dent & Sons Ltd., publishers, and the Trustees of the Joseph Conrad Estate.

The Malay only grunted, and went on looking fixedly at the river. The white man rested his chin on his crossed arms and gazed at the wake of the boat. At the end of the straight avenue of forests cut by the intense glitter of the river, the sun appeared unclouded and dazzling; poised low over the water that shone smoothly like a band of metal. The forests, somber and dull, stood motionless and silent on each side of the broad stream. At the foot of big, towering trees, trunkless nipa palms rose from the mud of the bank, in bunches of leaves enormous and heavy, that hung unstirring over the brown swirl of eddies. In the stillness of the air every tree, every leaf, every bough, every tendril of creeper and every petal of minute blossoms seemed to have been bewitched into an immobility perfect and final. Nothing moved on the river but the eight paddles that rose flashing regularly, dipped together with a single splash; while the steersman swept right and left with a periodic and sudden flourish of his blade describing a glinting semicircle above his head. The churned-up water frothed alongside with a confused murmur. And the white man's canoe, advancing upstream in the short-lived disturbance of its own making, seemed to enter the portals of a land from which the very memory of motion had forever departed.

The white man, turning his back upon the setting sun, looked along the empty and broad expanse of the sea-reach. For the last three miles of its course the wandering, hesitating river, as if enticed irresistibly by the freedom of an open horizon, flows straight into the sea, flows straight to the east—to the east that harbors both light and darkness. Astern of the boat the repeated call of some bird, a cry discordant and feeble, skipped along over the smooth water and lost itself, before it could reach the other shore, in the breathless silence of the world.

The steersman dug his paddle into the stream, and held hard with stiffened arms, his body thrown forward. The water gurgled aloud; and suddenly the long straight reach seemed to pivot on its center, the forests swung in a semicircle, and the slanting beams of sunset touched the broadside of the canoe with a fiery glow, throwing the slender and distorted shadows of its crew upon the streaked glitter of the river. The white man turned to look ahead. The course of the boat had been altered at right-angles to the stream, and the carved dragon-head of its prow was pointing now at a gap in the fringing bushes of the bank. It glided through, brushing the overhanging twigs, and disappeared from the river like some slim and amphibious creature leaving the water for its lair in the forests.

The narrow creek was like a ditch: tortuous, fabulously deep; filled with gloom under the thin strip of pure and shining blue of the heaven.

Immense trees soared up, invisible behind the festooned draperies of creepers. Here and there, near the glistening blackness of the water, a twisted root of some tall tree showed amongst the tracery of small ferns, black and dull, writhing and motionless, like an arrested snake. The short words of the paddlers reverberated loudly between the thick and somber walls of vegetation. Darkness oozed out from between the trees, through the tangled maze of the creepers, from behind the great fantastic and unstirring leaves; the darkness, mysterious and invincible; the darkness scented and poisonous of impenetrable forests.

The men poled in the shoaling water. The creek broadened, opening out into a wide sweep of a stagnant lagoon. The forests receded from the marshy bank, leaving a level strip of bright green, reedy grass to frame the reflected blueness of the sky. A fleecy pink cloud drifted high above, trailing the delicate coloring of its image under the floating leaves and the silvery blossoms of the lotus. A little house, perched on high poles, appeared black in the distance. Near it, two tall nibong palms, that seemed to have come out of the forests in the background, leaned slightly over the ragged roof, with a suggestion of sad tenderness and care in the droop of their leafy and soaring heads.

The steersman, pointing with his paddle, said, "Arsat is there. I see his canoe fast between the piles."

The polers ran along the sides of the boat, glancing over their shoulders at the end of the day's journey. They would have preferred to spend the night somewhere else than on this lagoon of weird aspect and ghostly reputation. Moreover, they disliked Arsat, first as a stranger, and also because he who repairs a ruined house, and dwells in it, proclaims that he is not afraid to live amongst the spirits that haunt the places abandoned by mankind. Such a man can disturb the course of fate by glances or words; while his familiar ghosts are not easy to propitiate by casual wayfarers upon whom they long to wreak the malice of their human master. White men care not for such things, being unbelievers and in league with the Father of Evil, who leads them unharmed through the invisible dangers of this world. To the warnings of the righteous they oppose an offensive pretense of disbelief. What is there to be done?

So they thought, throwing their weight on the

end of their long poles. The big canoe glided on swiftly, noiselessly, and smoothly, towards Arsat's clearing, till, in a great rattling of poles thrown down, and the loud murmurs of "Allah be praised!" it came with a gentle knock against the crooked piles below the house.

The boatmen with uplifted faces shouted discordantly, "Arsat! O Arsat!" Nobody came. The white man began to climb the rude ladder giving access to the bamboo platform before the house. The juragan of the boat said sulkily, "We will cook in the sampan, and sleep on the water."

"Pass my blankets and the basket," said the white man, curtly.

He knelt on the edge of the platform to receive the bundle. Then the boat shoved off, and the white man, standing up, confronted Arsat, who had come out through the low door of his hut. He was a man young, powerful, with broad chest and muscular arms. He had nothing on but his sarong. His head was bare. His big, soft eyes stared eagerly at the white man, but his voice and demeanor were composed as he asked, without any words of greeting—

"Have you medicine, Tuan?"

"No," said the visitor in a startled tone. "No. Why? Is there sickness in the house?"

"Enter and see," replied Arsat, in the same calm manner, and turning short round, passed again through the small doorway. The white man, dropping his bundles, followed.

In the dim light of the dwelling he made out on a couch of bamboos a woman stretched on her back under a broad sheet of red cotton cloth. She lay still, as if dead; but her big eyes, wide open, glittered in the gloom, staring upwards at the slender rafters, motionless and unseeing. She was in a high fever, and evidently unconscious. Her cheeks were sunk slightly, her lips were partly open, and on the young face there was the ominous and fixed expression—the absorbed, contemplating expression of the unconscious who are going to die. The two men stood looking down at her in silence.

"Has she been long ill?" asked the traveler.

"I have not slept for five nights," answered the Malay, in a deliberate tone. "At first she heard voices calling her from the water and struggled against me who held her. But since the sun of today rose she hears nothing—she hears not me. She sees nothing. She sees not me—me!"

He remained silent for a minute, then asked softly—

"Tuan, will she die?"

"I fear so," said the white man, sorrowfully. He had known Arsat years ago, in a far country in times of trouble and danger, when no friendship is to be despised. And since his Malay friend had come unexpectedly to dwell in the hut on the lagoon with a strange woman, he had slept many times there, in his journeys up and down the river. He liked the man who knew how to keep faith in council and how to fight without fear by the side of his white friend. He liked him—not so much perhaps as a man likes his favorite dog—but still he liked him well enough to help and ask no questions, to think sometimes vaguely and hazily in the midst of his own pursuits, about the lonely man and the long-haired woman with audacious face and triumphant eyes, who lived together hidden by the forest—alone and feared.

The white man came out of the hut in time to see the enormous conflagration of sunset put out by the swift and stealthy shadows that, rising like a black and impalpable vapor above the tree-tops, spread over the heaven, extinguishing the crimson glow of floating clouds and the red brilliance of departing daylight. In a few moments all the stars came out above the intense blackness of the earth and the great lagoon, gleaming suddenly with reflected lights, resembled an oval patch of night sky flung down into the hopeless and abysmal night of the wilderness. The white man had some supper out of the basket, then collecting a few sticks that lay about the platform, made up a small fire, not for warmth, but for the sake of the smoke, which would keep off the mosquitoes. He wrapped himself in the blankets and sat with his back against the reed wall of the house, smoking thoughtfully.

Arsat came through the doorway with noiseless steps and squatted down by the fire. The white man moved his outstretched legs a little.

"She breathes," said Arsat in a low voice, anticipating the expected question. "She breathes and burns as if with a great fire. She speaks not; she hears not—and burns!"

He paused for a moment, then asked in a quiet, incurious tone—

"Tuan . . . will she die?"

The white man moved his shoulders uneasily and muttered in a hesitating manner—

"If such is her fate."

"No, Tuan," said Arsat, calmly. "If such is my

fate. I hear, I see, I wait. I remember . . . Tuan, do you remember the old days? Do you remember my brother?"

"Yes," said the white man. The Malay rose suddenly and went in. The other, sitting still outside, could hear the voice in the hut. Arsat said: "Hear me! Speak!" His words were succeeded by a complete silence. "O Diamelen!" he cried, suddenly. After that cry there was a deep sigh. Arsat came out and sank down again in his old place.

They sat in silence before the fire. There was no sound within the house, there was no sound near them; but far away on the lagoon they could hear the voices of the boatmen ringing fitful and distinct on the calm water. The fire in the bows of the sampan shone faintly in the distance with a hazy red glow. Then it died out. The voices ceased. The land and the water slept invisible, unstirring and mute. It was as though there had been nothing left in the world but the glitter of stars streaming, ceaseless and vain, through the black stillness of the night.

The white man gazed straight before him into the darkness with wide-open eyes. The fear and fascination, the inspiration and the wonder of death—of death near, unavoidable, and unseen, soothed the unrest of his race and stirred the most indistinct, the most intimate of his thoughts. The ever-ready suspicion of evil, the gnawing suspicion that lurks in our hearts, flowed out into the stillness round him—into the stillness profound and dumb, and made it appear untrustworthy and infamous, like the placid and impenetrable mask of an unjustifiable violence. In that fleeting and powerful disturbance of his being the earth enfolded in the starlight peace became a shadowy country of inhuman strife, a battlefield of phantoms terrible and charming, august or ignoble, struggling ardently for the possession of our helpless hearts. An unquiet and mysterious country of inextinguishable desires and fears.

A plaintive murmur rose in the night; a murmur saddening and startling, as if the great solitudes of surrounding woods had tried to whisper into his ear the wisdom of their immense and lofty indifference. Sounds hesitating and vague floated in the air around him, shaped themselves slowly into words; and at last flowed on gently in a murmuring stream of soft and monotonous sentences. He stirred like a man waking up and changed his position slightly. Arsat, motionless

and shadowy, sitting with bowed head under the stars, was speaking in a low and dreamy tone—

". . . for where can we lay down the heaviness of our trouble but in a friend's heart? A man must speak of war and of love. You, Tuan, know what war is, and you have seen me in time of danger seek death as other men seek life! A writing may be lost; a lie may be written; but what the eye has seen is truth and remains in the mind!"

"I remember," said the white man, quietly. Arsat went on with mournful composure—

"Therefore I shall speak to you of love. Speak in the night. Speak before both night and love are gone—and the eye of day looks upon my sorrow and my shame; upon my blackened face; upon my burnt-up heart."

A sigh, short and faint, marked an almost imperceptible pause, and then his words flowed on, without a stir, without a gesture.

"After the time of trouble and war was over and you went away from my country in the pursuit of your desires, which we, men of the islands, cannot understand, I and my brother became again, as we had been before, the sword-bearers of the Ruler. You know we were men of family, belonging to a ruling race, and more fit than any to carry on our right shoulder the emblem of power. And in the time of prosperity Si Dendring showed us favor, as we, in time of sorrow, had showed to him the faithfulness of our courage. It was a time of peace. A time of deer-hunts and cock-fights; of idle talks and foolish squabbles between men whose bellies are full and weapons are rusty. But the sower watched the young rice-shoots grow up without fear, and the traders came and went, departed lean and returned fat into the river of peace. They brought news, too. Brought lies and truth mixed together, so that no man knew when to rejoice and when to be sorry. We heard from them about you also. They had seen you here and had seen you there. And I was glad to hear, for I remembered the stirring times, and I always remembered you, Tuan, till the time came when my eyes could see nothing in the past, because they had looked upon the one who is dying there—in the house."

He stopped to exclaim in an intense whisper, "O Mara bahia! O Calamity!" then went on speaking a little louder:

"There's no worse enemy and no better friend than a brother, Tuan, for one brother knows another, and in perfect knowledge is strength for good or evil. I loved my brother. I went to him and told him that I could see nothing but one face, hear nothing but one voice. He told me: 'Open your heart so that she can see what is in it—and wait. Patience is wisdom. Inchi Midah may die or our Ruler may throw off his fear of a woman!' . . . I waited! . . . You remember the lady with the veiled face, Tuan, and the fear of our Ruler before her cunning and temper. And if she wanted her servant, what could I do? But I fed the hunger of my heart on short glances and stealthy words. I loitered on the path to the bath-houses in the daytime, and when the sun had fallen behind the forest I crept along the jasmine hedges of the women's courtyard. Unseeing, we spoke to one another through the scent of flowers, through the veil of leaves, through the blades of long grass that stood still before our lips; so great was our prudence, so faint was the murmur of our great longing. The time passed swiftly . . . and there were whispers amongst women—and our enemies watched—my brother was gloomy, and I began to think of killing and of a fierce death. . . . We are of a people who take what they want—like you whites. There is a time when a man should forget loyalty and respect. Might and authority are given to rulers, but to all men is given love and strength and courage. My brother said, 'You shall take her from their midst. We are two who are like one.' And I answered, 'Let it be soon, for I find no warmth in sunlight that does not shine upon her.' Our time came when the Ruler and all the great people went to the mouth of the river to fish by torchlight. There were hundreds of boats, and on the white sand, between the water and the forests, dwellings of leaves were built for the households of the Rajahs. The smoke of cooking-fires was like a blue mist of the evening, and many voices rang in it joyfully. While they were making the boats ready to beat up the fish, my brother came to me and said, 'Tonight!' I looked to my weapons, and when the time came our canoe took its place in the circle of boats carrying the torches. The lights blazed on the water, but behind the boats there was darkness. When the shouting began and the excitement made them like mad we dropped out. The water swallowed our fire, and we floated back to the shore that was dark with only here and there the glimmer of embers. We could hear the talk of slave-girls amongst the sheds. Then we found a place deserted and silent. We waited there. She came. She came running along the shore, rapid and leaving no trace, like a leaf driven by the wind into the sea. My brother said gloomily, 'Go and take her; carry her into our boat.' I lifted her in my arms. She panted. Her heart was beating against my breast. I said, 'I take you from those people. You came to the cry of my heart, but my arms take you into my boat against the will of the great!' 'It is right,' said my brother. 'We are men who take what we want and can hold it against many. We should have taken her in daylight.' I said, 'Let us be off'; for since she was in my boat I began to think of our Ruler's many men. 'Yes. Let us be off,' said my brother. 'We are cast out and this boat is our country now— and the sea is our refuge.' He lingered with his foot on the shore, and I entreated him to hasten, for I remembered the strokes of her heart against my breast and thought that two men cannot withstand a hundred. We left, paddling downstream close to the bank; and as we passed by the creek where they were fishing, the great shouting had ceased, but the murmur of voices was loud like the humming of insects flying at noonday. The boats floated, clustered together, in the red light of torches, under a black roof of smoke; and men talked of their sport. Men that boasted, and praised, and jeered—men that would have been our friends in the morning, but on that night were already our enemies. We paddled swiftly past. We had no more friends in the country of our birth. She sat in the middle of the canoe with covered face; silent as she is now; unseeing as she is now—and I had no regret at what I was leaving because I could hear her breathing close to me—as I can hear her now."

He paused, listened with his ear turned to the doorway, then shook his head and went on:

"My brother wanted to shout the cry of challenge—one cry only—to let the people know we were freeborn robbers who trusted our arms and the great sea. And again I begged him in the name of our love to be silent. Could I not hear her breathing close to me? I knew the pursuit would come quick enough. My brother loved me. He dipped his paddle without a splash. He only said, 'There is half a man in you now—the other half is in that woman. I can wait. When you are a whole man again, you will come back with me here to shout defiance. We are sons of the same mother.' I made no answer. All my strength and all my spirit were in my hands that held the paddle—for I longed to be with her in a safe place beyond the reach of men's anger and of women's spite. My love was so great, that I thought it could guide me to a country where death was unknown, if I could only escape from Inchi Midah's fury and from our Ruler's sword. We paddled with haste, breathing through our teeth. The blades bit deep into the smooth water. We passed out of the river; we flew in clear channels amongst the shallows. We skirted the black coast; we skirted the sand beaches where the sea speaks in whispers to the land; and the gleam of white sand flashed back past our boat, so swiftly she ran upon the water. We spoke not. Only once I said, 'Sleep, Diamelen, for soon you may want all your strength.' I heard the sweetness of her voice, but I never turned my head. The sun rose and still we went on. Water fell from my face like rain from a cloud. We flew in the light and heat. I never looked back, but I knew that my brother's eyes, behind me, were looking steadily ahead, for the boat went as straight as a bushman's dart, when it leaves the end of the sumpitan. There was no better paddler, no better steersman than my brother. Many times, together, we had won races in that canoe. But we never had put out our strength as we did then—then, when for the last time we paddled together! There was no braver or stronger man in our country than my brother. I could not spare the strength to turn my head and look at him, but every moment I heard the hiss of his breath getting louder behind me. Still he did not speak. The sun was high. The heat clung to my back like a flame of fire. My ribs were ready to burst, but I could no longer get enough air into my chest. And then I felt I must cry out with my last breath, 'Let us rest!' . . . 'Good!' he answered; and his voice was firm. He was strong. He was brave. He knew not fear and no fatigue . . . My brother!"

A murmur powerful and gentle, a murmur vast and faint; the murmur of trembling leaves, of stirring boughs, ran through the tangled depths of the forests, ran over the starry smoothness of the lagoon, and the water between the piles lapped the slimy timber once with a sudden splash. A breath of warm air touched the two men's faces and passed on with a mournful sound—a breath loud and short like an uneasy sigh of the dreaming earth.

Arsat went on in an even, low voice.

"We ran our canoe on the white beach of a little bay close to a long tongue of land that seemed to bar our road; a long wooded cape going far into the sea. My brother knew that place. Beyond the cape a river has its entrance, and through the jungle of that land there is a narrow path. We made a fire and cooked rice. Then we lay down to sleep on the soft sand in the shade of our canoe, while she watched. No sooner had I closed my eyes than I heard her cry of alarm. We leaped up. The sun was halfway down the sky already, and coming in sight in the opening of the bay we saw a prau manned by many paddlers. We knew it at once; it was one of our Rajah's praus. They were watching the shore, and saw us. They beat the gong, and turned the head of the prau into the bay. I felt my heart become weak within my breast. Diamelen sat on the sand and covered her face. There was no escape by sea. My brother laughed. He had the gun you had given him, Tuan, before you went away, but there was only a handful of powder. He spoke to me quickly: 'Run with her along the path. I shall keep them back, for they have no firearms, and landing in the face of a man with a gun is certain death for some. Run with her. On the other side of that wood there is a fisherman's house—and a canoe. When I have fired all the shots I will follow. I am a great runner, and before they can come up we shall be gone. I will hold out as long as I can, for she is but a woman—that can neither run nor fight, but she has your heart in her weak hands.' He dropped behind the canoe. The prau was coming. She and I ran, and as we rushed along the path I heard shots. My brother fired—once—twice—and the booming of the gong ceased. There was silence behind us. That neck of land is narrow. Before I heard my brother fire the third shot I saw the shelving shore, and I saw the water again; the mouth of a broad river. We crossed a grassy glade. We ran down to the water. I saw a low hut above the black mud, and a small canoe hauled up. I heard another shot behind me. I thought, 'This is his last charge.' We rushed down to the canoe; a man came running from the hut, but I leaped on him, and we rolled together in the mud. Then I got up, and he lay still at my feet. I don't know whether I had killed him or not. I and Diamelen pushed the canoe afloat. I heard yells behind me, and I saw my brother run across the glade. Many men were bounding after him. I took her in my arms and threw her into the boat, then leaped in myself. When I looked back I saw that my brother had fallen. He fell and was up again, but the men were closing round him. He shouted, 'I am coming!' The men were close to him. I looked. Many men. Then I looked at her. Tuan, I pushed the canoe! I pushed it into deep water. She was kneeling forward looking at me, and I said, 'Take your paddle,' while I struck the water with mine. Tuan, I heard him cry. I heard him cry my name twice; and I heard voices shouting, 'Kill! Strike!' I never turned back. I heard him calling my name again with a great shriek, as when life is going out together with the voice—and I never turned my head. My own name! . . . My brother! Three times he called—but I was not afraid of life. Was she not there in that canoe? And could I not with her find a country where death is forgotten—where death is unknown!"

The white man sat up. Arsat rose and stood, an indistinct and silent figure above the dying embers of the fire. Over the lagoon a mist drifting and low had crept, erasing slowly the glittering images of the stars. And now a great expanse of white vapor covered the land: it flowed cold and gray in the darkness, eddied in noiseless whirls round the tree-trunks and about the platform of the house, which seemed to float upon a restless and impalpable illusion of a sea. Only far away the tops of the trees stood outlined on the twinkle of heaven, like a somber and forbidding shore—a coast deceptive, pitiless and black.

Arsat's voice vibrated loudly in the profound peace. "I had her there! I had her! To get her I would have faced all mankind. But I had her—and—"

His words went out ringing into the empty distances. He paused, and seemed to listen to them dying away very far—beyond help and beyond recall. Then he said quietly—

"Tuan, I loved my brother."

A breath of wind made him shiver. High above his head, high above the silent sea of mist the drooping leaves of the palms rattled together with a mournful and expiring sound. The white man stretched his legs. His chin rested on his

chest, and he murmured sadly without lifting his head—

"We all love our brothers."

Arsat burst out with an intense whispering violence—

"What did I care who died? I wanted peace in my own heart."

He seemed to hear a stir in the house—listened—then stepped in noiselessly. The white man stood up. A breeze was coming in fitful puffs. The stars shone paler as if they had retreated into the frozen depths of immense space. After a chill gust of wind there were a few seconds of perfect calm and absolute silence. Then from behind the black and wavy line of the forests a column of golden light shot up into the heavens and spread over the semicircle of the eastern horizon. The sun had risen. The mist lifted, broke into drifting patches, vanished into thin flying wreaths; and the unveiled lagoon lay, polished and black, in the heavy shadows at the foot of the wall of trees. A white eagle rose over it with a slanting and ponderous flight, reached the clear sunshine and appeared dazzlingly brilliant for a moment, then soaring higher, became a dark and motionless speck before it vanished into the blue as if it had left the earth forever. The white man, standing gazing upwards before the doorway, heard in the hut a confused and broken murmur of distracted words ending with a loud groan. Suddenly Arsat stumbled out with outstretched hands, shivered, and stood still for some time with fixed eyes. Then he said—

"She burns no more."

Before his face the sun showed its edge above the treetops rising steadily. The breeze freshened; a great brilliance burst upon the lagoon, sparkled on the rippling water. The forests came out of the clear shadows of the morning, became distinct, as if they had rushed nearer—to stop short in a great stir of leaves, of nodding boughs, of swaying branches. In the merciless sunshine the whisper of unconscious life grew louder, speaking in an incomprehensible voice round the dumb darkness of that human sorrow. Arsat's eyes wandered slowly, then stared at the rising sun.

"I can see nothing," he said half aloud to himself.

"There is nothing," said the white man, moving to the edge of the platform and waving his hand to his boat. A shout came faintly over the lagoon and the sampan began to glide towards the abode of the friend of ghosts.

"If you want to come with me, I will wait all the morning," said the white man, looking away upon the water.

"No, Tuan," said Arsat, softly. "I shall not eat or sleep in this house, but I must first see my road. Now I can see nothing—see nothing! There is no light and no peace in the world; but there is death—death for many. We are sons of the same mother—and I left him in the midst of enemies; but I am going back now."

He drew a long breath and went on in a dreamy tone:

"In a little while I shall see clear enough to strike—to strike. But she has died, and . . . now . . . darkness."

He flung his arms wide open, let them fall along his body, then stood still with unmoved face and stony eyes, staring at the sun. The white man got down into his canoe. The polers ran smartly along the sides of the boat, looking over their shoulders at the beginning of a weary journey. High in the stern, his head muffled up in white rags, the juragan sat moody, letting his paddle trail in the water. The white man, leaning with both arms over the grass roof of the little cabin, looked back at the shining ripple of the boat's wake. Before the sampan passed out of the lagoon into the creek he lifted his eyes. Arsat had not moved. He stood lonely in the searching sunshine; and he looked beyond the great light of a cloudless day into the darkness of a world of illusions.

## WILLIAM FAULKNER

# Spotted Horses

William Faulkner (1897–1962) spent most of his life near Oxford, Mississippi, which is the "Jefferson" of his novels and short stories. During World War I he was enlisted in the Canadian Air Force. After the war he returned to Oxford, taking a few courses at the University of Mississippi and supporting himself by doing odd jobs. In 1959 he was appointed lecturer on writing at the University of Virginia.

Faulkner's early novels brought him critical acclaim but little or no popularity or financial remuneration. *Sartoris*, 1929, was the first of his many novels centering on the Sartoris family, patterned after his own wealthy Southern ancestors, who had been reduced to genteel poverty after the Civil War. The Snopes family made their first appearance in this novel and began accumulating, by various rascalities, the wealth and power once held by the now degenerating aristocracy. In 1931 Faulkner published *Sanctuary*, which he said was deliberately made "horrific" in order to appeal to popular taste and earn enough money to support himself; in this aim he was successful. He wrote several other novels and many short stories; the latter were collected in a volume published in 1950. More recent publications are *The Town*, 1957; *The Long Hot Summer*, 1958, "a dramatic book" from *The Hamlet*, 1940; *The Mansion*, 1959, the third novel of the Snopes family; and *The Reivers*, 1962.

In 1939 Faulkner received the O. Henry Memorial Award; in 1949, after the publication in 1948 of *Intruder in the Dust*, he received the Nobel Prize for Literature "for his forceful and independently artistic contribution to modern American fiction"; and in 1954 he won a Pulitzer Prize for *A Fable*. In all, Faulkner, along with Hemingway, has received greater critical acclaim than any other contemporary American novelist.

Few writers achieve so much intense dramatic activity in a story as William Faulkner. In "Spotted Horses," for instance, every detail vibrates with a life of its own and gives added life to other details—the wild, odd-eyed horses, which symbolize the folly of Henry Armstid and his kind; the meek and passive Mrs. Armstid, who objectifies the results of ignorance and rascality; the taciturn and sneaking Flem Snopes; and the calm, sensible Mrs. Littlejohn, who is never deluded by the folly and madness of her neighbors.

Yes sir. Flem Snopes has filled that whole country full of spotted horses. You can hear folks running them all day and all night, whooping and hollering, and the horses running back and forth across them little wooden bridges ever now and then kind of like thunder. Here I was this morning pretty near halfway to town, with the team ambling along and me setting in the buckboard about half asleep, when all of a sudden something come swurging up outen the bushes and jumped the road clean, without touching hoof to it. It flew right over my team big as a billboard and flying through the air like a hawk. It taken me thirty minutes to stop my team and untangle the harness and the buckboard and hitch them up again.

That Flem Snopes. I be dog if he ain't a case, now. One morning about ten years ago the boys was just getting settled down on Varner's porch for a little talk and tobacco, when here come Flem out from behind the counter, with his coat off and his hair all parted, like he might have been clerking for Varner for ten years already. Folks all knowed him; it was a big family of them about five miles down the bottom. That year, at least. Share-cropping. They never stayed on any place over a year. Then they would move on to another place, with the chap or maybe the twins of that year's litter. It was a regular nest of them. But Flem. The rest of them stayed tenant farmers, moving ever year, but here come Flem one day, walking out from behind Jody Varner's counter like he owned it. And he wasn't there but a year or two before folks knowed that if him and Jody was both still in that store in ten years more it would be Jody clerking for Flem Snopes. Why, that fellow could make a nickel where it wasn't but four cents to begin with. He

skun me in two trades myself, and the fellow that can do that, I just hope he'll get rich before I do; that's all.

All right. So here Flem was, clerking at Varner's, making a nickel here and there and not telling nobody about it. No, sir. Folks never knowed when Flem got the better of somebody lessen the fellow he beat told it. He'd just set there in the store-chair, chewing his tobacco and keeping his own business to hisself, until about a week later we'd find out it was somebody else's business he was keeping to hisself—provided the fellow he trimmed was mad enough to tell it. That's Flem.

We give him ten years to own ever thing Jody Varner had. But he never waited no ten years. I reckon you-all know that gal of Uncle Billy Varner's, the youngest one, Eula. Jody's sister. Ever Sunday ever yellow-wheeled buggy and curried riding horse in that country would be hitched to Bill Varner's fence, and the young bucks setting on the porch, swarming around Eula like bees around a honey pot. One of these here kind of big, soft-looking gals that could giggle richer than plowed new-ground. Wouldn't none of them leave before the others, and so they would set there on the porch until time to go home, with some of them with nine and ten miles to ride and then get up tomorrow and go back to the field. So they would all leave together and they would ride in a clump down to the creek ford and hitch them curried horses and yellow-wheeled buggies and get out and fight one another. Then they would get in the buggies again and go on home.

Well, one day about a year ago, one of them yellow-wheeled buggies and one of them curried saddle-horses quit this country. We heard they was heading for Texas. The next day Uncle Billy and Eula and Flem come in to town in Uncle Bill's surrey, and when they come back, Flem and Eula was married. And on the next day we heard that two more of them yellow-wheeled buggies had left the country. They mought have gone to Texas, too. It's a big place.

Anyway, about a month after the wedding, Flem and Eula went to Texas, too. They was gone pretty near a year. Then one day last month, Eula come back, with a baby. We figered up, and we decided that it was as well-growed a three-months-old baby as we ever see. It can already pull up on a chair. I reckon Texas makes big men quick, being a big place. Anyway, if it keeps on like it started, it'll be chewing tobacco and voting time it's eight years old.

And so last Friday here come Flem himself. He was on a wagon with another fellow. The other fellow had one of these two-gallon hats and a ivory-handled pistol and a box of gingersnaps sticking out of his hind pocket, and tied to the tail-gate of the wagon was about two dozen of them Texas ponies, hitched to one another with barbed wire. They was colored like parrots and they was quiet as doves, and ere a one of them would kill you quick as a rattlesnake. Nere a one of them had two eyes the same color, and nere a one of them had ever see a bridle, I reckon; and when that Texas man got down offen the wagon and walked up to them to show how gentle they was, one of them cut his vest clean offen him, same as with a razor.

Flem had done already disappeared; he had went on to see his wife, I reckon, and to see if that ere baby had done gone on to the field to help Uncle Billy plow, maybe. It was the Texas man that taken the horses on to Mrs. Littlejohn's lot. He had a little trouble at first, when they come to the gate, because they hadn't never see a fence before, and when he finally got them in and taken a pair of wire cutters and unhitched them and got them into the barn and poured some shell corn into the trough, they durn nigh tore down the barn. I reckon they thought that shell corn was bugs, maybe. So he left them in the lot and he announced that the auction would begin at sunup tomorrow.

That night we was setting on Mrs. Littlejohn's porch. You-all mind the moon was nigh full that night, and we could watch them spotted varmints swirling along the fence and back and forth

across the lot same as minnows in a pond. And then now and then they would all kind of huddle up against the barn and rest themselves by biting and kicking one another. We would hear a squeal, and then a set of hoofs would go Bam! against the barn, like a pistol. It sounded just like a fellow with a pistol, in a nest of cattymounts, taking his time.

It wasn't ere a man knowed yet if Flem owned them things or not. They just knowed one thing: that they wasn't never going to know for sho if Flem did or not, or if maybe he didn't just get on that wagon at the edge of town, for the ride or not. Even Eck Snopes didn't know, Flem's own cousin. But wasn't nobody surprised at that. We knowed that Flem would skin Eck quick as he would ere a one of us.

They was there by sunup next morning, some of them come twelve and sixteen miles, with seed-money tied up in tobacco sacks in their overalls, standing along the fence, when the Texas man come out of Mrs. Littlejohn's after breakfast and clumb onto the gate post with that ere white pistol butt sticking outen his hind pocket. He taken a new box of gingersnaps outen his pocket and bit the end offen it like a cigar and spit out the paper, and said the auction was open. And still they was coming up in wagons and a horse- and mule-back and hitching the teams across the road and coming to the fence. Flem wasn't nowhere in sight.

But he couldn't get them started. He begun to work on Eck, because Eck holp him last night to get them into the barn and feed them that shell corn. Eck got out just in time. He come outen that barn like a chip on the crest of a busted dam of water, and clumb into the wagon just in time.

He was working on Eck when Henry Armstid come up in his wagon. Eck was saying he was skeered to bid on one of them, because he might get it, and the Texas man says, "Them ponies? Them little horses?" He clumb down offen the gate post and went toward the horses. They broke and run, and him following them, kind of chirping to them, with his hand out like he was fixing to catch a fly, until he got three or four of them cornered. Then he jumped into them, and then we couldn't see nothing for a while because of the dust. It was a big cloud of it, and them blare-eyed, spotted things swoaring outen it twenty foot to a jump, in forty directions without counting up. Then the dust settled and there they was, that Texas man and the horse. He had its head twisted clean around like a owl's head. Its legs was braced and it was trembling like a new bride and groaning like a sawmill, and him holding its head wrung clean around on its neck so it was snuffing sky. "Look it over," he says, with his heels dug too and that white pistol sticking outen his pocket and his neck swole up like a spreading adder's until you could just tell what he was saying, cussing the horse and talking to us all at once: "Look him over, the fiddle-headed son of fourteen fathers. Try him, buy him; you will get the best—" Then it was all dust again, and we couldn't see nothing but spotted hide and mane, and that ere Texas man's boot-heels like a couple of walnuts on two strings, and after a while that two-gallon hat come sailing out like a fat old hen crossing a fence.

When the dust settled again, he was just getting outen the far fence corner, brushing himself off. He come and got his hat and brushed it off and come and clumb onto the gate post again. He was breathing hard. The hammer-head horse was still running round and round the lot like a merry-go-round at a fair. That was when Henry Armstid come shoving up to the gate in them patched overalls and one of them dangle-armed shirts of hisn. Hadn't nobody noticed him until then. We was all watching the Texas man and the horses. Even Mrs. Littlejohn; she had done come out and built a fire under the wash-pot in her back yard, and she would stand at the fence a while and then go back into the house and come out again with a arm full of wash and stand at the fence again. Well, here come Henry shoving up, and then we see Mrs. Armstid right behind him, in that ere faded wrapper and sunbonnet and them tennis shoes. "Get on back to that wagon," Henry says.

"Henry," she says.

"Here, boys," the Texas man says; "make room for missus to git up and see. Come on, Henry," he says; "here's your chance to buy that saddlehorse missus has been wanting. What about ten dollars, Henry?"

"Henry," Mrs. Armstid says. She put her hand on Henry's arm. Henry knocked her hand down.

"Git on back to that wagon, like I told you," he says.

Mrs. Armstid never moved. She stood behind Henry, with her hands rolled into her dress, not looking at nothing. "He hain't no more despair than to buy one of them things," she says. "And us not five dollars ahead of the pore house, he hain't no more despair." It was the truth, too. They ain't never made more than a bare living offen that place of theirs, and them with four chaps and the very clothes they wears she earns by weaving by the firelight at night while Henry's asleep.

"Shut your mouth and git on back to that wagon," Henry says. "Do you want I taken a wagon stake to you here in the big road?"

Well, that Texas man taken one look at her. Then he begun on Eck again, like Henry wasn't even there. But Eck was skeered. "I can git me a snapping turtle or a water moccasin for nothing. I ain't going to buy none."

So the Texas man said he would give Eck a horse. "To start the auction, and because you holp me last night. If you'll start the bidding on the next horse," he says, "I'll give you that fiddle-head horse."

I wish you could have seen them, standing there with their seed-money in their pockets, watching that Texas man give Eck Snopes a live horse, all fixed to call him a fool if he taken it or not. Finally Eck says he'll take it. "Only I just starts the bidding," he says. "I don't have to buy the next one lessen I ain't overtopped." The Texas man said all right, and Eck bid a dollar on the next one, with Henry Armstid standing there with his mouth already open, watching Eck and the Texas man like a mad-dog or something. "A dollar," Eck says.

The Texas man looked at Eck. His mouth was already open too, like he had started to say something and what he was going to say had up and died on him. "A dollar? You mean, *one* dollar, Eck?"

"Durn it," Eck says; "two dollars, then."

Well, sir, I wish you could a seen that Texas man. He taken out that gingersnap box and held it up and looked into it, careful, like it might have been a diamond ring in it, or a spider. Then he throwed it away and wiped his face with a bandanna. "Well," he says. "Well. Two dollars. Two dollars. Is your pulse all right, Eck?" he says. "Do you have ager-sweats at night, maybe?" he says. "Well," he says, "I got to take it. But are you boys going to stand there and see Eck get two horses at a dollar a head?"

That done it. I be dog if he wasn't nigh as

smart as Flem Snopes. He hadn't no more than got the words outen his mouth before here was Henry Armstid, waving his hand. "Three dollars," Henry says. Mrs. Armstid tried to hold him again. He knocked her hand off, shoving up to the gate post.

"Mister," Mrs. Armstid says, "we got chaps in the house and not corn to feed the stock. We got five dollars I earned my chaps a-weaving after dark, and him snoring in the bed. And he hain't no more despair."

"Henry bid three dollars," the Texas man says. "Raise him a dollar, Eck, and the horse is yours."

"Henry," Mrs. Armstid says.

"Raise him, Eck," the Texas man says.

"Four dollars," Eck says.

"Five dollars," Henry says, shaking his fist. He shoved up right under the gate post. Mrs. Armstid was looking at the Texas man too.

"Mister," she says, "if you take that five dollars I earned my chaps a-weaving for one of them things, it'll be a curse onto you and yourn during all the time of man."

But it wasn't no stopping Henry. He had shoved up, waving his fist at the Texas man. He opened it; the money was in nickels and quarters, and one dollar bill that looked like a cow's cud. "Five dollars," he says. "And the man that raises it'll have to beat my head off, or I'll beat hisn."

"All right," the Texas man says. "Five dollars is bid. But don't you shake your hand at me."

It taken till nigh sundown before the last one was sold. He got them hotted up once and the bidding got up to seven dollars and a quarter, but most of them went around three or four dollars, him setting on the gate post and picking the horses out one at a time by mouth-word, and Mrs. Littlejohn pumping up and down at the tub and stopping and coming to the fence for a while and going back to the tub again. She had done got done too, and the wash was hung on the line in the back yard, and we could smell supper cooking. Finally they was all sold; he swapped the last two and the wagon for a buckboard.

We was all kind of tired, but Henry Armstid looked more like a mad-dog than ever. When he bought, Mrs. Armstid had went back to the wagon, setting in it behind them two rabbit-sized, bone-pore mules, and the wagon itself looking like it would fall all to pieces soon as the mules moved. Henry hadn't even waited to pull it outen the road; it was still in the middle

of the road and her setting in it, not looking at nothing, ever since this morning.

Henry was right up against the gate. He went up to the Texas man. "I bought a horse and I paid cash," Henry says. "And yet you expect me to stand around here until they are all sold before I can get my horse. I'm going to take my horse outen that lot."

The Texas man looked at Henry. He talked like he might have been asking for a cup of coffee at the table. "Take your horse," he says.

Then Henry quit looking at the Texas man. He begun to swallow, holding onto the gate. "Ain't you going to help me?" he says.

"It ain't my horse," the Texas man says.

Henry never looked at the Texas man again, he never looked at nobody. "Who'll help me catch my horse?" he says. Never nobody said nothing. "Bring the plowline," Henry says. Mrs. Armstid got outen the wagon and brought the plowline. The Texas man got down offen the post. The woman made to pass him, carrying the rope.

"Don't you go in there, missus," the Texas man says.

Henry opened the gate. He didn't look back. "Come on here," he says.

"Don't you go in there, missus," the Texas man says.

Mrs. Armstid wasn't looking at nobody, neither, with her hands across her middle, holding the rope. "I reckon I better," she says. Her and Henry went into the lot. The horses broke and run. Henry and Mrs. Armstid followed.

"Get him into the corner," Henry says. They got Henry's horse cornered finally, and Henry taken the rope, but Mrs. Armstid let the horse get out. They hemmed it up again, but Mrs. Armstid let it get out again, and Henry turned and hit her with the rope. "Why didn't you head him back?" Henry says. He hit her again. "Why didn't you?" It was about that time I looked around and see Flem Snopes standing there.

It was the Texas man that done something. He moved fast for a big man. He caught the rope before Henry could hit the third time, and Henry whirled and made like he would jump at the Texas man. But he never jumped. The Texas man went and taken Henry's arm and led him outen the lot. Mrs. Armstid come behind them and the Texas man taken some money outen his pocket and he give it into Mrs. Armstid's hand. "Get him into the wagon and take him on home," the Texas man says, like he might have been telling them he enjoyed his supper.

Then here come Flem. "What's that for, Buck?" Flem says.

"Thinks he bought one of them ponies," the Texas man says. "Get him on away, missus."

But Henry wouldn't go. "Give him back that money," he says. "I bought that horse and I aim to have him if I have to shoot him."

And there was Flem, standing there with his hands in his pockets, chewing, like he had just happened to be passing.

"You take your money and I take my horse," Henry says. "Give it back to him," he says to Mrs. Armstid.

"You don't own no horse of mine," the Texas man says. "Get him on home, missus."

Then Henry seen Flem. "You got something to do with these horses," he says. "I bought one. Here's the money for it." He taken the bill outen Mrs. Armstid's hand. He offered it to Flem. "I bought one. Ask him. Here. Here's the money," he says, giving the bill to Flem.

When Flem taken the money, the Texas man dropped the rope he had snatched outen Henry's hand. He had done sent Eck Snopes's boy up to the store for another box of gingersnaps, and he taken the box outen his pocket and looked into it. It was empty and he dropped it on the ground. "Mr. Snopes will have your money for you to-morrow," he says to Mrs. Armstid. "You can get it from him tomorrow. He don't own no horse. You get him into the wagon and get him on home." Mrs. Armstid went back to the wagon and got in. "Where's that ere buckboard I bought?" the Texas man says. It was after sun-down then. And then Mrs. Littlejohn come out on the porch and rung the supper bell.

I come on in and et supper. Mrs. Littlejohn would bring in a pan of bread or something, then she would go out to the porch a minute and come back and tell us. The Texas man had hitched his team to the buckboard he had swapped them last two horses for, and him and Flem had gone, and then she told that the rest of them that never had ropes had went back to the store with I. O. Snopes to get some ropes, and wasn't nobody at the gate but Henry Armstid, and Mrs. Armstid setting in the wagon in the road, and Eck Snopes and that boy of hisn. "I don't care how many of them fool men gets killed by them things,"

Mrs. Littlejohn says, "but I ain't going to let Eck Snopes take that boy into that lot again." So she went down to the gate, but she come back without the boy or Eck neither.

"It ain't no need to worry about that boy," I says. "He's charmed." He was right behind Eck last night when Eck went to help feed them. The whole drove of them jumped clean over that boy's head and never touched him. It was Eck that touched him. Eck snatched him into the wagon and taken a rope and frailed the tar outen him.

So I had done et and went to my room and was undressing, long as I had a long trip to make next day; I was trying to sell a machine to Mrs. Bundren up past Whiteleaf; when Henry Armstid opened that gate and went in by hisself. They couldn't make him wait for the balance of them to get back with their ropes. Eck Snopes said he tried to make Henry wait, but Henry wouldn't do it. Eck said Henry walked right up to them and that when they broke, they run clean over Henry like a hay-mow breaking down. Eck said he snatched that boy of hisn out of the way just in time and that them things went through that gate like a creek flood and into the wagons and teams hitched side the road, busting wagon tongues and snapping harness like it was fishing-line, with Mrs. Armstid still setting in their wagon in the middle of it like something carved outen wood. Then they scattered, wild horses and tame mules with pieces of harness and singletrees dangling offen them, both ways up and down the road.

"There goes ourn, paw!" Eck said his boy said. "There it goes, into Mrs. Littlejohn's house." Eck says it run right up the steps and into the house like a boarder late for supper. I reckon so. Any-way, I was in my room, in my underclothes, with one sock on and one sock in my hand, leaning out the window when the commotion busted out, when I heard something run into the melodeon in the hall; it sounded like a railroad engine. Then the door to my room come sailing in like when you throw a tin bucket top into the wind and I looked over my shoulder and see something that looked like a fourteen-foot pinwheel a-blar-ing its eyes at me. It had to blare them fast, because I was already done jumped out the win-dow.

I reckon it was anxious, too. I reckon it hadn't never seen barbed wire or shell corn before, but

I know it hadn't never seen underclothes before, or maybe it was a sewing-machine agent it hadn't never seen. Anyway, it whirled and turned to run back up the hall and outen the house, when it met Eck Snopes and that boy just coming in, carrying a rope. It swirled again and run down the hall and out the back door just in time to meet Mrs. Littlejohn. She had just gathered up the clothes she had washed, and she was coming onto the back porch with a armful of washing in one hand and a scrubbing-board in the other, when the horse skidded up to her, trying to stop and swirl again. It never taken Mrs. Littlejohn no time a-tall.

"Git outen here, you son," she says. She hit it across the face with the scrubbing-board; that ere scrubbing-board split as neat as ere a axe could have done it, and when the horse swirled to run back up the hall, she hit it again with what was left of the scrubbing-board, not on the head this time. "And stay out," she says.

Eck and that boy was halfway down the hall by this time. I reckon that horse looked like a pinwheel to Eck too. "Git to hell outen here, Ad!" Eck says. Only there wasn't time. Eck dropped flat on his face, but the boy never moved. The boy was about a yard tall maybe, in overalls just like Eck's; that horse swoared over his head without touching a hair. I saw that, because I was just coming back up the front steps, still carrying that ere sock and still in my underclothes, when the horse come onto the porch again. It taken one look at me and swirled again and run to the end of the porch and jumped the banisters and the lot fence like a hen-hawk and lit in the lot running and went out the gate again and jumped eight or ten upside-down wagons and went on down the road. It was a full moon then. Mrs. Armstid was still setting in the wagon like she had done been carved outen wood and left there and forgot.

That horse. It ain't never missed a lick. It was going about forty miles a hour when it come to the bridge over the creek. It would have had a clear road, but it so happened that Vernon Tull was already using the bridge when it got there. He was coming back from town; he hadn't heard about the auction; him and his wife and three daughters and Mrs. Tull's aunt, all setting in chairs in the wagon bed, and all asleep, including the mules. They waked up when the horse hit the bridge one time, but Tull said the first he knew was when the mules tried to turn the wagon around in the middle of the bridge and he seen that spotted varmint run right twixt the mules and run up the wagon tongue like a squirrel. He said he just had time to hit it across the face with his whip-stock, because about that time the mules turned the wagon around on that ere one-way bridge and that horse clumb across onto the bridge again and went on, with Vernon standing up in the wagon and kicking at it.

Tull said the mules turned in the harness and clumb back into the wagon too, with Tull trying to beat them out again, with the reins wrapped around his wrist. After that he says all he seen was overturned chairs and womenfolks' legs and white drawers shining in the moonlight, and his mules and that spotted horse going on up the road like a ghost.

The mules jerked Tull outen the wagon and drug him a spell on the bridge before the reins broke. They thought at first that he was dead, and while they was kneeling around him, picking the bridge splinters outen him, here come Eck and that boy, still carrying the rope. They was running and breathing a little hard. "Where'd he go?" Eck said.

I went back and got my pants and shirt and shoes on just in time to go and help get Henry Armstid outen the trash in the lot. I be dog if he didn't look like he was dead, with his head hanging back and his teeth showing in the moonlight, and a little rim of white under his eye-lids. We could still hear them horses, here and there; hadn't none of them got more than four-five miles away yet, not knowing the country, I reckon. So we could hear them and folks yelling now and then: "Whooey. Head him!"

We toted Henry into Mrs. Littlejohn's. She was in the hall; she hadn't put down the armful of clothes. She taken one look at us, and she laid down the busted scrubbing-board and taken up the lamp and opened a empty door. "Bring him in here," she says.

We toted him in and laid him on the bed. Mrs. Littlejohn set the lamp on the dresser, still carrying the clothes. "I'll declare, you men," she says. Our shadows was way up the wall, tiptoeing too; we could hear ourselves breathing. "Better get his wife," Mrs. Littlejohn says. She went out, carrying the clothes.

"I reckon we had," Quick says. "Go get her, somebody."

"Whyn't you go?" Winterbottom says.

"Let Ernest git her," Durley says. "He lives neighbors with them."

Ernest went to fetch her. I be dog if Henry didn't look like he was dead. Mrs. Littlejohn come back, with a kettle and some towels. She went to work on Henry, and then Mrs. Armstid and Ernest come in. Mrs. Armstid come to the foot of the bed and stood there, with her hands rolled into her apron, watching what Mrs. Littlejohn was doing, I reckon.

"You men get outen the way," Mrs. Littlejohn says. "Git outside," she says. "See if you can't find something else to play with that will kill some more of you."

"Is he dead?" Winterbottom says.

"It ain't your fault if he ain't," Mrs. Littlejohn says. "Go tell Will Varner to come up here. I reckon a man ain't so different from a mule, come long come short. Except maybe a mule's got more sense."

We went to get Uncle Billy. It was a full moon. We could hear them, now and then, four miles away: "Whooey. Head him." The country was full of them, one on ever wooden bridge in the land, running across it like thunder: "Whooey. There he goes. Head him."

We hadn't got far before Henry begun to scream. I reckon Mrs. Littlejohn's water had brung him to; anyway, he wasn't dead. We went on to Uncle Billy's. The house was dark. We called to him, and after a while the window opened and Uncle Billy put his head out, peart as a peckerwood, listening. "Are they still trying to catch them durn rabbits?" he says.

He come down, with his britches on over his night-shirt and his suspenders dangling, carrying his horse-doctoring grip. "Yes, sir," he says, cocking his head like a woodpecker; "they're still a-trying."

We could hear Henry before we reached Mrs. Littlejohn's. He was going Ah-Ah-Ah. We stopped in the yard. Uncle Billy went on in. We could hear Henry. We stood in the yard, hearing them on the bridges, this-a-way and that: "Whooey. Whooey."

"Eck Snopes ought to caught hisn," Ernest says.

"Looks like he ought," Winterbottom said.

Henry was going Ah-Ah-Ah steady in the house; then he begun to scream. "Uncle Billy's started," Quick says. We looked into the hall. We could see the light where the door was. Then Mrs. Littlejohn come out.

"Will needs some help," she says. "You, Ernest. You'll do." Ernest went into the house.

"Hear them?" Quick said. "That one was on Four Mile bridge." We could hear them; it sounded like thunder a long way off; it didn't last long:

"Whooey."

We could hear Henry: "Ah-Ah-Ah-Ah-Ah."

"They are both started now," Winterbottom says. "Ernest too."

That was early in the night. Which was a good thing, because it taken a long night for folks to chase them things right and for Henry to lay there and holler, being as Uncle Billy never had none of this here chloryfoam to set Henry's leg with. So it was considerate in Flem to get them started early. And what do you reckon Flem's com-ment was?

That's right. Nothing. Because he wasn't there. Hadn't nobody see him since that Texas man left.

That was Saturday night. I reckon Mrs. Armstid got home about daylight, to see about the chaps. I don't know where they thought her and Henry was. But lucky the oldest one was a gal, about twelve, big enough to take care of the little ones. Which she did for the next two days. Mrs. Armstid would nurse Henry all night and work in the kitchen for hern and Henry's keep, and in the afternoon she would drive home (it was about four miles) to see to the chaps. She would cook up a pot of victuals and leave it on the stove, and the gal would bar the house and keep the little ones quiet. I would hear Mrs. Littlejohn and Mrs. Armstid talking in the kitchen. "How are the chaps making out?" Mrs. Littlejohn says.

"All right," Mrs. Armstid says.

"Don't they git skeered at night?" Mrs. Littlejohn says.

"Ina May bars the door when I leave," Mrs. Armstid says. "She's got the axe in bed with her. I reckon she can make out."

I reckon they did. And I reckon Mrs. Armstid was waiting for Flem to come back to town; hadn't nobody seen him until this morning; to get her money the Texas man said Flem was keeping for her. Sho. I reckon she was.

Anyway, I heard Mrs. Armstid and Mrs. Littlejohn talking in the kitchen this morning while I was eating breakfast. Mrs. Littlejohn had just told Mrs. Armstid that Flem was in town. "You can ask him for that five dollars," Mrs. Littlejohn says.

"You reckon he'll give it to me?" Mrs. Armstid says.

Mrs. Littlejohn was washing dishes, washing them like a man, like they was made out of iron. "No," she says. "But asking him won't do no hurt. It might shame him. I don't reckon it will, but it might."

"If he wouldn't give it back, it ain't no use to ask," Mrs. Armstid says.

"Suit yourself," Mrs. Littlejohn says. "It's your money."

I could hear the dishes.

"Do you reckon he might give it back to me?" Mrs. Armstid says. "That Texas man said he would. He said I could get it from Mr. Snopes later."

"Then go and ask him for it," Mrs. Littlejohn says.

I could hear the dishes.

"He won't give it back to me," Mrs. Armstid says.

"All right," Mrs. Littlejohn says. "Don't ask him for it then."

I could hear the dishes; Mrs. Armstid was helping. "You don't reckon he would, do you?" she says. Mrs. Littlejohn never said nothing. It sounded like she was throwing the dishes at one another. "Maybe I better go and talk to Henry about it," Mrs. Armstid says.

"I would," Mrs. Littlejohn says. I be dog if it didn't sound like she had two plates in her hands, beating them together. "Then Henry can buy another five-dollar horse with it. Maybe he'll buy one next time that will out and out kill him. If I thought that, I'd give you back the money, myself."

"I reckon I better talk to him first," Mrs. Armstid said. Then it sounded like Mrs. Littlejohn taken up all the dishes and throwed them at the cook-stove, and I come away.

That was this morning. I had been up to Bundren's and back, and I thought that things would have kind of settled down. So after breakfast, I went up to the store. And there was Flem, setting in the store chair and whittling, like he might not have ever moved since he come to clerk for Jody Varner. I. O. was leaning in the door, in his shirt sleeves and with his hair parted too, same as Flem was before he turned the clerking

job over to I. O. It's a funny thing about them Snopes: they all looks alike, yet there ain't ere a two of them that claims brothers. They're always just cousins, like Flem and Eck and Flem and I. O. Eck was there too, squatting against the wall, him and that boy, eating cheese and crackers outen a sack; they told me that Eck hadn't been home a-tall. And that Lon Quick hadn't got back to town, even. He followed his horse clean down to Samson's Bridge, with a wagon and a camp outfit. Eck finally caught one of hisn. It run into a blind lane at Freeman's and Eck and the boy taken and tied their rope across the end of the lane, about three foot high. The horse come to the end of the lane and whirled and run back without ever stopping. Eck says it never seen the rope a-tall. He says it looked just like one of these here Christmas pinwheels. "Didn't it try to run again?" I says.

"No," Eck says, eating a bite of cheese offen his knife blade. "Just kicked some."

"Kicked some?" I says.

"It broke its neck," Eck says.

Well, they was squatting there, about six of them, talking, talking at Flem; never nobody knowed yet if Flem had ere a interest in them horses or not. So finally I come right out and asked him. "Flem's done skun all of us so much," I says, "that we're proud of him. Come on, Flem," I says, "how much did you and that Texas man make offen them horses? You can tell us. Ain't nobody here but Eck that bought one of them; the others ain't got back to town yet, and Eck's your own cousin; he'll be proud to hear, too. How much did you-all make?"

They was all whittling, not looking at Flem, making like they was studying. But you could a heard a pin drop. And I. O. He had been rubbing his back up and down on the door, but he stopped now, watching Flem like a pointing dog. Flem finished cutting the sliver offen his stick. He spit across the porch, into the road. "Twarn't none of my horses," he says.

I. O. cackled, like a hen, slapping his legs with both hands. "You boys might just as well quit trying to get ahead of Flem," he said.

Well, about that time I see Mrs. Armstid come outen Mrs. Littlejohn's gate, coming up the road. I never said nothing. I says, "Well, if a man can't take care of himself in a trade, he can't blame the man that trims him."

Flem never said nothing, trimming at the stick. He hadn't seen Mrs. Armstid. "Yes, sir," I says. "A fellow like Henry Armstid ain't got nobody but hisself to blame."

"Course he ain't," I. O. says. He ain't seen her, either. "Henry Armstid's a born fool. Always is been. If Flem hadn't got his money, somebody else would."

We looked at Flem. He never moved. Mrs. Armstid come on up the road.

"That's right," I says. "But come to think of it, Henry never bought no horse." We looked at Flem; you could a heard a match drop. "That Texas man told her to get that five dollars back from Flem next day. I reckon Flem's done already taken that money to Mrs. Littlejohn's and give it to Mrs. Armstid."

We watched Flem. I. O. quit rubbing his back against the door again. After a while Flem raised his head and spit across the porch, into the dust. I. O. cackled, just like a hen. "Ain't he a beating fellow, now?" I. O. says.

Mrs. Armstid was getting closer, so I kept on talking, watching to see if Flem would look up and see her. But he never looked up. I went on talking about Tull, about how he was going to sue Flem, and Flem setting there, whittling his stick, not saying nothing else after he said they wasn't none of his horses.

Then I. O. happened to look around. He seen Mrs. Armstid. "Pssssst!" he says. Flem looked up. "Here she comes!" I. O. says. "Go out the back. I'll tell her you done went in to town today."

But Flem never moved. He just sat there, whittling, and we watched Mrs. Armstid come up onto the porch, in that ere faded sunbonnet and wrapper and them tennis shoes that make a kind of hissing noise on the porch. She come onto the porch and stopped, her hands rolled into her dress in front, not looking at nothing.

"He said Saturday," she says, "that he wouldn't sell Henry no horse. He said I could get the money from you."

Flem looked up. The knife never stopped. It went on trimming off a sliver same as if he was watching it. "He taken that money off with him when he left," Flem says.

Mrs. Armstid never looked at nothing. We never looked at her, neither, except that boy of Eck's. He had a half-et cracker in his hand, watching her, chewing.

"He said Henry hadn't bought no horse," Mrs. Armstid says. "He said for me to get the money from you today."

"I reckon he forgot about it," Flem said. "He taken that money off with him Saturday." He whittled again. I. O. kept on rubbing his back, slow. He licked his lips. After a while the woman looked up the road, where it went on up the hill, toward the graveyard. She looked up that way for a while, with that boy of Eck's watching her and I. O. rubbing his back slow against the door. Then she turned back toward the steps.

"I reckon it's time to get dinner started," she says.

"How's Henry this morning, Mrs. Armstid?" Winterbottom says.

She looked at Winterbottom; she almost stopped. "He's resting, I thank you kindly," she says.

Flem got up, outen the chair, putting his knife away. He spit across the porch. "Wait a minute, Mrs. Armstid," he says. She stopped again. She didn't look at him. Flem went on into the store, with I. O. done quit rubbing his back now, with his head craned after Flem, and Mrs. Armstid standing there with her hands rolled into her dress, not looking at nothing. A wagon come up the road and passed; it was Freeman, on the way to town. Then Flem come out again, with I. O. still watching him. Flem had one of these little striped sacks of Jody Varner's candy; I bet he still owes Jody that nickel, too. He put the sack into Mrs. Armstid's hand, like he would have put it into a hollow stump. He spit again across the porch. "A little sweetening for the chaps," he says.

"You're right kind," Mrs. Armstid says. She held the sack of candy in her hand, not looking at nothing. Eck's boy was watching the sack, the half-et cracker in his hand; he wasn't chewing now. He watched Mrs. Armstid roll the sack into her apron. "I reckon I better get on back and help with dinner," she says. She turned and went back across the porch. Flem set down in the chair again and opened his knife. He spit across the porch again, past Mrs. Armstid where she hadn't went down the steps yet. Then she went on, in that ere sunbonnet and wrapper all the same color, back down the road toward Mrs. Little-john's. You couldn't see her dress move, like a natural woman walking. She looked like a old snag still standing up and moving along on a high water. We watched her turn in at Mrs. Littlejohn's and go outen sight. Flem was whittling. I. O. begun to rub his back on the door. Then he begun to cackle, just like a durn hen.

"You boys might just as well quit trying," I.

O. says. "You can't git ahead of Flem. You can't touch him. Ain't he a sight, now?"

I be dog if he ain't. If I had brung a herd of wild cattymounts into town and sold them to my neighbors and kinfolks, they would have lynched me. Yes, sir.

## THOMAS HARDY

# The Three Strangers

Thomas Hardy (1840–1928), born near Dorchester, England, began his working career as an architect. However, poetry was a compelling interest, and he began to write it. Because he was not able to attract an audience for his poetry, he turned to writing short stories and novels for a livelihood. His first success as a novelist came in 1874 with the publication of *Far from the Madding Crowd*. Then followed his masterpieces, *The Return of the Native*, 1878; *The Mayor of Casterbridge*, 1886; *Tess of the D'Urbervilles*, 1891; and *Jude the Obscure*, 1895. In 1896, discouraged by harsh criticism of *Jude the Obscure* and now financially secure because of his earlier successes, Hardy returned to writing poetry and became one of the great English poets.

Hardy's main concerns as a writer are clearly shown in "The Three Strangers"—the unpredictable character of man's fate, the irony of life, the warmth of natural human response, and the authentic detailing of scene.

Among the few features of agricultural England which retain an appearance but little modified by the lapse of centuries may be reckoned the high, grassy and furzy downs, coombs, or eweleases, as they are indifferently called, that fill a large area of certain counties in the south and south-west. If any mark of human occupation is met with hereon, it usually takes the form of the solitary cottage of some shepherd.

Fifty years ago such a lonely cottage stood on such a down, and may possibly be standing there now. In spite of its loneliness, however, the spot, by actual measurement, was not more than five miles from a county-town. Yet that affected it little. Five miles of irregular upland, during the long inimical seasons, with their sleets, snows, rains, and mists, afford withdrawing space

enough to isolate a Timon or a Nebuchadnezzar; much less, in fair weather, to please that less repellent tribe, the poets, philosophers, artists, and others who "conceive and meditate of pleasant things."

Some old earthen camp or barrow, some clump of trees, at least some starved fragment of ancient hedge is usually taken advantage of in the erection of these forlorn dwellings. But, in the present case, such a kind of shelter had been disregarded. Higher Crowstairs, as the house was called, stood quite detached and undefended. The only reason for its precise situation seemed to be the crossing of two footpaths at right angles hard by, which may have crossed there and thus for a good five hundred years. Hence the house was exposed to the elements on all sides. But, though the wind up here blew unmistakably when it did blow, and the rain hit hard whenever it fell, the various weathers of the winter season were not quite so formidable on the coomb as they were imagined to be by dwellers on low ground. The raw rimes were not so pernicious as in the hollows, and the frosts were scarcely so severe. When the shepherd and his family who tenanted the house were pitied for their sufferings from the exposure, they said that upon the whole they were less inconvenienced by "wuzzes and flames" (hoarses and phlegms) than when they had lived by the stream of a snug neighboring valley.

The night of March 28, 182– was precisely one of the nights that were wont to call forth these expressions of commiseration. The level rain-storm smote walls, slopes, and hedges like the clothyard shafts of Senlac and Crecy. Such sheep and outdoor animals as had no shelter stood with their buttocks to the winds; while the tails of little birds trying to roost on some scraggy thorn were blown inside-out like umbrellas. The gable-end of the cottage was stained with wet, and the eavesdroppings flapped against the wall. Yet never was commiseration for the shepherd more misplaced. For that cheerful rustic was entertaining a large party in glorification of the christening of his second girl.

The guests had arrived before the rain began to fall, and they were all now assembled in the chief or living room of the dwelling. A glance into the apartment at eight o'clock on this eventful evening would have resulted in the opinion that it was as cozy and comfortable a nook as could be wished for in boisterous weather. The calling of its inhabitant was proclaimed by a number of highly polished sheep-crooks without stems that were hung ornamentally over the fireplace, the curl of each shining crook varying from the antiquated type engraved in the patriarchal pictures of old family Bibles to the most approved fashion of the last local sheep-fair. The room was lighted by half-a-dozen candles, having wicks only a trifle smaller than the grease which enveloped them, in candlesticks that were never used but at high-days, holy-days, and family feasts. The lights were scattered about the room, two of them standing on the chimney-piece. This position of candles was in itself significant. Candles on the chimney-piece always meant a party.

On the hearth, in front of a back-brand to give

substance, blazed a fire of thorns, that crackled "like the laughter of the fool."

Nineteen persons were gathered here. Of these, five women, wearing gowns of various bright hues, sat in chairs along the wall; girls shy and not shy filled the window-bench; four men, including Charley Jake the hedge-carpenter, Elijah New the parish-clerk, and John Pitcher, a neighboring dairyman, the shepherd's father-in-law, lolled in the settle; a young man and maid, who were blushing over tentative pour-parlers on a life-companionship, sat beneath the corner-cupboard; and an elderly engaged man of fifty or upward moved restlessly about from spots where his betrothed was not to the spot where she was. Enjoyment was pretty general, and so much the more prevailed in being unhampered by conventional restrictions. Absolute confidence in each other's good opinion begat perfect ease, while the finishing stroke of manner, amounting to a truly princely serenity, was lent to the majority by the absence of any expression or trait denoting that they wished to get on in the world, enlarge their minds, or do any eclipsing thing whatever—which nowadays so generally nips the bloom and bonhomie of all except the two extremes of the social scale.

Shepherd Fennel had married well, his wife being a dairyman's daughter from a vale at a distance, who brought fifty guineas in her pocket—and kept them there, till they should be required for ministering to the needs of a coming family. This frugal woman had been somewhat exercised as to the character that should be given to the gathering. A sit-still party had its advantages; but an undisturbed position of ease in chairs and settles was apt to lead on the men to such an unconscionable deal of toping that they would sometimes fairly drink the house dry. A dancing-party was the alternative; but this, while avoiding the foregoing objection on the score of good drink, had a counterbalancing disadvantage in the matter of good victuals, the ravenous appetites engendered by the exercise causing immense havoc in the buttery. Shepherdess Fennel fell back upon the intermediate plan of mingling short dances with short periods of talk and singing, so as to hinder any ungovernable rage in either. But this scheme was entirely confined to her own gentle mind: the shepherd himself was in the mood to exhibit the most reckless phases of hospitality.

The fiddler was a boy of those parts, about twelve years of age, who had a wonderful dexterity in jigs and reels, though his fingers were so small and short as to necessitate a constant shifting for the high notes, from which he scrambled back to the first position with sounds not of unmixed purity of tone. At seven the shrill tweedle-dee of this youngster had begun, accompanied by a booming ground-bass from Elijah New, the parish-clerk, who had thoughtfully brought with him his favorite musical instrument, the serpent. Dancing was instantaneous, Mrs. Fennel privately enjoining the players on no account to let the dance exceed the length of a quarter of an hour.

But Elijah and the boy, in the excitement of their position, quite forgot the injunction. Moreover, Oliver Giles, a man of seventeen, one of the dancers, who was enamored of his partner, a fair girl of thirty-three rolling years, had recklessly handed a new crown-piece to the musicians, as a bribe to keep going as long as they had muscle and wind. Mrs. Fennel, seeing the steam begin to generate on the countenances of her guests, crossed over and touched the fiddler's elbow and put her hand on the serpent's mouth. But they took no notice, and fearing she might lose her character of genial hostess if she were to interfere too markedly, she retired and sat down helpless. And so the dance whizzed on with cumulative fury, the performers moving in their planet-like courses, direct and retrograde, from apogee to perigee, till the hand of the well-kicked clock at the bottom of the room had traveled over the circumference of an hour.

While these cheerful events were in course of enactment within Fennel's pastoral dwelling, an incident having considerable bearing on the party had occurred in the gloomy night without. Mrs. Fennel's concern about the growing fierceness of the dance corresponded in point of time with the ascent of a human figure to the solitary hill of Higher Crowstairs from the direction of the distant town. This personage strode on through the rain without a pause, following the little-worn path which, further on in its course, skirted the shepherd's cottage.

It was nearly the time of full moon, and on this account, though the sky was lined with a uniform sheet of dripping cloud, ordinary objects out of doors were readily visible. The sad wan light revealed the lonely pedestrian to be a man of supple frame; his gait suggested that he had somewhat passed the period of perfect and instinctive agility, though not so far as to be otherwise than rapid of motion when occasion required. At a rough guess, he might have been about forty years of age. He appeared tall, but a recruiting sergeant, or other person accustomed to the judging of men's heights by the eye, would have discerned that this was chiefly owing to his gauntness, and that he was not more than five-feet-eight or nine.

Notwithstanding the regularity of his tread, there was caution in it, as in that of one who mentally feels his way; and despite the fact that it was not a black coat nor a dark garment of any sort that he wore, there was something about him which suggested that he naturally belonged to the black-coated tribes of men. His clothes were of fustian, and his boots hobnailed, yet in his progress he showed not the mud-accustomed bearing of hobnailed and fustianed peasantry.

By the time that he had arrived abreast of the shepherd's premises the rain came down, or rather came along, with yet more determined violence. The outskirts of the little settlement partially broke the force of wind and rain, and this induced him to stand still. The most salient of the shepherd's domestic erections was an empty sty at the forward corner of his hedgeless garden, for in these latitudes the principle of masking the homelier features of your establishment by a conventional frontage was unknown. The traveler's eye was attracted to this small building by the pallid shine of the wet slates that covered it. He turned aside, and, finding it empty, stood under the pent-roof for shelter.

While he stood, the boom of the serpent within the adjacent house, and the lesser strains of the fiddler, reached the spot as an accompaniment to the surging hiss of the flying rain on the sod, its louder beating on the cabbage-leaves of the garden, on the eight or ten beehives just discernible by the path, and its dripping from the eaves into a row of buckets and pans that had been placed under the walls of the cottage. For at Higher Crowstairs, as at all such elevated domiciles, the grand difficulty of housekeeping was an insufficiency of water; and a casual rainfall was utilized by turning out, as catchers, every utensil that the house contained. Some queer stories might be told of the contrivances for economy in suds and dishwaters that are absolutely necessitated in upland habitations during the droughts of summer. But at this season there were no such exigencies; a mere acceptance of what the skies bestowed was sufficient for an abundant store.

At last the notes of the serpent ceased and the house was silent. This cessation of activity aroused the solitary pedestrian from the reverie into which he had lapsed, and, emerging from the shed, with an apparently new intention, he walked up the path to the house-door. Arrived here, his first act was to kneel down on a large stone beside the row of vessels, and to drink a copious draught from one of them. Having quenched his thirst he rose and lifted his hand to knock, but paused with his eye upon the panel. Since the dark surface of the wood revealed absolutely nothing, it was evident that he must be mentally looking through the door, as if he wished to measure thereby all the possibilities that a house of this sort might include, and how they might bear upon the question of his entry.

In his indecision he turned and surveyed the scene around. Not a soul was anywhere visible. The garden-path stretched downward from his feet, gleaming like the track of a snail; the roof of the little well (mostly dry), the well-cover, the top rail of the garden-gate, were varnished with the same dull liquid glaze; while, far away in the vale, a faint whiteness of more than usual extent showed that the rivers were high in the meads. Beyond all this winked a few bleared lamplights through the beating drops—lights that denoted the situation of the county-town from which he had appeared to come. The absence of all notes of life in that direction seemed to clinch his intentions, and he knocked at the door.

Within, a desultory chat had taken the place of movement and musical sound. The hedge-carpenter was suggesting a song to the company, which nobody just then was inclined to undertake, so that the knock afforded a not unwelcome diversion.

"Walk in!" said the shepherd promptly.

The latch clicked upward, and out of the night our pedestrian appeared upon the door-mat. The shepherd arose, snuffed two of the nearest candles, and turned to look at him.

Their light disclosed that the stranger was dark in complexion and not unprepossessing as to feature. His hat, which for a moment he did not remove, hung low over his eyes, without concealing that they were large, open, and determined, moving with a flash rather than a glance round the room. He seemed pleased with his survey, and, baring his shaggy head, said, in a rich deep voice, "The rain is so heavy, friends, that I ask leave to come in and rest awhile."

"To be sure, stranger," said the shepherd. "And faith, you've been lucky in choosing your time, for we are having a bit of a fling for a glad cause—though, to be sure, a man could hardly wish that glad cause to happen more than once a year."

"Nor less," spoke up a woman. "For 'tis best to get your family over and done with, as soon as you can, so as to be all the earlier out of the fag o't."

"And what may be this glad cause?" asked the stranger.

"A birth and christening," said the shepherd.

The stranger hoped his host might not be made unhappy, either by too many or too few of such episodes, and being invited by a gesture to a pull at the mug, he readily acquiesced. His manner, which, before entering, had been so dubious, was now altogether that of a careless and candid man.

"Late to be traipsing athwart this coomb—hey?" said the engaged man of fifty.

"Late it is, master, as you say.—I'll take a seat in the chimney-corner, if you have nothing to urge against it, ma'am; for I am a little moist on the side that was next the rain."

Mrs. Shepherd Fennel assented, and made room for the self-invited comer, who, having got completely inside the chimney-corner, stretched out his legs and his arms with the expansiveness of a person quite at home.

"Yes, I am rather cracked in the vamp," he said freely, seeing that the eyes of the shepherd's wife fell upon his boots, "and I am not well fitted either. I have had some rough times lately, and have been forced to pick up what I can get in the way of wearing, but I must find a suit better fit for working-days when I reach home."

"One of hereabouts?" she inquired.

"Not quite that—further up the country."

"I thought so. And so be I; and by your tongue you come from my neighborhood."

"But you would hardly have heard of me," he

said quickly. "My time would be long before yours, ma'am, you see."

This testimony to the youthfulness of his hostess had the effect of stopping her cross-examination.

"There is only one thing more wanted to make me happy," continued the new-comer. "And that is a little baccy, which I am sorry to say I am out of."

"I'll fill your pipe," said the shepherd.

"I must ask you to lend me a pipe likewise."

"A smoke, and no pipe about 'ee?"

"I have dropped it somewhere on the road."

The shepherd filled and handed him a new clay pipe, saying, as he did so, "Hand me your baccy-box—I'll fill that too, now I am about it."

The man went through the movement of searching his pockets.

"Lost that too?" said his entertainer, with some surprise.

"I am afraid so," said the man with some confusion. "Give it to me in a screw of paper." Lighting his pipe at the candle with a suction that drew the whole flame into the bowl, he resettled himself in the corner and bent his looks upon the faint stream from his damp legs, as if he wished to say no more.

Meanwhile the general body of guests had been taking little notice of this visitor by reason of an absorbing discussion in which they were engaged with the band about a tune for the next dance. The matter being settled, they were about to stand up when an interruption came in the shape of another knock at the door.

At sound of the same the man in the chimney-corner took up the poker and began stirring the brands as if doing it thoroughly were the one aim of his existence; and a second time the shepherd said, "Walk in!" In a moment another man stood upon the straw-woven door-mat. He too was a stranger.

This individual was one of a type radically different from the first. There was more of the commonplace in his manner, and a certain jovial cosmopolitanism sat upon his features. He was several years older than the first arrival, his hair being slightly frosted, his eyebrows bristly, and his whiskers cut back from his cheeks. His face was rather full and flabby, and yet it was not altogether a face without power. A few grog-blossoms marked the neighborhood of his nose. He flung back his long drab greatcoat, revealing

that beneath it he wore a suit of cinder-gray shade throughout, large heavy seals, of some metal or other that would take a polish, dangling from his fob as his only personal ornament. Shaking the water-drops from his low-crowned glazed hat, he said, "I must ask for a few minutes' shelter, comrades, or I shall be wetted to my skin before I get to Casterbridge."

"Make yourself at home, master," said the shepherd, perhaps a trifle less heartily than on the first occasion. Not that Fennel had the least tinge of niggardliness in his composition; but the room was far from large, spare chairs were not numerous, and damp companions were not altogether desirable at close quarters for the women and girls in their bright-colored gowns.

However, the second comer, after taking off his greatcoat, and hanging his hat on a nail in one of the ceiling-beams as if he had been specially invited to put it there, advanced and sat down at the table. This had been pushed so closely into the chimney-corner, to give all available room to the dancers, that its inner edge grazed the elbow of the man who had ensconced himself by the fire; and thus the two strangers were brought into close companionship. They nodded to each other by way of breaking the ice of unacquaintance, and the first stranger handed his neighbor the family mug—a huge vessel of brown ware, having its upper edge worn away like a threshold by the rub of whole generations of thirsty lips that had gone the way of all flesh, and bearing the following inscription burnt upon its rotund side in yellow letters:

THERE IS NO FUN
UNTILL I CUM

The other man, nothing loth, raised the mug to his lips, and drank on, and on, and on—till a curious blueness overspread the countenance of the shepherd's wife, who had regarded with no little surprise the first stranger's free offer to the second of what did not belong to him to dispense.

"I knew it!" said the toper to the shepherd with much satisfaction. "When I walked up your garden before coming in, and saw the hives all of a row, I said to myself, 'Where there's bees there's honey, and where there's honey there's mead.' But mead of such a truly comfortable sort as this I really didn't expect to meet in my older days." He took yet another pull at the mug, till it assumed an ominous elevation.

"Glad you enjoy it!" said the shepherd warmly.

"It is goodish mead," assented Mrs. Fennel, with an absence of enthusiasm which seemed to say that it was possible to buy praise for one's cellar at too heavy a price. "It is trouble enough to make—and really I hardly think we shall make any more. For honey sells well, and we ourselves can make shift with a drop o' small mead and metheglin for common use from the comb-washings."

"O, but you'll never have the heart!" reproachfully cried the stranger in cinder-gray, after taking up the mug a third time and setting it down empty. "I love mead, when 'tis old like this, as I love to go to church o' Sundays, or to relieve the needy any day of the week."

"Ha, ha, ha!" said the man in the chimney-corner, who, in spite of the taciturnity induced by the pipe of tobacco, could not or would not refrain from this slight testimony to his comrade's humor.

Now the old mead of those days, brewed of the purest first year or maiden honey, four pounds to the gallon—with its due complement of white of eggs, cinnamon, ginger, cloves, mace, rosemary, yeast, and processes of working, bottling and cellaring—tasted remarkably strong; but it did not taste so strong as it actually was. Hence, presently, the stranger in cinder-gray at the table, moved by its creeping influence, unbuttoned his waistcoat, threw himself back in his chair, spread his legs, and made his presence felt in various ways.

"Well, well, as I say," he resumed, "I am going to Casterbridge, and to Casterbridge I must go. I should have been almost there by this time; but the rain drove me into your dwelling, and I'm not sorry for it."

"You don't live in Casterbridge?" said the shepherd.

"Not as yet; though I shortly mean to move there."

"Going to set up in trade, perhaps?"

"No, no," said the shepherd's wife. "It is easy to see that the gentleman is rich, and don't want to work at anything."

The cinder-gray stranger paused, as if to consider whether he would accept that definition of himself. He presently rejected it by answering, "Rich is not quite the word for me, dame. I do

work, and I must work. And even if I only get to Casterbridge by midnight I must begin work there at eight tomorrow morning. Yes, het or wet, blow or snow, famine or sword, my day's work tomorrow must be done."

"Poor man! Then, in spite o' seeming, you be worse off than we?" replied the shepherd's wife.

"'Tis the nature of my trade, men and maidens. 'Tis the nature of my trade more than my poverty. . . . But really and truly I must up and off, or I shan't get a lodging in the town." However, the speaker did not move, and directly added, "There's time for one more draught of friendship before I go; and I'd perform it at once if the mug were not dry."

"Here's a mug o' small," said Mrs. Fennel. "Small, we call it, though to be sure 'tis only the first wash o' the combs."

"No," said the stranger disdainfully. "I won't spoil your first kindness by partaking o' your second."

"Certainly not," broke in Fennel. "We don't increase and multiply every day, and I'll fill the mug again." He went away to the dark place under the stairs where the barrel stood. The shepherdess followed him.

"Why should you do this?" she said reproachfully, as soon as they were alone. "He's emptied it once, though it held enough for ten people; and now he's not contented wi' the small, but must needs call for more o' the strong! And a stranger unbeknown to any of us. For my part, I don't like the look o' the man at all."

"But he's in the house, my honey; and 'tis a wet night, and a christening. Daze it, what's a cup of mead more or less? There'll be plenty more next bee-burning."

"Very well—this time, then," she answered, looking wistfully at the barrel. "But what is the man's calling, and where is he one of, that he should come in and join us like this?"

"I don't know. I'll ask him again."

The catastrophe of having the mug drained dry at one pull by the stranger in cinder-gray was effectually guarded against this time by Mrs. Fennel. She poured out his allowance in a small cup, keeping the large one at a discreet distance from him. When he had tossed off his portion the shepherd renewed his inquiry about the stranger's occupation.

The latter did not immediately reply, and the man in the chimney-corner, with sudden demonstrativeness, said, "Anybody may know my trade—I'm a wheelwright."

"A very good trade for these parts," said the shepherd.

"And anybody may know mine—if they've the sense to find it out," said the stranger in cinder-gray.

"You may generally tell what a man is by his claws," observed the hedge-carpenter, looking at his own hands. "My fingers be as full of thorns as an old pincushion is of pins."

The hands of the man in the chimney-corner instinctively sought the shade, and he gazed into the fire as he resumed his pipe. The man at the table took up the hedge-carpenter's remark, and added smartly, "True; but the oddity of my trade is that, instead of setting a mark upon me, it sets a mark upon my customers."

No observation being offered by anybody in elucidation of this enigma, the shepherd's wife once more called for a song. The same obstacles presented themselves as at the former time—one had no voice, another had forgotten the first verse. The stranger at the table, whose soul had now risen to a good working temperature, relieved the difficulty by exclaiming that, to start the company, he would sing himself. Thrusting one thumb into the arm-hole of his waistcoat, he waved the other hand in the air, and, with an extemporizing gaze at the shining sheep-crooks above the mantelpiece, began:

> O my trade it is the rarest one,
>     Simple shepherds all—
>     My trade is a sight to see;
> For my customers I tie, and take them up on high,
>     And waft 'em to a far countree!

The room was silent when he had finished the verse—with one exception, that of the man in the chimney-corner, who, at the singer's word, "Chorus!" joined him in a deep bass voice of musical relish:

> And waft 'em to a far countree!

Oliver Giles, John Pitcher the dairyman, the parish-clerk, the engaged man of fifty, the row of young women against the wall, seemed lost in thought not of the gayest kind. The shepherd looked meditatively on the ground, the shep-

herdess gazed keenly at the singer, and with some suspicion; she was doubting whether this stranger were merely singing an old song from recollection, or was composing one there and then for the occasion. All were as perplexed at the obscure revelation as the guests at Belshazzar's Feast, except the man in the chimney-corner, who quietly said, "Second verse, stranger," and smoked on.

The singer thoroughly moistened himself from his lips inwards, and went on with the next stanza as requested:

> My tools are but common ones,
>     Simple shepherds all—
>     My tools are no sight to see:
> A little hempen string, and a post whereon to swing,
>     Are implements enough for me!

Shepherd Fennel glanced round. There was no longer any doubt that the stranger was answering his question rhythmically. The guests one and all started back with suppressed exclamations. The young woman engaged to the man of fifty fainted half-way, and would have proceeded, but finding him wanting in alacrity for catching her she sat down trembling.

"O, he's the—!" whispered the people in the background, mentioning the name of an ominous public officer. "He's come to do it! 'Tis to be at Casterbridge jail tomorrow—the man for sheep-stealing—the poor clock-maker we heard of, who used to live away at Shottsford and had no work to do—Timothy Summers, whose family were a-starving, and so he went out of Shottsford by the high-road, and took a sheep in open daylight, defying the farmer and the farmer's wife and the farmer's lad, and every man jack among 'em. He" (and they nodded towards the stranger of the deadly trade) "is come from up the country to do it because there's not enough to do in his own county-town, and he's got the place here now our own county man's dead; he's going to live in the same cottage under the prison wall."

The stranger in cinder-gray took no notice of this whispered string of observations, but again wetted his lips. Seeing that his friend in the chimney-corner was the only one who reciprocated his joviality in any way, he held out his cup towards that appreciative comrade, who also held out his own. They clinked together, the eyes of the rest of the room hanging upon the singer's actions. He parted his lips for the third verse; but at that moment another knock was audible upon the door. This time the knock was faint and hesitating.

The company seemed scared; the shepherd looked with consternation towards the entrance, and it was with some effort that he resisted his alarmed wife's deprecatory glance, and uttered for the third time the welcoming words, "Walk in!"

The door was gently opened, and another man stood upon the mat. He, like those who had preceded him, was a stranger. This time it was a short, small personage, of fair complexion, and dressed in a decent suit of dark clothes.

"Can you tell me the way to——?" he began, when, gazing round the room to observe the nature of the company amongst whom he had fallen, his eyes lighted on the stranger in cinder-gray. It was just at the instant when the latter, who had thrown his mind into his song, with such a will that he scarcely heeded the interruption, silenced all whispers and inquiries by bursting into his third verse.

Tomorrow is my working day,
Simple shepherds all—
Tomorrow is a working day for me:
For the farmer's sheep is slain, and the lad who
did it ta'en,
And on his soul may God ha' merc-y!

The stranger in the chimney-corner, waving cups with the singer so heartily that his mead splashed over on the hearth, repeated in his bass voice as before:

And on his soul may God ha' merc-y!

All this time the third stranger had been standing in the doorway. Finding now that he did not come forward or go on speaking, the guests particularly regarded him. They noticed to their surprise that he stood before them the picture of abject terror—his knees trembling, his hand shaking so violently that the door-latch by which he supported himself rattled audibly: his white lips were parted, and his eyes fixed on the merry officer of justice in the middle of the room. A moment more and he had turned, closed the door, and fled.

"What a man can it be?" said the shepherd.

The rest, between the awfulness of their late discovery and the odd conduct of this third visitor, looked as if they knew not what to think, and said nothing. Instinctively they withdrew further and further from the grim gentleman in their midst, whom some of them seemed to take for the Prince of Darkness himself, till they formed a remote circle, an empty space of floor being left between them and him:

. . . circulus, cujus centrum diabolus.

The room was so silent—though there were more than twenty people in it—that nothing could be heard but the patter of the rain against the window-shutters, accompanied by the occasional hiss of a stray drop that fell down the chimney into the fire, and the steady puffing of the man in the corner, who had now resumed his pipe of long clay.

The stillness was unexpectedly broken. The distant sound of a gun reverberated through the air—apparently from the direction of the county-town.

"Be jiggered!" cried the stranger who had sung the song, jumping up.

"What does that mean?" asked several.

"A prisoner escaped from the jail—that's what it means."

All listened. The sound was repeated, and none of them spoke but the man in the chimney-corner, who said quietly, "I've often been told that in this county they fire a gun at such times; but I never heard it till now."

"I wonder if it is *my* man?" murmured the personage in cinder-gray.

"Surely it is!" said the shepherd involuntarily. "And surely we've zeed him! That little man who looked in at the door by now, and quivered like a leaf when he zeed ye and heard your song!"

"His teeth chattered, and the breath went out of his body," said the dairyman.

"And his heart seemed to sink within him like a stone," said Oliver Giles.

"And he bolted as if he'd been shot at," said the hedge-carpenter.

"True—his teeth chattered, and his heart seemed to sink; and he bolted as if he'd been shot at," slowly summed up the man in the chimney-corner.

"I didn't notice it," remarked the hangman.

"We were all a-wondering what made him run

off in such a fright," faltered one of the women against the wall, "and now 'tis explained!"

The firing of the alarm-gun went on at intervals, low and sullenly, and their suspicions became a certainty. The sinister gentleman in cinder-gray roused himself. "Is there a constable here?" he asked, in thick tones. "If so, let him step forward."

The engaged man of fifty stepped quavering out from the wall, his betrothed beginning to sob on the back of the chair.

"You are a sworn constable?"

"I be, sir."

"Then pursue the criminal at once, with assistance, and bring him back here. He can't have gone far."

"I will, sir, I will—when I've got my staff. I'll go home and get it, and come sharp here, and start in a body."

"Staff!—never mind your staff; the man'll be gone!"

"But I can't do nothing without my staff—can I, William, and John, and Charles Jake? No; for there's the king's royal crown a painted on en in yaller and gold, and the lion and the unicorn, so as when I raise en up and hit my prisoner, 'tis made a lawful blow thereby. I wouldn't 'tempt to take up a man without my staff—no, not I. If I hadn't the law to gie me courage, why, instead o' my taking up him he might take up me!"

"Now, I'm a king's man myself, and can give you authority enough for this," said the formidable officer in gray. "Now then, all of ye, be ready. Have ye any lanterns?"

"Yes—have ye any lanterns?—I demand it!" said the constable.

"And the rest of you able-bodied—"

"Able-bodied men—yes—the rest of ye!" said the constable.

"Have you some good stout staves and pitchforks—"

"Staves and pitchforks—in the name o' the law! And take 'em in yer hands and go in quest, and do as we in authority tell ye!"

Thus aroused, the men prepared to give chase. The evidence was, indeed, though circumstantial, so convincing, that but little argument was needed to show the shepherd's guests that after what they had seen it would look very much like connivance if they did not instantly pursue the unhappy third stranger who could not as yet

have gone more than a few hundred yards over such uneven country.

A shepherd is always well provided with lanterns; and, lighting these hastily, and with hurdle-staves in their hands, they poured out of the door, taking a direction along the crest of the hill, away from the town, the rain having fortunately a little abated.

Disturbed by the noise, or possibly by unpleasant dreams of her baptism, the child who had been christened began to cry heartbrokenly in the room overhead. These notes of grief came down through the chinks of the floor to the ears of the women below, who jumped up one by one, and seemed glad of the excuse to ascend and comfort the baby, for the incidents of the last half-hour greatly oppressed them. Thus in the space of two or three minutes the room on the ground-floor was deserted quite.

But it was not for long. Hardly had the sound of footsteps died away when a man returned round the corner of the house from the direction the pursuers had taken. Peeping in at the door, and seeing nobody there, he entered leisurely. It was the stranger of the chimney-corner, who had gone out with the rest. The motive of his return was shown by his helping himself to a cut piece of skimmer-cake that lay on a ledge beside where he had sat, and which he had apparently forgotten to take with him. He also poured out half a cup more mead from the quantity that remained, ravenously eating and drinking these as he stood. He had not finished when another figure came in just as quietly—his friend in cinder-gray.

"O—you here?" said the latter, smiling. "I thought you had gone to help in the capture." And this speaker also revealed the object of his return by looking solicitously round for the fascinating mug of old mead.

"And I thought you had gone," said the other, continuing his skimmer-cake with some effort.

"Well, on second thoughts, I felt there were enough without me," said the first confidentially, "and such a night as it is, too. Besides, 'tis the business o' the Government to take care of its criminals—not mine."

"True; so it is. And I felt as you did, that there were enough without me."

"I don't want to break my limbs running over the humps and hollows of this wild country."

"Nor I neither, between you and me."

"These shepherd-people are used to it—

simple-minded souls, you know, stirred up to anything in a moment. They'll have him ready for me before morning, and no trouble to me at all."

"They'll have him, and we shall have saved ourselves all labor in the matter."

"True, true. Well, my way is to Casterbridge; and 'tis as much as my legs will do to take me that far. Going the same way?"

"No, I am sorry to say! I have to get home over there" (he nodded indefinitely to the right), "and I feel as you do, that it is quite enough for my legs to do before bedtime."

The other had by this time finished the mead in the mug, after which, shaking hands heartily at the door, and wishing each other well, they went their several ways.

In the meantime the company of pursuers had reached the end of the hog's-back elevation which dominated this part of the down. They had decided on no particular plan of action; and, finding that the man of the baleful trade was no longer in their company, they seemed quite unable to form any such plan now. They descended in all directions down the hill, and straightway several of the party fell into the snare set by Nature for all misguided midnight ramblers over this part of the cretaceous formation. The "lanchets," or flint slopes, which belted the escarpment at intervals of a dozen yards, took the less cautious ones unawares, and losing their footing on the rubbly steep they slid sharply downwards, the lanterns rolling from their hands to the bottom, and there lying on their sides till the horn was scorched through.

When they had again gathered themselves together, the shepherd, as the man who knew the country best, took the lead, and guided them round these treacherous inclines. The lanterns, which seemed rather to dazzle their eyes and warn the fugitive than to assist them in the exploration, were extinguished, due silence was observed; and in this more rational order they plunged into the vale. It was a grassy, briery, moist defile, affording some shelter to any person who had sought it; but the party perambulated it in vain, and ascended on the other side. Here they wandered apart, and after an interval closed together again to report progress. At the second time of closing in they found themselves near a lonely ash, the single tree on this part of the coomb, probably sown there by a passing bird

some fifty years before. And here, standing a little to one side of the trunk, as motionless as the trunk itself, appeared the man they were in quest of, his outline being well defined against the sky beyond. The band noiselessly drew up and faced him.

"Your money or your life!" said the constable sternly to the still figure.

"No, no," whispered John Pitcher. "'Tisn't our side ought to say that. That's the doctrine of vagabonds like him, and we be on the side of the law."

"Well, well," replied the constable impatiently; "I must say something, mustn't I? and if you had all the weight o' this undertaking upon your mind, perhaps you'd say the wrong thing too!—Prisoner at the bar, surrender, in the name of the Father—the Crown, I mane!"

The man under the tree seemed now to notice them for the first time, and, giving them no opportunity whatever for exhibiting their courage, he strolled slowly towards them. He was, indeed, the little man, the third stranger; but his trepidation had in a great measure gone.

"Well, travelers," he said, "did I hear ye speak to me?"

"You did: you've got to come and be our prisoner at once!" said the constable. "We arrest 'ee on the charge of not biding in Casterbridge jail in a decent proper manner to be hung tomorrow morning. Neighbors, do your duty, and seize the culpet!"

On hearing the charge, the man seemed enlightened, and, saying not another word, resigned himself with preternatural civility to the search-party, who, with their staves in their hands, surrounded him on all sides, and marched him back towards the shepherd's cottage.

It was eleven o'clock by the time they arrived. The light shining from the open door, a sound of men's voices within, proclaimed to them as they approached the house that some new events had arisen in their absence. On entering they discovered the shepherd's living room to be invaded by two officers from the Casterbridge jail, and a well-known magistrate who lived at the nearest county-seat, intelligence of the escape having become generally circulated.

"Gentlemen," said the constable, "I have brought back your man—not without risk and danger; but every one must do his duty! He is inside this circle of able-bodied persons, who have lent me useful aid, considering their ignorance of Crown work. Men, bring forward your prisoner!" And the third stranger was led to the light.

"Who is this?" said one of the officials.

"The man," said the constable.

"Certainly not," said the turnkey; and the first corroborated his statement.

"But how can it be otherwise?" asked the constable. "Or why was he so terrified at sight o' the singing instrument of the law who sat there?" Here he related the strange behavior of the third stranger on entering the house during the hangman's song.

"Can't understand it," said the officer coolly. "All I know is that it is not the condemned man. He's quite a different character from this one; a gauntish fellow, with dark hair and eyes, rather good-looking, and with a musical bass voice that if you heard it once you'd never mistake as long as you lived."

"Why, souls—'twas the man in the chimney-corner!"

"Hey—what?" said the magistrate, coming forward after inquiring particulars from the shepherd in the background. "Haven't you got the man after all?"

"Well, sir," said the constable, "he's the man we were in search of, that's true; and yet he's not the man we were in search of. For the man we were in search of was not the man we wanted, sir, if you understand my every-day way; for 'twas the man in the chimney-corner!"

"A pretty kettle of fish altogether!" said the magistrate. "You had better start for the other man at once."

The prisoner now spoke for the first time. The mention of the man in the chimney-corner seemed to have moved him as nothing else could do. "Sir," he said, stepping forward to the magistrate, "take no more trouble about me. The time is come when I may as well speak. I have done nothing; my crime is that the condemned man is my brother. Early this afternoon I left home at Shottsford to tramp it all the way to Casterbridge jail to bid him farewell. I was benighted, and called here to rest and ask the way. When I opened the door I saw before me the very man, my brother, that I thought to see in the condemned cell at Casterbridge. He was in this chimney-corner; and jammed close to him, so that he could not have got out if he had tried,

was the executioner who'd come to take his life, singing a song about it and not knowing that it was his victim who was close by, joining in to save appearances. My brother looked a glance of agony at me, and I knew he meant, 'Don't reveal what you see; my life depends on it.' I was so terror-struck that I could hardly stand, and, not knowing what I did, I turned and hurried away."

The narrator's manner and tone had the stamp of truth, and his story made a great impression on all around. "And do you know where your brother is at the present time?" asked the magistrate.

"I do not. I have never seen him since I closed this door."

"I can testify to that, for we've been between ye ever since," said the constable.

"Where does he think to fly to?—what is his occupation?"

"He's a watch-and-clock-maker, sir."

"'A said 'a was a wheelwright—a wicked rogue," said the constable.

"The wheels of clocks and watches he meant, no doubt," said Shepherd Fennel. "I thought his hands were palish for's trade."

"Well, it appears to me that nothing can be gained by retaining this poor man in custody," said the magistrate; "your business lies with the other, unquestionably."

And so the little man was released off-hand; but he looked nothing the less sad on that account, it being beyond the power of magistrate or constable to raze out the written troubles in his brain, for they concerned another whom he regarded with more solicitude than himself. When this was done, and the man had gone his way, the night was found to be so far advanced that it was deemed useless to renew the search before the next morning.

Next day, accordingly, the quest for the clever sheep-stealer became general and keen, to all appearance at least. But the intended punishment was cruelly disproportioned to the transgression, and the sympathy of a great many country-folk in that district was strongly on the side of the fugitive. Moreover, his marvelous coolness and daring in hob-and-nobbing with the hangman, under the unprecedented circumstances of the shepherd's party, won their admiration. So that it may be questioned if all those who ostensibly made themselves so busy in exploring woods and fields and lanes were quite so thorough when it came to the private examination of their own lofts and outhouses. Stories were afloat of a mysterious figure being occasionally seen in some overgrown trackway or other, remote from turnpike roads; but when a search was instituted in any of these suspected quarters, nobody was found. Thus the days and weeks passed without tidings.

In brief, the bass-voiced man of the chimney-corner was never recaptured. Some said that he went across the sea, others that he did not, but buried himself in the depths of a populous city. At any rate, the gentleman in cinder-gray never did his morning's work at Casterbridge, nor met anywhere at all, for business purposes, the genial comrade with whom he had passed an hour of relaxation in the lonely house on the coomb.

The grass has long been green on the graves of Shepherd Fennel and his frugal wife; the guests who made up the christening party have mainly followed their entertainers to the tomb; the baby in whose honor they all had met is a matron in the sere and yellow leaf. But the arrival of the three strangers at the shepherd's that night, and the details connected therewith, is a story as well known as ever in the country about Higher Crowstairs.

# STEPHEN CRANE

# The Open Boat

Stephen Crane (1871–1900), novelist, poet, journalist, and biographer, began his literary career by writing a startlingly realistic novel, *Maggie: A Girl of the Streets*, 1892. His second novel, *The Red Badge of Courage*, published in 1895, brought him fame. He was a war correspondent for Hearst's New York *Journal* during the Greco-Turkish War. After returning from Greece, Crane married and went to live in England, where he became a friend of Joseph Conrad. In 1898 he distinguished himself by his objective reporting from Cuba of the Spanish-American War. He contracted tuberculosis and died when he was only twenty-nine.

Crane's strongly realistic style did much to revolutionize the technique and style of American fiction. Carl and Mark Van Doren have commented, "Modern American fiction may be said to begin with Stephen Crane." H. G. Wells called "The Open Boat" the "finest short story in English." The story is based on an actual experience of Crane's, as indicated in the original subtitle—"A Fate Intended to Be After the Fact: Being the Experience of Four Men from the Sunk Steamer *Commodore*." Thoughtful readers will agree with Conrad, who commented, "The simple humanity of its presentation seems somehow to illustrate the essentials of life itself, like a symbolic tale."

None of them knew the color of the sky. Their eyes glanced level, and were fastened upon the waves that swept toward them. These waves

THE OPEN BOAT  From *Stephen Crane; An Omnibus*, edited by Robert Wooster Stallman, by permission of Alfred A. Knopf, Inc. Copyright 1952 by Alfred A. Knopf, Inc.

were of the hue of slate, save for the tops, which were of foaming white, and all of the men knew the colors of the sea. The horizon narrowed and widened, and dipped and rose, and at all times its edge was jagged with waves that seemed thrust up in points like rocks.

Many a man ought to have a bath-tub larger than the boat which here rode upon the sea. These waves were most wrongfully and barbarously abrupt and tall, and each froth-top was a problem in small-boat navigation.

The cook squatted in the bottom and looked with both eyes at the six inches of gunwale which separated him from the ocean. His sleeves were rolled over his fat forearms, and the two flaps of his unbuttoned vest dangled as he bent to bail out the boat. Often he said: "Gawd! That was a narrow clip." As he remarked it he invariably gazed eastward over the broken sea.

The oiler, steering with one of the two oars in the boat, sometimes raised himself suddenly to keep clear of water that swirled in over the stern. It was a thin little oar and it seemed often ready to snap.

The correspondent, pulling at the other oar, watched the waves and wondered why he was there.

The injured captain, lying in the bow, was at this time buried in that profound dejection and indifference which comes, temporarily at least, to even the bravest and most enduring when, willy-nilly, the firm fails, the army loses, the ship goes down. The mind of the master of a vessel is rooted deep in the timbers of her, though he command for a day or a decade, and this captain had on him the stern impression of a scene in the grays of dawn of seven turned faces, and later a stump of a top-mast with a white ball on it that slashed to and fro at the waves, went low and lower, and down. Thereafter there was something strange in his voice. Although steady, it was deep with mourning, and of a quality beyond oration or tears.

"Keep 'er a little more south, Billie," said he.

"A little more south, sir," said the oiler in the stern.

A seat in this boat was not unlike a seat upon a bucking bronco, and, by the same token, a bronco is not much smaller. The craft pranced and reared, and plunged like an animal. As each wave came, and she rose for it, she seemed like a horse making at a fence outrageously high. The manner of her scramble over these walls of water is a mystic thing, and, moreover, at the top of them were ordinarily these problems in white water, the foam racing down from the summit of each wave, requiring a new leap, and a leap from the air. Then, after scornfully bumping a crest, she would slide, and race, and splash down a long incline, and arrive bobbing and nodding in front of the next menace.

A singular disadvantage of the sea lies in the fact that after successfully surmounting one wave you discover that there is another behind it just as important and just as nervously anxious to do something effective in the way of swamping boats. In a ten-foot dinghy one can get an idea of the resources of the sea in the line of waves that is not probable to the average experience which is never at sea in a dinghy. As each slaty wall of water approached, it shut all else from the view of the men in the boat, and it was not difficult to imagine that this particular wave was the final outburst of the ocean, the last effort of the grim water. There was a terrible grace in the move of the waves, and they came in silence, save for the snarling of the crests.

In the wan light, the faces of the men must have been gray. Their eyes must have glinted in strange ways as they gazed steadily astern. Viewed from a balcony, the whole thing would doubtless have been weirdly picturesque. But the men in the boat had no time to see it, and if they had had leisure there were other things to occupy their minds. The sun swung steadily up the sky, and they knew it was broad day because the color of the sea changed from slate to emerald-green, streaked with amber lights, and the foam was like tumbling snow. The process of the breaking day was unknown to them. They were aware only of this effect upon the color of the waves that rolled toward them.

In disjointed sentences the cook and the correspondent argued as to the difference between a life-saving station and a house of refuge. The cook had said: "There's a house of refuge just north of the Mosquito Inlet Light, and as soon as they see us, they'll come off in their boat and pick us up."

"As soon as who see us?" said the correspondent.

"The crew," said the cook.

"Houses of refuge don't have crews," said the correspondent. "As I understand them, they are only places where clothes and grub are stored for the benefit of shipwrecked people. They don't carry crews."

"Oh, yes, they do," said the cook.

"No, they don't," said the correspondent.

"Well, we're not there yet, anyhow," said the oiler, in the stern.

"Well," said the cook, "perhaps it's not a house of refuge that I'm thinking of as being near Mosquito Inlet Light. Perhaps it's a life-saving station."

"We're not there yet," said the oiler, in the stern.

## II

As the boat bounced from the top of each wave, the wind tore through the hair of the hatless men, and as the craft plopped her stern down again the spray slashed past them. The crest of each of these waves was a hill, from the top of which the men surveyed, for a moment, a broad tumultuous expanse, shining and wind-driven. It was probably splendid. It was probably glorious, this play of the free sea, wild with lights of emerald and white and amber.

"Bully good thing it's an on-shore wind," said the cook. "If not, where would we be? Wouldn't have a show."

"That's right," said the correspondent.

The busy oiler nodded his assent.

Then the captain, in the bow, chuckled in a way that expressed humor, contempt, tragedy, all in one. "Do you think we've got much of a show now, boys?" said he.

Whereupon the three were silent, save for a trifle of hemming and hawing. To express any particular optimism at this time they felt to be childish and stupid, but they all doubtless possessed this sense of the situation in their mind. A young man thinks doggedly at such times. On the other hand, the ethics of their condition was decidedly against any open suggestion of hopelessness. So they were silent.

"Oh, well," said the captain, soothing his children, "we'll get ashore all right."

But there was that in his tone which made them think, so the oiler quoth: "Yes! If this wind holds!"

The cook was bailing: "Yes! If we don't catch hell in the surf."

Canton flannel gulls flew near and far. Sometimes they sat down on the sea, near patches of brown seaweed that rolled over the waves with a movement like carpets on a line in a gale. The birds sat comfortably in groups, and they were envied by some in the dinghy, for the wrath of the sea was no more to them than it was to a covey of prairie chickens a thousand miles inland. Often they came very close and stared at the men with black bead-like eyes. At these times they were uncanny and sinister in their unblinking scrutiny, and the men hooted angrily at them, telling them to be gone. One came, and evidently decided to alight on the top of the captain's head. The bird flew parallel to the boat and did not circle, but made short sidelong jumps in the air in chicken-fashion. His black eyes were wistfully fixed upon the captain's head. "Ugly brute," said the oiler to the bird. "You look as if you were made with a jackknife." The cook and the correspondent swore darkly at the creature. The captain naturally wished to knock it away with the end of the heavy painter; but he did not dare do it, because anything resembling an emphatic gesture would have capsized this freighted boat, and so, with his open hand, the captain gently and carefully waved the gull away. After it had been discouraged from the pursuit the captain breathed easier on account of his hair, and others breathed easier because the bird struck their minds at this time as being somehow gruesome and ominous.

In the meantime the oiler and the correspondent rowed. And also they rowed.

They sat together in the same seat, and each rowed an oar. Then the oiler took both oars; then the correspondent took both oars; then the oiler; then the correspondent. They rowed and they rowed. The very ticklish part of the business was when the time came for the reclining one in the stern to take his turn at the oars. By the very last star of truth, it is easier to steal eggs from under a hen than it was to change seats in the dinghy. First the man in the stern slid his hand along the thwart and moved with care, as if he were of Sèvres. Then the man in the rowing seat slid his hand along the other thwart. It was all done with the most extraordinary care. As the two sidled past each other, the whole party kept watchful eyes on the coming wave, and the captain cried: "Look out now! Steady there!"

The brown mats of seaweed that appeared from time to time were like islands, bits of earth. They were traveling, apparently, neither one way nor the other. They were, to all intents, stationary. They informed the men in the boat that it was making progress slowly toward the land.

The captain, rearing cautiously in the bow, after the dinghy soared on a great swell, said that he had seen the lighthouse at Mosquito Inlet. Presently the cook remarked that he had seen it. The correspondent was at the oars then, and for some reason he too wished to look at the lighthouse, but his back was toward the far shore and the waves were important, and for some time he could not seize an opportunity to turn his head. But at last there came a wave more gentle than the others, and when at the crest of it he swiftly scoured the western horizon.

"See it?" said the captain.

"No," said the correspondent slowly, "I didn't see anything."

"Look again," said the captain. He pointed. "It's exactly in that direction."

At the top of another wave, the correspondent did as he was bid, and this time his eyes chanced on a small still thing on the edge of the swaying horizon. It was precisely like the point of a pin. It took an anxious eye to find a lighthouse so tiny.

"Think we'll make it, captain?"

"If this wind holds and the boat don't swamp, we can't do much else," said the captain.

The little boat, lifted by each towering sea, and splashed viciously by the crests, made progress that in the absence of seaweed was not apparent to those in her. She seemed just a wee thing wallowing, miraculously top up, at the mercy of five oceans. Occasionally, a great spread of water, like white flames, swarmed into her.

"Bail her, cook," said the captain serenely.

"All right, captain," said the cheerful cook.


III

It would be difficult to describe the subtle brotherhood of men that was here established on the seas. No one said that it was so. No one mentioned it. But it dwelt in the boat, and each man felt it warm him. They were a captain, an oiler, a cook, and a correspondent, and they were friends, friends in a more curiously iron-bound degree than may be common. The hurt captain, lying against the water-jar in the bow, spoke always in a low voice and calmly, but he could never command a more ready and swiftly obedient crew than the motley three of the dinghy. It was more than a mere recognition of what was best for the common safety. There was surely in it a quality that was personal and heartfelt. And after this devotion to the commander of the boat there was this comradeship that the correspondent, for instance, who had been taught to be cynical of men, knew even at the time was the best experience of his life. But no one said that it was so. No one mentioned it.

"I wish we had a sail," remarked the captain. "We might try my overcoat on the end of an oar and give you two boys a chance to rest." So the cook and the correspondent held the mast and spread wide the overcoat. The oiler steered, and the little boat made good way with her new rig. Sometimes the oiler had to scull sharply to keep a sea from breaking into the boat, but otherwise sailing was a success.

Meanwhile the lighthouse had been growing slowly larger. It had now almost assumed color, and appeared like a little gray shadow on the sky. The man at the oars could not be prevented from turning his head rather often to try for a glimpse of this little gray shadow.

At last, from the top of each wave the men in the tossing boat could see land. Even as the lighthouse was an upright shadow on the sky, this land seemed but a long black shadow on the sea. It certainly was thinner than paper. "We must be about opposite New Smyrna," said the cook, who had coasted this shore often in schooners. "Captain, by the way, I believe they abandoned that life-saving station there about a year ago."

"Did they?" said the captain.

The wind slowly died away. The cook and the correspondent were not now obliged to slave in order to hold high the oar. But the waves continued their old impetuous swooping at the dinghy, and the little craft, no longer under way, struggled woundily over them. The oiler or the correspondent took the oars again.

Shipwrecks are apropos of nothing. If men could only train for them and have them occur when the men had reached pink condition, there would be less drowning at sea. Of the four in the dinghy none had slept any time worth mentioning for two days and two nights previous to embarking in the dinghy, and in the excitement of clambering about the deck of a foundering ship they had also forgotten to eat heartily.

For these reasons, and for others, neither the oiler nor the correspondent was fond of rowing at this time. The correspondent wondered ingenuously how in the name of all that was sane could there be people who thought it amusing to row a boat. It was not an amusement; it was a diabolical punishment, and even a genius of mental aberrations could never conclude that it was anything but a horror to the muscles and a crime against the back. He mentioned to the boat in general how the amusement of rowing struck him, and the weary-faced oiler smiled in full sympathy. Previously to the foundering, by the way, the oiler had worked double-watch in the engine-room of the ship.

"Take her easy, now, boys," said the captain. "Don't spend yourselves. If we have to run a surf you'll need all your strength, because we'll sure have to swim for it. Take your time."

Slowly the land arose from the sea. From a black line it became a line of black and a line of white, trees and sand. Finally, the captain said that he could make out a house on the shore. "That's the house of refuge, sure," said the cook. "They'll see us before long, and come out after us."

The distant lighthouse reared high. "The keeper ought to be able to make us out now, if he's looking through a glass," said the captain. "He'll notify the life-saving people."

"None of those other boats could have got ashore to give word of the wreck," said the oiler, in a low voice. "Else the lifeboat would be out hunting us."

Slowly and beautifully the land loomed out of the sea. The wind came again, It had veered from the north-east to the south-east. Finally, a new sound struck the ears of the men in the boat. It was the low thunder of the surf on the shore. "We'll never be able to make the lighthouse now," said the captain. "Swing her head a little more north, Billie."

"A little more north, sir," said the oiler.

Whereupon the little boat turned her nose once more down the wind, and all but the oarsmen watched the shore grow. Under the influence of this expansion doubt and direful apprehension were leaving the minds of the men. The management of the boat was still most absorbing, but it could not prevent a quiet cheerfulness. In an hour, perhaps, they would be ashore.

Their backbones had become thoroughly used to balancing in the boat, and they now rode this wild colt of a dinghy like circus men. The correspondent thought that he had been drenched to the skin, but happening to feel in the top pocket of his coat, he found therein eight cigars. Four of them were soaked with sea-water; four were perfectly scatheless. After a search, somebody produced three dry matches, and thereupon the four waifs rode impudently in their little boat, and with an assurance of an impending rescue shining in their eyes, puffed at the big cigars and judged well and ill of all men. Everybody took a drink of water.

## IV

"Cook," remarked the captain, "there don't seem to be any signs of life about your house of refuge."

"No," replied the cook. "Funny they don't see us!"

A broad stretch of lowly coast lay before the eyes of the men. It was of low dunes topped with dark vegetation. The roar of the surf was plain, and sometimes they could see the white lip of a wave as it spun up the beach. A tiny house was blocked out black upon the sky. Southward, the slim lighthouse lifted its little gray length.

Tide, wind, and waves were swinging the dinghy northward. "Funny they don't see us," said the men.

The surf's roar was here dulled, but its tone was, nevertheless, thunderous and mighty. As the boat swam over the great rollers, the men sat listening to this roar. "We'll swamp sure," said everybody.

It is fair to say here that there was not a life-saving station within twenty miles in either direction, but the men did not know this fact, and in consequence they made dark and opprobrious remarks concerning the eyesight of the nation's life-savers. Four scowling men sat in the dinghy and surpassed records in the invention of epithets.

"Funny they don't see us."

The light-heartedness of a former time had completely faded. To their sharpened minds it was easy to conjure pictures of all kinds of incompetency and blindness and, indeed, cowardice. There was the shore of the populous land, and it was bitter and bitter to them that from it came no sign.

"Well," said the captain, ultimately, "I suppose we'll have to make a try for ourselves. If we stay out here too long, we'll none of us have strength left to swim after the boat swamps."

And so the oiler, who was at the oars, turned the boat straight for the shore. There was a sudden tightening of muscles. There was some thinking.

"If we don't all get ashore—" said the captain. "If we don't all get ashore, I suppose you fellows know where to send news of my finish?"

They then briefly exchanged some addresses and admonitions. As for the reflections of the men, there was a great deal of rage in them. Perchance they might be formulated thus: "If I am going to be drowned—if I am going to be drowned—if I am going to be drowned, why, in the name of the seven mad gods who rule the sea, was I allowed to come thus far and contemplate sand and trees? Was I brought here merely to have my nose dragged away as I was about to nibble the sacred cheese of life? It is preposterous. If this old ninny-woman, Fate, cannot do better than this, she should be deprived of the management of men's fortunes. She is an old hen who knows not her intention. If she has decided to drown me, why did she not do it in the beginning and save me all this trouble? The whole affair is absurd. . . . But no, she cannot mean to drown me. She dare not drown me. She cannot drown me. Not after all this work." Afterward the man might have had an impulse to shake his fist at the clouds: "Just you drown me, now, and then hear what I call you!"

The billows that came at this time were more formidable. They seemed always just about to break and roll over the little boat in a turmoil of foam. There was a preparatory and long growl in the speech of them. No mind unused to the sea would have concluded that the dinghy could ascend these sheer heights in time. The shore was still afar. The oiler was a wily surfman. "Boys," he said swiftly, "she won't live three minutes more, and we're too far out to swim. Shall I take her to sea again, captain?"

"Yes! Go ahead!" said the captain.

This oiler, by a series of quick miracles, and fast and steady oarsmanship, turned the boat in the middle of the surf and took her safely to sea again.

There was a considerable silence as the boat bumped over the furrowed sea to deeper water. Then somebody in gloom spoke. "Well, anyhow, they must have seen us from the shore by now."

The gulls went in slanting flight up the wind toward the gray desolate east. A squall, marked by dingy clouds, and clouds brick-red, like smoke from a burning building, appeared from the south-east.

"What do you think of those life-saving people? Ain't they peaches?"

"Funny they haven't seen us."

"Maybe they think we're out here for sport! Maybe they think we're fishin'. Maybe they think we're damned fools."

It was a long afternoon. A changed tide tried to force them southward, but wind and wave said northward. Far ahead, where coastline, sea, and sky formed their mighty angle, there were little dots which seemed to indicate a city on the shore.

"St. Augustine?"

The captain shook his head. "Too near Mosquito Inlet."

And the oiler rowed, and then the correspondent rowed. Then the oiler rowed. It was a weary business. The human back can become the seat of more aches and pains than are registered in books for the composite anatomy of a regiment. It is a limited area, but it can become the theater of innumerable muscular conflicts, tangles, wrenches, knots, and other comforts.

"Did you ever like to row, Billie?" asked the correspondent.

"No," said the oiler. "Hang it."

When one exchanged the rowing-seat for a place in the bottom of the boat, he suffered a bodily depression that caused him to be careless of everything save an obligation to wiggle one finger. There was cold sea-water swashing to and fro in the boat, and he lay in it. His head, pillowed on a thwart, was within an inch of the swirl of a wave crest, and sometimes a particularly obstreperous sea came in-board and drenched him once more. But these matters did not annoy him. It is almost certain that if the boat had capsized he would have tumbled comfortably out upon the ocean as if he felt sure that it was a great soft mattress.

"Look! There's a man on the shore!"

"Where?"

"There! See 'im? See 'im?"

"Yes, sure! He's walking along."

"Now he's stopped. Look! He's facing us!"

"He's waving at us!"

"So he is! By thunder!"

"Ah, now we're all right! Now we're all right! There'll be a boat out here for us in half an hour."

"He's going on. He's running. He's going up to that house there."

The remote beach seemed lower than the sea, and it required a searching glance to discern the little black figure. The captain saw a floating stick and they rowed to it. A bath-towel was by some weird chance in the boat, and, tying this on the stick, the captain waved it. The oarsman did not dare turn his head, so he was obliged to ask questions.

"What's he doing now?"

"He's standing still again. He's looking, I think. . . . There he goes again. Toward the house. . . . Now he stopped again."

"Is he waving at us?"

"No, not now! He was, though."

"Look! There comes another man!"

"He's running."

"Look at him go, would you!"

"Why, he's on a bicycle. Now he's met the other man. They're both waving at us. Look!"

"There comes something up the beach."

"What the devil is that thing?"

"Why, it looks like a boat."

"Why, certainly it's a boat."

"No, it's on wheels."

"Yes, so it is. Well, that must be the life-boat. They drag them along shore on a wagon."

"That's the life-boat, sure."

"No, by—, it's—it's an omnibus."

"I tell you it's a life-boat."

"It is not! It's an omnibus. I can see it plain. See? One of these big hotel omnibuses."

"By thunder, you're right. It's an omnibus, sure as fate. What do you suppose they are doing with an omnibus? Maybe they are going around collecting the life-crew, hey?"

"That's it, likely. Look! There's a fellow waving a little black flag. He's standing on the steps of the omnibus. There come those other two fellows. Now they're all talking together. Look at the fellow with the flag. Maybe he ain't waving it."

"That ain't a flag, is it? That's his coat. Why, certainly, that's his coat."

"So it is. It's his coat. He's taken it off and is waving it around his head. But would you look at him swing it."

"Oh, say, there isn't any life-saving station there. That's just a winter resort hotel omnibus that has brought over some of the boarders to see us drown."

"What's that idiot with the coat mean? What's he signaling, anyhow?"

"It looks as if he were trying to tell us to go north. There must be a life-saving station up there."

"No! He thinks we're fishing. Just giving us a merry hand. See? Ah, there, Billie."

"Well, I wish I could make something out of those signals. What do you suppose he means?"

"He don't mean anything. He's just playing."

"Well, if he'd just signal us to try the surf again, or to go to sea and wait, or go north, or go south, or go to hell—there would be some reason in it. But look at him. He just stands there and keeps his coat revolving like a wheel. The ass!"

"There come more people."

"Now there's quite a mob. Look! Isn't that a boat?"

"Where? Oh, I see where you mean. No, that's no boat."

"That fellow is still waving his coat."

"He must think we like to see him do that. Why don't he quit it? It don't mean anything."

"I don't know. I think he is trying to make us go north. It must be that there's a life-saving station there somewhere."

"Say, he ain't tired yet. Look at 'im wave."

"Wonder how long he can keep that up. He's been revolving his coat ever since he caught sight of us. He's an idiot. Why aren't they getting men to bring a boat out? A fishing boat—one of those big yawls—could come out here all right. Why don't he do something?"

"Oh, it's all right, now."

"They'll have a boat out here for us in less than no time, now that they've seen us."

A faint yellow tone came into the sky over the low land. The shadows on the sea slowly deepened. The wind bore coldness with it, and the men began to shiver.

"Holy smoke!" said one, allowing his voice to

express his impious mood, "if we keep on monkeying out here! If we've got to flounder out here all night!"

"Oh, we'll never have to stay here all night! Don't you worry. They've seen us now, and it won't be long before they'll come chasing out after us."

The shore grew dusky. The man waving a coat blended gradually into this gloom, and it swallowed in the same manner the omnibus and the group of people. The spray, when it dashed uproariously over the side, made the voyagers shrink and swear like men who were being branded.

"I'd like to catch the chump who waved that coat. I feel like soaking him one, just for luck."

"Why? What did he do?"

"Oh, nothing, but then he seemed so damned cheerful."

In the meantime the oiler rowed, and then the correspondent rowed, and then the oiler rowed. Gray-faced and bowed forward, they mechanically, turn by turn, plied the leaden oars. The form of the lighthouse had vanished from the southern horizon, but finally a pale star appeared, just lifting from the sea. The streaked saffron in the west passed before the all-merging darkness, and the sea to the east was black. The land had vanished, and was expressed only by the low and drear thunder of the surf.

"If I am going to be drowned—if I am going to be drowned—if I am going to be drowned, why, in the name of the seven mad gods who rule the sea, was I allowed to come thus far and contemplate sand and trees? Was I brought here merely to have my nose dragged away as I was about to nibble the sacred cheese of life?"

The patient captain, drooped over the water-jar, was sometimes obliged to speak to the oarsman.

"Keep her head up! Keep her head up!"

"'Keep her head up,' sir." The voices were weary and low.

This was surely a quiet evening. All save the oarsman lay heavily and listlessly in the boat's bottom. As for him, his eyes were just capable of noting the tall black waves that swept forward in a most sinister silence, save for an occasional subdued growl of a crest.

The cook's head was on a thwart, and he looked without interest at the water under his nose. He was deep in other scenes. Finally he

spoke. "Billie," he murmured, dreamfully, "what kind of pie do you like best?"

V

"Pie," said the oiler and the correspondent, agitatedly. "Don't talk about those things, blast you!"

"Well," said the cook, "I was just thinking about ham sandwiches, and—"

A night on the sea in an open boat is a long night. As darkness settled finally, the shine of the light, lifting from the sea in the south, changed to full gold. On the northern horizon a new light appeared, a small bluish gleam on the edge of the waters. These two lights were the furniture of the world. Otherwise there was nothing but waves.

Two men huddled in the stern, and distances were so magnificent in the dinghy that the rower was enabled to keep his feet partly warmed by thrusting them under his companions. Their legs indeed extended far under the rowing-seat until they touched the feet of the captain forward. Sometimes, despite the efforts of the tired oarsman, a wave came piling into the boat, an icy wave of the night, and the chilling water soaked them anew. They would twist their bodies for a moment and groan, and sleep the dead sleep once more, while the water in the boat gurgled about them as the craft rocked.

The plan of the oiler and the correspondent was for one to row until he lost the ability, and then arouse the other from his sea-water couch in the bottom of the boat.

The oiler plied the oars until his head drooped forward, and the overpowering sleep blinded him. And he rowed yet afterward. Then he touched a man in the bottom of the boat, and called his name. "Will you spell me for a little while?" he said, meekly.

"Sure, Billie," said the correspondent, awakening and dragging himself to a sitting position. They exchanged places carefully, and the oiler, cuddling down in the sea-water at the cook's side, seemed to go to sleep instantly.

The particular violence of the sea had ceased. The waves came without snarling. The obligation of the man at the oars was to keep the boat headed so that the tilt of the rollers would not capsize her, and to preserve her from filling when the crests rushed past. The black waves were silent and hard to be seen in the darkness. Often one was almost upon the boat before the oarsman was aware.

In a low voice the correspondent addressed the captain. He was not sure that the captain was awake, although this iron man seemed to be always awake. "Captain, shall I keep her making for that light north, sir?"

The same steady voice answered him. "Yes. Keep it about two points off the port bow."

The cook had tied a life-belt around himself in order to get even the warmth which this clumsy cork contrivance could donate, and he seemed almost stove-like when a rower, whose teeth invariably chattered wildly as soon as he ceased his labor, dropped down to sleep.

The correspondent, as he rowed, looked down at the two men sleeping underfoot. The cook's arm was around the oiler's shoulders, and, with their fragmentary clothing and haggard faces, they were the babes of the sea, a grotesque rendering of the old babes in the wood.

Later he must have grown stupid at his work, for suddenly there was a growling of water, and a crest came with a roar and a swash into the boat, and it was a wonder that it did not set the cook afloat in his life-belt. The cook continued to sleep, but the oiler sat up, blinking his eyes and shaking with the new cold.

"Oh, I'm awful sorry, Billie," said the correspondent, contritely.

"That's all right, old boy," said the oiler, and lay down again and was asleep.

Presently it seemed that even the captain dozed, and the correspondent thought that he was the one man afloat on all the oceans. The wind had a voice as it came over the waves, and it was sadder than the end.

There was a long, loud swishing astern of the boat, and a gleaming trail of phosphorescence, like blue flame, was furrowed on the black waters. It might have been made by a monstrous knife.

Then there came a stillness, while the correspondent breathed with open mouth and looked at the sea.

Suddenly there was another swish and another long flash of bluish light, and this time it was alongside the boat, and might almost have been reached with an oar. The correspondent saw an enormous fin speed like a shadow through the water, hurling the crystalline spray and leaving the long glowing trail.

The correspondent looked over his shoulder at the captain. His face was hidden, and he seemed to be asleep. He looked at the babes of the sea. They certainly were asleep. So, being bereft of sympathy, he leaned a little way to one side and swore softly into the sea.

But the thing did not then leave the vicinity of the boat. Ahead or astern, on one side or the other, at intervals long or short, fled the long sparkling streak, and there was to be heard the *whiroo* of the dark fin. The speed and power of the thing was greatly to be admired. It cut the water like a gigantic and keen projectile.

The presence of this biding thing did not affect the man with the same horror that it would if he had been a picnicker. He simply looked at the sea dully and swore in an undertone.

Nevertheless, it is true that he did not wish to be alone with the thing. He wished one of his companions to awaken by chance and keep him company with it. But the captain hung motionless over the water-jar, and the oiler and the cook in the bottom of the boat were plunged in slumber.

VI

"If I am going to be drowned—if I am going to be drowned—if I am going to be drowned, why, in the name of the seven mad gods who rule the sea, was I allowed to come thus far and contemplate sand and trees?"

During this dismal night, it may be remarked that a man would conclude that it was really the intention of the seven mad gods to drown him, despite the abominable injustice of it. For it was certainly an abominable injustice to drown a man who had worked so hard, so hard. The man felt it would be a crime most unnatural. Other people had drowned at sea since galleys swarmed with painted sails, but still—

When it occurs to a man that nature does not regard him as important, and that she feels she would not maim the universe by disposing of him, he at first wishes to throw bricks at the temple, and he hates deeply the fact that there are no bricks and no temples. Any visible expression of nature would surely be pelleted with his jeers.

Then, if there be no tangible thing to hoot he feels, perhaps, the desire to confront a personification and indulge in pleas, bowed to one knee, and with hands supplicant, saying: "Yes, but I love myself."

A high cold star on a winter's night is the word he feels that she says to him. Thereafter he knows the pathos of his situation.

The men in the dinghy had not discussed these matters, but each had, no doubt, reflected upon them in silence and according to his mind. There was seldom any expression upon their faces save the general one of complete weariness. Speech was devoted to the business of the boat.

To chime the notes of his emotion, a verse mysteriously entered the correspondent's head. He had even forgotten that he had forgotten this verse, but it suddenly was in his mind.

A soldier of the Legion lay dying in Algiers,
There was lack of woman's nursing, there was dearth of woman's tears;
But a comrade stood beside him, and he took that comrade's hand,
And he said: "I shall never see my own, my native land."

In his childhood, the correspondent had been made acquainted with the fact that a soldier of the Legion lay dying in Algiers, but he had never regarded the fact as important. Myriads of his school-fellows had informed him of the soldier's plight, but the dinning had naturally ended by making him perfectly indifferent. He had never considered it his affair that a soldier of the Legion lay dying in Algiers, nor had it appeared to him as a matter for sorrow. It was less to him than the breaking of a pencil's point.

Now, however, it quaintly came to him as a human, living thing. It was no longer merely a picture of a few throes in the breast of a poet, meanwhile drinking tea and warming his feet at the grate; it was an actuality—stern, mournful, and fine.

The correspondent plainly saw the soldier. He lay on the sand with his feet out straight and still. While his pale left hand was upon his chest in an attempt to thwart the going of his life, the blood came between his fingers.

In the far Algerian distance, a city of low square forms was set against a sky that was faint with the last sunset hues. The correspondent, plying the oars and dreaming of the slow and slower movements of the lips of the soldier, was moved by a profound and perfectly impersonal comprehension. He was sorry for the soldier of the Legion who lay dying in Algiers.

The thing which had followed the boat and waited had evidently grown bored at the delay. There was no longer to be heard the slash of the cutwater, and there was no longer the flame of the long trail. The light in the north still glimmered, but it was apparently no nearer to the boat. Sometimes the boom of the surf rang in the correspondent's ears, and he turned the craft seaward then and rowed harder. Southward, someone had evidently built a watch-fire on the beach. It was too low and too far to be seen, but it made a shimmering, roseate reflection upon the bluff back of it, and this could be discerned from the boat. The wind came stronger, and sometimes a wave suddenly raged out like a mountain-cat, and there was to be seen the sheen and sparkle of a broken crest.

The captain, in the bow, moved on his water-jar and sat erect. "Pretty long night," he observed to the correspondent. He looked at the shore. "Those life-saving people take their time."

"Did you see that shark playing around?"

"Yes, I saw him. He was a big fellow, all right."

"Wish I had known you were awake."

Later the correspondent spoke into the bottom of the boat.

"Billie!" There was a slow and gradual disentanglement. "Billie, will you spell me?"

"Sure," said the oiler.

As soon as the correspondent touched the cold comfortable sea-water in the bottom of the boat and had huddled close to the cook's life-belt he was deep in sleep, despite the fact that his teeth played all the popular airs. This sleep was so good to him that it was but a moment before he heard a voice call his name in a tone that demonstrated the last stages of exhaustion. "Will you spell me?"

"Sure, Billie."

The light in the north had mysteriously vanished, but the correspondent took his course from the wide-awake captain.

Later in the night they took the boat farther out to sea, and the captain directed the cook to take one oar at the stern and keep the boat facing the seas. He was to call out if he should hear the thunder of the surf. This plan enabled the

oiler and the correspondent to get respite together. "We'll give those boys a chance to get
into shape again," said the captain. They curled
down and, after a few preliminary chatterings
and trembles, slept once more the dead sleep.
Neither knew they had bequeathed to the cook
the company of another shark, or perhaps the
same shark.

As the boat caroused on the waves, spray occasionally bumped over the side and gave them
a fresh soaking, but this had no power to break
their repose. The ominous slash of the wind and
the water affected them as it would have affected
mummies.

"Boys," said the cook, with the notes of every
reluctance in his voice, "she's drifted in pretty
close. I guess one of you had better take her to
sea again." The correspondent, aroused, heard
the crash of the toppled crests.

As he was rowing, the captain gave him some
whisky-and-water, and this steadied the chills out
of him. "If I ever get ashore and anybody shows
me even a photograph of an oar—"

At last there was a short conversation.

"Billie . . . Billie, will you spell me?"

"Sure," said the oiler.

VII

When the correspondent again opened his
eyes, the sea and the sky were each of the gray
hue of the dawning. Later, carmine and gold was
painted upon the waters. The morning appeared
finally, in its splendor, with a sky of pure blue,
and the sunlight flamed on the tips of the waves.

On the distant dunes were set many little black
cottages, and a tall white windmill reared above
them. No man, nor dog, nor bicycle appeared
on the beach. The cottages might have formed
a deserted village.

The voyagers scanned the shore. A conference
was held in the boat. "Well," said the captain,
"if no help is coming, we might better try a run
through the surf right away. If we stay out here
much longer we will be too weak to do anything
for ourselves at all." The others silently acquiesced in this reasoning. The boat was headed for
the beach. The correspondent wondered if none
ever ascended the tall wind-tower, and if then
they never looked seaward. This tower was a

giant, standing with its back to the plight of the
ants. It represented in a degree, to the correspondent, the serenity of nature amid the struggles of the individual—nature in the wind, and
nature in the vision of men. She did not seem
cruel to him then, nor beneficent, nor treacherous, nor wise. But she was indifferent, flatly
indifferent. It is, perhaps, plausible that a man
in this situation, impressed with the unconcern
of the universe, should see the innumerable flaws
of his life, and have them taste wickedly in his
mind and wish for another chance. A distinction
between right and wrong seems absurdly clear
to him, then, in this new ignorance of the grave-
edge, and he understands that if he were given
another opportunity he would mend his conduct
and his words, and be better and brighter during
an introduction or at a tea.

"Now, boys," said the captain, "she is going
to swamp sure. All we can do is to work her in
as far as possible, and then when she swamps,
pile out and scramble for the beach. Keep cool
now, and don't jump until she swamps sure."

The oiler took the oars. Over his shoulders he
scanned the surf. "Captain," he said, "I think I'd
better bring her about, and keep her head-on to
the seas and back her in."

"All right, Billie," said the captain. "Back her
in." The oiler swung the boat then and, seated
in the stern, the cook and the correspondent
were obliged to look over their shoulders to
contemplate the lonely and indifferent shore.

The monstrous in-shore rollers heaved the boat
high until the men were again enabled to see the
white sheets of water scudding up the slanted
beach. "We won't get in very close," said the
captain. Each time a man could wrest his attention from the rollers, he turned his glance toward
the shore, and in the expression of the eyes during this contemplation there was a singular quality. The correspondent, observing the others,
knew that they were not afraid, but the full
meaning of their glances was shrouded.

As for himself, he was too tired to grapple
fundamentally with the fact. He tried to coerce
his mind into thinking of it, but the mind was
dominated at this time by the muscles, and the
muscles said they did not care. It merely occurred to him that if he should drown it would
be a shame.

There were no hurried words, no pallor, no
plain agitation. The men simply looked at the

shore. "Now, remember to get well clear of the boat when you jump," said the captain.

Seaward the crest of a roller suddenly fell with a thunderous crash, and the long white comber came roaring down upon the boat.

"Steady now," said the captain. The men were silent. They turned their eyes from the shore to the comber and waited. The boat slid up the incline, leaped at the furious top, bounced over it, and swung down the long back of the waves. Some water had been shipped and the cook bailed it out.

But the next crest crashed also. The tumbling boiling flood of white water caught the boat and whirled it almost perpendicular. Water swarmed in from all sides. The correspondent had his hands on the gunwale at this time, and when the water entered at that place he swiftly withdrew his fingers, as if he objected to wetting them.

The little boat, drunken with this weight of water, reeled and snuggled deeper into the sea.

"Bail her out, cook! Bail her out," said the captain.

"All right, captain," said the cook.

"Now, boys, the next one will do for us, sure," said the oiler. "Mind to jump clear of the boat."

The third wave moved forward, huge, furious, implacable. It fairly swallowed the dinghy, and almost simultaneously the men tumbled into the sea. A piece of life-belt had lain in the bottom of the boat, and as the correspondent went overboard he held this to his chest with his left hand.

The January water was icy, and he reflected immediately that it was colder than he had expected to find it off the coast of Florida. This appeared to his dazed mind as a fact important enough to be noted at the time. The coldness of the water was sad; it was tragic. This fact was somehow so mixed and confused with his opinion of his own situation that it seemed almost a proper reason for tears. The water was cold.

When he came to the surface he was conscious of little but the noisy water. Afterward he saw his companions in the sea. The oiler was ahead in the race. He was swimming strongly and rapidly. Off to the correspondent's left, the cook's great white and corked back bulged out of the water, and in the rear the captain was hanging with his one good hand to the keel of the overturned dinghy.

There is a certain immovable quality to a shore, and the correspondent wondered at it amid the confusion of the sea.

It seemed also very attractive, but the correspondent knew that it was a long journey, and he paddled leisurely. The piece of life-preserver lay under him, and sometimes he whirled down the incline of a wave as if he were on a hand-sled.

But finally he arrived at a place in the sea where travel was beset with difficulty. He did not pause swimming to inquire what manner of current had caught him, but there his progress ceased. The shore was set before him like a bit of scenery on a stage, and he looked at it and understood with his eyes each detail of it.

As the cook passed, much farther to the left, the captain was calling to him, "Turn over on your back, cook! Turn over on your back and use the oar."

"All right, sir." The cook turned on his back, and, paddling with an oar, went ahead as if he were a canoe.

Presently the boat also passed to the left of the correspondent with the captain clinging with one hand to the keel. He would have appeared like a man raising himself to look over a board fence, if it were not for the extraordinary gymnastics of the boat. The correspondent marveled that the captain could still hold to it.

They passed on, nearer to shore—the oiler, the cook, the captain—and following them went the water-jar, bouncing gaily over the seas.

The correspondent remained in the grip of this strange new enemy—a current. The shore, with its white slope of sand and its green bluff, topped with little silent cottages, was spread like a picture before him. It was very near to him then, but he was impressed as one who in a gallery looks at a scene from Brittany or Algiers.

He thought: "I am going to drown? Can it be possible? Can it be possible? Can it be possible?" Perhaps an individual must consider his own death to be the final phenomenon of nature.

But later a wave perhaps whirled him out of this small deadly current, for he found suddenly that he could again make progress toward the shore. Later still, he was aware that the captain, clinging with one hand to the keel of the dinghy, had his face turned away from the shore and toward him and was calling his name. "Come to the boat! Come to the boat!"

In his struggle to reach the captain and the boat, he reflected that when one gets properly wearied, drowning must really be a comfortable arrangement, a cessation of hostilities accompanied by a large degree of relief, and he was glad of it, for the main thing in his mind for some moments had been horror of the temporary agony. He did not wish to be hurt.

Presently he saw a man running along the shore. He was undressing with most remarkable speed. Coat, trousers, shirt, everything flew magically off him.

"Come to the boat," called the captain.

"All right, captain." As the correspondent paddled, he saw the captain let himself down to bottom and leave the boat. Then the correspondent performed his one little marvel of the voyage. A large wave caught him and flung him with ease and supreme speed completely over the boat and far beyond it. It struck him even then as an event in gymnastics, and a true miracle of the sea. An overturned boat in the surf is not a plaything to a swimming man.

The correspondent arrived in water that reached only to his waist, but his condition did not enable him to stand for more than a moment. Each wave knocked him into a heap, and the undertow pulled at him.

Then he saw the man who had been running and undressing, and undressing and running, come bounding into the water. He dragged ashore the cook, and then waded toward the captain, but the captain waved him away, and sent him to the correspondent. He was naked, naked as a tree in winter, but a halo was about his head, and he shone like a saint. He gave a strong pull, and a long drag, and a bully heave at the correspondent's hand. The correspondent, schooled in the minor formulae, said: "Thanks, old man." But suddenly the man cried: "What's that?" He pointed a swift finger. The correspondent said: "Go."

In the shallows, face downward, lay the oiler. His forehead touched sand that was periodically, between each wave, clear of the sea.

The correspondent did not know all that transpired afterward. When he achieved safe ground he fell, striking the sand with each particular part of his body. It was as if he had dropped from a roof, but the thud was grateful to him.

It seems that instantly the beach was populated with men, with blankets, clothes, and flasks, and women with coffee-pots and all the remedies sacred to their minds. The welcome of the land to the men from the sea was warm and generous, but a still and dripping shape was carried slowly up the beach, and the land's welcome for it could only be the different and sinister hospitality of the grave.

When it came night, the white waves paced to and fro in the moonlight, and the wind brought the sound of the great sea's voice to the men on shore, and they felt that they could then be interpreters.

Drama

**D**rama has its genesis in several closely related human characteristics, most important of which perhaps are the urge to imitate and the love of make-believe. Such tendencies are everywhere apparent, in the games small children play—cowboys and Indians, or cops and robbers—and in the entertainments older people often enjoy—masquerades and costume parties. To lose oneself for a short time within the identity of some imagined creature—a Lone Ranger or a Queen of the Pirates—seems to answer a deeply felt need in the human heart. And both the urge to imitate and the love of make-believe culminate in drama—the impulse to make a story live through action.

The ancient Greeks, an agricultural people, met on semiannual feast days to honor the god Dionysus, who ruled over the harvest and wine press. At first, their worship of Dionysus seems to have been expressed in choral songs and dances performed by elaborately trained and costumed choruses; but with time more and more of a dramatic element crept in. During an intermission, perhaps, the leader of the chorus would tell of some exploit in the life of Dionysus; later on he came to *represent* the god himself and tell his story in the first person. Finally, some minor member of the chorus answered the rhetorical utterances of Dionysus, and thus dramatic dialogue and impersonation came into being. To describe this activity, the word *drama*, derived from a Greek verb *dran* meaning *to act* or *to do*, was used. By its etymology, drama implies action, the essence of dramatic composition.

Greek comedy and tragedy both originated in seasonal festivals. From the broad jesting and burlesque natural to a rustic carnival developed comedy. From worship developed tragedy, which reached its culmination in three great writers—Aeschylus, Sophocles, and Euripides—all of whose works emphasize the Greek ideal of artistic restraint and balance.

During the Dark Ages, when Greek drama was forgotten, another form of drama emerged in western Europe—the morality plays of the medieval Christian Church. Everywhere confronted by ignorance and lack of schooling, the priests realized that the easiest way to tell the Christian story to the people was through dramatic representation of the Easter and Christmas stories in the cathedrals. What started as devices for religious instruction became so popular as entertainment that it was necessary to find a larger place for their presentation. Once outside the church, these plays soon fell into secular hands; the trade guilds in certain cities produced an elaborate series of pageants telling the Biblical story from the Creation to the Crucifixion and Resurrection.

Out of these religious plays of the late Middle Ages and out of the school and university revivals of long-neglected Greek and Roman dramas during the Renaissance grew the new drama of western Europe. In the English tradition this means pre-eminently the dramas of William Shakespeare; but there were many other playwrights in the sixteenth and seventeenth centuries who contributed their share toward making English drama worthy of comparison with drama anywhere in the world. After Oliver Goldsmith and Richard Brinsley Sheridan in the late eighteenth century, British drama went into a decline that lasted until Henrik Ibsen revolutionized the drama of all Europe. Profiting in part from this foreign influence, writers like George Bernard Shaw and Arthur Wing Pinero reestablished British drama in the world's esteem, and so it has continued to our own day. In the United States powerful and original drama did not completely emerge until after World War I, when Eugene O'Neill began producing the plays that were to win for him the Nobel Prize for Literature in 1936. By this time such writers as Maxwell Anderson, Sidney Howard, Robert Sherwood, and Thornton Wilder had clearly demonstrated that American drama could take its place among the best contemporary drama found anywhere in the world. More recently, Tennessee Williams and Arthur Miller have affirmed the psychological power and lyricism of the American theater. And both in America and in Europe in the years during and since World War II an alliance has developed between drama and contemporary philosophy. Out of the interaction of naturalism, surrealism, and existentialism has come a new kind of drama known as "theater of the absurd." Writers working in this dramatic mode have continued to move from the representational, with concern for psychological motivation, to the presentational, with emphasis on situation. Albert Camus and Jean-Paul Sartre are writers identified with the early days of the movement; Eugene Ionesco, Samuel Beckett, and, in America, Edward Albee are the well-known figures in this new theater.

Both comedy and tragedy are likely to be built around a central figure involved in some kind of conflict of will—the wills of two persons who oppose each other, the will of a person to win out over unfavorable circumstances, or the internally conflicting emotions of a person torn between two irreconcilable desires. Generally speaking, if the central character is in the end defeated, the play is tragic; if he is triumphant, the play is comic. Aristotle, the ancient Greek philosopher, believed that tragedy must excite the emotions of pity and fear and that to accomplish this end, it must present a single, complete action, must present a reversal of fortune involving persons renowned and of superior attainments, and, finally, must be written in poetry of the highest sort.

Later writers have modified some of these requirements. According to Aristotle, the interest aroused in tragic conflict is proportionate to the impressiveness of character displayed by the central figure in the drama. Comedies can be written about trivial people, but a tragedy usually centers around a great personality going down in defeat before forces too great for him to master. It is doubtless this need for magnitude in the central character that long compelled dramatists to center their tragedies around people of exalted rank, such as kings and princesses. Shakespeare to some extent demonstrated that people of humbler station can be fit subjects for tragedy, and Ibsen set the example for modern dramatists not only by choosing tragic characters from common life but by utilizing prose instead of poetry as the language of tragedy.

In contrast with tragedy, comedy, by conventional definition at least, is light and amusing; where amusement is its end, it becomes farce or burlesque. But comedy at its best is scarcely less serious in purpose than tragedy and is equally exacting in plot, dialogue, and characterization. Since the comic effect derives primarily from the exposure of some kind of incongruity, comedy reveals to us absurd, illogical, or pretentious speech, action, or character. The function of comedy, as George Meredith observed, is to provoke thoughtful laughter, the sort that arises out of our realization of human foibles and inconsistencies. Consequently, comedy lends itself well to satire and becomes a means whereby the dramatist chastises the world for its vices and shortcomings.

The drama selections included here offer considerable variety in style and subject matter and represent characteristic plays by five great dramatists. Sophocles' *Antigonê* exemplifies the classic Greek tragedy. Edith Hamilton says in "The Idea of Tragedy" that three of the four great writers of tragedy are Greek—Sophocles, Euripides, and Aeschylus—and that it was the Greeks who created tragedy and perfected it. Camus' *Caligula*, an existentialist drama, portays a poignant tragedy of the Emperor Caligula, who tries to exert his freedom without being destroyed by it. In the end he accepts death rather than gain his freedom at the expense of others. Arthur Miller's *The Crucible* is a tragedy set in the time of the Salem witchcraft trials but with intended application to social and psychological problems of modern times. *The Stronger* illustrates Strindberg's successful experimentation with simplifying the structure of drama and presenting psychological conflict solely through dialogue. This play has been said to mark the beginning of the modern one-act play. Modern comedy may assume the satiric, realistic form favored by Ben Jonson in the 1600's, which ridiculed the vices and follies of his contemporaries. So satirical and carefully drawn was Synge's portrait of the Irish in *The Playboy of the Western World* that its first audiences refused to allow the actors to be heard. Intense feelings of nationalism, together with the politics of the time, caused nightly disturbances at the Abbey Theatre in Dublin during the play's first week and were repeated when the play came to America.

Since most plays are written to be acted, the technique of play-reading is somewhat different from that of reading a short story or a novel; and the enjoyment of plays can therefore be increased greatly if one stops to consider some special problems that the reading of plays presents.

If plays are to be read successfully—that is, with the fullest degree of understanding and enjoyment—the reader is compelled to visualize with his own imagination, characters speaking, gesticulating, and moving about in a setting that playwrights, especially the modern ones, frequently describe in detail. From the cast of characters and from the stage directions, the reader can determine many things about the people of the play, particularly the main characters—what they look like, how old they are, what relationship exists among them, and what their special mannerisms and peculiarities imply. Another help to intelligent play-reading is to observe the play's structure. In the conventional play much of the first scene is devoted to getting the play under way. This portion—the "exposition" as it is technically called—should be read carefully in order to get one's bearings early. As soon as the exposition is finished, most playwrights start their main plot. In many modern dramas new scenes indicate the introduction of a new character or a new element in the story. The reader should watch for these developments.

## SOPHOCLES

# Antigonê

TRANSLATION BY DUDLEY FITTS AND ROBERT FITZGERALD

Sophocles (*c.* 496–406 B.C.), born near Athens, Greece, to a family of wealth and position, was a contemporary of the two other great Greek writers of tragedy, Aeschylus and Euripides. Only seven of his 123 plays have come down to us in complete form. His first successful tragedy was *Ajax. Antigonê* followed, then *Oedipus Rex* and *Electra.* Among the Greek dramatists of his time Sophocles was known for his innovations: increasing the size of the chorus, adding more actors, and introducing painted scenery.

*Antigonê* is the third and last play in Sophocles' Oedipus cycle, which also includes *Oedipus Rex* and *Oedipus at Colonus.* According to Greek legend, King Laios of Thebes and his descendants have been doomed by the god Apollo. Oedipus, supposedly killed as a baby, has survived in exile. Not knowing that he is the son of Laios and Iocastê, he kills his father. Several years later he solves the riddle of the Sphinx for the Thebans and becomes their king, marrying his mother, the widow Iocastê. When the truth is revealed, Oedipus, in horror, blinds himself and proclaims his own exile. His two sons, Eteoclês and Polyneicês, quarrel over the succession; the Thebans favor Eteoclês, and Polyneicês is driven from the city. He returns with an army, but he and Eteoclês kill each other in battle, and Creon, brother of Iocastê, succeeds to the throne. Antigonê and Ismenê, daughters of Oedipus, are discussing Creon's first official decree as the play opens.

*Antigonê* contains some of Sophocles' finest characterizations. The characters are more human than those in his other plays; they are governed less by the gods than by their own wills. Antigonê does not seem an unwitting victim of the gods; her tragedy arises from actions based on her own deep beliefs and emotions.

## PERSONS REPRESENTED

ANTIGONÊ
ISMENÊ
EURYDICÊ
CREON
HAIMON
TEIRESIAS

A SENTRY
A MESSENGER
A BOY
SERVANTS
GUARDS

    CHORUS (*with a* CHORAGOS, *or Leader*)

## SCENE

*Before the palace of* CREON, *King of Thebes. A central double door, and two lateral doors. A platform extends the length of the façade, and from this platform three steps lead down into the* orchestra, *or chorus-ground.*

    TIME: *Dawn of the day after the repulse of the Argive army from the assault on Thebes.*

## PROLOGUE

(ANTIGONÊ *and* ISMENÊ *enter from the central door of the Palace.*)

ANTIGONÊ:
Ismenê, dear sister,
You would think that we had already suffered enough
For the curse on Oedipus:
I cannot imagine any grief
That you and I have not gone through. And now—
Have they told you of the new decree of our King Creon?

ISMENÊ:
I have heard nothing: I know
That two sisters lost two brothers, a double death
In a single hour; and I know that the Argive army
Fled in the night; but beyond this, nothing.

ANTIGONÊ:
I thought so. And that is why I wanted you
To come out here with me. There is something we must do.

ISMENÊ:
Why do you speak so strangely?

ANTIGONÊ:
Listen, Ismenê:
Creon buried our brother Eteoclês
With military honors, gave him a soldier's funeral,
And it was right that he should; but Polyneicês,
Who fought as bravely and died as miserably,—
They say that Creon has sworn
No one shall bury him, no one mourn for him,
But his body must lie in the fields, a sweet treasure
For carrion birds to find as they search for food.
That is what they say, and our good Creon is coming here
To announce it publicly; and the penalty—
Stoning to death in the public square!
                There it is,
And now you can prove what you are:
A true sister, or a traitor to your family.

ISMENÊ:
Antigonê, you are mad! What could I possibly do?

ANTIGONÊ:
You must decide whether you will help me or not.

ISMENÊ:
I do not understand you. Help you in what?

ANTIGONÊ:
Ismenê, I am going to bury him. Will you come?

ISMENÊ:
Bury him! You have just said the new law forbids it.

ANTIGONÊ:
He is my brother. And he is your brother, too.

ISMENÊ:
But think of the danger! Think what Creon will do!

ANTIGONÊ:
Creon is not strong enough to stand in my way.

ISMENÊ:
Ah sister!
Oedipus died, everyone hating him
For what his own search brought to light, his
 eyes
Ripped out by his own hand; and Iocastê died,
His mother and wife at once: she twisted the
 cords
That strangled her life; and our two brothers
 died,
Each killed by the other's sword. And we are left:
But oh, Antigonê,
Think how much more terrible than these
Our own death would be if we should go against
 Creon
And do what he has forbidden! We are only
 women,
We cannot fight with men, Antigonê!
The law is strong, we must give in to the law
In this thing, and in worse. I beg the Dead
To forgive me, but I am helpless: I must yield
To those in authority. And I think it is dangerous
 business
To be always meddling.

ANTIGONÊ:
                    If that is what you think,
I should not want you, even if you asked to come.
You have made your choice, you can be what
 you want to be.
But I will bury him; and if I must die,
I say that this crime is holy: I shall lie down
With him in death, and I shall be as dear
To him as he to me.
                    It is the dead,
Not the living, who make the longest demands:
We die for ever . . .
                    You may do as you like,
Since apparently the laws of the gods mean
 nothing to you.

ISMENÊ:
They mean a great deal to me; but I have no
 strength
To break laws that were made for the public
 good.

ANTIGONÊ:
That must be your excuse, I suppose. But as for
 me,
I will bury the brother I love.

ISMENÊ:
                    Antigonê,
I am so afraid for you!

ANTIGONÊ:
                    You need not be:
You have yourself to consider, after all.

ISMENÊ:
But no one must hear of this, you must tell no
 one!
I will keep it a secret, I promise!

ANTIGONÊ:
                    Oh tell it! Tell everyone!
Think how they'll hate you when it all comes
 out
If they learn that you knew about it all the time!

ISMENÊ:
So fiery! You should be cold with fear.

ANTIGONÊ:
Perhaps. But I am doing only what I must.

ISMENÊ:
But can you do it? I say that you cannot.

ANTIGONÊ:
Very well: when my strength gives out, I shall
 do no more.

ISMENÊ:
Impossible things should not be tried at all.

ANTIGONÊ:
Go away, Ismenê:
I shall be hating you soon, and the dead will too,
For your words are hateful. Leave me my foolish
 plan:
I am not afraid of the danger; if it means death,
It will not be the worst of deaths—death without
 honor.

ISMENÊ:
Go then, if you feel that you must.
You are unwise,
But a loyal friend indeed to those who love you.

(*Exit into the Palace.* ANTIGONÊ *goes off,* L.
*Enter the* CHORUS.)

## PÁRODOS

### STROPHE 1

CHORUS:
Now the long blade of the sun, lying
Level east to west, touches with glory
Thebes of the Seven Gates. Open, unlidded
Eye of golden day! O marching light
Across the eddy and rush of Dircê's stream,

Striking the white shields of the enemy
Thrown headlong backward from the blaze of
   morning!

CHORAGOS:
Polyneicês their commander
Roused them with windy phrases,
He the wild eagle screaming
Insults above our land,
His wings their shields of snow,
His crest their marshalled helms.

ANTISTROPHE 1

CHORUS:
Against our seven gates in a yawning ring
The famished spears came onward in the night;
But before his jaws were sated with our blood,
Or pinefire took the garland of our towers,
He was thrown back; and as he turned, great
   Thebes—
No tender victim for his noisy power—
Rose like a dragon behind him, shouting war.

CHORAGOS:
For God hates utterly
The bray of bragging tongues;
And when he beheld their smiling,
Their swagger of golden helms,
The frown of his thunder blasted
Their first man from our walls.

STROPHE 2

CHORUS:
We heard his shout of triumph high in the air
Turn to a scream; far out in a flaming arc
He fell with his windy torch, and the earth struck
   him.
And others storming in fury no less than his
Found shock of death in the dusty joy of battle.

CHORAGOS:
Seven captains at seven gates
Yielded their clanging arms to the god
That bends the battle-line and breaks it.
These two only, brothers in blood,
Face to face in matchless rage,
Mirroring each the other's death,
Clashed in long combat.

ANTISTROPHE 2

CHORUS:
But now in the beautiful morning of victory
Let Thebes of the many chariots sing for joy!

With hearts for dancing we'll take leave of war:
Our temples shall be sweet with hymns of praise,
And the long night shall echo with our chorus.

SCENE I

CHORAGOS:
But now at last our new King is coming:
Creon of Thebes, Menoikeus' son.
In this auspicious dawn of his reign
What are the new complexities
That shifting Fate has woven for him?
What is his counsel? Why has he summoned
The old men to hear him?

(Enter CREON from the Palace, C. He addresses
the CHORUS from the top step.)

CREON:
   Gentlemen: I have the honor to inform you
that our Ship of State, which recent storms have
threatened to destroy, has come safely to harbor
at last, guided by the merciful wisdom of
Heaven. I have summoned you here this morning
because I know that I can depend upon you: your
devotion to King Laios was absolute; you never
hesitated in your duty to our late ruler Oedipus;
and when Oedipus died, your loyalty was transferred to his children. Unfortunately, as you
know, his two sons, the princes Eteoclês and
Polyneicês, have killed each other in battle; and
I, as the next in blood, have succeeded to the
full power of the throne.
   I am aware, of course, that no Ruler can expect
complete loyalty from his subjects until he has
been tested in office. Nevertheless, I say to you
at the very outset that I have nothing but contempt for the kind of Governor who is afraid,
for whatever reason, to follow the course that
he knows is best for the State; and as for the man
who sets private friendship above the public
welfare,—I have no use for him, either. I call
God to witness that if I saw my country headed
for ruin, I should not be afraid to speak out
plainly; and I need hardly remind you that I
would never have any dealings with an enemy
of the people. No one values friendship more
highly than I; but we must remember that friends
made at the risk of wrecking our Ship are not
real friends at all.
   These are my principles, at any rate, and that
is why I have made the following decision concerning the sons of Oedipus: Eteoclês, who died

as a man should die, fighting for his country, is to be buried with full military honors, with all the ceremony that is usual when the greatest heroes die; but his brother Polyneicês, who broke his exile to come back with fire and sword against his native city and the shrines of his fathers' gods, whose one idea was to spill the blood of his blood and sell his own people into slavery—Polyneicês, I say, is to have no burial: no man is to touch him or say the least prayer for him; he shall lie on the plain, unburied; and the birds and the scavenging dogs can do with him whatever they like.

This is my command, and you can see the wisdom behind it. As long as I am King, no traitor is going to be honored with the loyal man. But whoever shows by word and deed that he is on the side of the State, he shall have my respect while he is living, and my reverence when he is dead.

CHORAGOS:
If that is your will, Creon son of Menoikeus,
You have the right to enforce it: we are yours.

CREON:
That is my will. Take care that you do your part.

CHORAGOS:
We are old men: let the younger ones carry it out.

CREON:
I do not mean that: the sentries have been appointed.

CHORAGOS:
Then what is it that you would have us do?

CREON:
You will give no support to whoever breaks this law.

CHORAGOS:
Only a crazy man is in love with death!

CREON:
And death it is; yet money talks, and the wisest
Have sometimes been known to count a few coins too many.

(Enter SENTRY from L.)

SENTRY:
I'll not say that I'm out of breath from running, King, because every time I stopped to think about what I have to tell you, I felt like going back. And all the time a voice kept saying, "You fool, don't you know you're walking straight into trouble?"; and then another voice: "Yes, but if you let somebody else get the news to Creon first, it will be even worse than that for you!" But good sense won out, at least I hope it was good sense, and here I am with a story that makes no sense at all; but I'll tell it anyhow, because, as they say, what's going to happen's going to happen, and—

CREON:
Come to the point. What have you to say?

SENTRY:
I did not do it. I did not see who did it. You must not punish me for what someone else has done.

CREON:
A comprehensive defense! More effective, perhaps,
If I knew its purpose. Come: what is it?

SENTRY:
A dreadful thing . . . I don't know how to put it—

CREON:
Out with it!

SENTRY:
                    Well, then;
The dead man—
                    Polyneicês—

(Pause. The SENTRY is overcome, fumbles for words. CREON waits impassively.)

                                    out there—
                                            someone,—
New dust on the slimy flesh!

(Pause. No sign from CREON.)

Someone has given it burial that way, and
Gone . . .

(Long pause. CREON finally speaks with deadly control.)

CREON:
And the man who dared do this?

SENTRY:
                                    I swear I
Do not know! You must believe me!
                                    Listen:
The ground was dry, not a sign of digging, no,

SCENE I                                                  SOPHOCLES  123

Not a wheeltrack in the dust, no trace of anyone.
It was when they relieved us this morning: and
   one of them,
The corporal, pointed to it.
                                        There it was,
The strangest—
             Look:
The body, just mounded over with light dust: you
   see?
Not buried really, but as if they'd covered it
Just enough for the ghost's peace. And no sign
Of dogs or any wild animal that had been there.

And then what a scene there was! Every man
   of us
Accusing the other: we all proved the other man
   did it,
We all had proof that we could not have done
   it.
We were ready to take hot iron in our hands,
Walk through fire, swear by all the gods,
*It was not I!*
*I do not know who it was, but it was not I!*

   (CREON's *rage has been mounting steadily, but*
*the* SENTRY *is too intent upon his story to notice*
*it.*)

And then, when this came to nothing, someone
   said
A thing that silenced us and made us stare
Down at the ground: you had to be told the
   news,
And one of us had to do it! We threw the dice,
And the bad luck fell to me. So here I am,
No happier to be here than you are to have me:
Nobody likes the man who brings bad news.

CHORAGOS:
I have been wondering, King: can it be that the
   gods have done this?

CREON (*furiously*):
Stop!
Must you doddering wrecks
Go out of your heads entirely? "The gods!"
Intolerable!
The gods favor this corpse? Why? How had he
   served them?
Tried to loot their temples, burn their images,
Yes, and the whole State, and its laws with it!
Is it your senile opinion that the gods love to
   honor bad men?
A pious thought!—
                  No, from the very beginning

There have been those who have whispered together,
Stiff-necked anarchists, putting their heads together,
Scheming against me in alleys. These are the
   men,
And they have bribed my own guard to do this
   thing.

Money!
(*Sententiously*)
There's nothing in the world so demoralizing as
   money.
Down go your cities,
Homes gone, men gone, honest hearts corrupted,
Crookedness of all kinds, and all for money!
(*To* SENTRY)
                                    But you—!
I swear by God and by the throne of God,
The man who has done this thing shall pay for it!
Find that man, bring him here to me, or your
   death
Will be the least of your problems: I'll string you
   up
Alive, and there will be certain ways to make
   you
Discover your employer before you die;
And the process may teach you a lesson you seem
   to have missed:
The dearest profit is sometimes all too dear:
That depends on the source. Do you understand
   me?
A fortune won is often misfortune.

SENTRY:
King, may I speak?

CREON:
                  Your very voice distresses me.

SENTRY:
Are you sure that it is my voice, and not your
   conscience?

CREON:
By God, he wants to analyze me now!

SENTRY:
It is not what I say, but what has been done,
   that hurts you.

CREON:
You talk too much.

SENTRY:
                     Maybe; but I've done nothing.

CREON:

Sold your soul for some silver: that's all you've done.

SENTRY:

How dreadful it is when the right judge judges wrong!

CREON:

Your figures of speech
May entertain you now; but unless you bring me the man,
You will get little profit from them in the end.
(*Exit* CREON *into the Palace.*)

SENTRY:

"Bring me the man"—!
I'd like nothing better than bringing him the man!
But bring him or not, you have seen the last of me here.
At any rate, I am safe!
(*Exit* SENTRY.)

## ODE I

### STROPHE 1

CHORUS:

Numberless are the world's wonders, but none
More wonderful than man; the stormgray sea
Yields to his prows, the huge crests bear him high;
Earth, holy and inexhaustible, is graven
With shining furrows where his plows have gone
Year after year, the timeless labor of stallions.

### ANTISTROPHE 1

The lightboned birds and beasts that cling to cover,
The lithe fish lighting their reaches of dim water,
All are taken, tamed in the net of his mind;
The lion on the hill, the wild horse windy-maned,
Resign to him; and his blunt yoke has broken
The sultry shoulders of the mountain bull.

### STROPHE 2

Words also, and thought as rapid as air,
He fashions to his good use; statecraft is his,
And his the skill that deflects the arrows of snow,
The spears of winter rain: from every wind
He has made himself secure—from all but one:
In the late wind of death he cannot stand.

### ANTISTROPHE 2

O clear intelligence, force beyond all measure!
O fate of man, working both good and evil!
When the laws are kept, how proudly his city stands!
When the laws are broken, what of his city then?
Never may the anarchic man find rest at my hearth,
Never be it said that my thoughts are his thoughts.

## SCENE II

(*Re-enter* SENTRY *leading* ANTIGONÊ.)

CHORAGOS:

What does this mean? Surely this captive woman
Is the Princess Antigonê. Why should she be taken?

SENTRY:

Here is the one who did it! We caught her
In the very act of burying him.—Where is Creon?

CHORAGOS:

Just coming from the house.

(*Enter* CREON, *C.*)

CREON:

What has happened?
Why have you come back so soon?

SENTRY (*expansively*):

O King,
A man should never be too sure of anything:
I would have sworn
That you'd not see me here again: your anger
Frightened me so, and the things you threatened me with;
But how could I tell then
That I'd be able to solve the case so soon?

No dice-throwing this time: I was only too glad to come!

Here is this woman. She is the guilty one:
We found her trying to bury him.
Take her, then; question her; judge her as you will.
I am through with the whole thing now, and glad of it.

CREON:
But this is Antigonê! Why have you brought her
   here?

SENTRY:
She was burying him, I tell you!

CREON (severely):
                                          Is this the truth?

SENTRY:
I saw her with my own eyes. Can I say more?

CREON:
The details: come, tell me quickly!

SENTRY:
                                 It was like this:
After those terrible threats of yours, King,
We went back and brushed the dust away from
   the body.
The flesh was soft by now, and stinking,
So we sat on a hill to windward and kept guard.
No napping this time! We kept each other
   awake.
But nothing happened until the white round sun
Whirled in the center of the round sky over us:
Then, suddenly,
A storm of dust roared up from the earth, and
   the sky
Went out, the plain vanished with all its trees
In the stinging dark. We closed our eyes and
   endured it.
The whirlwind lasted a long time, but it passed;
And then we looked, and there was Antigonê!
I have seen
A mother bird come back to a stripped nest,
   heard
Her crying bitterly a broken note or two
For the young ones stolen. Just so, when this girl
Found the bare corpse, and all her love's work
   wasted,
She wept, and cried on heaven to damn the hands
That had done this thing.
                         And then she brought more dust
And sprinkled wine three times for her brother's
   ghost.

We ran and took her at once. She was not afraid,
Not even when we charged her with what she
   had done.
She denied nothing.
                    And this was a comfort to me,
And some uneasiness: for it is a good thing
To escape from death, but it is no great pleasure
To bring death to a friend.

                                 Yet I always say
There is nothing so comfortable as your own safe
   skin!

CREON (slowly, dangerously):
And you, Antigonê,
You with your head hanging, do you confess this
   thing?

ANTIGONÊ:
I do. I deny nothing.

CREON (to SENTRY):
                              You may go.

(Exit SENTRY.)

(To ANTIGONÊ)
Tell me, tell me briefly:
Had you heard my proclamation touching this
   matter?

ANTIGONÊ:
It was public. Could I help hearing it?

CREON:
And yet you dared defy the law.

ANTIGONÊ:
                              I dared.
It was not God's proclamation. That final Justice
That rules the world below makes no such laws.

Your edict, King, was strong,
But all your strength is weakness itself against
The immortal unrecorded laws of God.
They are not merely now: they were, and shall
   be,
Operative for ever, beyond man utterly.

I knew I must die, even without your decree:
I am only mortal. And if I must die
Now, before it is my time to die,
Surely this is no hardship: can anyone
Living, as I live, with evil all about me,
Think Death less than a friend? This death of
   mine
Is of no importance; but if I had left my brother
Lying in death unburied, I should have suffered.
Now I do not.
                         You smile at me. Ah Creon,
Think me a fool, if you like; but it may well be
That a fool convicts me of folly.

CHORAGOS:
Like father, like daughter: both headstrong, deaf
   to reason!
She has never learned to yield.

CREON:

She has much to learn.
The inflexible heart breaks first, the toughest iron
Cracks first, and the wildest horses bend their
  necks
At the pull of the smallest curb.

Pride? In a slave?
This girl is guilty of a double insolence,
Breaking the given laws and boasting of it.
Who is the man here,
She or I, if this crime goes unpunished?
Sister's child, or more than sister's child,
Or closer yet in blood—she and her sister
Win bitter death for this!
  (*To* SERVANTS)

Go, some of you,
Arrest Ismenê. I accuse her equally.
Bring her: you will find her sniffling in the house
  there.

Her mind's a traitor: crimes kept in the dark
Cry for light, and the guardian brain shudders;
But how much worse than this
Is brazen boasting of barefaced anarchy!

ANTIGONÊ:
Creon, what more do you want than my death?

CREON:

Nothing.
That gives me everything.

ANTIGONÊ:

Then I beg you: kill me.
This talking is a great weariness: your words
Are distasteful to me, and I am sure that mine
Seem so to you. And yet they should not seem
  so:
I should have praise and honor for what I have
  done.
All these men here would praise me
Were their lips not frozen shut with fear of
  you.
  (*Bitterly*)
Ah the good fortune of kings,
Licensed to say and do whatever they please!

CREON:
You are alone here in that opinion.

ANTIGONÊ:
No, they are with me. But they keep their tongues
  in leash.

CREON:
Maybe. But you are guilty, and they are not.

ANTIGONÊ:
There is no guilt in reverence for the dead.

CREON:
But Eteoclês—was he not your brother too?

ANTIGONÊ:
My brother too.

CREON:

And you insult his memory?

ANTIGONÊ (*softly*):
The dead man would not say that I insult it.

CREON:
He would: for you honor a traitor as much as
  him.

ANTIGONÊ:
His own brother, traitor or not, and equal in
  blood.

CREON:
He made war on his country. Eteoclês defended
  it.

ANTIGONÊ:
Nevertheless, there are honors due all the dead.

CREON:
But not the same for the wicked as for the just.

ANTIGONÊ:
Ah Creon, Creon,
Which of us can say what the gods hold wicked?

CREON:
An enemy is an enemy, even dead.

ANTIGONÊ:
It is my nature to join in love, not hate.

CREON (*finally losing patience*):
Go join them, then; if you must have your love,
Find it in hell!

CHORAGOS:
But see, Ismenê comes:

  (*Enter* ISMENÊ, *guarded*.)

Those tears are sisterly, the cloud
That shadows her eyes rains down gentle sorrow.

CREON:
You too, Ismenê,
Snake in my ordered house, sucking my blood
Stealthily—and all the time I never knew
That these two sisters were aiming at my throne!

Ismenê,

Do you confess your share in this crime, or deny
  it?
Answer me.

ISMENÊ:
Yes, if she will let me say so. I am guilty.

ANTIGONÊ    (coldly):
No, Ismenê. You have no right to say so.
You would not help me, and I will not have you
  help me.

ISMENÊ:
But now I know what you meant; and I am here
To join you, to take my share of punishment.

ANTIGONÊ:
The dead man and the gods who rule the dead
Know whose act this was. Words are not friends.

ISMENÊ:
Do you refuse me, Antigonê? I want to die with
  you:
I too have a duty that I must discharge to the
  dead.

ANTIGONÊ:
You shall not lessen my death by sharing it.

ISMENÊ:
What do I care for life when you are dead?

ANTIGONÊ:
Ask Creon. You're always hanging on his opinions.

ISMENÊ:
You are laughing at me. Why, Antigonê?

ANTIGONÊ:
It's a joyless laughter, Ismenê.

ISMENÊ:
                    But can I do nothing?

ANTIGONÊ:
Yes. Save yourself. I shall not envy you.
There are those who will praise you; I shall have
  honor, too.

ISMENÊ:
But we are equally guilty!

ANTIGONÊ:
                    No more, Ismenê.
You are alive, but I belong to Death.

CREON (to the CHORUS):
Gentlemen, I beg you to observe these girls:
One has just now lost her mind; the other,
It seems, has never had a mind at all.

ISMENÊ:
Grief teaches the steadiest minds to waver, King.

CREON:
Yours certainly did, when you assumed guilt with
  the guilty!

ISMENÊ:
But how could I go on living without her?

CREON:
                                        You are.
She is already dead.

ISMENÊ:
                    But your own son's bride!

CREON:
There are places enough for him to push his
  plow.
I want no wicked women for my sons!

ISMENÊ:
O dearest Haimon, how your father wrongs you!

CREON:
I've had enough of your childish talk of marriage!

CHORAGOS:
Do you really intend to steal this girl from your
  son?

CREON:
No; Death will do that for me.

CHORAGOS:
                            Then she must die?

CREON (ironically):
You dazzle me.
            —But enough of this talk!
(To GUARDS)
You, there, take them away and guard them well:
For they are but women, and even brave men
  run
When they see Death coming.

(Exeunt ISMENÊ, ANTIGONÊ, and GUARDS.)

## ODE II

### Strophe 1

CHORUS:
Fortunate is the man who has never tasted God's
  vengeance!
Where once the anger of heaven has struck, that
  house is shaken
For ever: damnation rises behind each child

Like a wave cresting out of the black northeast,
When the long darkness under sea roars up
And bursts drumming death upon the wind-
    whipped sand.

### Antistrophe 1

I have seen this gathering sorrow from time long
    past
Loom upon Oedipus' children: generation from
    generation
Takes the compulsive rage of the enemy god.
So lately this last flower of Oedipus' line
Drank the sunlight! but now a passionate word
And a handful of dust have closed up all its
    beauty.

### Strophe 2

What mortal arrogance
    Transcends the wrath of Zeus?
Sleep cannot lull him, nor the effortless long
    months
Of the timeless gods: but he is young for ever,
And his house is the shining day of high Olympos.
    All that is and shall be,
    And all the past, is his.
No pride on earth is free of the curse of heaven.

### Antistrophe 2

The straying dreams of men
    May bring them ghosts of joy:
But as they drowse, the waking embers burn
    them;
Or they walk with fixed eyes, as blind men walk.
But the ancient wisdom speaks for our own time:
    *Fate works most for woe*
    *With Folly's fairest show.*
Man's little pleasure is the spring of sorrow.

## SCENE III

CHORAGOS:
But here is Haimon, King, the last of all your
    sons.
Is it grief for Antigonê that brings him here,
And bitterness at being robbed of his bride?

    (*Enter* HAIMON.)

CREON:
We shall soon see, and no need of diviners.
                                        —Son,

You have heard my final judgment on that girl:
Have you come here hating me, or have you
    come
With deference and with love, whatever I do?

HAIMON:
I am your son, father. You are my guide.
You make things clear for me, and I obey you.
No marriage means more to me than your con-
    tinuing wisdom.

CREON:
Good. That is the way to behave: subordinate
Everything else, my son, to your father's will.
This is what a man prays for, that he may get
Sons attentive and dutiful in his house,
Each one hating his father's enemies,
Honoring his father's friends. But if his sons
Fail him, if they turn out unprofitably,
What has he fathered but trouble for himself
And amusement for the malicious?
                                    So you are right
Not to lose your head over this woman.
Your pleasure with her would soon grow cold,
    Haimon,
And then you'd have a hellcat in bed and else-
    where.
Let her find her husband in Hell!
Of all the people in this city, only she
Has had contempt for my law and broken it.

Do you want me to show myself weak before
    the people?
Or to break my sworn word? No, and I will not.
The woman dies.
I suppose she'll plead "family ties." Well, let her.
If I permit my own family to rebel,
How shall I earn the world's obedience?
Show me the man who keeps his house in hand,
He's fit for public authority.
                            I'll have no dealings
With law-breakers, critics of the government:
Whoever is chosen to govern should be obeyed—
Must be obeyed, in all things, great and small,
Just and unjust! O Haimon,
The man who knows how to obey, and that man
    only,
Knows how to give commands when the time
    comes.
You can depend on him, no matter how fast
The spears come: he's a good soldier, he'll stick
    it out.

Anarchy, anarchy! Show me a greater evil!

This is why cities tumble and the great houses
  rain down,
This is what scatters armies!
No, no: good lives are made so by discipline.
We keep the laws then, and the lawmakers,
And no woman shall seduce us. If we must lose,
Let's lose to a man, at least! Is a woman stronger
  than we?

CHORAGOS:
Unless time has rusted my wits,
What you say, King, is said with point and dig-
  nity.

HAIMON (boyishly earnest):
Father:
Reason is God's crowning gift to man, and you
  are right
To warn me against losing mine. I cannot say—
I hope that I shall never want to say!—that you
Have reasoned badly. Yet there are other men
Who can reason, too; and their opinions might
  be helpful.
You are not in a position to know everything
That people say or do, or what they feel:
Your temper terrifies them—everyone
Will tell you only what you like to hear.
But I, at any rate, can listen; and I have heard
  them
Muttering and whispering in the dark about this
  girl.
They say no woman has ever, so unreasonably,
Died so shameful a death for a generous act:
"She covered her brother's body. Is this inde-
  cent?
She kept him from dogs and vultures. Is this a
  crime?
Death?—She should have all the honor that we
  can give her!"

This is the way they talk out there in the city.

You must believe me:
Nothing is closer to me than your happiness.
What could be closer? Must not any son
Value his father's fortune as his father does his?
I beg you, do not be unchangeable:
Do not believe that you alone can be right.
The man who thinks that,
The man who maintains that only he has the
  power
To reason correctly, the gift to speak, the soul—
A man like that, when you know him, turns out
  empty.

It is not reason never to yield to reason!

In flood time you can see how some trees bend,
And because they bend, even their twigs are safe,
While stubborn trees are torn up, roots and all.
And the same thing happens in sailing:
Make your sheet fast, never slacken,—and over
  you go,
Head over heels and under: and there's your
  voyage.
Forget you are angry! Let yourself be moved!
I know I am young; but please let me say this:
The ideal condition
Would be, I admit, that men should be right by
  instinct;
But since we are all too likely to go astray,
The reasonable thing is to learn from those who
  can teach.

CHORAGOS:
You will do well to listen to him, King,
If what he says is sensible. And you, Haimon,
Must listen to your father.—Both speak well.

CREON:
You consider it right for a man of my years and
  experience
To go to school to a boy?

HAIMON:
                    It is not right
If I am wrong. But if I am young, and right,
What does my age matter?

CREON:
You think it right to stand up for an anarchist?

HAIMON:
Not at all. I pay no respect to criminals.

CREON:
Then she is not a criminal?

HAIMON:
The City would deny it, to a man.

CREON:
And the City proposes to teach me how to rule?

HAIMON:
Ah. Who is it that's talking like a boy now?

CREON:
My voice is the one voice giving orders in this
  City!

HAIMON:
It is no City if it takes orders from one voice.

CREON:
The State is the King!

HAIMON:
                    Yes, if the State is a desert.

(*Pause.*)

CREON:
This boy, it seems, has sold out to a woman.

HAIMON:
If you are a woman: my concern is only for you.

CREON:
So? Your "concern"! In a public brawl with your
    father!

HAIMON:
How about you, in a public brawl with justice?

CREON:
With justice, when all that I do is within my
    rights?

HAIMON:
You have no right to trample on God's right.

CREON (*completely out of control*):
Fool, adolescent fool! Taken in by a woman!

HAIMON:
You'll never see me taken in by anything vile.

CREON:
Every word you say is for her!

HAIMON (*quietly, darkly*):
                        And for you.
And for me. And for the gods under the earth.

CREON:
You'll never marry her while she lives.

HAIMON:
Then she must die.—But her death will cause
    another.

CREON:
Another?
Have you lost your senses? Is this an open threat?

HAIMON:
There is no threat in speaking to emptiness.

CREON:
I swear you'll regret this superior tone of yours!
You are the empty one!

HAIMON:
                    If you were not my father,
I'd say you were perverse.

CREON:
You girlstruck fool, don't play at words with me!

HAIMON:
I am sorry. You prefer silence.

CREON.
                        Now, by God—!
I swear, by all the gods in heaven above us,
You'll watch it, I swear you shall!
    (*To the* SERVANTS)
                        Bring her out!
Bring the woman out! Let her die before his eyes!
Here, this instant, with her bridegroom beside
    her!

HAIMON:
Not here, no; she will not die here, King.
And you will never see my face again.
Go on raving as long as you've a friend to endure
    you.
    (*Exit* HAIMON.)

CHORAGOS:
Gone, gone.
Creon, a young man in a rage is dangerous!

CREON:
Let him do, or dream to do, more than a man
    can.
He shall not save these girls from death.

CHORAGOS:
                        These girls?
You have sentenced them both?

CREON:
                        No, you are right.
I will not kill the one whose hands are clean.

CHORAGOS:
But Antigonê?

CREON (*somberly*):
                    I will carry her far away
Out there in the wilderness, and lock her
Living in a vault of stone. She shall have food,
As the custom is, to absolve the State of her
    death.
And there let her pray to the gods of hell:
They are her only gods:
Perhaps they will show her an escape from
    death,
Or she may learn,
                    though late,
That piety shown the dead is pity in vain.
    (*Exit* CREON.)

## ODE III

### STROPHE

CHORUS:
Love, unconquerable
Waster of rich men, keeper
Of warm lights and all-night vigil
In the soft face of a girl:
Sea-wanderer, forest-visitor!
Even the pure Immortals cannot escape you,
And mortal man, in his one day's dusk,
Trembles before your glory.

### ANTISTROPHE

Surely you swerve upon ruin
The just man's consenting heart,
As here you have made bright anger
Strike between father and son—
And none has conquered but Love!
A girl's glance working the will of heaven:
Pleasure to her alone who mocks us,
Merciless Aphroditê.

## SCENE IV

CHORAGOS (as ANTIGONÊ enters guarded):
But I can no longer stand in awe of this,
Nor, seeing what I see, keep back my tears.
Here is Antigonê, passing to that chamber
Where all find sleep at last.

### STROPHE 1

ANTIGONÊ:
Look upon me, friends, and pity me
Turning back at the night's edge to say
Good-by to the sun that shines for me no longer;
Now sleepy Death
Summons me down to Acheron, that cold shore:
There is no bridesong there, nor any music.

CHORUS:
Yet not unpraised, not without a kind of honor,
You walk at last into the underworld;
Untouched by sickness, broken by no sword.
What woman has ever found your way to death?

### ANTISTROPHE 1

ANTIGONÊ:
How often I have heard the story of Niobê,
Tantalos' wretched daughter, how the stone

Clung fast about her, ivy-close: and they say
The rain falls endlessly
And sifting soft snow; her tears are never done.
I feel the loneliness of her death in mine.

CHORUS:
But she was born of heaven, and you
Are woman, woman-born. If her death is yours,
A mortal woman's, is this not for you
Glory in our world and in the world beyond?

### STROPHE 2

ANTIGONÊ:
You laugh at me. Ah, friends, friends,
Can you not wait until I am dead? O Thebes,
O men many-charioted, in love with Fortune,
Dear springs of Dircê, sacred Theban grove,
Be witnesses for me, denied all pity,
Unjustly judged! and think a word of love
For her whose path turns
Under dark earth, where there are no more tears.

CHORUS:
You have passed beyond human daring and come
    at last
Into a place of stone where Justice sits.
I cannot tell
What shape of your father's guilt appears in this.

### ANTISTROPHE 2

ANTIGONÊ:
You have touched it at last: that bridal bed
Unspeakable, horror of son and mother mingling:
Their crime, infection of all our family!
O Oedipus, father and brother!
Your marriage strikes from the grave to murder
    mine.
I have been a stranger here in my own land:
All my life
The blasphemy of my birth has followed me.

CHORUS:
Reverence is a virtue, but strength
Lives in established law: that must prevail.
You have made your choice,
Your death is the doing of your conscious hand.

### EPODE

ANTIGONÊ:
Then let me go, since all your words are bitter,
And the very light of the sun is cold to me.
Lead me to my vigil, where I must have

Neither love nor lamentation; no song, but
  silence.

(CREON *interrupts impatiently.*)

CREON:
If dirges and planned lamentations could put off
  death,
Men would be singing for ever.
  (*To the* SERVANTS)
                              Take her, go!
You know your orders; take her to the vault
And leave her alone there. And if she lives or
  dies,
That's her affair, not ours: our hands are clean.

ANTIGONÊ:
O tomb, vaulted bride-bed in eternal rock,
Soon I shall be with my own again
Where Persephonê welcomes the thin ghosts
  underground:
And I shall see my father again, and you, mother,
And dearest Polyneicês—
                        dearest indeed
To me, since it was my hand
That washed him clean and poured the ritual
  wine:
And my reward is death before my time!

And yet, as men's hearts know, I have done no
  wrong,
I have not sinned before God. Or if I have,
I shall know the truth in death. But if the guilt
Lies upon Creon who judged me, then, I pray,
May his punishment equal my own.

CHORAGOS:
                        O passionate heart,
Unyielding, tormented still by the same winds!

CREON:
Her guards shall have good cause to regret their
  delaying.

ANTIGONÊ:
Ah! That voice is like the voice of death!

CREON:
I can give you no reason to think you are mistaken.

ANTIGONÊ:
Thebes, and you my father's gods,
And rulers of Thebes, you see me now, the last
Unhappy daughter of a line of kings,
Your kings, led away to death. You will remem-
  ber

What things I suffer, and at what men's hands,
Because I would not transgress the laws of
  heaven.
  (*To the* GUARDS, *simply*)
Come: let us wait no longer.

(*Exit* ANTIGONÊ, *L., guarded.*)

## ODE IV

### STROPHE 1

CHORUS:
All Danaê's beauty was locked away
In a brazen cell where the sunlight could not
  come:
A small room, still as any grave, enclosed her.
Yet she was a princess too,
And Zeus in a rain of gold poured love upon her.
O child, child,
No power in wealth or war
Or tough sea-blackened ships
Can prevail against untiring Destiny!

### ANTISTROPHE 1

And Dryas' son also, that furious king,
Bore the god's prisoning anger for his pride:
Sealed up by Dionysos in deaf stone,
His madness died among echoes.
So at the last he learned what dreadful power
His tongue had mocked:
For he had profaned the revels,
And fired the wrath of the nine
Implacable Sisters that love the sound of the
  flute.

### STROPHE 2

And old men tell a half-remembered tale
Of horror done where a dark ledge splits the sea
And a double surf beats on the gray shores:
How a king's new woman, sick
With hatred for the queen he had imprisoned,
Ripped out his two sons' eyes with her bloody
  hands
While grinning Arês watched the shuttle plunge
Four times: four blind wounds crying for re-
  venge,

### ANTISTROPHE 2

Crying, tears and blood mingled.—Piteously
  born,

Those sons whose mother was of heavenly birth!
Her father was the god of the North Wind
And she was cradled by gales,
She raced with young colts on the glittering hills
And walked untrammeled in the open light:
But in her marriage deathless Fate found means
To build a tomb like yours for all her joy.

## SCENE V

(*Enter blind* TEIRESIAS, *led by a* BOY. *The opening speeches of* TEIRESIAS *should be in singsong contrast to the realistic lines of* CREON.)

TEIRESIAS:
This is the way the blind man comes, Princes, Princes,
Lock-step, two heads lit by the eyes of one.

CREON:
What new thing have you to tell us, old Teiresias?

TEIRESIAS:
I have much to tell you: listen to the prophet, Creon.

CREON:
I am not aware that I have ever failed to listen.

TEIRESIAS:
Then you have done wisely, King, and ruled well.

CREON:
I admit my debt to you. But what have you to say?

TEIRESIAS:
This, Creon: you stand once more on the edge of fate.

CREON:
What do you mean? Your words are a kind of dread.

TEIRESIAS:
Listen, Creon:
I was sitting in my chair of augury, at the place
Where the birds gather about me. They were all a-chatter,
As is their habit, when suddenly I heard
A strange note in their jangling, a scream, a
Whirring fury; I knew that they were fighting,
Tearing each other, dying
In a whirlwind of wings clashing. And I was afraid.

I began the rites of burnt-offering at the altar,
But Hephaistos failed me: instead of bright flame,
There was only the sputtering slime of the fat thigh-flesh
Melting: the entrails dissolved in gray smoke,
The bare bone burst from the welter. And no blaze!

This was a sign from heaven. My boy described it,
Seeing for me as I see for others.

I tell you, Creon, you yourself have brought
This new calamity upon us. Our hearths and altars
Are stained with the corruption of dogs and carrion birds
That glut themselves on the corpse of Oedipus' son.
The gods are deaf when we pray to them, their fire
Recoils from our offering, their birds of omen
Have no cry of comfort, for they are gorged
With the thick blood of the dead.
                                        O my son,
These are no trifles! Think: all men make mistakes,
But a good man yields when he knows his course is wrong,
And repairs the evil. The only crime is pride.

Give in to the dead man, then: do not fight with a corpse—
What glory is it to kill a man who is dead?
Think, I beg you:
It is for your own good that I speak as I do.
You should be able to yield for your own good.

CREON:
It seems that prophets have made me their especial province.
All my life long
I have been a kind of butt for the dull arrows
Of doddering fortune-tellers!
                                        No, Teiresias:
If your birds—if the great eagles of God himself
Should carry him stinking bit by bit to heaven,
I would not yield. I am not afraid of pollution:
No man can defile the gods.
                                        Do what you will,
Go into business, make money, speculate
In India gold or that synthetic gold from Sardis,
Get rich otherwise than by my consent to bury him.

Teiresias, it is a sorry thing when a wise man
Sells his wisdom, lets out his words for hire!

TEIRESIAS:
Ah Creon! Is there no man left in the world—

CREON:
To do what?—Come, let's have the aphorism!

TEIRESIAS:
No man who knows that wisdom outweighs any
    wealth?

CREON:
As surely as bribes are baser than any baseness.

TEIRESIAS:
You are sick, Creon! You are deathly sick!

CREON:
As you say: it is not my place to challenge a
    prophet.

TEIRESIAS:
Yet you have said my prophecy is for sale.

CREON:
The generation of prophets has always loved
    gold.

TEIRESIAS:
The generation of kings has always loved brass.

CREON:
You forget yourself! You are speaking to your
    King:

TEIRESIAS:
I know it. You are a king because of me.

CREON:
You have a certain skill; but you have sold out.

TEIRESIAS:
King, you will drive me to words that—

CREON:
                              Say them, say them!
Only remember: I will not pay you for them.

TEIRESIAS:
No, you will find them too costly.

CREON:
                              No doubt. Speak:
Whatever you say, you will not change my will.

TEIRESIAS:
Then take this, and take it to heart!
The time is not far off when you shall pay back
Corpse for corpse, flesh of your own flesh.

You have thrust the child of this world into living
    night,
You have kept from the gods below the child that
    is theirs:
The one in a grave before her death, the other,
Dead, denied the grave. This is your crime:
And the Furies and the dark gods of Hell
Are swift with terrible punishment for you.

Do you want to buy me now, Creon?

                              Not many days,
And your house will be full of men and women
    weeping,
And curses will be hurled at you from far
Cities grieving for sons unburied, left to rot
Before the walls of Thebes.

These are my arrows, Creon: they are all for you.

    (*To* BOY)
But come, child: lead me home.
Let him waste his fine anger upon younger men.
Maybe he will learn at last
To control a wiser tongue in a better head.

    (*Exit* TEIRESIAS.)

CHORAGOS:
The old man has gone, King, but his words
Remain to plague us. I am old, too,
But I cannot remember that he was ever false.

CREON:
That is true. . . . It troubles me.
Oh it is hard to give in! but it is worse
To risk everything for stubborn pride.

CHORAGOS:
Creon: take my advice.

CREON:
                              What shall I do?

CHORAGOS:
Go quickly: free Antigonê from her vault
And build a tomb for the body of Polyneicês.

CREON:
You would have me do this?

CHORAGOS:
                              Creon, yes!
And it must be done at once: God moves
Swiftly to cancel the folly of stubborn men.

CREON:
It is hard to deny the heart! But I
Will do it: I will not fight with destiny.

CHORAGOS:
You must go yourself, you cannot leave it to
    others.

CREON:
I will go.
          —Bring axes, servants.
Come with me to the tomb. I buried her, I
Will set her free.
                   Oh quickly!
My mind misgives—
The laws of the gods are mighty, and a man must
    serve them
To the last day of his life!
    (*Exit* CREON.)

## PAEAN

### STROPHE 1

CHORAGOS:
God of many names

CHORUS:
                   O Iacchos
                            son
of Kadmeian Sémelê
                   O born of the Thunder!
Guardian of the West
                   Regent
of Eleusis' plain
                   O Prince of maenad Thebes
and the Dragon Field by rippling Ismenos:

### ANTISTROPHE 1

CHORAGOS:
God of many names

CHORUS:
                   the flame of torches
flares on our hills
                   the nymphs of Iacchos
dance at the spring of Castalia:
from the vine-close mountain
                            come ah come in ivy:
*Evohé evohé!* sings through the streets of Thebes

### STROPHE 2

CHORAGOS:
God of many names

CHORUS:
                   Iacchos of Thebes
heavenly Child
          of Sémelê bride of the Thunderer!

The shadow of plague is upon us:
                            come
with clement feet
                   oh come from Parnasos
down the long slopes
                   across the lamenting water

### ANTISTROPHE 2

CHORAGOS:
Iô Fire! Chorister of the throbbing stars!
O purest among the voices of the night!
Thou son of God, blaze for us!

CHORUS:
Come with choric rapture of circling Maenads
Who cry *Iô Iacche!*
                   *God of many names!*

## ÉXODOS

(*Enter* MESSENGER, *L.*)

MESSENGER:
Men of the line of Kadmos, you who live
Near Amphion's citadel:
                            I cannot say
Of any condition of human life "This is fixed,
This is clearly good, or bad." Fate raises up,
And Fate casts down the happy and unhappy
    alike:
No man can foretell his Fate.
                            Take the case of Creon:
Creon was happy once, as I count happiness:
Victorious in battle, sole governor of the land,
Fortunate father of children nobly born.
And now it has all gone from him! Who can say
That a man is still alive when his life's joy fails?
He is a walking dead man. Grant him rich,
Let him live like a king in his great house:
If his pleasure is gone, I would not give
So much as the shadow of smoke for all he owns.

CHORAGOS:
Your words hint at sorrow: what is your news
    for us?

MESSENGER:
They are dead. The living are guilty of their
    death.

CHORAGOS:
Who is guilty? Who is dead? Speak!

MESSENGER:

Haimon.
Haimon is dead; and the hand that killed him
Is his own hand.

CHORAGOS:

His father's? or his own?

MESSENGER:

His own, driven mad by the murder his father
had done.

CHORAGOS:

Teiresias, Teiresias, how clearly you saw it all!

MESSENGER:

This is my news: you must draw what conclusions
you can from it.

CHORAGOS:

But look: Eurydicê, our Queen:
Has she overheard us?

(*Enter* EURYDICÊ *from the Palace, C.*)

EURYDICÊ:

I have heard something, friends:
As I was unlocking the gate of Pallas' shrine,
For I needed her help today, I heard a voice
Telling of some new sorrow. And I fainted
There at the temple with all my maidens about
me.
But speak again: whatever it is, I can bear it:
Grief and I are no strangers.

MESSENGER:

Dearest Lady,
I will tell you plainly all that I have seen.
I shall not try to comfort you: what is the use,
Since comfort could lie only in what is not true?
The truth is always best.
I went with Creon
To the outer plain where Polyneicês was lying,
No friend to pity him, his body shredded by dogs.
We made our prayers in that place to Hecatê
And Pluto, that they would be merciful. And we
bathed
The corpse with holy water, and we brought
Fresh-broken branches to burn what was left of
it,
And upon the urn we heaped up a towering
barrow
Of the earth of his own land.
When we were done, we ran
To the vault where Antigonê lay on her couch
of stone.

One of the servants had gone ahead,
And while he was yet far off he heard a voice
Grieving within the chamber, and he came back
And told Creon. And as the King went closer,
The air was full of wailing, the words lost,
And he begged us to make all haste. "Am I a
prophet?"
He said, weeping, "And must I walk this road,
The saddest of all that I have gone before?
My son's voice calls me on. Oh quickly, quickly!
Look through the crevice there, and tell me
If it is Haimon, or some deception of the gods!"

We obeyed; and in the cavern's farthest corner
We saw her lying:
She had made a noose of her fine linen veil
And hanged herself. Haimon lay beside her,
His arms about her waist, lamenting her,
His love lost under ground, crying out
That his father had stolen her away from him.

When Creon saw him the tears rushed to his eyes
And he called to him: "What have you done,
child? Speak to me.
What are you thinking that makes your eyes so
strange?
O my son, my son, I come to you on my knees!"
But Haimon spat in his face. He said not a word,
Staring—
And suddenly drew his sword
And lunged. Creon shrank back, the blade
missed; and the boy,
Desperate against himself, drove it half its length
Into his own side, and fell. And as he died
He gathered Antigonê close in his arms again,
Choking, his blood bright red on her white
cheek.
And now he lies dead with the dead, and she
is his
At last, his bride in the houses of the dead.

(*Exit* EURYDICÊ *into the Palace.*)

CHORAGOS:

She has left us without a word. What can this
mean?

MESSENGER:

It troubles me, too; yet she knows what is best,
Her grief is too great for public lamentation,
And doubtless she has gone to her chamber to
weep
For her dead son, leading her maidens in his
dirge.

CHORAGOS:
It may be so; but I fear this deep silence.

*(Pause.)*

MESSENGER:
I will see what she is doing. I will go in.
*(Exit MESSENGER into the Palace.)*

*(Enter CREON with ATTENDANTS, bearing HAIMON's body.)*

CHORAGOS:
But here is the King himself: oh look at him,
Bearing his own damnation in his arms.

CREON:
Nothing you say can touch me any more.
My own blind heart has brought me
From darkness to final darkness. Here you see
The father murdering, the murdered son—
And all my civic wisdom!

Haimon my son, so young, so young to die,
I was the fool, not you; and you died for me.

CHORAGOS:
That is the truth; but you were late in learning
   it.

CREON:
This truth is hard to bear. Surely a god
Has crushed me beneath the hugest weight of
   heaven,
And driven me headlong a barbaric way
To trample out the thing I held most dear.

The pains that men will take to come to pain!

*(Enter MESSENGER from the Palace.)*

MESSENGER:
The burden you carry in your hands is heavy,
But it is not all: you will find more in your house.

CREON:
What burden worse than this shall I find there?

MESSENGER:
The Queen is dead.

CREON:
O port of death, deaf world,
Is there no pity for me? And you, Angel of evil,
I was dead, and your words are death again.
Is it true, boy? Can it be true?
Is my wife dead? Has death bred death?

MESSENGER:
You can see for yourself.

*(The doors are opened, and the body of EURYDICÊ is disclosed within.)*

CREON:
Oh pity!
All true, all true, and more than I can bear!
O my wife, my son!

MESSENGER:
She stood before the altar, and her heart
Welcomed the knife her own hand guided,
And a great cry burst from her lips for Megareus
   dead,
And for Haimon dead, her sons; and her last
   breath
Was a curse for their father, the murderer of her
   sons.
And she fell, and the dark flowed in through her
   closing eyes.

CREON:
O God, I am sick with fear.
Are there no swords here? Has no one a blow
   for me?

MESSENGER:
Her curse is upon you for the deaths of both.

CREON:
It is right that it should be. I alone am guilty.
I know it, and I say it. Lead me in,
Quickly, friends.
I have neither life nor substance. Lead me in.

CHORAGOS:
You are right, if there can be right in so much
   wrong.
The briefest way is best in a world of sorrow.

CREON:
Let it come,
Let death come quickly, and be kind to me.
I would not ever see the sun again.

CHORAGOS:
All that will come when it will; but we, mean-
   while,
Have much to do. Leave the future to itself.

CREON:
All my heart was in that prayer!

CHORAGOS:
Then do not pray any more: the sky is deaf.

CREON:
Lead me away. I have been rash and foolish.

I have killed my son and my wife.
I look for comfort; my comfort lies here dead.
Whatever my hands have touched has come to
    nothing.
Fate has brought all my pride to a thought of
    dust.

(As CREON *is being led into the house, the*

CHORAGOS *advances and speaks directly to the
audience.*)

CHORAGOS:
There is no happiness where there is no wisdom;
No wisdom but in submission to the gods.
Big words are always punished,
And proud men in old age learn to be wise.

TRANSLATORS' COMMENTARY

Et quod propriè dicitur in idiomate Picardorum
horrescit apud Burgundos, immò apud Gallicos
viciniores; quanto igitur magis accidet hoc
apud linguas diversas! Quapropter quod bene
factum est in unâ linguâ non est possibile ut
transferatur in aliam secundum ejus proprie-
tatem quam habuerit in priori.

—ROGER BACON

I

In the Commentary appended to our version of
Euripides' *Alcestis* we wrote:

Our object was to make the *Alcestis* clear and
credible in English. Since it is a poem, it had
to be made clear as a poem; and since it is
a play, it had to be made credible as a play.
We set for ourselves no fixed rules of translation
or of dramatic verse: often we found the best
English equivalent in a literalness which extended to the texture and rhythm of the Greek
phrasing; at other times we were forced to a
more or less free paraphrase in order to achieve
effects which the Greek conveyed in ways impossible to English. Consequently, this version
of the *Alcestis* is not a "translation" in the
classroom sense of the word. The careful
reader, comparing our text with the original,
will discover alterations, suppressions, expan-
sions—a word, perhaps, drawn out into a
phrase, or a phrase condensed to a word: a way
of saying things that is admittedly not Euripidean, if by Euripidean one means a translation *ad verbum expressa* of Euripides' poem.
In defense we can say only that our purpose
was to reach—and, if possible, to render precisely—the emotional and sensible meaning in
every speech in the play; we could not follow
the Greek word for word, where to do so would
have been weak and therefore false.

We have been guided by the same principles in
making this version of the *Antigonê*.

II

We have made cuts only when it seemed absolutely necessary. The most notable excision is
that of a passage of sixteen lines beginning with
904 (Antigonê's long speech near the end of
Scene IV), which has been bracketed as spurious,
either in whole or in part, by the best critics.
Aristotle quotes two verses from it, which proves,
as Professor Jebb points out, that if it is an inter-
polation it must have been made soon after
Sophocles' death, possibly by his son Iophon.
However that may be, it is dismal stuff. Antigonê
is made to interrupt her lamentation by a series
of limping verses whose sense is as discordant as
their sound. We quote the Oxford translation, the
style of which is for once wholly adequate to the
occasion:

And yet, in the opinion of those who have just
sentiments, I honoured you [Polyneicês] aright.
For neither, though I had been the mother of
children, nor though my husband dying, had
mouldered away, would I have undertaken this
toil against the will of the citizens. On account
of what law do I say this? There would have
been another husband for me if the first died,
and if I lost my child there would have been
another from another man! but my father and
my mother being laid in the grave, it is impossible a brother should ever be born to me. On
the principle of such a law, having preferred
you, my brother, to all other considerations, I
seemed to Creon to commit a sin, and to dare
what was dreadful. And now, seizing me by
force, he thus leads me away, having never
enjoyed the nuptial bed, nor heard the nuptial
lay, nor having gained the lot of marriage, nor

of rearing my children; but thus I, an unhappy woman, deserted by my friends, go, while alive, to the cavern of the dead.

There are other excisions of less importance. Perhaps the discussion of one of them will serve to explain them all. Near the end of the *Éxodos*, Creon is told of his wife's suicide. The Messenger has five very graphic lines describing Eurydicê's suicide, to which Creon responds with an outburst of dread and grief; yet two lines later, as if he had not heard the first time, he is asking the Messenger how Eurydicê died. The Messenger replies that she stabbed herself to the heart. There is no evidence that the question and reply are interpolations: on the contrary, they serve the definite purpose of filling out the iambic interlude between two lyric strophes; but in a modern version which does not attempt to reproduce the strophic structure of this *Kommos* they merely clog the dialogue. Therefore we have skipped them; and the occasional suppression of short passages throughout the play is based upon similar considerations.

### III

In a like manner, we have not hesitated to use free paraphrase when a literal rendering of the Greek would result in obscurity. Again, the discussion of a specific instance may illuminate the whole question.

After Antigonê has been led away to death, the Chorus, taking a hint from her having compared her own fate to that of Niobê, proceeds to elaborate the stories of mythological persons who have suffered similar punishment. The Fourth Ode cites Danaê, Lycurgos, the son of Dryas, and Cleopatra, the daughter of Boreas and wife of the Thracian king Phineus. Only Danaê is mentioned by name; the others are allusively identified. The difficulty arises from the allusive method. Sophocles' audience would be certain to recognize the allusions, but that is not true of ours. To what extent can we depend upon the audience's recognition in a day when, to quote Mr. I. A. Richards, "we can no longer refer with any confidence to any episode in the Bible or to any nursery tale or any piece of mythology"? We can assume that the story of Danaê is still current; but Lycurgos is forgotten now, and the sordid Phineus-Cleopatra-Eidothea affair no

longer stirs so much as an echo. Nevertheless, Sophocles devotes two of his four strophes to this Cleopatra, and he does it in so oblique a manner that "translation" is out of the question. We have therefore rendered these strophes with such slight additions to the Greek sense as might convey an equivalent suggestion of fable to a modern audience.

### IV

The Chorus is composed, says the Scholiast, of "certain old men of Thebes": leading citizens ("O men many-charioted, in love with Fortune") to whom Creon addresses his fatal decree, and from whom he later takes advice. Sophocles' Chorus numbered fifteen, including the Choragos, or Leader; its function was to chant the Odes and, in the person of the Choragos, to participate in the action. In a version designed for the modern stage certain changes are inevitable. It cannot be urged too strongly that the words of the Odes must be intelligible to the audience; and they are almost certain not to be intelligible if they are chanted in unison by so large a group, with or without musical accompaniment. It is suggested, then, that in producing this play no attempt be made to follow the ancient choric method. There should be no dancing. The *Párodos*, for example, should be a solemn but almost unnoticeable evolution of moving or still patterns accompanied by a drum-beat whose rhythm may be derived from the cadence of the Ode itself. The lines given to the Chorus in the Odes should probably be spoken by single voices. The only accompaniment should be percussion: we follow Allan Sly's score of the *Alcestis* in suggesting a large side drum, from which the snares have been removed, to be struck with two felt-headed tympani sticks, one hard, one soft.

### V

A careful production might make successful use of masks. They should be of the Benda type used in the production of O'Neill's *The Great God Brown*: lifelike, closely fitting the contours of the face, and valuable only as they give the effect of immobility to character. On no account should there be any attempt to reproduce the Greek mask, which was larger than life size and served a function non-existent on the modern stage—the amplification of voice and mood for projection to the distant seats of the outdoor theater.

If masks are used at all, they might well be allotted only to those characters who are somewhat depersonalized by official position or discipline: Creon, Teiresias, the Chorus and Choragos, possibly the Messenger. By this rule, Antigonê has no mask; neither has Ismenê, Haimon, nor Eurydicê. If Creon is masked, we see no objection, in art or feeling, to the symbolic removal of his mask before he returns with the dead body of his son.

### INDEX OF NAMES IN *Antigonê*

The transliteration of Greek names is an uncertain and—ultimately, perhaps—subjective matter. Certain of the entries below have more than one form, the first being that used in this translation.

ACHERON:  a river of Hades

AMPHION:  a prince of Orchomenos who married NIOBÊ, *q.v.*; hence, an ancestor of Oedipus

ANTIGONÊ:  a daughter of Oedipus; in *Antigonê* affianced to HAIMON, *q.v.*

APHRODITÊ:  goddess of love

APOLLO:  god of the sun

ARÊS:  god of war

ARGIVE:  Greek

ARGOS:  capital of Argolis, in the Peloponnesos

ARTEMIS:  goddess of the hunt, sister of Apollo

ATHENA, ATHENÊ:  daughter of Zeus, tutelary goddess of Athens

CASTALIA:  a spring sacred to the Muses, on Mount Parnassos

CREON, KREON:  brother of IOCASTÊ, *q.v.*; father of HAIMON and MEGAREUS, *qq.v.*; King of Thebes after the death of Polyneicês and Eteoclês

DANAÊ:  a princess of Argos, confined by her father in a brazen chamber underground (or, some say, in a brazen tower), where she was seduced by Zeus in the form of a golden rain and bore him Perseus

DELPHI, DELPHOI:  a city of Phokis, seat of a celebrated Oracle of Apollo

DEMÉTER:  a sister of Zeus, goddess of agriculture

DIONYSOS, DIONYSUS:  son of Zeus and SÉMELÊ, *q.v.*; god of wine

DIRCÊ, DIRKÊ:  a spring near Thebes

DRYAS:  a king of Thrace; father of Lykûrgos, who was driven mad by Dionysos

ELEUSIS:  a city in Attica, sacred to Deméter and Persephonê; hence the adjective ELEUSINIAN

ETEOCLÊS, ETEOKLÊS:  a son of Oedipus and Iocastê; brother of POLYNEICÊS, *q.v.*

EURYDICÊ, EURYDIKÊ:  wife of CREON, *q.v.*

FURIES:  the infernal spirits of Divine Vengeance

HAIMON, HAEMON:  a son of Creon; affianced to Antigonê

HECATÊ:  a goddess of the Titan race; identified with various other deities, as Selenê in heaven, Artemis on earth, and Persephonê in Hades; generally, a goddess of sorcery and witchcraft

HEPHAISTOS, HEPHAESTUS:  god of fire

IACCHOS:  a name for DIONYSOS, *q.v.*

IOCASTÊ, JOCASTA:  wife of LAÏOS, *q.v.*; after Laïos' death, wife of Oedipus, and, by him, mother of ANTIGONÊ, ISMENÊ, POLYNEICÊS and ETEOCLÊS, *qq.v.*

ISMENÊ:  a daughter of Oedipus and Iocastê; sister of Antigonê

ISMENOS:  a river of Thebes, sacred to Apollo

KADMOS, CADMUS:  the legendary founder of Thebes; father of SÉMELÊ, *q.v.*

LAÏOS, LAIUS:  a king of Thebes; father of Oedipus, killed by him in fulfillment of an oracle

MAENAD:  a priestess of DIONYSOS, *q.v.*

MEGAREUS:  a son of CREON, *q.v.*; died during the assault of the Seven against Thebes

MENOIKEUS:  father of CREON and IOCASTÊ, *qq.v.*

MUSES:  nine daughters of Zeus and the nymph Mnemosynê, goddesses presiding over the arts and sciences

NIOBÊ:  wife of AMPHION, *q.v.*; mother of fourteen children killed, because of her pride, by Apollo and Artemis; transformed into a rock on Mt. Sipylos

OEDIPUS:  son of LAÏOS and IOCASTÊ, *qq.v.*

OLYMPOS, OLYMPUS:  a Thessalian mountain, the seat of the gods

PALLAS:  an epithet of ATHENA, *q.v.*

PARNASSOS, PARNASOS, PARNASSUS:  a mountain sacred to Apollo; at its foot are Delphi and the Castalian Spring

PELOPS:  a son of Tantalos; father of Atreus

PERSEPHONÊ:  daughter of DEMÉTER, *q.v.*; Queen of Hades

PHOKIS:  a kingdom on the Gulf of Corinth

PLUTO:  brother of Zeus and Poseidon; King of Hades

POLYNEICÊS, POLYNEIKÊS: a son of Oedipus and Iocastê; killed by his brother Eteoclês, whom he killed at the same time, during the assault upon Thebes

SARDIS: a city in Lydia

SÉMELÊ: a daughter of KADMOS, *q.v.;* mother, by Zeus, of the god Dionysos

SPHINX: a riddling she-monster who killed herself when Oedipus solved her riddle

TANTALOS, TANTALUS: a king of Phrygia, father of PELOPS and NIOBÊ, *qq.v.*

TEIRESIAS, TIRESIAS: a blind prophet of Thebes, counsellor of Oedipus and Creon

ZEUS: father of gods and men

D.F.
R.F.

# ALBERT CAMUS

# Caligula

TRANSLATED BY STUART GILBERT

Albert Camus (1913–1960) was born in Algiers and had become an intellectual and artistic leader there by the age of twenty-one. Among the works for which he is best known are an essay, "The Myth of Sisyphus"; a novel, *The Plague,* 1947; a play, *Caligula,* 1943; and dramatic adaptations of two novels—Faulkner's *Requiem for a Nun,* 1956, and Dostoevsky's *The Possessed,* 1959.

*Caligula,* derived in part from the biography of the Emperor Caligula by the Roman historian Suetonius, is Camus's expression of the absurdity of life. The characterization of Caligula shows Camus's ability to portray the power of man's inner existence as he tries to assert freedom without being destroyed by it.

AUTHOR'S PREFACE (DECEMBER 1957)

The plays making up this collection were written between 1938 and 1950.[1] The first, *Caligula,* was composed in 1938 after a reading of Suetonius' *Twelve Caesars.* I intended the play for the little theater I had organized in Algiers, and my artless intention was to play the part of Caligula myself. Inexperienced actors often show such guileless-

ness. Besides, I was only twenty-five, the age when one doubts everything except oneself. The war forced me to modesty, and *Caligula* was first played in 1945 at the Théâtre-Hébertot in Paris.

Hence *Caligula* is an actor's and director's play. But of course it takes its inspiration from the concerns that were mine at that moment. French criticism, although it greeted the play very cordially, often astonished me by speaking of it as a philosophical play. Is there any truth in this?

Caligula, a relatively attractive prince up to then, becomes aware, on the death of Drusilla,

CALIGULA   From *Caligula and Three Other Plays* by Albert Camus, translated by Stuart Gilbert. Copyright © 1958 by Alfred A. Knopf, Inc. Reprinted by permission of the publisher.

[1] *Caligula and Three Other Plays.*

his sister and mistress, that this world is not satisfactory. Thenceforth, obsessed with the impossible and poisoned with scorn and horror, he tries, through murder and the systematic perversion of all values, to practice a liberty that he will eventually discover not to be the right one. He challenges friendship and love, common human solidarity, good and evil. He takes those about him at their word and forces them to be logical; he levels everything around him by the strength of his rejection and the destructive fury to which his passion for life leads him.

But, if his truth is to rebel against fate, his error lies in negating what binds him to mankind. One cannot destroy everything without destroying oneself. This is why Caligula depopulates the world around him and, faithful to his logic, does what is necessary to arm against him those who will eventually kill him. *Caligula* is the story of a superior suicide. It is the story of the most human and most tragic of errors. Unfaithful to mankind through fidelity to himself, Caligula accepts death because he has understood that no one can save himself all alone and that one cannot be free at the expense of others.

Consequently it is a tragedy of the intelligence. Whence the natural conclusion that the drama was intellectual. Personally, I think I am well aware of this work's shortcomings. But I look in vain for philosophy in these four acts. Or, if it exists, it stands on the level of this assertion by the hero: "Men die; and they are not happy." A very modest ideology, as you see, which I have the impression of sharing with Everyman. No, my ambition lay elsewhere. For the dramatist the passion for the impossible is just as valid a subject for study as avarice or adultery. Showing it in all its frenzy, illustrating the havoc it wreaks, bringing out its failure—such was my intention. And the work must be judged thereon.

One word more. Some found my play provocative who nevertheless consider it natural for Œdipus to kill his father and marry his mother and who accept the adulterous triangle if it is placed, to be sure, in the best society. Yet I have little regard for an art that deliberately aims to shock because it is unable to convince. And if I happened, by ill luck, to be scandalous, this would result solely from that immoderate devotion to truth which an artist cannot renounce without giving up his art itself.

· · ·

One word more to tell the reader what he will not find in this book. Although I have the most passionate attachment for the theater, I have the misfortune of liking only one kind of play, whether comic or tragic. After a rather long experience as director, actor, and dramatist, it seems to me that there is no true theater without language and style, nor any dramatic work which does not, like our classical drama and the Greek tragedians, involve human fate in all its simplicity and grandeur. Without claiming to equal them, these are at least the models to set oneself. Psychology, ingenious plot-devices, and spicy situations, though they may amuse me as a member of the audience, leave me indifferent as an author. I am willing to admit that such a conception is debatable. But it seems to me only fair to present myself, in this regard, as I am. Forewarned, the reader may, if he wishes, abstain from reading further. As for those who are not discouraged by such a bias, I am more likely to awaken in them that strange friendship which, over and above frontiers, joins reader and writer and, when it is devoid of misunderstanding, is the writer's royal reward.

(*Translated by* JUSTIN O'BRIEN)

## CHARACTERS IN THE PLAY

| | |
|---|---|
| CALIGULA | LEPIDUS |
| CÆSONIA | INTENDANT |
| HELICON | MEREIA |
| SCIPIO | MUCIUS |
| CHEREA | MUCIUS' WIFE |
| THE OLD PATRICIAN | PATRICIANS, KNIGHTS, |
| METELLUS | POETS, GUARDS, |
| | SERVANTS |

Caligula *was first presented at the Théâtre Hébertot, Paris, in 1945.*

## ACT ONE

*A number of patricians, one a very old man, are gathered in a state room of the imperial palace. They are showing signs of nervousness.*

FIRST PATRICIAN:  Still no news.

THE OLD PATRICIAN:  None last night, none this morning.

SECOND PATRICIAN: Three days without news. Strange indeed!

THE OLD PATRICIAN: Our messengers go out, our messengers return. And always they shake their heads and say: "Nothing."

SECOND PATRICIAN: They've combed the whole countryside. What more can be done?

FIRST PATRICIAN: We can only wait. It's no use meeting trouble halfway. Perhaps he'll return as abruptly as he left us.

THE OLD PATRICIAN: When I saw him leaving the palace, I noticed a queer look in his eyes.

FIRST PATRICIAN: Yes, so did I. In fact I asked him what was amiss.

SECOND PATRICIAN: Did he answer?

FIRST PATRICIAN: One word: "Nothing."

(*A short silence.* HELICON *enters. He is munching onions.*)

SECOND PATRICIAN (*in the same nervous tone*): It's all very perturbing.

FIRST PATRICIAN: Oh, come now! All young fellows are like that.

THE OLD PATRICIAN: You're right there. They take things hard. But time smooths everything out.

SECOND PATRICIAN: Do you really think so?

THE OLD PATRICIAN: Of course. For one girl dead, a dozen living ones.

HELICON: Ah? So you think that there's a girl behind it?

FIRST PATRICIAN: What else should there be? Anyhow—thank goodness!—grief never lasts forever. Is any one of us here capable of mourning a loss for more than a year on end?

SECOND PATRICIAN: Not I, anyhow.

FIRST PATRICIAN: No one can do that.

THE OLD PATRICIAN: Life would be intolerable if one could.

FIRST PATRICIAN: Quite so. Take my case. I lost my wife last year. I shed many tears, and then I forgot. Even now I feel a pang of grief at times. But, happily, it doesn't amount to much.

THE OLD PATRICIAN: Yes, Nature's a great healer.

(CHEREA *enters.*)

FIRST PATRICIAN: Well . . . ?

CHEREA: Still nothing.

HELICON: Come, gentlemen! There's no need for consternation.

FIRST PATRICIAN: I agree.

HELICON: Worrying won't mend matters—and it's lunchtime.

THE OLD PATRICIAN: That's so. We mustn't drop the prey for the shadow.

CHEREA: I don't like the look of things. But all was going too smoothly. As an emperor, he was perfection's self.

SECOND PATRICIAN: Yes, exactly the emperor we wanted; conscientious and inexperienced.

FIRST PATRICIAN: But what's come over you? There's no reason for all these lamentations. We've no ground for assuming he will change. Let's say he loved Drusilla. Only natural; she was his sister. Or say his love for her was something more than brotherly; shocking enough, I grant you. But it's really going too far, setting all Rome in a turmoil because the girl has died.

CHEREA: Maybe. But, as I said, I don't like the look of things; this escapade alarms me.

THE OLD PATRICIAN: Yes, there's never smoke without fire.

FIRST PATRICIAN: In any case, the interests of the State should prevent his making a public tragedy of . . . of, let's say, a regrettable attachment. No doubt such things happen; but the less said the better.

HELICON: How can you be sure Drusilla is the cause of all this trouble?

SECOND PATRICIAN: Who else should it be?

HELICON: Nobody at all, quite likely. When there's a host of explanations to choose from, why pick on the stupidest, most obvious one?

(*Young* SCIPIO *enters.* CHEREA *goes toward him.*)

CHEREA: Well?

SCIPIO: Still nothing. Except that some peasants think they saw him last night not far from Rome, rushing through the storm.

(CHEREA *comes back to the patricians,* SCIPIO *following him.*)

CHEREA: That makes three days, Scipio, doesn't it?

SCIPIO: Yes . . . I was there, following him as I usually do. He went up to Drusilla's body. He stroked it with two fingers, and seemed lost in thought for a long while. Then he swung round and walked out, calmly enough. . . . And ever since we've been hunting for him—in vain.

CHEREA (*shaking his head*): That young man was too fond of literature.

SECOND PATRICIAN: Oh, at his age, you know . . .

CHEREA: At his age, perhaps; but not in his position. An artistic emperor is an anomaly. I grant you we've had one or two; misfits happen in the best of empires. But the others had the good taste to remember they were public servants.

FIRST PATRICIAN:   It made things run more smoothly.

THE OLD PATRICIAN:   One man, one job—that's how it should be.

SCIPIO:   What can we do, Cherea?

CHEREA:   Nothing.

SECOND PATRICIAN:   We can only wait. If he doesn't return, a successor will have to be found. Between ourselves—there's no shortage of candidates.

FIRST PATRICIAN:   No, but there's a shortage of the right sort.

CHEREA:   Suppose he comes back in an ugly mood?

FIRST PATRICIAN:   Oh, he's a mere boy; we'll make him see reason.

CHEREA:   And what if he declines to see it?

FIRST PATRICIAN (*laughing*):   In that case, my friend, don't forget I once wrote a manual of revolutions. You'll find all the rules there.

CHEREA:   I'll look it up—if things come to that. But I'd rather be left to my books.

SCIPIO:   If you'll excuse me. . . . (*Goes out*)

CHEREA:   He's offended.

THE OLD PATRICIAN:   Scipio is young, and young people always hang together.

HELICON:   Scipio doesn't count, anyhow.

(*Enter a member of the imperial bodyguard.*)

THE GUARDSMAN:   Caligula has been seen in the palace gardens.

(*All leave the room. The stage is empty for some moments. Then* CALIGULA *enters stealthily from the left. His legs are caked with mud, his garments dirty; his hair is wet, his look distraught. He brings his hand to his mouth several times. Then he approaches a mirror, stopping abruptly when he catches sight of his reflected self. After muttering some unintelligible words, he sits down on the right, letting his arms hang limp between his knees.* HELICON *enters, left. On seeing* CALIGULA, *he stops at the far end of the stage and contemplates him in silence.* CALIGULA *turns and sees him. A short silence.*)

HELICON (*across the stage*):   Good morning, Caius.

CALIGULA (*in quite an ordinary tone*):   Good morning, Helicon.

(*A short silence*)

HELICON:   You're looking tired.

CALIGULA:   I've walked a lot.

HELICON:   Yes, you've been away for quite a while.

(*Another short silence*)

CALIGULA:   It was hard to find.

HELICON:   What was hard to find?

CALIGULA:   What I was after.

HELICON:   Meaning?

CALIGULA (*in the same matter-of-fact tone*): The moon.

HELICON:   What?

CALIGULA:   Yes, I wanted the moon.

HELICON:   Ah. . . . (*Another silence.* HELICON *approaches* CALIGULA.) And why did you want it?

CALIGULA:   Well . . . it's one of the things I haven't got.

HELICON:   I see. And now—have you fixed it up to your satisfaction?

CALIGULA:   No. I couldn't get it.

HELICON:   Too bad!

CALIGULA:   Yes, and that's why I'm tired. (*Pauses; then*) Helicon!

HELICON:   Yes, Caius?

CALIGULA:   No doubt, you think I'm crazy.

HELICON:   As you know well, I never think.

CALIGULA:   Ah, yes. . . . Now, listen! I'm not mad; in fact I've never felt so lucid. What happened to me is quite simple; I suddenly felt a desire for the impossible. That's all. (*Pauses*) Things as they are, in my opinion, are far from satisfactory.

HELICON:   Many people share your opinion.

CALIGULA:   That is so. But in the past I didn't realize it. *Now* I know. (*Still in the same matter-of-fact tone*) Really, this world of ours, the scheme of things as they call it, is quite intolerable. That's why I want the moon, or happiness, or eternal life—something, in fact, that may sound crazy, but which isn't of this world.

HELICON:   That's sound enough in theory. Only, in practice one can't carry it through to its conclusion.

CALIGULA (*rising to his feet, but still with perfect calmness*):   You're wrong there. It's just because no one *dares* to follow up his ideas to the end that nothing is achieved. All that's needed, I should say, is to be logical right through, at all costs. (*He studies* HELICON's *face.*) I can see, too, what you're thinking. What a fuss over a woman's death! But that's not it. True enough, I seem to remember that a woman died some days ago; a woman whom I loved. But love, what is it? A side issue. And I swear to you her death is not the point; it's no more than the symbol of a truth that makes the moon essential to me. A childishly simple, obvious, almost silly truth, but one that's hard to come by and heavy to endure.

HELICON: May I know what it is, this truth that you've discovered?

CALIGULA (*his eyes averted, in a toneless voice*): Men die; and they are not happy.

HELICON (*after a short pause*): Anyhow, Caligula, it's a truth with which one comes to terms, without much trouble. Only look at the people over there. This truth of yours doesn't prevent them from enjoying their meal.

CALIGULA (*with sudden violence*): All it proves is that I'm surrounded by lies and self-deception. But I've had enough of that; I wish men to live by the light of truth. And I've the power to make them do so. For I know what they need and haven't got. They're without understanding and they need a teacher; someone who knows what he's talking about.

HELICON: Don't take offense, Caius, if I give you a word of advice. . . . But that can wait. First, you should have some rest.

CALIGULA (*Sitting down. His voice is gentle again.*): That's not possible, Helicon. I shall never rest again.

HELICON: But—why?

CALIGULA: If I sleep, who'll give me the moon?

HELICON (*after a short silence*): That's true.

CALIGULA (*rising to his feet again, with an effort*): Listen, Helicon . . . I hear footsteps, voices. Say nothing—and forget you've seen me.

HELICON: I understand.

CALIGULA (*looking back, as he moves toward the door*): And please help me, from now on.

HELICON: I've no reason not to do so, Caius. But I know very few things, and few things interest me. In what way can I help you?

CALIGULA: In the way of . . . the impossible.

HELICON: I'll do my best.

(CALIGULA *goes out.* SCIPIO *and* CÆSONIA *enter hurriedly.*)

SCIPIO: No one! Haven't you seen him?

HELICON: No.

CÆSONIA: Tell me, Helicon. Are you quite sure he didn't say anything to you before he went away?

HELICON: I'm not a sharer of his secrets, I'm his public. A mere onlooker. It's more prudent.

CÆSONIA: Please don't talk like that.

HELICON: My dear Cæsonia, Caius is an idealist as we all know. He follows his bent, and no one can foresee where it will take him. . . . But, if you'll excuse me, I'll go to lunch.

(*Exit* HELICON)

CÆSONIA (*sinking wearily onto a divan*): One of the palace guards saw him go by. But all Rome sees Caligula everywhere. And Caligula, of course, sees nothing but his own idea.

SCIPIO: What idea?

CÆSONIA: How can I tell, Scipio?

SCIPIO: Are you thinking of Drusilla?

CÆSONIA: Perhaps. One thing is sure; he loved her. And it's a cruel thing to have someone die today whom only yesterday you were holding in your arms.

SCIPIO (*timidly*): And you . . . ?

CÆSONIA: Oh, I'm the old, trusted mistress. That's my role.

SCIPIO: Cæsonia, we must save him.

CÆSONIA: So you, too, love him?

SCIPIO: Yes. He's been very good to me. He encouraged me; I shall never forget some of the things he said. He told me life isn't easy, but it has consolations: religion, art, and the love one inspires in others. He often told me that the only mistake one makes in life is to cause others suffering. He tried to be a just man.

CÆSONIA (*rising*): He's only a child. (*She goes to the glass and scans herself.*) The only god I've ever had is my body, and now I shall pray this god of mine to give Caius back to me.

(CALIGULA *enters. On seeing* CÆSONIA *and* SCIPIO *he hesitates, and takes a backward step. At the same moment several men enter from the opposite side of the room: patricians and the* INTENDANT *of the palace. They stop short when they see* CALIGULA. CÆSONIA *turns. She and* SCIPIO *hurry toward* CALIGULA, *who checks them with a gesture.*)

INTENDANT (*in a rather quavering voice*): We . . . we've been looking for you, Cæsar, high and low.

CALIGULA (*in a changed, harsh tone*): So I see.

INTENDANT: We . . . I mean . . .

CALIGULA (*roughly*): What do you want?

INTENDANT: We were feeling anxious, Cæsar.

CALIGULA (*going toward him*): What business had you to feel anxious?

INTENDANT: Well . . . er . . . (*He has an inspiration.*) Well, as you know, there are points to be settled in connection with the Treasury.

CALIGULA (*bursting into laughter*): Ah, yes. The Treasury! That's so. The Treasury's of prime importance.

INTENDANT: Yes, indeed.

CALIGULA (*still laughing, to* CÆSONIA): Don't you agree, my dear? The Treasury is all-important.

CÆSONIA: No, Caligula. It's a secondary matter.

CALIGULA: That only shows your ignorance. We are extremely interested in our Treasury. Everything's important: our fiscal system, public morals, foreign policy, army equipment, and agrarian laws. Everything's of cardinal importance, I assure you. And everything's on an equal footing: the grandeur of Rome and your attacks of arthritis. . . . Well, well, I'm going to apply my mind to all that. And, to begin with . . . Now listen well, Intendant.

INTENDANT: We are listening, sir.

(*The patricians come forward.*)

CALIGULA: You're our loyal subjects, are you not?

INTENDANT (*in a reproachful tone*): Oh, Cæsar . . . !

CALIGULA: Well, I've something to propose to you. We're going to make a complete change in our economic system. In two moves. Drastic and abrupt. I'll explain, Intendant . . . when the patricians have left. (*The patricians go out.* CALIGULA *seats himself beside* CÆSONIA, *with his arm around her waist.*) Now mark my words. The first move's this. Every patrician, everyone in the Empire who has any capital—small or large, it's all the same thing—is ordered to disinherit his children and make a new will leaving his money to the State.

INTENDANT: But Cæsar . . .

CALIGULA: I've not yet given you leave to speak. As the need arises, we shall have these people die; a list will be drawn up by us fixing the order of their deaths. When the fancy takes us, we may modify that order. And, of course, we shall step into their money.

CÆSONIA (*freeing herself*): But—what's come over you?

CALIGULA (*imperturbably*): Obviously the order of their going has no importance. Or, rather, all these executions have an equal impor-

tance—from which it follows that none has any. Really all those fellows are on a par, one's as guilty as another. (*To the* INTENDANT, *peremptorily*) You are to promulgate this edict without a moment's delay and see it's carried out forthwith. The wills are to be signed by residents in Rome this evening; within a month at the latest by persons in the provinces. Send out your messengers.

INTENDANT: Cæsar, I wonder if you realize . . .

CALIGULA: Do I realize . . . ? Now, listen well, you fool! If the Treasury has paramount importance, human life has none. That should be obvious to you. People who think like you are bound to admit the logic of my edict, and since money is the only thing that counts, should set no value on their lives or anyone else's. I have resolved to be logical, and I have the power to enforce my will. Presently you'll see what logic's going to cost you! I shall eliminate contradictions and contradicters. If necessary, I'll begin with you.

INTENDANT: Cæsar, my good will can be relied on, that I swear.

CALIGULA: And mine, too; that I guarantee. Just see how ready I am to adopt your point of view, and give the Treasury the first place in my program. Really you should be grateful to me; I'm playing into your hand, and with your own cards. (*He pauses, before continuing in a flat, unemotional tone.*) In any case there is a touch of genius in the simplicity of my plan—which clinches the matter. I give you three seconds in which to remove yourself. One . . .

(*The* INTENDANT *hurries out.*)

CÆSONIA: I can't believe it's you! But it was just a joke, wasn't it?—all you said to him.

CALIGULA: Not quite that, Cæsonia. Let's say, a lesson in statesmanship.

SCIPIO: But, Caius, it's . . . it's impossible!

CALIGULA: That's the whole point.

SCIPIO: I don't follow.

CALIGULA: I repeat—that is my point. I'm exploiting the impossible. Or, more accurately, it's a question of making the impossible possible.

SCIPIO: But that game may lead to—to anything! It's a lunatic's pastime.

CALIGULA: No, Scipio. An emperor's vocation. (*He lets himself sink back wearily among the cushions.*) Ah, my dears, at last I've come to see the uses of supremacy. It gives impossibilities a run. From this day on, so long as life is mine, my freedom has no frontier.

CÆSONIA (*sadly*): I doubt if this discovery of yours will make us any happier.

CALIGULA: So do I. But, I suppose, we'll have to live it through.

(CHEREA *enters.*)

CHEREA: I have just heard of your return. I trust your health is all it should be.

CALIGULA: My health is duly grateful. (*A pause. Then, abruptly*) Leave us, Cherea. I don't want to see you.

CHEREA: Really, Caius, I'm amazed . . .

CALIGULA: There's nothing to be amazed at. I don't like literary men, and I can't bear lies.

CHEREA: If we lie, it's often without knowing it. I plead Not Guilty.

CALIGULA: Lies are never guiltless. And yours attribute importance to people and to things. That's what I cannot forgive you.

CHEREA: And yet—since this world is the only one we have, why not plead its cause?

CALIGULA: Your pleading comes too late, the verdict's given. . . . This world has no importance; once a man realizes that, he wins his freedom. (*He has risen to his feet.*) And that is why I hate you, you and your kind; because you are not free. You see in me the one free man in the whole Roman Empire. You should be glad to have at last among you an emperor who points the way to freedom. Leave me, Cherea; and you, too, Scipio, go—for what is friendship? Go, both of you, and spread the news in Rome that freedom has been given her at last, and with the gift begins a great probation.

(*They go out.* CALIGULA *has turned away, hiding his eyes.*)

CÆSONIA: Crying?

CALIGULA: Yes, Cæsonia.

CÆSONIA: But, after all, what's changed in your life? You may have loved Drusilla, but you loved many others—myself included—at the same time. Surely that wasn't enough to set you roaming the countryside for three days and nights and bring you back with this . . . this cruel look on your face?

CALIGULA (*swinging round on her*): What nonsense is this? Why drag in Drusilla? Do you imagine love's the only thing that can make a man shed tears?

CÆSONIA: I'm sorry, Caius. Only I was trying to understand.

CALIGULA: Men weep because . . . the world's all wrong. (*She comes toward him.*) No, Cæsonia. (*She draws back.*) But stay beside me.

CÆSONIA: I'll do whatever you wish. (*Sits down*) At my age one knows that life's a sad business. But why deliberately set out to make it worse?

CALIGULA: No, it's no good; you can't understand. But what matter? Perhaps I'll find a way out. Only, I feel a curious stirring within me, as if undreamed of things were forcing their way up into the light—and I'm helpless against them. (*He moves closer to her.*) Oh, Cæsonia, I knew that men felt anguish, but I didn't know what that word anguish meant. Like everyone else I fancied it was a sickness of the mind—no more. But no, it's my body that's in pain. Pain everywhere, in my chest, in my legs and arms. Even my skin is raw, my head is buzzing, I feel like vomiting. But worst of all is this queer taste in my mouth. Not blood, or death, or fever, but a mixture of all three. I've only to stir my tongue, and the world goes black, and everyone looks . . . horrible. How hard, how cruel it is, this process of becoming a man!

CÆSONIA: What you need, my dear, is a good, long sleep. Let yourself relax and, above all stop thinking. I'll stay by you while you sleep. And when you wake, you'll find the world's got back its savor. Then you must use your power to good effect—for loving better what you still find lovable. For the possible, too, deserves to be given a chance.

CALIGULA: Ah but for that I'd need to sleep, to let myself go—and that's impossible.

CÆSONIA: So one always thinks when one is overtired. A time comes when one's hand is firm again.

CALIGULA: But one must know where to place it. And what's the use to me of a firm hand, what use is the amazing power that's mine, if I can't have the sun set in the east, if I can't reduce the sum of suffering and make an end of death? No, Cæsonia, it's all one whether I sleep or keep awake, if I've no power to tamper with the scheme of things.

CÆSONIA: But that's madness, sheer madness. It's wanting to be a god on earth.

CALIGULA: So you, too, think I'm mad. And yet—what is a god that I should wish to be his equal? No, it's something higher, far above the gods, that I'm aiming at, longing for with all my heart and soul. I am taking over a kingdom where the impossible is king.

CÆSONIA: You can't prevent the sky from being the sky, or a fresh young face from aging, or a man's heart from growing cold.

CALIGULA (*with rising excitement*): I want . . . I want to drown the sky in the sea, to infuse ugliness with beauty, to wring a laugh from pain.

CÆSONIA (*facing him with an imploring gesture*): There's good and bad, high and low, justice and injustice. And I swear to you these will never change.

CALIGULA (*in the same tone*): And I'm resolved to change them . . . I shall make this age of ours a kingly gift—the gift of equality. And when all is leveled out, when the impossible has come to earth and the moon is in my hands—then, perhaps, I shall be transfigured and the world renewed; then men will die no more and at last be happy.

CÆSONIA (*with a little cry*): And love? Surely you won't go back on love!

CALIGULA (*in a wild burst of anger*): Love, Cæsonia! (*He grips her shoulders and shakes her.*) I've learned the truth about love; it's nothing, nothing! That fellow was quite right—you heard what he said, didn't you?—it's only the Treasury that counts. The fountainhead of all. Ah, now at last I'm going to live, really *live*. And living, my dear, is the opposite of loving. I know what I'm talking about—and I invite you to the most gorgeous of shows, a sight for gods to gloat on, a whole world called to judgment. But for that I must have a crowd—spectators, victims, criminals, hundreds and thousands of them. (*He rushes to the gong and begins hammering on it, faster and faster.*) Let the accused come forward. I want my criminals, and they all are criminals. (*Still striking the gong*) Bring in the condemned men. I must have my public. Judges, witnesses, accused—all sentenced to death without a hearing. Yes, Cæsonia, I'll show them something they have never seen before, the one free man in the Roman Empire. (*To the clangor of the gong the palace has been gradually filling with noises; the clash of arms, voices, footsteps slow or hurried, coming nearer, growing louder. Some soldiers enter, and leave hastily.*) And you, Cæsonia, shall obey me. You must stand by me to the end. It will be marvelous, you'll see. Swear to stand by me, Cæsonia.

CÆSONIA (*wildly, between two gong strokes*): I needn't swear. You know I love you.

CALIGULA (*in the same tone*): You'll do all I tell you.

CÆSONIA: All, all, Caligula—but do, please, stop. . . .

CALIGULA (*still striking the gong*): You will be cruel.

CÆSONIA (*sobbing*): Cruel.

CALIGULA (*still beating the gong*): Cold and ruthless.

CÆSONIA: Ruthless.

CALIGULA: And you will suffer, too.

CÆSONIA: Yes, yes—oh, no, please . . . I'm—I'm going mad, I think! (*Some patricians enter, followed by members of the palace staff. All look bewildered and perturbed.* CALIGULA *bangs the gong for the last time, raises his mallet, swings round and summons them in a shrill, half-crazy voice.*)

CALIGULA: Come here. All of you. Nearer. Nearer still. (*He is quivering with impatience.*) Your Emperor commands you to come nearer. (*They come forward, pale with terror.*) Quickly. And you, Cæsonia, come beside me. (*He takes her hand, leads her to the mirror, and with a wild sweep of his mallet effaces a reflection on its surface. Then gives a sudden laugh.*) All gone. You see, my dear? An end of memories; no more masks. Nothing, nobody left. Nobody? No, that's not true. Look, Cæsonia. Come here, all of you, and *look* . . .

(*He plants himself in front of the mirror in a grotesque attitude.*)

CÆSONIA (*staring, horrified, at the mirror*): Caligula!

(CALIGULA *lays a finger on the glass. His gaze steadies abruptly and when he speaks his voice has a new, proud ardor.*)

CALIGULA: Yes . . . Caligula.

*Curtain*

## ACT TWO

*Three years later.*

*A room in* CHEREA's *house, where the patricians have met in secret.*

FIRST PATRICIAN: It's outrageous, the way he's treating us.

THE OLD PATRICIAN: He calls me "darling"! In public, mind you—just to make a laughing-stock of me. Death's too good for him.

FIRST PATRICIAN: And fancy making us run beside his litter when he goes into the country.

SECOND PATRICIAN: He says the exercise will do us good.

THE OLD PATRICIAN: Conduct like that is quite inexcusable.

THIRD PATRICIAN: You're right. That's precisely the sort of thing one can't forgive.

FIRST PATRICIAN: He confiscated your property, Patricius. He killed your father, Scipio. He's taken your wife from you, Octavius, and forced her to work in his public brothel. He has killed your son, Lepidus. I ask you, gentlemen, can you endure this? I, anyhow, have made up my mind. I know the risks, but I also know this life of abject fear is quite unbearable. Worse than death, in fact. Yes, as I said, my mind's made up.

SCIPIO: He made my mind up for me when he had my father put to death.

FIRST PATRICIAN: Well? Can you still hesitate?

A KNIGHT: No. We're with you. He's transferred our stalls at the Circus to the public, and egged us on to fight with the rabble—just to have a pretext for punishing us, of course.

THE OLD PATRICIAN: He's a coward.

SECOND PATRICIAN: A bully.

THIRD PATRICIAN: A buffoon.

THE OLD PATRICIAN: He's impotent—that's his trouble, I should say.

(*A scene of wild confusion follows, weapons are brandished, a table is overturned, and there is a general rush toward the door. Just at this moment* CHEREA *strolls in, composed as usual, and checks their onrush.*)

CHEREA: What's all this about? Where are you going?

A PATRICIAN: To the palace.

CHEREA: Ah, yes. And I can guess why. But do you think you'll be allowed to enter?

THE PATRICIAN: There's no question of asking leave.

CHEREA: Lepidus, would you kindly shut that door? (*The door is shut.* CHEREA *goes to the overturned table and seats himself on a corner of it. The others turn toward him.*) It's not so simple as you think, my friends. You're afraid, but fear can't take the place of courage and deliberation. In short, you're acting too hastily.

A KNIGHT: If you're not with us, go. But keep your mouth shut.

CHEREA: I suspect I'm with you. But make no mistake. Not for the same reasons.

A VOICE: That's enough idle talk.

CHEREA (*standing up*): I agree. Let's get down to facts. But, first, let me make myself clear. Though I am *with* you, I'm not *for* you. That, indeed, is why I think you're going about it the wrong way. You haven't taken your enemy's measure; that's obvious, since you attribute petty motives to him. But there's nothing petty about Caligula, and you're riding for a fall. You'd be better placed to fight him if you would try to see him as he really is.

A VOICE: We see him as he is—a crazy tyrant.

CHEREA: No. We've had experience of mad emperors. But this one isn't mad enough. And what I loathe in him is this: that he knows what he wants.

FIRST PATRICIAN: And we, too, know it; he wants to murder us all.

CHEREA: You're wrong. Our deaths are only a side issue. He's putting his power at the service of a loftier, deadlier passion; and it imperils everything we hold most sacred. True, it's not the first time Rome has seen a man wielding unlimited power; but it's the first time he sets no limit to his use of it, and counts mankind, and the world we know, for nothing. That's what appalls me in Caligula; that's what I want to fight. To lose one's life is no great matter; when the time comes I'll have the courage to lose mine. But what's intolerable is to see one's life being drained of meaning, to be told there's no reason for existing. A man can't live without some reason for living.

FIRST PATRICIAN: Revenge is a good reason.

CHEREA: Yes, and I propose to share it with you. But I'd have you know that it's not on your account, or to help you to avenge your petty humiliations. No, if I join forces with you, it's to combat a big idea—an ideal, if you like—whose triumph would mean the end of everything. I can endure your being made a mock of, but I cannot endure Caligula's carrying out his theories to the end. He is converting his philosophy into corpses and—unfortunately for us—it's a philosophy that's logical from start to finish. And where one can't refute, one strikes.

A VOICE: Yes. We must *act*.

CHEREA: We must take action, I agree. But a frontal attack's quite useless when one is fighting an imperial madman in the full flush of his power. You can take arms against a vulgar tyrant, but cunning is needed to fight down disinterested malice. You can only urge it on to follow its bent, and bide your time until its logic founders in sheer lunacy. As you see, I prefer to be quite frank, and I warn you I'll be with you only for a time. Afterward, I shall do nothing to advance your interests; all I wish is to regain some peace of mind in a world that has regained a meaning. What spurs me on is not ambition but fear, my very reasonable fear of that inhuman vision in which my life means no more than a speck of dust.

FIRST PATRICIAN (*approaching him*):  I have an inkling of what you mean, Cherea. Anyhow, the great thing is that you, too, feel that the whole fabric of society is threatened. You, gentlemen, agree with me, I take it, that our ruling motive is of a moral order. Family life is breaking down, men are losing their respect for honest work, a wave of immorality is sweeping the country. Who of us can be deaf to the appeal of our ancestral piety in its hour of danger? Fellow conspirators, will you tolerate a state of things in which patricians are forced to run, like slaves, beside the Emperor's litter?

THE OLD PATRICIAN:  Will you allow them to be addressed as "darling"?

A VOICE:  And have their wives snatched from them?

ANOTHER VOICE:  No!

FIRST PATRICIAN:  Cherea, your advice is good, and you did well to calm our passion. The time is not yet ripe for action; the masses would still be against us. Will you join us in watching for the best moment to strike—and strike hard?

CHEREA:  Yes—and meanwhile let Caligula follow his dream. Or, rather, let's actively encourage him to carry out his wildest plans. Let's put method into his madness. And then, at last, a day will come when he's alone, a lonely man in an empire of the dead and kinsmen of the dead.

(*A general uproar. Trumpet calls outside. Then silence, but for whispers of a name:* "CALIGULA!" CALIGULA *enters with* CÆSONIA, *followed by* HELICON *and some soldiers. Pantomime.* CALIGULA *halts and gazes at the conspirators. Without a word he moves from one to the other, straightens a buckle on one man's shoulder, steps back to contemplate another, sweeps them with his gaze, then draws his hand over his eyes and walks out, still without a word.*)

CÆSONIA (*ironically, pointing to the disorder of the room*):  Were you having a fight?

CHEREA:  Yes, we were fighting.

CÆSONIA (*in the same tone*):  Really? Might I know what you were fighting about?

CHEREA:  About . . . nothing in particular.

CÆSONIA:  Ah? Then it isn't true.

CHEREA:  What isn't true?

CÆSONIA:  You were *not* fighting.

CHEREA:  Have it your own way. We weren't fighting.

CÆSONIA (*smiling*):  Perhaps you'd do better to tidy up the place. Caligula hates untidiness.

HELICON (*to the* OLD PATRICIAN):  You'll end by making him do something out of character.

THE OLD PATRICIAN:  Pardon . . . I don't follow. What have we done to him?

HELICON:  Nothing. Just nothing. It's fantastic being futile to that point; enough to get on anybody's nerves. Try to put yourselves in Caligula's place. (*A short pause*) I see; doing a bit of plotting, weren't you now?

THE OLD PATRICIAN:  Really, that's too absurd. I hope Caligula doesn't imagine . . .

HELICON:  He doesn't imagine. He *knows*. But, I suppose, at bottom, he rather wants it. . . . Well, we'd better set to tidying up.

(*All get busy.* CALIGULA *enters and watches them.*)

CALIGULA (*to the* OLD PATRICIAN):  Good day, darling. (*To the others*) Gentlemen, I'm on my way to an execution. But I thought I'd drop in at your place, Cherea, for a light meal. I've given orders to have food brought here for all of us. But send for your wives first. (*A short silence*) Rufius should thank his stars that I've been seized with hunger. (*Confidentially*) Rufius, I may tell you, is the knight who's going to be executed. (*Another short silence*) What's this? None of you asks me why I've sentenced him to death? (*No one speaks. Meanwhile slaves lay the table and bring food.*) Good for you! I see you're growing quite intelligent. (*He nibbles an olive.*) It has dawned on you that a man needn't have done anything for him to die. (*He stops eating and gazes at his guests with a twinkle in his eye.*) Soldiers, I am proud of you. (*Three or four women enter*) Good! Let's take our places. Anyhow. No order of precedence today. (*All are seated.*) There's no denying it, that fellow Rufius is in luck. But I wonder if he appreciates this short reprieve. A few hours gained on death, why, they're worth their weight in gold! (*He begins eating; the others follow suit. It becomes clear that* CALIGULA's *table manners are deplorable. There is no need for him to flick his olive stones onto his neighbors' plates, or to spit out bits of gristle over the dish, or to pick his teeth with his nails, or to scratch his head furiously. However, he indulges in these practices through-out the meal, without the least compunction. At one moment he stops eating, stares at* LEPIDUS, *one of the guests, and says roughly*) You're look-ing grumpy, Lepidus. I wonder, can it be because I had your son killed?

LEPIDUS (*thickly*):    Certainly not, Caius. Quite the contrary.

CALIGULA (*beaming at him*):    "Quite the con-trary!" It's always nice to see a face that hides the secrets of the heart. Your face is sad. But what about your heart? Quite the contrary—isn't that so, Lepidus?

LEPIDUS (*doggedly*):    Quite the contrary, Cæsar.

CALIGULA (*more and more enjoying the situa-tion*):    Really, Lepidus, there's no one I like better than you. Now let's have a laugh together, my dear friend. Tell me a funny story.

LEPIDUS (*who has overrated his endurance*): Please . . .

CALIGULA:    Good! Very good! Then it's I who'll tell the story. But you'll laugh, won't you, Lepidus? (*With a glint of malice*) If only for the sake of your other son. (*Smiling again*) In any case, as you've just told us, you're not in a bad humor. (*He takes a drink, then says in the tone of a teacher prompting a pupil*) Quite . . . quite the . . .

LEPIDUS (*wearily*):    Quite the contrary, Cæsar.

CALIGULA:    Splendid! (*Drinks again.*) Now lis-ten. (*In a gentle, faraway tone*) Once upon a time there was a poor young emperor whom nobody loved. He loved Lepidus, and to root out of his heart his love for Lepidus, he had his youngest son killed. (*In a brisker tone*) Needless to say, there's not a word of truth in it. Still it's a funny story, eh? But you're not laughing. Nobody's laughing. Now listen! (*In a burst of anger*) I insist on everybody's laughing. You, Lepidus, shall lead the chorus. Stand up, every one of you, and laugh. (*He thumps the table.*) Do you hear what I say? I wish to see you laughing, all of you. (*All rise to their feet. During this scene all the players,* CALIGULA *and* CÆSONIA *excepted, behave like marionettes in a puppet play.* CALIGULA *sinks back on his couch, beaming with delight, and bursts into a fit of laughter.*) Oh, Cæsonia! Just look at them! The game is up; honor, respect-ability, the wisdom of the nations, gone with the wind! The wind of fear has blown them all away. Fear, Cæsonia—don't you agree?—is a noble emotion, pure and simple, self-sufficient, like no other; it draws its patent of nobility straight from the guts. (*He strokes his forehead and drinks again. In a friendly tone*) Well, well, let's change the subject. What have you to say, Cherea? You've been very silent.

CHEREA:    I'm quite ready to speak, Caius. When you give me leave.

CALIGULA:    Excellent. Then—keep silent. I'd rather have a word from our friend Mucius.

MUCIUS (*reluctantly*):    As you will, Caius.

CALIGULA:    Then tell us something about your wife. And begin by sending her to this place, on my right. (MUCIUS' WIFE *seats herself beside* CA-LIGULA.) Well, Mucius? We're waiting.

MUCIUS (*hardly knowing what he says*):    My wife . . . but . . . I'm very fond of her.

(*General laughter*)

CALIGULA:    Why, of course, my friend, of course. But how ordinary of you! So unoriginal! (*He is leaning toward her, tickling her shoulder playfully with his tongue.*) By the way, when I came in just now, you were hatching a plot, weren't you? A nice bloody little plot?

OLD PATRICIAN:    Oh, Caius, how can you . . . ?

CALIGULA:    It doesn't matter in the least, my pet. Old age will be served. I won't take it seri-ously. Not one of you has the spunk for a heroic act. . . . Ah, it's just come to my mind, I have some affairs of state to settle. But, first, let the imperious desires that nature creates in us have their way.

(*He rises and leads* MUCIUS' WIFE *into an ad-joining room.* MUCIUS *starts up from his seat.*)

CÆSONIA (*amiably*):    Please, Mucius. Will you pour me out another glass of this excellent wine. (MUCIUS *complies; his movement of revolt is quelled. Everyone looks embarrassed. Chairs creak noisily. The ensuing conversation is in a strained tone.* CÆSONIA *turns to* CHEREA.) Now, Cherea, suppose you tell me why you people were fighting just now?

CHEREA (*coolly*):    With pleasure, my dear Cæsonia. Our quarrel arose from a discussion whether poetry should be bloodthirsty or not.

CÆSONIA:    An interesting problem. Somewhat beyond my feminine comprehension, of course. Still it surprises me that your passion for art should make you come to blows.

CHEREA (*in the same rather stilted tone*):    That I can well understand. But I remember Caligula's telling me the other day that all true passion has a spice of cruelty.

CÆSONIA (*helping herself from the dish in front of her*): There's truth in that. Don't you agree, gentlemen?

THE OLD PATRICIAN: Ah, yes. Caligula has a rare insight into the secret places of the heart.

FIRST PATRICIAN: And how eloquently he spoke just now of courage!

SECOND PATRICIAN: Really, he should put his ideas into writing. They would be most instructive.

CHEREA: And, what's more, it would keep him busy. It's obvious he needs something to occupy his leisure.

CÆSONIA (*still eating*): You'll be pleased to hear that Caligula shares your views; he's working on a book. Quite a big one, I believe.

(CALIGULA *enters, accompanied by* MUCIUS' WIFE.)

CALIGULA: Mucius, I return your wife, with many thanks. But excuse me, I've some orders to give.

(*He hurries out.* MUCIUS *has gone pale and risen to his feet.*)

CÆSONIA (*to* MUCIUS, *who is standing*): This book of his will certainly rank among our Latin Classics. Are you listening, Mucius?

MUCIUS (*his eyes still fixed on the door by which* CALIGULA *went out*): Yes. And what's the book about, Cæsonia?

CÆSONIA (*indifferently*): Oh, it's above my head, you know.

CHEREA: May we assume it deals with the murderous power of poetry?

CÆSONIA: Yes, something of that sort, I understand.

THE OLD PATRICIAN (*cheerfully*): Well anyhow, as our friend Cherea said, it will keep him busy.

CÆSONIA: Yes, my love. But I'm afraid there's one thing you won't like quite so much about this book, and that's its title.

CHEREA: What is it?

CÆSONIA: *Cold Steel.*

(CALIGULA *hurries in.*)

CALIGULA: Excuse me, but I've some urgent public work in hand. (*To the* INTENDANT) Intendant, you are to close the public granaries. I have signed a decree to that effect; you will find it in my study.

INTENDANT: But, sire . . .

CALIGULA: Famine begins tomorrow.

INTENDANT: But . . . but heaven knows what may happen—perhaps a revolution.

CALIGULA (*firmly and deliberately*): I repeat; famine begins tomorrow. We all know what famine means—a national catastrophe. Well, tomorrow there will be a catastrophe, and I shall end it when I choose. After all, I haven't so many ways of proving I am free. One is always free at someone else's expense. Absurd perhaps, but so it is. (*With a keen glance at* MUCIUS) Apply this principle to your jealousy—and you'll understand better. (*In a meditative tone*) Still, what an ugly thing is jealousy! A disease of vanity and the imagination. One pictures one's wife . . . (MUCIUS *clenches his fists and opens his mouth to speak. Before he can get a word out,* CALIGULA *cuts in.*) Now, gentlemen, let's go on with our meal. . . . Do you know, we've been doing quite a lot of work, with Helicon's assistance? Putting the final touches to a little monograph on execution—about which you will have much to say.

HELICON: Assuming we ask your opinion.

CALIGULA: Why not be generous, Helicon, and let them into our little secrets? Come now, give them a sample. Section Three, first paragraph.

HELICON (*standing, declaims in a droning voice*): "Execution relieves and liberates. It is universal, tonic, just in precept and in practice. A man dies because he is guilty. A man is guilty because he is one of Caligula's subjects. Now all men are Caligula's subjects. *Ergo*, all men are guilty and shall die. It is only a matter of time and patience."

CALIGULA (*laughing*): There's logic for you, don't you agree? That bit about patience was rather neat, wasn't it? Allow me to tell you, that's the quality I most admire in you . . . your patience. Now, gentlemen, you can disperse. Cherea doesn't need your presence any longer. Cæsonia, I wish you to stay. You too, Lepidus. Also our old friend Mereia. I want to have a little talk with you about our National Brothel. It's not functioning too well; in fact, I'm quite concerned about it.

(*The others file out slowly.* CALIGULA *follows* MUCIUS *with his eyes.*)

CHEREA: At your orders, Caius. But what's the trouble? Is the staff unsatisfactory?

CALIGULA: No, but the takings are falling off.

MEREIA: Then you should raise the entrance fee.

CALIGULA: There, Mereia, you missed a golden opportunity of keeping your mouth shut.

You're too old to be interested in the subject, and I don't want your opinion.

MEREIA: Then why ask me to stay?

CALIGULA: Because, presently, I may require some cool, dispassionate advice.

(MEREIA *moves away.*)

CHEREA: If you wish to hear my views on the subject, Caius, I'd say, neither coolly nor dispassionately, that it would be a blunder to raise the scale of charges.

CALIGULA: Obviously. What's needed is a bigger turnover. I've explained my plan of campaign to Cæsonia, and she will tell you all about it. As for me, I've had too much wine, I'm feeling sleepy.

(*He lies down and closes his eyes.*)

CÆSONIA: It's very simple. Caligula is creating a new order of merit.

CHEREA: Sorry, I don't see the connection.

CÆSONIA: No? But there is one. It will be called the Badge of Civic Merit and awarded to those who have patronized Caligula's National Brothel most assiduously.

CHEREA: A brilliant idea!

CÆSONIA: I agree. Oh, I forgot to mention that the badge will be conferred each month, after checking the admission tickets. Any citizen who has not obtained the badge within twelve months will be exiled, or executed.

CHEREA: Why "or executed"?

CÆSONIA: Because Caligula says it doesn't matter which—but it's important he should have the right of choosing.

CHEREA: Bravo! The Public Treasury will wipe out its deficit in no time.

(CALIGULA *has half opened his eyes and is watching old* MEREIA *who, standing in a corner, has produced a small flask and is sipping its contents.*)

CALIGULA (*still lying on the couch*): What's that you're drinking, Mereia?

MEREIA: It's for my asthma, Caius.

CALIGULA (*rises, and thrusting the others aside, goes up to* MEREIA *and sniffs his mouth*): No, it's an antidote.

MEREIA: What an idea, Caius! You must be joking. I have choking fits at night and I've been in the doctor's hands for months.

CALIGULA: So you're afraid of being poisoned?

MEREIA: My asthma . . .

CALIGULA: No. Why beat about the bush? You're afraid I'll poison you. You suspect me. You're keeping an eye on me.

MEREIA: Good heavens, no!

CALIGULA: You suspect me. I'm not to be trusted, eh?

MEREIA: Caius!

CALIGULA (*roughly*): Answer! (*In a cool, judicial tone*) If you take an antidote, it follows that you credit me with the intention of poisoning you. Q.E.D.

MEREIA: Yes . . . I mean . . . no!

CALIGULA: And thinking I intend to poison you, you take steps to frustrate my plan. (*He falls silent. Meanwhile* CÆSONIA *and* CHEREA *have moved away, backstage.* LEPIDUS *is watching the speakers with an air of consternation.*) That makes two crimes, Mereia, and a dilemma from which you can't escape. *Either* I have no wish to cause your death; in which case you are unjustly suspecting me, your emperor. *Or else* I desire your death; in which case, vermin that you are, you're trying to thwart my will. (*Another silence.* CALIGULA *contemplates the old man gloatingly.*) Well, Mereia, what have you to say to my logic?

MEREIA: It . . . it's sound enough, Caius. Only it doesn't apply to the case.

CALIGULA: A third crime. You take me for a fool. Now sit down and listen carefully. (*To* LEPIDUS) Let everyone sit down. (*To* MEREIA) Of these three crimes only one does you honor; the second one—because by crediting me with a certain wish and presuming to oppose it you are deliberately defying me. You are a rebel, a leader of revolt. And that needs courage. (*Sadly*) I've a great liking for you, Mereia. And that is why you'll be condemned for crime number two, and not for either of the others. You shall die nobly, a rebel's death. (*While he talks* MEREIA *is shrinking together on his chair.*) Don't thank me. It's quite natural. Here. (*Holds out a phial. His tone is amiable.*) Drink this poison. (MEREIA *shakes his head. He is sobbing violently.* CALIGULA *shows signs of impatience.*) Don't waste time. Take it. (MEREIA *makes a feeble attempt to escape. But* CALIGULA *with a wild leap is on him, catches him in the center of the stage and after a brief struggle pins him down on a low couch. He forces the phial between his lips and smashes it with a blow of his fist. After some convulsive movements* MEREIA *dies. His face is streaming with blood and tears.* CALIGULA *rises, wipes his hands absent-mindedly, then hands* MEREIA's *flask to* CÆSONIA.) What was it? An antidote?

CÆSONIA (*calmly*):  No, Caligula. A remedy for asthma.

(*A short silence*)

CALIGULA (*gazing down at* MEREIA):  No matter. It all comes to the same thing in the end. A little sooner, a little later. . . . (*He goes out hurriedly, still wiping his hands.*)

LEPIDUS (*in a horrified tone*):  What . . . what shall we do?

CÆSONIA (*cooly*):  Remove that body to begin with, I should say. It's rather a beastly sight.

(CHEREA *and* LEPIDUS *drag the body into the wings.*)

LEPIDUS (*to* CHEREA):  We must act quickly.

CHEREA:  We'll need to be two hundred.

(*Young* SCIPIO *enters. Seeing* CÆSONIA, *he makes as if to leave.*)

CÆSONIA:  Come.

SCIPIO:  What do you want?

CÆSONIA:  Come nearer. (*She pushes up his chin and looks him in the eyes. A short silence. Then, in a calm, unemotional voice*) He killed your father, didn't he?

SCIPIO:  Yes.

CÆSONIA:  Do you hate him?

SCIPIO:  Yes.

CÆSONIA:  And you'd like to kill him?

SCIPIO:  Yes.

CÆSONIA (*withdrawing her hand*):  But—why tell me this?

SCIPIO:  Because I fear nobody. Killing him or being killed—either way out will do. And anyhow you won't betray me.

CÆSONIA:  That's so. I won't betray you. But I want to tell you something—or, rather, I'd like to speak to what is best in you.

SCIPIO:  What's best in me is—my hatred.

CÆSONIA:  Please listen carefully to what I'm going to say. It may sound hard to grasp, but it's as clear as daylight, really. And it's something that would bring about the one real revolution in this world of ours, if people would only take it in.

SCIPIO:  Yes? What is it?

CÆSONIA:  Wait! Try to call up a picture of your father's death, of the agony on his face as they were tearing out his tongue. Think of the blood streaming from his mouth, and recall his screams, like a tortured animal's.

SCIPIO:  Yes.

CÆSONIA:  And now think of Caligula.

SCIPIO (*his voice rough with hatred*):  Yes.

CÆSONIA:  Now listen. *Try to understand him.* (*She goes out, leaving* SCIPIO *gaping after her in bewilderment.* HELICON *enters.*)

HELICON:  Caligula will be here in a moment. Suppose you go for your meal, young poet?

SCIPIO:  Helicon, help me.

HELICON:  Too dangerous, my lamb. And poetry means nothing to me.

SCIPIO:  You can help me. You know . . . so many things.

HELICON:  I know that the days go by—and growing boys should have their meals on time . . . I know, too, that you could kill Caligula . . . and he wouldn't greatly mind it.

(HELICON *goes out.* CALIGULA *enters.*)

CALIGULA:  Ah, it's you, Scipio. (*He pauses. One has the impression that he is somewhat embarrassed.*) It's quite a long time since I saw you last. (*Slowly approaches* SCIPIO) What have you been up to? Writing more poems, I suppose. Might I see your latest composition?

SCIPIO (*likewise ill at ease, torn between hatred and some less defined emotion*):  Yes, Cæsar, I've written some more poems.

CALIGULA:  On what subject?

SCIPIO:  Oh, on nothing in particular. Well, on Nature in a way.

CALIGULA:  A fine theme. And a vast one. And what has Nature done for you?

SCIPIO (*pulling himself together, in a somewhat truculent tone*):  It consoles me for not being Cæsar.

CALIGULA:  Really? And do you think Nature could console me for being Cæsar?

SCIPIO (*in the same tone*):  Why not? Nature has healed worse wounds than that.

CALIGULA (*in a curiously young, unaffected voice*):  Wounds, you said? There was anger in your voice. Because I put your father to death? . . . That word you used—if you only knew how apt it is! My wounds! (*In a different tone*) Well, well, there's nothing like hatred for developing the intelligence.

SCIPIO (*stiffly*):  I answered your question about Nature.

(CALIGULA *sits down, gazes at* SCIPIO, *then brusquely grips his wrists and forces him to stand up. He takes the young man's face between his hands.*)

CALIGULA:  Recite your poem to me, please.

SCIPIO:  No, please, don't ask me that.

CALIGULA:  Why not?

SCIPIO: I haven't got it on me.

CALIGULA: Can't you remember it?

SCIPIO: No.

CALIGULA: Anyhow you can tell me what it's about.

SCIPIO (*still hostile; reluctantly*): I spoke of a . . . a certain harmony . . .

CALIGULA (*breaking in; in a pensive voice*): . . . between one's feet and the earth.

SCIPIO (*looking surprised*): Yes, it's almost that . . . and it tells of the wavy outline of the Roman hills and the sudden thrill of peace that twilight brings to them . . .

CALIGULA: And the cries of swifts winding through the green dusk.

SCIPIO (*yielding more and more to his emotion*): Yes, yes! And that fantastic moment when the sky all flushed with red and gold swings round and shows its other side, spangled with stars.

CALIGULA: And the faint smell of smoke and trees and streams that mingles with the rising mist.

SCIPIO (*in a sort of ecstasy*): Yes, and the chirr of crickets, the coolness veining the warm air, the rumble of carts and the farmers' shouts, dogs barking . . .

CALIGULA: And the roads drowned in shadow winding through the olive groves . . .

SCIPIO: Yes, yes. That's it, exactly. . . . But how did you know?

CALIGULA (*drawing* SCIPIO *to his breast*): I wonder! Perhaps because the same eternal truths appeal to us both.

SCIPIO (*quivering with excitement, burying his head on* CALIGULA's *breast*): Anyhow, what does it matter! All I know is that everything I feel or think of turns to love.

CALIGULA (*stroking his hair*): That, Scipio, is a privilege of noble hearts—and how I wish I could share your . . . your limpidity! But my appetite for life's too keen; Nature can never sate it. You belong to quite another world, and you can't understand. You are single-minded for good; and I am single-minded—for evil.

SCIPIO: I *do* understand.

CALIGULA: No. There's something deep down in me—an abyss of silence, a pool of stagnant water, rotting weeds. (*With an abrupt change of manner*) Your poem sounds very good indeed, but, if you really want my opinion. . . .

SCIPIO (*his head on* CALIGULA's *breast, murmurs*): Yes?

CALIGULA: All that's a bit . . . anemic.

SCIPIO (*recoiling abruptly, as if stung by a serpent, and gazing, horrified, at* CALIGULA, *he cries hoarsely*): Oh, you brute! You loathsome brute! You've fooled me again. I know! You were playing a trick on me, weren't you? And now you're gloating over your success.

CALIGULA (*with a hint of sadness*): There's truth in what you say. I *was* playing a part.

SCIPIO (*in the same indignant tone*): What a foul, black heart you have! And how all that wickedness and hatred must make you suffer!

CALIGULA (*gently*): That's enough.

SCIPIO: How I loathe you! And how I pity you!

CALIGULA (*angrily*): Enough, I tell you.

SCIPIO: And how horrible a loneliness like yours must be!

CALIGULA (*in a rush of anger, gripping the boy by the collar, and shaking him*): Loneliness! What do *you* know of it? Only the loneliness of poets and weaklings. You prate of loneliness, but you don't realize that one is *never* alone. Always we are attended by the same load of the future and the past. Those we have killed are always with us. But *they* are no great trouble. It's those we have loved, those who loved us and whom we did not love; regrets, desires, bitterness and sweetness, whores and gods, the celestial gang! Always, always with us! (*He releases* SCIPIO *and moves back to his former place.*) Alone! Ah, if only in this loneliness, this ghoul-haunted wilderness of mine, I could know, but for a moment, real solitude, real silence, the throbbing stillness of a tree! (*Sitting down, in an access of fatigue*) Solitude? No, Scipio, mine is full of gnashings of teeth, hideous with jarring sounds and voices. And when I am with the women I make mine and darkness falls on us and I think, now my body's had its fill, that I can feel myself my own at last, poised between death and life—ah, then my solitude is fouled by the stale smell of pleasure from the woman sprawling at my side.

(*A long silence.* CALIGULA *seems weary and despondent.* SCIPIO *moves behind him and approaches hesitantly. He slowly stretches out a hand toward him, from behind, and lays it on his shoulder. Without looking round,* CALIGULA *places his hand on* SCIPIO's.)

SCIPIO: All men have a secret solace. It helps

them to endure, and they turn to it when life has wearied them beyond enduring.

CALIGULA:  Yes, Scipio.

SCIPIO:  Have you nothing of the kind in your life, no refuge, no mood that makes the tears well up, no consolation?

CALIGULA:  Yes, I have something of the kind.

SCIPIO:  What is it?

CALIGULA (*very quietly*):  Scorn.

*Curtain*

## ACT THREE

*A room in the imperial palace.*

*Before the curtain rises a rhythmic clash of cymbals and the thudding of a drum have been coming from the stage, and when it goes up we see a curtained-off booth, with a small proscenium in front, such as strolling players use at country fairs. On the little stage are* CÆSONIA *and* HELICON, *flanked by cymbal players. Seated on benches, with their backs to the audience, are some patricians and young* SCIPIO.

HELICON (*in the tone of a showman at a fair*): Walk up! Walk up! (*A clash of cymbals*) Once more the gods have come to earth. They have assumed the human form of our heaven-born emperor, known to men as Caligula. Draw near, mortals of common clay; a holy miracle is taking place before your eyes. By a divine dispensation peculiar to Caligula's hallowed reign, the secrets of the gods will be revealed to you. (*Cymbals*)

CÆSONIA:  Come, gentlemen. Come and adore him—and don't forget to give your alms. Today heaven and its mysteries are on show, at a price to suit every pocket.

HELICON:  For all to see, the secrets of Olympus, revelations in high places, featuring gods in undress, their little plots and pranks. Step this way! The whole truth about your gods! (*Cymbals*)

CÆSONIA:  Adore him, and give your alms. Come near, gentlemen. The show's beginning.

(*Cymbals. Slaves are placing various objects on the platform.*)

HELICON:  An epoch-making reproduction of the life celestial, warranted authentic in every detail. For the first time the pomp and splendor of the gods are presented to the Roman public.

You will relish our novel, breathtaking effects: flashes of lightning (*Slaves light Greek fires.*), peals of thunder (*They roll a barrel filled with stones.*), the divine event on its triumphal way. Now watch with all your eyes.

(*He draws aside the curtain. Grotesquely attired as Venus,* CALIGULA *beams down on them from a pedestal.*)

CALIGULA (*amiably*):  I'm Venus today.

CÆSONIA:  Now for the adoration. Bow down. (*All but* SCIPIO *bend their heads.*) And repeat after me the litany of Venus called Caligula.

"Our Lady of pangs and pleasures . . ."

THE PATRICIANS:  "Our Lady of pangs and pleasures . . ."

CÆSONIA:  "Born of the waves, bitter and bright with seafoam . . ."

THE PATRICIANS:  "Born of the waves, bitter and bright with seafoam . . ."

CÆSONIA:  "O Queen whose gifts are laughter and regrets . . ."

THE PATRICIANS:  "O Queen whose gifts are laughter and regrets . . ."

CÆSONIA:  "Rancors and raptures . . ."

THE PATRICIANS:  "Rancors and raptures . . ."

CÆSONIA:  "Teach us the indifference that kindles love anew . . ."

THE PATRICIANS:  "Teach us the indifference that kindles love anew . . ."

CÆSONIA:  "Make known to us the truth about this world—which is that it has none . . ."

THE PATRICIANS:  "Make known to us the truth about this world—which is that it has none . . ."

CÆSONIA:  "And grant us strength to live up to this verity of verities."

THE PATRICIANS:  "And grant us strength to live up to this verity of verities."

CÆSONIA:  Now, pause.

THE PATRICIANS:  Now, pause.

CÆSONIA (*after a short silence*):  "Bestow your gifts on us, and shed on our faces the light of your impartial cruelty, your wanton hatred; unfold above our eyes your arms laden with flowers and murders . . ."

THE PATRICIANS:  ". . . your arms laden with flowers and murders."

CÆSONIA:  "Welcome your wandering children home, to the bleak sanctuary of your heartless, thankless love. Give us your passions without object, your griefs devoid of reason, your raptures that lead nowhere . . ."

THE PATRICIANS:  ". . . your raptures that lead nowhere . . ."

CÆSONIA (*raising her voice*): "O Queen, so empty yet so ardent, inhuman yet so earthly, make us drunk with the wine of your equivalence, and surfeit us forever in the brackish darkness of your heart."

THE PATRICIANS: "Make us drunk with the wine of your equivalence, and surfeit us forever in the brackish darkness of your heart." (*When the patricians have said the last response, CALIGULA, who until now has been quite motionless, snorts and rises.*)

CALIGULA (*in a stentorian voice*): Granted, my children. Your prayer is heard. (*He squats cross-legged on the pedestal. One by one the patricians make obeisance, deposit their alms, and line up on the right. The last, in his flurry, forgets to make an offering. CALIGULA bounds to his feet.*) Steady! Steady on! Come here, my lad. Worship's very well, but almsgiving is better. Thank you. We are appeased. Ah, if the gods had no wealth other than the love you mortals give them, they'd be as poor as poor Caligula. Now, gentlemen, you may go, and spread abroad the glad tidings of the miracle you've been allowed to witness. You have seen Venus, seen her godhead with your fleshly eyes, and Venus herself has spoken to you. Go, most favored gentlemen. (*The patricians begin to move away.*) Just a moment. When you leave, mind you take the exit on your left. I have posted sentries in the others, with orders to kill you.

(*The patricians file out hastily, in some disorder. The slaves and musicians leave the stage.*)

HELICON (*pointing a threatening finger at* SCIPIO): Naughty boy, you've been playing the anarchist again.

SCIPIO (*to* CALIGULA): You spoke blasphemy, Caius.

CALIGULA: Blasphemy? What's that?

SCIPIO: You're befouling heaven, after bloodying the earth.

HELICON: How this youngster loves big words! (*He stretches himself on a couch*)

CÆSONIA (*composedly*): You should watch your tongue, my lad. At this moment men are dying in Rome for saying much less.

SCIPIO: Maybe—but I've resolved to tell Caligula the truth.

CÆSONIA: Listen to him, Caligula! That was the one thing missing in your Empire—a bold young moralist.

CALIGULA (*giving* SCIPIO *a curious glance*): Do you really believe in the gods, Scipio?

SCIPIO: No.

CALIGULA: Then I fail to follow. If you don't believe, why be so keen to scent out blasphemy?

SCIPIO: One may deny something without feeling called on to besmirch it, or deprive others of the right of believing in it.

CALIGULA: But that's humility, the real thing, unless I'm much mistaken. Ah, my dear Scipio, how glad I am on your behalf—and a trifle envious, too. Humility's the one emotion I may never feel.

SCIPIO: It's not I you're envious of; it's the gods.

CALIGULA: If you don't mind, that will remain our secret—the great enigma of our reign. Really, you know, there's only one thing for which I might be blamed today—and that's this small advance I've made upon the path of freedom. For someone who loves power the rivalry of the gods is rather irksome. Well, I've proved to these imaginary gods that any man, without previous training, if he applies his mind to it, can play their absurd parts to perfection.

SCIPIO: That, Caius, is what I meant by blasphemy.

CALIGULA: No, Scipio, it's clear-sightedness. I've merely realized that there's only one way of getting even with the gods. All that's needed is to be as cruel as they.

SCIPIO: All that's needed is to play the tyrant.

CALIGULA: Tell me, my young friend. What exactly *is* a tyrant?

SCIPIO: A blind soul.

CALIGULA: That's a moot point. I should say the real tyrant is a man who sacrifices a whole nation to his ideal or his ambition. But I have no ideal, and there's nothing left for me to covet by way of power or glory. If I use this power of mine, it's to compensate.

SCIPIO: For what?

CALIGULA: For the hatred and stupidity of the gods.

SCIPIO: Hatred does not compensate for hatred. Power is no solution. Personally I know only one way of countering the hostility of the world we live in.

CALIGULA: Yes? And what is it?

SCIPIO: Poverty.

CALIGULA (*bending over his feet and scrutinizing his toes*): I must try that, too.

SCIPIO: Meanwhile many men round you are dying.

CALIGULA: Oh, come! Not so many as all that.

Do you know how many wars I've refused to embark on?

SCIPIO:  No.

CALIGULA:  Three. And do you know why I refused?

SCIPIO:  Because the grandeur of Rome means nothing to you.

CALIGULA:  No. Because I respect human life.

SCIPIO:  You're joking, Caius.

CALIGULA:  Or, anyhow, I respect it more than I respect military triumphs. But it's a fact that I don't respect it more than I respect my own life. And if I find killing easy, it's because dying isn't hard for me. No, the more I think about it, the surer I feel that I'm no tyrant.

SCIPIO:  What does it matter, if it costs us quite as dear as if you were one?

CALIGULA (with a hint of petulance):  If you had the least head for figures you'd know that the smallest war a tyrant—however levelheaded he might be—indulged in would cost you a thousand times more than all my vagaries (shall we call them?) put together.

SCIPIO:  Possibly. But at least there'd be some sense behind a war; it would be understandable—and to understand makes up for much.

CALIGULA:  There's no understanding fate; therefore I choose to play the part of fate. I wear the foolish, unintelligible face of a professional god. And that is what the men who were here with you have learned to adore.

SCIPIO:  That, too, Caius, is blasphemy.

CALIGULA:  No, Scipio, it's dramatic art. The great mistake you people make is not to take the drama seriously enough. If you did, you'd know that any man can play lead in the divine comedy and become a god. All he needs do is to harden his heart.

SCIPIO:  You may be right, Caius. But I rather think you've done everything that was needed to rouse up against you a legion of human gods, ruthless as yourself, who will drown in blood your godhead of a day.

CÆSONIA:  Really, Scipio!

CALIGULA (peremptorily):  No, don't stop him, Cæsonia. Yes, Scipio, you spoke truer than you knew; I've done everything needed to that end. I find it hard to picture the event you speak of—but I sometimes dream it. And in all those faces surging up out of the angry darkness, convulsed with fear and hatred, I see, and I rejoice

to see, the only god I've worshipped on this earth; foul and craven as the human heart. (Irritably) Now go. I've had enough of you, more than enough. (In a different tone) I really must attend to my toenails; they're not nearly red enough, and I've no time to waste. (All go, with the exception of HELICON. He hovers round CALIGULA, who is busy examining his toes.) Helicon!

HELICON:  Yes?

CALIGULA:  Getting on with your task?

HELICON:  What task?

CALIGULA:  You know . . . the moon.

HELICON:  Ah yes, the moon. . . . It's a matter of time and patience. But I'd like to have a word with you.

CALIGULA:  I might have patience; only I have not much time. So you must make haste.

HELICON:  I said I'd do my utmost. But, first, I have something to tell you. Very serious news.

CALIGULA (as if he has not heard):  Mind you, I've had her already.

HELICON:  Whom?

CALIGULA:  The moon.

HELICON:  Yes, yes. . . . Now listen, please. Do you know there's a plot being hatched against your life?

CALIGULA:  What's more, I had her thoroughly. Only two or three times, to be sure. Still, I had her all right.

HELICON:  For the last hour I've been trying to tell you about it, only—

CALIGULA:  It was last summer. I'd been gazing at her so long, and stroking her so often on the marble pillars in the gardens that evidently she'd come to understand.

HELICON:  Please stop trifling, Caius. Even if you refuse to listen, it's my duty to tell you this. And if you shut your ears, it can't be helped.

CALIGULA (applying red polish to his toenails):  This varnish is no good at all. But, to come back to the moon—it was a cloudless August night. (HELICON looks sulkily away, and keeps silence.) She was coy, to begin with. I'd gone to bed. First she was blood-red, low on the horizon. Then she began rising, quicker and quicker, growing brighter and brighter all the while. And the higher she climbed, the paler she grew, till she was like a milky pool in a dark wood rustling with stars. Slowly, shyly, she approached, through the warm night air, soft, light as gossamer, naked in beauty. She crossed the threshold of my room, glided to my bed, poured herself into it, and flooded me with her smiles and sheen. . . . No, really this new varnish is a failure. . . . So you see, Helicon, I can say, without boasting, that I've had her.

HELICON: Now will you listen, and learn the danger that's threatening you?

CALIGULA (*ceasing to fiddle with his toes, and gazing at him fixedly*): All I want, Helicon, is—the moon. For the rest, I've always known what will kill me. I haven't yet exhausted all that is to keep me living. That's why I want the moon. And you must not return till you have secured her for me.

HELICON: Very well. . . . Now I'll do my duty and tell you what I've learned. There's a plot against you. Cherea is the ringleader. I came across this tablet which tells you all you need to know. See, I put it here. (*He places the tablet on one of the seats and moves away.*)

CALIGULA: Where are you off to, Helicon?

HELICON (*from the threshold*): To get the moon for you.

(*There is a mouselike scratching at the opposite door.* CALIGULA *swings round and sees the* OLD PATRICIAN.)

THE OLD PATRICIAN (*timidly*): May I, Caius . . .

CALIGULA (*impatiently*): Come in! Come in! (*Gazes at him.*) So, my pet, you've returned to have another look at Venus.

THE OLD PATRICIAN: Well . . . no. It's not quite that. Ssh! Oh, sorry, Caius! I only wanted to say . . . You know I'm very, very devoted to you—and my one desire is to end my days in peace.

CALIGULA: Be quick, man. Get it out!

THE OLD PATRICIAN: Well, it's . . . it's like this. (*Hurriedly*) It's terribly serious, that's what I meant to say.

CALIGULA: No, it isn't serious.

THE OLD PATRICIAN: But—I don't follow. *What* isn't serious?

CALIGULA: But what are we talking about, my love?

THE OLD PATRICIAN (*Glancing nervously round the room*): I mean to say . . . (*Wriggles, shuffles, then bursts out with it*) There's a plot afoot, against you.

CALIGULA: There! You see. Just as I said; it isn't serious.

THE OLD PATRICIAN: But, Caius, they mean to kill you.

CALIGULA (*approaching him and grasping his shoulders*): Do you know why I can't believe you?

THE OLD PATRICIAN (*raising an arm, as if to take an oath*): The gods bear witness, Caius, that . . .

CALIGULA (*gently but firmly pressing him back toward the door*): Don't swear. I particularly ask you not to swear. Listen, instead. Suppose it were true, what you are telling me—I'd have to assume you were betraying your friends, isn't that so?

THE OLD PATRICIAN (*flustered*): Well, Caius, considering the deep affection I have for you . . .

CALIGULA (*in the same tone as before*): And I cannot assume *that*. I've always loathed baseness of that sort so profoundly that I could never restrain myself from having a betrayer put to death. But I know the man you are, my worthy friend. And I'm convinced you neither wish to play the traitor nor to die.

THE OLD PATRICIAN: Certainly not, Caius. Most certainly not.

CALIGULA: So you see I was right in refusing to believe you. You wouldn't stoop to baseness, would you?

THE OLD PATRICIAN: Oh, no, indeed!

CALIGULA: Nor betray your friends?

THE OLD PATRICIAN: I need hardly tell you that, Caius.

CALIGULA. Therefore it follows that there isn't any plot. It was just a joke—between ourselves, rather a silly joke—what you've just been telling me, eh?

THE OLD PATRICIAN (*feebly*): Yes, yes. A joke, merely a joke.

CALIGULA: Good. So now we know where we are. Nobody wants to kill me.

THE OLD PATRICIAN: Nobody. That's it. Nobody at all.

CALIGULA (*drawing a deep breath; in measured tones*): Then—leave me, sweetheart. A man of honor is an animal so rare in the present-day world that I couldn't bear the sight of one too long. I must be left alone to relish this unique experience. (*For some moments he gazes, without moving, at the tablet. He picks it up and reads it. Then, again, draws a deep breath. Then summons a palace guard.*)

CALIGULA: Bring Cherea to me. (*The man starts to leave.*) Wait! (*The man halts.*) Treat him politely. (*The man goes out.* CALIGULA *falls to pacing the room. After a while he approaches the mirror.*) You decided to be logical, didn't you, poor simpleton? Logic for ever! The question now is: Where will that take you? (*Ironically*) Suppose the moon were brought here, everything would be different. That was the idea, wasn't it? Then the impossible would become possible, in a flash the Great Change come, and all things be transfigured. After all, why shouldn't Helicon bring it off? One night, perhaps, he'll catch her sleeping in a lake, and carry her here, trapped in a glistening net, all slimy with weeds and water, like a pale bloated fish drawn from the depths. Why not, Caligula? Why not, indeed? (*He casts a glance round the room.*) Fewer and fewer people round me; I wonder why. (*Addressing the mirror, in a muffled voice*) Too many dead, too many dead—that makes an emptiness. . . . No, even if the moon were mine, I could not retrace my way. Even were those dead men thrilling again under the sun's caress, the murders wouldn't go back underground for that. (*Angrily*) Logic, Caligula; follow where logic leads. Power to the uttermost; wilfulness without end. Ah, I'm the only man on earth to know the secret—that power can never be complete without a total self-surrender to the dark impulse of one's destiny. No, there's no return. I must go on and on, until the consummation.

(CHEREA *enters.* CALIGULA *is slumped in his chair, the cloak drawn tightly round him.*)

CHEREA:  You sent for me, Caius?

CALIGULA (*languidly*):  Yes, Cherea.

(*A short silence*)

CHEREA:  Have you anything particular to tell me?

CALIGULA:  No, Cherea.

(*Another silence*)

CHEREA (*with a hint of petulance*):  Are you sure you really need my presence?

CALIGULA:  Absolutely sure, Cherea. (*Another silence. Then, as if suddenly recollecting himself*) I'm sorry for seeming so inhospitable. I was following up my thoughts, and—Now do sit down, we'll have a friendly little chat. I'm in a mood for some intelligent conversation. (CHEREA *sits down. For the first time since the play began,* CALIGULA *gives the impression of being his natural self.*) Do you think, Cherea, that it's possible for two men of much the same temperament and equal pride to talk to each other with complete frankness—if only once in their lives? Can they

strip themselves naked, so to speak, and shed their prejudices, their private interests, the lies by which they live?

CHEREA:  Yes, Caius, I think it possible. But I don't think you'd be capable of it.

CALIGULA:  You're right. I only wished to know if you agreed with me. So let's wear our masks, and muster up our lies. And we'll talk as fencers fight, padded on all the vital parts. Tell me, Cherea, why don't you like me?

CHEREA:  Because there's nothing likeable about you, Caius. Because such feelings can't be had to order. And because I understand you far too well. One cannot like an aspect of oneself which one always tries to keep concealed.

CALIGULA:  But why is it you hate me?

CHEREA:  There, Caius, you're mistaken. I do not hate you. I regard you as noxious and cruel, vain and selfish. But I cannot hate you, because I don't think you are happy. And I cannot scorn you, because I know you are no coward.

CALIGULA:  Then why wish to kill me?

CHEREA:  I've told you why; because I regard you as noxious, a constant menace. I like, and need, to feel secure. So do most men. They resent living in a world where the most preposterous fancy may at any moment become a reality, and the absurd transfix their lives, like a dagger in the heart. I feel as they do; I refuse to live in a topsy-turvy world. I want to know where I stand, and to stand secure.

CALIGULA:  Security and logic don't go together.

CHEREA:  Quite true. My plan of life may not be logical, but at least it's sound.

CALIGULA:  Go on.

CHEREA:  There's no more to say. I'll be no party to your logic. I've a very different notion of my duties as a man. And I know that the majority of your subjects share my view. You outrage their deepest feelings. It's only natural that you should . . . disappear.

CALIGULA:  I see your point, and it's legitimate enough. For most men, I grant you, it's obvious. But *you*, I should have thought, would have known better. You're an intelligent man, and given intelligence, one has a choice: either to pay its price or to disown it. Why do you shirk the issue and neither disown it nor consent to pay its price?

CHEREA:  Because what I want is to live, and to be happy. Neither, to my mind, is possible if one pushes the absurd to its logical conclusions. As you see, I'm quite an ordinary sort of man. True, there are moments when, to feel free of them, I desire the death of those I love, or I hanker after women from whom the ties of family or friendship debar me. Were logic everything, I'd kill or fornicate on such occasions. But I consider that these passing fancies have no great importance. If everyone set to gratifying them, the world would be impossible to live in, and happiness, too, would go by the board. And these, I repeat, are the things that count, for me.

CALIGULA: So, I take it, you believe in some higher principle?

CHEREA: Certainly I believe that some actions are—shall I say?—more praiseworthy than others.

CALIGULA: And *I* believe that all are on an equal footing.

CHEREA: I know it, Caius, and that's why I don't hate you. I understand, and, to a point, agree with you. But you're pernicious, and you've got to go.

CALIGULA: True enough. But why risk your life by telling me this?

CHEREA: Because others will take my place, and because I don't like lying.

(*A short silence*)

CALIGULA: Cherea!

CHEREA: Yes, Caius?

CALIGULA: Do you think that two men of similar temperament and equal pride can, if only once in their lives, open their hearts to each other?

CHEREA: That, I believe, is what we've just been doing.

CALIGULA: Yes, Cherea. But you thought I was incapable of it.

CHEREA: I was wrong, Caius. I admit it, and I thank you. Now I await your sentence.

CALIGULA: My sentence? Ah, I see. (*Producing the tablet from under his cloak*) You know what this is, Cherea?

CHEREA: I knew you had it.

CALIGULA (*passionately*): You knew I had it! So your frankness was all a piece of play acting. The two friends did *not* open their hearts to each other. Well, well! It's no great matter. Now we can stop playing at sincerity, and resume life on the old footing. But first I'll ask you to make just one more effort; to bear with my caprices and my tactlessness a little longer. Listen well,

Cherea. This tablet is the one and only piece of evidence against you.

CHEREA: Caius, I'd rather go. I'm sick and tired of all these antics. I know them only too well, and I've had enough. Let me go, please.

CALIGULA (*in the same tense, passionate voice*): No, stay. This tablet is the only evidence. Is that clear?

CHEREA: Evidence? I never knew you needed evidence to send a man to his death.

CALIGULA: That's true. Still, for once I wish to contradict myself. Nobody can object to that. It's so pleasant to contradict oneself occasionally; so restful. And I need rest, Cherea.

CHEREA: I don't follow . . . and, frankly, I've no taste for these subtleties.

CALIGULA: I know, Cherea, I know. You're not like me; you're an ordinary man, sound in mind and body. And naturally you've no desire for the extraordinary. (*With a burst of laughter*) You want to live and to be happy. That's all!

CHEREA: I think, Caius, we'd better leave it at that. . . . Can I go?

CALIGULA: Not yet. A little patience, if you don't mind—I shall not keep you long. You see this thing—this piece of evidence? I choose to assume that I can't sentence you to death without it. That's my idea . . . and my repose. Well! See what becomes of evidence in an emperor's hands. (*He holds the tablet to a torch.* CHEREA *approaches. The torch is between them. The tablet begins to melt.*) You see, conspirator! The tablet's melting, and as it melts a look of innocence is dawning on your face. What a handsome forehead you have, Cherea! And how rare, how beautiful a sight is an innocent man! Admire my power. Even the gods cannot restore innocence without first punishing the culprit. But your emperor needs only a torch flame to absolve you and give you a new lease of hope. So carry on, Cherea; follow out the noble precepts we've been hearing, wherever they may take you. Meanwhile your emperor awaits his repose. It's his way of living and being happy.

(CHEREA *stares, dumfounded, at* CALIGULA. *He makes a vague gesture, seems to understand, opens his mouth to speak—and walks abruptly away. Smiling, holding the tablet to the flame,* CALIGULA *follows the receding figure with his gaze.*)

*Curtain*

## ACT FOUR

*A room in the imperial palace.*

*The stage is in semidarkness.* CHEREA *and* SCIPIO *enter.* CHEREA *crosses to the right, then comes back left to* SCIPIO.

SCIPIO (*sulkily*):  What do you want of me?

CHEREA:  There's no time to lose. And we must know our minds, we must be resolute.

SCIPIO:  Who says I'm not resolute?

CHEREA:  You didn't attend our meeting yesterday.

SCIPIO (*looking away*):  That's so, Cherea.

CHEREA:  Scipio, I am older than you, and I'm not in the habit of asking others' help. But, I won't deny it, I need you now. This murder needs honorable men to sponsor it. Among all these wounded vanities and sordid fears, our motives only, yours and mine, are disinterested. Of course I know that, if you leave us, we can count on your silence. But that is not the point. What I want is—for you to stay with us.

SCIPIO:  I understand. But I can't, oh, no, I *cannot* do as you wish.

CHEREA:  So you are with him?

SCIPIO:  No. But I cannot be against him. (*Pauses. Then in a muffled voice*) Even if I killed him, my heart would still be with him.

CHEREA:  And yet—he killed your father!

SCIPIO:  Yes—and that's how it all began. But that, too, is how it ends.

CHEREA:  He denies what you believe in. He tramples on all that you hold sacred.

SCIPIO:  I know, Cherea. And yet something inside me is akin to him. The same fire burns in both our hearts.

CHEREA:  There are times when a man must make his choice. As for me, I have silenced in my heart all that might be akin to him.

SCIPIO:  But—*I*—I cannot make a choice. I have my own sorrow, but I suffer with him, too; I share his pain. I understand all—that is my trouble.

CHEREA:  So that's it. You have chosen to take his side.

SCIPIO (*passionately*):  No, Cherea. I beg you, don't think that. I can never, never again take anybody's side.

CHEREA (*affectionately; approaching* SCIPIO):

Do you know, I hate him even more for having made of you—what he has made.

SCIPIO:  Yes, he has taught me to expect everything of life.

CHEREA:  No, he has taught you despair. And to have instilled despair into a young heart is fouler than the foulest of the crimes he has committed up to now. I assure you, *that* alone would justify me in killing him out of hand.

(*He goes toward the door.* HELICON *enters.*)

HELICON:  I've been hunting for you high and low, Cherea. Caligula's giving a little party here, for his personal friends only. Naturally he expects you to attend it. (*To* SCIPIO) You, my boy, aren't wanted. Off you go!

SCIPIO (*looking back at* CHEREA *as he goes out*):  Cherea.

CHEREA (*gently*):  Yes, Scipio?

SCIPIO:  Try to understand.

CHEREA (*in the same gentle tone*):  No, Scipio.

(SCIPIO *and* HELICON *go out. A clash of arms in the wings. Two soldiers enter at right, escorting the* OLD PATRICIAN *and the* FIRST PATRICIAN, *who show signs of alarm.*)

FIRST PATRICIAN (*to one of the soldiers, in a tone which he vainly tries to steady*):  But . . . but what *can* he want with us at this hour of the night?

SOLDIER:  Sit there. (*Points to the chairs on the right.*)

FIRST PATRICIAN:  If it's only to have us killed—like so many others—why all these preliminaries?

SOLDIER:  Sit down, you old mule.

THE OLD PATRICIAN:  Better do as he says. It's clear he doesn't know anything.

SOLDIER:  Yes, darling, quite clear. (*Goes out*)

FIRST PATRICIAN:  We should have acted sooner; I always said so. Now we're in for the torture chamber.

(*The* SOLDIER *comes back with* CHEREA, *then goes out.*)

CHEREA (*Seating himself. He shows no sign of apprehension.*):  Any idea what's happening?

FIRST PATRICIAN AND THE OLD PATRICIAN (*speaking together*):  He's found out about the conspiracy.

CHEREA:  Yes? And then?

THE OLD PATRICIAN (*shuddering*):  The torture chamber for us all.

CHEREA (*still unperturbed*):  I remember that

Caligula once gave eighty-one thousand sesterces to a slave who, though he was tortured nearly to death, wouldn't confess to a theft he had committed.

FIRST PATRICIAN: A lot of consolation that is—for us!

CHEREA: Anyhow, it shows that he appreciates courage. You ought to keep that in mind. (*To the* OLD PATRICIAN) Would you very much mind not chattering with your teeth? It's a noise I particularly dislike.

THE OLD PATRICIAN: I'm sorry, but—

FIRST PATRICIAN: Enough trifling! Our lives are at stake.

CHEREA (*coolly*): Do you know Caligula's favorite remark?

THE OLD PATRICIAN (*on the verge of tears*): Yes. He says to the executioner: "Kill him slowly, so that he feels what dying's like!"

CHEREA: No, there's a better one. After an execution he yawns, and says quite seriously: "What I admire most is my imperturbability."

FIRST PATRICIAN: Do you hear . . . ?

(*A clanking of weapons is heard off stage.*)

CHEREA: That remark betrays a weakness in his make-up.

THE OLD PATRICIAN: Would you be kind enough to stop philosophizing? It's something I particularly dislike.

(*A slave enters and deposits a sheaf of knives on a seat.*)

CHEREA (*who has not noticed him*): Still, there's no denying it's remarkable, the effect this man has on all with whom he comes in contact. He forces one to think. There's nothing like insecurity for stimulating the brain. That, of course, is why he's so much hated.

THE OLD PATRICIAN (*pointing a trembling finger*): Look!

CHEREA (*noticing the knives, in a slightly altered tone*): Perhaps you were right.

FIRST PATRICIAN: Yes, waiting was a mistake. We should have acted at once.

CHEREA: I agree. Wisdom's come too late.

THE OLD PATRICIAN: But it's . . . it's crazy. I don't want to die.

(*He rises and begins to edge away. Two soldiers appear, and, after slapping his face, force him back onto his seat. The* FIRST PATRICIAN *squirms in his chair.* CHEREA *utters some inaudible words. Suddenly a queer music begins behind the curtain at the back of the stage; a thrumming and tinkling of zithers and cymbals. The patricians gaze at each other in silence. Outlined on the illuminated curtain, in shadow play,* CALIGULA *appears, makes some grotesque dance movements, and retreats from view. He is wearing ballet dancer's skirts and his head is garlanded with flowers. A moment later a* SOLDIER *announces gravely:* "Gentlemen, the performance is over." *Meanwhile* CÆSONIA *has entered soundlessly behind the watching patricians. She speaks in an ordinary voice, but none the less they give a start on hearing it.*)

CÆSONIA: Caligula has instructed me to tell you that, whereas in the past he always summoned you for affairs of state, today he invited you to share with him an artistic emotion. (*A short pause. Then she continues in the same tone.*) He added, I may say, that anyone who has not shared in it will be beheaded. (*They keep silent.*) I apologize for insisting, but I must ask you if you found that dance beautiful.

FIRST PATRICIAN (*after a brief hesitation*): Yes, Cæsonia. It was beautiful.

THE OLD PATRICIAN (*effusively*): Lovely! Lovely!

CÆSONIA: And you, Cherea?

CHEREA (*icily*): It was . . . very high art.

CÆSONIA: Good. Now I can describe your artistic emotions to Caligula. (CÆSONIA *goes out.*)

CHEREA: And now we must act quickly. You two stay here. Before the night is out there'll be a hundred of us. (*He goes out.*)

THE OLD PATRICIAN: No, no. *You* stay. Let me go, instead. (*Sniffs the air*) It smells of death here.

FIRST PATRICIAN: And of lies. (*Sadly*) I said that dance was beautiful!

THE OLD PATRICIAN (*conciliatingly*): And so it was, in a way. Most original.

(*Some patricians and knights enter hurriedly.*)

SECOND PATRICIAN: What's afoot? Do you know anything? The Emperor's summoned us here.

THE OLD PATRICIAN (*absent-mindedly*): For the dance, maybe.

SECOND PATRICIAN: What dance?

THE OLD PATRICIAN: Well, I mean . . . er . . . the artistic emotion.

THIRD PATRICIAN: I've been told Caligula's very ill.

FIRST PATRICIAN: He's a sick man, yes . . .

THIRD PATRICIAN:    What's he suffering from? (*In a joyful tone*) By God, is he going to die?

FIRST PATRICIAN:    I doubt it. His disease is fatal—to others only.

THE OLD PATRICIAN:    That's one way of putting it.

SECOND PATRICIAN:    Quite so. But hasn't he some other disease less serious, and more to our advantage?

FIRST PATRICIAN:    No. That malady of his excludes all others.

(*He goes out.* CÆSONIA *enters. A short silence*)

CÆSONIA (*in a casual tone*):    If you want to know, Caligula has stomach trouble. Just now he vomited blood.

(*The patricians crowd round her.*)

SECOND PATRICIAN:    O mighty gods, I vow, if he recovers, to pay the Treasury two hundred thousand sesterces as a token of my joy.

THIRD PATRICIAN (*with exaggerated eagerness*):    O Jupiter, take my life in place of his!

(CALIGULA *has entered, and is listening.*)

CALIGULA (*going up to the* SECOND PATRICIAN): I accept your offer, Lucius. And I thank you. My Treasurer will call on you tomorrow. (*Goes to the* THIRD PATRICIAN *and embraces him.*) You can't imagine how touched I am. (*A short silence. Then, tenderly*) So you love me, Cassius, as much as that?

THIRD PATRICIAN (*emotionally*):    Oh, Cæsar, there's nothing, nothing I wouldn't sacrifice for your sake.

CALIGULA (*embracing him again*):    Ah, Cassius, this is really too much; I don't deserve all this love. (CASSIUS *makes a protesting gesture.*) No, no, really I don't! I'm not worthy of it. (*He beckons to two soldiers.*) Take him away. (*Gently, to* CASSIUS) Go, dear friend, and remember that Caligula has lost his heart to you.

THIRD PATRICIAN (*vaguely uneasy*):    But— where are they taking me?

CALIGULA:    Why, to your death, of course. Your generous offer was accepted, and I feel better already. Even that nasty taste of blood in my mouth has gone. You've cured me, Cassius. It's been miraculous, and how proud you must feel of having worked the miracle by laying your life down for your friend—especially when that friend's none other than Caligula! So now you see me quite myself again, and ready for a festive night.

THIRD PATRICIAN (*shrieking, as he is dragged away*):    No! No! I don't want to die. You can't be serious!

CALIGULA (*in a thoughtful voice, between the shrieks*):    Soon the sea roads will be golden with mimosas. The women will wear their lightest dresses. And the sky! Ah, Cassius, what a blaze of clean, swift sunshine! The smiles of life. (CASSIUS *is near the door.* CALIGULA *gives him a gentle push. Suddenly his tone grows serious.*) Life, my friend, is something to be cherished. Had you cherished it enough, you wouldn't have gambled it away so rashly. (CASSIUS *is led off.* CALIGULA *returns to the table.*) The loser must pay. There's no alternative. (*A short silence*) Come, Cæsonia. (*He turns to the others.*) By the way, an idea has just waylaid me, and it's such an apt one that I want to share it with you. Until now my reign has been too happy. There's been no world-wide plague, no religious persecution, not even a rebellion—nothing in fact to make us memorable. And that, I'd have you know, is why I try to remedy the stinginess of fate. I mean—I don't know if you've followed me—that, well (*He gives a little laugh.*), it's I who replace the epidemics that we've missed. (*In a different tone*) That's enough. I see Cherea's coming. Your turn, Cæsonia. (CALIGULA *goes out.* CHEREA *and the* FIRST PATRICIAN *enter.* CÆSONIA *hurries toward* CHEREA)

CÆSONIA:    Caligula is dead.

(*She turns her head, as if to hide her tears; her eyes are fixed on the others, who keep silence. Everyone looks horrified, but for different reasons.*)

FIRST PATRICIAN:    You . . . you're *sure* this dreadful thing has happened? It seems incredible. Only a short while ago he was dancing.

CÆSONIA:    Quite so—and the effort was too much for him. (CHEREA *moves hastily from one man to the other. No one speaks.*) You've nothing to say, Cherea?

CHEREA (*in a low voice*):    It's a great misfortune for us all, Cæsonia.

(CALIGULA *bursts in violently and goes up to* CHEREA.)

CALIGULA:    Well played, Cherea. (*He spins round and stares at the others. Petulantly*) Too bad! It didn't come off. (*To* CÆSONIA) Don't forget what I told you.

(CALIGULA *goes out.* CÆSONIA *stares after him without speaking.*)

THE OLD PATRICIAN (*hoping against hope*):   Is he ill, Cæsonia?

CÆSONIA (*with a hostile look*):   No, my pet. But what you don't know is that the man never has more than two hours' sleep and spends the best part of the night roaming about the corridors in his palace. Another thing you don't know—and you've never given a thought to—is what may pass in this man's mind in those deadly hours between midnight and sunrise. Is he ill? No, not ill—unless you invent a name and medicine for the black ulcers that fester in his soul.

CHEREA (*seemingly affected by her words*): You're right, Cæsonia. We all know that Caius . . .

CÆSONIA (*breaking in emotionally*):   Yes, you know it—in your fashion. But, like all those who have none, you can't abide anyone who has too much soul. Healthy people loathe invalids. Happy people hate the sad. Too much soul! That's what bites you, isn't it? You prefer to label it a disease; that way all the dolts are justified and pleased. (*In a changed tone*) Tell me, Cherea. Has love ever meant anything to you?

CHEREA (*himself again*):   I'm afraid we're too old now, Cæsonia, to learn the art of love-making. And anyhow it's highly doubtful if Caligula will give us time to do so.

CÆSONIA (*who has recovered her composure*): True enough. (*She sits down.*) Oh, I was forgetting. . . . Caligula asked me to impart some news to you. You know, perhaps, that it's a red-letter day today, consecrated to art.

THE OLD PATRICIAN:   According to the calendar?

CÆSONIA:   No, according to Caligula. He's convoked some poets. He will ask them to improvise a poem on a set theme. And he particularly wants those of you who are poets to take part in the competition. He specially mentioned young Scipio and Metellus.

METELLUS:   But we're not ready.

CÆSONIA (*in a level tone, as if she has not heard him*):   Needless to say there are prizes. There will be penalties, too. (*Looks of consternation*) Between ourselves, the penalties won't be so very terrible.

(CALIGULA *enters, looking gloomier than ever.*)

CALIGULA:   All ready?

CÆSONIA:   Yes. (*To a soldier*) Bring in the poets.

(*Enter, two by two, a dozen poets, keeping step; they line up on the right of the stage.*)

CALIGULA:   And the others?

CÆSONIA:   Metellus! Scipio!

(*They cross the stage and take their stand beside the poets.* CALIGULA *seats himself, backstage on the left, with* CÆSONIA *and the patricians. A short silence*)

CALIGULA:   Subject: death. Time limit: one minute.

(*The poets scribble feverishly on their tablets.*)

THE OLD PATRICIAN:   Who will compose the jury?

CALIGULA:   I. Isn't that enough?

THE OLD PATRICIAN:   Oh, yes, indeed. Quite enough.

CHEREA:   Won't you take part in the competition, Caius?

CALIGULA:   Unnecessary. I made my poem on that theme long ago.

THE OLD PATRICIAN (*eagerly*):   Where can one get a copy of it?

CALIGULA:   No need to get a copy. I recite it every day, after my fashion. (CÆSONIA *eyes him nervously.* CALIGULA *rounds on her almost savagely.*) Is there anything in my appearance that displeases you?

CÆSONIA (*gently*):   I'm sorry. . . .

CALIGULA:   No meekness, please. For heaven's sake, no meekness. You're exasperating enough as it is, but if you start being humble . . . (CÆSONIA *slowly moves away.* CALIGULA *turns to* CHEREA.) I continue. It's the only poem I have made. And it's proof that I'm the only true artist Rome has known—the only one, believe me—to match his inspiration with his deeds.

CHEREA:   That's only a matter of having the power.

CALIGULA:   Quite true. Other artists create to compensate for their lack of power. I don't need to make a work of art; I *live* it. (*Roughly*) Well, poets, are you ready?

METELLUS:   I think so.

THE OTHERS:   Yes.

CALIGULA:   Good. Now listen carefully. You are to fall out of line and come forward one by one. I'll whistle. Number One will start reading his poem. When I whistle, he must stop, and the next begin. And so on. The winner, naturally, will be the one whose poem hasn't been cut short by the whistle. Get ready. (*Turning to* CHEREA, *he whispers*) You see, organization's needed for everything, even for art. (*Blows his whistle*)

FIRST POET:   Death, when beyond thy darkling shore . . . (*A blast of the whistle. The poet steps briskly to the left. The others will follow the same procedure. These movements should be made with mechanical precision.*)

SECOND POET:   In their dim cave, the Fatal Sisters Three . . .

(*Whistle*)

THIRD POET:   Come to me death, beloved . . .

(*A shrill blast of the whistle. The* FOURTH POET *steps forward and strikes a dramatic posture. The whistle goes before he has opened his mouth.*)

FIFTH POET:   When I was in my happy infancy . . .

CALIGULA (*yelling*):   Stop that! What earthly connection has a blockhead's happy infancy with the theme I set? The connection! Tell me the connection!

FIFTH POET:   But, Caius, I've only just begun, and . . .

(*Shrill blast*)

SIXTH POET (*in a high-pitched voice*):   Ruthless, he goes his hidden ways . . .

(*Whistle*)

SEVENTH POET (*mysteriously*):   Oh, long, abstruse orison . . .

(*Whistle, broken off as* SCIPIO *comes forward without a tablet*)

CALIGULA:   You haven't a tablet?

SCIPIO:   I do not need one.

CALIGULA:   Well, let's hear you. (*He chews at his whistle.*)

SCIPIO (*Standing very near* CALIGULA, *he recites listlessly, without looking at him.*)

Pursuit of happiness that purifies the heart,
Skies rippling with light,
O wild, sweet, festal joys, frenzy without hope!

CALIGULA (*gently*):   Stop, please. The others needn't compete. (*To* SCIPIO) You're very young to understand so well the lessons we can learn from death.

SCIPIO (*gazing straight at* CALIGULA):   I was very young to lose my father.

CALIGULA (*turning hastily*):   Fall in, the rest of you. No, really a sham poet is too dreadful an infliction. Until now I'd thought of enrolling you as my allies; I sometimes pictured a gallant band of poets defending me in the last ditch. Another illusion gone! I shall have to relegate you to my enemies. So now the poets are against me—and that looks much like the end of all. March out in good order. As you go past you are to lick your tablets so as to efface the atrocities you scrawled on them. Attention! Forward! (*He blows his whistle in short rhythmic jerks. Keeping step, the poets file out by the right, tonguing their immortal tablets.* CALIGULA *adds in a lower tone*) Now leave me, everyone.

(*In the doorway, as they are going out,* CHEREA *touches the* FIRST PATRICIAN'S *shoulder, and speaks in his ear*)

CHEREA:   Now's our opportunity.

(SCIPIO, *who has overheard, halts on the threshold and walks back to* CALIGULA.)

CALIGULA (*acidly*):   Can't you leave me in peace—as your father's doing?

SCIPIO:   No, Caius, all that serves no purpose now. For now I know, I *know* that you have made your choice.

CALIGULA:   Won't you leave me in peace!

SCIPIO:   Yes, you shall have your wish; I am going to leave you, for I think I've come to understand you. There's no way out left to us, neither to you nor to me—who am like you in so many ways. I shall go away, far away, and try to discover the meaning of it all. (*He gazes at* CALIGULA *for some moments. Then, with a rush of emotion*) Good-by, dear Caius. When all is ended, remember that I loved you. (*He goes out.* CALIGULA *makes a vague gesture. Then, almost savagely, he pulls himself together and takes some steps toward* CÆSONIA.)

CÆSONIA:   What did he say?

CALIGULA:   Nothing you'd understand.

CÆSONIA:   What are you thinking about?

CALIGULA:   About him. And about you, too. But it amounts to the same thing.

CÆSONIA:   What is the matter?

CALIGULA (*staring at her*):   Scipio has gone. I am through with his friendship. But you, I wonder why you are still here. . . .

CÆSONIA:   Why, because you're fond of me.

CALIGULA:   No. But I think I'd understand—if I had you killed.

CÆSONIA:   Yes, that would be a solution. Do so, then. . . . But why, oh, why can't you relax, if only for a moment, and live freely, without constraint?

CALIGULA: I have been doing that for several years; in fact I've made a practice of it.

CÆSONIA: I don't mean that sort of freedom. I mean—Oh, don't you realize what it can be to live and love quite simply, naturally, in . . . in purity of heart?

CALIGULA: This purity of heart you talk of— every man acquires it, in his own way. Mine has been to follow the essential to the end. . . . Still all that needn't prevent me from putting you to death. (*Laughs*) It would round off my career so well, the perfect climax. (*He rises and swings the mirror round toward himself. Then he walks in a circle, letting his arms hang limp, almost without gestures; there is something feral in his gait as he continues speaking.*) How strange! When I don't kill, I feel alone. The living don't suffice to people my world and dispel my boredom. I have an impression of an enormous void when you and the others are here, and my eyes see nothing but empty air. No, I'm at ease only in the company of my dead. (*He takes his stand facing the audience, leaning a little forward. He has forgotten* CÆSONIA's *presence.*) Only the dead are real. They are of my kind. I see them waiting for me, straining toward me. And I have long talks with this man or that, who screamed to me for mercy and whose tongue I had cut out.

CÆSONIA: Come. Lie down beside me. Put your head on my knees. (CALIGULA *does so.*) That's better, isn't it? Now rest. How quiet it is here!

CALIGULA: Quiet? You exaggerate, my dear. Listen! (*Distant metallic tinklings, as of swords or armor*) Do you hear those thousands of small sounds all around us, hatred stalking its prey? (*Murmuring voices, footsteps*)

CÆSONIA: Nobody would dare. . . .

CALIGULA: Yes, stupidity.

CÆSONIA: Stupidity doesn't kill. It makes men slow to act.

CALIGULA. It can be murderous, Cæsonia. A fool stops at nothing when he thinks his dignity offended. No, it's not the men whose sons or fathers I have killed who'll murder me. *They*, anyhow, have understood. They're with me, they have the same taste in their mouths. But the others—those I made a laughingstock of—I've no defense against their wounded vanity.

CÆSONIA (*passionately*): *We* will defend you. There are many of us left who love you.

CALIGULA: Fewer every day. It's not surpris-

ing. I've done all that was needed to that end. And then—let's be fair—it's not only stupidity that's against me. There's the courage and the simple faith of men who ask to be happy.

CÆSONIA (*in the same tone*): No, *they* will not kill you. Or, if they tried, fire would come down from heaven and blast them, before they laid a hand on you.

CALIGULA: From heaven! There is no heaven, my poor dear woman! (*He sits down.*) But why this sudden access of devotion? It wasn't provided for in our agreement, if I remember rightly.

CÆSONIA (*who has risen from the couch and is pacing the room*): Don't you understand? Hasn't it been enough to see you killing others, without my also knowing you'll be killed as well? Isn't it enough to feel you hard and cruel, seething with bitterness, when I hold you in my arms; to breathe a reek of murder when you lie on me? Day after day I see all that's human in you dying out, little by little. (*She turns toward him.*) Oh, I know. I know I'm getting old, my beauty's on the wane. But it's you only I'm concerned for now; so much so that I've ceased troubling whether you love me. I only want you to get well, quite well again. You're still a boy, really; you've a whole life ahead of you. And, tell me, what greater thing can you want than a whole life?

CALIGULA (*rising, looks at her fixedly*): You've been with me a long time now, a very long time.

CÆSONIA: Yes. . . . But you'll keep me, won't you?

CALIGULA: I don't know. I only know that, if you're with me still, it's because of all those nights we've had together, nights of fierce, joyless pleasure; it's because you alone know me as I am. (*He takes her in his arms, bending her head back a little with his right hand.*) I'm twenty-nine. Not a great age really. But today when none the less my life seems so long, so crowded with scraps and shreds of my past selves, so complete in fact, you remain the last witness. And I can't avoid a sort of shameful tenderness for the old woman that you soon will be.

CÆSONIA: Tell me that you mean to keep me with you.

CALIGULA: I don't know. All I know—and it's the most terrible thing of all—is that this shameful tenderness is the one sincere emotion that my life has given up to now. (CÆSONIA *frees herself from his arms.* CALIGULA *follows her. She presses her back to his chest and he puts his arms round her.*) Wouldn't it be better that the last witness should disappear?

CÆSONIA:   That has no importance. All I know is: I'm happy. What you've just said has made me very happy. But why can't I share my happiness with you?

CALIGULA:   Who says I'm unhappy?

CÆSONIA:   Happiness is kind. It doesn't thrive on bloodshed.

CALIGULA:   Then there must be two kinds of happiness, and I've chosen the murderous kind. For I *am* happy. There was a time when I thought I'd reached the extremity of pain. But, no, one can go farther yet. Beyond the frontier of pain lies a splendid, sterile happiness. Look at me. (*She turns toward him.*) It makes me laugh, Cæsonia, when I think how for years and years all Rome carefully avoided uttering Drusilla's name. Well, all Rome was mistaken. Love isn't enough for me; I realized it then. And I realize it again today, when I look at you. To love someone means that one's willing to grow old beside that person. That sort of love is right outside my range. Drusilla old would have been far worse than Drusilla dead. Most people imagine that a man suffers because out of the blue death snatches away the woman he loves. But his real suffering is less futile; it comes from the discovery that grief, too, cannot last. Even grief is vanity.

You see, I had no excuses, not the shadow of a real love, neither bitterness nor profound regret. Nothing to plead in my defense! But today—you see me still freer than I have been for years; freed as I am from memories and illusion. (*He laughs bitterly.*) I know now that nothing, *nothing* lasts. Think what that knowledge means! There have been just two or three of us in history who really achieved this freedom, this crazy happiness. Well, Cæsonia, you have seen out a most unusual drama. It's time the curtain fell, for you. (*He stands behind her again, linking his forearm round* CÆSONIA's *neck.*)

CÆSONIA (*terrified*):   No, it's impossible! How can you call it happiness, this terrifying freedom?

CALIGULA (*gradually tightening his grip on* CÆSONIA's *throat*):   Happiness it is, Cæsonia; I know what I'm saying. But for this freedom I'd have been a contented man. Thanks to it, I have won the godlike enlightenment of the solitary.

(*His exaltation grows as little by little he strangles* CÆSONIA, *who puts up no resistance, but holds her hands half opened, like a suppliant's, before her. Bending his head, he goes on speaking, into her ear.*) I live, I kill, I exercise the rapturous power of a destroyer, compared with which the power of a creator is merest child's play. And this, *this* is happiness; this and nothing else—this intolerable release, devastating scorn, blood, hatred all around me; the glorious isolation of a man who all his life long nurses and gloats over the ineffable joy of the unpunished murderer; the ruthless logic that crushes out human lives (*He laughs.*), that's crushing yours out, Cæsonia, so as to perfect at last the utter loneliness that is my heart's desire.

CÆSONIA (*struggling feebly*):   Oh, Caius . . .

CALIGULA (*more and more excitedly*):   No. No sentiment. I must have done with it, for the time is short. My time is very short, dear Cæsonia. CÆSONIA *is gasping, dying.* CALIGULA *drags her to the bed and lets her fall on it. He stares wildly at her; his voice grows harsh and grating.*) You, too, were guilty. But killing is not the solution. (*He spins round and gazes crazily at the mirror.*) Caligula! You, too; you, too, are guilty. Then what of it—a little more, a little less? Yet who can condemn me in this world where there is no judge, where nobody is innocent? (*He brings his eyes close to his reflected face. He sounds genuinely distressed.*) You see, my poor friend. Helicon has failed you. I won't have the moon. Never, never, never! But how bitter it is to know all, and to have to go through to the consummation! Listen! That was a sound of weapons. Innocence arming for the fray—and innocence will triumph. Why am I not in their place, among them? And I'm afraid. That's cruelest of all, after despising others, to find oneself as cowardly as they. Still, no matter. Fear, too, has an end. Soon I shall attain that emptiness beyond all understanding, in which the heart has rest. (*He steps back a few paces, then returns to the mirror. He seems calmer. When he speaks again his voice is steadier, less shrill.*)

Yet, really, it's quite simple. If I'd had the moon, if love were enough, all might have been different. But where could I quench this thirst? What human heart, what god, would have for me the depth of a great lake? (*Kneeling, weeping*) There's nothing in this world, or in the other, made to my stature. And yet I know, and you, too, know (*still weeping, he stretches out his arms toward the mirror*) that all I need is for the impossible to be. The impossible! I've searched for it at the confines of the world, in the secret places of my heart. I've stretched out my hands (*his voice rises to a scream*); see, I stretch out my hands, but it's always you I find, you only, confronting me, and I've come to hate you. I have chosen a wrong path, a path that leads to nothing. My freedom isn't the right one. . . . Nothing, nothing yet. Oh, how oppressive is this darkness! Helicon has not come; we shall be forever guilty. The air tonight is heavy as the sum of human sorrows. (*A clash of arms and whisperings are heard in the wings.* CALIGULA *rises, picks up a* stool, *and returns to the mirror, breathing heavily. He contemplates himself, makes a slight leap forward, and, watching the symmetrical movement of his reflected self, hurls the stool at it, screaming.*) To history, Caligula! Go down to history! (*The mirror breaks and at the same moment armed conspirators rush in.* CALIGULA *swings round to face them with a mad laugh.* SCIPIO *and* CHEREA, *who are in front, fling themselves at him and stab his face with their daggers.* CALIGULA'*s laughter turns to gasps. All strike him, hurriedly, confusedly. In a last gasp, laughing and choking,* CALIGULA *shrieks.*) I'm still alive!

*Curtain*

# ARTHUR MILLER

# The Crucible

Arthur Miller (1915–        ) was born to a middle-class Jewish family in the Harlem district of New York. While he was attending the University of Michigan, his talent for playwriting won him the Hopwood Prize for Drama in 1936. He won the Theatre Guild National Award in 1938, the year of his graduation.

In 1945 Miller wrote an ironic novel, *Focus*, about racial prejudice. His first successful play on Broadway was *All My Sons*, 1947, which deals with a father, who, during World War II, uses faulty parts in the airplane equipment that he supplies to the government. Like much of Miller's work, it is critical of a social evil—in this case, war profiteering. *Death of a Salesman*, 1949, has become one of the classics of the American theater. It has won five awards, including the New York Drama Critics' Circle Award and the Pulitzer Prize, and has been performed innumerable times by college drama departments and amateur little-theater groups. *Death of a Salesman* has grown in stature in the nearly two decades since its long Broadway run.

In 1950 Miller wrote an adaptation of Ibsen's *An Enemy of the People;* in 1953 he wrote *The Crucible*. In 1955 two one-act plays were produced under the title *A View from the Bridge*, which again won him the New York Drama Critics' Circle Award and the Pulitzer Prize. He then wrote and helped direct the successful movie *The Misfits*, 1961. Early in 1964 Miller's autobiographical drama *After the Fall* was the first play to be presented by the newly established Repertory Company of Lincoln Center in New York. In December 1964 Miller's most recent play *Incident at Vichy* was produced in New York. His newest work is *I Don't Need You Anymore*, 1967, a collection of short stories that includes "The Misfits," from which the screen play of the movie was developed.

A reader survey report in the London *Observer* in 1966 put *Death of a Salesman* and *The Crucible* on a list of twenty plays written since 1900 that show the main trends of the theater in this century.

*The Crucible* deals with that dark period of the Salem witch trials in seventeenth-century New England. Miller saw the so-called witch hunting of the post-World War II years, led by Senator Joseph McCarthy, as similar to the hysterical forces at work in Salem. The play is also a psychological and social dramatization of people destroyed by prejudice, guilt, and greed.

## CAST OF CHARACTERS

| | |
|---|---|
| REVEREND PARRIS | GILES COREY |
| BETTY PARRIS | REVEREND JOHN HALE |
| TITUBA | ELIZABETH PROCTOR |
| ABIGAIL WILLIAMS | FRANCIS NURSE |
| SUSANNA WALCOTT | EZEKIEL CHEEVER |
| MRS. ANN PUTNAM | MARSHAL HERRICK |
| THOMAS PUTNAM | JUDGE HATHORNE |
| MERCY LEWIS | DEPUTY GOVERNOR |
| MARY WARREN | DANFORTH |
| JOHN PROCTOR | SARAH GOOD |
| REBECCA NURSE | HOPKINS |

### A NOTE ON THE HISTORICAL ACCURACY OF THIS PLAY

This play is not history in the sense in which the word is used by the academic historian. Dramatic purposes have sometimes required many characters to be fused into one; the number of girls involved in the "crying-out" has been reduced; Abigail's age has been raised; while there were several judges of almost equal authority, I have symbolized them all in Hathorne and Danforth. However, I believe that the reader will discover here the essential nature of one of the strangest and most awful chapters in human history. The fate of each character is exactly that of his historical model, and there is no one in the drama who did not play a similar—and in some cases exactly the same—role in history.

As for the characters of the persons, little is known about most of them excepting what may be surmised from a few letters, the trial record, certain broadsides written at the time, and references to their conduct in sources of varying reliability. They may therefore be taken as crea-

tions of my own, drawn to the best of my ability in conformity with their known behavior, except as indicated in the commentary I have written for this text.

## ACT ONE
### (AN OVERTURE)

*A small upper bedroom in the home of* REVEREND SAMUEL PARRIS, *Salem, Massachusetts, in the spring of the year* 1692.

*There is a narrow window at the left. Through its leaded panes the morning sunlight streams. A candle still burns near the bed, which is at the right. A chest, a chair, and a small table are the other furnishings. At the back a door opens on the landing of the stairway to the ground floor. The room gives off an air of clean spareness. The roof rafters are exposed, and the wood colors are raw and unmellowed.*

*As the curtain rises,* REVEREND PARRIS *is discovered kneeling beside the bed, evidently in prayer. His daughter,* BETTY PARRIS, *aged ten, is lying on the bed, inert.*

At the time of these events Parris was in his middle forties. In history he cut a villainous path, and there is very little good to be said for him. He believed he was being persecuted wherever he went, despite his best efforts to win people and God to his side. In meeting, he felt insulted if someone rose to shut the door without first asking his permission. He was a widower with no interest in children, or talent with them. He regarded them as young adults, and until this strange crisis he, like the rest of Salem, never conceived that the children were anything but thankful for being permitted to walk straight, eyes slightly lowered, arms at the sides, and mouths shut until bidden to speak.

His house stood in the "town"—but we today would hardly call it a village. The meeting house was nearby, and from this point outward—toward the bay or inland—there were a few small-windowed, dark houses snuggling against the raw Massachusetts winter. Salem had been established hardly forty years before. To the European world the whole province was a barbaric frontier inhabited by a sect of fanatics who, nevertheless, were shipping out products of slowly increasing quantity and value.

No one can really know what their lives were like. They had no novelists—and would not have permitted anyone to read a novel if one were handy. Their creed forbade anything resembling a theater or "vain enjoyment." They did not celebrate Christmas, and a holiday from work meant only that they must concentrate even more upon prayer.

Which is not to say that nothing broke into this strict and somber way of life. When a new farmhouse was built, friends assembled to "raise the roof," and there would be special foods cooked and probably some potent cider passed around. There was a good supply of ne'er-do-wells in Salem, who dallied at the shovelboard in Bridget Bishop's tavern. Probably more than the creed, hard work kept the morals of the place from spoiling, for the people were forced to fight the land like heroes for every grain of corn, and no man had very much time for fooling around.

That there were some jokers, however, is indicated by the practice of appointing a two-man patrol whose duty was to "walk forth in the time of God's worship to take notice of such as either lye about the meeting house, without attending to the word and ordinances, or that lye at home or in the fields without giving good account thereof, and to take the names of such persons, and to present them to the magistrates, whereby they may be accordingly proceeded against." This predilection for minding other people's business was time-honored among the people of Salem, and it undoubtedly created many of the suspicions which were to feed the coming madness. It was also, in my opinion, one of the things that a John Proctor would rebel against, for the time of the armed camp had almost passed, and since the country was reasonably—although not

wholly—safe, the old disciplines were beginning to rankle. But, as in all such matters, the issue was not clearcut, for danger was still a possibility, and in unity still lay the best promise of safety.

The edge of the wilderness was close by. The American continent stretched endlessly west, and it was full of mystery for them. It stood, dark and threatening, over their shoulders night and day, for out of it Indian tribes marauded from time to time, and Reverend Parris had parishioners who had lost relatives to these heathen.

The parochial snobbery of these people was partly responsible for their failure to convert the Indians. Probably they also preferred to take land from heathens rather than from fellow Christians. At any rate, very few Indians were converted, and the Salem folk believed that the virgin forest was the Devil's last preserve, his home base and the citadel of his final stand. To the best of their knowledge the American forest was the last place on earth that was not paying homage to God.

For these reasons, among others, they carried about an air of innate resistance, even of persecution. Their fathers had, of course, been persecuted in England. So now they and their church found it necessary to deny any other sect its freedom, lest their New Jerusalem be defiled and corrupted by wrong ways and deceitful ideas.

They believed, in short, that they held in their steady hands the candle that would light the world. We have inherited this belief, and it has helped and hurt us. It helped them with the discipline it gave them. They were a dedicated folk, by and large, and they had to be to survive the life they had chosen or been born into in this country.

The proof of their belief's value to them may be taken from the opposite character of the first Jamestown settlement, farther south, in Virginia. The Englishmen who landed there were motivated mainly by a hunt for profit. They had thought to pick off the wealth of the new country and then return rich to England. They were a band of individualists, and a much more ingratiating group than the Massachusetts men. But Virginia destroyed them. Massachusetts tried to kill off the Puritans, but they combined; they set up a communal society which, in the beginning, was little more than an armed camp with an autocratic and very devoted leadership. It was, however, an autocracy by consent, for they were united from top to bottom by a commonly held ideology whose perpetuation was the reason and justification for all their sufferings. So their self-denial, their purposefulness, their suspicion of all vain pursuits, their hard-handed justice, were altogether perfect instruments for the conquest of this space so antagonistic to man.

But the people of Salem in 1692 were not quite the dedicated folk that arrived on the *Mayflower*. A vast differentiation had taken place, and in their own time a revolution had unseated the royal government and substituted a junta which was at this moment in power. The times, to their eyes, must have been out of joint, and to the common folk must have seemed as insoluble and complicated as do ours today. It is not hard to see how easily many could have been led to believe that the time of confusion had been brought upon them by deep and darkling forces. No hint of such speculation appears on the court record, but social disorder in any age breeds such mystical suspicions, and when, as in Salem, wonders are brought forth from below the social surface, it is too much to expect people to hold back very long from laying on the victims with all the force of their frustrations.

The Salem tragedy, which is about to begin in these pages, developed from a paradox. It is a paradox in whose grip we still live, and there is no prospect yet that we will discover its resolution. Simply, it was this: for good purposes, even high purposes, the people of Salem developed a theocracy, a combine of state and religious power whose function was to keep the community together, and to prevent any kind of disunity that might open it to destruction by material or ideological enemies. It was forged for a necessary purpose and accomplished that purpose. But all organization is and must be grounded on the idea of exclusion and prohibition, just as two objects cannot occupy the same space. Evidently the time came in New England when the repressions of order were heavier than seemed warranted by the dangers against which the order was organized. The witch-hunt was a perverse manifestation of the panic which set in among all classes when the balance began to turn toward greater individual freedom.

When one rises above the individual villainy displayed, one can only pity them all, just as we shall be pitied someday. It is still impossible for man to organize his social life without repres-

sions, and the balance has yet to be struck between order and freedom.

The witch-hunt was not, however, a mere repression. It was also, and as importantly, a long overdue opportunity for everyone so inclined to express publicly his guilt and sins, under the cover of accusations against the victims. It suddenly became possible—and patriotic and holy—for a man to say that Martha Corey had come into his bedroom at night, and that, while his wife was sleeping at his side, Martha laid herself down on his chest and "nearly suffocated him." Of course it was her spirit only, but his satisfaction at confessing himself was no lighter than if it had been Martha herself. One could not ordinarily speak such things in public.

Long-held hatreds of neighbors could now be openly expressed, and vengeance taken, despite the Bible's charitable injunctions. Land-lust which had been expressed before by constant bickering over boundaries and deeds, could now be elevated to the arena of morality; one could cry witch against one's neighbor and feel perfectly justified in the bargain. Old scores could be settled on a plane of heavenly combat between Lucifer and the Lord; suspicions and the envy of the miserable toward the happy could and did burst out in the general revenge.

REVEREND PARRIS *is praying now, and, though we cannot hear his words, a sense of his confusion hangs about him. He mumbles, then seems about to weep; then he weeps, then prays again; but his daughter does not stir on the bed.*

*The door opens, and his Negro slave enters.* TITUBA *is in her forties.* PARRIS *brought her with him from Barbados, where he spent some years as a merchant before entering the ministry. She enters as one does who can no longer bear to be barred from the sight of her beloved, but she is also very frightened because her slave sense has warned her that, as always, trouble in this house eventually lands on her back.*

TITUBA (*already taking a step backward*): My Betty be hearty soon?

PARRIS: Out of here!

TITUBA (*backing to the door*): My Betty not goin' die . . .

PARRIS (*scrambling to his feet in a fury*): Out of my sight! (*She is gone.*) Out of my—(*He is overcome with sobs. He clamps his teeth against them and closes the door and leans against it, exhausted.*) Oh, my God! God help me! (*Quaking with fear, mumbling to himself through his sobs, he goes to the bed and gently takes* BETTY's *hand.*) Betty. Child. Dear child. Will you wake, will you open up your eyes! Betty, little one . . .

(*He is bending to kneel again when his niece,* ABIGAIL WILLIAMS, *seventeen, enters—a strikingly beautiful girl, an orphan, with an endless capacity for dissembling. Now she is all worry and apprehension and propriety.*)

ABIGAIL: Uncle? (*He looks to her.*) Susanna Walcott's here from Doctor Griggs.

PARRIS: Oh? Let her come, let her come.

ABIGAIL (*leaning out the door to call to* SUSANNA, *who is down the hall a few steps*): Come in, Susanna.

(SUSANNA WALCOTT, *a little younger than* ABIGAIL, *a nervous, hurried girl, enters.*)

PARRIS (*eagerly*): What does the doctor say, child?

SUSANNA (*craning around* PARRIS *to get a look at* BETTY): He bid me come and tell you, reverend sir, that he cannot discover no medicine for it in his books.

PARRIS: Then he must search on.

SUSANNA: Aye, sir, he have been searchin' his books since he left you, sir. But he bid me tell you, that you might look to unnatural things for the cause of it.

PARRIS (*his eyes going wide*): No—no. There be no unnatural cause here. Tell him I have sent for Reverend Hale of Beverly, and Mr. Hale will surely confirm that. Let him look to medicine and put out all thought of unnatural causes here. There be none.

SUSANNA: Aye, sir. He bid me tell you. (*She turns to go.*)

ABIGAIL: Speak nothin' of it in the village, Susanna.

PARRIS: Go directly home and speak nothing of unnatural causes.

SUSANNA: Aye, sir. I pray for her. (*She goes out.*)

ABIGAIL: Uncle, the rumor of witchcraft is all about; I think you'd best go down and deny it yourself. The parlor's packed with people, sir. I'll sit with her.

PARRIS (*pressed, turns on her*): And what shall I say to them? That my daughter and my niece I discovered dancing like heathen in the forest?

ABIGAIL: Uncle, we did dance; let you tell them I confessed it—and I'll be whipped if I must be. But they're speakin' of witchcraft. Betty's not witched.

PARRIS: Abigail, I cannot go before the congregation when I know you have not opened with me. What did you do with her in the forest?

ABIGAIL: We did dance, uncle, and when you leaped out of the bush so suddenly, Betty was frightened and then she fainted. And there's the whole of it.

PARRIS. Child. Sit you down.

ABIGAIL (*quavering, as she sits*): I would never hurt Betty. I love her dearly.

PARRIS: Now look you, child, your punishment will come in its time. But if you trafficked with spirits in the forest I must know it now, for surely my enemies will, and they will ruin me with it.

ABIGAIL: But we never conjured spirits.

PARRIS: Then why can she not move herself since midnight? This child is desperate! (ABIGAIL *lowers her eyes.*) It must come out—my enemies will bring it out. Let me know what you done there. Abigail, do you understand that I have many enemies?

ABIGAIL: I have heard of it, uncle.

PARRIS: There is a faction that is sworn to drive me from my pulpit. Do you understand that?

ABIGAIL: I think so, sir.

PARRIS: Now then, in the midst of such disruption, my own household is discovered to be the very center of some obscene practice. Abominations are done in the forest—

ABIGAIL: It were sport, uncle!

PARRIS (*pointing at* BETTY): You call this sport? (*She lowers her eyes. He pleads.*) Abigail, if you know something that may help the doctor, for God's sake tell it to me. (*She is silent.*) I saw Tituba waving her arms over the fire when I came on you. Why was she doing that? And I heard a screeching and gibberish coming from her mouth. She were swaying like a dumb beast over that fire!

ABIGAIL: She always sings her Barbados songs, and we dance.

PARRIS: I cannot blink what I saw, Abigail, for my enemies will not blink it. I saw a dress lying on the grass.

ABIGAIL (*innocently*): A dress?

PARRIS (*It is very hard to say.*): Aye, a dress.

And I thought I saw—someone naked running through the trees!

ABIGAIL (*in terror*): No one was naked! You mistake yourself, uncle!

PARRIS (*with anger*): I saw it! (*He moves from her. Then, resolved*) Now tell me true, Abigail. And I pray you feel the weight of truth upon you, for now my ministry's at stake, my ministry and perhaps your cousin's life. Whatever abomination you have done, give me all of it now, for I dare not be taken unaware when I go before them down there.

ABIGAIL: There is nothin' more. I swear it, uncle.

PARRIS (*studies her, then nods, half convinced*): Abigail, I have fought here three long years to bend these stiff-necked people to me, and now, just now when some good respect is rising for me in the parish, you compromise my very character. I have given you a home, child, I have put clothes upon your back—now give me upright answer. Your name in the town—it is entirely white, is it not?

ABIGAIL (*with an edge of resentment*): Why, I am sure it is, sir. There be no blush about my name.

PARRIS (*to the point*): Abigail, is there any other cause than you have told me, for your being discharged from Goody Proctor's service? I have heard it said, and I tell you as I heard it, that she comes so rarely to the church this year for she will not sit so close to something soiled. What signified that remark?

ABIGAIL: She hates me, uncle, she must, for I would not be her slave. It's a bitter woman, a lying, cold, sniveling woman, and I will not work for such a woman!

PARRIS: She may be. And yet it has troubled me that you are now seven month out of their house, and in all this time no other family has ever called for your service.

ABIGAIL: They want slaves, not such as I. Let them send to Barbados for that. I will not black my face for any of them! (*With ill-concealed resentment at him*) Do you begrudge my bed, uncle?

PARRIS: No—no.

ABIGAIL (*in a temper*): My name is good in the village! I will not have it said my name is soiled! Goody Proctor is a gossiping liar!

(*Enter* MRS. ANN PUTNAM. *She is a twisted soul of forty-five, a death-ridden woman, haunted by dreams.*)

PARRIS (*as soon as the door begins to open*): No—no, I cannot have anyone. (*He sees her, and a certain deference springs into him, although his worry remains.*) Why, Goody Putnam, come in.

MRS. PUTNAM (*full of breath, shiny-eyed*): It is a marvel. It is surely a stroke of hell upon you.

PARRIS: No, Goody Putnam, it is—

MRS. PUTNAM (*glancing at* BETTY): How high did she fly, how high?

PARRIS: No, no, she never flew—

MRS. PUTNAM (*very pleased with it*): Why, it's sure she did. Mr. Collins saw her goin' over Ingersoll's barn, and come down light as a bird, he says!

PARRIS: Now, look you, Goody Putnam, she never—(*Enter* THOMAS PUTNAM, *a well-to-do, hard-handed landowner, near fifty.*) Oh, good morning, Mr. Putnam.

PUTNAM: It is a providence the thing is out now! It is a providence. (*He goes directly to the bed.*)

PARRIS: What's out, sir, what's—?

(MRS. PUTNAM *goes to the bed.*)

PUTNAM (*looking down at Betty*): Why, *her* eyes is closed! Look you, Ann.

MRS. PUTNAM: Why, that's strange. (*To Parris*) Ours is open.

PARRIS (*shocked*): Your Ruth is sick?

MRS. PUTNAM (*with vicious certainty*): I'd not call it sick; the Devil's touch is heavier than sick. It's death, y'know, it's death drivin' into them, forked and hoofed.

PARRIS: Oh, pray not! Why, how does Ruth ail?

MRS. PUTNAM: She ails as she must—she never waked this morning, but her eyes open and she walks, and hears naught, sees naught, and cannot eat. Her soul is taken, surely.

(PARRIS *is struck.*)

PUTNAM (*as though for further details*): They say you've sent for Reverend Hale of Beverly?

PARRIS (*with dwindling conviction now*): A precaution only. He has much experience in all demonic arts, and I—

MRS. PUTNAM: He has indeed; and found a witch in Beverly last year, and let you remember that.

PARRIS: Now, Goody Ann, they only thought

that were a witch, and I am certain there be no element of witchcraft here.

PUTNAM: No witchcraft! Now look you, Mr. Parris—

PARRIS: Thomas, Thomas, I pray you, leap not to witchcraft. I know that you—you least of all, Thomas, would ever wish so disastrous a charge laid upon me. We cannot leap to witchcraft. They will howl me out of Salem for such corruption in my house.

A word about Thomas Putnam. He was a man with many grievances, at least one of which appears justified. Some time before, his wife's brother-in-law, James Bayley, had been turned down as minister at Salem. Bayley had all the qualifications, and a two-thirds vote into the bargain, but a faction stopped his acceptance, for reasons that are not clear.

Thomas Putnam was the eldest son of the richest man in the village. He had fought the Indians at Narragansett, and was deeply interested in parish affairs. He undoubtedly felt it poor payment that the village should so blatantly disregard his candidate for one of its more important offices, especially since he regarded himself as the intellectual superior of most of the people around him.

His vindictive nature was demonstrated long before the witchcraft began. Another former Salem minister, George Burroughs, had had to borrow money to pay for his wife's funeral, and, since the parish was remiss in his salary, he was soon bankrupt. Thomas and his brother John had Burroughs jailed for debts the man did not owe. The incident is important only in that Burroughs succeeded in becoming minister where Bayley, Thomas Putnam's brother-in-law, had been rejected; the motif of resentment is clear here. Thomas Putnam felt that his own name and the honor of his family had been smirched by the village, and he meant to right matters however he could.

Another reason to believe him a deeply embittered man was his attempt to break his father's will, which left a disproportionate amount to a stepbrother. As with every other public cause in which he tried to force his way, he failed in this.

So it is not surprising to find that so many accusations against people are in the handwriting of Thomas Putnam, or that his name is so often found as a witness corroborating the supernatural testimony, or that his daughter led the crying-out at the most opportune junctures of the trials, especially when—But we'll speak of that when we come to it.

PUTNAM (*At the moment he is intent upon getting* PARRIS, *for whom he has only contempt, to move toward the abyss.*): Mr. Parris, I have taken your part in all contention here, and I would continue; but I cannot if you hold back in this. There are hurtful, vengeful spirits layin' hands on these children.

PARRIS: But, Thomas, you cannot—

PUTNAM: Ann! Tell Mr. Parris what you have done.

MRS. PUTNAM: Reverend Parris, I have laid seven babies unbaptized in the earth. Believe me, sir, you never saw more hearty babies born. And yet, each would wither in my arms the very night of their birth. I have spoke nothin', but my heart has clamored intimations. And now, this year, my Ruth, my only—I see her turning strange. A secret child she has become this year, and shrivels like a sucking mouth were pullin' on her life too. And so I thought to send her to your Tituba—

PARRIS: To Tituba! What may Tituba—?

MRS. PUTNAM: Tituba knows how to speak to the dead, Mr. Parris.

PARRIS: Goody Ann, it is a formidable sin to conjure up the dead!

MRS. PUTNAM: I take it on my soul, but who else may surely tell us what person murdered my babies?

PARRIS (*horrified*): Woman!

MRS. PUTNAM: They were murdered, Mr. Parris! And mark this proof! Mark it! Last night my Ruth were ever so close to their little spirits; I know it, sir. For how else is she struck dumb now except some power of darkness would stop her mouth? It is a marvelous sign, Mr. Parris!

PUTNAM: Don't you understand it, sir? There is a murdering witch among us, bound to keep herself in the dark. (PARRIS *turns to* BETTY, *a frantic terror rising in him.*) Let your names make of it what they will, you cannot blink it more.

PARRIS (*to* ABIGAIL): Then you were conjuring spirits last night.

ABIGAIL (*whispering*): Not I, sir—Tituba and Ruth.

PARRIS (*turns now, with new fear, and goes to

BETTY, *looks down at her, and then, gazing off*): Oh, Abigail, what proper payment for my charity! Now I am undone.

PUTNAM:   You are not undone! Let you take hold here. Wait for no one to charge you—declare it yourself. You have discovered witchcraft—

PARRIS:   In my house? In my house, Thomas? They will topple me with this! They will make of it a—

(*Enter* MERCY LEWIS, *the* PUTNAMS' *servant, a fat, sly, merciless girl of eighteen.*)

MERCY:   Your pardons. I only thought to see how Betty is.

PUTNAM:   Why aren't you home? Who's with Ruth?

MERCY:   Her grandma come. She's improved a little, I think—she give a powerful sneeze before.

MRS. PUTNAM:   Ah, there's a sign of life!

MERCY:   I'd fear no more, Goody Putnam. It were a grand sneeze; another like it will shake her wits together, I'm sure. (*She goes to the bed to look.*)

PARRIS:   Will you leave me now, Thomas? I would pray a while alone.

ABIGAIL:   Uncle, you've prayed since midnight. Why do you not go down and—

PARRIS:   No—no. (*To* PUTNAM) I have no answer for that crowd. I'll wait till Mr. Hale arrives. (*To get* MRS. PUTNAM *to leave*) If you will, Goody Ann . . .

PUTNAM:   Now look you, sir. Let you strike out against the Devil, and the village will bless you for it! Come down, speak to them—pray with them. They're thirsting for your word, Mister! Surely you'll pray with them.

PARRIS (*swayed*):   I'll lead them in a psalm, but let you say nothing of witchcraft yet. I will not discuss it. The cause is yet unknown. I have had enough contention since I came; I want no more.

MRS. PUTNAM:   Mercy, you go home to Ruth, d'y'hear?

MERCY:   Aye, mum.

(MRS. PUTNAM *goes out.*)

PARRIS (*to* ABIGAIL):   If she starts for the window, cry for me at once.

ABIGAIL:   I will, uncle.

PARRIS (*to* PUTNAM):   There is a terrible power in her arms today. (*He goes out with* PUTNAM.)

ABIGAIL (*with hushed trepidation*):   How is Ruth sick?

MERCY:   It's weirdish, I know not—she seems to walk like a dead one since last night.

ABIGAIL (*turns at once and goes to* BETTY, *and now, with fear in her voice*):   Betty? (BETTY *doesn't move. She shakes her.*) Now stop this! Betty! Sit up now!

(BETTY *doesn't stir.* MERCY *comes over.*)

MERCY:   Have you tried beatin' her? I gave Ruth a good one and it waked her for a minute. Here, let me have her.

ABIGAIL (*holding* MERCY *back*):   No, he'll be comin' up. Listen, now; if they be questioning us, tell them we danced—I told him as much already.

MERCY:   Aye. And what more?

ABIGAIL:   He knows Tituba conjured Ruth's sisters to come out of the grave.

MERCY:   And what more?

ABIGAIL:   He saw you naked.

MERCY (*clapping her hands together with a frightened laugh*):   Oh, Jesus!

(*Enter* MARY WARREN, *breathless. She is seventeen, a subservient, naive, lonely girl.*)

MARY WARREN:   What'll we do? The village is out! I just come from the farm; the whole country's talkin' witchcraft! They'll be callin' us witches, Abby!

MERCY (*pointing and looking at* MARY WARREN):   She means to tell, I know it.

MARY WARREN:   Abby, we've got to tell. Witchery's a hangin' error, a hangin' like they done in Boston two year ago! We must tell the truth, Abby! You'll only be whipped for dancin', and the other things!

ABIGAIL:   Oh, *we'll* be whipped!

MARY WARREN:   I never done none of it, Abby. I only looked!

MERCY (*moving menacingly toward* MARY):   Oh, you're a great one for lookin', aren't you, Mary Warren? What a grand peeping courage you have!

(BETTY, *on the bed, whimpers.* ABIGAIL *turns to her at once.*)

ABIGAIL:   Betty? (*She goes to* BETTY.) Now, Betty, dear, wake up now. It's Abigail. (*She sits* BETTY *up and furiously shakes her.*) I'll beat you, Betty! (BETTY *whimpers.*) My, you seem improving. I talked to your papa and I told him everything. So there's nothing to—

BETTY (*darts off the bed, frightened of* ABIGAIL,

*and flattens herself against the wall*): I want my mama!

ABIGAIL (*with alarm, as she cautiously approaches* BETTY): What ails you, Betty? Your mama's dead and buried.

BETTY: I'll fly to Mama. Let me fly! (*She raises her arms as though to fly, and streaks for the window, gets one leg out.*)

ABIGAIL (*pulling her away from the window*): I told him everything; he knows now, he knows everything we—

BETTY: You drank blood, Abby! You didn't tell him that!

ABIGAIL: Betty, you never say that again! You will never—

BETTY: You did, you did! You drank a charm to kill John Proctor's wife! You drank a charm to kill Goody Proctor!

ABIGAIL (*smashes her across the face*): Shut it! Now shut it!

BETTY (*collapsing on the bed*) Mama, Mama! (*She dissolves into sobs.*)

ABIGAIL: Now look you. All of you. We danced. And Tituba conjured Ruth Putnam's dead sisters. And that is all. And mark this. Let either of you breathe a word, or the edge of a word, about the other things, and I will come to you in the black of some terrible night and I will bring a pointy reckoning that will shudder you. And you know I can do it; I saw Indians smash my dear parents' heads on the pillow next to mine, and I have seen some reddish work done at night, and I can make you wish you had never seen the sun go down! (*She goes to* BETTY *and roughly sits her up.*) Now, you—sit up and stop this!

(*But* BETTY *collapses in her hands and lies inert on the bed.*)

MARY WARREN (*with hysterical fright*): What's got her? (ABIGAIL *stares in fright at* BETTY.) Abby, she's going to die! It's a sin to conjure, and we—

ABIGAIL (*starting for* MARY): I say shut it, Mary Warren!

(*Enter* JOHN PROCTOR. *On seeing him,* MARY WARREN *leaps in fright.*)

Proctor was a farmer in his middle thirties. He need not have been a partisan of any faction in the town, but there is evidence to suggest that he had a sharp and biting way with hypocrites. He was the kind of man—powerful of body, even-tempered, and not easily led—who cannot refuse support to partisans without drawing their deepest resentment. In Proctor's presence a fool felt his foolishness instantly—and a Proctor is always marked for calumny therefore.

But as we shall see, the steady manner he displays does not spring from an untroubled soul. He is a sinner, a sinner not only against the moral fashion of the time, but against his own vision of decent conduct. These people had no ritual for the washing away of sins. It is another trait we inherited from them, and it has helped to discipline us as well as to breed hypocrisy among us. Proctor, respected and even feared in Salem, has come to regard himself as a kind of fraud. But no hint of this has yet appeared on the surface, and as he enters from the crowded parlor below it is a man in his prime we see, with a quiet confidence and an unexpressed, hidden force. Mary Warren, his servant, can barely speak for embarrassment and fear.

MARY WARREN: Oh! I'm just going home, Mr. Proctor.

PROCTOR: Be you foolish, Mary Warren? Be you deaf? I forbid you leave the house, did I not? Why shall I pay you? I am looking for you more often than my cows!

MARY WARREN: I only come to see the great doings in the world.

PROCTOR: I'll show you a great doin' on your arse one of these days. Now get you home; my wife is waitin' with your work! (*Trying to retain a shred of dignity, she goes slowly out.*)

MERCY LEWIS (*both afraid of him and strangely titillated*): I'd best be off. I have my Ruth to watch. Good morning, Mr. Proctor.

(MERCY *sidles out. Since* PROCTOR'S *entrance,* ABIGAIL *has stood as though on tiptoe, absorbing his presence, wide-eyed. He glances at her then goes to* BETTY *on the bed.*)

ABIGAIL: Gad. I'd almost forgot how strong you are, John Proctor!

PROCTOR (*looking at* ABIGAIL *now, the faintest suggestion of a knowing smile on his face*): What's this mischief here?

ABIGAIL (*with a nervous laugh*): Oh, she's only gone silly somehow.

PROCTOR: The road past my house is a pilgrimage to Salem all morning. The town's mumbling witchcraft.

ABIGAIL: Oh, posh! (*Winningly she comes a little closer, with a confidential, wicked air.*) We were dancin' in the woods last night, and my uncle leaped in on us. She took fright, is all.

PROCTOR (*his smile widening*): Ah, you're wicked yet, aren't y'! (*A thrill of expectant laughter escapes her, and she dares come closer, feverishly looking into his eyes.*) You'll be clapped in the stocks before you're twenty.

(*He takes a step to go, and she springs into his path.*)

ABIGAIL: Give me a word, John. A soft word. (*Her concentrated desire destroys his smile.*)

PROCTOR: No, no, Abby. That's done with.

ABIGAIL (*tauntingly*): You come five mile to see a silly girl fly? I know you better.

PROCTOR (*setting her firmly out of his path*): I come to see what mischief your uncle's brewin' now. (*With final emphasis*) Put it out of mind, Abby.

ABIGAIL (*grasping his hand before he can release her*): John—I am waitin' for you every night.

PROCTOR: Abby, I never give you hope to wait for me.

ABIGAIL (*now beginning to anger—she can't believe it*): I have something better than hope, I think!

PROCTOR: Abby, you'll put it out of mind. I'll not be comin' for you more.

ABIGAIL: You're surely sportin' with me.

PROCTOR: You know me better.

ABIGAIL: I know how you clutched my back behind your house and sweated like a stallion whenever I come near! Or did I dream that? It's she put me out, you cannot pretend it were you. I saw your face when she put me out, and you loved me then and you do now!

PROCTOR: Abby, that's a wild thing to say—

ABIGAIL: A wild thing may say wild things. But not so wild, I think. I have seen you since she put me out; I have seen you nights.

PROCTOR: I have hardly stepped off my farm this seven-month.

ABIGAIL: I have a sense for heat, John, and yours has drawn me to my window, and I have seen you looking up, burning in your loneliness. Do you tell me you've never looked up at my window?

PROCTOR: I may have looked up.

ABIGAIL (*now softening*): And you must. You are no wintry man. I know you, John. I *know* you. (*She is weeping.*) I cannot sleep for dreamin'; I cannot dream but I wake and walk about the house as though I'd find you comin' through some door. (*She clutches him desperately.*)

PROCTOR (*gently pressing her from him, with great sympathy but firmly*): Child—

ABIGAIL (*with a flash of anger*): How do you call me child!

PROCTOR: Abby, I think of you softly from time to time. But I will cut off my hand before I'll ever reach for you again. Wipe it out of mind. We never touched, Abby.

ABIGAIL: Aye, but we did.

PROCTOR: Aye, but we did not.

ABIGAIL (*with a bitter anger*): Oh, I marvel how such a strong man may let such a sickly wife be—

PROCTOR (*angered—at himself as well*): You'll speak nothin' of Elizabeth!

ABIGAIL: She is blackening my name in the village! She is telling lies about me! She is a cold, sniveling woman, and you bend to her! Let her turn you like a—

PROCTOR (*shaking her*): Do you look for whippin'?

(*A psalm is heard being sung below.*)

ABIGAIL (*in tears*): I look for John Proctor that took me from my sleep and put knowledge in my heart! I never knew what pretense Salem was, I never knew the lying lessons I was taught by all these Christian women and their covenanted men! And now you bid me tear the light out of my eyes? I will not, I cannot! You loved me, John Proctor, and whatever sin it is, you love me yet! (*He turns abruptly to go out. She rushes to him.*) John, pity me, pity me!

(*The words "going up to Jesus" are heard in the psalm, and* BETTY *claps her ears suddenly and whines loudly.*)

ABIGAIL: Betty? (*She hurries to* BETTY, *who is now sitting up and screaming.* PROCTOR *goes to* BETTY *as* ABIGAIL *is trying to pull her hands down, calling "Betty!"*)

PROCTOR (*growing unnerved*): What's she doing? Girl, what ails you? Stop that wailing!

(*The singing has stopped in the midst of this, and now* PARRIS *rushes in.*)

PARRIS: What happened? What are you doing to her? Betty! (*He rushes to the bed, crying, "Betty, Betty!"* MRS. PUTNAM *enters, feverish with curiosity, and with her* THOMAS PUTNAM *and* MERCY LEWIS. PARRIS, *at the bed, keeps lightly slapping* BETTY's *face, while she moans and tries to get up.*)

ABIGAIL: She heard you singin' and suddenly she's up and screamin'.

MRS. PUTNAM: The psalm! The psalm! She cannot bear to hear the Lord's name!

PARRIS: No, God forbid. Mercy, run to the doctor! Tell him what's happened here! (MERCY LEWIS *rushes out.*)

MRS. PUTNAM: Mark it for a sign, mark it! (REBECCA NURSE, *seventy-two, enters. She is white-haired, leaning upon her walking-stick.*)

PUTNAM (*pointing at the whimpering* BETTY): That is a notorious sign of witchcraft afoot, Goody Nurse, a prodigious sign!

MRS. PUTNAM: My mother told me that! When they cannot bear to hear the name of—

PARRIS (*trembling*): Rebecca, Rebecca, go to her, we're lost. She suddenly cannot bear to hear the Lord's—

(GILES COREY, *eighty-three, enters. He is knotted with muscle, canny, inquisitive, and still powerful.*)

REBECCA: There is hard sickness here, Giles Cory, so please to keep the quiet.

GILES: I've not said a word. No one here can testify I've said a word. Is she going to fly again? I hear she flies.

PUTNAM: Man, be quiet now!

(*Everything is quiet.* REBECCA *walks across the room to the bed. Gentleness exudes from her.* BETTY *is quietly whimpering, eyes shut.* REBECCA *simply stands over the child, who gradually quiets.*)

And while they are so absorbed, we may put a word in for Rebecca. Rebecca was the wife of Francis Nurse, who, from all accounts, was one of those men for whom both sides of the argument had to have respect. He was called upon to arbitrate disputes as though he were an unofficial judge, and Rebecca also enjoyed the high opinion most people had for him. By the time of the delusion, they had three hundred acres, and their children were settled in separate homesteads within the same estate. However, Francis had originally rented the land, and one theory has it that, as he gradually paid for it and raised his social status, there were those who resented his rise.

Another suggestion to explain the systematic campaign against Rebecca, and inferentially against Francis, is the land war he fought with his neighbors, one of whom was a Putnam. This squabble grew to the proportions of a battle in the woods between partisans of both sides, and it is said to have lasted for two days. As for Rebecca herself, the general opinion of her character was so high that to explain how anyone dared cry her out for a witch—and more, how adults could bring themselves to lay hands on her—we must look to the fields and boundaries of that time.

As we have seen, Thomas Putnam's man for the Salem ministry was Bayley. The Nurse clan had been in the faction that prevented Bayley's taking office. In addition, certain families allied to the Nurses by blood or friendship, and whose farms were contiguous with the Nurse farm or close to it, combined to break away from the Salem town authority and set up Topsfield, a new and independent entity whose existence was resented by old Salemites.

That the guiding hand behind the outcry was Putnam's is indicated by the fact that, as soon as it began, this Topsfield-Nurse faction absented themselves from church in protest and disbelief. It was Edward and Jonathan Putnam who signed the first complaint against Rebecca; and Thomas Putnam's little daughter was the one who fell into a fit at the hearing and pointed to Rebecca as her attacker. To top it all, Mrs. Putnam—who is now staring at the bewitched child on the bed—soon accused Rebecca's spirit of "tempting her to iniquity," a charge that had more truth in it than Mrs. Putnam could know.

MRS. PUTNAM (*astonished*): What have you done?

(REBECCA, *in thought, now leaves the bedside and sits.*)

PARRIS (*wondrous and relieved*): What do you make of it, Rebecca?

PUTNAM (*eagerly*): Goody Nurse, will you go to my Ruth and see if you can wake her?

REBECCA (*sitting*): I think she'll wake in time. Pray calm yourselves. I have eleven children, and I am twenty-six times a grandma, and I have seen them all through their silly seasons, and when it comes on them they will run the Devil bow-legged keeping up with their mischief. I think she'll wake when she tires of it. A child's spirit is like a child, you can never catch it by running after it; you must stand still, and, for love, it will soon itself come back.

PROCTOR: Aye, that's the truth of it, Rebecca.

MRS. PUTNAM:  This is no silly season, Rebecca. My Ruth is bewildered, Rebecca; she cannot eat.

REBECCA:  Perhaps she is not hungered yet. (*To* PARRIS) I hope you are not decided to go in search of loose spirits, Mr. Parris. I've heard promise of that outside.

PARRIS:  A wide opinion's running in the parish that the Devil may be among us, and I would satisfy them that they are wrong.

PROCTOR:  Then let you come out and call them wrong. Did you consult the wardens before you called this minister to look for devils?

PARRIS:  He is not coming to look for devils!

PROCTOR:  Then what's he coming for?

PUTNAM:  There be children dyin' in the village, Mister!

PROCTOR:  I see none dyin'. This society will not be a bag to swing around your head, Mr. Putnam. (*To* PARRIS.) Did you call a meeting before you—?

PUTNAM:  I am sick of meetings; cannot the man turn his head without he have a meeting?

PROCTOR:  He may turn his head, but not to Hell!

REBECCA:  Pray, John, be calm. (*Pause. He defers to her.*) Mr. Parris, I think you'd best send Reverend Hale back as soon as he come. This will set us all to arguin' again in the society, and we thought to have peace this year. I think we ought rely on the doctor now, and good prayer.

MRS. PUTNAM:  Rebecca, the doctor's baffled!

REBECCA:  If so he is, then let us go to God for the cause of it. There is prodigious danger in the seeking of loose spirits. I fear it, I fear it. Let us rather blame ourselves and—

PUTNAM:  How may we blame ourselves? I am one of nine sons; the Putnam seed have peopled this province. And yet I have but one child left of eight—and now she shrivels!

REBECCA:  I cannot fathom that.

MRS. PUTNAM (*with a growing edge of sarcasm*):  But I must! You think it God's work you should never lose a child, nor grandchild either, and I bury all but one? There are wheels within wheels in this village, and fires within fires!

PUTNAM (*to* PARRIS):  When Reverend Hale comes, you will proceed to look for signs of witchcraft here.

PROCTOR (*to* PUTNAM):  You cannot command Mr. Parris. We vote by name in this society, not by acreage.

PUTNAM:  I never heard you worried so on this society, Mr. Proctor. I do not think I saw you at Sabbath meeting since snow flew.

PROCTOR:  I have trouble enough without I come five mile to hear him preach only hellfire and bloody damnation. Take it to heart, Mr. Parris. There are many others who stay away from church these days because you hardly ever mention God any more.

PARRIS (*now aroused*):  Why, that's a drastic charge!

REBECCA:  It's somewhat true; there are many that quail to bring their children—

PARRIS:  I do not preach for children, Rebecca. It is not the children who are unmindful of their obligations toward this ministry.

REBECCA:  Are there really those unmindful?

PARRIS:  I should say the better half of Salem village—

PUTNAM:  And more than that!

PARRIS:  Where is my wood? My contract provides I be supplied with all my firewood. I am waiting since November for a stick, and even in November I had to show my frostbitten hands like some London beggar!

GILES:  You are allowed six pound a year to buy your wood, Mr. Parris.

PARRIS:  I regard that six pound as part of my salary. I am paid little enough without I spend six pound on firewood.

PROCTOR:  Sixty, plus six for firewood—

PARRIS:  The salary is sixty-six pound, Mr. Proctor! I am not some preaching farmer with a book under my arm; I am a graduate of Harvard College.

GILES:  Aye, and well instructed in arithmetic!

PARRIS:  Mr. Corey, you will look far for a man of my kind at sixty pound a year! I am not used to this poverty; I left a thrifty business in the Barbados to serve the Lord. I do not fathom it, why am I persecuted here? I cannot offer one proposition but there be a howling riot of argument. I have often wondered if the Devil be in it somewhere; I cannot understand you people otherwise.

PROCTOR:  Mr. Parris, you are the first minister ever did demand the deed to this house—

PARRIS:  Man! Don't a minister deserve a house to live in?

PROCTOR:  To live in, yes. But to ask ownership is like you shall own the meeting house itself; the last meeting I were at you spoke so long on deeds and mortgages I thought it were an auction.

PARRIS: I want a mark of confidence, is all! I am your third preacher in seven years. I do not wish to be put out like the cat whenever some majority feels the whim. You people seem not to comprehend that a minister is the Lord's man in the parish; a minister is not to be so lightly crossed and contradicted—

PUTNAM: Aye!

PARRIS: There is either obedience or the church will burn like Hell is burning!

PROCTOR: Can you speak one minute without we land in Hell again? I am sick of Hell!

PARRIS: It is not for you to say what is good for you to hear!

PROCTOR: I may speak my heart, I think!

PARRIS (in a fury): What, are we Quakers? We are not Quakers here yet, Mr. Proctor. And you may tell that to your followers!

PROCTOR: My followers!

PARRIS (Now he's out with it.): There is a party in this church. I am not blind; there is a faction and a party.

PROCTOR: Against you?

PUTNAM: Against him and all authority!

PROCTOR: Why, then I must find it and join it.

(There is shock among the others.)

REBECCA: He does not mean that.

PUTNAM: He confessed it now!

PROCTOR: I mean it solemnly, Rebecca; I like not the smell of this "authority."

REBECCA: No, you cannot break charity with your minister. You are another kind, John. Clasp his hand, make your peace.

PROCTOR: I have a crop to sow and lumber to drag home. (He goes angrily to the door and turns to COREY with a smile.) What say you, Giles, let's find the party. He says there's a party.

GILES: I've changed my opinion of this man, John. Mr. Parris, I beg your pardon. I never thought you had so much iron in you.

PARRIS (surprised): Why, thank you, Giles!

GILES: It suggests to the mind what the trouble be among us all these years. (To all) Think on it. Wherefore is everybody suing everybody else? Think on it now, it's a deep thing, and dark as a pit. I have been six time in court this year—

PROCTOR (familiarly, with warmth, although he knows he is approaching the edge of GILES' tolerance with this): Is it the Devil's fault that a man cannot say you good morning without you clap him for defamation? You're old, Giles, and you're not hearin' so well as you did.

GILES (He cannot be crossed.): John Proctor, I have only last month collected four pound damages for you publicly sayin' I burned the roof off your house, and I—

PROCTOR (laughing): I never said no such thing, but I've paid you for it, so I hope I can call you deaf without charge. Now come along, Giles, and help me drag my lumber home.

PUTNAM: A moment, Mr. Proctor. What lumber is that you're draggin', if I may ask you?

PROCTOR: My lumber. From out my forest by the riverside.

PUTNAM: Why, we are surely gone wild this year. What anarchy is this? That tract is in my bounds, it's in my bounds, Mr. Proctor.

PROCTOR: In your bounds! (Indicating REBECCA) I bought that tract from Goody Nurse's husband five months ago.

PUTNAM: He had no right to sell it. It stands clear in my grandfather's will that all the land between the river and—

PROCTOR: Your grandfather had a habit of willing land that never belonged to him, if I may say it plain.

GILES: That's God's truth; he nearly willed away my north pasture but he knew I'd break his fingers before he'd set his name to it. Let's get your lumber home, John. I feel a sudden will to work coming on.

PUTNAM: You load one oak of mine and you'll fight to drag it home!

GILES: Aye, and we'll win too, Putnam—this fool and I. Come on! (He turns to PROCTOR and starts out.)

PUTNAM: I'll have my men on you, Corey! I'll clap a writ on you!

(Enter REVEREND JOHN HALE of Beverly.)

Mr. Hale is nearing forty, a tight-skinned, eager-eyed intellectual. This is a beloved errand for him; on being called here to ascertain witchcraft he felt the pride of the specialist whose unique knowledge has at last been publicly called for. Like almost all men of learning, he spent a good deal of his time pondering the invisible world, especially since he had himself encountered a witch in his parish not long before. That woman, however, turned into a mere pest under his searching scrutiny, and the child she had allegedly been afflicting recovered her normal behavior after Hale had given her his kindness and a few days of rest in his own house. However, that experience never raised a doubt in his mind as to the reality of the underworld or the existence of Lucifer's many-faced lieutenants. And his belief is not to his discredit. Better minds than Hale's were—and still are—convinced that there is a society of spirits beyond our ken. One cannot help noting that one of his lines has never yet raised a laugh in any audience that has seen this play; it is his assurance that "We cannot look to superstition in this. The Devil is precise." Evidently we are not quite certain even now whether diabolism is holy and not to be scoffed at. And it is no accident that we should be so bemused.

Like Reverend Hale and the others on this stage, we conceive the Devil as a necessary part of a respectable view of cosmology. Ours is a divided empire in which certain ideas and emotions and actions are of God, and their opposites are of Lucifer. It is as impossible for most men to conceive of a morality without sin as of an earth without "sky." Since 1692 a great but superficial change has wiped out God's beard and the Devil's horns, but the world is still gripped between two diametrically opposed absolutes. The concept of unity, in which positive and negative are attributes of the same force, in which good and evil are relative, ever-changing, and always joined to the same phenomenon— such a concept is still reserved to the physical sciences and to the few who have grasped the history of ideas. When it is recalled that until the Christian era the underworld was never regarded as a hostile area, that all gods were useful and essentially friendly to man despite occasional lapses; when we see the steady and methodical inculcation into humanity of the idea of man's worthlessness—until redeemed—the necessity of the Devil may become evident as a weapon, a weapon designed and used time and time again in every age to whip men into a surrender to a particular church or church-state.

Our difficulty in believing the—for want of a better word—political inspiration of the Devil is due in great part to the fact that he is called up and damned not only by our social antagonists but by our own side, whatever it may be. The Catholic Church, through its Inquisition, is famous for cultivating Lucifer as the arch-fiend, but the Church's enemies relied no less upon the Old Boy to keep the human mind enthralled. Luther was himself accused of alliance with Hell, and he in turn accused his enemies. To complicate matters further, he believed that he had had contact with the Devil and had argued theology with him. I am not surprised at this, for at my own university a professor of history—a Lutheran, by the way—used to assemble his graduate students, draw the shades, and commune in the classroom with Erasmus. He was never, to my knowledge, officially scoffed at for this, the reason being that the university officials, like most of us, are the children of a history which still sucks at the Devil's teats. At this writing, only England has held back before the temptations of contemporary diabolism. In the countries of the Communist ideology, all resistance of any import is linked to the totally malign capitalist succubi, and in America any man who is not reactionary in his views is open to the charge of alliance with the Red hell. Political opposition, thereby, is given an inhumane overlay which then justifies the abrogation of all normally applied customs of civilized intercourse. A political policy is equated with moral right, and opposition to it with diabolical malevolence. Once such an equation is effectively made, society becomes a congerie of plots and counterplots, and the main role of government changes from that of the arbiter to that of the scourge of God.

The results of this process are no different now from what they ever were, except sometimes in the degree of cruelty inflicted, and not always even in that department. Normally the actions and deeds of a man were all that society felt comfortable in judging. The secret intent of an action was left to the ministers, priests, and rabbis to deal with. When diabolism rises, however, actions are the least important manifests of the true nature of a man. The Devil, as Reverend Hale said, is a wily one, and until an hour before he fell, even God thought him beautiful in Heaven.

The analogy, however, seems to falter when one considers that, while there were no witches then, there are Communists and capitalists now, and in each camp there is certain proof that spies of each side are at work undermining the other. But this is a snobbish objection and not at all warranted by the facts. I have no doubt that people *were* communing with, and even worshiping, the Devil in Salem, and if the whole truth could be known in this case, as it is in others, we should discover a regular and conventionalized propitiation of the dark spirit. One certain evidence of this is the confession of Tituba, the slave of Reverend Parris, and another is the behavior of the children who were known to have indulged in sorceries with her.

There are accounts of similar *klatches* in Europe, where the daughters of the towns would assemble at night and, sometimes with fetishes, sometimes with a selected young man, give themselves to love, with some bastardly results. The Church, sharp-eyed as it must be when gods long dead are brought to life, condemned these orgies as witchcraft and interpreted them, rightly, as a resurgence of the Dionysiac forces it had crushed long before. Sex, sin, and the Devil were early linked, and so they continued to be in Salem, and are today. From all accounts there are no more puritanical mores in the world than those enforced by the Communists in Russia, where women's fashions, for instance, are as prudent and all-covering as any American Baptist would desire. The divorce laws lay a tremendous responsibility on the father for the care of his children. Even the laxity of divorce regulations in the early years of the revolution was undoubtedly a revulsion from the nineteenth-century Victorian immobility of marriage and the consequent hypocrisy that developed from it. If for no other reasons, a state so powerful, so jealous of the uniformity of its citizens, cannot long tolerate the atomization of the family. And yet, in American eyes at least, there remains the conviction that the Russian attitude toward women is lascivious. It is the Devil working again, just as he is working within the Slav who is shocked at the very idea of a woman's disrobing herself in a burlesque show. Our opposites are always robed in sexual sin, and it is from this unconscious conviction that demonology gains both its attractive sensuality and its capacity to infuriate and frighten.

Coming into Salem now, Reverend Hale conceives of himself much as a young doctor on his first call. His painfully acquired armory of symptoms, catchwords, and diagnostic procedures are now to be put to use at last. The road from Beverly is unusually busy this morning, and he has passed a hundred rumors that make him smile at the ignorance of the yeomanry in this most precise science. He feels himself allied with the best minds of Europe—kings, philosophers, scientists, and ecclesiasts of all churches. His goal is light, goodness and its preservation, and he knows the exaltation of the blessed whose intelligence, sharpened by minute examinations of enormous tracts, is finally called upon to face what may be a bloody fight with the Fiend himself.

(*He appears loaded down with half a dozen heavy books.*)

HALE:  Pray you, someone take these!

PARRIS (*delighted*):  Mr. Hale! Oh! it's good to see you again! (*Taking some books*) My, they're heavy!

HALE (*setting down his books*):  They must be; they are weighted with authority.

PARRIS (*a little scared*):  Well, you do come prepared!

HALE:  We shall need hard study if it comes to tracking down the Old Boy. (*Noticing* REBECCA) You cannot be Rebecca Nurse?

REBECCA:  I am, sir. Do you know me?

HALE:  It's strange how I knew you, but I suppose you look as such a good soul should. We have all heard of your great charities in Beverly.

PARRIS:  Do you know this gentleman? Mr. Thomas Putnam. And his good wife Ann.

HALE:  Putnam! I had not expected such distinguished company, sir.

PUTNAM (*pleased*):  It does not seem to help us today, Mr. Hale. We look to you to come to our house and save our child.

HALE:  Your child ails too?

MRS. PUTNAM:  Her soul, her soul seems flown away. She sleeps and yet she walks . . .

PUTNAM:  She cannot eat.

HALE:  Cannot eat! (*Thinks on it. Then, to* PROCTOR *and* GILES COREY) Do you men have afflicted children?

PARRIS:  No, no, these are farmers John Proctor—

GILES COREY:  He don't believe in witches.

PROCTOR (*to* HALE):  I never spoke on witches one way or the other. Will you come, Giles?

GILES:  No—no, John, I think not. I have some few queer questions of my own to ask this fellow.

PROCTOR:  I've heard you to be a sensible man,

Mr. Hale. I hope you'll leave some of it in Salem.

(PROCTOR *goes.* HALE *stands embarrassed for an instant.*)

PARRIS (*quickly*): Will you look at my daughter, sir? (*Leads* HALE *to the bed.*) She has tried to leap out the window; we discovered her this morning on the highroad, waving her arms as though she'd fly.

HALE (*narrowing his eyes*): Tries to fly.

PUTNAM: She cannot bear to hear the Lord's name, Mr. Hale; that's a sure sign of witchcraft afloat.

HALE (*holding up his hands*): No, no. Now let me instruct you. We cannot look to superstition in this. The Devil is precise; the marks of his presence are definite as stone, and I must tell you all that I shall not proceed unless you are prepared to believe me if I should find no bruise of hell upon her.

PARRIS: It is agreed, sir—it is agreed—we will abide by your judgment.

HALE: Good then. (*He goes to the bed, looks down at* BETTY. *To* PARRIS) Now, sir, what were your first warning of this strangeness?

PARRIS: Why, sir—I discovered her—(*indicating* ABIGAIL)—and my niece and ten or twelve of the other girls, dancing in the forest last night.

HALE (*surprised*): You permit dancing?

PARRIS: No, no, it were secret—

MRS. PUTNAM (*unable to wait*): Mr. Parris's slave has knowledge of conjurin', sir.

PARRIS (*to* MRS. PUTNAM): We cannot be sure of that, Goody Ann—

MRS. PUTNAM (*frightened, very softly*): I know it, sir. I sent my child—she should learn from Tituba who murdered her sisters.

REBECCA (*horrified*): Goody Ann! You sent a child to conjure up the dead?

MRS. PUTNAM: Let God blame me, not you, not you, Rebecca! I'll not have you judging me any more! (*To* HALE) Is it a natural work to lose seven children before they live a day?

PARRIS: Ssh!

(REBECCA, *with great pain, turns her face away. There is a pause.*)

HALE: Seven dead in childbirth.

MRS. PUTNAM (*softly*): Aye. (*Her voice breaks; she looks up at him. Silence.* HALE *is impressed.* PARRIS *looks to him. He goes to his books, opens one, turns pages, then reads. All wait, avidly.*)

PARRIS (*hushed*): What book is that?

MRS. PUTNAM: What's there, sir?

HALE (*with a tasty love of intellectual pursuit*): Here is all the invisible world, caught, defined, and calculated. In these books the Devil stands stripped of all his brute disguises. Here are all your familiar spirits—your incubi and succubi; your witches that go by land, by air, and by sea; your wizards of the night and of the day. Have no fear now—we shall find him out if he has come among us, and I mean to crush him utterly if he has shown his face! (*He starts for the bed.*)

REBECCA: Will it hurt the child, sir?

HALE: I cannot tell. If she is truly in the Devil's grip we may have to rip and tear to get her free.

REBECCA: I think I'll go, then. I am too old for this. (*She rises.*)

PARRIS (*striving for conviction*): Why, Rebecca, we may open up the boil of all our troubles today!

REBECCA: Let us hope for that. I go to God for you, sir.

PARRIS (*with trepidation—and resentment*): I hope you do not mean to go to Satan here! (*Slight pause.*)

REBECCA: I wish I knew. (*She goes out; they feel resentful of her note of moral superiority.*)

PUTNAM (*abruptly*): Come, Mr. Hale, let's get on. Sit you here.

GILES: Mr. Hale, I have always wanted to ask a learned man—what signifies the readin' of strange books?

HALE: What books?

GILES: I cannot tell; she hides them.

HALE: Who does this?

GILES: Martha, my wife. I have waked at night many a time and found her in a corner, readin' of a book. Now what do you make of that?

HALE: Why, that's not necessarily—

GILES: It discomfits me! Last night—mark this—I tried and tried and could not say my prayers. And then she close her book and walks out of the house, and suddenly—mark this—I could pray again!

Old Giles must be spoken for, if only because his fate was to be so remarkable and so different from that of all the others. He was in his early eighties at this time, and was the most comical hero in the history. No man has ever been blamed for so much. If a cow was missed, the first thought was to look for her around Corey's house; a fire blazing up at night brought suspicion of arson to his door. He didn't give a hoot for public opinion, and only in his last years—after he had married Martha—did he bother much with the church. That she stopped his prayer is very probable, but he forgot to say that he'd only recently learned any prayers and it didn't take much to make him stumble over them. He was a crank and a nuisance, but withal a deeply innocent and brave man. In court, once, he was asked if it were true that he had been frightened by the strange behavior of a hog and had then said he knew it to be the Devil in an animal's shape. "What frighted you?" he was asked. He forgot everything but the word "frighted," and instantly replied, "I do not know that I ever spoke that word in my life."

HALE: Ah! The stoppage of prayer—that is strange. I'll speak further on that with you.

GILES: I'm not sayin' she's touched the Devil, now, but I'd admire to know what books she reads and why she hides them. She'll not answer me, y' see.

HALE: Aye, we'll discuss it. (*To all*) Now mark me, if the Devil is in her you will witness some frightful wonders in this room, so please to keep your wits about you. Mr. Putnam, stand close in case she flies. Now, Betty, dear, will you sit up? (PUTNAM *comes in closer, ready-handed.* HALE *sits* BETTY *up, but she hangs limp in his hands.*) Hmmm. (*He observes her carefully. The others watch breathlessly.*) Can you hear me? I am John Hale, minister of Beverly. I have come to help you, dear. Do you remember my two little girls in Beverly? (*She does not stir in his hands.*)

PARRIS (*in fright*): How can it be the Devil? Why would he choose my house to strike? We have all manner of licentious people in the village!

HALE: What victory would the Devil have to win a soul already bad? It is the best the Devil wants, and who is better than the minister?

GILES: That's deep, Mr. Parris, deep, deep!

PARRIS (*with resolution now*): Betty! Answer Mr. Hale! Betty!

HALE: Does someone afflict you, child? It need not be a woman, mind you, or a man. Perhaps some bird invisible to others comes to you—perhaps a pig, a mouse, or any beast at all. Is there some figure bids you fly? (*The child remains limp in his hands. In silence he lays her back on the pillow. Now, holding out his hands toward her, he intones.*) In nomine Domini Sabaoth sui filiique ite ad infernos. (*She does not stir. He turns to* ABIGAIL, *his eyes narrowing.*) Abigail, what sort of dancing were you doing with her in the forest?

ABIGAIL: Why—common dancing is all.

PARRIS: I think I ought to say that I—I saw a kettle in the grass where they were dancing.

ABIGAIL: That were only soup.

HALE: What sort of soup were in this kettle, Abigail?

ABIGAIL: Why, it were beans—and lentils, I think, and—

HALE: Mr. Parris, you did not notice, did you, any living thing in the kettle? A mouse, perhaps, a spider, a frog—?

PARRIS (*fearfully*): I—do believe there were some movement—in the soup.

ABIGAIL: That jumped in, we never put it in!

HALE (*quickly*): What jumped in?

ABIGAIL: Why, a very little frog jumped—

PARRIS: A frog, Abby!

HALE (*grasping* ABIGAIL): Abigail, it may be your cousin is dying. Did you call the Devil last night?

ABIGAIL: I never called him! Tituba, Tituba . . .

PARRIS (*blanched*): She called the Devil?

HALE: I should like to speak with Tituba.

PARRIS: Goody Ann, will you bring her up? (MRS. PUTNAM *exits.*)

HALE: How did she call him?

ABIGAIL: I know not—she spoke Barbados.

HALE: Did you feel any strangeness when she called him? A sudden cold wind, perhaps? A trembling below the ground?

ABIGAIL: I didn't see no Devil! (*Shaking* BETTY) Betty, wake up. Betty! Betty!

HALE: You cannot evade me, Abigail. Did your cousin drink any of the brew in that kettle?

ABIGAIL: She never drank it!

HALE: Did you drink it?

ABIGAIL: No, sir!

HALE: Did Tituba ask you to drink it?

ABIGAIL: She tried, but I refused.

HALE: Why are you concealing? Have you sold yourself to Lucifer?

ABIGAIL: I never sold myself! I'm a good girl! I'm a proper girl!

(MRS. PUTNAM *enters with* TITUBA, *and instantly* ABIGAIL *points at* TITUBA.)

ABIGAIL: She made me do it! She made Betty do it!

TITUBA (*shocked and angry*): Abby!

ABIGAIL: She makes me drink blood!

PARRIS: Blood!!

MRS. PUTNAM: My baby's blood?

TITUBA: No, no, chicken blood. I give she chicken blood!

HALE: Woman, have you enlisted these children for the Devil?

TITUBA: No, no, sir, I don't truck with no Devil!

HALE: Why can she not wake? Are you silencing this child?

TITUBA: I love me Betty!

HALE: You have sent your spirit out upon this child, have you not? Are you gathering souls for the Devil?

ABIGAIL: She sends her spirit on me in church; she makes me laugh at prayer!

PARRIS: She have often laughed at prayer!

ABIGAIL: She comes to me every night to go and drink blood!

TITUBA: You beg *me* to conjure! She beg *me* make charm—

ABIGAIL: Don't lie! (*To* HALE) She comes to me while I sleep; she's always making me dream corruptions!

TITUBA: Why you say that, Abby?

ABIGAIL: Sometimes I wake and find myself standing in the open doorway and not a stitch on my body! I always hear her laughing in my sleep. I hear her singing her Barbados songs and tempting me with—

TITUBA: Mister Reverend, I never—

HALE (*resolved now*): Tituba, I want you to wake this child.

TITUBA: I have no power on this child, sir.

HALE: You most certainly do, and you will free her from it now! When did you compact with the Devil?

TITUBA: I don't compact with no Devil!

PARRIS: You will confess yourself or I will take you out and whip you to your death, Tituba!

PUTNAM: This woman must be hanged! She must be taken and hanged!

TITUBA (*terrified, falls to her knees*): No, no, don't hang Tituba! I tell him I don't desire to work for him, sir.

PARRIS: The Devil?

HALE: Then you saw him! (*Tituba weeps.*) Now Tituba, I know that when we bind ourselves to Hell it is very hard to break with it. We are going to help you tear yourself free—

TITUBA (*frightened by the coming process*): Mister Reverend, I do believe somebody else be witchin' these children.

HALE: Who?

TITUBA: I don't know, sir, but the Devil got him numerous witches.

HALE: Does he! (*It is a clue.*) Tituba, look into my eyes. Come, look into me. (*She raises her eyes to his fearfully.*) You would be a good Christian woman, would you not, Tituba?

TITUBA: Aye, sir, a good Christian woman.

HALE: And you love these little children?

TITUBA: Oh, yes, sir, I don't desire to hurt little children.

HALE: And you love God, Tituba?

TITUBA: I love God with all my bein'.

HALE: Now, in God's holy name—

TITUBA: Bless Him. Bless Him. (*She is rocking on her knees, sobbing in terror.*)

HALE: And to His glory—

TITUBA: Eternal glory. Bless Him—bless God . . .

HALE: Open yourself, Tituba—open yourself and let God's holy light shine on you.

TITUBA: Oh, bless the Lord.

HALE: When the Devil comes to you does he ever come—with another person? (*She stares up into his face.*) Perhaps another person in the village? Someone you know.

PARRIS: Who came with him?

PUTNAM: Sarah Good? Did you ever see Sarah Good with him? Or Osburn?

PARRIS: Was it man or woman came with him?

TITUBA: Man or woman. Was—was woman.

PARRIS: What woman? A woman, you said. What woman?

TITUBA: It was black dark, and I—

PARRIS: You could see him, why could you not see her?

TITUBA: Well, they was always talking; they was always runnin' round and carryin' on—

PARRIS: You mean out of Salem? Salem witches?

TITUBA: I believe so, yes, sir.

(*Now* HALE *takes her hand. She is surprised.*)

HALE: Tituba. You must have no fear to tell us who they are, do you understand? We will protect you. The Devil can never overcome a minister. You know that, do you not?

TITUBA (*kisses* HALE's *hand*): Aye, sir, oh, I do.

HALE: You have confessed yourself to witchcraft, and that speaks a wish to come to Heaven's side. And we will bless you, Tituba.

TITUBA (*deeply relieved*): Oh, God bless you, Mr. Hale!

HALE (*with rising exaltation*): You are God's instrument put in our hands to discover the Devil's agent among us. You are selected, Tituba, you are chosen to help us cleanse our village. So speak utterly, Tituba, turn your back on him and face God—face God, Tituba, and God will protect you.

TITUBA (*joining with him*): Oh, God, protect Tituba!

HALE (*kindly*): Who came to you with the Devil? Two? Three? Four? How many?

(TITUBA *pants, and begins rocking back and forth again, staring ahead.*)

TITUBA: There was four. There was four.

PARRIS (*pressing in on her*): Who? Who? Their names, their names!

TITUBA (*suddenly bursting out*): Oh, how many times he bid me kill you, Mr. Parris!

PARRIS: Kill me!

TITUBA (*in a fury*): He say Mr. Parris must be kill! Mr. Parris no goodly man, Mr. Parris mean man and no gentle man, and he bid me rise out of my bed and cut your throat! (*They gasp.*) But I tell him, "No! I don't hate that man. I don't want kill that man." But he say, "You work for me, Tituba, and I make you free! I give you pretty dress to wear, and put you way high up in the air, and you gone fly back to Barbados!" And I say, "You lie, Devil, you lie!" And then he come one stormy night to me, and he say, "Look! I have *white* people belong to me." And I look—and there was Goody Good.

PARRIS: Sarah Good!

TITUBA (*rocking and weeping*): Aye, sir, and Goody Osburn.

MRS. PUTNAM: I knew it! Goody Osburn were midwife to me three times. I begged you, Thomas, did I not? I begged him not to call Osburn because I feared her. My babies always shriveled in her hands!

HALE: Take courage, you must give us all their names. How can you bear to see this child suffering? Look at her, Tituba. (*He is indicating* BETTY *on the bed.*) Look at her God-given innocence; her soul is so tender; we must protect her,

Tituba; the Devil is out and preying on her like a beast upon the flesh of the pure lamb. God will bless you for your help.

(ABIGAIL *rises, staring as though inspired, and cries out.*)

ABIGAIL: I want to open myself! (*They turn to her, startled. She is enraptured, as though in a pearly light.*) I want the light of God, I want the sweet love of Jesus! I danced for the Devil; I saw him; I wrote in his book; I go back to Jesus; I kiss His hand. I saw Sarah Good with the Devil! I saw Goody Osburn with the Devil! I saw Bridget Bishop with the Devil!

(*As she is speaking,* BETTY *is rising from the bed, a fever in her eyes, and picks up the chant.*)

BETTY (*staring too*): I saw George Jacobs with the Devil! I saw Goody Howe with the Devil!

PARRIS: She speaks! (*He rushes to embrace* BETTY.) She speaks!

HALE: Glory to God! It is broken, they are free!

BETTY (*calling out hysterically and with great relief*): I saw Martha Bellows with the Devil!

ABIGAIL: I saw Goody Sibber with the Devil! (*It is rising to a great glee.*)

PUTNAM: The marshal, I'll call the marshal! (PARRIS *is shouting a prayer of thanksgiving.*)

BETTY: I saw Alice Barrow with the Devil! (*The curtain begins to fall.*)

HALE (*as* PUTNAM *goes out*): Let the marshal bring irons!

ABIGAIL: I saw Goody Hawkins with the Devil!

BETTY: I saw Goody Bibber with the Devil!

ABIGAIL: I saw Goody Booth with the Devil! (*On their ecstatic cries the curtain falls.*)

## ACT TWO

*The common room of* PROCTOR's *house, eight days later.*

*At the right is a door opening on the fields outside. A fireplace is at the left, and behind it a stairway leading upstairs. It is the low, dark, and rather long living room of the time. As the curtain rises, the room is empty. From above,* ELIZABETH *is heard softly singing to the children. Presently the door opens and* JOHN PROCTOR *enters, carrying his gun. He glances about the room as he comes toward the fireplace, then halts for an instant as he hears her singing. He con-*

*tinues on to the fireplace, leans the gun against the wall as he swings a pot out of the fire and smells it. Then he lifts out the ladle and tastes. He is not quite pleased. He reaches to a cupboard, takes a pinch of salt, and drops it into the pot. As he is tasting again, her footsteps are heard on the stair. He swings the pot into the fireplace and goes to a basin and washes his hands and face.*
ELIZABETH *enters.*

ELIZABETH:   What keeps you so late? It's almost dark.

PROCTOR:   I were planting far out to the forest edge.

ELIZABETH:   Oh, you're done then.

PROCTOR:   Aye, the farm is seeded. The boys asleep?

ELIZABETH:   They will be soon. (*And she goes to the fireplace, proceeds to ladle up stew in a dish.*)

PROCTOR:   Pray now for a fair summer.

ELIZABETH:   Aye.

PROCTOR:   Are you well today?

ELIZABETH:   I am. (*She brings the plate to the table, and, indicating the food*) It is a rabbit.

PROCTOR: (*going to the table*):   Oh, is it! In Jonathan's trap?

ELIZABETH:   No, she walked into the house this afternoon, I found her sittin' in the corner like she come to visit.

PROCTOR:   Oh, that's a good sign walkin' in.

ELIZABETH:   Pray God. It hurt my heart to strip her, poor rabbit. (*She sits and watches him taste it.*)

PROCTOR:   It's well seasoned.

ELIZABETH (*blushing with pleasure*):   I took great care. She's tender?

PROCTOR:   Aye. (*He eats. She watches him.*) I think we'll see green fields soon. It's warm as blood beneath the clods.

ELIZABETH:   That's well.

(PROCTOR *eats, then looks up.*)

PROCTOR:   If the crop is good I'll buy George Jacob's heifer. How would that please you?

ELIZABETH:   Aye, it would.

PROCTOR (*with a grin*):   I mean to please you, Elizabeth.

ELIZABETH (*It is hard to say.*)   I know it, John.

(*He gets up, goes to her, kisses her. She receives it. With a certain disappointment, he returns to the table.*)

PROCTOR (*as gently as he can*):   Cider?

ELIZABETH (*with a sense of reprimanding her-self for having forgot*):   Aye! (*She gets up and goes and pours a glass for him. He now arches his back.*)

PROCTOR:   This farm's a continent when you go foot by foot droppin' seeds in it.

ELIZABETH (*coming with the cider*):   It must be.

PROCTOR (*drinks a long draught, then, putting the glass down*):   You ought to bring some flowers in the house.

ELIZABETH:   Oh! I forgot! I will tomorrow.

PROCTOR:   It's winter in here yet. On Sunday let you come with me, and we'll walk the farm together; I never see such a load of flowers on the earth. (*With good feeling he goes and looks up at the sky through the open doorway.*) Lilacs have a purple smell. Lilac is the smell of night-fall, I think. Massachusetts is a beauty in the spring!

ELIZABETH:   Aye, it is.

(*There is a pause. She is watching him from the table as he stands there absorbing the night. It is as though she would speak but cannot. Instead, now, she takes up his plate and glass and fork and goes with them to the basin. Her back is turned to him. He turns to her and watches her. A sense of their separation rises.*)

PROCTOR:   I think you're sad again. Are you?

ELIZABETH (*She doesn't want friction, and yet she must.*):   You come so late I thought you'd gone to Salem this afternoon.

PROCTOR:   Why? I have no business in Salem.

ELIZABETH:   You did speak of going, earlier this week.

PROCTOR (*He knows what she means.*):   I thought better of it since.

ELIZABETH:   Mary Warren's there today.

PROCTOR:   Why'd you let her? You heard me forbid her go to Salem any more!

ELIZABETH:   I couldn't stop her.

PROCTOR (*holding back a full condemnation of her*):   It is a fault, it is a fault, Elizabeth—you're the mistress here, not Mary Warren.

ELIZABETH:   She frightened all my strength away.

PROCTOR:   How may that mouse frighten you, Elizabeth? You—

ELIZABETH:   It is a mouse no more. I forbid her go, and she raises up her chin like the daughter of a prince and says to me, "I must go to Salem, Goody Proctor; I am an official of the court!"

PROCTOR:   Court! What court?

ELIZABETH: Aye, it is a proper court they have now. They've sent four judges out of Boston, she says, weighty magistrates of the General Court, and at the head sits the Deputy Governor of the Province.

PROCTOR (*astonished*): Why, she's mad.

ELIZABETH: I would to God she were. There be fourteen people in the jail now, she says. (PROCTOR *simply looks at her, unable to grasp it.*) And they'll be tried, and the court have power to hang them too, she says.

PROCTOR (*scoffing, but without conviction*): Ah, they'd never hang—

ELIZABETH: The Deputy Governor promise hangin' if they'll not confess, John. The town's gone wild, I think. She speak of Abigail, and I thought she were a saint, to hear her. Abigail brings the other girls into the court, and where she walks the crowd will part like the sea for Israel. And folks are brought before them, and if they scream and howl and fall to the floor—the person's clapped in the jail for bewitchin' them.

PROCTOR (*wide-eyed*): Oh, it is a black mischief.

ELIZABETH: I think you must go to Salem, John. (*He turns to her.*) I think so. You must tell them it is a fraud.

PROCTOR (*thinking beyond this*): Aye, it is, it is surely.

ELIZABETH: Let you go to Ezekiel Cheever—he knows you well. And tell him what she said to you last week in her uncle's house. She said it had naught to do with witchcraft, did she not?

PROCTOR (*in thought*): Aye, she did, she did. (*Now, a pause.*)

ELIZABETH (*quietly, fearing to anger him by prodding.*): God forbid you keep that from the court, John. I think they must be told.

PROCTOR (*quietly, struggling with his thought*): Aye, they must, they must. It is a wonder they do believe her.

ELIZABETH: I would go to Salem now, John—let you go tonight.

PROCTOR: I'll think on it.

ELIZABETH (*with her courage now*): You cannot keep it, John.

PROCTOR (*angering*): I know I cannot keep it. I say I will think on it!

ELIZABETH (*hurt, and very coldly*): Good, then, let you think on it. (*She stands and starts to walk out of the room.*)

PROCTOR: I am only wondering how I may prove what she told me, Elizabeth. If the girl's a saint now, I think it is not easy to prove she's fraud, and the town gone so silly. She told it to me in a room alone—I have no proof for it.

ELIZABETH: You were alone with her?

PROCTOR (*stubbornly*): For a moment alone, aye.

ELIZABETH: Why, then, it is not as you told me.

PROCTOR (*his anger rising*): For a moment, I say. The others come in soon after.

ELIZABETH (*Quietly. She has suddenly lost all faith in him.*): Do as you wish, then. (*She starts to turn.*)

PROCTOR: Woman. (*She turns to him.*) I'll not have your suspicion any more.

ELIZABETH (*a little loftily*): I have no—

PROCTOR: I'll not have it!

ELIZABETH: Then let you not earn it.

PROCTOR (*with a violent undertone*): You doubt me yet?

ELIZABETH (*with a smile, to keep her dignity*): John, if it were not Abigail that you must go to hurt, would you falter now? I think not.

PROCTOR: Now look you—

ELIZABETH: I see what I see, John.

PROCTOR (*with solemn warning*): You will not judge me more, Elizabeth. I have good reason to think before I charge fraud on Abigail, and I will think on it. Let you look to your own improvement before you go to judge your husband any more. I have forgot Abigail, and—

ELIZABETH: And I.

PROCTOR: Spare me! You forget nothin' and forgive nothin'. Learn charity, woman. I have gone tiptoe in this house all seven month since she is gone. I have not moved from there to there without I think to please you, and still an everlasting funeral marches round your heart. I cannot speak but I am doubted, every moment judged for lies, as though I come into a court when I come into this house!

ELIZABETH: John, you are not open with me. You saw her with a crowd, you said. Now you—

PROCTOR: I'll plead my honesty no more, Elizabeth.

ELIZABETH (*Now she would justify herself.*): John, I am only—

PROCTOR: No more! I should have roared you down when first you told me your suspicion. But I wilted, and, like a Christian, I confessed. Confessed! Some dream I had must have mistaken you for God that day. But you're not, you're not, and let you remember it! Let you look sometimes for the goodness in me, and judge me not.

ELIZABETH: I do not judge you. The magistrate sits in your heart that judges you. I never thought you but a good man, John— (*with a smile*)—only somewhat bewildered.

PROCTOR (*laughing bitterly*): Oh, Elizabeth, your justice would freeze beer! (*He turns suddenly toward a sound outside. He starts for the door as* MARY WARREN *enters. As soon as he sees her, he goes directly to her and grabs her by the cloak, furious.*) How do you go to Salem when I forbid it? Do you mock me? (*Shaking her*) I'll whip you if you dare leave this house again!

(*Strangely, she doesn't resist him, but hangs limply by his grip.*)

MARY WARREN: I am sick, I am sick, Mr. Proctor. Pray, pray, hurt me not. (*Her strangeness throws him off, and her evident pallor and weakness. He frees her.*) My insides are all shuddery; I am in the proceedings all day, sir.

PROCTOR (*With draining anger—his curiosity is draining it.*): And what of these proceedings here? When will you proceed to keep this house, as you are paid nine pound a year to do—and my wife not wholly well?

(*As though to compensate,* MARY WARREN *goes to* ELIZABETH *with a small rag doll.*)

MARY WARREN: I made a gift for you today, Goody Proctor. I had to sit long hours in a chair, and passed the time with sewing.

ELIZABETH (*perplexed, looking at the doll*): Why, thank you, it's a fair poppet.

MARY WARREN (*with a trembling, decayed voice*): We must all love each other now, Goody Proctor.

ELIZABETH (*amazed at her strangeness*): Aye, indeed we must.

MARY WARREN (*glancing at the room*): I'll get up early in the morning and clean the house. I must sleep now. (*She turns and starts off.*)

PROCTOR: Mary. (*She halts.*) Is it true? There be fourteen women arrested?

MARY WARREN: No, sir. There be thirty-nine now—(*She suddenly breaks off and sobs and sits down, exhausted.*)

ELIZABETH: Why, she's weepin'! What ails you, child?

MARY WARREN: Goody Osburn—will hang! (*There is a shocked pause, while she sobs.*)

PROCTOR: Hang! (*He calls into her face.*) Hang, y'say?

MARY WARREN (*through her weeping*): Aye.

PROCTOR: The Deputy Governor will permit it?

MARY WARREN: He sentenced her. He must. (*To ameliorate it*) But not Sarah Good. For Sarah Good confessed, y'see.

PROCTOR: Confessed! To what?

MARY WARREN: That she—(*in horror at the memory*)—she sometimes made a compact with Lucifer, and wrote her name in his black book—with her blood—and bound herself to torment Christians till God's thrown down—and we all must worship Hell forevermore.

(*Pause.*)

PROCTOR: But—surely you know what a jabberer she is. Did you tell them that?

MARY WARREN: Mr. Proctor, in open court she near to choked us all to death.

PROCTOR: How, choked you?

MARY WARREN: She sent her spirit out.

ELIZABETH: Oh, Mary, Mary, surely you—

MARY WARREN (*with an indignant edge*): She tried to kill me many times, Goody Proctor!

ELIZABETH: Why, I never heard you mention that before.

MARY WARREN: I never knew it before. I never knew anything before. When she come into the court I say to myself, I must not accuse this woman, for she sleep in ditches, and so very old and poor. But then—then she sit there, denying and denying, and I feel a misty coldness climbin' up my back, and the skin on my skull begin to creep, and I feel a clamp around my neck and I cannot breathe air; and then—(*entranced*)—I hear a voice, a screamin' voice, and it were my voice—and all at once I remembered everything she done to me!

PROCTOR: Why? What did she do to you?

MARY WARREN (*like one awakened to a marvelous secret insight*): So many time, Mr. Proctor, she come to this very door, beggin' bread and a cup of cider—and mark this: whenever I turned her away empty, she *mumbled*.

ELIZABETH: Mumbled! She may mumble if she's hungry.

MARY WARREN: But *what* does she mumble? You must remember, Goody Proctor. Last month—a Monday, I think—she walked away, and I thought my guts would burst for two days after. Do you remember it?

ELIZABETH: Why—I do, I think, but—

MARY WARREN: And so I told that to Judge

Hathorne, and he asks her so. "Goody Osburn," says he, "what curse do you mumble that this girl must fall sick after turning you away?" And then she replies—(mimicking an old crone)—"Why, your excellence, no curse at all. I only say my commandments; I hope I may say my commandments," says she!

ELIZABETH: And that's an upright answer.

MARY WARREN: Aye, but then Judge Hathorne say, "Recite for us your commandments!"—(leaning avidly toward them)—and of all the ten she could not say a single one. She never knew no commandments, and they had her in a flat lie!

PROCTOR: And so condemned her?

MARY WARREN (now a little strained, seeing his stubborn doubt): Why, they must when she condemned herself.

PROCTOR: But the proof, the proof!

MARY WARREN (with greater impatience with him): I told you the proof. It's hard proof, hard as rock, the judges said.

PROCTOR (pauses an instant, then): You will not go to court again, Mary Warren.

MARY WARREN: I must tell you, sir, I will be gone every day now. I am amazed you do not see what weighty work we do.

PROCTOR: What work you do! It's strange work for a Christian girl to hang old women!

MARY WARREN: But, Mr. Proctor, they will not hang them if they confess. Sarah Good will only sit in jail some time—(recalling)—and here's a wonder for you; think on this. Goody Good is pregnant!

ELIZABETH: Pregnant! Are they mad? The woman's near to sixty!

MARY WARREN: They had Doctor Griggs examine her, and she's full to the brim. And smokin' a pipe all these years, and no husband either! But she's safe, thank God, for they'll not hurt the innocent child. But be that not a marvel? You must see it, sir, it's God's work we do. So I'll be gone every day for some time. I'm—I am an official of the court, they say, and I—(She has been edging toward offstage.)

PROCTOR: I'll official you! (He strides to the mantel, takes down the whip hanging there.)

MARY WARREN (terrified, but coming erect, striving for her authority): I'll not stand whipping any more!

ELIZABETH (hurriedly, as PROCTOR approaches): Mary, promise you'll stay at home—

MARY WARREN (backing from him, but keeping her erect posture, striving, striving for her way): The Devil's loose in Salem, Mr. Proctor; we must discover where he's hiding!

PROCTOR: I'll whip the Devil out of you! (With whip raised he reaches out for her, and she streaks away and yells.)

MARY WARREN (pointing at ELIZABETH): I saved her life today!

(Silence. His whip comes down.)

ELIZABETH (softly): I am accused?

MARY WARREN (quaking): Somewhat mentioned. But I said I never see no sign you ever sent your spirit out to hurt no one, and seeing I do live so closely with you, they dismissed it.

ELIZABETH: Who accused me?

MARY WARREN: I am bound by law, I cannot tell it. (To PROCTOR) I only hope you'll not be so sarcastical no more. Four judges and the King's deputy sat to dinner with us but an hour ago. I—I would have you speak civilly to me, from this out.

PROCTOR (in horror, muttering in disgust at her): Go to bed.

MARY WARREN (with a stamp of her foot): I'll not be ordered to bed no more, Mr. Proctor! I am eighteen and a woman, however single!

PROCTOR: Do you wish to sit up? Then sit up.

MARY WARREN: I wish to go to bed!

PROCTOR (in anger): Good night, then!

MARY WARREN: Good night. (Dissatisfied, uncertain of herself, she goes out. Wide-eyed, both, PROCTOR and ELIZABETH stand staring.)

ELIZABETH (quietly): Oh, the noose, the noose is up!

PROCTOR: There'll be no noose.

ELIZABETH: She wants me dead. I knew all week it would come to this!

PROCTOR (without conviction): They dismissed it. You heard her say—

ELIZABETH: And what of tomorrow? She will cry me out until they take me!

PROCTOR: Sit you down.

ELIZABETH: She wants me dead, John, you know it!

PROCTOR: I say sit down. (She sits, trembling. He speaks quickly, trying to keep his wits.) Now we must be wise, Elizabeth.

ELIZABETH (with sarcasm, and a sense of being lost): Oh, indeed, indeed!

PROCTOR: Fear nothing. I'll find Ezekiel Cheever. I'll tell him she said it were all sport.

ELIZABETH: John, with so many in the jail, more than Cheever's help is needed now, I think. Would you favor me with this? Go to Abigail.

PROCTOR (*his soul hardening as he senses . . .*): What have I say to Abigail?

ELIZABETH (*delicately*): John—grant me this. You have a faulty understanding of young girls. There is a promise made in any bed—

PROCTOR (*striving against his anger*): What promise!

ELIZABETH: Spoke or silent, a promise is surely made. And she may dote on it now—I am sure she does—and thinks to kill me, then to take my place.

(PROCTOR's *anger is rising; he cannot speak.*)

ELIZABETH: It is her dearest hope, John, I know it. There be a thousand names; why does she call mine? There be a certain danger in calling such a name—I am no Goody Good that sleeps in ditches, nor Osburn, drunk and half-witted. She'd dare not call out such a farmer's wife but there be monstrous profit in it. She thinks to take my place, John.

PROCTOR: She cannot think it! (*He knows it is true.*)

ELIZABETH ("*reasonably*"): John, have you ever shown her somewhat of contempt? She cannot pass you in the church but you will blush—

PROCTOR: I may blush for my sin.

ELIZABETH: I think she sees another meaning in that blush.

PROCTOR: And what see you? What see you, Elizabeth?

ELIZABETH ("*conceding*"): I think you be somewhat ashamed, for I am there, and she so close.

PROCTOR: When will you know me, woman? Were I stone I would have cracked for shame this seven month!

ELIZABETH: Then go and tell her she's a whore. Whatever promise she may sense—break it, John, break it.

PROCTOR (*between his teeth*): Good, then. I'll go. (*He starts for his rifle.*)

ELIZABETH (*trembling, fearfully*): Oh, how unwillingly!

PROCTOR (*turning on her, rifle in hand*): I will curse her hotter than the oldest cinder in hell. But pray, begrudge me not my anger!

ELIZABETH: Your anger! I only ask you—

PROCTOR: Woman, am I so base? Do you truly think me base?

ELIZABETH: I never called you base.

PROCTOR: Then how do you charge me with such a promise? The promise that a stallion gives a mare I gave that girl!

ELIZABETH: Then why do you anger with me when I bid you break it?

PROCTOR: Because it speaks deceit, and I am honest! But I'll plead no more! I see now your spirit twists around the single error of my life, and I will never tear it free!

ELIZABETH (*crying out*): You'll tear it free— when you come to know that I will be your only wife, or no wife at all! She has an arrow in you yet, John Proctor, and you know it well!

(*Quite suddenly, as though from the air, a figure appears in the doorway. They start slightly. It is* MR. HALE. *He is different now—drawn a little, and there is a quality of deference, even of guilt, about his manner now.*)

HALE: Good evening.

PROCTOR (*still in his shock*): Why, Mr. Hale! Good evening to you, sir. Come in, come in.

HALE (*to* ELIZABETH): I hope I do not startle you.

ELIZABETH: No, no, it's only that I heard no horse—

HALE: You are Goodwife Proctor.

PROCTOR: Aye; Elizabeth.

HALE (*nods, then*): I hope you're not off to bed yet.

PROCTOR (*setting down his gun*): No, no.

(HALE *comes further into the room. And* PROCTOR, *to explain his nervousness*) We are not used to visitors after dark, but you're welcome here. Will you sit you down, sir?

HALE: I will. (*He sits.*) Let you sit, Goodwife Proctor.

(*She does, never letting him out of her sight. There is a pause as* HALE *looks about the room.*)

PROCTOR (*to break the silence*): Will you drink cider, Mr. Hale?

HALE: No, it rebels my stomach; I have some further traveling yet tonight. Sit you down, sir. (PROCTOR *sits.*) I will not keep you long, but I have some business with you.

PROCTOR: Business of the court?

HALE: No—no, I come of my own, without the court's authority. Hear me. (*He wets his lips.*) I know not if you are aware, but your wife's name is—mentioned in the court.

PROCTOR: We know it, sir. Our Mary Warren told us. We are entirely amazed.

HALE: I am a stranger here, as you know. And in my ignorance I find it hard to draw a clear opinion of them that come accused before the court. And so this afternoon, and now tonight, I go from house to house—I come now from Rebecca Nurse's house and—

ELIZABETH (*shocked*): Rebecca's charged!

HALE: God forbid such a one be charged. She is, however—mentioned somewhat.

ELIZABETH (*with an attempt at a laugh*): You will never believe, I hope, that Rebecca trafficked with the Devil.

HALE: Woman, it is possible.

PROCTOR (*taken aback*): Surely you cannot think so.

HALE: This is a strange time, Mister. No man may longer doubt the powers of the dark are gathered in monstrous attack upon this village. There is too much evidence now to deny it. You will agree, sir?

PROCTOR (*evading*): I—have no knowledge in that line. But it's hard to think so pious a woman to be secretly a Devil's bitch after seventy year of such good prayer.

HALE: Aye. But the Devil is a wily one, you cannot deny it. However, she is far from accused, and I know she will not be. (*Pause.*) I thought, sir, to put some questions as to the Christian character of this house, if you'll permit me.

PROCTOR (*coldly, resentful*): Why, we—have no fear of questions, sir.

HALE: Good, then. (*He makes himself more comfortable.*) In the book of record that Mr. Parris keeps, I note that you are rarely in the church on Sabbath Day.

PROCTOR: No, sir, you are mistaken.

HALE: Twenty-six time in seventeen month, sir. I must call that rare. Will you tell me why you are so absent?

PROCTOR: Mr. Hale, I never knew I must account to that man for I come to church or stay at home. My wife were sick this winter.

HALE: So I am told. But you, Mister, why could you not come alone?

PROCTOR: I surely did come when I could, and when I could not I prayed in this house.

HALE: Mr. Proctor, your house is not a church; your theology must tell you that.

PROCTOR: It does, sir, it does; and it tells me that a minister may pray to God without he have golden candlesticks upon the altar.

HALE: What golden candlesticks?

PROCTOR: Since we built the church there were pewter candlesticks upon the altar; Francis Nurse made them, y'know, and a sweeter hand never touched the metal. But Parris came, and for twenty week he preach nothin' but golden candlesticks until he had them. I labor the earth from dawn of day to blink of night, and I tell you true, when I look to heaven and see my money glaring at his elbows—it hurt my prayer, sir, it hurt my prayer. I think, sometimes, the man dreams cathedrals, not clapboard meetin' houses.

HALE (*thinks, then*): And yet, Mister, a Christian on Sabbath Day must be in church. (*Pause.*) Tell me—you have three children?

PROCTOR: Aye, Boys.

HALE: How comes it that only two are baptized?

PROCTOR (*starts to speak, then stops, then, as though unable to restrain this*): I like it not that Mr. Parris should lay his hand upon my baby. I see no light of God in that man. I'll not conceal it.

HALE: I must say it, Mr. Proctor; that is not for you to decide. The man's ordained, therefore the light of God is in him.

PROCTOR (*flushed with resentment but trying to smile*): What's your suspicion, Mr. Hale?

HALE: No, no, I have no—

PROCTOR: I nailed the roof upon the church, I hung the door—

HALE: Oh, did you! That's a good sign, then.

PROCTOR: It may be I have been too quick to bring the man to book, but you cannot think we ever desired the destruction of religion. I think that's in your mind, is it not?

HALE (*not altogether giving way*): I—have—there is a softness in your record, sir, a softness.

ELIZABETH: I think, maybe, we have been too hard with Mr. Parris. I think so. But sure we never loved the Devil here.

HALE (*nods, deliberating this; then, with the voice of one administering a secret test*): Do you know your Commandments, Elizabeth?

ELIZABETH (*without hesitation, even eagerly*): I surely do. There be no mark of blame upon my life, Mr. Hale. I am a covenanted, Christian woman.

HALE: And you, Mister?

PROCTOR (*a trifle unsteadily*): I—am sure I do, sir.

HALE (*glances at her open face, then at* JOHN, *then*):   Let you repeat them, if you will.

PROCTOR:   The Commandments.

HALE:   Aye.

PROCTOR (*looking off, beginning to sweat*): Thou shalt not kill.

HALE:   Aye.

PROCTOR (*counting on his fingers*):   Thou shalt not steal. Thou shalt not covet thy neighbor's goods, nor make unto thee any graven image. Thou shalt not take the name of the Lord in vain; thou shalt have no other gods before me. (*With some hesitation*) Thou shalt remember the Sabbath Day and keep it holy. (*Pause. Then*) Thou shalt honor thy father and mother. Thou shalt not bear false witness. (*He is stuck. He counts back on his fingers, knowing one is missing.*) Thou shalt not make unto thee any graven image.

HALE:   You have said that twice, sir.

PROCTOR (*lost*):   Aye. (*He is flailing for it.*)

ELIZABETH (*delicately*):   Adultery, John.

PROCTOR (*as though a secret arrow had pained his heart*):   Aye. (*Trying to grin it away—to* HALE) You see, sir, between the two of us we do know them all. (HALE *only looks at* PROCTOR, *deep in his attempt to define this man.* PROCTOR *grows more uneasy.*) I think it be a small fault.

HALE:   Theology, sir, is a fortress; no crack in a fortress may be accounted small. (*He rises; he seems worried now. He paces a little, in deep thought.*)

PROCTOR:   There be no love for Satan in this house, Mister.

HALE:   I pray it, I pray it dearly. (*He looks to both of them, an attempt at a smile on his face, but his misgivings are clear.*) Well, then— I'll bid you good night.

ELIZABETH (*unable to restrain herself*):   Mr. Hale. (*He turns.*) I do think you are suspecting me somewhat? Are you not?

HALE (*obviously disturbed—and evasive*): Goody Proctor, I do not judge you. My duty is to add what I may to the godly wisdom of the court. I pray you both good health and good fortune. (*To* JOHN) Good night, sir. (*He starts out.*)

ELIZABETH (*with a note of desperation*):   I think you must tell him, John.

HALE:   What's that?

ELIZABETH (*restraining a call*):   Will you tell him?

(*Slight pause.* HALE *looks questioningly at* JOHN.)

PROCTOR (*with difficulty*):   I—I have no witness and cannot prove it, except my word be taken. But I know the children's sickness had naught to do with witchcraft.

HALE (*stopped, struck*):   Naught to do—?

PROCTOR:   Mr. Parris discovered them sportin' in the woods. They were startled and took sick. (*Pause.*)

HALE:   Who told you this?

PROCTOR (*hesitates, then*):   Abigail Williams.

HALE:   Abigail!

PROCTOR:   Aye.

HALE (*his eyes wide*):   Abigail Williams told you it had naught to do with witchcraft!

PROCTOR:   She told me the day you came, sir.

HALE (*suspiciously*):   Why—why did you keep this?

PROCTOR:   I never knew until tonight that the world is gone daft with this nonsense.

HALE:   Nonsense! Mister, I have myself examined Tituba, Sarah Good, and numerous others that have confessed to dealing with the Devil. They have *confessed* it.

PROCTOR:   And why not, if they must hang for denyin' it? There are them that will swear to anything before they'll hang; have you never thought of that?

HALE:   I have. I—I have indeed. (*It is his own suspicion, but he resists it. He glances at* ELIZABETH, *then at* JOHN.) And you—would you testify to this in court?

PROCTOR:   I—had not reckoned with goin' into court. But if I must I will.

HALE:   Do you falter here?

PROCTOR:   I falter nothing, but I may wonder if my story will be credited in such a court. I do wonder on it, when such a steady-minded minister as you will suspicion such a woman that never lied, and cannot, and the world knows she cannot! I may falter somewhat, Mister; I am no fool.

HALE (*Quietly—it has impressed him.*):   Proctor, let you open with me now, for I have a rumor that troubles me. It's said you hold no belief that there may even be witches in the world. Is that true, sir?

PROCTOR (*He knows this is critical, and is striving against his disgust with* HALE *and with himself for even answering.*):   I know not what I have said, I may have said it. I have wondered if there be witches in the world—although I cannot believe they come among us now.

HALE: Then you do not believe—

PROCTOR: I have no knowledge of it; the Bible speaks of witches, and I will not deny them.

HALE: And you, woman?

ELIZABETH: I—I cannot believe it.

HALE (*shocked*): You cannot!

PROCTOR: Elizabeth, you bewilder him!

ELIZABETH (*to HALE*): I cannot think the Devil may own a woman's soul, Mr. Hale, when she keeps an upright way, as I have. I am a good woman, I know it; and if you believe I may do only good work in the world, and yet be secretly bound to Satan, then I must tell you, sir, I do not believe it.

HALE: But, woman, you do believe there are witches in—

ELIZABETH: If you think that I am one, then I say there are none.

HALE: You surely do not fly against the Gospel, the Gospel—

PROCTOR: She believe in the Gospel, every word!

ELIZABETH: Question Abigail Williams about the Gospel, not myself!

(HALE *stares at her.*)

PROCTOR: She do not mean to doubt the Gospel, sir, you cannot think it. This be a Christian house, sir, a Christian house.

HALE: God keep you both; let the third child be quickly baptized, and go you without fail each Sunday in to Sabbath prayer; and keep a solemn, quiet way among you. I think—

(GILES COREY *appears in doorway.*)

GILES: John!

PROCTOR: Giles! What's the matter?

GILES: They take my wife.

(FRANCIS NURSE *enters.*)

GILES: And his Rebecca!

PROCTOR (*to FRANCIS*): Rebecca's in the *jail!*

FRANCIS: Aye, Cheever come and take her in his wagon. We've only now come from the jail, and they'll not even let us in to see them.

ELIZABETH: They've surely gone wild now, Mr. Hale!

FRANCES (*going to HALE*): Reverend Hale! Can you not speak to the Deputy Governor? I'm sure he mistakes these people—

HALE: Pray calm yourself, Mr. Nurse.

FRANCIS: My wife is the very brick and mortar of the church, Mr. Hale—(*indicating Giles*)—and Martha Corey, there cannot be a woman closer yet to God than Martha.

HALE: How is Rebecca charged, Mr. Nurse?

FRANCIS (*with a mocking, half-hearted laugh*): For murder, she's charged! (*Mockingly quoting the warrant*) "For the marvelous and supernatural murder of Goody Putnam's babies." What am I to do, Mr. Hale?

HALE (*turns from FRANCIS, deeply troubled, then*): Believe me, Mr. Nurse, if Rebecca Nurse be tainted, then nothing's left to stop the whole green world from burning. Let you rest upon the justice of the court; the court will send her home, I know it.

FRANCIS: You cannot mean she will be tried in court!

HALE (*pleading*): Nurse, though our hearts break, we cannot flinch; these are new times, sir. There is a misty plot afoot so subtle we should be criminal to cling to old respects and ancient friendships. I have seen too many frightful proofs in court—the Devil is alive in Salem, and we dare not quail to follow wherever the accusing finger points!

PROCTOR (*angered*): How may such a woman murder children?

HALE (*in great pain*): Man, remember, until an hour before the Devil fell, God thought him beautiful in Heaven.

GILES: I never said my wife were a witch, Mr. Hale; I only said she were reading books!

HALE: Mr. Corey, exactly what complaint were made on your wife?

GILES: That bloody mongrel Walcott charge her. Y'see, he buy a pig of my wife four or five year ago, and the pig died soon after. So he come dancin' in for his money back. So my Martha, she says to him, "Walcott, if you haven't the wit to feed a pig properly, you'll not live to own many," she says. Now he goes to court and claims that from that day to this he cannot keep a pig alive for more than four weeks because my Martha bewitch them with her books!

(*Enter* EZEKIEL CHEEVER. *A shocked silence.*)

CHEEVER: Good evening to you, Proctor.

PROCTOR: Why, Mr. Cheever. Good evening.

CHEEVER: Good evening, all. Good evening, Mr. Hale.

PROCTOR: I hope you come not on business of the court.

CHEEVER: I do, Proctor, aye, I am clerk of the court now, y'know.

(*Enter* MARSHAL HERRICK, *a man in his early*

*thirties, who is somewhat shamefaced at the moment.)*

GILES:   It's a pity, Ezekiel, that an honest tailor might have gone to Heaven must burn in Hell. You'll burn for this, do you know it?

CHEEVER:   You know yourself I must do as I'm told. You surely know that, Giles. And I'd as lief you'd not be sending me to Hell. I like not the sound of it, I tell you; I like not the sound of it. (*He fears* PROCTOR, *but starts to reach inside his coat.*) Now believe me, Proctor, how heavy be the law, all its tonnage I do carry on my back tonight. (*He takes out a warrant.*) I have a warrant for your wife.

PROCTOR (*to* HALE):   You said she were not charged!

HALE:   I know nothin' of it. (*To* CHEEVER) When were she charged?

CHEEVER:   I am given sixteen warrant tonight, sir, and she is one.

PROCTOR:   Who charged her?

CHEEVER:   Why, Abigail Williams charge her.

PROCTOR:   On what proof, what proof?

CHEEVER (*looking about the room*):   Mr. Proctor, I have little time. The court bid me search your house, but I like not to search a house. So will you hand me any poppets that your wife may keep here?

PROCTOR:   Poppets?

ELIZABETH:   I never kept no poppets, not since I were a girl.

CHEEVER (*embarrassed, glancing toward the mantel where sits* MARY WARREN's *poppet*):   I spy a poppet, Goody Proctor.

ELIZABETH:   Oh! (*Going for it*) Why, this is Mary's.

CHEEVER (*shyly*):   Would you please to give it to me?

ELIZABETH (*handing it to him, asks* HALE):   Has the court discovered a text in poppets now?

CHEEVER (*carefully holding the poppet*):   Do you keep any others in this house?

PROCTOR:   No, nor this one either till tonight. What signifies a poppet?

CHEEVER:   Why, a poppet—(*he gingerly turns the poppet over*)—a poppet may signify—Now, woman, will you please to come with me?

PROCTOR:   She will not! (*To* ELIZABETH) Fetch Mary here.

CHEEVER (*ineptly reaching toward* ELIZABETH):   No, no, I am forbid to leave her from my sight.

PROCTOR (*pushing his arm away*):   You'll leave her out of sight and out of mind, Mister. Fetch Mary, Elizabeth. (ELIZABETH *goes upstairs.*)

HALE:   What signifies a poppet, Mr. Cheever?

CHEEVER (*turning the poppet over in his hands*):   Why, they say it may signify that she—(*He has lifted the poppet's skirt, and his eyes widen in astonished fear.*) Why, this, this—

PROCTOR (*reaching for the poppet*):   What's there?

CHEEVER:   Why—(*he draws out a long needle from the poppet*)—it is a needle! Herrick, Herrick, it is a needle!

(HERRICK *comes toward him.*)

PROCTOR (*angrily, bewildered*):   And what signifies a needle!

CHEEVER (*his hands shaking*):   Why, this go hard with her, Proctor, this—I had my doubts, Proctor, I had my doubts, but here's calamity. (*To* HALE, *showing the needle*) You see it, sir, it is a needle!

HALE:   Why? What meanin' has it?

CHEEVER (*wide-eyed, trembling*):   The girl, the Williams girl, Abigail Williams, sir. She sat to dinner in Reverend Parris's house tonight, and without word nor warnin' she falls to the floor. Like a struck beast, he says, and screamed a scream that a bull would weep to hear. And he goes to save her, and, stuck two inches in the flesh of her belly, he draw a needle out. And demandin' of her how she come to be so stabbed, she—(*to* PROCTOR *now*)—testify it were your wife's familiar spirit pushed it in.

PROCTOR:   Why, she done it herself! (*To* HALE):   I hope you're not takin' this for proof, Mister!

CHEEVER:   'Tis hard proof! (*To* HALE) I find here a poppet Goody Proctor keeps. I have found it, sir. And in the belly of the poppet a needle's stuck. I tell you true, Proctor, I never warranted to see such proof of Hell, and I bid you obstruct me not, for I—

(*Enter* ELIZABETH *with* MARY WARREN. PROCTOR, *seeing* MARY WARREN, *draws her by the arm to* HALE.)

PROCTOR:   Here now! Mary, how did this poppet come into my house?

MARY WARREN (*frightened for herself, her voice very small*):   What poppet's that, sir?

PROCTOR (*impatiently, points at the doll in* CHEEVER's *hand*):   This poppet, this poppet.

MARY WARREN (*evasively, looking at it*):   Why, I—I think it is mine.

PROCTOR: It is your poppet, is it not?

MARY WARREN (*not understanding the direction of this*): It—is, sir.

PROCTOR: And how did it come into this house?

MARY WARREN (*glancing about at the avid faces*): Why—I made it in the court, sir, and—give it to Goody Proctor tonight.

PROCTOR (*to HALE*): Now, sir—do you have it?

HALE: Mary Warren, a needle have been found inside this poppet.

MARY WARREN (*bewildered*): Why, I meant no harm by it, sir.

PROCTOR (*quickly*): You stuck that needle in yourself?

MARY WARREN: I—I believe I did, sir, I—

PROCTOR (*to HALE*): What say you now?

HALE (*watching MARY WARREN closely*): Child, you are certain this be your natural memory? May it be, perhaps, that someone conjures you even now to say this?

MARY WARREN: Conjures me? Why, no, sir, I am entirely myself, I think. Let you ask Susanna Walcott—she saw me sewin' it in court. (*Or better still*) Ask Abby, Abby sat beside me when I made it.

PROCTOR (*to HALE, of CHEEVER*): Bid him begone. Your mind is surely settled now. Bid him out, Mr. Hale.

ELIZABETH: What signifies a needle?

HALE: Mary—you charge a cold and cruel murder on Abigail.

MARY WARREN: Murder! I charge no—

HALE: Abigail were stabbed tonight; a needle were found stuck into her belly—

ELIZABETH: And she charges me?

HALE: Aye.

ELIZABETH (*her breath knocked out*): Why—! The girl is murder! She must be ripped out of the world!

CHEEVER (*pointing at ELIZABETH*): You've heard that, sir! Ripped out of the world! Herrick, you heard it!

PROCTOR (*suddenly snatching the warrant out of CHEEVER's hands*): Out with you.

CHEEVER: Proctor, you dare not touch the warrant.

PROCTOR (*ripping the warrant*): Out with you!

CHEEVER: You've ripped the Deputy Governor's warrant, man!

PROCTOR: Damn the Deputy Governor! Out of my house!

HALE: Now, Proctor, Proctor!

PROCTOR: Get y'gone with them! You are a broken minister.

HALE: Proctor, if she is innocent, the court—

PROCTOR: If *she* is innocent! Why do you never wonder if Parris may be innocent, or Abigail? Is the accuser always holy now? Were they born this morning as clean as God's fingers? I'll tell you what's walking Salem—vengeance is walking Salem. We are what we always were in Salem, but now the little crazy children are jangling the keys of the kingdom, and common vengeance writes the law! This warrant's vengeance! I'll not give my wife to vengeance!

ELIZABETH: I'll go, John—

PROCTOR: You will not go!

HERRICK: I have nine men outside. You cannot keep her. The law binds me, John, I cannot budge.

PROCTOR (*to HALE, ready to break him*): Will you see her taken?

HALE: Proctor, the court is just—

PROCTOR: Pontius Pilate! God will not let you wash your hands of this!

ELIZABETH: John—I think I must go with them. (*He cannot bear to look at her.*) Mary, there is bread enough for the morning; you will bake, in the afternoon. Help Mr. Proctor as you were his daughter—you owe me that, and much more. (*She is fighting her weeping. To PROCTOR*) When the children wake, speak nothing of witchcraft—it will frighten them. (*She cannot go on.*)

PROCTOR: I will bring you home. I will bring you soon.

ELIZABETH: Oh, John, bring me soon!

PROCTOR: I will fall like an ocean on that court! Fear nothing, Elizabeth.

ELIZABETH (*with great fear*): I will fear nothing. (*She looks about the room, as though to fix it in her mind.*) Tell the children I have gone to visit someone sick.

(*She walks out the door, HERRICK and CHEEVER behind her. For a moment, PROCTOR watches from the doorway. The clank of chain is heard.*)

PROCTOR: Herrick! Herrick, don't chain her! (*He rushes out the door. From outside*) Damn you, man, you will not chain her! Off with them! I'll not have it! I will not have her chained!

(*There are other men's voices against his. HALE, in a fever of guilt and uncertainty, turns from the door to avoid the sight; MARY WARREN bursts into tears and sits weeping. GILES COREY calls to HALE.*)

GILES: And yet silent, minister? It is fraud, you know it is fraud! What keeps you, man?

(PROCTOR *is half braced, half pushed into the room by two deputies and* HERRICK.)

PROCTOR: I'll pay you, Herrick, I will surely pay you!

HERRICK (*panting*): In God's name, John, I cannot help myself. I must chain them all. Now let you keep inside this house till I am gone! (*He goes out with his deputies.*)

(PROCTOR *stands there, gulping air. Horses and a wagon creaking are heard.*)

HALE (*in great uncertainty*): Mr. Proctor—

PROCTOR: Out of my sight!

HALE: Charity, Proctor, charity. What I have heard in her favor, I will not fear to testify in court. God help me, I cannot judge her guilty or innocent—I know not. Only this consider: the world goes mad, and it profit nothing you should lay the cause to the vengeance of a little girl.

PROCTOR: You are a coward! Though you be ordained in God's own tears, you are a coward now!

HALE: Proctor, I cannot think God be provoked so grandly by such a petty cause. The jails are packed—our greatest judges sit in Salem now—and hangin's promised. Man, we must look to cause proportionate. Were there murder done, perhaps, and never brought to light? Abomination? Some secret blasphemy that stinks to Heaven? Think on cause, man, and let you help me to discover it. For there's your way, believe it, there is your only way, when such confusion strikes upon the world. (*He goes to* GILES *and* FRANCIS.) Let you counsel among yourselves; think on your village and what may have drawn from heaven such thundering wrath upon you all. I shall pray God open up our eyes.

(HALE *goes out.*)

FRANCIS (*struck by* HALE's *mood*): I never heard no murder done in Salem.

PROCTOR (*He has been reached by* HALE's *words.*): Leave me, Francis, leave me.

GILES (*shaken*): John—tell me, are we lost?

PROCTOR: Go home now, Giles. We'll speak on it tomorrow.

GILES: Let you think on it. We'll come early, eh?

PROCTOR: Aye. Go now, Giles.

GILES: Good night, then.

(GILES COREY *goes out. After a moment*)

MARY WARREN (*in a fearful squeak of a voice*): Mr. Proctor, very likely they'll let her come home once they're given proper evidence.

PROCTOR: You're coming to the court with me, Mary. You will tell it in the court.

MARY WARREN: I cannot charge murder on Abigail.

PROCTOR (*moving menacingly toward her*): You will tell the court how that poppet come here and who stuck the needle in.

MARY WARREN: She'll kill me for sayin' that! (PROCTOR *continues toward her.*) Abby'll charge lechery on you, Mr. Proctor!

PROCTOR (*halting*): She's told you!

MARY WARREN: I have known it, sir. She'll ruin you with it, I know she will.

PROCTOR (*hesitating, and with deep hatred of himself*): Good. Then her saintliness is done with. (MARY *backs from him.*) We will slide together into our pit; you will tell the court what you know.

MARY WARREN (*in terror*): I cannot, they'll turn on me—

(PROCTOR *strides and catches her, and she is repeating, "I cannot, I cannot!"*)

PROCTOR: My wife will never die for me! I will bring your guts into your mouth but that goodness will not die for me!

MARY WARREN (*struggling to escape him*): I cannot do it, I cannot!

PROCTOR (*grasping her by the throat as though he would strangle her*): Make your peace with it! Now Hell and Heaven grapple on our backs, and all our old pretense is ripped away—make your peace! (*He throws her to the floor, where she sobs, "I cannot, I cannot . . ." And now, half to himself, staring, and turning to the open door*) Peace. It is a providence, and no great change; we are only what we always were, but naked now. (*He walks as though toward a great horror, facing the open sky.*) Aye, naked! And the wind, God's icy wind, will blow!

(*And she is over and over again sobbing, "I cannot, I cannot, I cannot," as the curtain falls.*)


## ACT THREE

*The vestry room of the Salem meeting house, now serving as the anteroom of the General Court.*

*As the curtain rises, the room is empty, but for sunlight pouring through two high windows in the back wall. The room is solemn, even forbid-*

*ding. Heavy beams jut out, boards of random widths make up the walls. At the right are two doors leading into the meeting house proper, where the court is being held. At the left another door leads outside.*

*There is a plain bench at the left, and another at the right. In the center a rather long meeting table, with stools and a considerable armchair snugged up to it.*

*Through the partitioning wall at the right we hear a prosecutor's voice,* JUDGE HATHORNE'S, *asking a question; then a woman's voice,* MARTHA COREY'S, *replying.*

HATHORNE'S VOICE:   Now, Martha Corey, there is abundant evidence in our hands to show that you have given yourself to the reading of fortunes. Do you deny it?

MARTHA COREY'S VOICE:   I am innocent to a witch. I know not what a witch is.

HATHORNE'S VOICE:   How do you know, then, that you are not a witch?

MARTHA COREY'S VOICE:   If I were, I would know it.

HATHORNE'S VOICE:   Why do you hurt these children?

MARTHA COREY'S VOICE:   I do not hurt them. I scorn it!

GILES' VOICE (*roaring*):   I have evidence for the court!

(*Voices of townspeople rise in excitement.*)

DANFORTH'S VOICE:   You will keep your seat!

GILES' VOICE:   Thomas Putnam is reaching out for land!

DANFORTH'S VOICE:   Remove that man, Marshal!

GILES' VOICE:   You're hearing lies, lies!

(*A roaring goes up from the people.*)

HATHORNE'S VOICE:   Arrest him, excellency!

GILES' VOICE:   I have evidence. Why will you not hear my evidence?

(*The door opens and* GILES *is half carried into the vestry room by* HERRICK.)

GILES:   Hands off, damn you, let me go!

HERRICK:   Giles, Giles!

GILES:   Out of my way, Herrick! I bring evidence—

HERRICK:   You cannot go in there, Giles! it's a court!

(*Enter* HALE *from the court.*)

HALE:   Pray be calm a moment.

GILES:   You, Mr. Hale, go in there and demand I speak.

HALE:   A moment, sir, a moment.

GILES:   They'll be hangin' my wife!

(JUDGE HATHORNE *enters. He is in his sixties, a bitter, remorseless Salem judge.*)

HATHORNE:   How do you dare come roarin' into this court! Are you gone daft, Corey?

GILES:   You're not a Boston judge, Hathorne. You'll not call me daft!

(*Enter* DEPUTY GOVERNOR DANFORTH *and, behind him,* EZEKIEL CHEEVER *and* PARRIS. *On his appearance, silence falls.* DANFORTH *is a grave man in his sixties, of some humor and sophistication that does not, however, interfere with an exact loyalty to his position and his cause. He comes down to* GILES, *who awaits his wrath.*)

DANFORTH (*looking directly at* GILES):   Who is this man?

PARRIS:   Giles Corey, sir, and a more contentious—

GILES (*to* PARRIS):   I am asked the question, and I am old enough to answer it! (*To* DANFORTH, *who impresses him and to whom he smiles through his strain*) My name is Corey, sir, Giles Corey. I have six hundred acres, and timber in addition. It is my wife you be condemning now. (*He indicates the courtroom.*)

DANFORTH:   And how do you imagine to help her cause with such contemptuous riot? Now be gone. Your old age alone keeps you out of jail for this.

GILES (*beginning to plead*):   They be tellin' lies about my wife, sir, I—

DANFORTH:   Do you take it upon yourself to determine what this court shall believe and what it shall set aside?

GILES:   Your Excellency, we mean no disrespect for—

DANFORTH:   Disrespect indeed! It is disruption, Mister. This is the highest court of the supreme government of this province, do you know it?

GILES (*beginning to weep*):   Your Excellency, I only said she were readin' books, sir, and they come and take her out of my house for—

DANFORTH (*mystified*):   Books! What books?

GILES (*through helpless sobs*):   It is my third wife, sir; I never had no wife that be so taken with books, and I thought to find the cause of it, d'y'see, but it were no witch I blamed her for. (*He is openly weeping.*) I have broke charity with the woman, I have broke charity with her.

(*He covers his face, ashamed.* DANFORTH *is respectfully silent.*)

HALE:   Excellency, he claims hard evidence for his wife's defense. I think that in all justice you must—

DANFORTH:   Then let him submit his evidence in proper affidavit. You are certainly aware of our procedure here, Mr. Hale. (*To* HERRICK) Clear this room.

HERRICK:   Come now, Giles. (*He gently pushes* COREY *out.*)

FRANCIS:   We are desperate, sir; we come here three days now and cannot be heard.

DANFORTH:   Who is this man?

FRANCIS:   Francis Nurse, Your Excellency.

HALE:   His wife's Rebecca that were condemned this morning.

DANFORTH:   Indeed! I am amazed to find you in such uproar. I have only good report of your character, Mr. Nurse.

HATHORNE:   I think they must both be arrested in contempt, sir.

DANFORTH (*to* FRANCIS):   Let you write your plea, and in due time I will—

FRANCIS:   Excellency, we have proof for your eyes; God forbid you shut them to it. The girls, sir, the girls are frauds.

DANFORTH:   What's that?

FRANCIS:   We have proof of it, sir. They are all deceiving you.

(DANFORTH *is shocked, but studying* FRANCIS.)

HATHORNE:   This is contempt, sir, contempt!

DANFORTH:   Peace, Judge Hathorne. Do you know who I am, Mr. Nurse?

FRANCIS:   I surely do, sir, and I think you must be a wise judge to be what you are.

DANFORTH:   And do you know that near to four hundred are in the jails from Marblehead to Lynn, and upon my signature?

FRANCIS:   I—

DANFORTH:   And seventy-two condemned to hang by that signature?

FRANCIS:   Excellency, I never thought to say it to such a weighty judge, but you are deceived.

(*Enter* GILES COREY *from left. All turn to see as he beckons in* MARY WARREN *with* PROCTOR. MARY *is keeping her eyes to the ground;* PROCTOR *has her elbow as though she were near collapse.*)

PARRIS (*on seeing her, in shock*):   Mary Warren! (*He goes directly to bend close to her face.*) What are you about here?

PROCTOR (*pressing* PARRIS *away from her with*

a gentle but firm motion of protectiveness):   She would speak with the Deputy Governor.

DANFORTH (*shocked by this, turns to* HERRICK):   Did you not tell me Mary Warren were sick in bed?

HERRICK:   She were, Your Honor. When I go to fetch her to the court last week, she said she were sick.

GILES:   She has been strivin' with her soul all week, Your Honor; she comes now to tell the truth of this to you.

DANFORTH:   Who is this?

PROCTOR:   John Proctor, sir. Elizabeth Proctor is my wife.

PARRIS:   Beware this man, Your Excellency, this man is mischief.

HALE (*excitedly*):   I think you must hear the girl, sir, she—

DANFORTH (*who has become very interested in* MARY WARREN *and only raises a hand toward* HALE):   Peace. What would you tell us, Mary Warren?

(PROCTOR *looks at her, but she cannot speak.*)

PROCTOR:   She never saw no spirits, sir.

DANFORTH (*with great alarm and surprise, to* MARY):   Never saw no spirits!

GILES (*eagerly*):   Never.

PROCTOR (*reaching into his jacket*):   She has signed a deposition, sir—

DANFORTH (*instantly*):   No, no, I accept no depositions. (*He is rapidly calculating this; he turns from her to* PROCTOR.):   Tell me, Mr. Proctor, have you given out this story in the village?

PROCTOR:   We have not.

PARRIS:   They've come to overthrow the court, sir! This man is—

DANFORTH:   I pray you, Mr. Parris. Do you know, Mr. Proctor, that the entire contention of the state in these trials is that the voice of Heaven is speaking through the children?

PROCTOR:   I know that, sir.

DANFORTH (*thinks, staring at* PROCTOR, *then turns to* MARY WARREN):   And you, Mary Warren, how came you to cry out people for sending their spirits against you?

MARY WARREN:   It were pretense, sir.

DANFORTH:   I cannot hear you.

PROCTOR:   It were pretense, she says.

DANFORTH:   Ah? And the other girls? Susanna Walcott, and—the others? They are also pretending?

MARY WARREN:   Aye, sir.

DANFORTH (*wide-eyed*): Indeed. (*Pause. He is baffled by this. He turns to study* PROCTOR's *face.*)

PARRIS (*in a sweat*): Excellency, you surely cannot think to let so vile a lie be spread in open court.

DANFORTH: Indeed not, but it strike hard upon me that she will dare come here with such a tale. Now, Mr. Proctor, before I decide whether I shall hear you or not, it is my duty to tell you this. We burn a hot fire here; it melts down all concealment.

PROCTOR: I know that, sir.

DANFORTH: Let me continue. I understand well, a husband's tenderness may drive him to extravagance in defense of a wife. Are you certain in your conscience, Mister, that your evidence is the truth?

PROCTOR: It is. And you will surely know it.

DANFORTH: And you thought to declare this revelation in the open court before the public?

PROCTOR: I thought I would, aye—with your permission.

DANFORTH (*his eyes narrowing*): Now, sir, what is your purpose in so doing?

PROCTOR: Why, I—I would free my wife, sir.

DANFORTH: There lurks nowhere in your heart, nor hidden in your spirit, any desire to undermine this court?

PROCTOR (*with the faintest faltering*): Why, no, sir.

CHEEVER (*clears his throat, awakening*): I—Your Excellency.

DANFORTH: Mr. Cheever.

CHEEVER: I think it be my duty, sir—(*Kindly, to* PROCTOR) You'll not deny it, John. (*To* DANFORTH) When we come to take his wife, he damned the court and ripped your warrant.

PARRIS: Now you have it!

DANFORTH: He did that, Mr. Hale?

HALE (*takes a breath*): Aye, he did.

PROCTOR: It were a temper, sir. I knew not what I did.

DANFORTH (*studying him*): Mr. Proctor.

PROCTOR: Aye, sir.

DANFORTH (*straight into his eyes*): Have you ever seen the Devil?

PROCTOR: No, sir.

DANFORTH: You are in all respects a Gospel Christian?

PROCTOR: I am, sir.

PARRIS: Such a Christian that will not come to church but once in a month!

DANFORTH (*Restrained—he is curious.*): Not come to church?

PROCTOR: I—I have no love for Mr. Parris. It is no secret. But God I surely love.

CHEEVER: He plow on Sunday, sir.

DANFORTH: Plow on Sunday!

CHEEVER (*apologetically*): I think it be evidence, John. I am an official of the court, I cannot keep it.

PROCTOR: I—I have once or twice plowed on Sunday. I have three children, sir, and until last year my land give little.

GILES: You'll find other Christians that do plow on Sunday if the truth be known.

HALE: Your Honor, I cannot think you may judge the man on such evidence.

DANFORTH: I judge nothing. (*Pause. He keeps watching* PROCTOR, *who tries to meet his gaze.*) I tell you straight, Mister—I have seen marvels in this court. I have seen people choked before my eyes by spirits; I have seen them stuck by pins and slashed by daggers. I have until this moment not the slightest reason to suspect that the children may be deceiving me. Do you understand my meaning?

PROCTOR: Excellency, does it not strike upon you that so many of these women have lived so long with such upright reputation, and—

PARRIS: Do you read the Gospel, Mr. Proctor?

PROCTOR: I read the Gospel.

PARRIS: I think not, or you should surely know that Cain were an upright man, and yet he did kill Abel.

PROCTOR: Aye, God tells us that. (*To* DANFORTH) But who tells us Rebecca Nurse murdered seven babies by sending out her spirit on them? It is the children only, and this one will swear she lied to you.

(DANFORTH *considers, then beckons* HATHORNE *to him.* HATHORNE *leans in, and he speaks in his ear.* HATHORNE *nods.*)

HATHORNE: Aye, she's the one.

DANFORTH: Mr. Proctor, this morning, your wife send me a claim in which she states that she is pregnant now.

PROCTOR: My wife pregnant!

DANFORTH: There be no sign of it—we have examined her body.

PROCTOR: But if she say she is pregnant, then she must be! That woman will never lie, Mr. Danforth.

DANFORTH: She will not?

PROCTOR:   Never, sir, never.

DANFORTH:   We have thought it too convenient to be credited. However, if I should tell you now that I will let her be kept another month; and if she begin to show her natural signs, you shall have her living yet another year until she is delivered—what say you to that? (JOHN PROCTOR *is struck silent.*) Come now. You say your only purpose is to save your wife. Good, then, she is saved at least this year, and a year is long. What say you, sir? It is done now. (*In conflict,* PROCTOR *glances at* FRANCIS *and* GILES.) Will you drop this charge?

PROCTOR:   I—I think I cannot.

DANFORTH (*now an almost imperceptible hardness in his voice*):   Then your purpose is somewhat larger.

PARRIS:   He's come to overthrow this court, Your Honor!

PROCTOR:   These are my friends. Their wives are also accused—

DANFORTH (*with a sudden briskness of manner*):   I judge you not, sir. I am ready to hear your evidence.

PROCTOR:   I come not to hurt the court; I only—

DANFORTH (*cutting him off*):   Marshal, go into the court and bid Judge Stoughton and Judge Sewall declare recess for one hour. And let them go to the tavern, if they will. All witnesses and prisoners are to be kept in the building.

HERRICK:   Aye, sir. (*Very deferentially*) If I may say it, sir, I know this man all my life. It is a good man, sir.

DANFORTH (*It is the reflection on himself he resents.*):   I am sure of it, Marshal. (HERRICK *nods, then goes out.*) Now, what deposition do you have for us, Mr. Proctor? And I beg you be clear, open as the sky, and honest.

PROCTOR (*as he takes out several papers*):   I am no lawyer, so I'll—

DANFORTH:   The pure in heart need no lawyers. Proceed as you will.

PROCTOR (*handing* DANFORTH *a paper*):   Will you read this first, sir? It's a sort of testament. The people signing it declare their good opinion of Rebecca, and my wife, and Martha Corey. (DANFORTH *looks down at the paper.*)

PARRIS (*to enlist* DANFORTH's *sarcasm*):   Their good opinion! (*But* DANFORTH *goes on reading, and* PROCTOR *is heartened.*)

PROCTOR:   These are all landholding farmers, members of the church. (*Delicately, trying to point out a paragraph*) If you'll notice, sir—they've known the women many years and never saw no sign they had dealings with the Devil.

(PARRIS *nervously moves over and reads over* DANFORTH's *shoulder.*)

DANFORTH (*glancing down a long list*):   How many names are here?

FRANCIS:   Ninety-one, Your Excellency.

PARRIS (*sweating*):   These people should be summoned. (DANFORTH *looks up at him questioningly.*) For questioning.

FRANCIS (*trembling with anger*):   Mr. Danforth, I gave them all my word no harm would come to them for signing this.

PARRIS:   This is a clear attack upon the court!

HALE (*to* PARRIS, *trying to contain himself*):   Is every defense an attack upon the court? Can no one—?

PARRIS:   All innocent and Christian people are happy for the courts in Salem! These people are gloomy for it. (*To* DANFORTH *directly*) And I think you will want to know, from each and every one of them, what discontents them with you!

HATHORNE:   I think they ought to be examined, sir.

DANFORTH:   It is not necessarily an attack, I think. Yet—

FRANCIS:   These are all covenanted Christians, sir.

DANFORTH:   Then I am sure they may have nothing to fear. (*Hands* CHEEVER *the paper*) Mr. Cheever, have warrants drawn for all of these—arrest for examination. (*To* PROCTOR) Now, Mister, what other information do you have for us? (FRANCIS *is still standing, horrified.*) You may sit, Mr. Nurse.

FRANCIS:   I have brought trouble on these people; I have—

DANFORTH:   No, old man, you have not hurt these people if they are of good conscience. But you must understand, sir, that a person is either with this court or he must be counted against it, there be no road between. This is a sharp time, now, a precise time—we live no longer in the dusky afternoon when evil mixed itself with good and befuddled the world. Now, by God's grace, the shining sun is up, and them that fear not light will surely praise it. I hope you will be one of those. (MARY WARREN *suddenly sobs.*) She's not hearty, I see.

PROCTOR:   No, she's not, sir. (*To* MARY, *bending*

*to her, holding her hand, quietly*) Now remember what the angel Raphael said to the boy Tobias. Remember it.

MARY WARREN (*hardly audible*):  Aye.

PROCTOR:  "Do that which is good, and no harm shall come to thee."

MARY WARREN:  Aye.

DANFORTH:  Come, man, we wait you.

(MARSHAL HERRICK *returns, and takes his post at the door.*)

GILES:  John, my deposition, give him mine.

PROCTOR:  Aye. (*He hands* DANFORTH *another paper.*) This is Mr. Corey's deposition.

DANFORTH:  Oh? (*He looks down at it. Now* HATHORNE *comes behind him and reads with him.*)

HATHORNE (*suspiciously*):  What lawyer drew this, Corey?

GILES:  You know I never hired a lawyer in my life, Hathorne.

DANFORTH (*finishing the reading*):  It is very well phrased. My compliments. Mr. Parris, if Mr. Putnam is in the court, will you bring him in? (HATHORNE *takes the deposition, and walks to the window with it.* PARRIS *goes into the court.*) You have no legal training, Mr. Corey?

GILES (*very pleased*):  I have the best, sir—I am thirty-three time in court in my life. And always plaintiff, too.

DANFORTH:  Oh, then you're much put-upon.

GILES:  I am never put-upon; I know my rights, sir, and I will have them. You know, your father tried a case of mine—might be thirty-five year ago, I think.

DANFORTH:  Indeed.

GILES:  He never spoke to you of it?

DANFORTH:  No, I cannot recall it.

GILES:  That's strange, he give me nine pound damages. He were a fair judge, your father. Y'see, I had a white mare that time, and this fellow come to borrow the mare—(*Enter* PARRIS *with* THOMAS PUTNAM. *When he sees* PUTNAM, GILES' *ease goes; he is hard.*) Aye, there he is.

DANFORTH:  Mr. Putnam, I have here an accusation by Mr. Corey against you. He states that you coldly prompted your daughter to cry witchery upon George Jacobs that is now in jail.

PUTNAM:  It is a lie.

DANFORTH (*turning to* GILES):  Mr. Putnam states your charge is a lie. What say you to that?

GILES (*furious, his fists clenched*):  A fart on Thomas Putnam, that is what I say to that!

DANFORTH:  What proof do you submit for your charge, sir?

GILES:  My proof is there! (*Pointing to the paper*) If Jacobs hangs for a witch he forfeit up his property—that's law! And there is none but Putnam with the coin to buy so great a piece. This man is killing his neighbors for their land!

DANFORTH:  But proof, sir, proof.

GILES (*pointing at his deposition*):  The proof is there! I have it from an honest man who heard Putnam say it! The day his daughter cried out on Jacobs, he said she'd given him a fair gift of land.

HATHORNE:  And the name of this man?

GILES (*taken aback*):  What name?

HATHORNE:  The man that give you this information.

GILES (*hesitates, then*):  Why, I—I cannot give you his name.

HATHORNE:  And why not?

GILES (*hesitates, then bursts out*):  You know well why not! He'll lay in jail if I give his name!

HATHORNE:  This is contempt of the court, Mr. Danforth!

DANFORTH (*to avoid that*):  You will surely tell us the name.

GILES:  I will not give you no name. I mentioned my wife's name once and I'll burn in hell long enough for that. I stand mute.

DANFORTH:  In that case, I have no choice but to arrest you for contempt of this court, do you know that?

GILES:  This is a hearing; you cannot clap me for contempt of a hearing.

DANFORTH:  Oh, it is a proper lawyer! Do you wish me to declare the court in full session here? Or will you give me good reply?

GILES (*faltering*):  I cannot give you no name, sir, I cannot.

DANFORTH:  You are a foolish old man. Mr. Cheever, begin the record. The court is now in session. I ask you, Mr. Corey—

PROCTOR (*breaking in*):  Your Honor—he has the story in confidence, sir, and he—

PARRIS:  The Devil lives on such confidences! (*To* DANFORTH) Without confidences there could be no conspiracy, Your Honor!

HATHORNE:  I think it must be broken, sir.

DANFORTH (*to* GILES):  Old man, if your informant tells the truth let him come here openly like a decent man. But if he hide in anonymity I must know why. Now sir, the government and central church demand of you the name of him who reported Mr. Thomas Putnam a common murderer.

HALE: Excellency—

DANFORTH: Mr. Hale.

HALE: We cannot blink it more. There is a prodigious fear of this court in the country—

DANFORTH: Then there is a prodigious guilt in the country. Are *you* afraid to be questioned here?

HALE: I may only fear the Lord, sir, but there is fear in the country nevertheless.

DANFORTH (*angered now*): Reproach me not with the fear in the country; there is fear in the country because there is a moving plot to topple Christ in the country!

HALE: But it does not follow that everyone accused is part of it.

DANFORTH: No uncorrupted man may fear this court, Mr. Hale! None! (*To* GILES): You are under arrest in contempt of this court. Now sit you down and take counsel with yourself, or you will be set in the jail until you decide to answer all questions.

(GILES COREY *makes a rush for* PUTNAM. PROCTOR *lunges and holds him.*)

PROCTOR: No, Giles!

GILES (*over* PROCTOR's *shoulder at* PUTNAM): I'll cut your throat, Putnam, I'll kill you yet!

PROCTOR (*forcing him into a chair*): Peace, Giles, peace. (*Releasing him.*) We'll prove ourselves. Now we will. (*He starts to turn to* DANFORTH.)

GILES: Say nothin' more, John. (*Pointing at* DANFORTH) He's only playin' you! He means to hang us all!

(MARY WARREN *bursts into sobs.*)

DANFORTH: This is a court of law, Mister. I'll have no effrontery here!

PROCTOR: Forgive him, sir, for his old age. Peace, Giles, we'll prove it all now. (*He lifts up* MARY's *chin.*) You cannot weep, Mary. Remember the angel, what he say to the boy. Hold to it, now; there is your rock. (MARY *quiets. He takes out a paper, and turns to* DANFORTH.) This is Mary Warren's deposition. I—I would ask you remember, sir, while you read it, that until two week ago she were no different than the other children are today. (*He is speaking reasonably, restraining all his fears, his anger, his anxiety.*) You saw her scream, she howled, she swore familiar spirits choked her; she even testified that

Satan, in the form of women now in jail, tried to win her soul away, and then when she refused—

DANFORTH: We know all this.

PROCTOR: Aye, sir. She swears now that she never saw Satan; nor any spirit, vague or clear, that Satan may have sent to hurt her. And she declares her friends are lying now.

(PROCTOR *starts to hand* DANFORTH *the deposition, and* HALE *comes up to* DANFORTH *in a trembling state.*)

HALE: Excellency, a moment. I think this goes to the heart of the matter.

DANFORTH (*with deep misgivings*): It surely does.

HALE: I cannot say he is an honest man; I know him little. But in all justice, sir, a claim so weighty cannot be argued by a farmer. In God's name, sir, stop here; send him home and let him come again with a lawyer—

DANFORTH (*patiently*): Now look you, Mr. Hale—

HALE: Excellency, I have signed seventy-two death warrants; I am a minister of the Lord, and I dare not take a life without there be a proof so immaculate no slightest qualm of conscience may doubt it.

DANFORTH: Mr. Hale, you surely do not doubt my justice.

HALE: I have this morning signed away the soul of Rebecca Nurse, Your Honor. I'll not conceal it, my hand shakes yet as with a wound! I pray you, sir, *this* argument let lawyers present to you.

DANFORTH: Mr. Hale, believe me; for a man of such terrible learning you are most bewildered—I hope you will forgive me. I have been thirty-two year at the bar, sir, and I should be confounded were I called upon to defend these people. Let you consider, now—(*To* PROCTOR *and the others*) And I bid you all do likewise. In an ordinary crime, how does one defend the accused? One calls up witnesses to prove his innocence. But witchcraft is *ipso facto*, on its face and by its nature, an invisible crime, is it not? Therefore, who may possibly be witness to it? The witch and the victim. None other. Now we cannot hope the witch will accuse herself; granted? Therefore, we must rely upon her victims—and they do testify, the children certainly do testify. As for the witches, none will deny that we are most eager for all their confessions. Therefore, what is left for a lawyer to bring out? I think I have made my point. Have I not?

HALE: But this child claims the girls are not truthful, and if they are not—

DANFORTH: That is precisely what I am about to consider, sir. What more may you ask of me? Unless you doubt my probity?

HALE (defeated): I surely do not, sir. Let you consider it, then.

DANFORTH: And let you put your heart to rest. Her deposition, Mr. Proctor.

(PROCTOR hands it to him. HATHORNE rises, goes beside DANFORTH, and starts reading. PARRIS comes to his other side. DANFORTH looks at JOHN PROCTOR, then proceeds to read. HALE gets up, finds position near the JUDGE, reads too. PROCTOR glances at GILES. FRANCIS prays silently, hands pressed together. CHEEVER waits placidly, the sublime official, dutiful. MARY WARREN sobs once. JOHN PROCTOR touches her head reassuringly. Presently DANFORTH lifts his eyes, stands up, takes out a kerchief and blows his nose. The others stand aside as he moves in thought toward the window.)

PARRIS (hardly able to contain his anger and fear): I should like to question—

DANFORTH (his first real outburst, in which his contempt for PARRIS is clear): Mr. Parris, I bid you be silent! (He stands in silence, looking out the window. Now, having established that he will set the gait) Mr. Cheever, will you go into the court and bring the children here? (CHEEVER gets up and goes out upstage. DANFORTH now turns to MARY.) Mary Warren, how came you to this turnabout? Has Mr. Proctor threatened you for this deposition?

MARY WARREN: No, sir.

DANFORTH: Has he ever threatened you?

MARY WARREN (weaker): No, sir.

DANFORTH (sensing a weakening): Has he threatened you?

MARY WARREN: No, sir.

DANFORTH: Then you tell me that you sat in my court, callously lying, when you knew that people would hang by your evidence? (She does not answer.) Answer me!

MARY WARREN (almost inaudibly): I did, sir.

DANFORTH: How were you instructed in your life? Do you not know that God damns all liars? (She cannot speak.) Or is it now that you lie?

MARY WARREN: No, sir—I am with God now.

DANFORTH: You are with God now.

MARY WARREN: Aye, sir.

DANFORTH (containing himself): I will tell you this—you are either lying now, or you were lying in the court, and in either case you have committed perjury and you will go to jail for it. You cannot lightly say you lied, Mary. Do you know that?

MARY WARREN: I cannot lie no more. I am with God, I am with God.

(But she breaks into sobs at the thought of it, and the right door opens, and enter SUSANNA WALCOTT, MERCY LEWIS, BETTY PARRIS, and finally ABIGAIL. CHEEVER comes to DANFORTH.)

CHEEVER: Ruth Putnam's not in the court, sir, nor the other children.

DANFORTH: These will be sufficient. Sit you down, children. (Silently they sit.) Your friend, Mary Warren, has given us a deposition. In which she swears that she never saw familiar spirits, apparitions, nor any manifest of the Devil. She claims as well that none of you have seen these things either. (Slight pause.) Now, children, this is a court of law. The law, based upon the Bible, and the Bible, writ by Almighty God, forbid the practice of witchcraft, and describe death as the penalty thereof. But likewise, children, the law and Bible damn all bearers of false witness. (Slight pause.) Now then. It does not escape me that this deposition may be devised to blind us; it may well be that Mary Warren has been conquered by Satan, who sends her here to distract our sacred purpose. If so, her neck will break for it. But if she speak true, I bid you now drop your guile and confess your pretense, for a quick confession will go easier with you. (Pause.) Abigail Williams, rise. (Abigail slowly rises.) Is there any truth in this?

ABIGAIL: No, sir.

DANFORTH (thinks, glances at MARY, then back to ABIGAIL): Children, a very augur bit will now be turned into your souls until your honesty is proved. Will either of you change your positions now, or do you force me to hard questioning?

ABIGAIL: I have naught to change, sir. She lies.

DANFORTH (to MARY): You would still go on with this?

MARY WARREN (faintly): Aye, sir.

DANFORTH (turning to Abigail): A poppet were discovered in Mr. Proctor's house, stabbed by a needle. Mary Warren claims that you sat beside her in the court when she made it, and that you saw her make it and witnessed how she herself stuck the needle into it for safe-keeping. What say you to that?

ABIGAIL (*with a slight note of indignation*): It is a lie, sir.

DANFORTH (*after a slight pause*):   While you worked for Mr. Proctor, did you see poppets in that house?

ABIGAIL:   Goody Proctor always kept poppets.

PROCTOR:   Your Honor, my wife never kept no poppets. Mary Warren confesses it was her poppet.

CHEEVER:   Your Excellency.

DANFORTH:   Mr. Cheever.

CHEEVER:   When I spoke with Goody Proctor in that house, she said she never kept no poppets. But she said she did keep poppets when she were a girl.

PROCTOR:   She has not been a girl these fifteen years, Your Honor.

HATHORNE:   But a poppet will keep fifteen years, will it not?

PROCTOR:   It will keep if it is kept, but Mary Warren swears she never saw no poppets in my house, nor anyone else.

PARRIS:   Why could there not have been poppets hid where no one ever saw them?

PROCTOR (*furious*):   There might also be a dragon with five legs in my house, but no one has ever seen it.

PARRIS:   We are here, Your Honor, precisely to discover what no one has ever seen.

PROCTOR:   Mr. Danforth, what profit this girl to turn herself about? What may Mary Warren gain but hard questioning and worse?

DANFORTH:   You are charging Abigail Williams with a marvelous cool plot to murder, do you understand that?

PROCTOR:   I do, sir. I believe she means to murder.

DANFORTH (*pointing at* ABIGAIL, *incredulously*):   This child would murder your wife?

PROCTOR:   It is not a child. Now hear me, sir. In the sight of the congregation she were twice this year put out of this meetin' house for laughter during prayer.

DANFORTH (*shocked, turning to* ABIGAIL):   What's this? Laughter during—!

PARRIS:   Excellency, she were under Tituba's power at that time, but she is solemn now.

GILES:   Aye, now she is solemn and goes to hang people!

DANFORTH:   Quiet, man.

HATHORNE:   Surely it have no bearing on the question, sir. He charges contemplation of murder.

DANFORTH:   Aye. (*He studies* ABIGAIL *for a moment. Then*) Continue, Mr. Proctor.

PROCTOR:   Mary. Now tell the Governor how you danced in the woods.

PARRIS (*instantly*):   Excellency, since I come to Salem this man is blackening my name. He—

DANFORTH:   In a moment, sir. (*To* MARY WARREN, *sternly, and surprised*) What is this dancing?

MARY WARREN:   I—(*She glances at* ABIGAIL, *who is staring down at her remorselessly. Then, appealing to* PROCTOR) Mr. Proctor—

PROCTOR (*taking it right up*):   Abigail leads the girls to the woods, Your Honor, and they have danced there naked—

PARRIS:   Your Honor, this—

PROCTOR (*at once*):   Mr. Parris discovered them himself in the dead of night! There's the "child" she is!

DANFORTH (*It is growing into a nightmare, and he turns, astonished, to* PARRIS.):   Mr. Parris—

PARRIS:   I can only say, sir, that I never found any of them naked, and this man is—

DANFORTH:   But you discovered them dancing in the woods? (*Eyes on Parris, he points at* ABIGAIL.) Abigail?

HALE:   Excellency, when I first arrived from Beverly, Mr. Parris told me that.

DANFORTH:   Do you deny it, Mr. Parris?

PARRIS:   I do not, sir, but I never saw any of them naked.

DANFORTH:   But she have *danced?*

PARRIS (*unwillingly*):   Aye, sir.

(DANFORTH, *as though with new eyes, looks at* ABIGAIL.)

HATHORNE:   Excellency, will you permit me? (*He points at* MARY WARREN.)

DANFORTH (*with great worry*):   Pray, proceed.

HATHORNE:   You say you never saw no spirits, Mary, were never threatened or afflicted by any manifest of the Devil or the Devil's agents.

MARY WARREN (*very faintly*):   No, sir.

HATHORNE (*with a gleam of victory*):   And yet, when people accused of witchery confronted you in court, you would faint, saying their spirits came out of their bodies and choked you—

MARY WARREN:   That were pretense, sir.

DANFORTH:   I cannot hear you.

MARY WARREN:   Pretense, sir.

PARRIS:   But you did turn cold, did you not? I myself picked you up many times, and your skin were icy. Mr. Danforth, you—

DANFORTH:   I saw that many times.

PROCTOR:   She only pretended to faint, Your Excellency. They're all marvelous pretenders.

HATHORNE:   Then can she pretend to faint now?

PROCTOR:   Now?

PARRIS:   Why not? Now there are no spirits attacking her, for none in this room is accused of witchcraft. So let her turn herself cold now, let her pretend she is attacked now, let her faint. (*He turns to* MARY WARREN.) Faint!

MARY WARREN:   Faint?

PARRIS:   Aye, faint. Prove to us how you pretended in the court so many times.

MARY WARREN (*looking to* PROCTOR):   I—cannot faint now, sir.

PROCTOR (*alarmed, quietly*):   Can you not pretend it?

MARY WARREN:   I—(*She looks about as though searching for the passion to faint.*) I—have no *sense* of it now, I—

DANFORTH:   Why? What is lacking now?

MARY WARREN:   I—cannot tell, sir, I—

DANFORTH:   Might it be that here we have no afflicting spirit loose, but in the court there were some?

MARY WARREN:   I never saw no spirits.

PARRIS:   Then see no spirits now, and prove to us that you can faint by your own will, as you claim.

MARY WARREN (*stares, searching for the emotion of it, and then shakes her head*):   I—cannot do it.

PARRIS:   Then you will confess, will you not? It were attacking spirits made you faint!

MARY WARREN:   No, sir, I—

PARRIS:   Your Excellency, this is a trick to blind the court!

MARY WARREN:   It's not a trick! (*She stands.*) I—I used to faint because I—I thought I saw spirits.

DANFORTH:   *Thought* you saw them!

MARY WARREN:   But I did not, Your Honor.

HATHORNE:   How could you think you saw them unless you saw them?

MARY WARREN:   I—I cannot tell how, but I did. I—I heard the other girls screaming, and you, Your Honor, you seemed to believe them,

and I—It were only sport in the beginning, sir, but then the whole world cried spirits, spirits, and I—I promise you, Mr. Danforth, I only thought I saw them but I did not.

(DANFORTH *peers at her.*)

PARRIS (*smiling, but nervous because* DANFORTH *seems to be struck by* MARY WARREN's *story*):   Surely Your Excellency is not taken by this simple lie.

DANFORTH (*turning worriedly to* ABIGAIL):   Abigail. I bid you now search your heart and tell me this—and beware of it, child, to God every soul is precious and His vengeance is terrible on them that take life without cause. Is it possible, child, that the spirits you have seen are illusion only, some deception that may cross your mind when—

ABIGAIL:   Why, this—this—is a base question, sir.

DANFORTH:   Child, I would have you consider it—

ABIGAIL:   I have been hurt, Mr. Danforth; I have seen my blood runnin' out! I have been near to murdered every day because I done my duty pointing out the Devil's people—and this is my reward? To be mistrusted, denied, questioned like a—

DANFORTH (*weakening*):   Child, I do not mistrust you—

ABIGAIL (*in an open threat*):   Let *you* beware, Mr. Danforth. Think you to be so mighty that the power of Hell may not turn *your* wits? Beware of it! There is—(*Suddenly, from an accusatory attitude, her face turns, looking into the air above—it is truly frightened.*)

DANFORTH (*apprehensively*):   What is it, child?

ABIGAIL (*looking about in the air, clasping her arms about her as though cold*):   I—I know not. A wind, a cold wind, has come. (*Her eyes fall on* MARY WARREN.)

MARY WARREN (*terrified, pleading*):   Abby!

MERCY LEWIS (*shivering*):   Your Honor, I freeze!

PROCTOR:   They're pretending!

HATHORNE (*touching* ABIGAIL's *hand*):   She is cold, Your Honor, touch her!

MERCY LEWIS (*through chattering teeth*):   Mary, do you send this shadow on me?

MARY WARREN:   Lord, save me!

SUSANNA WALCOTT:   I freeze, I freeze!

ABIGAIL (*shivering visibly*):   It is a wind, a wind!

MARY WARREN: Abby, don't do that!

DANFORTH (*himself engaged and entered by* ABIGAIL): Mary Warren, do you witch her? I say to you, do you send your spirit out?

(*With a hysterical cry* MARY WARREN *starts to run.* PROCTOR *catches her.*)

MARY WARREN (*almost collapsing*): Let me go, Mr. Proctor, I cannot, I cannot—

ABIGAIL (*crying to Heaven*): Oh, Heavenly Father, take away this shadow!

(*Without warning or hesitation,* PROCTOR *leaps at* ABIGAIL *and, grabbing her by the hair, pulls her to her feet. She screams in pain.* DANFORTH, *astonished, cries, "What are you about?" and* HATHORNE *and* PARRIS *call, "Take your hands off her!" and out of it all comes* PROCTOR's *roaring voice.*)

PROCTOR: How do you call Heaven! Whore! Whore!

(HERRICK *breaks* PROCTOR *from her.*)

HERRICK: John!

DANFORTH: Man! Man, what do you—

PROCTOR (*breathless and in agony*): It is a whore!

DANFORTH (*dumfounded*): You charge—?

ABIGAIL: Mr. Danforth, he is lying!

PROCTOR: Mark her! Now she'll suck a scream to stab me with, but—

DANFORTH: You will prove this! This will not pass!

PROCTOR (*trembling, his life collapsing about him*): I have known her, sir. I have known her.

DANFORTH: You—you are a lecher?

FRANCIS (*horrified*): John, you cannot say such a—

PROCTOR: Oh, Francis, I wish you had some evil in you that you might know me! (*To* DANFORTH) A man will not cast away his good name. You surely know that.

DANFORTH (*dumfounded*): In—in what time? In what place?

PROCTOR (*his voice about to break, and his shame great*): In the proper place—where my beasts are bedded. On the last night of my joy, some eight months past. She used to serve me in my house, sir. (*He has to clamp his jaw to keep from weeping.*) A man may think God sleeps, but God sees everything. I know it now. I beg you, sir, I beg you—see her what she is. My wife, my dear good wife, took this girl soon after, sir, and put her out on the highroad. And being what she is, a lump of vanity, sir—(*He is being overcome.*)

Excellency, forgive me, forgive me. (*Angrily against himself, he turns away from the governor for a moment. Then, as though to cry out is his only means of speech left*) She thinks to dance with me on my wife's grave! And well she might, for I thought of her softly. God help me, I lusted, and there *is* a promise in such sweat. But it is a whore's vengeance, and you must see it; I set myself entirely in your hands. I know you must see it now.

DANFORTH (*blanched, in horror, turning to* ABIGAIL): You deny every scrap and tittle of this?

ABIGAIL: If I must answer that, I will leave and I will not come back again!

(DANFORTH *seems unsteady.*)

PROCTOR: I have a bell of my honor! I have rung the doom of my good name—you will believe me, Mr. Danforth! My wife is innocent, except she knew a whore when she saw one!

ABIGAIL (*stepping up to* DANFORTH): What look do you give me? (DANFORTH *cannot speak.*) I'll not have such looks! (*She turns and starts for the door.*)

DANFORTH: You will remain where you are! (HERRICK *steps into her path. She comes up short, fire in her eyes.*) Mr. Parris, go into the court and bring Goodwife Proctor out.

PARRIS (*objecting*): Your Honor, this is all a—

DANFORTH (*sharply to* PARRIS): Bring her out! And tell her not one word of what's been spoken here. And let you knock before you enter. (PARRIS *goes out.*) Now we shall touch the bottom of this swamp. (*To* PROCTOR) Your wife, you say, is an honest woman.

PROCTOR: In her life, sir, she have never lied. There are them that cannot sing, and them that cannot weep—my wife cannot lie. I have paid much to learn it, sir.

DANFORTH: And when she put this girl out of your house, she put her out for a harlot?

PROCTOR: Aye, sir.

DANFORTH: And knew her for a harlot?

PROCTOR: Aye, sir, she knew her for a harlot.

DANFORTH: Good then. (*To* ABIGAIL) And if she tell me, child, it were for harlotry, may God spread His mercy on you! (*There is a knock. He calls to the door.*) Hold! (*To* ABIGAIL) Turn your back. Turn your back. (*To* PROCTOR) Do likewise. (*Both turn their backs—*ABIGAIL *with indignant slowness.*) Now let neither of you turn to face Goody Proctor. No one in this room is to speak one word, or raise a gesture aye or nay. (*He turns toward the door, calls.*) Enter! (*The door opens.* ELIZABETH *enters with* PARRIS. PARRIS *leaves her. She stands alone, her eyes looking for* PROCTOR.) Mr. Cheever, report this testimony in all exactness. Are you ready?

CHEEVER:  Ready, sir.

DANFORTH:  Come here, woman. (ELIZABETH *comes to him, glancing at* PROCTOR'*s back.*) Look at me only, not at your husband. In my eyes only.

ELIZABETH ( *faintly*):  Good, sir.

DANFORTH:  We are given to understand that at one time you dismissed your servant, Abigail Williams.

ELIZABETH:  That is true, sir.

DANFORTH:  For what cause did you dismiss her? (*Slight pause. Then* ELIZABETH *tries to glance at* PROCTOR.) You will look in my eyes only and not at your husband. The answer is in your memory and you need no help to give it to me. Why did you dismiss Abigail Williams?

ELIZABETH (*not knowing what to say, sensing a situation, wetting her lips to stall for time*):  She—dissatisfied me. (*Pause.*) And my husband.

DANFORTH:  In what way dissatisfied you?

ELIZABETH:  She were—(*She glances at* PROCTOR *for a cue.*)

DANFORTH:  Woman, look at me! (ELIZABETH *does.*) Were she slovenly? Lazy? What disturbance did she cause?

ELIZABETH:  Your Honor, I—in that time I were sick. And I—My husband is a good and righteous man. He is never drunk as some are, nor wastin' his time at the shovelboard, but always at his work. But in my sickness—you see, sir, I were a long time sick after my last baby, and I thought I saw my husband somewhat turning from me. And this girl—(*She turns to* ABIGAIL.)

DANFORTH:  Look at me.

ELIZABETH:  Aye, sir. Abigail Williams—(*She breaks off.*)

DANFORTH:  What of Abigail Williams?

ELIZABETH:  I came to think he fancied her. And so one night I lost my wits, I think, and put her out on the highroad.

DANFORTH:  Your husband—did he indeed turn from you?

ELIZABETH (*in agony*):  My husband—is a goodly man, sir.

DANFORTH:  Then he did not turn from you.

ELIZABETH (*starting to glance at* Proctor):  He—

DANFORTH (*reaches out and holds her face, then*):  Look at me! To your own knowledge, has John Proctor ever committed the crime of lechery? (*In a crisis of indecision she cannot speak.*) Answer my question! Is your husband a lecher!

ELIZABETH (*faintly*):  No, sir.

DANFORTH:  Remove her, Marshal.

PROCTOR:  Elizabeth, tell the truth!

DANFORTH:  She has spoken. Remove her!

PROCTOR (*crying out*):  Elizabeth, I have confessed it!

ELIZABETH:  Oh, God! (*The door closes behind her.*)

PROCTOR:  She only thought to save my name!

HALE:  Excellency, it is a natural lie to tell; I beg you, stop now before another is condemned! I may shut my conscience to it no more—private vengeance is working through this testimony! From the beginning this man has struck me true. By my oath to Heaven, I believe him now, and I pray you call back his wife before we—

DANFORTH:  She spoke nothing of lechery, and this man has lied!

HALE:  I believe him! (*Pointing at* ABIGAIL) This girl has always struck me false! She has—

(ABIGAIL, *with a weird, wild, chilling cry, screams up to the ceiling.*)

ABIGAIL:  You will not! Begone! Begone, I say!

DANFORTH:  What is it, child? (*But* ABIGAIL, *pointing with fear, is now raising up her frightened eyes, her awed face, toward the ceiling—the girls are doing the same—and now* HATHORNE, HALE, PUTNAM, CHEEVER, HERRICK, *and* DANFORTH *do the same.*) What's there? (*He lowers his eyes from the ceiling, and now he is frightened; there is real tension in his voice.*) Child! (*She is transfixed—with all the girls, she is whimpering open-mouthed, agape at the ceiling.*) Girls! Why do you—?

MERCY LEWIS (*pointing*):  It's on the beam! Behind the rafter!

DANFORTH (*looking up*):  Where!

ABIGAIL:  Why—? (*She gulps.*) Why do you come, yellow bird?

PROCTOR:  Where's a bird? I see no bird!

ABIGAIL (*to the ceiling*):  My face? My face?

PROCTOR:  Mr. Hale—

DANFORTH:  Be quiet!

PROCTOR (*to* HALE):  Do you see a bird?

DANFORTH:  Be quiet!!

ABIGAIL (*to the ceiling, in a genuine conversation with the "bird," as though trying to talk it out of attacking her*):  But God made my face; you cannot want to tear my face. Envy is a deadly sin, Mary.

MARY WARREN (*on her feet with a spring, and horrified, pleading*):  Abby!

ABIGAIL (*unperturbed, continuing to the "bird"*):  Oh, Mary, this is a black art to change your shape. No, I cannot, I cannot stop my mouth; it's God's work I do.

MARY WARREN:  Abby, I'm *here!*

PROCTOR (*frantically*):  They're pretending, Mr. Danforth!

ABIGAIL (*Now she takes a backward step, as though in fear the bird will swoop down momentarily.*):  Oh, please, Mary! Don't come down.

SUSANNA WALCOTT:  Her claws, she's stretching her claws!

PROCTOR:  Lies, lies.

ABIGAIL (*backing further, eyes still fixed above*):  Mary, please don't hurt me!

MARY WARREN (*to* DANFORTH):  I'm not hurting her!

DANFORTH (*to* MARY WARREN):  Why does she see this vision?

MARY WARREN:  She sees nothin'!

ABIGAIL (*now staring full front as though hypnotized, and mimicking the exact tone of* MARY WARREN'*s cry*):  She sees nothin'!

MARY WARREN (*pleading*):  Abby, you mustn't!

ABIGAIL AND ALL THE GIRLS (*all transfixed*):  Abby, you mustn't!

MARY WARREN (*to all the girls*):  I'm here, I'm here!

GIRLS:  I'm here, I'm here!

DANFORTH (*horrified*):  Mary Warren! Draw back your spirit out of them!

MARY WARREN:  Mr. Danforth!

GIRLS (*cutting her off*):  Mr. Danforth!

DANFORTH:  Have you compacted with the Devil? Have you?

MARY WARREN:  Never, never!

GIRLS:  Never, never!

DANFORTH (*growing hysterical*):  Why can they only repeat you?

PROCTOR:  Give me a whip—I'll stop it!

MARY WARREN:  They're sporting. They—!

GIRLS:  They're sporting!

MARY WARREN (*turning on them all hysterically and stamping her feet*):  Abby, stop it!

GIRLS (*stamping their feet*):  Abby, stop it!

MARY WARREN:  Stop it!

GIRLS:  Stop it!

MARY WARREN (*screaming it out at the top of her lungs, and raising her fists*):  Stop it!!

GIRLS (*raising their fists*):  Stop it!!

(MARY WARREN, *utterly confounded, and becoming overwhelmed by* ABIGAIL'*s—and the girls'—utter conviction, starts to whimper, hands half raised, powerless, and all the girls begin whimpering exactly as she does.*)

DANFORTH:  A little while ago you were afflicted. Now it seems you afflict others; where did you find this power?

MARY WARREN (*staring at* ABIGAIL):  I—have no power.

GIRLS:  I have no power.

PROCTOR:  They're gulling you, Mister!

DANFORTH:  Why did you turn about this past two weeks? You have seen the Devil, have you not?

HALE (*indicating* ABIGAIL *and the girls*):  You cannot believe them!

MARY WARREN:  I—

PROCTOR (*sensing her weakening*):  Mary, God damns all liars!

DANFORTH (*pounding it into her*):  You have seen the Devil, you have made compact with Lucifer, have you not?

PROCTOR:  God damns liars, Mary!

(MARY *utters something unintelligible, staring at* ABIGAIL, *who keeps watching the "bird" above.*)

DANFORTH:  I cannot hear you. What do you say? (MARY *utters again unintelligibly.*) You will confess yourself or you will hang? (*He turns her roughly to face him.*) Do you know who I am? I say you will hang if you do not open with me!

PROCTOR:  Mary, remember the angel Raphael—do that which is good and—

ABIGAIL (*pointing upward*):  The wings! Her wings are spreading! Mary, please, don't, don't—!

HALE:  I see nothing, Your Honor!

DANFORTH:  Do you confess this power! (*He is an inch from her face.*) Speak!

ABIGAIL:  She's going to come down! She's walking the beam!

DANFORTH:  Will you speak!

MARY WARREN (*staring in horror*): I cannot!

GIRLS: I cannot!

PARRIS: Cast the Devil out! Look him in the face! Trample him! We'll save you, Mary, only stand fast against him and—

ABIGAIL (*looking up*): Look out! She's coming down!

(*She and all the girls run to one wall, shielding their eyes. And now, as though cornered, they let out a gigantic scream, and* MARY, *as though infected, opens her mouth and screams with them. Gradually* ABIGAIL *and the girls leave off, until only* MARY *is left there, staring up at the "bird," screaming madly. All watch her, horrified by this evident fit.* PROCTOR *strides to her.*)

PROCTOR: Mary, tell the Governor what they—(*He has hardly got a word out, when, seeing him coming for her, she rushes out of his reach, screaming in horror.*)

MARY WARREN: Don't touch me—don't touch me! (*At which the girls halt at the door.*)

PROCTOR (*astonished*): Mary!

MARY WARREN (*pointing at* PROCTOR): You're the Devil's man!

(*He is stopped in his tracks.*)

PARRIS: Praise God!

GIRLS: Praise God!

PROCTOR (*numbed*): Mary, how—?

MARY WARREN: I'll not hang with you! I love God, I love God.

DANFORTH (*to* MARY): He bid you do the Devil's work?

MARY WARREN (*hysterically, indicating* PROCTOR): He come at me by night and every day to sign, to sign, to—

DANFORTH: Sign what?

PARRIS: The Devil's book? He come with a book?

MARY WARREN (*hysterically, pointing at* PROCTOR, *fearful of him*): My name, he want my name. "I'll murder you," he says, "if my wife hangs! We must go and overthrow the court," he says!

(DANFORTH's *head jerks toward* PROCTOR, *shock and horror in his face.*)

PROCTOR (*turning, appealing to* HALE): Mr. Hale!

MARY WARREN (*her sobs beginning*): He wake me every night, his eyes were like coals and his fingers claw my neck, and I sign, I sign . . .

HALE: Excellency, this child's gone wild!

PROCTOR (*as* DANFORTH's *wide eyes pour on him*): Mary, Mary!

MARY WARREN (*screaming at him*): No, I love God; I go your way no more. I love God, I bless God. (*Sobbing, she rushes to* ABIGAIL.) Abby, Abby, I'll never hurt you more! (*They all watch, as* ABIGAIL, *out of her infinite charity, reaches out and draws the sobbing* MARY *to her, and then looks up to* DANFORTH.)

DANFORTH (*to* PROCTOR): What are you? (PROCTOR *is beyond speech in his anger.*) You are combined with anti-Christ, are you not? I have seen your power; you will not deny it! What say you, Mister?

HALE: Excellency—

DANFORTH: I will have nothing from you, Mr. Hale! (*To* PROCTOR) Will you confess yourself befouled with Hell, or do you keep that black allegiance yet? What say you?

PROCTOR (*his mind wild, breathless*): I say—I say—God is dead!

PARRIS: Hear it, hear it!

PROCTOR (*laughs insanely, then*): A fire, a fire is burning! I hear the boot of Lucifer, I see his filthy face! And it is my face, and yours, Danforth! For them that quail to bring men out of ignorance, as I have quailed, and as you quail now when you know in all your black hearts that this be fraud—God damns our kind especially, and we will burn, we will burn together.

DANFORTH: Marshal! Take him and Corey with him to the jail!

HALE (*starting across to the door*): I denounce these proceedings!

PROCTOR: You are pulling Heaven down and raising up a whore!

HALE: I denounce these proceedings, I quit this court! (*He slams the door to the outside behind him.*)

DANFORTH (*calling to him in a fury*): Mr. Hale! Mr. Hale!

(*The curtain falls.*)

## ACT FOUR

*A cell in Salem jail, that fall.*

*At the back is a high barred window; near it, a great, heavy door. Along the walls are two benches.*

*The place is in darkness but for the moonlight seeping through the bars. It appears empty. Pres-*

*ently footsteps are heard coming down a corridor beyond the wall, keys rattle, and the door swings open.* MARSHAL HERRICK *enters with a lantern.*

*He is nearly drunk, and heavy-footed. He goes to a bench and nudges a bundle of rags lying on it.*

HERRICK:  Sarah, wake up! Sarah Good! (*He then crosses to the other bench.*)

SARAH GOOD (*rising in her rags*):  Oh, Majesty! Comin', comin'! Tituba, he's here, His Majesty's come!

HERRICK:  Go to the north cell; this place is wanted now. (*He hangs his lantern on the wall.* TITUBA *sits up.*)

TITUBA:  That don't look to me like His Majesty; look to me like the marshal.

HERRICK (*taking out a flask*):  Get along with you now, clear this place. (*He drinks, and* SARAH GOOD *comes and peers up into his face.*)

SARAH GOOD:  Oh, is it you, Marshal! I thought sure you be the devil comin' for us. Could I have a sip of cider for me goin'-away?

HERRICK (*handing her the flask*):  And where are you off to, Sarah?

TITUBA (*as* SARAH *drinks*):  We goin' to Barbados, soon the Devil gits here with the feathers and the wings.

HERRICK:  Oh? A happy voyage to you.

SARAH GOOD:  A pair of bluebirds wingin' southerly, the two of us! Oh, it be a grand transformation, Marshal! (*She raises the flask to drink again.*)

HERRICK (*taking the flask from her lips*): You'd best give me that or you'll never rise off the ground. Come along now.

TITUBA:  I'll speak to him for you, if you desires to come along, Marshal.

HERRICK:  I'd not refuse it, Tituba; it's the proper morning to fly into Hell.

TITUBA:  Oh, it be no Hell in Barbados. Devil, him be pleasureman in Barbados, him be singin' and dancin' in Barbados. It's you folks—you riles him up 'round here; it be too cold 'round here for that Old Boy. He freeze his soul in Massachusetts, but in Barbados he just as sweet and—(*A bellowing cow is heard, and* TITUBA *leaps up and calls to the window.*) Aye, sir! That's him, Sarah!

SARAH GOOD:  I'm here, Majesty! (*They hurriedly pick up their rags as* HOPKINS, *a guard, enters.*)

HOPKINS:  The Deputy Governor's arrived.

HERRICK (*grabbing* TITUBA): Come along, come along.

TITUBA (*resisting him*):  No, he comin' for me. I goin' home!

HERRICK (*pulling her to the door*):  That's not Satan, just a poor old cow with a hatful of milk. Come along now, out with you!

TITUBA (*calling to the window*):  Take me home, Devil! Take me home!

SARAH GOOD (*following the shouting* TITUBA *out*):  Tell him I'm goin', Tituba! Now you tell him Sarah Good is goin' too!

(*In the corridor outside* TITUBA *calls on*—"*Take me home, Devil; Devil take me home!*" *and* HOPKINS' *voice orders her to move on.* HERRICK *returns and begins to push old rags and straw into a corner. Hearing footsteps, he turns, and enter* DANFORTH *and* JUDGE HATHORNE. *They are in greatcoats and wear hats against the bitter cold. They are followed in by* CHEEVER, *who carries a dispatch case and a flat wooden box containing his writing materials.*)

HERRICK:  Good morning, Excellency.

DANFORTH:  Where is Mr. Parris?

HERRICK:  I'll fetch him. (*He starts for the door.*)

DANFORTH:  Marshal. (HERRICK *stops.*) When did Reverend Hale arrive?

HERRICK:  It were toward midnight, I think.

DANFORTH (*suspiciously*):  What is he about here?

HERRICK:  He goes among them that will hang, sir. And he prays with them. He sits with Goody Nurse now. And Mr. Parris with him.

DANFORTH:  Indeed. That man have no authority to enter here, Marshal. Why have you let him in?

HERRICK:  Why, Mr. Parris command me, sir. I cannot deny him.

DANFORTH:  Are you drunk, Marshal?

HERRICK:  No, sir; it is a bitter night, and I have no fire here.

DANFORTH (*containing his anger*):  Fetch Mr. Parris.

HERRICK:  Aye, sir.

DANFORTH:  There is a prodigious stench in this place.

HERRICK:  I have only now cleared the people out for you.

DANFORTH:  Beware hard drink, Marshal.

HERRICK:  Aye, sir. (*He waits an instant for further orders. But* DANFORTH, *in dissatisfaction, turns his back on him, and* HERRICK *goes out. There is a pause.* DANFORTH *stands in thought.*)

HATHORNE: Let you question Hale, Excellency; I should not be surprised he have been preaching in Andover lately.

DANFORTH: We'll come to that; speak nothing of Andover. Parris prays with him. That's strange. (*He blows on his hands, moves toward the window, and looks out.*)

HATHORNE: Excellency, I wonder if it be wise to let Mr. Parris so continuously with the prisoners. (DANFORTH *turns to him, interested.*) I think, sometimes, the man has a mad look these days.

DANFORTH: Mad?

HATHORNE: I met him yesterday coming out of his house, and I bid him good morning—and he wept and went his way. I think it is not well the village sees him so unsteady.

DANFORTH: Perhaps he have some sorrow.

CHEEVER (*stamping his feet against the cold*): I think it be the cows, sir.

DANFORTH: Cows?

CHEEVER: There be so many cows wanderin' the highroads, now their masters are in the jails, and much disagreement who they will belong to now. I know Mr. Parris be arguin' with farmers all yesterday—there is great contention, sir, about the cows. Contention make him weep, sir; it were always a man that weep for contention. (*He turns, as do* HATHORNE *and* DANFORTH, *hearing someone coming up the corridor.* Danforth *raises his head as* PARRIS *enters. He is gaunt, frightened, and sweating in his greatcoat.*)

PARRIS (*to* DANFORTH, *instantly*): Oh, good morning, sir, thank you for coming. I beg your pardon wakin' you so early. Good morning, Judge Hathorne.

DANFORTH: Reverend Hale have no right to enter this—

PARRIS: Excellency, a moment. (*He hurries back and shuts the door.*)

HATHORNE: Do you leave him alone with the prisoners?

DANFORTH: What's his business here?

PARRIS (*prayerfully holding up his hands*): Excellency, hear me. It is a providence. Reverend Hale has returned to bring Rebecca Nurse to God.

DANFORTH (*surprised*): He bids her confess?

PARRIS (*sitting*): Hear me. Rebecca have not given me a word this three month since she came. Now she sits with him, and her sister and Martha Corey and two or three others, and he pleads with them, confess their crimes and save their lives.

DANFORTH: Why—this is indeed a providence. And they soften, they soften?

PARRIS: Not yet, not yet. But I thought to summon you, sir, that we might think on whether it be not wise, to—(*He dares not say it.*) I had thought to put a question, sir, and I hope you will not—

DANFORTH: Mr. Parris, be plain, what troubles you?

PARRIS: There is news, sir, that the court—the court must reckon with. My niece, sir, my niece—I believe she has vanished.

DANFORTH: Vanished!

PARRIS: I had thought to advise you of it earlier in the week, but—

DANFORTH: Why? How long is she gone?

PARRIS: This be the third night. You see, sir, she told me she would stay a night with Mercy Lewis. And next day, when she does not return, I send to Mr. Lewis to inquire. Mercy told him she would sleep in *my* house for a night.

DANFORTH: They are both gone?!

PARRIS (*in fear of him*): They are, sir.

DANFORTH (*alarmed*): I will send a party for them. Where may they be?

PARRIS: Excellency, I think they be aboard a ship. (DANFORTH *stands agape.*) My daughter tells me how she heard them speaking of ships last week, and tonight I discover my—my strongbox is broke into. (*He presses his fingers against his eyes to keep back tears.*)

HATHORNE (*astonished*): She have robbed you?

PARRIS: Thirty-one pound is gone. I am penniless. (*He covers his face and sobs.*)

DANFORTH: Mr. Parris, you are a brainless man! (*He walks in thought, deeply worried.*)

PARRIS: Excellency, it profit nothing you should blame me. I cannot think they would run off except they fear to keep in Salem any more. (*He is pleading.*) Mark it, sir, Abigail had close knowledge of the town, and since the news of Andover has broken here—

DANFORTH: Andover is remedied. The court returns there on Friday, and will resume examinations.

PARRIS: I am sure of it, sir. But the rumor here speaks rebellion in Andover, and it—

DANFORTH: There is no rebellion in Andover!

PARRIS: I tell you what is said here, sir. Andover have thrown out the court, they say, and will have no part of witchcraft. There be a faction here, feeding on that news, and I tell you true, sir, I fear there will be riot here.

HATHORNE: Riot! Why at every execution I have seen naught but high satisfaction in the town.

PARRIS: Judge Hathorne—it were another sort that hanged till now. Rebecca Nurse is no Bridget that lived three year with Bishop before she married him. John Proctor is not Isaac Ward that drank his family to ruin. (*To* DANFORTH) I would to God it were not so, Excellency, but these people have great weight yet in the town. Let Rebecca stand upon the gibbet and send up some righteous prayer, and I fear she'll wake a vengeance on you.

HATHORNE: Excellency, she is condemned a witch. The court have—

DANFORTH (*in deep concern, raising a hand to* HATHORNE): Pray you. (*To* PARRIS) How do you propose, then?

PARRIS: Excellency, I would postpone these hangin's for a time.

DANFORTH: There will be no postponement.

PARRIS: Now Mr. Hale's returned, there is hope, I think—for if he bring even one of these to God, that confession surely damns the others in the public eye, and none may doubt more that they are all linked to Hell. This way, unconfessed and claiming innocence, doubts are multiplied, many honest people will weep for them, and our good purpose is lost in their tears.

DANFORTH (*after thinking a moment, then going to* CHEEVER): Give me the list.

(CHEEVER *opens the dispatch case, searches.*)

PARRIS: It cannot be forgot, sir, that when I summoned the congregation for John Proctor's excommunication there were hardly thirty people come to hear it. That speak a discontent, I think, and—

DANFORTH (*studying the list*): There will be no postponement.

PARRIS: Excellency—

DANFORTH: Now, sir—which of these in your opinion may be brought to God? I will myself strive with him till dawn. (*He hands the list to* PARRIS, *who merely glances at it.*)

PARRIS: There is not sufficient time till dawn.

DANFORTH: I shall do my utmost. Which of them do you have hope for?

PARRIS (*not even glancing at the list now, and in a quavering voice, quietly*): Excellency—a dagger—(*He chokes up.*)

DANFORTH: What do you say?

PARRIS: Tonight, when I open my door to leave my house—a dagger clattered to the ground. (*Silence.* DANFORTH *absorbs this. Now* PARRIS *cries out.*) You cannot hang this sort. There is danger for me. I dare not step outside at night!

(REVEREND HALE *enters. They look at him for an instant in silence. He is steeped in sorrow, exhausted, and more direct than he ever was.*)

DANFORTH: Accept my congratulations, Reverend Hale; we are gladdened to see you returned to your good work.

HALE (*coming to* DANFORTH *now*): You must pardon them. They will not budge.

(HERRICK *enters, waits.*)

DANFORTH (*conciliatory*): You misunderstand, sir; I cannot pardon these when twelve are already hanged for the same crime. It is not just.

PARRIS (*with failing heart*): Rebecca will not confess?

HALE: The sun will rise in a few minutes. Excellency, I must have more time.

DANFORTH: Now hear me, and beguile yourselves no more. I will not receive a single plea for pardon or postponement. Them that will not confess will hang. Twelve are already executed; the names of these seven are given out, and the village expects to see them die this morning. Postponement now speaks a floundering on my part; reprieve or pardon must cast doubt upon the guilt of them that died till now. While I speak God's law, I will not crack its voice with whimpering. If retaliation is your fear, know this—I should hang ten thousand that dared to rise against the law, and an ocean of salt tears could not melt the resolution of the statutes. Now draw yourselves up like men and help me, as you are bound by Heaven to do. Have you spoken with them all, Mr. Hale?

HALE: All but Proctor. He is in the dungeon.

DANFORTH (*to* HERRICK): What's Proctor's way now?

HERRICK: He sits like some great bird; you'd not know he lived except he will take food from time to time.

DANFORTH (*after thinking a moment*): His wife—his wife must be well on with child now.

HERRICK: She is, sir.

DANFORTH: What think you, Mr. Parris? You have closer knowledge of this man; might her presence soften him?

PARRIS: It is possible, sir. He have not laid eyes on her these three months. I should summon her.

DANFORTH (*to* HERRICK): Is he yet adamant? Has he struck at you again?

HERRICK: He cannot, sir, he is chained to the wall now.

DANFORTH (*after thinking on it*): Fetch Goody Proctor to me. Then let you bring him up.

HERRICK: Aye, sir. (HERRICK *goes. There is silence.*)

HALE: Excellency, if you postpone a week and publish to the town that you are striving for their confessions, that speak mercy on your part, not faltering.

DANFORTH: Mr. Hale, as God have not empowered me like Joshua to stop this sun from rising, so I cannot withhold from them the perfection of their punishment.

HALE (*harder now*): If you think God wills you to raise rebellion, Mr. Danforth, you are mistaken!

DANFORTH (*instantly*): You have heard rebellion spoken in the town?

HALE: Excellency, there are orphans wandering from house to house; abandoned cattle bellow on the highroads, the stink of rotting crops hangs everywhere, and no man knows when the harlots' cry will end his life—and you wonder yet if rebellion's spoke? Better you should marvel how they do not burn your province!

DANFORTH: Mr. Hale, have you preached in Andover this month?

HALE: Thank God they have no need of me in Andover.

DANFORTH: You baffle me, sir. Why have you returned here?

HALE: Why, it is all simple. I come to do the Devil's work. I come to counsel Christians they should belie themselves. (*His sarcasm collapses.*) There is blood on my head! Can you not see the blood on my head!

PARRIS: Hush! (*For he has heard footsteps. They all face the door.* HERRICK *enters with* ELIZABETH. *Her wrists are linked by heavy chain, which* HERRICK *now removes. Her clothes are dirty; her face is pale and gaunt.* HERRICK *goes out.*)

DANFORTH (*very politely*): Goody Proctor. (*She is silent.*) I hope you are hearty?

ELIZABETH (*as a warning reminder*): I am yet six months before my time.

DANFORTH: Pray be at your ease, we come not for your life. We—(*uncertain how to plead, for he is not accustomed to it*) Mr. Hale, will you speak with the woman?

HALE: Goody Proctor, your husband is marked to hang this morning.

(*Pause.*)

ELIZABETH (*quietly*): I have heard it.

HALE: You know, do you not, that I have no connection with the court? (*She seems to doubt it.*) I come of my own, Goody Proctor. I would save your husband's life, for if he is taken I count myself his murderer. Do you understand me?

ELIZABETH: What do you want of me?

HALE: Goody Proctor, I have gone this three month like our Lord into the wilderness. I have sought a Christian way, for damnation's doubled on a minister who counsels men to lie.

HATHORNE: It is no lie, you cannot speak of lies.

HALE: It is a lie! They are innocent!

DANFORTH: I'll hear no more of that!

HALE (*continuing to* ELIZABETH): Let you not mistake your duty as I mistook my own. I came into this village like a bridegroom to his beloved, bearing gifts of high religion; the very crowns of holy law I brought, and what I touched with my bright confidence, it died; and where I turned the eye of my great faith, blood flowed up. Beware, Goody Proctor—cleave to no faith when faith brings blood. It is mistaken law that leads you to sacrifice. Life, woman, life is God's most precious gift; no principle, however glorious, may justify the taking of it. I beg you, woman, prevail upon your husband to confess. Let him give his lie. Quail not before God's judgment in this, for it may well be God damns a liar less than he that throws his life away for pride. Will you plead with him? I cannot think he will listen to another.

ELIZABETH: (*quietly*): I think that be the Devil's argument.

HALE (*with a climactic desperation*): Woman,

before the laws of God we are as swine! We cannot read His will!

ELIZABETH: I cannot dispute with you, sir; I lack learning for it.

DANFORTH (*going to her*): Goody Proctor, you are not summoned here for disputation. Be there no wifely tenderness within you? He will die with the sunrise. Your husband. Do you understand it? (*She only looks at him.*) What say you? Will you contend with him? (*She is silent.*) Are you stone? I tell you true, woman, had I no other proof of your unnatural life, your dry eyes now would be sufficient evidence that you delivered up your soul to Hell! A very ape would weep at such calamity! Have the devil dried up any tear of pity in you? (*She is silent.*) Take her out. It profit nothing she should speak to him!

ELIZABETH (*quietly*): Let me speak with him, Excellency.

PARRIS (*with hope*): You'll strive with him? (*She hesitates.*)

DANFORTH: Will you plead for his confession or will you not?

ELIZABETH: I promise nothing. Let me speak with him.

(*A sound—the sibilance of dragging feet on stone. They turn. A pause.* HERRICK *enters with* JOHN PROCTOR. *His wrists are chained. He is another man, bearded, filthy, his eyes misty as though webs had overgrown them. He halts inside the doorway, his eye caught by the sight of* ELIZABETH. *The emotion flowing between them prevents anyone from speaking for an instant. Now* HALE, *visibly affected, goes to* DANFORTH *and speaks quietly.*)

HALE: Pray, leave them, Excellency.

DANFORTH (*pressing* HALE *impatiently aside*): Mr. Proctor, you have been notified, have you not? (PROCTOR *is silent, staring at* ELIZABETH.) I see light in the sky, Mister; let you counsel with your wife, and may God help you turn your back on Hell. (PROCTOR *is silent, staring at* ELIZABETH.)

HALE (*quietly*): Excellency, let—

(DANFORTH *brushes past* HALE *and walks out.* HALE *follows.* CHEEVER *stands and follows,* HATHORNE *behind.* HERRICK *goes.* PARRIS, *from a safe distance, offers:*)

PARRIS: If you desire a cup of cider, Mr. Proctor, I am sure I—(PROCTOR *turns an icy stare at him, and he breaks off.* PARRIS *raises his palms toward* PROCTOR.) God lead you now. (PARRIS *goes out.*)

(*Alone.* PROCTOR *walks to her, halts. It is as though they stood in a spinning world. It is beyond sorrow, above it. He reaches out his hand as though toward an embodiment not quite real, and as he touches her, a strange soft sound, half laughter, half amazement, comes from his throat. He pats her hand. She covers his hand with hers. And then, weak, he sits. Then she sits, facing him.*)

PROCTOR: The child?

ELIZABETH: It grows.

PROCTOR: There is no word of the boys?

ELIZABETH: They're well. Rebecca's Samuel keeps them.

PROCTOR: You have not seen them?

ELIZABETH: I have not. (*She catches a weakening in herself and downs it.*)

PROCTOR: You are a—marvel, Elizabeth.

ELIZABETH: You—have been tortured?

PROCTOR: Aye. (*Pause. She will not let herself be drowned in the sea that threatens her.*) They come for my life now.

ELIZABETH: I know it.

(*Pause.*)

PROCTOR: None—have yet confessed?

ELIZABETH: There be many confessed.

PROCTOR: Who are they?

ELIZABETH: There be a hundred or more, they say. Goody Ballard is one; Isaiah Goodkind is one. There be many.

PROCTOR: Rebecca?

ELIZABETH: Not Rebecca. She is one foot in Heaven now; naught may hurt her more.

PROCTOR: And Giles?

ELIZABETH: You have not heard of it?

PROCTOR: I hear nothin', where I am kept.

ELIZABETH: Giles is dead.

(*He looks at her incredulously.*)

PROCTOR: When were he hanged?

ELIZABETH (*quietly, factually*): He were not hanged. He would not answer aye or nay to his indictment; for if he denied the charge they'd hang him surely, and auction out his property. So he stand mute, and died Christian under the law. And so his sons will have his farm. It is the law, for he could not be condemned a wizard without he answer the indictment, aye or nay.

PROCTOR: Then how does he die?

ELIZABETH (*gently*): They press him, John.

PROCTOR: Press?

ELIZABETH: Great stones they lay upon his chest until he plead aye or nay. (*With a tender smile for the old man*) They say he give them but two words. "More weight," he says. And died.

PROCTOR (*numbed—a thread to weave into his agony*): "More weight."

ELIZABETH: Aye. It were a fearsome man, Giles Corey.

(*Pause.*)

PROCTOR (*with great force of will, but not quite looking at her*): I have been thinking I would confess to them, Elizabeth. (*She shows nothing.*) What say you? If I give them that?

ELIZABETH: I cannot judge you, John.

(*Pause.*)

PROCTOR (*simply—a pure question*): What would you have me do?

ELIZABETH: As you will, I would have it. (*Slight pause*) I want you living, John. That's sure.

PROCTOR (*pauses, then with a flailing of hope*): Giles' wife? Have she confessed?

ELIZABETH: She will not.

(*Pause.*)

PROCTOR: It is a pretense, Elizabeth.

ELIZABETH: What is?

PROCTOR: I cannot mount the gibbet like a saint. It is a fraud. I am not that man. (*She is silent.*) My honesty is broke, Elizabeth; I am no good man. Nothing's spoiled by giving them this lie that were not rotten long before.

ELIZABETH: And yet you've not confessed till now. That speak goodness in you.

PROCTOR: Spite only keeps me silent. It is hard to give a lie to dogs. (*Pause. For the first time he turns directly to her.*) I would have your forgiveness, Elizabeth.

ELIZABETH: It is not for me to give, John, I am—

PROCTOR: I'd have you see some honesty in it. Let them that never lied die now to keep their souls. It is pretense for me, a vanity that will not blind God nor keep my children out of the wind. (*Pause.*) What say you?

ELIZABETH (*upon a heaving sob that always threatens*): John, it come to naught that I should forgive you, if you'll not forgive yourself. (*Now he turns away a little, in great agony.*) It is not my soul, John, it is yours. (*He stands, as though in physical pain, slowly rising to his feet with a great immortal longing to find his answer. It is difficult to say, and she is on the verge of tears.*) Only be sure of this, for I know it now: Whatever you will do, it is a good man does it. (*He turns his doubting, searching gaze upon her.*) I have read my heart this three month, John. (*Pause.*) I have sins of my own to count. It needs a cold wife to prompt lechery.

PROCTOR (*in great pain*): Enough, enough—

ELIZABETH (*now pouring out her heart*): Better you should know me!

PROCTOR: I will not hear it! I know you!

ELIZABETH: You take my sins upon you, John—

PROCTOR (*in agony*): No, I take my own, my own!

ELIZABETH: John, I counted myself so plain, so poorly made, no honest love could come to me! Suspicion kissed you when I did; I never knew how I should say my love. It were a cold house I kept! (*In fright, she swerves, as* HATHORNE *enters.*)

HATHORNE: What say you, Proctor? The sun is soon up.

(PROCTOR, *his chest heaving, stares, turns to* ELIZABETH. *She comes to him as though to plead, her voice quaking.*)

ELIZABETH: Do what you will. But let none be your judge. There be no higher judge under Heaven than Proctor is! Forgive me, forgive me, John—I never knew such goodness in the world! (*She covers her face, weeping.*)

(PROCTOR *turns from her to* HATHORNE; *he is off the earth, his voice hollow.*)

PROCTOR: I want my life.

HATHORNE (*electrified, surprised*): You'll confess yourself?

PROCTOR: I will have my life.

HATHORNE (*with a mystical tone*): God be praised! It is a providence! (*He rushes out the door, and his voice is heard calling down the corridor.*) He will confess! Proctor will confess!

PROCTOR (*with a cry, as he strides to the door*): Why do you cry it? (*In great pain he turns back to her.*) It is evil, is it not? It is evil.

ELIZABETH (*in terror, weeping*): I cannot judge you, John, I cannot!

PROCTOR: Then who will judge me? (*Suddenly clasping his hands*) God in Heaven, what is John Proctor, what is John Proctor? (*He moves as an animal, and a fury is riding in him, a tantalized search.*) I think it is honest, I think so; I am no saint. (*As though she had denied this he calls angrily at her.*) Let Rebecca go like a saint; for me it is fraud!

(*Voices are heard in the hall, speaking together in suppressed excitement.*)

ELIZABETH:   I am not your judge, I cannot be. (*As though giving him release*) Do as you will, do as you will!

PROCTOR:   Would you give them such a lie? Say it. Would you ever give them this? (*She cannot answer.*) You would not; if tongs of fire were singeing you you would not! It is evil. Good, then—it is evil, and I do it!

(HATHORNE *enters with* DANFORTH, *and, with them,* CHEEVER, PARRIS, *and* HALE. *It is a businesslike, rapid entrance, as though the ice had been broken.*)

DANFORTH (*with great relief and gratitude*): Praise to God, man, praise to God; you shall be blessed in Heaven for this. (CHEEVER *has hurried to the bench with pen, ink, and paper.* PROCTOR *watches him.*) Now then, let us have it. Are you ready, Mr. Cheever?

PROCTOR (*with a cold, cold horror at their efficiency*):   Why must it be written?

DANFORTH:   Why, for the good instruction of the village, Mister; this we shall post upon the church door! (*To* PARRIS, *urgently*) Where is the marshal?

PARRIS (*runs to the door and calls down the corridor*):   Marshal! Hurry!

DANFORTH:   Now, then, Mister, will you speak slowly, and directly to the point, for Mr. Cheever's sake. (*He is on record now, and is really dictating to* CHEEVER, *who writes.*) Mr. Proctor, have you seen the Devil in your life? (PROCTOR's *jaws lock.*) Come, man, there is light in the sky; the town waits at the scaffold; I would give out this news. Did you see the Devil?

PROCTOR:   I did.

PARRIS:   Praise God!

DANFORTH:   And when he come to you, what were his demand? (PROCTOR *is silent.* DANFORTH *helps.*) Did he bid you to do his work upon the earth?

PROCTOR:   He did.

DANFORTH:   (And you bound yourself to his service? (DANFORTH *turns, as* REBECCA NURSE *enters, with* HERRICK *helping to support her. She is barely able to walk.*) Come in, come in, woman!

REBECCA (*brightening as she sees* PROCTOR): Ah, John! You are well, then, eh?

(PROCTOR *turns his face to the wall.*)

DANFORTH:   Courage, man, courage—let her witness your good example that she may come to God herself. Now hear it, Goody Nurse! Say on, Mr. Proctor. Did you bind yourself to the Devil's service?

REBECCA (*astonished*):   Why, John!

PROCTOR (*through his teeth, his face turned from* REBECCA):   I did.

DANFORTH:   Now, woman, you surely see it profit nothin' to keep this conspiracy any further. Will you confess yourself with him?

REBECCA:   Oh, John—God send his mercy on you!

DANFORTH:   I say, will you confess yourself, Goody Nurse?

REBECCA:   Why, it is a lie, it is a lie; how may I damn myself? I cannot, I cannot.

DANFORTH:   Mr. Proctor. When the Devil came to you did you see Rebecca Nurse in his company? (PROCTOR *is silent.*) Come, man, take courage—did you ever see her with the Devil?

PROCTOR (*almost inaudibly*):   No.

(DANFORTH, *now sensing trouble, glances at* JOHN *and goes to the table, and picks up a sheet—the list of condemned.*)

DANFORTH:   Did you ever see her sister, Mary Easty, with the Devil?

PROCTOR:   No, I did not.

DANFORTH (*his eyes narrow on* PROCTOR): Did you ever see Martha Corey with the Devil?

PROCTOR:   I did not.

DANFORTH (*realizing, slowly putting the sheet down*):   Did you ever see anyone with the Devil?

PROCTOR:   I did not.

DANFORTH:   Proctor, you mistake me. I am not empowered to trade your life for a lie. You have most certainly seen some person with the Devil. (*Proctor is silent.*) Mr. Proctor, a score of people have already testified they saw this woman with the Devil.

PROCTOR: Then it is proved. Why must I say it?

DANFORTH:   Why "must" you say it! Why, you should rejoice to say it if your soul is truly purged of any love for Hell!

PROCTOR:   They think to go like saints. I like not to spoil their names.

DANFORTH (*inquiring, incredulous*):   Mr. Proctor, do you think they go like saints?

PROCTOR (*evading*):   This woman never thought she done the Devil's work.

DANFORTH:   Look you, sir. I think you mistake your duty here. It matters nothing what she thought—she is convicted of the unnatural murder of children, and you for sending your spirit out upon Mary Warren. Your soul alone is the issue here, Mister, and you will prove its whiteness or you cannot live in a Christian country. Will you tell me now what persons conspired with you in the Devil's company? (PROCTOR *is silent.*) To your knowledge was Rebecca Nurse ever—

PROCTOR: I speak my own sins; I cannot judge another. (*Crying out, with hatred*) I have no tongue for it.

HALE (*quickly to* DANFORTH): Excellency, it is enough he confess himself. Let him sign it, let him sign it.

PARRIS (*feverishly*): It is a great service, sir. It is a weighty name; it will strike the village that Proctor confess. I beg you, let him sign it. The sun is up, Excellency!

DANFORTH (*considers; then with dissatisfaction*): Come, then, sign your testimony. (*To* CHEEVER) Give it to him. (CHEEVER *goes to* PROCTOR, *the confession and a pen in hand.* PROCTOR *does not look at it.*) Come, man, sign it.

PROCTOR (*after glancing at the confession*): You have all witnessed it—it is enough.

DANFORTH: You will not sign it?

PROCTOR: You have all witnessed it; what more is needed?

DANFORTH: Do you sport with me? You will sign your name or it is no confession, Mister! (*His breast heaving with agonized breathing,* PROCTOR *now lays the paper down and signs his name.*)

PARRIS: Praise be to the Lord!

(PROCTOR *has just finished signing when* DANFORTH *reaches for the paper. But* PROCTOR *snatches it up, and now a wild terror is rising in him, and a boundless anger.*)

DANFORTH (*perplexed, but politely extending his hand*): If you please, sir.

PROCTOR: No.

DANFORTH (*as though* PROCTOR *did not understand*): Mr. Proctor, I must have—

PROCTOR: No, no. I have signed it. You have seen me. It is done! You have no need for this.

PARRIS: Proctor, the village must have proof that—

PROCTOR: Damn the village! I confess to God, and God has seen my name on this! It is enough!

DANFORTH: No, sir, it is—

PROCTOR: You came to save my soul, did you not? Here! I have confessed myself; it is enough!

DANFORTH: You have not con—

PROCTOR: I have confessed myself! Is there no good penitence but it be public? God does not need my name nailed upon the church! God sees my name; God knows how black my sins are! It is enough!

DANFORTH: Mr. Proctor—

PROCTOR: You will not use me! I am no Sarah Good or Tituba, I am John Proctor! You will not use me! It is no part of salvation that you should use me!

DANFORTH: I do not wish to—

PROCTOR: I have three children—how may I teach them to walk like men in the world, and I sold my friends?

DANFORTH: You have not sold your friends—

PROCTOR: Beguile me not! I blacken all of them when this is nailed to the church the very day they hang for silence!

DANFORTH: Mr. Proctor, I must have good and legal proof that you—

PROCTOR: You are the high court, your word is good enough! Tell them I confessed myself; say Proctor broke his knees and wept like a woman; say what you will, but my name cannot—

DANFORTH (*with suspicion*): It is the same, is it not? If I report it or you sign to it?

PROCTOR (*He knows it is insane.*) No, it is not the same! What others say and what I sign to is not the same!

DANFORTH: Why? Do you mean to deny this confession when you are free?

PROCTOR: I mean to deny nothing!

DANFORTH: Then explain to me, Mr. Proctor, why you will not let—

PROCTOR (*with a cry of his whole soul*): Because it is my name! Because I cannot have another in my life! Because I lie and sign myself to lies! Because I am not worth the dust on the feet of them that hang! How may I live without my name? I have given you my soul; leave me my name!

DANFORTH (*pointing at the confession in* PROCTOR's *hand*): Is that document a lie? If it is a lie I will not accept it! What say you? I will not deal in lies, Mister! (PROCTOR *is motionless.*) You will give me your honest confession in my hand, or I cannot keep you from the rope. (PROCTOR *does not reply.*) Which way do you go, Mister?

(*His breast heaving, his eyes staring,* PROCTOR *tears the paper and crumples it, and he is weeping in fury, but erect.*)

DANFORTH: Marshal!

PARRIS (*hysterically, as though the tearing paper were his life*): Proctor, Proctor!

HALE:   Man, you will hang! You cannot!

PROCTOR (*his eyes full of tears*):   I can. And there's your first marvel, that I can. You have made your magic now, for now I do think I see some shred of goodness in John Proctor. Not enough to weave a banner with, but white enough to keep it from such dogs. (ELIZABETH, *in a burst of terror, rushes to him and weeps against his hand.*) Give them no tear! Tears pleasure them! Show honor now, show a stony heart and sink them with it! (*He has lifted her, and kisses her now with great passion.*)

REBECCA:   Let you fear nothing! Another judgment waits us all!

DANFORTH:   Hang them high over the town! Who weeps for these, weeps for corruption! (*He sweeps out past them.* HERRICK *starts to lead* REBECCA, *who almost collapses, but* PROCTOR *catches her, and she glances up at him apologetically.*)

REBECCA:   I've had no breakfast.

HERRICK:   Come, man.

(HERRICK *escorts them out,* HATHORNE *and* CHEEVER *behind them.* ELIZABETH *stands staring at the empty doorway.*)

PARRIS (*in deadly fear, to* ELIZABETH):   Go to him, Goody Proctor! There is yet time!

(*From outside a drumroll strikes the air.* PARRIS *is startled.* ELIZABETH *jerks about toward the window.*)

PARRIS:   Go to him! (*He rushes out the door, as though to hold back his fate.*) Proctor! Proctor!

(*Again, a short burst of drums.*)

HALE:   Woman, plead with him! (*He starts to rush out the door, and then goes back to her.*) Woman! It is pride, it is vanity. (*She avoids his eyes, and moves to the window. He drops to his knees.*) Be his helper!—What profit him to bleed? Shall the dust praise him? Shall the worms declare his truth? Go to him, take his shame away!

ELIZABETH (*supporting herself against collapse, grips the bars of the window, and with a cry*):   He have his goodness now. God forbid I take it from him!

(*The final drumroll crashes, then heightens violently.* HALE *weeps in frantic prayer, and the new sun is pouring in upon her face, and the drums rattle like bones in the morning air. The curtain falls.*)

## JOHN MILLINGTON SYNGE

# The Playboy of the Western World

John Millington Synge (1871–1910), was born in Dublin, attended Trinity College, Dublin, and studied for six years in Paris. In 1899 he returned to Ireland, partly at the persuasion of the poet W. B. Yeats. He was to live as one of the Aran Islanders, learn their peasant dialect, and write of their experiences. He brought with him, however, the balancing effect of a sound classical education and extensive travel and study on the Continent.

Synge's first prose work, *The Aran Islands*, recounts his journeys to the four islands that lie off the west coast of Ireland; his second, not completed, is a series of essays about the surrounding countryside. His first play, *In the Shadow of the Glen*, 1903, with a theme similar to that of Ibsen's *A Doll House*, renders a story he had heard and recounted in *The Aran Islands*. It was followed by the five plays on which his reputation as a playwright rests: *Riders to the Sea*, 1904, a story of fate and the implacable sea; *The Well of the Saints*, 1905, his first three-act drama; *The Playboy of the Western World*, 1907; *The Tinker's Wedding*, 1908, not produced in Dublin during the poet's lifetime because of its controversial nature; and the unfinished *Deirdre of the Sorrows*, 1910, his first play based on Irish legendary material. In a reader survey reported in the London *Observer* in 1966, *The Playboy of the Western World* was included as one of the twenty plays written since 1900 in which the main trends of the theater in this century could be most clearly discerned.

*The Playboy of the Western World* is based on a story Synge heard in the Aran Islands. Deceptively simple, the story clearly demonstrates his dramatic theory: that one must listen to and use the imaginative language of the people; that "one must have reality, and one must have joy."

## PREFACE

In writing *The Playboy of the Western World*, as in my other plays, I have used one or two words only that I have not heard among the country people of Ireland, or spoken in my own nursery before I could read the newspapers. A certain number of the phrases I employ I have heard also from herds and fishermen along the coast from Kerry to Mayo, or from beggarwomen and ballad singers near Dublin; and I am glad to acknowledge how much I owe to the folk imagination of these fine people. Anyone who has lived in real intimacy with the Irish peasantry will know that the wildest sayings and ideas in this play are tame indeed, compared with the fancies one may hear in any little hillside cabin in Geesala, or Carraroe, or Dingle Bay. All art is a collaboration! and there is little doubt that in the happy ages of literature, striking and beautiful phrases were as ready to the storyteller's or the playwright's hand, as the rich cloaks and dresses of his time. It is probable that when the Elizabethan dramatist took his inkhorn and sat down to his work he used many phrases that he had just heard, as he sat at dinner, from his mother or his children. In Ireland, those of us who know the people have the same privilege. When I was writing *The Shadow of the Glen*, some years ago, I got more aid than any learning could have given me from a chink in the floor of the old Wicklow house where I was staying, that let me hear what was being said by the servant girls in the kitchen. This matter, I think, is of importance, for in countries where the imagination of the people, and the language they use, is rich and living, it is possible for a writer to be rich and copious in his words, and at the same time to give the reality, which is the root of all poetry, in a comprehensive and natural form. In the modern literature of towns, however, richness is found only in sonnets, or prose poems, or in one or two elaborate books that are far away from the profound and common interests of life. One has, on one side, Mallarmé and Huysmans[1] producing this literature; and, on the other, Ibsen and Zola dealing with the reality of life in joyless and pallid words. On the stage one must have reality, and one must have joy; and that is why the intellectual modern drama has failed, and people have grown sick of the false joy of the musical comedy that has been given them in place of the rich joy found only in what is superb and wild in reality. In a good play every speech should be as fully flavored as a nut or apple, and such speeches cannot be written by anyone who works among people who have shut their lips on poetry. In Ireland, for a few years more, we have a popular imagination that is fiery and magnificent, and tender; so that those who wish to write start with a chance that is not given to writers in places where the springtime of the local life has been forgotten, and the harvest is a memory only, and the straw has been turned into bricks.

*1907*

## CAST OF CHARACTERS

CHRISTOPHER MAHON
OLD MAHON, *his father—a squatter*
MICHAEL JAMES FLAHERTY, *called* MICHAEL JAMES, *a publican*
MARGARET FLAHERTY, *called* PEGEEN MIKE, *his daughter*
WIDOW QUIN, *a woman of about thirty*

---

[1] Joris Karl Huysmans (1848–1907), French novelist and poet, most famous for *Against the Grain*.

SHAWN KEOGH, *her cousin, a young farmer*

PHILLY CULLEN *and* JIMMY FARRELL, *small farmers*

SARA TANSEY, SUSAN BRADY, *and* HONOR BLAKE, *village girls*

A BELLMAN

SOME PEASANTS

*The action takes place near a village, on a wild coast of Mayo. The first act passes on an evening of autumn, the other two acts on the following day.*

### ACT ONE

*SCENE*

*Country public-house or shebeen, very rough and untidy. There is a sort of counter on the right with shelves, holding many bottles and jugs, just seen above it. Empty barrels stand near the counter. At back, a little to left of counter, there is a door into the open air, then, more to the left, there is a settle with shelves above it, with more jugs, and a table beneath a window. At the left there is a large open fireplace, with turf fire, and a small door into inner room.* PEGEEN, *a wild-looking but fine girl, of about twenty, is writing at table. She is dressed in the usual peasant dress.*

PEGEEN (*slowly as she writes*): Six yards of stuff for to make a yellow gown. A pair of lace boots with lengthy heels on them and brassy eyes. A hat is suited for a wedding day. A fine tooth comb. To be sent with three barrels of porter in Jimmy Farrell's creel cart on the evening of the coming Fair to Mister Michael James Flaherty. With the best compliments of this season. Margaret Flaherty.

SHAWN KEOUGH (*a fat and fair young man, comes in as she signs, looks round awkwardly, when he sees she is alone*): Where's himself?

PEGEEN (*without looking at him*): He's coming. (*She directs the letter.*) To Mister Sheamus Mulroy, Wine and Spirit Dealer, Castlebar.

SHAWN (*uneasily*): I didn't see him on the road.

PEGEEN: How would you see him (*licks stamp and puts it on letter*) and it dark night this half hour gone by?

SHAWN (*turning towards the door again*): I stood a while outside wondering would I have

a right to pass on or to walk in and see you, Pegeen Mike (*comes to fire*), and I could hear the cows breathing, and sighing in the stillness of the air, and not a step moving any place from this gate to the bridge.

PEGEEN (*putting letter in envelope*): It's above at the cross-roads he is, meeting Philly Cullen; and a couple more are going along with him to Kate Cassidy's wake.

SHAWN (*looking at her blankly*): And he's going that length in the dark night?

PEGEEN (*impatiently*): He is surely, and leaving me lonesome on the scruff of the hill. (*She gets up and puts envelope on dresser, then winds clock.*) Isn't it long the nights are now, Shawn Keogh, to be leaving a poor girl with her own self counting the hours to the dawn of day?

SHAWN (*with awkward humor*): If it is, when we're wedded in a short while you'll have no call to complain, for I've little will to be walking off to wakes or weddings in the darkness of the night.

PEGEEN (*with rather scornful good humor*): You're making mighty certain, Shaneen, that I'll wed you now.

SHAWN: Aren't we after making a good bargain, the way we're only waiting these days on Father Reilly's dispensation from the bishops, or the Court of Rome.

PEGEEN (*looking at him teasingly, washing up at dresser*): It's a wonder, Shaneen, the Holy Father'd be taking notice of the likes of you; for if I was him I wouldn't bother with this place where you'll meet none but Red Linahan, has a squint in his eye, and Patcheen is lame in his heel, or the mad Mulrannies were driven from California and they lost in their wits. We're a queer lot these times to go troubling the Holy Father on his sacred seat.

SHAWN (*scandalized*): If we are, we're as good this place as another, maybe, and as good these times as we were for ever.

PEGEEN (*with scorn*): As good, is it? Where now will you meet the like of Daneen Sullivan knocked the eye from a peeler, or Marcus Quin, God rest him, got six months for maiming ewes, and he a great warrant to tell stories of holy Ireland till he'd have the old women shedding down tears about their feet. Where will you find the like of them, I'm saying?

SHAWN (*timidly*): If you don't, it's a good job,

maybe; for (*with peculiar emphasis on the words*) Father Reilly has small conceit to have that kind walking around and talking to the girls.

PEGEEN (*impatiently, throwing water from basin out of the door*): Stop tormenting me with Father Reilly (*imitating his voice*) when I'm asking only what way I'll pass these twelve hours of dark, and not take my death with the fear. (*Looking out of door.*)

SHAWN (*timidly*): Would I fetch you the Widow Quin, maybe?

PEGEEN: Is it the like of that murderer? You'll not, surely.

SHAWN (*going to her, soothingly*): Then I'm thinking himself will stop along with you when he sees you taking on, for it'll be a long night-time with great darkness, and I'm after feeling a kind of fellow above in the furzy ditch, groaning wicked like a maddening dog, the way it's good cause you have, maybe, to be fearing now.

PEGEEN (*turning on him sharply*): What's that? Is it a man you seen?

SHAWN (*retreating*): I couldn't see him at all; but I heard him groaning out, and breaking his heart. It should have been a young man from his words speaking.

PEGEEN (*going after him*): And you never went near to see was he hurted or what ailed him at all?

SHAWN: I did not, Pegeen Mike. It was a dark, lonesome place to be hearing the like of him.

PEGEEN: Well, you're a daring fellow, and if they find his corpse stretched above in the dews of dawn, what'll you say then to the peelers, or the Justice of the Peace?

SHAWN (*thunderstruck*): I wasn't thinking of that. For the love of God, Pegeen Mike, don't let on I was speaking of him. Don't tell your father and the men is coming above; for if they heard that story, they'd have great blabbing this night at the wake.

PEGEEN: I'll maybe tell them, and I'll maybe not.

SHAWN: They are coming at the door. Will you whisht, I'm saying?

PEGEEN: Whisht yourself.

(*She goes behind counter.* MICHAEL JAMES, *fat jovial publican, comes in followed by* PHILLY CULLEN, *who is thin and mistrusting, and* JIMMY FARRELL, *who is fat and amorous, about forty-five.*)

MEN (*together*): God bless you. The blessing of God on this place.

PEGEEN: God bless you kindly.

MICHAEL (*to men who go to the counter*): Sit down now, and take your rest. (*Crosses to* SHAWN *at the fire*) And how is it you are, Shawn Keogh? Are you coming over the sands to Kate Cassidy's wake?

SHAWN: I am not, Michael James. I'm going home the short cut to my bed.

PEGEEN (*speaking across the counter*): He's right, too, and have you no shame, Michael James, to be quitting off for the whole night, and leaving myself lonesome in the shop?

MICHAEL (*good-humoredly*): Isn't it the same whether I go for the whole night or a part only? and I'm thinking it's a queer daughter you are if you'd have me crossing backward through the Stooks of the Dead Women, with a drop taken.

PEGEEN: If I am a queer daughter, it's a queer father'd be leaving me lonesome these twelve hours of dark, and I piling the turf with the dogs barking, and the calves mooing, and my own teeth rattling with the fear.

JIMMY (*flatteringly*): What is there to hurt you, and you a fine, hardy girl would knock the head of any two men in the place?

PEGEEN (*working herself up*): Isn't there the harvest boys with their tongues red for drink, and the ten tinkers is camped in the east glen, and the thousand militia—bad cess to them!—walking idle through the land. There's lots surely to hurt me, and I won't stop alone in it, let himself do what he will.

MICHAEL: If you're that afeard, let Shawn Keogh stop along with you. It's the will of God, I'm thinking, himself should be seeing to you now.

(*They all turn on* SHAWN.)

SHAWN (*in horrified confusion*): I would and welcome, Michael James, but I'm afeard of Father Reilly; and what at all would the Holy Father and the Cardinals of Rome be saying if they heard I did the like of that?

MICHAEL (*with contempt*): God help you! Can't you sit in by the hearth with the light lit and herself beyond in the room? You'll do that surely, for I've heard tell there's a queer fellow above, going mad or getting his death, maybe, in the gripe of the ditch, so she'd be safer this night with a person here.

SHAWN (*with plaintive despair*): I'm afeard of Father Reilly, I'm saying. Let you not be tempting me, and we near married itself.

PHILLY (*with cold contempt*): Lock him in the west room. He'll stay then and have no sin to be telling to the priest.

MICHAEL (*to* SHAWN, *getting between him and the door*): Go up now.

SHAWN (*at the top of his voice*): Don't stop me, Michael James. Let me out of the door, I'm saying, for the love of the Almighty God. Let me out. (*Trying to dodge past him*) Let me out of it, and may God grant you His indulgence in the hour of need.

MICHAEL (*loudly*): Stop your noising, and sit down by the hearth. (*Gives him a push and goes to counter laughing.*)

SHAWN (*turning back, wringing his hands*): Oh, Father Reilly and the saints of God, where will I hide myself to-day? Oh, St. Joseph and St. Patrick and St. Brigid, and St. James, have mercy on me now!

(SHAWN *turns round, sees door clear, and makes a rush for it.*)

MICHAEL (*catching him by the coat tail*): You'd be going, is it?

SHAWN (*screaming*): Leave me go, Michael James, leave me go, you old Pagan, leave me go, or I'll get the curse of the priests on you, and of the scarlet-coated bishops of the courts of Rome.

(*With a sudden movement he pulls himself out of his coat, and disappears out of the door, leaving his coat in* MICHAEL's *hands.*)

MICHAEL (*turning round, and holding up coat*): Well, there's the coat of a Christian man. Oh, there's sainted glory this day in the lonesome west; and by the will of God I've got you a decent man, Pegeen, you'll have no call to be spying after if you've a score of young girls, maybe, weeding in your fields.

PEGEEN (*taking up the defence of her property*): What right have you to be making game of a poor fellow for minding the priest, when it's your own the fault is, not paying a penny pot-boy to stand along with me and give me courage in the doing of my work? (*She snaps the coat away from him, and goes behind counter with it.*)

MICHAEL (*taken aback*): Where would I get a pot-boy? Would you have me send the bellman screaming in the streets of Castlebar?

SHAWN (*opening the door a chink and putting in his head, in a small voice*): Michael James!

MICHAEL (*imitating him*): What ails you?

SHAWN: The queer dying fellow's beyond looking over the ditch. He's come up, I'm thinking, stealing your hens. (*Looks over his shoulder*) God help me, he's following me now (*he runs into room*), and if he's heard what I said, he'll be having my life, and I going home lonesome in the darkness of the night.

(*For a perceptible moment they watch the door with curiosity. Some one coughs outside. Then* CHRISTY MAHON, *a slight young man, comes in very tired and frightened and dirty.*)

CHRISTY (*in a small voice*): God save all here!

MEN: God save you kindly.

CHRISTY (*going to the counter*): I'd trouble you for a glass of porter, woman of the house. (*He puts down coin.*)

PEGEEN (*serving him*): You're one of the tinkers, young fellow, is beyond camped in the glen?

CHRISTY: I am not; but I'm destroyed walking.

MICHAEL (*patronizingly*): Let you come up then to the fire. You're looking famished with the cold.

CHRISTY: God reward you. (*He takes up his glass and goes a little way across to the left, then stops and looks about him.*) Is it often the police do be coming into this place, master of the house?

MICHAEL: If you'd come in better hours, you'd have seen "Licensed for the sale of Beer and Spirits, to be consumed on the premises," written in white letters above the door, and what would the polis want spying on me, and not a decent house within four miles, the way every living Christian is a bona fide, saving one widow alone?

CHRISTY (*with relief*): It's a safe house, so.

(*He goes over to the fire, sighing and moaning. Then he sits down, putting his glass beside him, and begins gnawing a turnip, too miserable to feel the others staring at him with curiosity.*)

MICHAEL (*going after him*): Is it yourself is fearing the polis? You're wanting, maybe?

CHRISTY: There's many wanting.

MICHAEL: Many surely, with the broken harvest and the ended wars. (*He picks up some stockings, etc., that are near the fire, and carries them away furtively.*) It should be larceny, I'm thinking?

CHRISTY (*dolefully*): I had it in my mind it was a different word and a bigger.

PEGEEN: There's a queer lad. Were you never slapped in school, young fellow, that you don't know the name of your deed?

CHRISTY (*bashfully*): I'm slow at learning, a middling scholar only.

MICHAEL: If you're a dunce itself, you'd have a right to know that larceny's robbing and stealing. Is it for the like of that you're wanting?

CHRISTY (*with a flash of family pride*): And I the son of a strong farmer (*with a sudden qualm*), God rest his soul, could have bought up the whole of your old house a while since, from the butt of his tailpocket, and not have missed the weight of it gone.

MICHAEL (*impressed*): If it's not stealing, it's maybe something big.

CHRISTY (*flattered*): Aye, it's maybe something big.

JIMMY: He's a wicked-looking young fellow. Maybe he followed after a young woman on a lonesome night.

CHRISTY (*shocked*): Oh, the saints forbid, mister; I was all times a decent lad.

PHILLY (*turning on* JIMMY): You're a silly man, Jimmy Farrell. He said his father was a farmer a while since, and there's himself now in a poor state. Maybe the land was grabbed from him, and he did what any decent man would do.

MICHAEL (*to* CHRISTY, *mysteriously*): Was it bailiffs?

CHRISTY: The divil a one.

MICHAEL: Agents?

CHRISTY: The divil a one.

MICHAEL: Landlords?

CHRISTY (*peevishly*): Ah, not at all, I'm saying. You'd see the like of them stories on any little paper of a Munster town. But I'm not calling to mind any person, gentle, simple, judge or jury, did the like of me.

(*They all draw nearer with delighted curiosity.*)

PHILLY: Well, that lad's a puzzle-the-world.

JIMMY: He'd beat Dan Davies' circus, or the holy missioners making sermons on the villainy of man. Try him again, Philly.

PHILLY: Did you strike golden guineas out of solder, young fellow, or shilling coins itself?

CHRISTY: I did not, mister, not sixpence nor a farthing coin.

JIMMY: Did you marry three wives maybe? I'm told there's a sprinkling have done that

among the holy Luthers of the preaching north.

CHRISTY (*shyly*): I never married with one, let alone with a couple or three.

PHILLY: Maybe he went fighting for the Boers, the like of the man beyond, was judged to be hanged, quartered and drawn. Were you off east, young fellow, fighting bloody wars for Kruger and the freedom of the Boers?

CHRISTY: I never left my own parish till Tuesday was a week.

PEGEEN (*coming from counter*): He's done nothing, so. (*To* CHRISTY) If you didn't commit murder or a bad, nasty thing, or false coining, or robbery, or butchery, or the like of them, there isn't anything that would be worth your troubling for to run from now. You did nothing at all.

CHRISTY (*his feelings hurt*): That's an unkindly thing to be saying to a poor orphaned traveller, has a prison behind him, and hanging before, and hell's gap gaping below.

PEGEEN (*with a sign to the men to be quiet*): You're only saying it. You did nothing at all. A soft lad the like of you wouldn't slit the windpipe of a screeching sow.

CHRISTY (*offended*): You're not speaking the truth.

PEGEEN (*in mock rage*): Not speaking the truth, is it? Would you have me knock the head of you with the butt of the broom?

CHRISTY (*twisting round on her with a sharp cry of horror*): Don't strike me. I killed my poor father, Tuesday was a week, for doing the like of that.

PEGEEN (*with black amazement*): Is it killed your father?

CHRISTY (*subsiding*): With the help of God I did surely, and that the Holy Immaculate Mother may intercede for his soul.

PHILLY (*retreating with* JIMMY): There's a daring fellow.

JIMMY: Oh, glory be to God!

MICHAEL (*with great respect*): That was a hanging crime, mister honey. You should have had good reason for doing the like of that.

CHRISTY (*in a very reasonable tone*): He was a dirty man, God forgive him, and he getting old and crusty, the way I couldn't put up with him at all.

PEGEEN: And you shot him dead?

CHRISTY (*shaking his head*): I never used

weapons. I've no license, and I'm a law-fearing man.

MICHAEL: It was with a hilted knife maybe? I'm told, in the big world it's bloody knives they use.

CHRISTY (*loudly, scandalized*): Do you take me for a slaughter-boy?

PEGEEN: You never hanged him, the way Jimmy Farrell hanged his dog from the license, and had it screeching and wriggling three hours at the butt of a string, and himself swearing it was a dead dog, and the peelers swearing it had life?

CHRISTY: I did not then. I just riz the loy and let fall the edge of it on the ridge of his skull, and he went down at my feet like an empty sack, and never let a grunt or groan from him at all.

MICHAEL (*making a sign to PEGEEN to fill CHRISTY's glass*): And what way weren't you hanged, mister? Did you bury him then?

CHRISTY (*considering*): Aye. I buried him then. Wasn't I digging spuds in the field?

MICHAEL: And the peelers never followed after you the eleven days that you're out?

CHRISTY (*shaking his head*): Never a one of them, and I walking forward facing hog, dog, or divil on the highway of the road.

PHILLY (*nodding wisely*): It's only with a common week-day kind of a murderer them lads would be trusting their carcase, and that man should be a great terror when his temper's roused.

MICHAEL: He should then. (*To CHRISTY*): And where was it, mister honey, that you did the deed?

CHRISTY (*looking at him with suspicion*): Oh, a distant place, master of the house, a windy corner of high, distant hills.

PHILLY (*nodding with approval*): He's a close man, and he's right, surely.

PEGEEN: That'd be a lad with a sense of Solomon to have for a pot-boy, Michael James, if it's the truth you're seeking one at all.

PHILLY: The peelers is fearing him, and if you'd that lad in the house there isn't one of them would come smelling around if the dogs itself were lapping poteen from the dung-pit of the yard.

JIMMY: Bravery's a treasure in a lonesome place, and a lad would kill his father, I'm thinking, would face a foxy divil with a pitchpike on the flags of hell.

PEGEEN: It's the truth they're saying, and if I'd that lad in the house, I wouldn't be fearing the loosed kharki cut-throats, or the walking dead.

CHRISTY (*swelling with surprise and triumph*): Well, glory be to God!

MICHAEL (*with deference*): Would you think well to stop here and be pot-boy, mister honey, if we gave you good wages, and didn't destroy you with the weight of work?

SHAWN (*coming forward uneasily*): That'd be a queer kind to bring into a decent quiet household with the like of Pegeen Mike.

PEGEEN (*very sharply*): Will you whisht? Who's speaking to you?

SHAWN (*retreating*): A bloody-handed murderer the like of . . .

PEGEEN (*snapping at him*): Whisht I am saying: we'll take no fooling from your like at all. (*To CHRISTY with a honeyed voice*) And you, young fellow, you'd have a right to stop, I'm thinking, for we'd do our all and utmost to content your needs.

CHRISTY (*overcome with wonder*): And I'd be safe in this place from the searching law?

MICHAEL: You would, surely. If they're not fearing you, itself, the peelers in this place is decent droughty poor fellows, wouldn't touch a cur dog and not give warning in the dead of night.

PEGEEN (*very kindly and persuasively*): Let you stop a short while anyhow. Aren't you destroyed walking with your feet in bleeding blisters, and your whole skin needing washing like a Wicklow sheep.

CHRISTY (*looking round with satisfaction*): It's a nice room, and if it's not humbugging me you are, I'm thinking that I'll surely stay.

JIMMY (*jumps up*): Now, by the grace of God, herself will be safe this night, with a man killed his father holding danger from the door, and let you come on, Michael James, or they'll have the best stuff drunk at the wake.

MICHAEL (*going to the door with men*): And begging your pardon, mister, what name will we call you, for we'd like to know?

CHRISTY: Christopher Mahon.

MICHAEL: Well, God bless you, Christy, and a good rest till we meet again when the sun'll be rising to the noon of day.

CHRISTY: God bless you all.

MEN: God bless you.

*(They go out except* SHAWN, *who lingers at door.)*

SHAWN *(to* PEGEEN*):* Are you wanting me to stop along with you to keep you from harm?

PEGEEN *(gruffly):* Didn't you say you were fearing Father Reilly?

SHAWN: There'd be no harm staying now, I'm thinking, and himself in it too.

PEGEEN: You wouldn't stay when there was need for you, and let you step off nimble this time when there's none.

SHAWN: Didn't I say it was Father Reilly . . .

PEGEEN: Go on, then, to Father Reilly *(in a jeering tone),* and let him put you in the holy brotherhoods, and leave that lad to me.

SHAWN: If I meet the Widow Quin . . .

PEGEEN: Go on, I'm staying, and don't be waking this place with your noise. *(She hustles him out and bolts the door.)* That lad would wear the spirits from the saints of peace. *(Bustles about, then takes off her apron and pins it up in the window as a blind,* CHRISTY *watching her timidly. Then she comes to him and speaks with bland good humor.)* Let you stretch out now by the fire, young fellow. You should be destroyed travelling.

CHRISTY *(shyly again, drawing off his boots):* I'm tired, surely, walking wild eleven days, and waking fearful in the night. *(He holds up one of his feet, feeling his blisters, and looking at them with compassion.)*

PEGEEN *(standing beside him, watching him with delight):* You should have had great people in your family, I'm thinking, with the little, small feet you have, and you with a kind of a quality name, the like of what you'd find on the great powers and potentates of France and Spain.

CHRISTY *(with pride):* We were great surely, with wide and windy acres of rich Munster land.

PEGEEN: Wasn't I telling you, and you a fine, handsome young fellow with a noble brow?

CHRISTY *(with a flash of delighted surprise):* Is it me?

PEGEEN: Aye. Did you never hear that from the young girls where you come from in the west or south?

CHRISTY *(with venom):* I did not then. Oh, they're bloody liars in the naked parish where I grew a man.

PEGEEN: If they are itself, you've heard it these days, I'm thinking, and you walking the world telling out your story to young girls or old.

CHRISTY: I've told my story no place till this night, Pegeen Mike, and it's foolish I was here, maybe, to be talking free, but you're decent people, I'm thinking, and yourself a kindly woman, the way I wasn't fearing you at all.

PEGEEN *(filling a sack with straw):* You've said the like of that, maybe, in every cot and cabin where you've met a young girl on your way.

CHRISTY *(going over to her, gradually raising his voice):* I've said it nowhere till this night, I'm telling you, for I've seen none the like of you the eleven long days I am walking the world, looking over a low ditch or a high ditch on my north or my south, into stony scattered fields, or scribes of bog, where you'd see young, limber girls, and fine prancing women making laughter with the men.

PEGEEN: If you weren't destroyed travelling, you'd have as much talk and streeleen, I'm thinking, as Owen Roe O'Sullivan or the poets of the Dingle Bay, and I've heard all times it's the poets are your like, fine fiery fellows with great rages when their temper's roused.

CHRISTY *(drawing a little nearer to her):* You've a power of rings, God bless you, and would there be any offense if I was asking are you single now?

PEGEEN: What would I want wedding so young?

CHRISTY *(with relief):* We're alike, so.

PEGEEN *(She puts sack on settle and beats it up.):* I never killed my father. I'd be afeard to do that, except I was the like of yourself with blind rages tearing me within, for I'm thinking you should have had great tussling when the end was come.

CHRISTY *(expanding with delight at the first confidential talk he has ever had with a woman):* We had not then. It was a hard woman was come over the hill, and if he was always a crusty kind when he'd a hard woman setting him on, not the divil himself or his four fathers could put up with him at all.

PEGEEN *(with curiosity):* And isn't it a great wonder that one wasn't fearing you?

CHRISTY *(very confidentially):* Up to the day I killed my father, there wasn't a person in Ireland knew the kind I was, and I there drinking, waking, eating, sleeping, a quiet, simple poor fellow with no man giving me heed.

PEGEEN *(getting a quilt out of the cupboard and putting it on the sack):* It was the girls were giving you heed maybe, and I'm thinking it's most conceit you'd have to be gaming with their like.

CHRISTY (*shaking his head, with simplicity*): Not the girls itself, and I won't tell you a lie. There wasn't anyone heeding me in that place saving only the dumb beasts of the field. (*He sits down at fire.*)

PEGEEN (*with disappointment*): And I thinking you should have been living the like of a king of Norway or the Eastern world. (*She comes and sits beside him after placing bread and mug of milk on the table.*)

CHRISTY (*laughing piteously*): The like of a king, is it? And I after toiling, moiling, digging, dodging from the dawn till dusk with never a sight of joy or sport saving only when I'd be abroad in the dark night poaching rabbits on hills, for I was a devil to poach, God forgive me, (*very naïvely*) and I near got six months for going with a dung fork and stabbing a fish.

PEGEEN: And it's that you'd call sport, is it, to be abroad in the darkness with yourself alone?

CHRISTY: I did, God help me, and there I'd be as happy as the sunshine of St. Martin's Day, watching the light passing the north or the patches of fog, till I'd hear a rabbit starting to screech and I'd go running in the furze. Then when I'd my full share I'd come walking down where you'd see the ducks and geese stretched sleeping on the highway of the road, and before I'd pass the dunghill, I'd hear himself snoring out, a loud lonesome snore he'd be making all times, the while he was sleeping, and he a man 'd be raging all times, the while he was waking, like a gaudy officer you'd hear cursing and damning and swearing oaths.

PEGEEN: Providence and Mercy, spare us all!

CHRISTY: It's that you'd say surely if you seen him and he after drinking for weeks, rising up in the red dawn, or before it maybe, and going out into the yard as naked as an ash tree in the moon of May, and shying clods against the visage of the stars till he'd put the fear of death into the banbhs and the screeching sows.

PEGEEN: I'd be well-nigh afeard of that lad myself, I'm thinking. And there was no one in it but the two of you alone?

CHRISTY: The divil a one, though he'd sons and daughters walking all great states and territories of the world, and not a one of them, to

this day, but would say their seven curses on him, and they rousing up to let a cough or sneeze, maybe, in the deadness of the night.

PEGEEN (*nodding her head*): Well, you should have been a queer lot. I never cursed my father the like of that, though I'm twenty and more years of age.

CHRISTY: Then you'd have cursed mine, I'm telling you, and he a man never gave peace to any, saving when he'd get two months or three, or be locked in the asylums for battering peelers or assaulting men (*with depression*) the way it was a bitter life he led me till I did up a Tuesday and halve his skull.

PEGEEN (*putting her hand on his shoulder*): Well, you'll have peace in this place, Christy Mahon, and none to trouble you, and it's near time a fine lad like you should have your good share of the earth.

CHRISTY: It's time surely, and I a seemly fellow with great strength in me and bravery of . . .

(*Someone knocks.*)

CHRISTY (*clinging to* PEGEEN): Oh, glory! it's late for knocking, and this last while I'm in terror of the peelers, and the walking dead.

(*Knocking again.*)

PEGEEN: Who's there?

VOICE (*outside*): Me.

PEGEEN: Who's me?

VOICE: The Widow Quin.

PEGEEN (*jumping up and giving him the bread and milk*): Go on now with your supper, and let on to be sleepy, for if she found you were such a warrant to talk, she'd be stringing gabble till the dawn of day.

(*He takes bread and sits shyly with his back to the door.*)

PEGEEN (*opening door, with temper*): What ails you, or what is it you're wanting at this hour of the night?

WIDOW QUIN (*coming in a step and peering at* CHRISTY): I'm after meeting Shawn Keogh and Father Reilly below, who told me of your curiosity man, and they fearing by this time he was maybe roaring, romping on your hands with drink.

PEGEEN (*pointing to* CHRISTY): Look now is he roaring, and he stretched away drowsy with his supper and his mug of milk. Walk down and tell that to Father Reilly and to Shaneen Keogh.

WIDOW QUIN (*coming forward*): I'll not see them again, for I've their word to lead that lad forward for to lodge with me.

PEGEEN (*in blank amazement*): This night, is it?

WIDOW QUIN (*going over*): This night. "It isn't fitting," says the priesteen, "to have his likeness lodging with an orphaned girl." (*To* CHRISTY) God save you, mister!

CHRISTY (*shyly*): God save you kindly.

WIDOW QUIN (*looking at him with half-amazed curiosity*): Well, aren't you a little smiling fellow? It should have been great and bitter torments did arouse your spirits to a deed of blood.

CHRISTY (*doubtfully*): It should, maybe.

WIDOW QUIN: It's more than "maybe" I'm saying, and it'd soften my heart to see you sitting so simple with your cup and cake, and you fitter to be saying your catechism than slaying your da.

PEGEEN (*at counter, washing glasses*): There's talking when any'd see he's fit to be holding his head high with the wonders of the world. Walk on from this, for I'll not have him tormented and he destroyed travelling since Tuesday was a week.

WIDOW QUIN (*peaceably*): We'll be walking surely when his supper's done, and you'll find we're great company, young fellow, when it's of the like of you and me you'd hear the penny poets singing in an August Fair.

CHRISTY (*innocently*): Did you kill your father?

PEGEEN (*contemptuously*): She did not. She hit himself with a worn pick, and the rusted poison did corrode his blood the way he never overed it, and died after. That was a sneaky kind of murder did win small glory with the boys itself. (*She crosses to* CHRISTY's *left*.)

WIDOW QUIN (*with good humor*): If it didn't, maybe all knows a widow woman has buried her children and destroyed her man is a wiser comrade for a young lad than a girl, the like of you, who'd go helter-skeltering after any man would let you a wink upon the road.

PEGEEN (*breaking out into wild rage*): And you'll say that, Widow Quin, and you gasping with the rage you had racing the hill beyond to look on his face.

WIDOW QUIN (*laughing derisively*): Me, is it? Well, Father Reilly has cuteness to divide you

now. (*She pulls* CHRISTY *up.*) There's great temptation in a man did slay his da, and we'd best be going, young fellow; so rise up and come with me.

PEGEEN (*seizing his arm*): He'll not stir. He's pot-boy in this place, and I'll not have him stolen off and kidnabbed while himself's abroad.

WIDOW QUIN: It'd be a crazy pot-boy'd lodge him in the shebeen where he works by day, so you'd have a right to come on, young fellow, till you see my little houseen, a perch off on the rising hill.

PEGEEN: Wait till morning, Christy Mahon. Wait till you lay eyes on her leaky thatch is growing more pasture for her buck goat than her square of fields, and she without a tramp itself to keep in order her place at all.

WIDOW QUIN: When you see me contriving in my little gardens, Christy Mahon, you'll swear the Lord God formed me to be living lone, and that there isn't my match in Mayo for thatching, or mowing, or shearing a sheep.

PEGEEN (*with noisy scorn*): It's true the Lord God formed you to contrive indeed. Doesn't the world know you reared a black lamb at your own breast, so that the Lord Bishop of Connaught felt the elements of a Christian, and he eating it after in a kidney stew? Doesn't the world know you've been seen shaving the foxy skipper from France for a threepenny bit and a sop of grass tobacco would wring the liver from a mountain goat you'd meet leaping the hills?

WIDOW QUIN (*with amusement*): Do you hear her now young fellow? Do you hear the way she'll be rating at your own self when a week is by?

PEGEEN (*to* CHRISTY): Don't heed her. Tell her to go into her pigsty and not plague us here.

WIDOW QUIN: I'm going; but he'll come with me.

PEGEEN (*shaking him*): Are you dumb, young fellow?

CHRISTY (*timidly, to* WIDOW QUIN): God increase you; but I'm pot-boy in this place, and it's here I'd liefer stay.

PEGEEN (*triumphantly*): Now you have heard him, and go on from this.

WIDOW QUIN (*looking round the room*): It's lonesome this hour crossing the hill, and if he won't come along with me, I'd have a right maybe to stop this night with yourselves. Let me

stretch out on the settle, Pegeen Mike; and himself can lie by the hearth.

PEGEEN (*short and fiercely*):   Faith, I won't.
Quit off or I will send you now.

WIDOW QUIN (*gathering her shawl up*):   Well,
it's a terror to be aged a score. (*To* CHRISTY) God
bless you now, young fellow, and let you be
wary, or there's right torment will await you
here if you go romancing with her like, and she
waiting only, as they bade me say, on a sheepskin
parchment to be wed with Shawn Keogh of
Killakeen.

CHRISTY (*going to* PEGEEN *as she bolts the
door*):   What's that she's after saying?

PEGEEN:   Lies and blather, you've no call to
mind. Well, isn't Shawn Keogh an impudent
fellow to send up spying on me? Wait till I lay
hands on him. Let him wait, I'm saying.

CHRISTY:   And you're not wedding him at all?

PEGEEN:   I wouldn't wed him if a bishop came
walking for to join us here.

CHRISTY:   That God in glory may be thanked
for that.

PEGEEN:   There's your bed now. I've put a
quilt upon you I'm after quilting a while since
with my own two hands, and you'd best stretch
out now for your sleep, and may God give you
a good rest till I call you in the morning when
the cocks will crow.

CHRISTY (*as she goes to inner room*):   May God
and Mary and St. Patrick bless you and reward
you, for your kindly talk. (*She shuts the door
behind her. He settles his bed slowly, feeling the
quilt with immense satisfaction.*)   Well, it's a
clean bed and soft with it, and it's great luck and
company I've won me in the end of time—two
fine women fighting for the likes of me—till I'm
thinking this night wasn't I a foolish fellow not
to kill my father in the years gone by.

## ACT TWO

*SCENE*

As before. Brilliant morning light. CHRISTY, looking bright and cheerful, is cleaning a girl's boots.

CHRISTY (*to himself, counting jugs on dresser*):
Half a hundred beyond. Ten there. A score that's
above. Eighty jugs. Six cups and a broken one.
Two plates. A power of glasses. Bottles, a
school-master'd be hard set to count, and enough

in them I'm thinking, to drunken all the wealth
and wisdom of the County Clare. (*He puts down
the boot carefully.*) There's her boots now, nice
and decent for her evening use, and isn't it grand
brushes she has? (*He puts them down and goes
by degrees to the looking-glass.*) Well, this'd be
a fine place to be my whole life talking out with
swearing Christians, in place of my old dogs and
cat, and I stalking around, smoking my pipe and
drinking my fill, and never a day's work but
drawing a cork an odd time, or wiping a glass,
or rinsing out a shiny tumbler for a decent man.
(*He takes the looking-glass from the wall and puts
it on the back of a chair; then sits down in front
of it and begins washing his face.*) Didn't I know
rightly I was handsome, though it was the divil's
own mirror we had beyond, would twist a squint
across an angel's brow; and I'll be growing fine
from this day, the way I'll have a soft lovely skin
on me and won't be the like of the clumsy young
fellows do be ploughing all times in the earth
and dung. (*He starts.*) Is she coming again? (*He
looks out.*) Stranger girls. God help me, where'll
I hide myself away and my long neck naked to
the world? (*He looks out.*) I'd best go to the room
maybe till I'm dressed again. (*He gathers up his
coat and the looking-glass and runs into the
inner room. The door is pushed open, and* SUSAN
BRADY *looks in, and knocks on door.*)

SUSAN:   There's nobody in it. (*Knocks again.*)

NELLY (*pushing her in and following her, with
HONOR BLAKE and SARA TANSEY*):   It'd be early
for them both to be out walking the hill.

SUSAN:   I'm thinking Shawn Keogh was making game of us and there's no such man in it at
all.

HONOR (*pointing to straw and quilt*):   Look at
that. He's been sleeping there in the night. Well,
it'll be a hard case if he's gone off now, the way
we'll never set our eyes on a man killed his
father, and we after rising early and destroying
ourselves running fast on the hill.

NELLY:   Are you thinking them's his boots?

SARA (*taking them up*):   If they are, there
should be his father's track on them. Did you
never read in the papers the way murdered men
do bleed and drip?

SUSAN:   Is that blood there, Sara Tansey?

SARA (*smelling it*):   That's bog water, I'm
thinking, but it's his own they are surely, for I
never seen the like of them for whity mud, and
red mud, and turf on them, and the fine sands

of the sea. That man's been walking, I'm telling you. (*She goes down right, putting on one of his boots.*)

SUSAN (*going to window*): Maybe he's stolen off to Belmullet with the boots of Michael James, and you'd have a right so to follow after him, Sara Tansey, and you the one yoked the ass cart and drove ten miles to set your eyes on the man bit the yellow lady's nostril on the northern shore. (*She looks out.*)

SARA (*running to window with one boot on*): Don't be talking, and we fooled today (*putting on other boot.*) There's a pair do fit me well, and I'll be keeping them for walking to the priest, when you'd be ashamed this place, going up winter and summer with nothing worth while to confess at all.

HONOR (*who has been listening at the door*): Whisht! there's someone inside the room. (*She pushes door a chink open.*) It's a man.

(SARA *kicks off boots and puts them where they were. They all stand in a line looking through chink.*)

SARA: I'll call him. Mister! Mister! (*He puts in his head.*) Is Pegeen within?

CHRISTY (*coming in as meek as a mouse, with the looking-glass held behind his back*): She's above on the cnuceen, seeking the nanny goats, the way she'd have a sup of goat's milk for to color my tea.

SARA: And asking your pardon, is it you's the man killed his father?

CHRISTY (*sidling toward the nail where the glass was hanging*): I am, God help me!

SARA (*taking eggs she has brought*): Then my thousand welcomes to you, and I've run up with a brace of duck's eggs for your food today. Pegeen's ducks is no use, but these are the real rich sort. Hold out your hand and you'll see it's no lie I'm telling you.

CHRISTY (*coming forward shyly, and holding out his left hand*): They're a great and weighty size.

SUSAN: And I run up with a pat of butter, for it'd be a poor thing to have you eating your spuds dry, and you after running a great way since you did destroy your da.

CHRISTY: Thank you kindly.

HONOR: And I brought you a little cut of cake, for you should have a thin stomach on you, and you that length walking the world.

NELLY: And I brought you a little laying pullet—boiled and all she is—was crushed at the fall of night by the curate's car. Feel the fat of that breast, mister.

CHRISTY: It's bursting, surely. (*He feels it with the back of his hand, in which he holds the presents.*)

SARA: Will you pinch it? Is your right hand too sacred for to use at all? (*She slips round behind him.*) It's a glass he has. Well, I never seen to this day a man with a looking-glass held to his back. Them that kills their fathers is a vain lot surely.

(*Girls giggle.*)

CHRISTY (*smiling innocently and piling presents on glass*): I'm very thankful to you all today. . . .

WIDOW QUIN (*coming in quickly, at door*): Sara Tansey, Susan Brady, Honor Blake! What in glory has you here at this hour of day?

GIRLS (*giggling*): That's the man killed his father.

WIDOW QUIN (*coming to them*): I know well it's the man; and I'm after putting him down in the sports below for racing, leaping, pitching, and the Lord knows what.

SARA (*exuberantly*): That's right, Widow Quin. I'll bet my dowry that he'll lick the world.

WIDOW QUIN: If you will, you'd have a right to have him fresh and nourished in place of, nursing a feast. (*Taking presents.*) Are you fasting or fed, young fellow?

CHRISTY: Fasting, if you please.

WIDOW QUIN (*loudly*): Well, you're the lot. Stir up now and give him his breakfast. (*To* CHRISTY) Come here to me (*she puts him on bench beside her while the girls make tea and get his breakfast*) and let you tell us your story before Pegeen will come, in place of grinning your ears off like the moon of May.

CHRISTY (*beginning to be pleased*): It's a long story; you'd be destroyed listening.

WIDOW QUIN: Don't be letting on to be shy, a fine, gamey, treacherous lad the like of you. Was it in your house beyond you cracked his skull?

CHRISTY (*shy but flattered*): It was not. We were digging spuds in his cold, sloping stony, divil's patch of a field.

WIDOW QUIN: And you went asking money of him, or making talk of getting a wife would drive him from his farm?

CHRISTY: I did not, then; but there I was,

digging and digging, and "You squinting idiot," says he, "let you walk down now and tell the priest you'll wed the Widow Casey in a score of days."

WIDOW QUIN: And what kind was she?

CHRISTY (*with horror*): A walking terror from beyond the hills, and she two score and two hundredweights and five pounds in the weighing scales, with a limping leg on her, and a blinded eye, and she a woman of noted misbehavior with the old and young.

GIRLS (*clustering round him, serving him*): Glory be.

WIDOW QUIN: And what did he want driving you to wed with her? (*She takes a bit of the chicken.*)

CHRISTY (*eating with growing satisfaction*): He was letting on I was wanting a protector from the harshness of the world, and he without a thought the whole while but how he'd have her hut to live in and her gold to drink.

WIDOW QUIN: There's maybe worse than a dry hearth and a widow woman and your glass at night. So you hit him then?

CHRISTY (*getting almost excited*): I did not. "I won't wed her," says I, "when all know she did suckle me for six weeks when I came into the world, and she a hag this day with a tongue on her has the crows and seabirds scattered, the way they wouldn't cast a shadow on her garden with the dread of her curse."

WIDOW QUIN (*teasingly*): That one should be right company.

SARA (*eagerly*): Don't mind her. Did you kill him then?

CHRISTY: "She's too good for the like of you," says he, "and go on now or I'll flatten you out like a crawling beast has passed under a dray." "You will not if I can help it," says I. "Go on," says he, "or I'll have the divil making garters of your limbs tonight." "You will not if I can help it," says I. (*He sits up, brandishing his mug.*)

SARA: You were right surely.

CHRISTY (*impressively*): With that the sun came out between the cloud and the hill, and it shining green in my face. "God have mercy on your soul," says he, lifting a scythe; "or on your own," says I, raising the loy.

SUSAN: That's a grand story.

HONOR: He tells it lovely.

CHRISTY (*flattered and confident, waving bone*): He gave a drive with the scythe, and I gave a lep to the east. Then I turned around with my back to the north, and I hit a blow on the ridge of his skull, laid him stretched out, and he split to the knob of his gullet. (*He raises the chicken bone to his Adam's apple.*)

GIRLS (*together*): Well, you're a marvel! Oh, God bless you! You're the lad surely!

SUSAN: I'm thinking the Lord God sent him this road to make a second husband to the Widow Quin, and she with a great yearning to be wedded, though all dread her here. Lift him on her knee, Sara Tansey.

WIDOW QUIN: Don't tease him.

SARA (*going over to dresser and counter very quickly, and getting two glasses and porter*): You're heroes surely, and let you drink a supeen with your arms linked like the outlandish lovers in the sailor's song. (*She links their arms and gives them the glasses.*) There now. Drink a health to the wonders of the western world, the pirates, preachers, poteen-makers, with the jobbing jockies; parching peelers, and the juries fill their stomachs selling judgments of the English law. (*Brandishing the bottle.*)

WIDOW QUIN: That's a right toast, Sara Tansey. Now Christy.

(*They drink with their arms linked, he drinking with his left hand, she with her right. As they are drinking, PEGEEN MIKE comes in with a milk can and stands aghast. They all spring away from CHRISTY. He goes down left. WIDOW QUIN remains seated.*)

PEGEEN (*angrily, to SARA*): What is it you're wanting?

SARA (*twisting her apron*): A ounce of tobacco.

PEGEEN: Have you tuppence?

SARA: I've forgotten my purse.

PEGEEN: Then you'd best be getting it and not fooling us here. (*To the WIDOW QUIN, with more elaborate scorn*) And what is it you're wanting, Widow Quin?

WIDOW QUIN (*insolently*): A penn'orth of starch.

PEGEEN (*breaking out*): And you without a white shift or a shirt in your whole family since the drying of the flood. I've no starch for the like of you, and let you walk on now to Killamuck.

WIDOW QUIN (*turning to CHRISTY, as she goes out with the girls*): Well, you're mighty huffy this day, Pegeen Mike, and, you young fellow, let you not forget the sports and racing when the noon is by.

(*They go out.*)

PEGEEN (*imperiously*): Fling out that rubbish and put them cups away. (CHRISTY *tidies away in great haste.*) Shove in the bench by the wall. (*He does so.*) And hang that glass on the nail. What disturbed it at all?

CHRISTY (*very meekly*): I was making myself decent only, and this a fine country for young lovely girls.

PEGEEN (*sharply*): Whisht your talking of girls. (*Goes to counter—right.*)

CHRISTY: Wouldn't any wish to be decent in a place . . .

PEGEEN: Whisht I'm saying.

CHRISTY (*Looks at her face for a moment with great misgivings, then as a last effort takes up a loy, and goes towards her, with feigned assurance.*): It was with a loy the like of that I killed my father.

PEGEEN (*still sharply*): You've told me that story six times since the dawn of day.

CHRISTY (*reproachfully*): It's a queer thing you wouldn't care to be hearing it and them girls after walking four miles to be listening to me now.

PEGEEN (*turning round astonished*): Four miles.

CHRISTY (*apologetically*): Didn't himself say there were only four bona fides living in this place?

PEGEEN: It's bona fides by the road they are, but that lot came over the river lepping the stones. It's not three perches when you go like that, and I was down this morning looking on the papers the post-boy does have in his bag. (*With meaning and emphasis*) For there was great news this day, Christopher Mahon. (*She goes into room left.*)

CHRISTY (*suspiciously*): Is it news of my murder?

PEGEEN (*inside*): Murder, indeed.

CHRISTY (*loudly*): A murdered da?

PEGEEN (*coming in again and crossing right*): There was not, but a story filled half a page of the hanging of a man. Ah, that should be a fearful end, young fellow, and it worst of all for a man who destroyed his da, for the like of him would get small mercies, and when it's dead he is, they'd put him in a narrow grave, with cheap sacking wrapping him round, and pour down quicklime

on his head, the way you'd see a woman pouring any frish-frash from a cup.

CHRISTY (*very miserably*): Oh, God help me. Are you thinking I'm safe? You were saying at the fall of night, I was shut of jeopardy and I here with yourselves.

PEGEEN (*severely*): You'll be shut of jeopardy no place if you go talking with a pack of wild girls the like of them do be walking abroad with the peelers, talking whispers at the fall of night.

CHRISTY (*with terror*): And you're thinking they'd tell?

PEGEEN (*with mock sympathy*): Who knows, God help you.

CHRISTY (*loudly*): What joy would they have to bring hanging to the likes of me?

PEGEEN: It's queer joys they have, and who knows the thing they'd do, if it'd make the green stones cry itself to think of you swaying and swiggling at the butt of a rope, and you with a fine, stout neck, God bless you! the way you'd be a half an hour, in great anguish, getting your death.

CHRISTY (*getting his boots and putting them on*): If there's that terror of them, it'd be best, maybe, I went on wandering like Esau or Cain and Abel on the sides of Neifin or the Erris plain.

PEGEEN (*beginning to play with him*): It would, maybe, for I've heard the Circuit Judges this place is a heartless crew.

CHRISTY (*bitterly*): It's more than Judges this place is a heartless crew. (*Looking up at her*) And isn't it a poor thing to be starting again and I a lonesome fellow will be looking out on women and girls the way the needy fallen spirits do be looking on the Lord?

PEGEEN: What call have you to be that lonesome when there's poor girls walking Mayo in their thousands now?

CHRISTY (*grimly*): It's well you know what call I have. It's well you know it's a lonesome thing to be passing small towns with the lights shining sideways when the night is down, or going in strange places with a dog noising before you and a dog noising behind, or drawn to the cities where you'd hear a voice kissing and talking deep love in every shadow of the ditch, and you passing on with an empty, hungry stomach failing from your heart.

PEGEEN: I'm thinking you're an odd man, Christy Mahon. The oddest walking fellow I ever set my eyes on to this hour today.

CHRISTY: What would any be but odd men and they living lonesome in the world?

PEGEEN: I'm not odd, and I'm my whole life with my father only.

CHRISTY (*with infinite admiration*): How would a lovely handsome woman the like of you be lonesome when all men should be thronging around to hear the sweetness of your voice, and the little infant children should be pestering your steps I'm thinking, and you walking the roads.

PEGEEN: I'm hard set to know what way a coaxing fellow the like of yourself should be lonesome either.

CHRISTY: Coaxing?

PEGEEN: Would you have me think a man never talked with the girls would have the words you've spoken today? It's only letting on you are to be lonesome, the way you'd get around me now.

CHRISTY: I wish to God I was letting on; but I was lonesome all times, and born lonesome, I'm thinking, as the moon of dawn. (*Going to door.*)

PEGEEN (*puzzled by his talk*): Well, it's a story I'm not understanding at all why you'd be worse than another, Christy Mahon, and you a fine lad with the great savagery to destroy your da.

CHRISTY: It's little I'm understanding myself, saving only that my heart's scalded this day, and I going off stretching out the earth between us, the way I'll not be waking near you another dawn of the year till the two of us do arise to hope or judgment with the saints of God, and now I'd best be going with my wattle in my hand, for hanging is a poor thing (*turning to go*), and it's little welcome only is left me in this house today.

PEGEEN (*sharply*): Christy! (*He turns round.*) Come here to me. (*He goes towards her.*) Lay down that switch and throw some sods on the fire. You're pot-boy in this place, and I'll not have you mitch off from us now.

CHRISTY: You were saying I'd be hanged if I stay.

PEGEEN (*quite kindly at last*): I'm after going down and reading the fearful crimes of Ireland for two weeks or three, and there wasn't a word of your murder. (*Getting up and going over to the counter*) They've likely not found the body. You're safe so with ourselves.

CHRISTY (*astonished, slowly*): It's making game of me you were (*following her with fearful joy*), and I can stay so, working at your side, and I not lonesome from this mortal day.

PEGEEN: What's to hinder you from staying, except the widow woman or the young girls would inveigle you off?

CHRISTY (*with rapture*): And I'll have your words from this day filling my ears, and that look is come upon you meeting my two eyes, and I watching you loafing around in the warm sun, or rinsing your ankles when the night is come.

PEGEEN (*kindly, but a little embarrassed*): I'm thinking you'll be a loyal young lad to have working around, and if you vexed me a while since with your leaguing with the girls, I wouldn't give a thraneen for a lad hadn't a mighty spirit in him and a gamey heart.

(SHAWN KEOGH *runs in carrying a cleeve on his back, followed by the* WIDOW QUIN.)

SHAWN (*to* PEGEEN): I was passing below, and I seen your mountainy sheep eating cabbages in Jimmy's field. Run up or they'll be bursting surely.

PEGEEN: Oh, God mend them! (*She puts a shawl over her head and runs out.*)

CHRISTY (*looking from one to the other. Still in high spirits*): I'd best go to her aid maybe. I'm handy with ewes.

WIDOW QUIN (*closing the door*): She can do that much, and there is Shaneen has long speeches for to tell you now. (*She sits down with an amused smile.*)

SHAWN (*taking something from his pocket and offering it to* CHRISTY): Do you see that, mister?

CHRISTY (*looking at it*): The half of a ticket to the Western States!

SHAWN (*trembling with anxiety*): I'll give it to you and my new hat (*pulling it out of hamper*); and my breeches with the double seat (*pulling it off*); and my new coat is woven from the blackest shearings for three miles around (*giving him the coat*); I'll give you the whole of them, and my blessing, and the blessing of Father Reilly itself, maybe, if you'll quit from this and leave us in the peace we had till last night at the fall of dark.

CHRISTY (*with a new arrogance*): And for what is it you're wanting to get shut of me?

SHAWN (*looking to the* WIDOW *for help*): I'm a poor scholar with middling faculties to coin a lie, so I'll tell you the truth, Christy Mahon. I'm wedding with Pegeen beyond, and I don't think well of having a clever fearless man the like of you dwelling in her house.

CHRISTY (*almost pugnaciously*): And you'd be using bribery for to banish me?

SHAWN (*in an imploring voice*): Let you not take it badly mister honey, isn't beyond the best place for you where you'll have golden chains and shiny coats and you riding upon hunters with the ladies of the land. (*He makes an eager sign to the* WIDOW QUIN *to come to help him.*)

WIDOW QUIN (*coming over*): It's true for him, and you'd best quit off and not have that poor girl setting her mind on you, for there's Shaneen thinks she wouldn't suit you though all is saying that she'll wed you now.

(CHRISTY *beams with delight.*)

SHAWN (*in terrified earnest*): She wouldn't suit you, and she with the divil's own temper the way you'd be strangling one another in a score of days. (*He makes the movement of strangling with his hands.*) It's the like of me only that she's fit for, a quiet simple fellow wouldn't raise a hand upon her if she scratched itself.

WIDOW QUIN (*putting* SHAWN'*s hat on* CHRISTY): Fit them clothes on you anyhow, young fellow, and he'd maybe loan them to you for the sports. (*Pushing him towards inner door*) Fit them on and you can give your answer when you have them tried.

CHRISTY (*beaming, delighted with the clothes*): I will then. I'd like herself to see me in them tweeds and hat. (*He goes into room and shuts the door.*)

SHAWN (*in great anxiety*): He'd like herself to see them. He'll not leave us, Widow Quin. He's a score of divils in him the way it's well nigh certain he will wed Pegeen.

WIDOW QUIN (*jeeringly*): It's true all girls are fond of courage and do hate the like of you.

SHAWN (*walking about in desperation*): Oh, Widow Quin, what'll I be doing now? I'd inform again him, but he'd burst from Kilmainham and he'd be sure and certain to destroy me. If I wasn't so God-fearing, I'd near have courage to come behind him and run a pike into his side. Oh, it's a hard case to be an orphan and not to have your father that you're used to, and you'd easy kill and make yourself a hero in the sight of all. (*Coming up to her*) Oh, Widow Quin, will you find me some contrivance when I've promised you a ewe?

WIDOW QUIN: A ewe's a small thing, but what would you give me if I did wed him and did save you so?

SHAWN (*with astonishment*): You?

WIDOW QUIN: Aye. Would you give me the red cow you have and the mountainy ram, and the right of way across your rye path, and a load of dung at Michaelmas, and turbary upon the western hill?

SHAWN (*radiant with hope*): I would surely, and I'd give you the wedding ring I have, and the loan of a new suit, the way you'd have him decent on the wedding day. I'd give you two kids for your dinner, and a gallon of poteen, and I'd call the piper on the long car to your wedding from Crossmolina or from Ballina. I'd give you . . .

WIDOW QUIN: That'll do so, and let you whisht, for he's coming now again.

(CHRISTY *comes in very natty in the new clothes.* WIDOW QUIN *goes to him admiringly.*)

WIDOW QUIN: If you seen yourself now, I'm thinking you'd be too proud to speak to us at all, and it'd be a pity surely to have your like sailing from Mayo to the Western World.

CHRISTY (*as proud as a peacock*): I'm not going. If this is a poor place itself, I'll make myself contented to be lodging here.

(WIDOW QUIN *makes a sign to* SHAWN *to leave them.*)

SHAWN: Well, I'm going measuring the racecourse while the tide is low, so I'll leave you the garments and my blessing for the sports today. God bless you! (*He wriggles out.*)

WIDOW QUIN (*admiring* CHRISTY): Well, you're mighty spruce, young fellow. Sit down now while you're quiet till you talk with me.

CHRISTY (*swaggering*): I'm going abroad on the hillside for to seek Pegeen.

WIDOW QUIN: You'll have time and plenty for to seek Pegeen, and you heard me saying at the fall of night the two of us should be great company.

CHRISTY: From this out I'll have no want of company when all sorts is bringing me their food and clothing (*he swaggers to the door, tightening his belt*), the way they'd set their eyes upon a gallant orphan cleft his father with one blow to the breeches belt. (*He opens door, then staggers back.*) Saints of glory! Holy angels from the throne of light!

WIDOW QUIN (*going over*):   What ails you?

CHRISTY:   It's the walking spirit of my murdered da?

WIDOW QUIN (*looking out*):   Is it that tramper?

CHRISTY (*wildly*):   Where'll I hide my poor body from that ghost of hell?

(*The door is pushed open, and old* MAHON *appears on threshold.* CHRISTY *darts in behind door.*)

WIDOW QUIN (*in great amusement*):   God save you, my poor man.

MAHON (*gruffly*):   Did you see a young lad passing this way in the early morning or the fall of night?

WIDOW QUIN:   You're a queer kind to walk in not saluting at all.

MAHON:   Did you see the young lad?

WIDOW QUIN (*stiffly*):   What kind was he?

MAHON:   An ugly young streeler with a murderous gob on him, and a little switch in his hand. I met a tramper seen him coming this way at the fall of night.

WIDOW QUIN:   There's harvest hundreds do be passing these days for the Sligo boat. For what is it you're wanting him, my poor man?

MAHON:   I want to destroy him for breaking the head on me with the clout of a loy. (*He takes off a big hat, and shows his head in a mass of bandages and plaster, with some pride.*) It was he did that, and amn't I a great wonder to think I've traced him ten days with that rent in my crown?

WIDOW QUIN (*taking his head in both hands and examining it with extreme delight*):   That was a great blow. And who hit you? A robber maybe?

MAHON:   It was my own son hit me, and he the divil a robber, or anything else, but a dirty, stuttering lout.

WIDOW QUIN (*letting go his skull and wiping her hands in her apron*):   You'd best be wary of a mortified scalp, I think they call it, lepping around with that wound in the splendor of the sun. It was a bad blow surely, and you should have vexed him fearful to make him strike that gash in his da.

MAHON:   Is it me?

WIDOW QUIN (*amusing herself*):   Aye. And isn't it a great shame when the old and hardened do torment the young?

MAHON (*raging*):   Torment him is it? And I after holding out with the patience of a martyred saint till there's nothing but destruction on, and I'm driven out in my old age with none to aid me.

WIDOW QUIN (*greatly amused*):   It's a sacred wonder the way that wickedness will spoil a man.

MAHON:   My wickedness, is it? Amn't I after saying it is himself has me destroyed, and he a liar on walls, a talker of folly, a man you'd see stretched the half of the day in the brown ferns with his belly to the sun.

WIDOW QUIN:   Not working at all?

MAHON:   The divil a work, or if he did itself, you'd see him raising up a haystack like the stalk of a rush, or driving our last cow till he broke her leg at the hip, and when he wasn't at that he'd be fooling over little birds he had—finches and felts—or making mugs at his own self in the bit of a glass we had hung on the wall.

WIDOW QUIN (*looking at* CHRISTY):   What way was he so foolish? It was running wild after the girls may be?

MAHON (*with a shout of derision*):   Running wild, is it? If he seen a red petticoat coming swinging over the hill, he'd be off to hide in the sticks, and you'd see him shooting out his sheep's eyes between the little twigs and the leaves, and his two ears rising like a hare looking out through a gap. Girls, indeed!

WIDOW QUIN:   It was drink maybe?

MAHON:   And he a poor fellow would get drunk on the smell of a pint. He'd a queer rotten stomach, I'm telling you, and when I gave him three pulls from my pipe a while since, he was taken with contortions till I had to send him in the ass cart to the females' nurse.

WIDOW QUIN (*clasping her hands*):   Well, I never till this day heard tell of a man the like of that!

MAHON:   I'd take a mighty oath you didn't surely, and wasn't he the laughing joke of every female woman where four baronies meet, the way the girls would stop their weeding if they seen him coming the road to let a roar at him, and call him the looney of Mahon's.

WIDOW QUIN:   I'd give the world and all to see the like of him. What kind was he?

MAHON:   A small low fellow.

WIDOW QUIN:   And dark?

MAHON:   Dark and dirty.

WIDOW QUIN (*considering*):   I'm thinking I seen him.

MAHON (*eagerly*):  An ugly young blackguard.

WIDOW QUIN:  A hideous, fearful villain, and the spit of you.

MAHON:  What way is he fled?

WIDOW QUIN:  Gone over the hills to catch a coasting steamer to the north or south.

MAHON:  Could I pull up on him now?

WIDOW QUIN:  If you'll cross the sands below where the tide is out, you'll be in it as soon as himself, for he had to go round ten miles by the top of the bay. (*She points to the door.*) Strike down by the head beyond and then follow on the roadway to the north and east.

(MAHON *goes abruptly.*)

WIDOW QUIN (*shouting after him*):  Let you give him a good vengeance when you come up with him, but don't put yourself in the power of the law, for it'd be a poor thing to see a judge in his black cap reading out his sentence on a civil warrior the like of you. (*She swings the door to and looks at* CHRISTY, *who is cowering in terror, for a moment, then she bursts into a laugh.*)

WIDOW QUIN:  Well, you're the walking Playboy of the Western World, and that's the poor man you had divided to his breeches belt.

CHRISTY (*looking out: then, to her*):  What'll Pegeen say when she hears that story? What'll she be saying to me now?

WIDOW QUIN:  She'll knock the head of you, I'm thinking, and drive you from the door. God help her to betaking you for a wonder, and you a little schemer making up the story you destroyed your da.

CHRISTY (*turning to the door, nearly speechless with rage, half to himself*):  To be letting on he was dead, and coming back to his life, and following after me like an old weasel tracing a rat, and coming in here laying desolation between my own self and the fine women of Ireland, and he a kind of carcase that you'd fling upon the sea. . . .

WIDOW QUIN (*more soberly*):  There's talking for a man's one only son.

CHRISTY (*breaking out*):  His one son, is it? May I meet him with one tooth and it aching, and one eye to be seeing seven and seventy divils in the twists of the road, and one old timber leg on him to limp into the scalding grave. (*Looking out*) There he is now crossing the strands, and that the Lord God would send a high wave to wash him from the world.

WIDOW QUIN (*scandalized*):  Have you no shame? (*Putting her hand on his shoulder and turning him round*) What ails you? Near crying, is it?

CHRISTY (*in despair and grief*):  Amn't I after seeing the love-light of the star of knowledge shining from her brow, and hearing words would put you thinking on the holy Brigid speaking to the infant saints, and now she'll be turning again, and speaking hard words to me, like an old woman with a spavindy ass she'd have, urging on a hill.

WIDOW QUIN:  There's poetry talk for a girl you'd see itching and scratching, and she with a stale stink of poteen on her from selling in the shop.

CHRISTY (*impatiently*):  It's her like is fitted to be handling merchandise in the heavens above, and what'll I be doing now, I ask you, and I a kind of wonder was jilted by the heavens when a day was by.

(*There is a distant noise of girls' voices.* WIDOW QUIN *looks from window and comes to him, hurriedly.*)

WIDOW QUIN:  You'll be doing like myself, I'm thinking, when I did destroy my man, for I'm above many's the day, odd times in great spirits, abroad in the sunshine, darning a stocking or stitching a shift; and odd times again looking out on the schooners, hookers, trawlers is sailing the sea, and I thinking on the gallant hairy fellows are drifting beyond, and myself long years living alone.

CHRISTY (*interested*):  You're like me, so.

WIDOW QUIN:  I am your like, and it's for that I'm taking a fancy to you, and I with my little houseen above where there'd be myself to tend you, and none to ask were you a murderer or what at all.

CHRISTY:  And what would I be doing if I left Pegeen?

WIDOW QUIN:  I've nice jobs you could be doing, gathering shells to make a whitewash for our hut within, building up a little goosehouse, or stretching a new skin on an old curragh I have, and if my hut is far from all sides, it's there you'll meet the wisest old men, I tell you, at the corner of my wheel, and it's there yourself and me will have great times whispering and hugging. . . .

VOICES (*outside, calling far away*):  Christy! Christy Mahon! Christy!

CHRISTY:  Is it Pegeen Mike?

WIDOW QUIN:  It's the young girls, I'm thinking, coming to bring you to the sports below, and what is it you'll have me to tell them now?

CHRISTY:  Aid me for to win Pegeen. It's herself only that I'm seeking now. (WIDOW QUIN *gets up and goes to window.*) Aid me for to win her, and I'll be asking God to stretch a hand to you in the hour of death, and lead you short cuts through the Meadows of Ease, and up the floor of Heaven to the Footstool of the Virgin's Son.

WIDOW QUIN:  There's praying.

VOICES (*nearer*):  Christy! Christy Mahon!

CHRISTY (*with agitation*):  They're coming. Will you swear to aid and save me for the love of Christ?

WIDOW QUIN (*looks at him for a moment*):  If I aid you, will you swear to give me a right of way I want, and a mountainy ram, and a load of dung at Michaelmas, the time that you'll be master here?

CHRISTY:  I will, by the elements and stars of night.

WIDOW QUIN:  Then we'll not say a word of the old fellow, the way Pegeen won't know your story till the end of time.

CHRISTY:  And if he chances to return again?

WIDOW QUIN:  We'll swear he's a maniac and not your da. I could take an oath I seen him raving on the sands today.

(*Girls run in.*)

SUSAN:  Come on to the sports below. Pegeen says you're to come.

SARA TANSEY:  The lepping's beginning, and we've a jockey's suit to fit upon you for the mule race on the sands below.

HONOR:  Come on, will you?

CHRISTY:  I will then if Pegeen's beyond.

SARA TANSEY:  She's in the boreen making game of Shaneen Keogh.

CHRISTY:  Then I'll be going to her now. (*He runs out followed by the girls.*)

WIDOW QUIN:  Well, if the worst comes in the end of all, it'll be great game to see there's none to pity him but a widow woman, the like of me, has buried her children and destroyed her man. (*She goes out.*)

## ACT THREE

*SCENE*

As before. Later in the day. JIMMY comes in, slightly drunk.

JIMMY (*calls*):  Pegeen! (*Crosses to inner door.*) Pegeen Mike! (*Comes back again into the room.*) Pegeen! (PHILLY *comes in in the same state.*) (*To* PHILLY) Did you see herself?

PHILLY:  I did not; but I sent Shawn Keogh with the ass cart for to bear him home. (*Trying cupboards which are locked*) Well, isn't he a nasty man to get into such staggers at a morning wake? and isn't herself the divil's daughter for locking, and she so fussy after that young gaffer, you might take your death with drought and none to heed you?

JIMMY:  It's little wonder she'd be fussy, and he after bringing bankrupt ruin on the roulette man, and the trick-o'-the-loop man, and breaking the nose of the cockshot-man, and winning all in the sports below, racing, lepping, dancing, and the Lord knows what! He's right luck, I'm telling you.

PHILLY:  If he has, he'll be rightly hobbled yet, and he not able to say ten words without making a brag of the way he killed his father, and the great blow he hit with the loy.

JIMMY:  A man can't hang by his own informing, and his father should be rotten by now.

(OLD MAHON *passes window slowly.*)

PHILLY:  Supposing a man's digging spuds in that field with a long spade, and supposing he flings up the two halves of that skull, what'll be said then in the papers and the courts of law?

JIMMY:  They'd say it was an old Dane, maybe, was drowned in the flood. (OLD MAHON *comes in and sits down near door listening.*) Did you never tell of the skulls they have in the city of Dublin, ranged out like blue jugs in a cabin of Connaught?

PHILLY:  And you believe that?

JIMMY (*pugnaciously*):  Didn't a lad see them and he after coming from harvesting in the Liverpool boat? "They have them there," says he, "making a show of the great people there was one time walking the world. White skulls and black skulls and yellow skulls, and some with full teeth, and some haven't only but one."

PHILLY:  It was no lie, maybe, for when I was a young lad there was a graveyard beyond the house with the remnants of a man who had thighs as long as your arm. He was a horrid man, I'm telling you, and there was many a fine Sunday I'd put him together for fun, and he with shiny bones, you wouldn't meet the like of these days in the cities of the world.

MAHON (*getting up*): You wouldn't, is it? Lay your eyes on that skull, and tell me where and when there was another the like of it, is splintered only from the blow of a loy.

PHILLY: Glory be to God! And who hit you at all?

MAHON (*triumphantly*): It was my own son hit me. Would you believe that?

JIMMY: Well, there's wonders hidden in the heart of man!

PHILLY (*suspiciously*): And what way was it done?

MAHON (*wandering about the room*): I'm after walking hundreds and long scores of miles, winning clean beds and the fill of my belly four times in the day, and I doing nothing but telling stories of that naked truth. (*He comes to them a little aggressively.*) Give me a supeen and I'll tell you now.

(WIDOW QUIN *comes in and stands aghast behind him. He is facing* JIMMY *and* PHILLY, *who are on the left.*)

JIMMY: Ask herself beyond. She's the stuff hidden in her shawl.

WIDOW QUIN (*coming to* MAHON *quickly*): You here, is it? You didn't go far at all?

MAHON: I seen the coasting steamer passing, and I got a drought upon me and a cramping leg, so I said, "The divil go along with him," and turned again. (*Looking under her shawl*) And let you give me a supeen, for I'm destroyed travelling since Tuesday was a week.

WIDOW QUIN (*getting a glass, in a cajoling tone*): Sit down then by the fire and take your ease for a space. You've a right to be destroyed indeed, with your walking, and fighting, and facing the sun (*giving him poteen from a stone jar she has brought in*). There now is a drink for you, and may it be to your happiness and length of life.

MAHON (*taking glass greedily and sitting down by fire*): God increase you!

WIDOW QUIN (*taking men to the right stealthily*): Do you know what? That man's raving from his wound today, for I met him a while since telling a rambling tale of a tinker had him destroyed. Then he heard of Christy's deed, and he up and says it was his son had cracked his skull. O isn't madness a fright, for he'll go killing someone yet, and he thinking it's the man has struck him so?

JIMMY (*entirely convinced*): It's a fright, surely. I knew a party was kicked in the head by a red mare, and he went killing horses a great while, till he eat the insides of a clock and died after.

PHILLY (*with suspicion*): Did he see Christy?

WIDOW QUIN: He didn't. (*With a warning gesture*) Let you not be putting him in mind of him, or you'll be likely summoned if there's murder done. (*Looking round at* MAHON) Whisht! He's listening. Wait now till you hear me taking him easy and unravelling all. (*She goes to* MAHON.) And what way are you feeling, mister? Are you in contentment now?

MAHON (*slightly emotional from his drink*): I'm poorly only, for it's a hard story the way I'm left today, when it was I did tend him from his hour of birth, and he a dunce never reached his second book, the way he'd come from school, many's the day, with his legs lamed under him, and he blackened with his beatings like a tinker's ass. It's a hard story, I'm saying, the way some do have their next and nighest raising up a hand of murder on them, and some is lonesome getting their death with lamentation in the dead of night.

WIDOW QUIN (*not knowing what to say*): To hear you talking so quiet, who'd know you were the same fellow we seen pass today?

MAHON: I'm the same surely. The wrack and ruin of three score years; and it's a terror to live that length, I tell you, and to have your sons going to the dogs against you, and you wore out scolding them, and skelping them, and God knows what.

PHILLY (*to* JIMMY): He's not raving. (*To* WIDOW QUIN) Will you ask him what kind was his son?

WIDOW QUIN (*to* MAHON, *with a peculiar look*): Was your son that hit you a lad of one year and a score maybe, a great hand at racing and lepping and licking the world?

MAHON (*turning on her with a roar of rage*): Didn't you hear me say he was the fool of men, the way from this out he'll know the orphan's lot with old and young making game of him and they swearing, raging, kicking at him like a mangy cur.

(*A great burst of cheering outside, some way off.*)

MAHON (*putting his hands to his ears*): What in the name of God do they want roaring below?

WIDOW QUIN (*with the shade of a smile*):

They're cheering a young lad, the champion Playboy of the Western World.

(*More cheering.*)

MAHON (*going to window*): It'd split my heart to hear them, and I with pulses in my brain-pan for a week gone by. Is it racing they are?

JIMMY (*looking from door*): It is then. They are mounting him for the mule race will be run upon the sands. That's the playboy on the winkered mule.

MAHON (*puzzled*): That lad, is it? If you said it was a fool he was, I'd have laid a mighty oath he was the likeness of my wandering son (*uneasily, putting his hand to his head*). Faith, I'm thinking I'll go walking for to view the race.

WIDOW QUIN (*stopping him, sharply*): You will not. You'd best take the road to Belmullet, and not be dilly-dallying in this place where there isn't a spot you could sleep.

PHILLY (*coming forward*): Don't mind her. Mount there on the bench and you'll have a view of the whole. They're hurrying before the tide will rise, and it'd be near over if you went down the pathway through the crags below.

MAHON (*mounts on bench,* WIDOW QUIN *beside him*): That's a right view again the edge of the sea. They're coming now from the point. He's leading. Who is he at all?

WIDOW QUIN: He's the champion of the world, I tell you, and there isn't a hop'orth isn't falling lucky to his hands today.

PHILLY (*looking out, interested in the race*): Look at that. They're pressing him now.

JIMMY: He'll win it yet.

PHILLY: Take your time, Jimmy Farrell. It's too soon to say.

WIDOW QUIN (*shouting*): Watch him taking the gate. There's riding.

JIMMY (*cheering*): More power to the young lad!

MAHON: He's passing the third.

JIMMY: He'll lick them yet!

WIDOW QUIN: He'd lick them if he was running races with a score itself.

MAHON: Look at the mule he has, kicking the stars.

WIDOW QUIN: There was a lep! (*Catching hold of* MAHON *in her excitement*) He's fallen! He's mounted again! Faith, he's passing them all!

JIMMY: Look at him skelping her!

PHILLY: And the mountain girls hooshing him on!

JIMMY: It's the last turn! The post's cleared for them now!

MAHON: Look at the narrow place. He'll be into the bogs! (*With a yell*) Good rider! He's through it again!

JIMMY: He's neck and neck!

MAHON: Good boy to him! Flames, but he's in!

(*Great cheering, in which all join.*)

MAHON (*with hesitation*): What's that? They're raising him up. They're coming this way. (*With a roar of rage and astonishment*) It's Christy! by the stars of God! I'd know his way of spitting and he astride the moon.

(*He jumps down and makes for the door, but* WIDOW QUIN *catches him and pulls him back.*)

WIDOW QUIN: Stay quiet, will you. That's not your son. (*To* JIMMY) Stop him, or you'll get a month for the abetting of manslaughter and be fined as well.

JIMMY: I'll hold him.

MAHON (*struggling*): Let me out! Let me out, the lot of you! till I have my vengeance on his head today.

WIDOW QUIN (*shaking him, vehemently*): That's not your son. That's a man is going to make a marriage with the daughter of this house, a place with fine trade, with a license, and with poteen too.

MAHON (*amazed*): That man marrying a decent and a moneyed girl! Is it mad yous are? Is it in a crazy house for females that I'm landed now?

WIDOW QUIN: It's mad yourself is with the blow upon your head. That lad is the wonder of the Western World.

MAHON: I seen it's my son.

WIDOW QUIN: You seen that you're mad. (*Cheering outside*) Do you hear them cheering him in the zig-zags of the road? Aren't you after saying that your son's a fool, and how would they be cheering a true idiot born?

MAHON (*getting distressed*): It's maybe out of reason that that man's himself. (*Cheering again*) There's none surely will go cheering him. Oh, I'm raving with a madness that would fright the world! (*He sits down with his hand to his head.*) There was one time I seen ten scarlet divils letting on they'd cork my spirit in a gallon can; and one time I seen rats as big as badgers sucking the life blood from the butt of my lug; but I never till this day confused that dribbling idiot with a likely man. I'm destroyed surely.

WIDOW QUIN:  And who'd wonder when it's your brain-pan that is gaping now?

MAHON:  Then the blight of the sacred drought upon myself and him, for I never went mad to this day, and I not three weeks with the Limerick girls drinking myself silly, and parlatic from the dusk to dawn. (*To* WIDOW QUIN, *suddenly*) Is my visage astray?

WIDOW QUIN:  It is then. You're a sniggering maniac, a child could see.

MAHON (*getting up more cheerfully*):  Then I'd best be going to the union beyond, and there'll be a welcome before me, I tell you (*with great pride*), and I a terrible and fearful case, the way that there I was one time, screeching in a strait-ened waistcoat, with seven doctors writing out my sayings in a printed book. Would you believe that?

WIDOW QUIN:  If you're a wonder itself, you'd best be hasty, for them lads caught a maniac one time and pelted the poor creature till he ran out, raving and foaming, and was drowned in the sea.

MAHON (*with philosophy*):  It's true mankind is the divil when your head's astray. Let me out now and I'll slip down the boreen, and not see them so.

WIDOW QUIN (*showing him out*):  That's it. Run to the right, and not a one will see.

(*He runs off.*)

PHILLY (*wisely*):  You're at some gaming, Widow Quin; but I'll walk after him and give him his dinner and a time to rest, and I'll see then if he's raving or as sane as you.

WIDOW QUIN (*annoyed*):  If you go near that lad, let you be wary of your head, I'm saying. Didn't you hear him telling he was crazed at times?

PHILLY:  I heard him telling a power; and I'm thinking we'll have right sport, before night will fall. (*He goes out.*)

JIMMY:  Well, Philly's a conceited and foolish man. How could that madman have his senses and his brain-pan slit? I'll go after them and see him turn on Philly now.

(*He goes;* WIDOW QUIN *hides poteen behind counter. Then hubbub outside.*)

VOICES:  There you are! Good jumper! Grand lepper! Darlint boy! He's the racer! Bear him on, will you!

(CHRISTY *comes in, in Jockey's dress, with* PEGEEN MIKE, SARA, *and other girls, and men.*)

PEGEEN (*to crowd*):  Go on now and don't destroy him and he drenching with sweat. Go along, I'm saying, and have your tug-of-warring till he's dried his skin.

CROWD:  Here's his prizes! A bagpipes! A fiddle was played by a poet in the years gone by! A flat and three-thorned blackthorn would lick the scholars out of Dublin town!

CHRISTY (*taking prizes from the men*):  Thank you kindly, the lot of you. But you'd say it was little only I did this day if you'd seen me a while since striking my one single blow.

TOWN CRIER (*outside, ringing a bell*):  Take notice, last event of this day! Tug-of-warring on the green below! Come on, the lot of you! Great achievements for all Mayo men!

PEGEEN:  Go on, and leave him for to rest and dry. Go on, I tell you, for he'll do no more.

(*She hustles crowd out;* WIDOW QUIN *following them.*)

MEN (*going*):  Come on then. Good luck for the while!

PEGEEN (*radiantly, wiping his face with her shawl*):  Well, you're the lad, and you'll have great times from this out when you could win that wealth of prizes, and you sweating in the heat of noon!

CHRISTY (*looking at her with delight*):  I'll have great times if I win the crowning prize I'm seek-ing now, and that's your promise that you'll wed me in a fortnight, when our banns is called.

PEGEEN (*backing away from him*):  You're right daring to go ask me that, when all knows you'll be starting to some girl in your own town-land, when your father's rotten in four months, or five.

CHRISTY (*indignantly*):  Starting from you, is it? (*He follows her.*) I will not, then, and when the airs is warming in four months, or five, it's then yourself and me should be pacing Neifin in the dews of night, the times sweet smells do be rising, and you'd see a little shiny new moon, maybe, sinking on the hills.

PEGEEN (*looking at him playfully*):  And it's that kind of a poacher's love you'd make, Christy Mahon, on the sides of Neifin, when the night is down?

CHRISTY:  It's little you'll think if my love's a poacher's, or an earl's itself, when you'll feel my two hands stretched around you, and I squeezing kisses on your puckered lips, till I'd feel a kind of pity for the Lord God is all ages sitting lonesome in his golden chair.

PEGEEN:   That'll be right fun, Christy Mahon, and any girl would walk her heart out before she'd meet a young man was your like for eloquence, or talk, at all.

CHRISTY (*encouraged*):   Let you wait, to hear me talking, till we're astray in Erris, when Good Friday's by, drinking a sup from a well, and making mighty kisses with our wetted mouths, or gaming in a gap or sunshine, with yourself stretched back onto your necklace, in the flowers of the earth.

PEGEEN (*in a lower voice, moved by his tone*): I'd be nice so, is it?

CHRISTY (*with rapture*):   If the mitred bishops seen you that time, they'd be the like of the holy prophets, I'm thinking, do be straining the bars of Paradise to lay eyes on the Lady Helen of Troy, and she abroad, pacing back and forward, with a nosegay in her golden shawl.

PEGEEN (*with real tenderness*):   And what is it I have, Christy Mahon, to make me fitting entertainment for the like of you, that has such poet's talking, and such bravery of heart?

CHRISTY (*in a low voice*):   Isn't there the light of seven heavens in your heart alone, the way you'll be an angel's lamp to me from this out, and I abroad in the darkness, spearing salmons in the Owen, or the Carrowmore?

PEGEEN:   If I was your wife, I'd be along with you those nights, Christy Mahon, the way you'd see I was a great hand at coaxing bailiffs, or coining funny nick-names for the stars of night.

CHRISTY:   You, is it? Taking your death in the hailstones, or in the fogs of dawn.

PEGEEN:   Yourself and me would shelter easy in a narrow bush (*with a qualm of dread*), but we're only talking, maybe, for this would be a poor, thatched place to hold a fine lad is the like of you.

CHRISTY (*putting his arm around her*):   If I wasn't a good Christian, it's on my naked knees I'd be saying my prayers and paters to every jackstraw you have roofing your head, and every stony pebble is paving the laneway to your door.

PEGEEN (*radiantly*):   If that's the truth, I'll be burning candles from this out to the miracles of God that have brought you from the south today, and I, with my gowns bought ready, the way that I can wed you, and not wait at all.

CHRISTY:   It's miracles, and that's the truth.

Me there toiling a long while, and walking a long while, not knowing at all I was drawing all times nearer to this holy day.

PEGEEN:   And myself, a girl, was tempted often to go sailing the seas till I'd marry a Jew-man, with ten kegs of gold, and I not knowing at all there was the like of you drawing nearer, like the stars of God.

CHRISTY:   And to think I'm long years hearing women talking that talk, to all bloody fools, and this the first time I've heard the like of your voice talking sweetly for my own delight.

PEGEEN:   And to think it's me is talking sweetly, Christy Mahon, and I the fright of seven townlands for my biting tongue. Well, the heart's a wonder; and, I'm thinking, there won't be our like in Mayo, for gallant lovers, from this hour, today. (*Drunken singing is heard outside.*) There's my father coming from the wake, and when he's had his sleep we'll tell him, for he's peaceful then.

(*They separate.*)

MICHAEL (*singing outside*):

The jailor and the turnkey
They quickly ran us down,
And brought us back as prisoners
Once more to Cavan town.

(*He comes in supported by* SHAWN.)

There we lay bewailing
All in a prison bound. . . .

(*He sees* CHRISTY. *Goes and shakes him drunkenly by the hand, while* PEGEEN *and* SHAWN *talk on the left.*)

MICHAEL (*to* CHRISTY):   The blessing of God and the holy angels on your head, young fellow. I hear tell you're after winning all in the sports below; and wasn't it a shame I didn't bear you along with me to Kate Cassidy's wake, a fine, stout lad, the like of you, for you'd never see the match of it for flows of drink, the way when we sunk her bones at noonday in her narrow grave, there were five men, aye, and six men, stretched out retching speechless on the holy stones.

CHRISTY (*uneasily, watching* PEGEEN):   Is that the truth?

MICHAEL:   It is then, and aren't you a louty schemer to go burying your poor father unbeknownst when you'd a right to throw him on the crupper of a Kerry mule and drive him westwards, like holy Joseph in the days gone by, the way we could have given him a decent burial, and not have him rotting beyond, and not a Christian drinking a smart drop to the glory of his soul?

CHRISTY (*gruffly*): It's well enough he's lying, for the likes of him.

MICHAEL (*slapping him on the back*): Well, aren't you a hardened slayer? It'll be a poor thing for the household man where you go sniffing for a female wife; and (*pointing to* SHAWN) look beyond at that shy and decent Christian I have chosen for my daughter's hand, and I after getting the gilded dispensation this day for to wed them now.

CHRISTY: And you'll be wedding them this day, is it?

MICHAEL (*drawing himself up*): Aye. Are you thinking, if I'm drunk itself, I'd leave my daughter living single with a little frisky rascal is the like of you?

PEGEEN (*breaking away from* SHAWN): Is it the truth the dispensation's come?

MICHAEL (*triumphantly*): Father Reilly's after reading it in gallous Latin, and "It's come in the nick of time," says he; "so I'll wed them in a hurry, dreading that young gaffer who'd capsize the stars."

PEGEEN (*fiercely*): He's missed his nick of time, for it's that lad, Christy Mahon, that I'm wedding now.

MICHAEL (*loudly with horror*): You'd be making him a son to me, and he wet and crusted with his father's blood?

PEGEEN: Aye. Wouldn't it be a bitter thing for a girl to go marrying the like of Shaneen, and he a middling kind of a scarecrow, with no savagery or fine words in him at all?

MICHAEL (*gasping and sinking on a chair*): Oh, aren't you a heathen daughter to go shaking the fat of my heart, and I swamped and drowned with the weight of drink? Would you have them turning on me the way that I'd be roaring to the dawn of day with the wind upon my heart? Have you not a word to aid me, Shaneen? Are you not jealous at all?

SHAWN (*in great misery*): I'd be afeard to be jealous of a man did slay his da.

PEGEEN: Well, it'd be a poor thing to go marrying your like. I'm seeing there's a world of peril for an orphan girl, and isn't it a great blessing I didn't wed you, before himself came walking from the west or south?

SHAWN: It's a queer story you'd go picking a dirty tramp up from the highways of the world.

PEGEEN (*playfully*): And you think you're a likely beau to go straying along with, the shiny Sundays of the opening year, when it's sooner on a bullock's liver you'd put a poor girl thinking than on the lily or the rose?

SHAWN: And have you no mind of my weight of passion, and the holy dispensation, and the drift of heifers I am giving, and the golden ring?

PEGEEN: I'm thinking you're too fine for the like of me, Shawn Keogh of Killakeen, and let you go off till you'd find a radiant lady with droves of bullocks on the plains of Meath, and herself bedizened in the diamond jewelleries of Pharaoh's ma. That'd be your match, Shaneen. So God save you now! (*She retreats behind* CHRISTY.)

SHAWN: Won't you hear me telling you . . . ?

CHRISTY (*with ferocity*): Take yourself from this, young fellow, or I'll maybe add a murder to my deeds today.

MICHAEL (*springing up with a shriek*): Murder is it? Is it mad yous are? Would you go making murder in this place, and it piled with poteen for our drink tonight? Go on to the foreshore if it's fighting you want, where the rising tide will wash all traces from the memory of man. (*Pushing* SHAWN *towards* CHRISTY.)

SHAWN (*shaking himself free, and getting behind* MICHAEL): I'll not fight him, Michael James. I'd liefer live a bachelor, simmering in passions to the end of time, than face a lepping savage the like of him has descended from the Lord knows where. Strike him yourself, Michael James, or you'll lose my drift of heifers and my blue bull from Sneem.

MICHAEL: Is it me fight him, when it's father-slaying he's bred to now? (*Pushing* SHAWN) Go on you fool and fight him now.

SHAWN (*coming forward a little*): Will I strike him with my hand?

MICHAEL: Take the loy is on your western side.

SHAWN: I'd be afeard of the gallows if I struck him with that.

CHRISTY (*taking up the loy*): Then I'll make you face the gallows or quit off from this.

(SHAWN *flies out of the door*.)

CHRISTY: Well, fine weather be after him, (*going to* MICHAEL, *coaxingly*): and I'm thinking you wouldn't wish to have that quaking blackguard in your house at all. Let you give us your blessing and hear her swear her faith to me, for I'm mounted on the springtide of the stars of luck, the way it'll be good for any to have me in the house.

PEGEEN (*at the other side of* MICHAEL): Bless us now, for I swear to God I'll wed him, and I'll not renege.

MICHAEL (*standing up in the center, holding on to both of them*): It's the will of God, I'm thinking, that all should win an easy or a cruel end, and it's the will of God that all should rear up lengthy families for the nurture of the earth. What's a single man, I ask you, eating a bit in one house and drinking a sup in another, and he with no place of his own, like an old braying jackass strayed upon the rocks? (*To* CHRISTY) It's many would be in dread to bring your like into their house for to end them, maybe, with a sudden end; but I'm a decent man of Ireland, and I liefer face the grave untimely and I seeing a score of grandsons growing up little gallant swearers by the name of God, than go peopling my bedside with puny weeds the like of what you'd breed, I'm thinking, out of Shaneen Keogh. (*He joins their hands.*) A daring fellow is the jewel of the world, and a man did split his father's middle with a single clout, should have the bravery of ten, so may God and Mary and St. Patrick bless you, and increase you from this mortal day.

CHRISTY *and* PEGEEN:   Amen, O Lord!

(*Hubbub outside.* OLD MAHON *rushes in, followed by all the crowd, and* WIDOW QUIN. *He makes a rush at* CHRISTY, *knocks him down, and begins to beat him.*)

PEGEEN (*dragging back his arm*):   Stop that, will you. Who are you at all?

MAHON:   His father, God forgive me!

PEGEEN (*drawing back*):   Is it rose from the dead?

MAHON:   Do you think I look so easy quenched with the tap of a loy? (*Beats* CHRISTY *again.*)

PEGEEN (*glaring at* CHRISTY):   And it's lies you told, letting on you had him slitted, and you nothing at all.

CHRISTY (*catching* MAHON's *stick*):   He's not my father. He's a raving maniac would scare the world. (*Pointing to* WIDOW QUIN) Herself knows it is true.

CROWD:   You're fooling Pegeen! The Widow Quin seen him this day, and you likely knew! You're a liar!

CHRISTY (*dumbfounded*):   It's himself was a liar, lying stretched out with an open head on him, letting on he was dead.

MAHON:   Weren't you off racing the hills before I got my breath with the start I had seeing you turn on me at all?

PEGEEN:   And to think of the coaxing glory we had given him, and he after doing nothing but hitting a soft blow and chasing northward in a sweat of fear. Quit off from this.

CHRISTY (*piteously*):   You've seen my doings this day, and let you save me from the old man; for why would you be in such a scorch of haste to spur me to destruction now?

PEGEEN:   It's there your treachery is spurring me, till I'm hard set to think you're the one I'm after lacing in my heart-strings half-an-hour gone by. (*To* MAHON) Take him on from this, for I think bad the world should see me raging for a Munster liar, and the fool of men.

MAHON:   Rise up now to retribution, and come on with me.

CROWD (*jeeringly*):   There's the playboy! There's the lad thought he'd rule the roost in Mayo. Slate him now, mister.

CHRISTY (*getting up in shy terror*):   What is it drives you to torment me here, when I'd asked the thunders of the might of God to blast me if I ever did hurt to any saving only that one single blow.

MAHON (*loudly*):   If you didn't, you're a poor good-for-nothing, and isn't it by the like of you the sins of the whole world are committed?

CHRISTY (*raising his hands*):   In the name of the Almighty God. . . .

MAHON:   Leave troubling the Lord God. Would you have him sending down droughts, and fevers, and the old hen and the cholera morbus?

CHRISTY (*to* WIDOW QUIN):   Will you come between us and protect me now?

WIDOW QUIN:   I've tried a lot, God help me, and my share is done.

CHRISTY (*looking round in desperation*):   And I must go back into my torment is it, or run off like a vagabond straying through the Unions with the dusts of August making mudstains in the gullet of my throat, or the winds of March blowing on me till I'd take an oath I felt them making whistles of my ribs within?

SARA:   Ask Pegeen to aid you. Her like does often change.

CHRISTY:   I will not then, for there's torment in the splendor of her like, and she a girl any moon of midnight would take pride to meet, facing southwards on the heaths of Keel. But what did I want crawling forward to scorch my understanding at her flaming brow?

PEGEEN (*to* MAHON, *vehemently, fearing she will break into tears*): Take him on from this or I'll set the young lads to destroy him here.

MAHON (*going to him, shaking his stick*): Come on now if you wouldn't have the company to see you skelped.

PEGEEN (*half laughing, through her tears*): That's it, now the world will see him pandied, and he an ugly liar was playing off the hero, and the fright of men.

CHRISTY (*to* MAHON, *very sharply*): Leave me go!

CROWD: That's it. Now Christy. If them two set fighting, it will lick the world.

MAHON (*making a grab at* CHRISTY): Come here to me.

CHRISTY (*more threateningly*): Leave me go, I'm saying.

MAHON: I will maybe, when your legs is limping, and your back is blue.

CROWD: Keep it up, the two of you. I'll back the old one. Now the playboy.

CHRISTY (*in low and intense voice*): Shut your yelling, for if you're after making a mighty man of me this day by the power of a lie, you're setting me now to think if it's a poor thing to be lonesome, it's worse maybe to go mixing with the fools of earth.

(MAHON *makes a movement towards him.*)

CHRISTY (*almost shouting*): Keep off . . . lest I do show a blow unto the lot of you would set the guardian angels winking in the clouds above. (*He swings round with a sudden rapid movement and picks up a loy.*)

CROWD (*half frightened, half amused*): He's going mad! Mind yourselves! Run from the idiot!

CHRISTY: If I am an idiot, I'm after hearing my voice this day saying words would raise the topknot on a poet in a merchant's town. I've won your racing, and your lepping, and . . .

MAHON: Shut your gullet and come on with me.

CHRISTY: I'm going, but I'll stretch you first.

(*He runs at old* MAHON *with the loy, chases him out of the door, followed by* CROWD *and* WIDOW QUIN. *There is a great noise outside, then a yell, and dead silence for a moment.* CHRISTY *comes in, half dazed, and goes to fire.*)

WIDOW QUIN (*coming in, hurriedly, and going to him*): They're turning again you. Come on, or you'll be hanged, indeed.

CHRISTY: I'm thinking, from this out, Pegeen'll be giving me praises the same as in the hours gone by.

WIDOW QUIN (*impatiently*): Come by the back door. I'd think bad to have you stifled on the gallows tree.

CHRISTY (*indignantly*): I will not, then. What good'd be my life-time, if I left Pegeen?

WIDOW QUIN: Come on, and you'll be no worse than you were last night; and you with a double murder this time to be telling to the girls.

CHRISTY: I'll not leave Pegeen Mike.

WIDOW QUIN (*impatiently*): Isn't there the match of her in every parish public, from Binghamstown unto the plain of Meath? Come on, I tell you, and I'll find you finer sweethearts at each waning moon.

CHRISTY: It's Pegeen I'm seeking only, and what'd I care if you brought me a drift of chosen females, standing in their shifts itself, maybe, from this place to the Eastern World?

SARA (*runs in, pulling off one of her petticoats*): They're going to hang him. (*Holding out petticoat and shawl*) Fit these upon him, and let him run off to the east.

WIDOW QUIN: He's raving now; but we'll fit them on him, and I'll take him, in the ferry, to the Achill boat.

CHRISTY (*struggling feebly*): Leave me go, will you? When I'm thinking of my luck today, for she will wed me surely, and I a proven hero in the end of all.

(*They try to fasten petticoat round him.*)

WIDOW QUIN: Take his left hand, and we'll pull him now. Come on, young fellow.

CHRISTY (*suddenly starting up*): You'll be taking me from her? You're jealous, is it, of her wedding me? Go on from this. (*He snatches up a stool, and threatens them with it.*)

WIDOW QUIN (*going*): It's in the mad-house they should put him, not in jail, at all. We'll go by the back door, to call the doctor, and we'll save him so.

(*She goes out, with* SARA, *through inner room. Men crowd in the doorway.* CHRISTY *sits down again by the fire.*)

MICHAEL (*in a terrified whisper*): Is the old lad killed surely?

PHILLY: I'm after feeling the last gasps quitting his heart.

(*They peer in at* CHRISTY.)

MICHAEL (*with a rope*): Look at the way he is. Twist a hangman's knot on it, and slip it over his head, while he's not minding at all.

PHILLY: Let you take it, Shaneen. You're the soberest of all that's here.

SHAWN: Is it me to go near him, and he the wickedest and worst with me? Let you take it, Pegeen Mike.

PEGEEN: Come on, so.

(*She goes forward with the others, and they drop the double hitch over his head.*)

CHRISTY: What ails you?

SHAWN (*triumphantly, as they pull the rope tight on his arms*): Come on to the peelers, till they stretch you now.

CHRISTY: Me!

MICHAEL: If we took pity on you, the Lord God would, maybe, bring us ruin from the law today, so you'd best come easy, for hanging is an easy and a speedy end.

CHRISTY: I'll not stir. (*To* PEGEEN) And what is it you'll say to me, and I after doing it this time in the face of all?

PEGEEN: I'll say, a strange man is a marvel, with his mighty talk; but what's a squabble in your back yard, and the blow of a loy, have taught me that there's a great gap between a gallous story and a dirty deed. (*To* MEN) Take him on from this, or the lot of us will be likely put on trial for his deed today.

CHRISTY (*with horror in his voice*): And it's yourself will send me off, to have a horny-fingered hangman hitching his bloody slipknots at the butt of my ear.

MEN (*pulling rope*): Come on, will you?

(*He is pulled down on the floor.*)

CHRISTY (*twisting his legs round the table*): Cut the rope, Pegeen, and I'll quit the lot of you, and live from this out, like the madmen of Keel, eating muck and green weeds, on the faces of the cliffs.

PEGEEN: And leave us to hang, is it, for a saucy liar, the like of you? (*To* MEN) Take him on, out from this.

SHAWN: Pull a twist on his neck, and squeeze him so.

PHILLY: Twist yourself. Sure he cannot hurt you, if you keep your distance from his teeth alone.

SHAWN: I'm afeard of him. (*To* PEGEEN) Lift a lighted sod, will you, and scorch his leg.

PEGEEN (*blowing the fire, with a bellows*):

Leave go now, young fellow, or I'll scorch your shins.

CHRISTY: You're blowing for to torture me. (*His voice rising and growing stronger*) That's your kind, is it? Then let the lot of you be wary, for, if I've to face the gallows, I'll have a gay march down, I tell you, and shed the blood of some of you before I die.

SHAWN (*in terror*): Keep a good hold, Philly. Be wary, for the love of God. For I'm thinking he would liefest wreak his pains on me.

CHRISTY (*almost gaily*): If I do lay my hands on you, it's the way you'll be at the fall of night, hanging as a scarecrow for the fowls of hell. Ah, you'll have a gallous jaunt I'm saying, coaching out through Limbo with my father's ghost.

SHAWN (*to* PEGEEN): Make haste, will you? Oh, isn't he a holy terror, and isn't it true for Father Reilly, that all drink's a curse that has the lot of you so shaky and uncertain now?

CHRISTY: If I can wring a neck among you, I'll have a royal judgment looking on the trembling jury in the courts of law. And won't there be crying out in Mayo the day I'm stretched upon the rope with ladies in their silks and satins snivelling in their lacy kerchiefs, and they rhyming songs and ballads on the terror of my fate? (*He squirms round on the floor and bites* SHAWN's *leg.*)

SHAWN (*shrieking*): My leg's bit on me. He's the like of a mad dog, I'm thinking, the way that I will surely die.

CHRISTY (*delighted with himself*): You will then, the way you can shake out hell's flags of welcome for my coming in two weeks or three, for I'm thinking Satan hasn't many have killed their da in Kerry, and in Mayo too.

(OLD MAHON *comes in behind on all fours and looks on unnoticed.*)

MEN (*to* PEGEEN): Bring the sod, will you?

PEGEEN (*coming over*): God help him so. (*Burns his leg.*)

CHRISTY (*kicking and screaming*): O, glory be to God!

(*He kicks loose from the table, and they all drag him towards the door.*)

JIMMY (*seeing old* MAHON): Will you look what's come in?

(*They all drop* CHRISTY *and run left.*)

CHRISTY (*scrambling on his knees face to face with old* MAHON): Are you coming to be killed a third time, or what ails you now?

MAHON: For what is it they have you tied?

CHRISTY: They're taking me to the peelers to have me hanged for slaying you.

MICHAEL (*apologetically*): It is the will of God that all should guard their little cabins from the treachery of law, and what would my daughter be doing if I was ruined or was hanged itself?

MAHON (*grimly, loosening* CHRISTY): It's little I care if you put a bag on her back, and went picking cockles till the hour of death; but my son and myself will be going our own way, and we'll have great times from this out telling stories of the villainy of Mayo, and the fools is here. (*To* CHRISTY, *who is freed*) Come on now.

CHRISTY: Go with you, is it? I will then, like a gallant captain with his heathen slave. Go on now and I'll see you from this day stewing my oatmeal and washing my spuds, for I'm master of all fights from now. (*Pushing* MAHON) Go on, I'm saying.

MAHON: Is it me?

CHRISTY: Not a word out of you. Go on from this.

MAHON (*walking out and looking back at* CHRISTY *over his shoulder*): Glory be to God! (*With a broad smile*) I am crazy again! (*Goes.*)

CHRISTY: Ten thousand blessings upon all that's here, for you've turned me a likely gaffer in the end of all, the way I'll go romancing through a romping lifetime from this hour to the drawing of the judgment day. (*He goes out.*)

MICHAEL: By the will of God, we'll have peace now for our drinks. Will you draw the porter, Pegeen?

SHAWN (*going up to her*): It's a miracle Father Reilly can wed us in the end of all, and we'll have none to trouble us when his vicious bite is healed.

PEGEEN (*hitting him a box on the ear*): Quit my sight. (*Putting her shawl over her head and breaking out into wild lamentations*): Oh my grief, I've lost him surely. I've lost the only Playboy of the Western World.

# AUGUST STRINDBERG

# The Stronger

TRANSLATION BY ANTS ORAS

August Strindberg (1849–1912) was one of the most influential dramatists of the late nineteenth century. Born in Stockholm, Sweden, he was the fourth in a family of eleven children, and his life, from the beginning, was filled with poverty, hardship, and fear. In 1867 he spent a term at the University of Upsala; then he briefly attended the University of Stockholm, left to try teaching and acting, but soon returned to study literature and science. Finally King Charles XV of Sweden gave him a financial reward for one of his plays, and he left the university for a writing career. Although his first full-length play, *Master Olof*, was rejected by publishers, he received for it an appointment to the Royal Library, where he read, studied Chinese, and wrote his first novel. Many short stories, novels, and plays followed. Among his most influential plays are *The Father*, 1887; *Miss Julie*, 1888; *There Are Crimes and Crimes*, 1898; and *A Dream Play*, 1902.

THE STRONGER    Reprinted by permission of Ants Oras.

Although Strindberg began by writing realistic drama, he moved to the naturalistic and finally to the symbolistic. He became preoccupied with innovation in the structure of drama, reducing the amount of exposition included, relying more and more on dialogue to present the psychological conflict, and abolishing the division of the play into acts.

*The Stronger*, 1889, which represents a breaking away from the conventional dramatic form, displays Strindberg's concern with the presentation of psychological conflict through dialogue alone and with the reduction of a play's structure to its simplest form, the brief monologue.

*PERSONS*

MME. X, *actress, married*
MLLE. Y, *actress, single*
A WAITRESS

*A corner in a ladies' café; two small iron tables, a red velvet sofa and some chairs.* MME. X *enters in winter clothing, wearing a hat and a cloak and carrying a fine Japanese basket on her arm.* MLLE. Y *sits with a half-empty beer bottle in front of her, reading an illustrated paper, then changing it for another.*

MME. X:  How are you, little Amelie?—You're sitting alone here on Christmas Eve like a disconsolate old bachelor.

(MLLE. Y *looks up from the paper, nods, goes on reading.*)

MME. X:  You know, I am heartily sorry to see you like this, alone, all alone in a café on Christmas Eve. I feel quite as sorry as that evening in a Paris restaurant when I saw a bridal party, with the bride sitting and reading a comic paper and the groom playing billiards with the witnesses. Goodness, I thought, with such a beginning how is this to continue and to end!

He played billiards on his wedding evening!—Yes, and she read a comic paper! Well, but that is hardly the same situation as here.

(*The* WAITRESS *enters, places a cup of hot chocolate before* MME. X *and goes out.*)

MME. X:  I tell you what, Amelie! Now I really believe you would have done better to have kept him. Remember, I was the first to urge you "Forgive him!" Don't you recall it?—You could have been married to him, with a home of your own. Don't you remember last Christmas, how happy you felt out in the country with your fiancé's parents; how you praised the happiness of a home and how you longed to get away from the theater?—Yes, darling Amelie, a home is the best of all things—next to the theater—a home and some brats too—but that you wouldn't understand.

(MLLE. Y *looks contemptuous.*)

MME. X (*drinks a few spoonfuls from her cup, opens her basket and shows her Christmas presents*):  Now you'll see what I've bought for my piglets. (*Shows a doll*) Look at this. This is for Lisa. Look how it rolls its eyes and turns its neck. There! And here is Maja's pop gun. (*Loads it and shoots at* MLLE. Y.)

(MLLE. Y *makes a scared gesture.*)

MME. X:  Did this startle you? Did you fear I'd shoot you? What?—Good heavens, I don't believe you could possibly have thought that. I'd be less surprised if you were shooting me, since I got in your way—I know you can't forget that—although I was completely innocent. You still believe I eased you out of the theater with my intrigues, but I didn't! I didn't, even though you think I did!—But what is the use of telling you, for you still believe I did it. (*Takes out a pair of embroidered slippers*) And these are for my old man. With tulips embroidered by myself—I abhor tulips, you understand, but he wants tulips on everything.

(MLLE. Y *looks up from her paper, ironically and with some curiosity.*)

MME. X (*puts a hand in each slipper*):  Look how small Bob's feet are. Well? And you ought to see how daintily he walks. You've never seen him in his slippers.

(MLLE. Y *laughs aloud.*)

MME. X:  Look, I'll show you. (*Makes the slippers walk along the table.*)

(MLLE. Y *laughs aloud.*)

MME. X:  Now look, and when he is out of sorts he stamps with his foot like this. "What! Damn those servants, they'll never learn how to make coffee! Goodness! Now those morons haven't clipped the lamp wick properly." And then there's a draught from the floor and his feet freeze: "Blast it, how cold it is, and these unspeakable idiots can't keep the fire going." (*Rubs one slipper's sole against the other's upper.*)

(MLLE. Y *bursts out laughing.*)

MME. X:  And then he comes home and has

to search for his slippers, which Marie has put under the chiffonier . . . Oh, but it is sinful to sit thus and make a fool of one's old man. Whatever he is, he is nice, a decent little fellow—you ought to've had such a husband, Amelie.—Why are you laughing? Why? Why?—And look here, I know he is faithful to me; yes, I do know that, for he told me himself . . . What are you grinning at? . . . When I was on my Norway tour, that nasty Frédérique came and tried to seduce him—Could you imagine such an infamy? (*Pause.*) But I'd have scratched out her eyes if she'd come near me after my return! (*Pause.*) What a good thing Bob told me about it himself rather than let me hear it through gossip! (*Pause.*) But Frédérique was not the only one, believe me! I don't know why, but the women are positively crazy about my husband—perhaps they think he has some say about theater engagements because he is in the government department!—Who knows but you yourself may have been chasing him!—I never trusted you more than just so much—but now I do know he doesn't care for you, and I always thought you were bearing him some grudge.

(*Pause. They view each other, both embarrassed.*)

MME. X:    Come to see us in the evening, Amelie, and show you aren't cross with us, at least not with me! I don't know why, but it is so uncomfortable to be at loggerheads with you, of all people. Possibly because I got in your way that time—(*rallentando*) or—I just don't know why in particular!

(*Pause.* MLLE. Y *gazes curiously at* MME. X.)

MME. X (*pensively*):    Our acquaintance was such an odd one—when I first saw you I was afraid of you, so afraid that I couldn't risk letting you out of my sight; whenever I came or went I was always near you—I couldn't afford to have you for an enemy, so I became your friend. But there was always something discordant in the air when you came to our home, for I saw my husband couldn't stand you—it all felt somehow awkward, like ill-fitting clothes—and I did what I could to make him take to you but to no purpose—until you got yourself engaged to be married! Then a violent friendship flared up so that for a moment it looked as though the two of you had only now ventured to show your real feelings because you were safe—and so what?—What happened?—I wasn't jealous—how queer!—And I recall the christening when

you stood godmother to our baby—I made Bob kiss you—and he did, but you were so confused—that is to say, I didn't notice at the time—haven't thought about it since—not once until—this moment. (*Gets up furiously.*)

Why are you silent? You haven't said a word all this time, you've only let me sit and talk. You've been sitting and staring and making me unwind all these thoughts which lay like raw silk in their cocoon—thoughts—maybe suspicious ones—let me see.—Why did you break off your engagement? Why haven't you been to our house since that happened? Why aren't you coming to see us tonight?

(MLLE. Y *seems on the point of speaking.*)

MME. X:    Be quiet! You needn't say a word, for now I grasp it all myself. It was because—because—because!—Yes indeed!—Every bit of it falls into its place! That's it!—Shame! Shame! I won't sit at the same table with you. (*Moves her things to the other table.*)

So that was why I had to embroider tulips on his slippers although I hate tulips—because you like them! That was why—(*throws the slippers on the floor*)—that was why we had to spend the summer on Lake Mälar—because you couldn't bear the sea at Saltsiö; that was why my son had to be christened Eskil—because such was the name of your father; that was why I had to wear your colors, read your authors, eat your favorite dishes, drink your drinks—your chocolate, for example; that was why—Oh, my God—this is frightful to think of, frightful!—Everything came from you to me, even your passions and addictions!—Your soul slithered into mine like a worm into an apple, eating and eating, digging and digging, until all that was left was a rind with some black, messy substance inside! I wanted to escape from you but couldn't; you lay like a snake bewitching me with your black eyes—I felt how my wings rose only to drag me down; I lay with tied feet in the water, and the harder my hands struck out, the more I worked myself down, down right to the bottom where you lay like an enormous crab in order to grip me with your claws—and this is where I now am.

Shame, shame! How I hate you, how I hate you, how I hate you! Yet you only sit, silent, calm, uncaring; not caring whether the moon is waxing or waning, whether it is Christmas or New Year's, whether people are happy or unhappy; incapable of love or hatred; rigid like a stork over a mousehole—unable to grab your quarry, unable to chase it, yet well able to wait until it comes into your clutches. Here you sit in your corner—do you know that it is because of you that it's called the Rat-trap?—Here you scan your paper to find out whether anybody has got into trouble or is wretched or must give up the theater; here you sit, watching out for victims, calculating your chances like a pilot planning a shipwreck, and collecting your tribute!

Poor Amelie, do you know that I pity you because you are unhappy, unhappy like a hurt beast and full of malice because you are hurt?—I can't feel angry with you although I would like to—you are the cornered one after all—well yes, that affair with Bob, why should I bother about it?—In what way does it harm me?—And whether it was you or somebody else who taught me to drink chocolate, what of it? (*Drinks a spoonful from her cup; knowingly*) After all, chocolate is good for one's health. And if I learned from you how to dress—*tant mieux*—that only strengthened my husband's affection for me—and so you lost what I won—Yes, there are indications that you really have lost him. Yet of course you intended me to fade out of the picture—as you have done, sitting here as you do and regretting what you did—but look here, I just won't do it!—We shan't be petty, don't you agree? And why should I take only what no one else wants!

Perhaps, all things considered, I may indeed be the stronger—for you never got anything out of me, you only gave—and now I am like that thief—as you woke up you found I had all the things you missed.

How else could it come about that everything turned worthless and barren in your hand? With all your tulips and fine affections you never managed to keep a man's love—as I have done; you never learned the art of living from your writers, as I did; nor did you ever get any little Eskil of your own, even though Eskil is the name of your father!

And why are you always silent, silent, silent? Yes, I mistook this for strength; but perhaps all it meant was that you hadn't anything to say— that you never were able to think a thought. (*Gets up and takes the slippers from the floor*) Now I'm going home—with the tulips—*your* tulips! You were unable to learn anything from people—unable to bend—and so you snapped like a dry stalk—but I won't snap.

Thanks ever so much, Amelie, for all your kind lessons; thanks for teaching my husband how to love! Now I'm going home to love him. (*Goes.*)

Poetry

Bingham

Poetry is a form of literature that many readers hold in a special kind of affectionate admiration. From the earliest times, probably even before the time of recorded language, poets have been the oracles and prophets of their peoples. Poets have always reflected the temper of the ages in which they live: Homer epitomizes a glorious epoch in Greek history, as Hardy epitomizes the perplexity and despair of late Victorian England.

*The nature of poetry.* Poetry cannot be precisely defined, but some of its distinguishing characteristics can be described. Poetry deals in matters beyond direct statement—in meanings conditioned by emotional attitudes—and its intention is to evoke the full flavor and impact of experience. Poetry often achieves its effects by the selection of words that are suggestive not only of sensory experience but of emotional attitudes, by the use of figurative comparisons, and by rime and rhythm. Finally, the most distinctive feature of poetry is the organic quality achieved by the close organization of its component parts. The poet in a sense is a maker of experiences. (The Old English word for poet is *scop*, "the maker.") Life is so cluttered with detail that to most of us it often seems chaotic. Like other artists, the poet discards the confusing detail, selects and arranges the remainder to communicate his impression, and thereby creates a meaningful experience for his reader.

What one receives from a poem, then, is an experience. I. A. Richards, perhaps the most stimulating of the contemporary critics of poetry, has pointed out that a poem has a "Total Meaning" which is a blend of the poet's *sense* (what the poem is apparently about), his *feeling* (the poet's attitude toward his subject matter), his *tone* (attitude toward his reader), and his *intention* (aim, or effect). A poet is more or less aware of this fact and, as he writes, expresses all the meanings as fully as his ability and his medium will permit. The reader, in turn, will profit by considering all of them when trying to arrive at a full realization of a poem.

Consider, for example, the following occasional poem by Thomas Hardy, "On an Invitation to the United States." [1]

[1]Reprinted with permission of the publisher from *Collected Poems* by Thomas Hardy. Copyright 1925 by The Macmillan Company.

My ardours for emprize nigh lost
Since life has bared its bones to me,
I shrink to seek a modern coast
Whose riper times have yet to be;
For, wonning in these ancient lands,
Enchased and lettered as a tomb,
And scored with prints of perished
　　hands,
And chronicled with dates of doom,

Where the new regions claim them
　　free
From that long drip of human tears
Which peoples old in tragedy
Have left upon the centuried years.
Though my own Being bear no bloom
I trace the lives such scenes enshrine,
Give past exemplars present room,
And their experience count as mine.

Obviously, the poem is about Hardy's declining an invitation to visit the United States—his reaction to an invitation to come to a land with a more promising future but a less historic past. But statement of the *sense* of the poem is not the equivalent of the poem. In fact, even the following full paraphrase of the sense of the poem falls far short of the poem itself: "I have almost lost my taste for adventure since I discovered how grim life is; I hesitate to seek a new country that has not yet reached full fruition, and has not had a tragic-storied past. Living in this old land, which is much like a tombstone with its inscriptions, I—even though I do not prosper personally—study the lives of the great people of England's history and consider their experience as mine."

For full comprehension we need to absorb the poet's *feeling* about the material. Hardy presents that feeling by implying a contrast between the pasts of the United States and England and by suggesting a relationship between his own past and that of his country. He hints some mild doubt of the United States—a country raw and untried by a long history of adversities and tribulations, though perhaps with a promising future. Just as indirectly he communicates, without sentimentality, his love of England by imagery that pictures her long and tragic history, full of adversities, trials, and struggles; and he makes clear his desire to share what he feels is England's unhappy lot.

We need also to grasp his *tone*, or his attitude toward his reader. His tone, like his feeling, is complex, for, though he is addressing himself particularly to the people of the United States, the people who extended to him the invitation that occasioned the poem, in the background he includes among his audience English compatriots. With neither condescension to the inviters nor depreciation of the worth of their regard, he courteously declines. Though he reminds his background audience, the English, of their mournful history, and indirectly rededicates them as well as himself to his resolve to endure and to be proud of enduring, he steers as widely clear of national conceit and chauvinism as he does of a defensive attitude that would be uncomfortable to English and American alike.

Hardy's full poetic *intention* is to comment feelingly on the individual's relation to his country's history and on his goal in life. Furthermore, he intends to imply the judgment that to assume a share of the unhappy human lot may be a greater act than to achieve purely personal well-being, the attitude of a true pessimist.

The total meaning of "On an Invitation to the United States," therefore, depends on its *sense*, *feeling*, *tone*, and *intention*. Briefly, Hardy says that he cannot accept the invitation, acknowledges the favorable prospects of America and expresses his love of England, shows to those who invited him a courteous but not deferential appreciation, and takes the opportunity to comment on the value of tradition. In other words, the communication of this complex meaning provides an experience for the reader, an experience which *is* the poem.

*The method of poetry.* As "On an Invitation to the United States" reveals, there is more to a poem than the *sense* which can be translated into direct prose statement or paraphrase. Poets characteristically communicate by suggestion or implication; that is, they say more than their words and word combinations literally mean. Perhaps *indirection* is the best term to summarize the way by which poets say so much in so few words.

DICTION.    The words of poetry are for the most part the same words that people use to carry on the plain business of living. Individually those words stand for about the same things and have approximately the same sounds in poems as they have in everyday speech. But in poetry words are used more precisely and are ordered more carefully than in conversation. Moreover, a poem does not depend solely upon denotative meanings of words; what the words suggest—their connotative rather than their denotative values—may be even more important to its effect. Consider the implications of some of the words in "On an Invitation to the United States": *modern, riper, emprize, wonning.* In context *modern* has just a slightly unfavorable overtone; it suggests, though faintly, that Hardy had in mind an overmodernity, an excessive degree of modernity. Much the same is true of the word *riper* in its context here: Hardy seems to imply that the United States is presently lacking the maturity he cherishes in England. *Emprize* and *wonning* are also highly implicative words. Their effect here is to promote, by supplying atmosphere, Hardy's intention of getting the reader to understand and approve his cherishing of the past. Both are archaic—*emprize* having been supplanted by the modern form *enterprise* or *adventure;* and *wonning,* by *dwelling, residing, living.* By using these archaisms along with such other words as *old, centuried, ancient, chronicled, dates of doom,* Hardy reminds the reader of Norse and Norman invaders, the Anglo-Saxon Chronicle, Alfred and Harold, the Domesday Book, and Runnymede and Magna Charta.

IMAGERY.    The selection of language in poetry is governed primarily by the poet's desire to give his reader sensory experience—as Coleridge says, "to instill that energy into the mind, which compels the imagination to produce the picture." By appealing to one or more of the physical senses, the poet arouses both the mind and the emotion of the reader so that he in a measure experiences physical sensation. These things imaginatively sensed are collectively known as *imagery.*

THE CONCRETE WORD.    Doubtless the simplest device to evoke imagery is the single concrete word, a word such as *scored* or *chronicled* in Hardy's poem. Hardy might have written *marked* "with prints of perished hands" instead of "*scored* with prints of perished hands." But he chose *scored* because it supplies to the reader's imagination the image Hardy desired, that of signs much deeper and more permanent than mere surface "marks." So with *chronicled.* Hardy chose a word to suggest a whole complex of meaning, the Anglo-Saxon Chronicle and even England's whole history.

FIGURATIVE LANGUAGE.    Another device poets use to create imagery is figurative language. Basically, most figures are comparisons, expressed or implied, of things not ordinarily thought of as being alike—comparisons that do not on the surface seem logical but that on closer inspection prove illuminating. For instance, Hardy says "life has bared its bones to me." He is using a *metaphor* here, an implied comparison that not only suggests his interpretation of the true character of life, but vividly reveals Hardy's state of mind. Again, Hardy, in a *simile*, directly compares England to a tomb—"ancient lands,/Enchased and lettered as a tomb." Thus he suggests to the reader the richness of England's past—the multitude of deeds and personages that make up England's history. As the inscriptions on tombs record the deeds and exploits (as well as the vital statistics) of the persons buried in the tombs, so England is filled with places, monuments, and shrines that recall the richness of her past.

RHYTHM AND RIME.    Another kind of indirection prominent in the method of poetry is the use of sound effects to intensify meaning. Along with the attempt to communicate his total meaning by choosing words and images which convey his sense, feeling, and tone, the poet attempts to organize his words into a pattern of sound that is a part of that total meaning. The sound of poetry, then, like the diction and the imagery, is to be considered only in relation to the total design of the poem.

Sound effects are the products of organized repetitions. *Rhythm* is the result of systematically *stressing* or *accenting* words and syllables, whereas *rime* repeats similar sounds in some apparent scheme. Both rhythm and rime arouse interest in the reader, for as soon as he grasps their pattern he unconsciously expects them to continue. Expecting their continuation, he is more attentive not only to the sound itself but to the sense, feeling, and tone of the poet.

Different rhythms tend to arouse different emotions.

> Scots, wha hae wi' Wallace bled,
> Scots, wham Bruce has aften led,
> Welcome to your gory bed,
>   Or to victory!
>
> Now's the day, and now's the hour:
> See the front o' battle lour;
> See approach proud Edward's power—
>   Chains and slavery![2]

The rhythmic beat here, along with the sense of the words, sounds a grim, determined battle cry and stirs the reader to a quicker beating of the blood.

> They sat them down upon the yellow sand,
> Between the sun and moon upon the shore;
> And sweet it was to dream of Fatherland,
> Of child, and wife, and slave; but evermore
> Most weary seemed the sea, weary the oar,
> Weary the wandering fields of barren foam.

[2] From "Scots, Wha Hae wi' Wallace Bled" by Robert Burns.

Then some one said, "We will return no more;"
And all at once they sang, "Our island home
Is far beyond the wave; we will no longer roam." [3]

Here the rhythm, aided by the heavy frequency of liquids and nasals, helps to induce in the reader a sense of the dreaminess and lack of ambition that, according to the myth, characterized all those who ate the lotus.

Rhythms exist for the full gamut of emotions, since the only limitation upon the variety of rhythms is that which word-meaning imposes. Thus rhythms can easily be found for those quieter emotions accompanying meditation and reflection:

"A cold coming we had of it,
Just the worst time of the year
For a journey, and such a long journey:
The ways deep and the weather sharp,
The very dead of winter."
And the camels galled, sore-footed, refractory,
Lying down in the melting snow. [4]

This rhythm is less patterned than the preceding two. The poet here has departed from a strict rhythmic movement much more frequently and prominently than has either of the two preceding poets. These departures, while preserving a reflective mood, make for informality and a conversational tone. Variation from a rigid metrical pattern is often found in poetry, especially in modern poetry.

Rime—a patterned recurrence of like or similar sounds—also functions indirectly to intensify meaning. It is a further impressing of design upon material in order to achieve an intention in sense, feeling, and tone. It serves as a binding and unifying element and lends continuity. It may also be used for emphasis, especially when, as often occurs, the rime word at the end of a line concludes a phrase or clause. And rime, like rhythm, affords pleasure at the fulfillment of a pattern the reader has unconsciously recognized. When Tennyson writes

They sat them down upon the yellow sand,

the reader recognizes the likelihood that Tennyson will somewhere, perhaps in the very next line, come back to a sound similar to the one on which he stopped the first, and is pleased when he finds that expectation fulfilled:

They sat them down upon the yellow sand,
Between the sun and moon upon the shore;
And sweet it was to dream of Fatherland.

Closely allied to metrical and rime pattern are a number of textural devices— devices that are similar to rime in that they involve correspondence of sounds. These

[3] From "The Lotos-Eaters" by Alfred, Lord Tennyson. See pages 274–75.
[4] From "Journey of the Magi" by T. S. Eliot. See page 263 for the full text.

devices tend to occur within the line unit of poetry but affect the total sound pattern. *Alliteration, assonance, consonance* give ease and speed to pronunciation, stepping up melody and tempo. Such pleasantness of sound is called euphony. Not always, however, is euphony desirable. In fact, cacophony, its opposite, may better achieve the poet's intention. For instance, in Eliot's line

And the camels galled, sore-footed, refractory

the last three words, *galled, sore-footed, refractory,* cause a sense of strain and slowing of tempo appropriate to the experience he is describing.

The nature of poetry and the method of poetry are so dependent upon each other that one cannot be conceived without the other. Their relationship is organic; it is not a mere mechanical association. In other words, the way of saying a thing is a large part of what is said. A poem does much more than say or state. It transmutes sense, feeling, tone, and intention into experience, into being itself.

# THE POET AS STORYTELLER

ANONYMOUS

## Brennan on the Moor

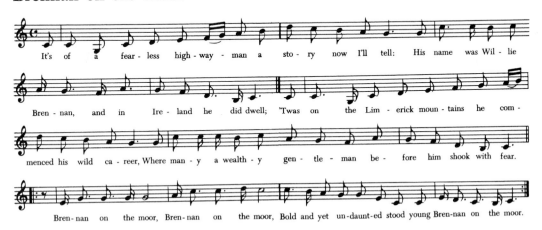

It's of a fearless high-way-man a sto-ry now I'll tell: His name was Wil-lie Bren-nan, and in Ire-land he did dwell; 'Twas on the Lim-erick moun-tains he com-menced his wild ca-reer, Where man-y a wealth-y gen-tle-man be-fore him shook with fear. Bren-nan on the moor, Bren-nan on the moor, Bold and yet un-daunt-ed stood young Bren-nan on the moor.

It's of a fearless highwayman a story now I'll
tell:
His name was Willie Brennan, and in Ireland
he did dwell;
'Twas on the Limerick mountains he
commenced his wild career,
Where many a wealthy gentleman before him
shook with fear.
*Brennan on the moor, Brennan on the moor,*
*Bold and yet undaunted stood young Brennan*
*on the moor.*

A brace of loaded pistols he carried night and
day,
He never robb'd a poor man upon the King's
highway;
But what he'd taken from the rich, like Turpin
and Black Bess,
He always did divide it with the widow in
distress.                                                    10

One night he robbed a packman, his name was
Pedlar Bawn;
They travelled on together, till day began to
dawn;
The pedlar seeing his money gone, likewise his
watch and chain,

He at once encountered Brennan and robbed
him back again.

When Brennan saw the pedlar was as good a
man as he,
He took him on the highway, his companion for
to be;
The pedlar threw away his pack without any
more delay,
And proved a faithful comrade until his dying
day.

One day upon the highway Willie he sat down,
He met the Mayor of Cashel, a mile outside the
town;                                                           20
The Mayor he knew his features, "I think,
young man," said he,
"Your name is Willie Brennan, you must come
along with me."

As Brennan's wife had gone to town provisions
for to buy,
When she saw her Willie, she began to weep
and cry;
He says, "Give me that tenpence"; as soon as
Willie spoke,
She handed him the blunderbuss from
underneath her cloak.

Then with his loaded blunderbuss, the truth I
  will unfold,
He made the Mayor to tremble, and robbed
  him of his gold;
One hundred pounds was offered for his
  apprehension there,
And with his horse and saddle to the mountains
  did repair.                                              30

Then Brennan being an outlaw upon the
  mountain high,
Where cavalry and infantry to take him they
  did try,
He laughed at them with scorn, until at length,
  it's said,
By a false-hearted young man he was basely
  betrayed.

In the County of Tipperary, in a place they
  called Clonmore,
Willie Brennan and his comrade that day did
  suffer sore;
He lay among the fern which was thick upon
  the field,
And nine wounds he had received before that
  he did yield.

Then Brennan and his companion knowing they
  were betrayed,
He with the mounted cavalry a noble battle
  made;                                                    40
He lost his foremost finger, which was shot off
  by a ball;
So Brennan and his comrade they were taken
  after all.

So they were taken prisoners, in irons they were
  bound,
And conveyed to Clonmel jail, strong walls did
  them surround;
They were tried and found guilty, the judge
  made this reply,
"For robbing on the King's highway you are
  both condemned to die."

Farewell unto my wife, and to my children
  three,
Likewise my aged father, he may shed tears
  for me,
And to my loving mother, who tore her gray
  locks and cried,
Saying, "I wish, Willie Brennan, in your cradle
  you had died."                                           50

ANONYMOUS

# The Three Ravens

There were three ravens sat on a tree,
  Downe a downe, hay downe, hay downe.
There were three ravens sat on a tree,
  With a downe.

There were three ravens sat on a tree,
They were as blacke as they might be.
  With a downe derrie, derrie, derrie, downe,
    downe.

The one of them said to his mate,
"Where shall we our breakfast take?"

"Downe in yonder greene field,                             10
There lies a knight slain under his shield.

"His hounds they lie downe at his feete,
So well they can their master keepe.

"His haukes they flie so eagerly,
There's no fowle dare him come nie."

Downe there comes a fallow doe,
As great with yong as she might goe.

She lift up his bloudy hed,
And kist his wounds that were so red.

She got him up upon her backe,                             20
And carried him to earthen lake.[1]

She buried him before the prime,
She was dead herselfe ere euen-song time.

God send every gentleman,
Such haukes, such hounds, and such a leman.[2]

ANONYMOUS

# The Twa Corbies

As I was walking all alane,
I heard twa corbies making a mane;[3]
The tane[4] unto the t'other say,
"Where sall we gang[5] and dine today?"

[1]pit.    [2]lover.    [3]moan.    [4]one.    [5]go.

"In behint yon auld fail dyke,[6]
I wot[7] there lies a new slain knight;
And naebody kens[8] that he lies there
But his hawk, his hound, and lady fair.

"His hound is to the hunting gane,
His hawk to fetch the wild-fowl hame,      10
His lady's ta'en another mate,
So we may mak our dinner sweet.

"Ye'll sit on his white hause-bane,[9]
And I'll pike out his bonny blue een;
Wi' ae lock o' his gowden hair
We'll theek[10] our nest when it grows bare.

"Mony a one for him makes mane,
But nane sall ken where he is gane;
O'er his white banes, when they are bare,
The wind sall blaw for evermair."      20

EZRA POUND

# Ballad of the Goodly Fere

*Simon Zelotes speaketh it somewhile after the
    Crucifixion.*

Ha' we lost the goodliest fere o' all
For the priests and the gallows tree?
Aye, lover he was of brawny men,
O' ships and the open sea.

When they came wi' a host to take Our Man
His smile was good to see;
"First let these go!" quo' our Goodly Fere,
"Or I'll see ye damned," says he.

Aye, he sent us out through the crossed high
    spears,
And the scorn of his laugh rang free;      10
"Why took ye not me when I walked about
Alone in the town?" says he.

Oh, we drunk his "Hale" in the good red wine
When we last made company;

No capon priest was the Goodly Fere
But a man o' men was he.

I ha' seen him drive a hundred men
Wi' a bundle o' cords swung free,
That they took the high and holy house
For their pawn and treasury.      20

They'll no' get him a' in a book I think,
Though they write it cunningly;
No mouse of the scrolls was the Goodly Fere
But aye loved the open sea.

If they think they ha' snared our Goodly Fere
They are fools to the last degree.
"I'll go to the feast," quo' our Goodly Fere,
"Though I go to the gallows tree."

"Ye ha' seen me heal the lame and blind,
And wake the dead," says he;      30
"Ye shall see one thing to master all:
'Tis how a brave man dies on the tree."

A son of God was the Goodly Fere
That bade us his brothers be.
I ha' seen him cow a thousand men.
I have seen him upon the tree.

He cried no cry when they drave the nails
And the blood gushed hot and free;
The hounds of the crimson sky gave tongue
But never a cry cried he.      40

I ha' seen him cow a thousand men
On the hills o' Galilee;
They whined as he walked out calm between,
Wi' his eyes like the grey o' the sea,

Like the sea that brooks no voyaging
With the winds unleashed and free,
Like the sea that he cowed at Genseret
Wi' twey words spoke' suddently.

A master of men was the Goodly Fere,
A mate of the wind and sea;      50
If they think they ha' slain our Goodly Fere
They are fools eternally.

I ha' seen him eat o' the honey-comb
Sin' they nailed him to the tree.

JOHN CROWE RANSOM

# Captain Carpenter

Captain Carpenter rose up in his prime
Put on his pistols and went riding out
But had got wellnigh nowhere at that time
Till he fell in with ladies in a rout.

It was a pretty lady and all her train
That played with him so sweetly but before
An hour she'd taken a sword with all her main
And twined him of his nose for evermore.

Captain Carpenter mounted up one day
And rode straightway into a stranger rogue          10
That looked unchristian but be that as may
The Captain did not wait upon prologue.

But drew upon him out of his great heart
The other swung against him with a club
And cracked his two legs at the shinny part
And let him roll and stick like any tub.

Captain Carpenter rode many a time
From male and female took he sundry harms
He met the wife of Satan crying "I'm
The she-wolf bids you shall bear no more arms."  20

Their strokes and counters whistled in the wind
I wish he had delivered half his blows
But where she should have made off like a hind
The bitch bit off his arms at the elbows.

And Captain Carpenter parted with his ears
To a black devil that used him in this wise
O Jesus ere his threescore and ten years
Another had plucked out his sweet blue eyes.

Captain Carpenter got up on his roan
And sallied from the gate in hell's despite          30
I heard him asking in the grimmest tone
If any enemy yet there was to fight?

"To any adversary it is fame
If he risk to be wounded by my tongue
Or burnt in two beneath my red heart's flame
Such are the perils he is cast among.

"But if he can he has a pretty choice
From an anatomy with little to lose

Whether he cut my tongue and take my voice
Or whether it be my round red heart he
      choose."                                                 40

It was the neatest knave that ever was seen
Stepping in perfume from his lady's bower
Who at this word put in his merry mien
And fell on Captain Carpenter like a tower.

I would not knock old fellows in the dust
But there lay Captain Carpenter on his back
His weapons were the old heart in his bust
And a blade shook between rotten teeth alack.

The rogue in scarlet and grey soon knew his
      mind
He wished to get his trophy and depart          50
With gentle apology and touch refined
He pierced him and produced the Captain's heart.

God's mercy rest on Captain Carpenter now
I thought him Sirs an honest gentleman
Citizen husband soldier and scholar enow
Let jangling kites eat of him if they can.

But God's deep curses follow after those
That shore him of his goodly nose and ears
His legs and strong arms at the two elbows
And eyes that had not watered seventy years.     60

The curse of hell upon the sleek upstart
That got the Captain finally on his back
And took the red red vitals of his heart
And made the kites to whet their beaks clack
      clack.

JOHN MANIFOLD

# The Griesly[1] Wife

"Lie still, my newly married wife,
   Lie easy as you can.
You're young and ill accustomed yet
   To sleeping with a man."

The snow lay thick, the moon was full
   And shone across the floor.

[1] ghastly, grisly, uncanny

The young wife went with never a word
  Barefooted to the door.

He up and followed sure and fast,
  The moon shone clear and white.                    10
But before his coat was on his back
  His wife was out of sight.

He trod the trail wherever it turned
  By many a mound and scree,
And still the barefoot track led on,
  And an angry man was he.

He followed fast, he followed slow,
  And still he called her name,
But only the dingoes of the hills
  Yowled back at him again.                           20

His hair stood up along his neck,
  His angry mood was gone,
For the track of the two bare feet gave out
  And a four-foot track went on.

Her nightgown lay upon the snow
  As it might upon the sheet,
But the track that led from where it lay
  Was never of human feet.

His heart turned over in his chest,
  He looked from side to side,                        30
And he thought more of his gumwood fire
  Than he did of his griesly bride.

And first he started walking back
  And then began to run,
And his quarry wheeled at the end of her track
  And hunted him in turn.

Oh, long the fire may burn for him
  And open stand the door,
And long the bed may wait empty:
  He'll not be back any more.                         40

T. S. ELIOT

# Journey of the Magi

"A cold coming we had of it,
Just the worst time of the year

JOURNEY OF THE MAGI  From *Collected Poems 1909–1962* by
T. S. Eliot, copyright, 1936, by Harcourt Brace Jovanovich,
Inc.; copyright, ©, 1963, 1964, by T. S. Eliot. Reprinted by
permission of the publisher.

For a journey, and such a long journey:
The ways deep and the weather sharp,
The very dead of winter."
And the camels galled, sore-footed, refractory,
Lying down in the melting snow.
There were times we regretted
The summer palaces on slopes, the terraces,
And the silken girls bringing sherbet.                10
Then the camel men cursing and grumbling
And running away, and wanting their liquor
  and women,
And the night-fires going out, and the lack of
  shelters,
And the cities hostile and the towns unfriendly
And the villages dirty and charging high prices:
A hard time we had of it.
At the end we preferred to travel all night,
Sleeping in snatches,
With the voices singing in our ears, saying
That this was all folly.                              20

Then at dawn we came down to a temperate
  valley,
Wet, below the snow line, smelling of
  vegetation;
With a running stream and a water-mill beating
  the darkness,
And three trees on the low sky,
And an old white horse galloped away in the
  meadow.
Then we came to a tavern with vine-leaves over
  the lintel,
Six hands at an open door dicing for pieces of
  silver,
And feet kicking the empty wine-skins.
But there was no information, and so we
  continued
And arrived at evening, not a moment too soon   30
Finding the place; it was (you may say)
  satisfactory.

All this was a long time ago, I remember,
And I would do it again, but set down
This set down
This: were we led all that way for
Birth or Death? There was a Birth, certainly,
We had evidence and no doubt. I had seen
  birth and death,
But had thought they were different; this Birth
  was
Hard and bitter agony for us, like Death, our
  death.
We returned to our places, these Kingdoms,      40
But no longer at ease here, in the old
  dispensation,
With an alien people clutching their gods.
I should be glad of another death.

WILLIAM MORRIS

# The Haystack in the Floods

Had she come all the way for this,
To part at last without a kiss?
Yea, had she borne the dirt and rain
That her own eyes might see him slain
Beside the haystack in the floods?

Along the dripping, leafless woods,
The stirrup touching either shoe,
She rode astride as troopers do;
With kirtle kilted to her knee,
To which the mud splashed wretchedly;            10
And the wet dripped from every tree
Upon her head and heavy hair,
And on her eyelids broad and fair;
The tears and rain ran down her face.
By fits and starts they rode apace,
And very often was his place
Far off from her; he had to ride
Ahead, to see what might betide
When the roads crossed; and sometimes, when
There rose a murmuring from his men,            20
Had to turn back with promises.
Ah me! she had but little ease;
And often for pure doubt and dread
She sobbed, made giddy in the head
By the swift riding; while, for cold,
Her slender fingers scarce could hold
The wet reins; yea, and scarcely, too,
She felt the foot within her shoe
Against the stirrup: all for this,
To part at last without a kiss                   30
Beside the haystack in the floods.

For when they neared that old soaked hay,
They saw across the only way
That Judas, Godmar, and the three
Red running lions dismally
Grinned from his pennon, under which
In one straight line along the ditch,
They counted thirty heads.

                    So then
While Robert turned round to his men,
She saw at once the wretched end,               40
And, stooping down, tried hard to rend
Her coif the wrong way from her head,
And hid her eyes; while Robert said,
"Nay, love, 'tis scarcely two to one;
At Poitiers where we made them run
So fast—why, sweet my love, good cheer,
The Gascon frontier is so near,
Naught after us."

                    But: "O!" she said,
"My God; my God! I have to tread
The long way back without you; then              50
The court at Paris; those six men;
The gratings of the Chatelet;
The swift Seine on some rainy day
Like this, and people standing by,
And laughing, while my weak hands try
To recollect how strong men swim.
All this, or else a life with him,
For which I should be damned at last;
Would God that this next hour were past!"

He answered not, but cried his cry,              60
"St. George for Marny!" cheerily;
And laid his hand upon her rein.
Alas! no man of all his train
Gave back that cheery cry again;
And, while for rage his thumb beat fast
Upon his sword-hilt, someone cast
About his neck a kerchief long,
And bound him.

                    Then they went along
To Godmar; who said: "Now, Jehane,
Your lover's life is on the wane                  70
So fast, that, if this very hour
You yield not as my paramour,
He will not see the rain leave off;
Nay, keep your tongue from gibe and scoff,
Sir Robert, or I slay you now."

She laid her hand upon her brow,
Then gazed upon the palm, as though
She thought her forehead bled, and "No!"
She said, and turned her head away,
As there was nothing else to say,                80
And everything was settled; red
Grew Godmar's face from chin to head—
"Jehane, on yonder hill there stands
My castle, guarding well my lands;
What hinders me from taking you,
And doing that I list to do
To your fair willful body, while
Your knight lies dead?"

                    A wicked smile
Wrinkled her face, her lips grew thin,
A long way out she thrust her chin:              90
"You know that I should strangle you
While you were sleeping; or bite through
Your throat, by God's help; ah!" she said,
"Lord Jesus pity your poor maid!
For in such wise they hem me in,
I cannot choose but sin and sin,
Whatever happens; yet I think
They could not make me eat or drink,

And so should I just reach my rest."
"Nay, if you do not my behest,                                    100
O Jehane! though I love you well,"
Said Godmar, "would I fail to tell
All that I know?" "Foul lies," she said.
"Eh? lies, my Jehane? by God's head,
At Paris folks would deem them true!
Do you know, Jehane, they cry for you:
'Jehane the brown! Jehane the brown!
Give us Jehane to burn or drown!'
Eh!—gag me Robert!—sweet my friend,
This were indeed a piteous end
For those long fingers, and long feet,
And long neck, and smooth shoulders sweet;
An end that few men would forget
That saw it. So, an hour yet—
Consider, Jehane, which to take
Of life or death!"

            So, scarce awake,
Dismounting, did she leave that place,
And totter some yards; with her face
Turned upward to the sky she lay,                                 120
Her head on a wet heap of hay,
And fell asleep; and while she slept,
And did not dream, the minutes crept
Round to the twelve again; but she,
Being waked at last, sighed quietly,
And strangely childlike came, and said:
"I will not." Straightway Godmar's head,
As though it hung on strong wires, turned
Most sharply round, and his face burned.

For Robert, both his eyes were dry—
He could not weep—but gloomily                                   130
He seemed to watch the rain; yea, too,
His lips were firm; he tried once more
To touch her lips; she reached out, sore
And vain desire so tortured them,
The poor gray lips, and now the hem
Of his sleeve brushed them.

            With a start
Up Godmar rose, thrust them apart;
From Robert's throat he loosed the bands
Of silk and mail; with empty hands
Held out, she stood and gazed, and saw,                          140
The long bright blade without a flaw
Glide out from Godmar's sheath, his hand
In Robert's hair; she saw him bend
Back Robert's head; she saw him send
The thin steel down; the blow told well—
Right backward the knight Robert fell,
And moaned as dogs do, being half dead,
Unwitting, as I deem; so then
Godmar turned grinning to his men,

Who ran, some five or six, and beat                              150
His head to pieces at their feet.

Then Godmar turned again and said:
"So, Jehane, the first fitte is read!
Take note, my lady, that your way
Lies backward to the Chatelet!"
She shook her head and gazed awhile
At her cold hands with a rueful smile,
As though this thing had made her mad.

This was the parting that they had
Beside the haystack in the floods.                               160

# W. H. AUDEN

# O What Is That Sound?

O what is that sound which so thrills the ear
    Down in the valley drumming, drumming?
Only the scarlet soldiers, dear,
    The soldiers coming.

O what is that light I see flashing so clear
    Over the distance brightly, brightly?
Only the sun on their weapons, dear,
    As they step lightly.

O what are they doing with all that gear;
    What are they doing this morning, this
        morning?                                       10
Only the usual maneuvers, dear,
    Or perhaps a warning.

O why have they left the road down there;
    Why are they suddenly wheeling, wheeling?
Perhaps a change in the orders, dear;
    Why are you kneeling?

O haven't they stopped for the doctor's care;
    Haven't they reined their horses, their horses?
Why, they are none of them wounded, dear,
    None of these forces.                                       20

O is it the parson they want, with white hair;
    Is it the parson, is it, is it?

No, they are passing his gateway, dear,
  Without a visit.

O it must be the farmer who lives so near,
  It must be the farmer, so cunning, cunning;
They have passed the farm already, dear,
  And now they are running.

O where are you going? stay with me here.

Were the vows you swore me deceiving,
  deceiving?                                        30
No, I promised to love you, my dear,
  But I must be leaving.

O it's broken the lock and splintered the door,
  O it's the gate where they're turning, turning;
Their feet are heavy on the floor
  And their eyes are burning.

THOMAS HARDY

## When I Set Out for Lyonnesse

When I set out for Lyonnesse,
  A hundred miles away,
  The rime was on the spray,
And starlight lit my lonesomeness
When I set out for Lyonnesse
  A hundred miles away.

What could bechance at Lyonnesse
  While I should sojourn there
  No prophet durst declare,
Nor did the wisest wizard guess                    10
What would bechance at Lyonnesse
  While I should sojourn there.

When I came back from Lyonnesse
  With magic in my eyes,
  All marked with mute surmise
My radiance rare and fathomless,
When I came back from Lyonnesse
  With magic in my eyes.

JOHN FANDEL

## Reading the News

I will lock my door for good,
Go to live in a green wood.

There I will learn my ABCs
All over, and Hesperides.

Birds turning ancient trees to song . . .
I will listen all day long.

I will wade each silver stream,
Dawdle in golden dells, and dream

To write a verse, and little heed
No one else is there to read—

But you, I mean. I would not go
Unless you come along, and know.

GERARD MANLEY HOPKINS

## Pied Beauty

Glory be to God for dappled things—
    For skies of couple-color as a brinded cow;
      For rose-moles all in stipple upon trout
    that swim;
Fresh-firecoal chestnut-falls; finches' wings;
    Landscape plotted and pieced—fold, fallow,
    and plow;
      And all trades, their gear and tackle and
    trim.
All things counter, original, spare, strange;
    Whatever is fickle, freckled (who knows how?)
      With swift, slow; sweet, sour; adazzle, dim;
He fathers-forth whose beauty is past change:      10
          Praise him.

WILLIAM BUTLER YEATS

## For Anne Gregory

"Never shall a young man,
Thrown into despair
By those great honey-coloured
Ramparts at your ear,
Love you for yourself alone
And not your yellow hair.

WHEN I SET OUT FOR LYONNESSE  Reprinted with permission of The Macmillan Company from *Collected Poems* by Thomas Hardy. Copyright 1925 by The Macmillan Company. READING THE NEWS  Originally appeared in *The Lyric*, Vol. 49, no. 2 (Spring, 1969). Reprinted by permission of *The Lyric*.

PIED BEAUTY  From *Poems of Gerard Manley Hopkins*, Third Edition, edited by W. H. Gardner. Copyright 1948 by Oxford University Press, Inc. Reprinted by permission. FOR ANNE GREGORY  Reprinted with permission of The Macmillan Company from *Collected Poems* by William Butler Yeats. Copyright 1933 by The Macmillan Company, renewed 1961 by Bertha Georgie Yeats.

"But I can get hair-dye
And set such colour there,
Brown, or black, or carrot,
That young men in despair                          10
May love me for myself alone
And not my yellow hair."

"I heard an old religious man
But yesternight declare
That he had found a text to prove
That only God, my dear,
Could love you for yourself alone
And not your yellow hair."

## WILLIAM BUTLER YEATS

# Down by the Salley Gardens

Down by the salley gardens my love and I did
    meet;
She passed the salley gardens with little
    snow-white feet.
She bid me take love easy, as the leaves grow
    on the tree;
But I, being young and foolish, with her would
    not agree.

In a field by a river my love and I did stand,
And on my leaning shoulder she laid her
    snow-white hand.
She bid me take life easy, as the grass grows on
    the weirs
But I was young and foolish, and now am full of
    tears.

## ANDREW MARVELL

# To His Coy Mistress

Had we but world enough, and time,
This coyness, Lady, were no crime.
We would sit down and think which way
To walk and pass our long love's day.
Thou by the Indian Ganges' side

Shouldst rubies find; I by the tide
Of Humber would complain. I would
Love you ten years before the Flood,
And you should, if you please, refuse
Till the conversion of the Jews.                   10
My vegetable love would grow
Vaster than empires, and more slow;
An hundred years would go to praise
Thine eyes and on thy forehead gaze;
Two hundred to adore each breast,
But thirty thousand to the rest;
An age at least to every part,
And the last age should show your heart.
For, Lady, you deserve this state,
Nor would I love at lower rate.                     20

But at my back I always hear
Time's wingèd chariot hurrying near;
And yonder all before us lie
Deserts of vast eternity.
Thy beauty shall no more be found,
Nor, in thy marble vault, shall sound
My echoing song; then worms shall try
That long preserved virginity,
And your quaint honor turn to dust,
And into ashes all my lust:                         30
The grave's a fine and private place,
But none, I think, do there embrace.

Now therefore, while the youthful hue
Sits on thy skin like morning dew,
And while thy willing soul transpires
At every pore with instant fires,
Now let us sport us while we may,
And now, like amorous birds of prey
Rather at once our time devour
Than languish in his slow-chapped power.            40
Let us roll all our strength and all
Our sweetness up into one ball,
And tear our pleasures with rough strife
Thorough the iron gates of life:
Thus, though we cannot make our sun
Stand still, yet we will make him run.

## ROBERT HERRICK

# Upon Julia's Clothes

Whenas in silks my Julia goes,
Then, then, methinks, how sweetly flows
The liquefaction of her clothes.

Next, when I cast mine eyes, and see
That brave vibration, each way free,
Oh, how that glittering taketh me!

Love alters not with his brief hours and weeks,
But bears it out even to the edge of doom.
   If this be error and upon me proved,
   I never writ, nor no man ever loved.

EDNA ST. VINCENT MILLAY

# I Know I Am But Summer

I know I am but summer to your heart,
And not the full four seasons of the year;
And you must welcome from another part
Such noble moods as are not mine, my dear.
No gracious weight of golden fruits to sell
Have I, nor any wise and wintry thing;
And I have loved you all too long and well
To carry still the high sweet breast of Spring.
Wherefore I say: O love, as summer goes,
I must be gone, steal forth with silent drums,   10
That you may hail anew the bird and rose
When I come back to you, as summer comes.
Else will you seek, at some not distant time,
Even your summer in another clime.

ELINOR WYLIE

# I Hereby Swear That to Uphold Your House

I hereby swear that to uphold your house
I would lay my bones in quick destroying lime
Or turn my flesh to timber for all time;
Cut down my womanhood; lop off the boughs
Of that perpetual ecstasy that grows
From the heart's core; condemn it as a crime
If it be broader than a beam, or climb
Above the stature that your roof allows.
I am not the hearthstone nor the cornerstone
Within this noble fabric you have builded;   10
Not by my beauty was its cornice gilded;
Not on my courage were its arches thrown:
My lord, adjudge my strength, and set me
   where
I bear a little more than I can bear.

WILLIAM SHAKESPEARE

# Let Me Not to the Marriage of True Minds

Let me not to the marriage of true minds
Admit impediments. Love is not love
Which alters when it alteration finds,
Or bends with the remover to remove.
O, no! it is an ever-fixèd mark
That looks on tempests and is never shaken.
It is the star to every wand'ring bark,
Whose worth's unknown, although his height be
   taken.
Love's not Time's fool, though rosy lips and
   cheeks
Within his bending sickle's compass come.   10

E. E. CUMMINGS

# if i have made, my lady, intricate

if i have made, my lady, intricate
imperfect various things chiefly which wrong
your eyes (frailer than most deep dreams are
   frail)
songs less firm than your body's whitest song
upon my mind—if i have failed to snare
the glance too shy—if through my singing slips
the very skillful strangeness of your smile

I HEREBY SWEAR THAT TO UPHOLD YOUR HOUSE Copyright
1919 by Alfred A. Knopf, Inc. Renewed 1957 by Edwina C.
Rubenstein. Reprinted from Collected Poems, by Elinor
Wylie, by permission of the publisher.
IF I HAVE MADE, MY LADY, INTRICATE Copyright, 1926, by
Horace Liveright; copyright, 1954, by E. E. Cummings.
Reprinted from his Poems 1923–1954 by permission of
Harcourt Brace Jovanovich, Inc.

I KNOW I AM BUT SUMMER From Collected Poems of Edna
St. Vincent Millay, Harper & Row. Copyright 1921, 1928,
1948, 1955 by Edna St. Vincent Millay and Norma Millay
Ellis. Reprinted by permission of Norma Millay Ellis.

the keen primeval silence of your hair
—let the world say "his most wise music stole
nothing from death"—
                    you only will create          10
(who are so perfectly alive) my shame:
lady through whose profound and fragile lips
the sweet small clumsy feet of April came

into the ragged meadow of my soul.


CARL SANDBURG

# For You

The peace of great doors be for you.
Wait at the knobs, at the panel oblongs.
Wait for the great hinges.

The peace of great churches be for you,
Where the players of lofty pipe organs
Practice old lovely fragments, alone.

The peace of great books be for you,
Stains of pressed clover leaves on pages,
Bleach of the light of years held in leather.

The peace of great prairies be for you.          10
Listen among windplayers in cornfields,
The wind leaning over its oldest music.

The peace of great seas be for you.
Wait on a hook of land, a rock footing
For you, wait in the salt wash.

The peace of great mountains be for you,
The sleep and the eyesight of eagles,
Sheet mist shadows and the long look across.

The peace of great hearts be for you,
Valves of the blood of the sun,                   20
Pumps of the strongest wants we cry.

The peace of great silhouettes be for you,
Shadow dancers alive in your blood now,
Alive and crying, "Let us out, let us out."

FOR YOU  From *Smoke and Steel* by Carl Sandburg, copyright, 1920, by Harcourt Brace Jovanovich, Inc.; copyright 1948, by Carl Sandburg. Reprinted by permission of the publisher.

The peace of great changes be for you.
Whispers, Oh beginners in the hills.
Tumble, Oh cubs—tomorrow belongs to you.

The peace of great loves be for you.
Rain, soak these roots; wind, shatter the dry rot.
Bars of sunlight, grips of the earth, hug these.   30

The peace of great ghosts be for you,
Phantoms of night-gray eyes, ready to go
To the fog-star dumps, to the fire-white doors.

Yes, the peace of great phantoms be for you,
Phantom iron men, mothers of bronze,
Keepers of the lean clean breeds.


ANONYMOUS

# The Maidens Came

The maidens came
When I was in my mother's bower:
I had all that I would.
The bailey[1] beareth the bell away:
The lily, the rose, the rose I lay.

The silver is white, red is the gold:
The robes they lay in fold.
The bailey beareth the bell away:
The lily, the rose, the rose I lay.

And through the glass window shines the sun.   10
How should I love, and I so young?
The bailey beareth the bell away:
The lily, the lily, the rose I lay.


JOHN STILL

# Jolly Good Ale and Old

Back and side go bare, go bare,
    Both foot and hand go cold;
But, belly, God send thee good ale enough,
    Whether it be new or old.

[1] bailiff or steward.

I cannot eat but little meat,
  My stomach is not good;
But sure I think that I can drink
  With him that wears a hood.
Though I go bare, take ye no care,
  I am nothing a-cold;          10
I stuff my skin so full within
  Of jolly good ale and old.

Back and side go bare, &c.

I love no roast but a nutbrown toast,
  And a crab laid in the fire;
A little bread shall do me stead,
  Much bread I not desire.        20
No frost nor snow, no wind, I trow,
  Can hurt me if I would,
I am so wrapped, and thoroughly lapped
  Of jolly good ale and old.

Back and side go bare, &c.

Now let them drink, till they nod and wink,
  Even as good fellows should do;        30
They shall not miss to have the bliss
  Good ale doth bring men to;
And all poor souls that have scoured bowls
  Or have them lustily trolled,
God save the lives of them and their wives,
  Whether they be young or old.

Back and side go bare, go bare,
  Both foot and hand go cold;
But, belly, God send thee good ale enough,
  Whether it be new or old.        40

## WALT WHITMAN

# The Commonplace

The commonplace I sing;
How cheap is health! how cheap nobility!
Abstinence, no falsehood, no gluttony, lust;
The open air I sing, freedom, toleration,
(Take here the mainest lesson—less from
  books—less from the schools,)
The common day and night—the common earth
  and waters,
Your farm—your work, trade, occupation,
The democratic wisdom underneath, like solid
  ground for all.

## THOM GUNN

# On the Move

*"Man, you gotta Go."*

The blue jay scuffling in the bushes follows
Some hidden purpose, and the gust of birds
That spurts across the field, the wheeling
  swallows,
Have nested in the trees and undergrowth.
Seeking their instinct, or their poise, or both,
One moves with an uncertain violence
Under the dust thrown by a baffled sense
Or the dull thunder of approximate words.

On motorcycles, up the road, they come:
Small, black, as flies hanging in heat, the Boys,  10
Until the distance throws them forth, their hum
Bulges to thunder held by calf and thigh.
In goggles, donned impersonality,
In gleaming jackets trophied with the dust,
They strap in doubt—by hiding it, robust—
And almost hear a meaning in their noise.

Exact conclusion of their hardiness
Has no shape yet, but from known whereabouts
They ride, direction where the tires press.
They scare a flight of birds across the field:  20
Much that is natural, to the will must yield.
Men manufacture both machine and soul,
And use what they imperfectly control
To dare a future from the taken routes.

It is a part solution, after all.
One is not necessarily discord
On earth; or damned because, half animal,
One lacks direct instinct, because one wakes
Afloat on movement that divides and breaks.
One joins the movement in a valueless world,  30
Choosing it, till, both hurler and the hurled,
One moves as well, always toward, toward.

A minute holds them, who have come to go:
The self-defined, astride the created will
They burst away; the towns they travel through
Are home for neither bird nor holiness,
For birds and saints complete their purposes.
At worst, one is in motion; and at best,
Reaching no absolute, in which to rest,
One is always nearer by not keeping still.  40

ON THE MOVE  From *The Sense of Movement* by Thom Gunn.
Reprinted by permission of Faber and Faber Ltd.

ROBERT FROST

# A Soldier

He is that fallen lance that lies as hurled,
That lies unlifted now, come dew, come rust,
But still lies pointed as it plowed the dust.
If we who sight along it round the world
See nothing worthy to have been its mark,
It is because like men we look too near,
Forgetting that as fitted to the sphere,
Our missiles always make too short an arc.
They fall, they rip the grass, they intersect
The curve of earth, and striking, break their
    own;
They make us cringe for metal-point on stone.
But this we know, the obstacle that checked
And tripped the body, shot the spirit on
Further than target ever showed or shone.


ROBERT FROST

# In Hardwood Groves

The same leaves over and over again!
They fall from giving shade above,
To make one texture of faded brown
And fit the earth like a leather glove.

Before the leaves can mount again
To fill the trees with another shade,
They must go down past things coming up.
They must go down into the dark decayed.

They *must* be pierced by flowers and put
Beneath the feet of dancing flowers.          10
However it is in some other world
I know that this is the way in ours.

WALLACE STEVENS

# Domination of Black

At night, by the fire,
The colors of the bushes
And of the fallen leaves,
Repeating themselves,
Turned in the room,
Like the leaves themselves
Turning in the wind.
Yes: but the color of the heavy hemlocks
Came striding.
And I remembered the cry of the peacocks.      10

The colors of their tails
Were like the leaves themselves
Turning in the wind,
In the twilight wind.
They swept over the room,
Just as they flew from the boughs of the hemlocks
Down to the ground.
I heard them cry—the peacocks.
Was it a cry against the twilight
Or against the leaves themselves           20
Turning in the wind,
Turning as the flames
Turned in the fire,
Turning as the tails of the peacocks
Turned in the loud fire,
Loud as the hemlocks
Full of the cry of the peacocks?
Or was it a cry against the hemlocks?

Out of the window,
I saw how the planets gathered            30
Like the leaves themselves
Turning in the wind.
I saw how the night came,
Came striding like the color of the heavy hemlocks.
I felt afraid.
And I remembered the cry of the peacocks.


WALTER DE LA MARE

# Silver

Slowly, silently, now the moon
Walks the night in her silver shoon;
This way, and that, she peers, and sees
Silver fruit upon silver trees;

One by one the casements catch
Her beams beneath the silvery thatch;
Couched in his kennel, like a log,
With paws of silver sleeps the dog;
From their shadowy cote the white breasts peep
Of doves in a silver-feathered sleep;          10
A harvest mouse goes scampering by,
With silver claws, and silver eye;
And moveless fish in the water gleam,
By silver reeds in a silver stream.

CONRAD AIKEN

# Morning Song from Senlin

It is morning, Senlin says, and in the morning
When the light drips through the shutters like
    the dew,
I arise, I face the sunrise,
And do the things my fathers learned to do.
Stars in the purple dusk above the rooftops
Pale in a saffron mist and seem to die,
And I myself on a swiftly tilting planet
Stand before a glass and tie my tie.

Vine leaves tap my window,
Dew-drops sing to the garden stones,          10
The robin chirps in the chinaberry tree
Repeating three clear tones.

It is morning. I stand by the mirror
And tie my tie once more.
While waves far off in a pale rose twilight
Crash on a coral shore.
I stand by a mirror and comb my hair:
How small and white my face!—
The green earth tilts through a sphere of air
And bathes in a flame of space.          20

There are houses hanging above the stars
And stars hung under a sea.
And a sun far off in a shell of silence
Dapples my walls for me.

It is morning, Senlin says, and in the morning
Should I not pause in the light to remember
    god?
Upright and firm I stand on a star unstable,
He is immense and lonely as a cloud.
I will dedicate this moment before my mirror
To him alone, for him I will comb my hair.          30
Accept these humble offerings, cloud of silence!
I will think of you as I descend the stair.

Vine leaves tap my window,
The snail-track shines on the stones,
Dew-drops flash from the chinaberry tree
Repeating two clear tones.

It is morning, I awake from a bed of silence,
Shining I rise from the starless waters of sleep.
The walls are about me still as in the evening,
I am the same, and the same name still I keep          40
The earth revolves with me, yet makes no
    motion,
The stars pale silently in a coral sky.
In a whistling void I stand before my mirror,
Unconcerned, and tie my tie.

There are horses neighing on far-off hills
Tossing their long white manes,
And mountains flash in the rose-white dusk,
Their shoulders black with rains.
It is morning. I stand by the mirror
And surprise my soul once more;          50
The blue air rushes above my ceiling,
There are suns beneath my floor.

. . . It is morning, Senlin says, I ascend from
    darkness
And depart on the winds of space for I know
    not where,
My watch is wound, a key is in my pocket,
And the sky is darkened as I descend the stair.
There are shadows across the windows, clouds
    in heaven,
And a god among the stars; and I will go
Thinking of him as I might think of daybreak
And humming a tune I know.          60

Vine leaves tap at the window,
Dew-drops sing to the garden stones,
The robin chirps in the chinaberry tree
Repeating three clear tones.

W. H. AUDEN

# Look, Stranger,
# on This Island Now

Look, stranger, on this island now
The leaping light for your delight discovers,
Stand stable here
And silent be,
That through the channels of the ear
May wander like a river
The swaying sound of the sea.

Here at the small field's ending pause
When the chalk wall falls to the foam and its
    tall ledges
Oppose the pluck                                                    10
And knock of the tide,
And the shingle scrambles after the sucking
    surf,
And the gull lodges
A moment on its sheer side.

Far off like floating seeds the ships
Diverge on urgent voluntary errands,
And the full view
Indeed may enter
And move in memory as now these clouds do,
That pass the harbour mirror                                        20
And all the summer through the water saunter.

A. E. HOUSMAN

# Loveliest of Trees

Loveliest of trees, the cherry now
Is hung with bloom along the bough,
And stands about the woodland ride
Wearing white for Eastertide.

Now, of my threescore years and ten,
Twenty will not come again,
And take from seventy springs a score,
It only leaves me fifty more.

And since to look at things in bloom
Fifty springs are little room,                                      10
About the woodlands I will go
To see the cherry hung with snow.

ELINOR WYLIE

# August

Why should this Negro insolently stride
Down the red noonday on such noiseless feet?
Piled in his barrow, tawnier than wheat,
Lie heaps of smoldering daisies, somber-eyed,
Their copper petals shriveled up with pride,
Hot with a superfluity of heat,
Like a great brazier borne along the street
By captive leopards, black and burning pied.
Are there no water-lilies, smooth as cream,
With long stems dripping crystal? Are there
    none                                                       10
Like those white lilies, luminous and cool,
Plucked from some hemlock-darkened northern
    stream
By fair-haired swimmers, diving where the sun
Scarce warms the surface of the deepest pool?

ALFRED, LORD TENNYSON

# from The Lotos-Eaters

"Courage!" he said, and pointed toward the
    land,
"This mounting wave will roll us shoreward
    soon."
In the afternoon they came unto a land
In which it seemèd always afternoon.
All round the coast the languid air did swoon,
Breathing like one that hath a weary dream.

Full-faced above the valley stood the moon;
And, like a downward smoke, the slender
  stream
Along the cliff to fall and pause and fall did
  seem.

A land of streams! some, like a downward
  smoke,                                          10
Slow-drooping veils of thinnest lawn, did go;
And some through wavering lights and shadows
  broke,
Rolling a slumbrous sheet of foam below.
They saw the gleaming river seaward flow
From the inner land; far off, three
  mountain-tops,
Three silent pinnacles of aged snow,
Stood sunset-flushed; and, dewed with showery
  drops,
Up-clomb the shadowy pine above the woven
  copse.

The charmèd sunset lingered low adown
In the red West; through mountain clefts the
  dale                                            20
Was seen far inland, and the yellow down
Bordered with palm, and many a winding vale
And meadow, set with slender galingale;
A land where all things always seemed the
  same!
And round about the keel with faces pale,
Dark faces pale against that rosy flame,
The mild-eyed melancholy Lotos-eaters came.

Branches they bore of that enchanted stem,
Laden with flowers and fruit, whereof they gave
To each, but whoso did receive of them          30
And taste, to him the gushing of the wave
Far far away did seem to mourn and rave
On alien shores; and if his fellow spake,
His voice was thin, as voices from the grave;
And deep-asleep he seemed, yet all awake.
And music in his ears his beating heart did
  make.

They sat them down upon the yellow sand,
Between the sun and moon upon the shore;
And sweet it was to dream of Fatherland,
Of child, and wife, and slave; but evermore     40
Most weary seemed the sea, weary the oar,
Weary the wandering fields of barren foam.
Then some one said, "We will return no more";
And all at once they sang, "Our island home
Is far beyond the wave; we will no longer
  roam."

THE DONKEY  From the book *The Wild Knight and Other Poems*, 1900, by G. K. Chesterton. Published by E. P. Dutton & Co., Inc., and reprinted with their permission.

## G. K. CHESTERTON

# The Donkey

When fishes flew and forests walked
  And figs grew upon thorn,
Some moment when the moon was blood,
  Then surely I was born;

With monstrous head and sickening cry
  And ears like errant wings,
The devil's walking parody
  On all four-footed things.

The tattered outlaw of the earth,
  Of ancient crooked will;                        10
Starve, scourge, deride me: I am dumb;
  I keep my secret still.

Fools! For I also had my hour;
  One far, fierce hour and sweet.
There was a shout about my ears,
  And palms before my feet.

## EMILY DICKINSON

# I Never Saw a Moor

I never saw a moor,
I never saw the sea;
Yet know I how the heather looks,
And what a wave must be.

I never spoke with God,
Nor visited in heaven;
Yet certain am I of the spot
As if the chart were given.

I NEVER SAW A MOOR  From *The Complete Poems of Emily Dickinson*, Little, Brown and Company, 1960.

## JOHN DONNE

# Death Be Not Proud

Death be not proud, though some have called
  thee
Mighty and dreadful, for, thou are not soe,
For, those, whom thou think'st, thou dost
  overthrow,

Die not, poore Death, nor yet canst thou kill
    mee;
From rest and sleepe, which but thy pictures
    bee,
Much pleasure, then from thee, much more
    must flow,
And soonest our best men with thee doe goe,
Rest of their bones, and soules deliverie.
Thou art slave to Fate, chance, kings, and
    desperate men,
And dost with poyson, warre, and sicknesse
    dwell,                                          10
And poppie, or charmes can make us sleepe as
    well,
And better than thy stroake; why swell'st thou
    then?
One short sleepe past, wee wake eternally,
And Death shall be no more, Death thou shalt
    die.


JULIAN SYMONS

# Pub

The glasses are raised, the voices drift into
    laughter,
The clock hands have stopped, the beer in the
    hands of the soldiers
Is blond, the faces are calm and the fingers can
    feel
The wet touch of glasses, the glasses print rings
    on the table,
The smoke rings curl and go up and dissolve
    near the ceiling,
        This moment exists and is real.

What is reality? Do not ask that. At this
    moment
Look at the butterfly eyes of the girls, watch
    the barmaid's
Precision in pouring a Scotch, and remember
    this day,

PUB From *The Second Man* by Julian Symons, 1943. Reprinted by permission of Routledge & Kegan Paul Ltd.

This day at this moment you were no longer an
    island,                                         10
People were friendly, the clock in the hands of
    the soldiers
        For this moment had nothing to say.

And nothing to say and the glasses are raised,
    we are happy
Drinking through time, and a world that is
    gentle and helpless
Survives in the pub and goes up in the smoke of
    our breath,
The regulars doze in the corner, the talkers are
    fluent;
Look now in the faces of those you love and
    remember
        That you are not thinking of death.

But thinking of death as the lights go out and
    the glasses
Are lowered, the people go out and the evening 20
Goes out, ah, goes out like a light and leaves
    you alone,
As the heart goes out, the door opens out into
    darkness,
The foot takes a step, and the moment, the
    moment of falling
        Is here, you go down like a stone,

Are you able to meet the disaster, able to meet
    the
Cold air of the street and the touch of
    corruption, the rotting
Fingers that murder your own in the grip of
    love?
Can you bear to find hateful the faces you once
    thought were lovely,
Can you bear to find comfort alone in the evil
    and stunted,
        Can you bear to abandon the dove?        30

The houses are shut and the people go home,
    we are left in
Our island of pain, the clocks start to move and
    the powerful
To act, there is nothing now, nothing at all
To be done: for the trouble is real: and the
    verdict is final
Against us. The clocks go round faster and
    faster. And fast as confetti
        The days are beginning to fall.

# THE POET AS WIT AND HUMORIST

## ROBERT HOGAN

## After Sending Freshmen to Describe a Tree

Twenty inglorious Miltons looked at a tree and
    saw God,
Noted its "clutching fingers groping in the sod,"
Heard "Zephyr's gentle breezes wafting through
    her hair,"
Saw "a solemn statue," heard "a growing woody
    prayer,"
Saw "dancing skirts" and "the Lord's design,"
"Green arrows to God" instead of pine,
Saw symbols in squirrels, heard musings in bees;
Not one of the Miltons saw any trees.

If you must see a tree, clean, clear, and bright,
For God's sake and mine, look *outside* your
    heart and write.      ·   10

## HILAIRE BELLOC

## Epitaph on the Politician

Here, richly, with ridiculous display,
The Politician's corpse was laid away.
While all of his acquaintance sneered and
    slanged,
I wept: for I had longed to see him hanged.

## FREDERICK WINSOR

## Little Jack Horner

    Little Jack Horner
    Sits in a corner
Extracting cube roots to infinity,
    An assignment for boys
    This will minimize noise
And produce a more peaceful vicinity.

## ARTHUR GUITERMAN

## On the Vanity of Earthly Greatness

The tusks that clashed in mighty brawls
Of mastodons, are billiard balls.

The sword of Charlemagne the Just
Is ferric oxide, known as rust.

The grizzly bear whose potent hug
Was feared by all, is now a rug.

Great Caesar's bust is on the shelf,
And I don't feel so well myself!

## ANONYMOUS

## The Modern Hiawatha

He killed the noble Mudjokivis.
Of the skin he made him mittens,
Made them with the fur side inside,
Made them with the skin side outside;

LITTLE JACK HORNER From *The Space Child's Mother Goose*
by Frederick Winsor. Reprinted by permission of Simon and
Schuster. Copyright, 1956, 1957, 1958 by Frederick Winsor
and Marian Parry.
ON THE VANITY OF EARTHLY GREATNESS From the book *Gaily
the Troubadour* by Arthur Guiterman. Copyright, 1936, by
E. P. Dutton & Co., Inc. Renewed by Vida Lindo Guiterman.
Reprinted by permission of Vida Lindo Guiterman.

AFTER SENDING FRESHMEN TO DESCRIBE A TREE From the
*American Association of University Professors Bulletin*, Win-
ter 1957. Reprinted by permission of the publishers.
EPITAPH ON THE POLITICIAN Reprinted by permission of A.
D. Peters, for the estate of Hilaire Belloc.

He, to get the warm side inside,
Put the inside skin side outside;
He, to get the cold side outside,
Put the warm side fur side inside.
That's why he put the fur side inside,
Why he put the skin side outside,                    10
Why he turned them inside outside.


## MORRIS BISHOP

# $E = mc^2$

What was our trust, we trust not,
    What was our faith, we doubt;
Whether we must or must not
    We may debate about.
The soul perhaps is a gust of gas
And wrong is a form of right—
But we know that Energy equals Mass
    By the Square of the Speed of Light.

What we have known, we know not,
    What we have proved, abjure.                     10
Life is a tangled bow-knot,
    But one thing still is sure.
Come, little lad; come, little lass,
    Your docile creed recite:
"We know that Energy equals Mass
    By the Square of the Speed of Light."


## ROBERT FROST

# The Hardship of Accounting

Never ask of money spent
Where the spender thinks it went.
Nobody was ever meant
To remember or invent
What he did with every cent.

## ROBERT FROST

# Forgive, O Lord

Forgive, O Lord, my little jokes on Thee
And I'll forgive Thy great big one on me.


## ROBERT GRAVES

# Traveller's Curse
# After Misdirection

*(from the Welsh)*

May they stumble, stage by stage
On an endless pilgrimage,
Dawn and dusk, mile after mile,
At each and every step, a stile;
At each and every step withal
May they catch their feet and fall;
At each and every fall they take
May a bone within them break;
And may the bone that breaks within
Not be, for variation's sake,                        10
Now rib, now thigh, now arm, now shin,
But always, without fail THE NECK.


## JAMES STEPHENS

# A Glass of Beer

The lanky hank of a she in the inn over there
Nearly killed me for asking the loan of a glass
    of beer;

May the devil grip the whey-faced slut by the
    hair,
And beat bad manners out of her skin for a
    year.

That parboiled ape, with the toughest jaw you
    will see
On virtue's path, and a voice that would rasp
    the dead,
Came roaring and raging the minute she looked
    at me,
And threw me out of the house on the back of
    my head!

If I asked her master he'd give me a cask a day;
But she, with the beer at hand, not a gill would
    arrange!                       10
May she marry a ghost and bear him a kitten,
    and may
The High King of Glory permit her to get the
    mange.

## LOUIS SIMPSON

# The Custom of the World

O, we loved long and happily, God knows!
The ocean danced, the green leaves tossed, the
    air
Was filled with petals, and pale Venus rose
When we began to kiss. Kisses brought care,
And closeness caused the taking off of clothes,
O, we loved long and happily, God knows!

"The watchdogs are asleep, the doormen
    doze. . . ."
We huddled in the corners of the stair,
And then we climbed it. What had we to lose?
What would we gain? The best way to compare   10
And quickest, was by taking off our clothes.
O, we loved long and happily, God knows!

Between us two a silent treason grows,
Our pleasures have been changed into despair.
Wild is the wind, from a cold country blows,
In which these tender blossoms disappear.
And did this come of taking off our clothes?
O, we loved long and happily, God knows!

Mistress, my song is drawing to a close.
Put on your rumpled skirt and comb your hair,   20
And when we meet again let us suppose
We never loved or ever naked were.
For though this nakedness was good, God knows
The custom of the world is wearing clothes.

## LUCIAN

# On Magical Whiskers

If by growing a goatee you hope to come upon
    wisdom,
then, O wise friend, any smelly goat in
                        a handsome beard
is at once Plato.

## OGDEN NASH

# Mother Isn't Well

I do not like the sound of "additive,"
The current video pitchman's fadditive.
From scrutiny of a thousand screens
I've now decided what it means:
You add a syllable, as in "moderen,"
"Prince Charels," "westeren," or "squaderon."
The additive, as a matter of factitive,
Logically leads to the subtractitive,
By eminent announcers endorsed,
In which the forest becomes the forst.         10
When I hear an orange called an ornch
I feel forgotten and forlornch—

Yet whom am I to cavil thus?
My own faults are preposterous.
I've caught me, even without imbibery,
Referring to my reference libary.
Occasionally, if still you follow me,
I prefer to pronounce the "P" in Ptolemy.
I also admit that almost half the
Time I omit the "h" in naphtha.        20

HOWARD NEMEROV

# To David,
# about His Education

The world is full of mostly invisible things,
And there is no way but putting the mind's eye,
Or its nose, in a book, to find them out,
Things like the square root of Everest
Or how many times Byron goes into Texas,
Or whether the law of the excluded middle
Applies west of the Rockies. For these
And the like reasons, you have to go to school
And study books and listen to what you are
    told,
And sometimes try to remember. Though I
    don't know                                          10
What you will do with the mean annual rainfall
On Plato's Republic, or the calorie content
Of the Diet of Worms, such things are said to
    be
Good for you, and you will have to learn them
In order to become one of the grown-ups
Who sees invisible things neither steadily nor
    whole,
But keeps gravely the grand confusion of the
    world
Under his hat, which is where it belongs,
And teaches small children to do this in their
    turn.

L. E. SISSMAN

# Clever Women

Clever women live and die on our attention.
They make us feel that we are their invention.
Perhaps we are. They scale us like a tower,
Hand over hand, their eyebeams locked on ours,
Until they overrun our slower brains.

Then what confusion, what cerebral pains!
We drown in borrowed wit and rented reading,
Tags, quotes, allusions, maxims, special pleading,
Polemics, set pieces, and syllogisms
Designed to tax us for our sins and schisms         10
In spurning each one of those nobly sexed
And fashionably gownèd intellects
Who wear the Empress's new clothes. Alas,
We can't accommodate their weight on us,
Who weighed on them until at length we
    sprang,
Relieved, to life, and joined the shabby gang
Of men, our dumb, companionable brothers,
Leaving behind those weeping, waving mothers,
Who now, refleshed as a small-breasted race
Of long-haired daughters, press their aching
    case                                               20
Against our flabby front at every arty
Show, opening, dance, happening, and party.

JOHN UPDIKE

# V. B. Nimble, V. B. Quick

V. B. Wigglesworth wakes at noon,
Washes, shaves, and very soon
Is at the lab; he reads his mail,
Swings a tadpole by the tail,
Undoes his coat, removes his hat,
Dips a spider in a vat
Of alkaline, phones the press,
Tells them he is F.R.S.,
Subdivides six protocells,
Kills a rat by ringing bells,                        10
Writes a treatise, edits two
Symposia on "Will Man Do?,"
Gives a lecture, audits three,
Has the Sperm Club in for tea,
Pensions off an aging spore,
Cracks a test tube, takes some pure
Science and applies it, finds
His hat, adjusts it, pulls the blinds,
Instructs the jellyfish to spawn,
And, by one o'clock, is gone.                        20

WEARE HOLBROOK

# Varitalk

When Very was a celibate,
It meant "in high degree;"
Its emphasis was moderate
But quite enough for me.
It never thumped its little chest
Or raised its voice unduly,
And always looked its level best
When flanked by Yours and Truly.

But in an age of shrill extremes
One adverb's ineffective,
So now the Verys trot in teams
To gain the same objective,    10

And no one can be mortified,
Or sad, or shy, or merry,
Unless the mood is fortified
By Very comma Very.

I hope this twosome will suffice
For purposes emphatic.
But mated words may breed like mice
Sequestered in an attic    20
And thus produce a corollary
—the intensified intensive—
A triple threat that makes me Very,
Very, *Very* apprehensive.

# THE POET AS PORTRAYER OF CHARACTER

EDWIN ARLINGTON ROBINSON

## Mr. Flood's Party

Old Eben Flood, climbing alone one night
Over the hill between the town below
And the forsaken upland hermitage
That held as much as he should ever know
On earth again of home, paused warily.
The road was his with not a native near;
And Eben, having leisure, said aloud,
For no man else in Tilbury Town to hear:

"Well, Mr. Flood, we have the harvest moon
Again, and we may not have many more;          10
The bird is on the wing, the poet says,
And you and I have said it here before.
Drink to the bird." He raised up to the light
The jug that he had gone so far to fill,
And answered huskily: "Well, Mr. Flood,
Since you propose it, I believe I will."

Alone, as if enduring to the end
A valiant armor of scarred hopes outworn,
He stood there in the middle of the road
Like Roland's ghost winding a silent horn.      20
Below him, in the town among the trees,
Where friends of other days had honored him,
A phantom salutation of the dead
Rang thinly till old Eben's eyes were dim.

Then, as a mother lays her sleeping child
Down tenderly, fearing it may awake,
He set the jug down slowly at his feet
With trembling care, knowing that most things
    break;
And only when assured that on firm earth
It stood, as the uncertain lives of men          30
Assuredly did not, he paced away,
And with his hand extended paused again:

"Well, Mr. Flood, we have not met like this
In a long time; and many a change has come

To both of us, I fear, since last it was
We had a drop together. Welcome home!"
Convivially returning with himself,
Again he raised the jug up to the light;
And with an acquiescent quaver said:
"Well, Mr. Flood, if you insist, I might.          40

"Only a very little, Mr. Flood—
For auld lang syne. No more, sir; that will do."
So, for the time, apparently it did,
And Eben evidently thought so too;
For soon amid the silver loneliness
Of night he lifted up his voice and sang,
Secure, with only two moons listening,
Until the whole harmonious landscape rang—

"For auld lang syne." The weary throat gave
    out,
The last word wavered; and the song being
    done,                                         50
He raised again the jug regretfully
And shook his head, and was again alone.
There was not much that was ahead of him,
And there was nothing in the town below—
Where strangers would have shut the many
    doors
That many friends had opened long ago.

E. E. CUMMINGS

## "next to of course god america i

"next to of course god america i
love you land of the pilgrims' and so forth oh
say can you see by the dawn's early my
country 'tis of centuries come and go

and are no more what of it we should worry
in every language even deafanddumb
thy sons acclaim your glorious name by gorry
by jingo by gee by gosh by gum
why talk of beauty what could be more beautiful than these heroic happy dead          10
who rushed like lions to the roaring slaughter
they did not stop to think they died instead
then shall the voice of liberty be mute?"

He spoke. And drank rapidly a glass of water

EMILY DICKINSON

# He Preached upon "Breadth"

He preached upon "breadth" til it argued him
    narrow,—
The broad are too broad to define;
And of "truth" until it proclaimed him a liar,—
The truth never flaunted a sign.

Simplicity fled from his counterfeit presence
As gold the pyrites would shun.
What confusion would cover the innocent Jesus
To meet so enabled a man!

PHYLLIS MC GINLEY

# Simeon Stylites

On top of a pillar Simeon sat.
He wore no mantle,
He had no hat,
But bare as a bird
Sat night and day.
And hardly a word
Did Simeon say.

Under the sun of the desert sky
He sat on a pillar
Nine feet high          10
When Fool and his brother
Came round to admire,
He raised it another
Nine feet high'r.

The seasons circled about his head.
He lived on water
And crusts of bread
(Or so one hears)
From pilgrims' store,
For thirty years          20
And a little more.

And why did Simeon sit like that,
Without a garment,
Without a hat,
In a holy rage
For the world to see?
It puzzles the age,
It puzzles me.
It puzzled many
A Desert Father.          30
And I think it puzzled the Good Lord, rather.

GWENDOLYN BROOKS

# We Real Cool

The Pool Players.
Seven at the Golden Shovel.

We real cool. We
Left school. We

Lurk late. We
Strike straight. We

Sing sin. We
Thin gin. We

Jazz June. We
Die soon.

HE PREACHED UPON "BREADTH" From *The Complete Poems of Emily Dickinson*, Little, Brown and Company, 1960.
SIMEON STYLITES From *Times Three* by Phyllis McGinley. Copyright © 1954 by Phyllis McGinley. Reprinted by permission of The Viking Press, Inc.

WE REAL COOL From *The World of Gwendolyn Brooks* (1971). Copyright © 1959 by Gwendolyn Brooks. Reprinted by permission of Harper & Row, Publishers, Inc.

GWENDOLYN BROOKS

# Weaponed Woman

Well, life has been a baffled vehicle
And baffling. But she fights, and
Has fought, according to her lights and
The lenience of her whirling-place.

She fights with semi-folded arms,
Her strong bag, and the stiff
Frost of her face (that challenges "When" and
   "If").
And altogether she does Rather Well.

GWENDOLYN BROOKS

# Bronzeville Man with a Belt in the Back

In such an armor he may rise and raid
The dark cave after midnight, unafraid,
And slice the shadows with his able sword
Of good broad nonchalance, hashing them down.

And come out and accept the gasping crowd,
Shake off the praises with an airiness.
And, searching, see love shining in an eye,
But never smile.

In such an armor he cannot be slain.

TED HUGHES

# Hawk Roosting

I sit in the top of the wood, my eyes closed.
Inaction, no falsifying dream
Between my hooked head and hooked feet:
Or in sleep rehearse perfect kills and eat.

The convenience of the high trees!
The air's buoyancy and the sun's ray
Are of advantage to me;
And the earth's face upward for my inspection.

My feet are locked upon the rough bark.
It took the whole of Creation      10
To produce my foot, my each feather:
Now I hold Creation in my foot

Or fly up, and revolve it all slowly—
I kill where I please because it is all mine.
There is no sophistry in my body:
My manners are tearing off heads—

The allotment of death.
For the one path of my flight is direct
Through the bones of the living.
No arguments assert my right:      20

The sun is behind me.
Nothing has changed since I began.
My eye has permitted no change.
I am going to keep things like this.

LUCILLE CLIFTON

# in the inner city

in the inner city
or
like we call it
home
we think a lot about uptown
and the silent nights
and the houses straight as
dead men
and the pastel lights
and we hang on to our no place      10
happy to be alive
and in the inner city
or
like we call it
home

ROBERT HAYDEN

# Homage to the Empress of the Blues

Because there was a man somewhere in a
  candystripe silk shirt,
gracile and dangerous as a jaguar and because a
  woman moaned
for him in sixty-watt gloom and mourned him
  Faithless Love
Twotiming Love Oh Love Oh Careless
  Aggravating Love,

    She came out on the stage in yards of
      pearls, emerging like
    a favorite scenic view, flashed her golden
      smile and sang.

Because grey laths began somewhere to show
  from underneath
torn hurdygurdy lithographs of dollfaced
  heaven;
and because there were those who feared
  alarming fists of snow
on the door and those who feared the riot-squad
  of statistics,                                                    10

    She came out on the stage in ostrich
      feathers, beaded satin,
    and shone that smile on us and sang.

WILLIAM STAFFORD

# So Long

At least at night, a streetlight
is better than a star.
And better good shoes on a
long walk than a good friend.

Often, in winter, with my old
cap, I slip away into the gloom
like a happy fish, at home
with all I touch, at the level of love.

No one can surface till far,
far on, and all that we'll have                                     10
to love may be what's near
in the cold, even then.

ALASTAIR REID

# Curiosity

may have killed the cat; more likely
the cat was just unlucky, or else curious
to see what death was like, having no cause
to go on licking paws, or fathering
litter on litter of kittens, predictably.

Nevertheless, to be curious
is dangerous enough. To distrust
what is always said, what seems,
to ask odd questions, interfere in dreams,
leave home, smell rats, have hunches                               10
do not endear cats to those doggy circles
where well-smelt baskets, suitable wives, good
  lunches
are the order of things, and where prevails
much wagging of incurious heads and tails.

Face it. Curiosity
will not cause us to die—
only lack of it will.
Never to want to see
the other side of the hill
or that improbable country                                          20
where living is an idyll
(although a probable hell)
would kill us all.
Only the curious
have, if they live, a tale
worth telling at all.

Dogs say cats love too much, are
  irresponsible,
are changeable, marry too many wives,
desert their children, chill all dinner tables
with tales of their nine lives.                                      30
Well, they are lucky. Let them be
nine-lived and contradictory,
curious enough to change, prepared to pay
the cat price, which is to die

and die again and again,
each time with no less pain.
A cat minority of one
is all that can be counted on
to tell the truth. And what cats have to tell
on each return from hell                                          40
is this: that dying is what the living do,
that dying is what the loving do,
and that dead dogs are those who do not know
that dying is what, to live, each has to do.


BIRON WALKER

# How Now

Said: Go jump in the lake.
I jumped into the lake.
It made my lips turn blue
and all my body ache.

Said: Go climb a tree.
I took the apt advice;
I tried a burred oak, blued
and blacked my flesh twice.

Said: Shove off. Blow.
As soon as said, enacted:                                         10
shoved, buffed, from shaking shore
exactly as instructed.

Said: Get lost.
So then for quite a spell
far wandering I went,
edged the edge of hell.

Presently crawled out to sun.
After a while shinned down.
Breezed back one more. Shoved in.
Turned up again—sound.                                            20

Silent, eyes lowered now.
I think I might guess why—
I think they do not know
what to say for me to do
or where to say to go
or what to say to try.

JOHN CIARDI

# Suburban Homecoming

As far as most of what you call people, my
    darling, are
concerned, I don't care who or what gets into
    the phone. I
am not home and not expected and I even,
    considerably, doubt I live here.


I mean this town and its everlasting
    katzenjammer when-
ever whoever dials again, is going to hell, or to
    some other
perpetual buffet, in a wheelbarrowful of bad
    martinis: and you, my


legal sweet, forever in the act of putting your
    hat on
as I come in the door to be told I have exactly
    five—
or, on good days, ten—minutes to change in
    because here we go


again to some collection of never-quite-the-
    same-but-                                                      10
always-no-different faces; you, my moth-brained
    flutter
from bright cup to cup, no matter what nothing
    is in them; you, my own


brand-named, laboratory-tested, fair-trade-
    priced, wedded
(as advertised in *Life*) feather-duster, may go
    jump into
twenty fathoms of Advice to the Lovelorn and
    pull it in after you—


but I have not arrived, am not in, the phone did
    not ring
and was not answered, we have not really, I
    believe, met, and
if we do and if I stay to be (I doubt it)
    introduced, I'm still not going.

HOW NOW  From *The Georgia Review*, XXII, 2 (Summer, 1968). Reprinted by permission of *The Georgia Review*.

SUBURBAN HOMECOMING  From *In Fact* by John Ciardi. © 1962 by Rutgers, The State University. Reprinted by permission of the author.

JAMES DICKEY

# To Landrum Guy, Beginning To Write at Sixty

One man in a house
Consumed by the effort of listening,
Sets down a worried phrase upon a paper.
It is poor, though it has come

From the table as out of a wall,
From his hand as out of his heart.

To sixty years it has come
At the same rate of time as he.
He cannot tell it, ever, what he thinks.
It is time, he says, he must                    10

Be thinking of nothing but singing,
Be singing of nothing but love.

But the right word cannot arrive
Through the dark, light house of one man
With his savage hand on a book,
With a cricket seizing slowly on his ear:

One man in a house cannot hear
His ear, with his hair falling out from the quick.

Even to himself he cannot say
Except with not one word,                        20
How he hears there is no more light
Than this, nor any word

More anywhere: how he is drunk
On hope, and why he calls himself mad.

Weeping is steadily built, and does not fall
From the shadow sitting slowly behind him
On the wall, like an angel who writes him a
    letter
To tell him his only talent is too late

To tell, to weep, to speak, or to begin
Here, or ever. Here, where he begins.            30

ROBERT BROWNING

# Soliloquy of the Spanish Cloister

Gr-r-r—there go, my heart's abhorrence!
    Water your damned flower-pots, do!
If hate killed men, Brother Lawrence,
    God's blood, would not mine kill you!
What? your myrtle-bush wants trimming?
    Oh, that rose has prior claims—
Needs its leaden vase filled brimming?
    Hell dry you up with its flames!

At the meal we sit together:
    *Salve tibi!* I must hear                    10
Wise talk of the kind of weather,
    Sort of season, time of year:
*Not a plenteous cork-crop: scarcely
    Dare we hope oak-galls, I doubt:*
*What's the Latin name for "parsley"?*
    What's the Greek name for Swine's Snout?

Whew! We'll have our platter burnished,
    Laid with care on our own shelf!
With a fire-new spoon we're furnished,
    And a goblet for ourself,                    20
Rinsed like something sacrificial
    Ere 'tis fit to touch our chaps—
Marked with L for our initial!
    (He-he! There his lily snaps!)

*Saint,* forsooth! While brown Dolores
    Squats outside the Convent bank
With Sanchicha, telling stories,
    Steeping tresses in the tank,
Blue-black, lustrous, thick like horse-hairs,
    —Can't I see his dead eye glow,              30
Bright as 'twere a Barbary corsair's?
    (That is, if he'd let it show!)

When he finishes refection,
    Knife and fork he never lays
Cross-wise, to my recollection,
    As do I, in Jesu's praise.
I the Trinity illustrate,
    Drinking watered orange-pulp—
In three sips the Arian frustrate;
    While he drains his at one gulp.             40

Oh, those melons! If he's able
    We're to have a feast! so nice!
One goes to the Abbott's table,
    All of us get each a slice.

How go on your flowers? None double?
   Not one fruit-sort can you spy?
Strange!—And I, too, at such trouble
   Keep them close-nipped on the sly!

There's a great text in Galatians,
   Once you trip on it, entails          50
Twenty-nine distinct damnations,
   One sure, if another fails:
If I trip him just a-dying,
   Sure of heaven as sure can be,
Spin him round and send him flying
   Off to hell, a Manichee!

Or, my scrofulous French novel
   On gray paper with blunt type!
Simply glance at it, you grovel
   Hand and foot in Belial's gripe:      60
If I double down its pages
   At the woeful sixteenth print,
When he gathers his greengages,
   Ope a sieve and slip it in't?

Or, there's Satan! one might venture
   Pledge one's soul to him, yet leave
Such a flaw in the indenture
   As he'd miss till, past retrieve,
Blasted lay that rose-acacia
   We're so proud of! *Hy, Zy, Hine . . .*   70
'St, there's Vespers! *Plena gratia,*
   *Ave, Virgo!* Gr-r-r—you swine!

## CARL SANDBURG

# Limited

I am riding on a limited express, one of the crack
   trains of the nation.
Hurtling across the prairie into blue haze and dark
   air go fifteen all-steel coaches holding a thousand
   people.
(All the coaches shall be scrap and rust and all the
   men and women laughing in the diners and
   sleepers shall pass to ashes.)
I ask a man in the smoker where he is going and
   he answers: "Omaha."

## ALAN DUGAN

# Morning Song

Look, it's morning, and a little water gurgles in the
   tap.
I wake up waiting, because it's Sunday, and turn
   twice more
than usual in bed, before I rise to cereal and comic
   strips.
I have risen to the morning danger and feel proud,
and after shaving off the night's disguises, after
   searching
close to the bone for blood, and finding only a
   little,
I shall walk out bravely into the daily accident.

## WILLIAM BUTLER YEATS

# That the Night Come

She lived in storm and strife,
Her soul had such desire
For what proud death may bring
That it could not endure
The common good of life,
But lived as 'twere a king
That packed his marriage day
With banneret and pennon,
Trumpet and kettle drum,
And the outrageous cannon          10
To bundle time away
That the night come.

## ROBERT FROST

# The Silken Tent

She is as in a field a silken tent
At midday when a sunny summer breeze
Has dried the dew and all its ropes relent,
So that in guys it gently sways at ease,

And its supporting central cedar pole,
That is its pinnacle to heavenward
And signifies the sureness of the soul,
Seems to owe naught to any single cord,
But strictly held by none, is loosely bound
By countless silken ties of love and thought 10
To everything on earth the compass round,
And only by one's going slightly taut
In the capriciousness of summer air
Is of the slightest bondage made aware.

HENRY REED

# Lessons Of War: Judging Distances

Not only how far away, but the way that you
    say it
Is very important. Perhaps you may never get
The knack of judging a distance, but at least
    you know
How to report on a landscape: the central
    sector,
The right of arc and that, which we had last
    Tuesday,
        And at least you know

That maps are of time, not place, so far as the
    army
Happens to be concerned—the reason being,
Is one which need not delay us. Again, you
    know
There are three kinds of tree, three only, the fir
    and the poplar, 10
And those which have bushy tops too; and
    lastly
        That things only seem to be things.

A barn is not called a barn, to put it more
    plainly,
Or a field in the distance, where sheep may be
    safely grazing.

THE SILKEN TENT From *The Poetry of Robert Frost*, edited by Edward Connery Lathem. Copyright 1923, 1928, 1934, © 1969 by Holt, Rinehart and Winston, Inc. Copyright 1936, 1942, 1951, © 1956, 1962 by Robert Frost. Copyright © 1964, 1970 by Lesley Frost Ballantine. Reprinted by permission of Holt, Rinehart and Winston, Inc.

You must never be over-sure. You must say,
    when reporting:
At five o'clock in the central sector is a dozen
Of what appear to be animals; whatever you do,
        Don't call the bleeders *sheep.*

I am sure that's quite clear; and suppose, for
    the sake of example,
The one at the end, asleep, endeavours to
    tell us 20
What he sees over there to the west, and how
    far away,
After first having come to attention. There to
    the west,
On the fields of summer the sun and the
    shadows bestow
        Vestments of purple and gold.

The still white dwellings are like a mirage in
    the heat,
And under the swaying elms a man and a
    woman
Lie gently together. Which is, perhaps, only to
    say
That there is a row of houses to the left of arc,
And that under some poplars a pair of what
    appears to be humans
        Appear to be loving. 30

Well that, for an answer, is what we might
    rightly call
Moderately satisfactory only, the reason being,
Is that two things have been omitted, and those
    are important.
The human beings, now: in what direction are
    they,
And how far away, would you say? And do not
    forget
        There may be dead ground in between.

There may be dead ground in between; and I
    may not have got
The knack of judging a distance; I will only
    venture
A guess that perhaps between me and the
    apparent lovers,
(Who, incidentally, appear by now to have
    finished,) 40
At seven o'clock from the houses, is roughly a
    distance
        Of about one year and a half.

JUDGING DISTANCES From *A Map of Verona and Other Poems*, copyright, 1947, by Henry Reed. Reprinted by permission of Harcourt Brace Jovanovich, Inc.

JOHN FREDERICK NIMS

# Love Poem

My clumsiest dear, whose hands shipwreck vases,
At whose quick touch all glasses chip and ring,
Whose palms are bulls in china, burs in linen,
And have no cunning with any soft thing

Except all ill-at-ease fidgeting people:
The refugee uncertain at the door
You make at home; deftly you steady
The drunk clambering on his undulant floor.

Unpredictable dear, the taxi drivers' terror,
Shrinking from far headlights pale as a dime        10
Yet leaping before red apoplectic streetcars—
Misfit in any space. And never on time.

A wrench in clocks and the solar system. Only
With words and people and love you move at
    ease.
In traffic of wit expertly manoeuvre
And keep us, all devotion, at your knees.

Forgetting your coffee spreading on our flannel,
Your lipstick grinning on our coat,
So gayly in love's unbreakable heaven
Our souls on glory of spilt bourbon float.        20

Be with me, darling, early and late. Smash
    glasses—
I will study wry music for your sake.
For should your hands drop white and empty
All the toys of the world would break.


JOANNE CHILDERS

# Children in an Empty House

Children with wet red boots and frozen faces
Went where they had never been before,
Into the empty house whose disrepair
Stared lazily from blank and broken spaces.

Children who added up dried nests of birds,
Dead matches, bits of paper, shards of glass,
Were certain they at last had found their place,
Themselves most silent at their echoing words.

Though they had beds to fill before the night,
They lay on straw and read the half-burnt
    letters                                       10
Of nameless men, and by the banging shutters
They guessed the haunts were sightless to their
    sight.

They guessed the lovers here by intimation,
Lurking like shadows in dark shadows hidden.
They guessed the tramps, the coupling cats
    unbidden
In phantom vacancy of habitation.

Because they loved the life they barely found
They knew full ownership of emptiness
In matters which could tempt them to a sense
Of unseen shadow and of unheard sound.        20


THEODORE ROETHKE

# I Knew a Woman

I knew a woman, lovely in her bones,
When small birds sighed, she would sigh back
    at them;
Ah, when she moved, she moved more ways
    than one:
The shapes a bright container can contain!
Of her choice virtues only gods should speak,
Or English poets who grew up on Greek
(I'd have them sing in chorus, cheek to cheek).

How well her wishes went! She stroked my
    chin,
She taught me Turn, and Counter-turn, and
    Stand;
She taught me Touch, that undulant white skin;  10
I nibbled meekly from her proffered hand;
She was the sickle; I, poor I, the rake,
Coming behind her for her pretty sake
(But what prodigious mowing we did make).

Love likes a gander, and adores a goose:
Her full lips pursed, the errant note to seize;
She played it quick, she played it light and
    loose;

My eyes, they dazzled at her flowing knees;
Her several parts could keep a pure repose,
Or one hip quiver with a mobile nose                20
(She moved in circles, and those circles moved).

Let seed be grass, and grass turn into hay:
I'm martyr to a motion not my own;
What's freedom for? To know eternity.
I swear she cast a shadow white as stone.
But who would count eternity in days?
These old bones live to learn her wanton ways:
(I measure time by how a body sways).


ROBERT SWARD

# Grandma Refreshed!

Grandma was out
upon the porch,
sipping catsup
through a straw.

The catsup
was made
with pineapple:
and distilled vinegar.

My sister, absorbed
in the pineapple, sucked                10

GRANDMA REFRESHED  From *The Carolina Quarterly*, Spring 1958. Copyright 1958 by *The Carolina Quarterly* and reprinted with the permission of *The Carolina Quarterly* and the author.

sometimes, at grandma's tight-
round, yellow-sour hair.

Poor grandma!
the first thing we said
to her was:
Where's grandpa?

Grandma wasn't one
for lipstick, nor for
grandpa; however,
she looked as if she were.                20

A shirt, a pair of pants
and socks
were lying there
beside the hamburger-buns.

Now, then, will anyone
have a pickle?
Grandma accepted one
herself, and smacked her lips.

Hot-damn! Grandpa's dead!! Yes,
evidently, said my mother.                30
And there was grandma, in her
little black bikini, sipping coke.

# THE POET AS ELEGIST

EMILY DICKINSON

## Because I Could Not Stop for Death

Because I could not stop for Death,
He kindly stopped for me;
The carriage held but just ourselves
And Immortality.

We slowly drove; he knew no haste,
And I had put away
My labor and my leisure too,
For his civility.

We passed the school, where children strove,
At recess, in the ring,                                           10
We passed the fields of gazing grain,
We passed the setting sun.

Or rather, he passed us;
The dews drew quivering and chill;
For only gossamer, my gown;
My tippet, only tulle.

We paused before a house that seemed
A swelling of the ground;
The roof was scarcely visible,
The cornice, in the ground.                                      20

Since then, 'tis centuries, and yet
Feels shorter than the day
I first surmised the horses' heads
Were toward eternity.

DYLAN THOMAS

## Do Not Go Gentle into That Good Night

Do not go gentle into that good night,
Old age should burn and rave at close of day;
Rage, rage against the dying of the light.

Though wise men at their end know dark is
  right,
Because their words had forked no lightning
  they
Do not go gentle into that good night.

Good men, the last wave by, crying how bright
Their frail deeds might have danced in a green
  bay,
Rage, rage against the dying of the light.

Wild men who caught and sang the sun in
  flight,                                                         10
And learn, too late, they grieved it on its way,
Do not go gentle into that good night.

Grave men, near death, who see with blinding
  sight
Blind eyes could blaze like meteors and be gay,
Rage, rage against the dying of the light.

And you, my father, there on the sad height,
Curse, bless, me now with your fierce tears, I
  pray.
Do not go gentle into that good night.
Rage, rage against the dying of the light.

A. E. HOUSMAN

## Epitaph on an Army of Mercenaries

These, in the day when heaven was falling,
  The hour when earth's foundations fled,
Followed their mercenary calling
  And took their wages and are dead.

BECAUSE I COULD NOT STOP FOR DEATH  From *The Complete Poems of Emily Dickinson*, Little, Brown and Company, 1960.
DO NOT GO GENTLE INTO THAT GOOD NIGHT  From Dylan Thomas, *The Poems of Dylan Thomas*. Copyright 1952 by Dylan Thomas. Reprinted by permission of New Directions Publishing Corporation.

Their shoulders held the sky suspended;
   They stood, and earth's foundations stay;
What God abandoned, these defended,
   And saved the sum of things for pay.

## WILLIAM WORDSWORTH
# A Slumber Did My Spirit Seal

A slumber did my spirit seal;
   I had no human fears:
She seemed a thing that could not feel
   The touch of earthly years.

No motion has she now, no force;
   She neither hears nor sees;
Rolled round in earth's diurnal course,
   With rocks, and stones, and trees.

## JOHN CROWE RANSOM
# Bells for John Whiteside's Daughter

There was such speed in her little body,
And such lightness in her footfall,
It is no wonder her brown study
Astonishes us all.

Her wars were bruited in our high window.
We looked among orchard trees and beyond,
Where she took arms against her shadow,
Or harried unto the pond

The lazy geese, like a snow cloud
Dripping their snow on the green grass,    10
Tricking and stopping, sleepy and proud,
Who cried in goose, Alas,

For the tireless heart within the little
Lady with rod that made them rise
From their noon apple-dreams and scuttle
Goose-fashion under the skies!

But now go the bells, and we are ready,
In one house we are sternly stopped
To say we are vexed at her brown study,
Lying so primly propped.    20

## W. H. AUDEN
# In Memory of W. B. Yeats

1

He disappeared in the dead of winter:
The brooks were frozen, the airports almost
   deserted,
The snow disfigured the public statues;
The mercury sank in the mouth of the dying
   day.
O all the instruments agree
The day of his death was a dark cold day.

Far from his illness
The wolves ran on through the evergreen
   forests,
The peasant river was untempted by the
   fashionable quays;
By mourning tongues    10
The death of the poet was kept from his poems.

But for him it was his last afternoon as himself,
An afternoon of nurses and rumors;
The provinces of his body revolted,
The squares of his mind were empty,
Silence invaded the suburbs,
The current of his feeling failed: he became his
   admirers.

Now he is scattered among a hundred cities
And wholly given over to unfamiliar affections;
To find his happiness in another kind of wood    20
And be punished under a foreign code of
   conscience.
The words of a dead man
Are modified in the guts of the living.

But in the importance and noise of tomorrow
When the brokers are roaring like beasts on the
    floor of the Bourse,
And the poor have the sufferings to which they
    are fairly accustomed,
And each in the cell of himself is almost
    convinced of his freedom;
A few thousand will think of this day
As one thinks of a day when one did something
    slightly unusual.

O all the instruments agree             30
The day of his death was a dark cold day.


2

You were silly like us: your gift survived it all;
The parish of rich women, physical decay,
Yourself; mad Ireland hurt you into poetry.
Now Ireland has her madness and her weather
    still,
For poetry makes nothing happen: it survives
In the valley of its saying where executives
Would never want to tamper; it flows south
From ranches of isolation and the busy griefs,
Raw towns that we believe and die in; it
    survives,      40
A way of happening, a mouth.


3

Earth, receive an honored guest;
William Yeats is laid to rest:
Let the Irish vessel lie
Emptied of its poetry.

Time that is intolerant
Of the brave and innocent,
And indifferent in a week
To a beautiful physique,

Worships language and forgives      50
Everyone by whom it lives;
Pardons cowardice, conceit,
Lays its honors at their feet.

Time that with this strange excuse
Pardoned Kipling and his views,
And will pardon Paul Claudel,
Pardons him for writing well.

In the nightmare of the dark
All the dogs of Europe bark,
And the living nations wait,      60
Each sequestered in its hate;

Intellectual disgrace
Stares from every human face,
And the seas of pity lie
Locked and frozen in each eye.

Follow, poet, follow right
To the bottom of the night,
With your unconstraining voice
Still persuade us to rejoice;

With the farming of a verse      70
Make a vineyard of the curse,
Sing of human unsuccess
In a rapture of distress;

In the deserts of the heart
Let the healing fountain start,
In the prison of his days
Teach the free man how to praise.


RICHARD EBERHART

# The Groundhog

In June, amid the golden fields,
I saw a groundhog lying dead.
Dead lay he; my senses shook,
And mind outshot our naked frailty.
There lowly in the vigorous summer
His form began its senseless change,
And made my senses waver dim
Seeing nature ferocious in him.
Inspecting close his maggots' might
And seething cauldron of his being,      10
Half with loathing, half with a strange love,
I poked him with an angry stick.
The fever rose, became a flame
And Vigour circumscribed the skies,
Immense energy in the sun,
And through my frame a sunless trembling.
My stick had done nor good nor harm.
Then stood I silent in the day
Watching the object, as before;
And kept my reverence for knowledge      20
Trying for control, to be still,
To quell the passion of the blood;
Until I had bent down on my knees
Praying for joy in the sight of decay.
And so I left; and I returned
In Autumn strict of eye, to see
The sap gone out of the groundhog,
But the bony sodden hulk remained.

But the year had lost its meaning,
And in intellectual chains                                    30
I lost both love and loathing,
Mured up in the wall of wisdom.
Another summer took the fields again
Massive and burning, full of life,
But when I chanced upon the spot
There was only a little hair left,
And bones bleaching in the sunlight
Beautiful as architecture;
I watched them like a geometer,
And cut a walking stick from a birch.                         40
It has been three years, now.
There is no sign of the groundhog.
I stood there in the whirling summer,
My hand capped a withered heart,
And thought of China and of Greece,
Of Alexander in his tent;
Of Montaigne in his tower,
Of Saint Theresa in her wild lament.

THE GROUNDHOG    From *Collected Poems 1930–1960* by Richard Eberhart. © 1960 by Richard Eberhart. Reprinted by permission of Oxford University Press, Inc.

DYLAN THOMAS

# Twenty-Four Years

Twenty-four years remind the tears of my eyes.
(Bury the dead for fear that they walk to the grave
    in labour.)
In the groin of the natural doorway I crouched like
    a tailor
Sewing a shroud for a journey
By the light of the meat-eating sun.
Dressed to die, the sensual strut begun,
With my red veins full of money,
In the final direction of the elementary town
I advance for as long as forever is.

TWENTY-FOUR YEARS    From Dylan Thomas, *Collected Poems*. Copyright 1939 by New Directions Publishing Corporation. Reprinted by permission by New Directions Publishing Corporation.

# THE POET AS CRITIC AND PHILOSOPHER

OLGA CABRAL

## Dead Sister of the Moon

Take the grand tour of the planet:
the busses are leaving for the badlands of
    bottletops.
See the petrified seaports! Visit the skeletal
    ships
moored on the shores of cinders.
Observe these sharp grids of footprints:
cybernetic man was here and gone.
He left his glyph on the dry ocean beds
in the dust of the bones of starfish.

A pity the planet's last President
could not attend his own inauguration                    10
but sent a xerox copy of himself
for thalidomide posterity.
A pair of Custer's last boots took the oath of
    office
and stands to this day in the Presidential
    Pantheon
where a myth machine still grinds missing a
    generator:
"It was the biggest barbecue ever!"

There was a god of this place: they called it
Huitzilopochitli or Gross National Product.
We are still decoding their history
from missing documents found in the mummy
    wrappings                                            20
of Cabinet members. Long ago
it was all declared a disaster area
when the god fell broken and blind in the
    market place
among dead croupiers and rusted bottletops.

ROBERT CREELEY

## I Know a Man

As I sd to my
friend, because I am
always talking,—John, I

sd, which was not his
name, the darkness sur-
rounds us, what

can we do against
it, or else, shall we &
why not, buy a goddamn big car,

drive, he sd, for                                        10
christ's sake, look
out where yr going.

PETER DAVISON

## The Gun Hand

You have been looking out for me. I held
A pistol to the ear of the Saigon captive.
It's been a busy year. I plugged the preacher
As he leaned on the lattice railing of his motel
And drilled the senator as he strode among the
    busboys.
I have aimed a thousand killers of all calibres
At television pictures, egg-hatted cops,
At the pulsing cartilage of a child's temple,
At the upstart cars that pass mine on the right.
I have squeezed so often you might think me
    weary,                                               10
But my hand is poised and clenched to squeeze
    again
At the next sweet target of opportunity.

ALAN DUGAN

# Tribute to Kafka
# for Someone Taken

The party is going strong.
The doorbell rings. It's
for someone named me.
I'm coming. I take
a last drink, a last
puff on a cigarette,
a last kiss at a girl,
and step into the hall,
                              bang,
shutting out the laughter. "Is          10
your name you?" "Yes."
"Well come along then."
"See here. See here. See here."

ANNE SEXTON

# The Farmer's Wife

From the hodge porridge
of their country lust,
their local life in Illinois,
where all their acres look
like a sprouting broom factory,
they name just ten years now
that she has been his habit;
as again tonight he'll say
honey bunch let's go
and she will not say how there     10
must be more to living
than this brief bright bridge
of the raucous bed or even
the slow braille touch of him
like a heavy god grown light,
that old pantomime of love
that she wants although
it leaves her still alone,
built back again at last,
minds apart from him, living       20

her own self in her own words
and hating the sweat of the house
they keep when they finally lie
each in separate dreams
and then how she watches him,
still strong in the blowzy bag
of his usual sleep while
her young years bungle past
their same marriage bed
and she wishes him cripple, or poet,     30
or even lonely, or sometimes,
better, my lover, dead.

DENNIS TRUDELL

# Going to Pittsburgh

In and between the cities
the go-go girls are bluffing.
They really will not step down
and lie on a corner table.

The men prefer the ones
who look most like coeds.
The men have come there
from factories or softball.

Their eyes do not love
one another's eyes; their              10
wives or girlfriends are home
changing sheets or channels.

Their in-laws fail to
understand them, their sons
wear faggoty hair—Something
is hungry; it is not fed.

———

In and between the cities
the night is ungenerous.
The pizza and hamburgers
are thin; hitchhikers freeze.          20

The car-hops don't jounce.
The motels are unfriendly,
their flies bite. Their walls
are sick of self-abortions.

Something is hungry; it is
not fed—In the soft suburbs
the martinis aren't working.
The heads of industry are sad.

Their candidates don't win.
Their alma maters won't let     30
them re-enroll; their suicide
notes have comma splices.

In and between the cities
the stares of the blacks
are causing cigarette burns
in beds of the middle class.

The husbands do not know
how to load the small arms
they have bought for summer.
They think often of Sweden.     40

They think that in rooms
behind drapes in Negro bars
the Navajos learn karate.
They fear for their stereos.

Something in and between
the cities is hungry; it is
not fed. This is no season
to learn the names of birds—

It is no time for that.

Soft fists insist on     10
Heaving the needles,
The leafy bedding,

Even the paving.
Our hammers, our rams,
Earless and eyeless,

Perfectly voiceless,
Widen the crannies,
Shoulder through holes. We

Diet on water,
On crumbs of shadow,     20
Bland-mannered, asking

Little or nothing.
So many of us!
So many of us!

We are shelves, we are
Tables, we are meek,
We are edible,

Nudgers and shovers     30
In spite of ourselves.
Our kind multiplies:

We shall by morning
Inherit the earth.
Our foot's in the door.

SYLVIA PLATH

# Mushrooms

Overnight, very
Whitely, discreetly,
Very quietly

Our toes, our noses
Take hold on the loam,
Acquire the air.

Nobody sees us,
Stops us, betrays us;
The small grains make room.

PERCY BYSSHE SHELLEY

# Ozymandias

I met a traveler from an antique land
Who said: Two vast and trunkless legs of stone
Stand in the desert. Near them, on the sand,
Half sunk, a shattered visage lies, whose frown,
And wrinkled lip, and sneer of cold command,
Tell that its sculptor well those passions read
Which yet survive, stamped on these lifeless
    things,
The hand that mocked them, and the heart that
    fed.
And on the pedestal these words appear:
"My name is Ozymandias, king of kings;     10
Look on my works, ye Mighty, and despair!"
Nothing beside remains. Round the decay
Of that colossal wreck, boundless and bare,
The lone and level sands stretch far away.

RANDALL JARRELL

# The Death of the Ball Turret Gunner

From my mother's sleep I fell into the State,
And I hunched in its belly till my wet fur froze.
Six miles from earth, loosed from its dream of life,
I woke to black flak and the nightmare fighters.
When I died they washed me out of the turret
    with a hose.


ROBINSON JEFFERS

# The Bloody Sire

It is not bad. Let them play.
Let the guns bark and the bombing-plane
Speak his prodigious blasphemies.
It is not bad, it is high time,
Stark violence is still the sire of all the world's
    values.
What but the wolf's tooth whittled so fine
The fleet limbs of the antelope?
What but fear winged the birds, and hunger
Jeweled with such eyes the great goshawk's
    head?
Violence has been the sire of all the world's          10
    values.
Who would remember Helen's face
Lacking the terrible halo of spears?
Who formed Christ but Herod and Caesar,
The cruel and bloody victories of Caesar?
Violence, the bloody sire of all the world's
    values.

Never weep, let them play,
Old violence is not too old to beget new values.


ROBINSON JEFFERS

# Science

Man, introverted man, having crossed
In passage and but a little with the nature of
    things this latter century
Has begot giants; but being taken up
Like a maniac with self-love and inward
    conflicts cannot manage his hybrids.

Being used to deal with edgeless dreams,
Now he's bred knives on nature turns them also
    inward: they have thirsty points though.
His mind forebodes his own destruction;
Actaeon who saw the goddess naked among
    leaves and his hounds tore him.
A little knowledge, a pebble from the shingle,
A drop from the oceans: who would have
    dreamed this infinitely little too much?          10


A. E. HOUSMAN

# "Terence, This Is Stupid Stuff . . ."

"Terence, this is stupid stuff:
You eat your victuals fast enough;
There can't be much amiss, 'tis clear,
To see the rate you drink your beer.
But oh, good Lord, the verse you make,
It gives a chap the belly-ache.
The cow, the old cow, she is dead;
It sleeps well, the horned head:
We poor lads, 'tis our turn now
To hear such tunes as killed the cow.          10
Pretty friendship 'tis to rhyme
Your friends to death before their time
Moping melancholy mad:
Come, pipe a tune to dance to, lad."

Why, if 'tis dancing you would be,
There's brisker pipes than poetry.
Say, for what were hop-yards meant,
Or why was Burton built on Trent?
Oh many a peer of England brews
Livelier liquor than the Muse,          20
And malt does more than Milton can
To justify God's ways to man.
Ale, man, ale's the stuff to drink
For fellows whom it hurts to think:

THE DEATH OF THE BALL TURRET GUNNER  From *Little Friend, Little Friend*, 1945, by Randall Jarrell. Reprinted by permission of the author.
THE BLOODY SIRE  Reprinted from *Be Angry at the Sun and Other Poems*, by Robinson Jeffers. Copyright 1941 by Robinson Jeffers. Reprinted by permission of Random House, Inc.
SCIENCE  Copyright 1925 and renewed 1953 by Robinson Jeffers. Reprinted from *The Selected Poetry of Robinson Jeffers* by permission of Random House, Inc.
"TERENCE, THIS IS STUPID STUFF . . ."  From "A Shropshire Lad"—Authorised Edition—from *The Collected Poems of A. E. Housman*. Copyright 1939, 1940, © 1959 by Holt, Rinehart and Winston, Inc. Copyright © 1967, 1968 by Robert E. Symons. Reprinted by permission of Holt, Rinehart and Winston, Inc.

Look into the pewter pot
To see the world as the world's not.
And faith, 'tis pleasant till 'tis past:
The mischief is that 'twill not last.
Oh I have been to Ludlow fair
And left my necktie God knows where,
And carried half-way home, or near,
Pints and quarts of Ludlow beer:
Then the world seemed none so bad,
And I myself a sterling lad;
And down in lovely muck I've lain,
Happy till I woke again.
Then I saw the morning sky:
Heigho, the tale was all a lie;
The world, it was the old world yet,
I was I, my things were wet,
And nothing now remained to do
But begin the game anew.

Therefore, since the world has still
Much good, but much less good than ill,
And while the sun and moon endure
Luck's a chance, but trouble's sure,
I'd face it as a wise man would,
And train for ill and not for good.
'Tis true, the stuff I bring for sale
Is not so brisk a brew as ale:
Out of a stem that scored the hand
I wrung it in a weary land.
But take it: if the smack is sour,
The better for the embittered hour;
It should do good to heart and head
When your soul is in my soul's stead;
And I will friend you, if I may,
In the dark and cloudy day.

There was a king reigned in the East:
There, when kings will sit to feast,
They get their fill before they think
With poisoned meat and poisoned drink.
He gathered all that springs to birth
From the many-venomed earth;
First a little, thence to more,
He sampled all her killing store;
And easy, smiling, seasoned sound
Sate the king when healths went round.
They put arsenic in his meat
And stared aghast to watch him eat;
They poured strychnine in his cup
And shook to see him drink it up:
They shook, they stared as white's their shirt:
Them it was their poison hurt.
—I tell the tale that I heard told.
Mithridates, he died old.

MATTHEW ARNOLD

# Dover Beach

The sea is calm tonight,
The tide is full, the moon lies fair
Upon the straits;—on the French coast the light
Gleams and is gone; the cliffs of England stand,
Glimmering and vast, out in the tranquil bay.
Come to the window, sweet is the night-air!
Only, from the long line of spray
Where the sea meets the moon-blanched land,
Listen! you hear the grating roar
Of pebbles which the waves draw back, and fling,
At their return, up the high strand,
Begin, and cease, and then again begin,
With tremulous cadence slow, and bring
The eternal note of sadness in.
Sophocles long ago
Heard it on the Aegean, and it brought
Into his mind the turbid ebb and flow
Of human misery; we
Find also in the sound a thought,
Hearing it by this distant northern sea.

The Sea of Faith
Was once, too, at the full, and round earth's shore
Lay like the folds of a bright girdle furled.
But now I only hear
Its melancholy, long, withdrawing roar,
Retreating, to the breath
Of the night-wind, down the vast edges drear
And naked shingles of the world.

Ah, love, let us be true
To one another! for the world, which seems
To lie before us like a land of dreams,
So various, so beautiful, so new,
Hath really neither joy, nor love, nor light,
Nor certitude, nor peace, nor help for pain;
And we are here as on a darkling plain
Swept with confused alarms of struggle and flight,
Where ignorant armies clash by night.

DYLAN THOMAS

# In My Craft or Sullen Art

In my craft or sullen art
Exercised in the still night
When only the moon rages

And the lovers lie abed
With all their griefs in their arms,
I labour by singing light
Not for ambition or bread
Or the strut and trade of charms
On the ivory stages
But for the common wages          10
Of their most secret heart.
Not for the proud man apart
From the raging moon I write
On these spindrift pages
Not for the towering dead
With their nightingales and psalms
But for the lovers, their arms
Round the griefs of the ages,
Who pay no praise or wages
Nor heed my craft or art.          20

## ROBERT FROST

# Sand Dunes

Sea waves are green and wet,
But up from where they die
Rise others vaster yet,
And those are brown and dry.

They are the sea made land
To come at the fisher town
And bury in solid sand
The men she could not drown.

She may know cove and cape,
But she does not know mankind     10
If by any change of shape
She hopes to cut off mind.

Men left her a ship to sink:
They can leave her a hut as well;
And be but more free to think
For the one more cast-off shell.

## EDWIN ARLINGTON ROBINSON

# Karma

Christmas was in the air and all was well
With him, but for a few confusing flaws
In divers of God's images. Because
A friend of his would neither buy nor sell,
Was he to answer for the axe that fell?
He pondered; and the reason for it was,
Partly, a slowly freezing Santa Claus
Upon the corner, with his beard and bell.

Acknowledging an improvident surprise,
He magnified a fancy that he wished          10
The friend whom he had wrecked were here
    again.
Not sure of that, he found a compromise;
And from the fullness of his heart he fished
A dime for Jesus who had died for men.

## COUNTEE CULLEN

# Ultimatum

I hold not with the fatalist creed
Of what must be must be;
There is enough to meet my need
In this most meagre me.

These two slim arms were made to rein
My steed, to ward and fend;
There is more gold in this small brain
Than I can ever spend.

The seed I plant is chosen well;
Ambushed by no sly sweven,          10
I plant it if it droops to hell,
Or if it blooms to heaven.

IN MY CRAFT OR SULLEN ART  From Dylan Thomas, *Collected Poems.* Copyright 1946, 1952 by Dylan Thomas. Reprinted by permission of New Directions Publishing Corporation.
SAND DUNES  From *The Poetry of Robert Frost* edited by Edward Connery Lathem. Copyright 1923, 1928, 1934, © 1969 by Holt, Rinehart and Winston, Inc. Copyright 1936, 1942, 1951, © 1956, 1962 by Robert Frost. Copyright © 1964, 1970 by Lesley Frost Ballantine. Reprinted by permission of Holt, Rinehart and Winston, Inc.

KARMA  Reprinted with permission of The Macmillan Company from *Collected Poems* by Edwin Arlington Robinson. Copyright 1925 by Edwin Arlington Robinson. Copyright renewed 1953 by Ruth Nivison and Barbara R. Holt.
ULTIMATUM  From *On These I Stand* (1947) by Countee Cullen. Copyright, 1927 by Harper & Row, Publishers, Inc.; renewed 1955 by Ida M. Cullen. Reprinted by permission of Harper & Row, Publishers.

COUNTEE CULLEN

# From the Dark Tower

We shall not always plant while others reap
The golden increment of bursting fruit,
Not always countenance, abject and mute,
That lesser men should hold their brothers
    cheap;
Not everlastingly while others sleep
Shall we beguile their limbs with mellow flute,
Not always bend to some more subtle brute;
We were not made eternally to weep.

The night whose sable breast relieves the stark,
White stars is no less lovely being dark,                                  10
And there are buds that cannot bloom at all
In light, but crumple, piteous, and fall;
So in the dark we hide the heart that bleeds,
And wait, and tend our agonizing seeds.

WILLIAM CARLOS WILLIAMS

# Poem

As the cat
climbed over
the top of

the jamcloset
first the right
forefoot

carefully
then the hind
stepped down

into the pit of                                  10
the empty
flowerpot

WILLIAM CARLOS WILLIAMS

# The Term

A rumpled sheet
of brown paper
about the length

and apparent bulk
of a man was
rolling with the

wind slowly over
and over in
the street as

a car drove down                                  10
upon it and
crushed it to

the ground. Unlike
a man it rose
again rolling

with the wind over
and over to be as
it was before.

HART CRANE

# Voyages I

Above the fresh ruffles of the surf
Bright striped urchins flay each other with sand.
They have contrived a conquest for shell shucks,
And their fingers crumble fragments of baked
    weed
Gaily digging and scattering.

And in answer to their treble interjections
The sun beats lightning on the waves,
The waves fold thunder on the sand;
And could they hear me I would tell them:

O brilliant kids, frisk with your dog,                     10
Fondle your shells and sticks, bleached
By time and the elements; but there is a line
You must not cross nor ever trust beyond it
Spry cordage of your bodies to caresses
Too lichen-faithful from too wide a breast.
The bottom of the sea is cruel.

Loose the flood, you shall find it patent,
  Gush after gush, reserved for you;
Scarlet experiment! sceptic Thomas,
  Now, do you doubt that your bird was true?

HENRY WADSWORTH LONGFELLOW

# Nature

As a fond mother, when the day is o'er,
Leads by the hand her little child to bed,
Half willing, half reluctant to be led
And leave his broken playthings on the floor,
Still gazing at them through the open door,
Nor wholly reassured and comforted
By promises of others in their stead,
Which, though more splendid, may not please
  him more:
So Nature deals with us, and takes away
Our playthings one by one, and by the hand          10
Leads us to rest so gently that we go
Scarce knowing if we wish to go or stay,
Being too full of sleep to understand
How far the unknown transcends the what we
  know.

EMILY DICKINSON

# Success Is Counted Sweetest

Success is counted sweetest
By those who ne'er succeed.
To comprehend a nectar
Requires sorest need.

Not one of all the purple host
Who took the Flag today
Can tell the definition,
So clear of victory

As he, defeated—dying—
On whose forbidden ear                          10
The distant strains of triumph
Burst agonized and clear!

JOHN MILTON

# On His Blindness

When I consider how my light is spent
  Ere half my days in this dark world and wide,
  And that one talent which is death to hide
  Lodged with me useless, though my soul
    more bent
To serve therewith my Maker, and present
  My true account, lest He returning chide,
  "Doth God exact day-labor, light denied?"
  I fondly ask. But Patience, to prevent
That murmur, soon replies, "God doth not need
  Either man's work or his own gifts. Who best
  Bear His mild yoke, they serve Him best. His
    state                                        10
Is kingly: thousands at His bidding speed
  And post o'er land and ocean without rest;
  They also serve who only stand and wait."

EMILY DICKINSON

# Split the Lark and
# You'll Find the Music

Split the lark and you'll find the music,
  Bulb after bulb, in silver rolled,
Scantily dealt to the summer morning,
  Saved for your ear when lutes be old.

SUCCESS IS COUNTED SWEETEST  From *The Complete Poems of Emily Dickinson*, Little, Brown and Company, 1960.
SPLIT THE LARK AND YOU'LL FIND THE MUSIC  From *The Complete Poems of Emily Dickinson*, Little, Brown and Company, 1960.

304 POETRY

THOMAS HARDY

# Hap

If but some vengeful god would call to me
From up the sky, and laugh: "Thou suffering
 thing,
Know that thy sorrow is my ecstasy,
That thy love's loss is my hate's profiting!"

Then would I bear it, clench myself, and die,
Steeled by the sense of ire unmerited;
Half-eased in that a Powerfuller than I
Had willed and meted me the tears I shed.

But not so. How arrives it joy lies slain,
And why unblooms the best hope ever sown? 10
—Crass Casualty obstructs the sun and rain,
And dicing Time for gladness casts a moan. . . .
These purblind Doomsters had as readily strown
Blisses about my pilgrimage as pain.

THOMAS HARDY

# The Convergence of the Twain

(*Lines on the loss of the* Titanic)

 In a solitude of the sea
 Deep from human vanity,
And the Pride of Life that planned her, stilly
 couches she.

 Steel chambers, late the pyres
 Of her salamandrine fires,
Cold currents thrid, and turn to rhythmic tidal
 lyres.

 Over the mirrors meant
 To glass the opulent
The sea-worm crawls—grotesque, slimed, dumb,
 indifferent.

 Jewels in joy designed 10
 To ravish the sensuous mind
Lie lightless, all their sparkles bleared and black
 and blind.

 Dim moon-eyed fishes near
 Gaze at the gilded gear
And query: "What does this vaingloriousness
 down here?" . . .

 Well: while was fashioning
 This creature of cleaving wing,
The Immanent Will that stirs and urges
 everything

 Prepared a sinister mate
 For her—so gaily great— 20
A Shape of Ice, for the time far and dissociate.

 And as the smart ship grew
 In stature, grace, and hue,
In shadowy silent distance grew the Iceberg
 too.

 Alien they seemed to be:
 No mortal eye could see
The intimate welding of their later history,

 Or sign that they were bent
 By paths coincident
On being anon twin halves of one august event, 30

 Till the Spinner of the Years
 Said "Now!" And each one hears,
And consummation comes, and jars two
 hemispheres.

THOMAS HARDY

# The Man He Killed

 Had he and I but met
 By some old ancient inn,
We should have sat us down to wet
 Right many a nipperkin!

 But ranged as infantry,
 And staring face to face,
I shot at him as he at me,
 And killed him in his place.

HAP Reprinted with permission of The Macmillan Company from *Collected Poems* by Thomas Hardy. Copyright 1925 by The Macmillan Company.
THE CONVERGENCE OF THE TWAIN Reprinted with permission of The Macmillan Company from *Collected Poems* by Thomas Hardy. Copyright 1925 by The Macmillan Company.
THE MAN HE KILLED Reprinted with permission of The Macmillan Company from *Collected Poems* by Thomas Hardy. Copyright 1925 by The Macmillan Company.

I shot him dead because—
Because he was my foe,                                    10
Just so: my foe of course he was;
     That's clear enough; although

He thought he'd 'list, perhaps
Off-hand-like—just as I—
Was out of work—had sold his traps—
     No other reason why.

Yes; quaint and curious war is!
You shoot a fellow down
You'd treat if met where any bar is,
     Or help to half-a-crown.                             20

RICHARD WILBUR

# Year's End

Now winter downs the dying of the year,
And night is all a settlement of snow;
From the soft street the rooms of houses show
A gathered light, a shapen atmosphere,
Like frozen-over lakes whose ice is thin
And still allows some stirring down within.

I've known the wind by water banks to shake
The late leaves down, which frozen where they
     fell
And held in ice as dancers in a spell
Fluttered all winter long into a lake;            10
Graved on the dark in gestures of descent,
They seemed their own most perfect monument.

There was perfection in the death of ferns
Which laid their fragile cheeks against the
     stone
A million years. Great mammoths overthrown
Composedly have made their long sojourns,
Like palaces of patience, in the gray
And changeless lands of ice. And at Pompeii

The little dog lay curled and did not rise
But slept the deeper as the ashes rose            20
And found the people incomplete, and froze
The random hands, the loose unready eyes

Of men expecting yet another sun
To do the shapely thing they had not done.

These sudden ends of time must give us pause.
We fray into the future, rarely wrought
Save in the tapestries of afterthought.
More time, more time. Barrages of applause
Come muffled from a buried radio.
The New-year bells are wrangling with the
     snow.                                           30

RICHARD WILBUR

# Lamarck Elaborated

*"The environment creates the organ"*

The Greeks were wrong who said our eyes have
     rays;
Not from these sockets or these sparkling poles
Comes the illumination of our days.
It was the sun that bored these two blue holes.

It was the song of doves begot the ear
And not the ear that first conceived of sound:
That organ bloomed in vibrant atmosphere,
As music conjured Ilium from the ground.

The yielding water, the repugnant stone,
The poisoned berry and the flaring rose           10
Attired in sense the tactless finger-bone
And set the taste-buds and inspired the nose.

Out of our vivid ambiance came unsought
All sense but that most formidably dim.
The shell of balance rolls in seas of thought.
It was the mind that taught the head to swim.

Newtonian numbers set to cosmic lyres
Whelmed us in whirling worlds we could not
     know,
And by the imagined floods of our desires
The voice of Sirens gave us vertigo.              20

YEAR'S END  From *Ceremony and Other Poems*, copyright, 1948, 1949, 1950, by Richard Wilbur. Reprinted by permission of Harcourt Brace Jovanovich, Inc.

LAMARCK ELABORATED  From *Things of This World*, © 1956, by Richard Wilbur. Reprinted by permission of Harcourt Brace Jovanovich, Inc.

## MARIANNE MOORE

# Silence

My father used to say,
"Superior people never make long visits,
have to be shown Longfellow's grave
or the glass flowers at Harvard.
Self-reliant like the cat—
that takes its prey to privacy,
the mouse's limp tail hanging like a shoelace
    from its mouth—
they sometimes enjoy solitude,
and can be robbed of speech
by speech which has delighted them.                          10
The deepest feeling always shows itself in
    silence;
not in silence, but restraint."
Nor was he insincere in saying, "Make my
    house your inn."
Inns are not residences.

## JOHN BETJEMAN

# Senex

Oh would I could subdue the flesh
    Which sadly troubles me!
And then perhaps could view the flesh
As though I never knew the flesh
    And merry misery.

To see the golden hiking girl
    With wind about her hair,
The tennis-playing, biking girl,
The wholly-to-my-liking girl,
    To see and not to care.                                 10

At sundown on my tricycle
    I tour the Borough's edge,
And icy as an icicle
See bicycle by bicycle
    Stacked waiting in the hedge.

SILENCE  Reprinted with permission of The Macmillan Company from *Collected Poems* by Marianne Moore. Copyright 1935 by Marianne Moore, renewed 1963 by Marianne Moore and T. S. Eliot.

SENEX  From *John Betjeman's Collected Poems*, Houghton Mifflin Company, 1959. Reprinted by permission of John Murray Ltd.

Get down from me! I thunder there,
    You spaniels! Shut your jaws!
Your teeth are stuffed with underwear,
Suspenders torn asunder there
    And buttocks in your paws!                              20

Oh whip the dogs away, my Lord,
    They make me ill with lust.
Bend bare knees down to pray, my Lord,
Teach sulky lips to say, my Lord,
    That flaxen hair is dust.

## EDNA ST. VINCENT MILLAY

# Sonnet to Gath

Country of hunchbacks!—where the strong,
    straight spine,
Jeered at by crooked children, makes his way
Through by-streets at the kindest hour of day,
Till he deplore his stature, and incline
To measure manhood with a gibbous line;
Till out of loneliness, being flawed with clay,
He stoop into his neighbour's house and say,
"Your roof is low for me—the fault is mine."
Dust in an urn long since, dispersed and dead
Is great Apollo; and the happier he;                        10
Since who amongst you all would lift a head
At a god's radiance on the mean door-tree,
Saving to run and hide your dates and bread,
And cluck your children in about your knee?

## RALPH WALDO EMERSON

# The Rhodora: On Being Asked, Whence Is the Flower?

In May, when sea-winds pierced our solitudes,
I found the fresh Rhodora in the woods,
Spreading its leafless blooms in a damp nook,
To please the desert and the sluggish brook.
The purple petals, fallen in the pool,
Made the black water with their beauty gay;
Here might the red-bird come his plumes to
    cool,

SONNET TO GATH  From *Collected Poems* of Edna St. Vincent Millay, Harper & Row. Copyright 1921, 1928, 1948, 1955 by Edna St. Vincent Millay and Norma Millay Ellis. Reprinted by permission of Norma Millay Ellis.

And court the flower that cheapens his array.
Rhodora! if the sages ask thee why
This charm is wasted on the earth and sky, 10
Tell them, dear, that if eyes were made for
 seeing,
Then Beauty is its own excuse for being:
Why thou wert there, O rival of the rose!
I never thought to ask, I never knew;
But, in my simple ignorance, suppose
The self-same Power that brought me there
 brought you.

## T. S. ELIOT

# Animula

"Issues from the hand of God, the simple soul"
To a flat world of changing lights and noise,
To light, dark, dry or damp, chilly or warm;
Moving between the legs of tables and of
 chairs,
Rising or falling, grasping at kisses and toys,
Advancing boldly, sudden to take alarm,
Retreating to the corner of arm and knee,
Eager to be reassured, taking pleasure
In the fragrant brilliance of the Christmas tree,
Pleasure in the wind, the sunlight and the sea; 10
Studies the sunlit pattern on the floor
And running stags around a silver tray;
Confounds the actual and the fanciful,
Content with playing-cards and kings and
 queens,
What the fairies do and what the servants say.
The heavy burden of the growing soul
Perplexes and offends more, day by day;
Week by week, offends and perplexes more
With the imperatives of "is and seems"
And may and may not, desire and control. 20
The pain of living and the drug of dreams
Curl up the small soul in the window seat
Behind the *Encyclopaedia Britannica*.
Issues from the hand of time the simple soul
Irresolute and selfish, misshapen, lame,
Unable to fare forward or retreat,
Fearing the warm reality, the offered good,
Denying the importunity of the blood,
Shadow of its own shadows, spectre in its own
 gloom,
Leaving disordered papers in a dusty room; 30
Living first in the silence after the viaticum.

Pray for Guiterriez, avid of speed and power,
For Boudin, blown to pieces,
For this one who made a great fortune,
And that one who went his own way.
Pray for Floret, by the boarhound slain between
 the yew trees,
Pray for us now and at the hour of our birth.

## THEODORE ROETHKE

# The Waking

I wake to sleep, and take my waking slow.
I feel my fate in what I cannot fear.
I learn by going where I have to go.

We think by feeling. What is there to know?
I hear my being dance from ear to ear.
I wake to sleep, and take my waking slow.

Of those so close beside me, which are you?
God bless the ground! I shall walk softly there,
And learn by going where I have to go.

Light takes the tree; but who can tell us how? 10
The lowly worm climbs up a winding stair;
I wake to sleep, and take my waking slow.

Great Nature has another thing to do
To you and me; so take the lively air,
And, lovely, learn by going where to go.

This shaking keeps me steady. I should know.
What falls away is always. And is near.
I wake to sleep, and take my waking slow.
I learn by going where I have to go.

## WALLACE STEVENS

# Anecdote of the Jar

I placed a jar in Tennessee,
And round it was, upon a hill.
It made the slovenly wilderness
Surround that hill.

The wilderness rose up to it,
And sprawled around, no longer wild.
The jar was round upon the ground
And tall and of a port in air.

It took dominion everywhere.
The jar was gray and bare.                    10
It did not give of bird or bush,
Like nothing else in Tennessee.

RICHARD EBERHART

# Rumination

When I can hold a stone within my hand
And feel time make it sand and soil, and see
The roots of living things grow in this land,
Pushing between my fingers flower and tree,
Then I shall be as wise as death,
For death has done this and he will
Do this to me, and blow his breath
To fire my clay, when I am still.

WILLIAM BUTLER YEATS

# Crazy Jane Talks
# with the Bishop

I met the Bishop on the road
And much said he and I.
"Those breasts are flat and fallen now,
Those veins must soon be dry;
Live in a heavenly mansion,
Not in some foul sty."

"Fair and foul are near of kin,
And fair needs foul," I cried.
"My friends are gone, but that's a truth

Nor grave nor bed denied,                     10
Learned in bodily lowliness
And in the heart's pride.

"A woman can be proud and stiff
When on love intent;
But Love has pitched his mansion in
The place of excrement;
For nothing can be sole or whole
That has not been rent."

WILLIAM BUTLER YEATS

# The Second Coming

Turning and turning in the widening gyre
The falcon cannot hear the falconer;
Things fall apart; the centre cannot hold;
Mere anarchy is loosed upon the world,
The blood-dimmed tide is loosed, and
    everywhere
The ceremony of innocence is drowned;
The best lack all conviction, while the worst
Are full of passionate intensity.

Surely some revelation is at hand;
Surely the Second Coming is at hand.         10
The Second Coming! Hardly are those words
    out
When a vast image out of *Spiritus Mundi*
Troubles my sight: somewhere in sands of the
    desert
A shape with lion body and the head of a man,
A gaze blank and pitiless as the sun,
Is moving its slow thighs, while all about it
Reel shadows of the indignant desert birds.
The darkness drops again; but now I know
That twenty centuries of stony sleep
Were vexed to nightmare by a rocking cradle,  20
And what rough beast, its hour come round at
    last,
Slouches towards Bethlehem to be born?

JOSEPHINE MILES

# Government Injunction Restraining Harlem Cosmetic Co.

They say La Jac Brite Pink Skin Bleach avails
    not,
They say its Orange Beauty Glow does not
    glow,
Nor the face grow five shades lighter nor the
    heart
Five shades lighter. They say no.

They deny good luck, love, power, romance,
    and inspiration
From La Jac Brite ointment and incense of all
    kinds,
And condemn in writing skin brightening and
    whitening
And whitening of minds.

There is upon the federal trade commission a
    burden of glory
So to defend the fact, so to impel                 10
The plucking of hope from the hand, honor
    from the complexion,
Sprite from the spell.


HOWARD NEMEROV

# Writing

The cursive crawl, the squared-off characters,
these by themselves delight, even without
a meaning, in a foreign language, in
Chinese, for instance, or when skaters curve
all day across the lake, scoring their white
records in ice. Being intelligible,
these winding ways with their audacities
and delicate hesitations, they become
miraculous, so intimately, out there
at the pen's point or brush's tip, do world      10
and spirit wed. The small bones of the wrist

balance against great skeletons of stars
exactly; the blind bat surveys his way
by echo alone. Still, the point of style
is character. The universe induces
a different tremor in every hand, from the
check-forger's to that of the Emperor
Hui Tsung, who called his own calligraphy
the 'Slender Gold.' A nervous man
writes nervously of a nervous world, and so on.  20

Miraculous. It is as though the world
were a great writing. Having said so much,
let us allow there is more to the world
than writing; continental faults are not
bare convoluted fissures in the brain.
Not only must the skaters soon go home;
also the hard inscription of their skates
is scored across the open water, which long
remembers nothing, neither wind nor wake.


E. E. CUMMINGS

# pity this busy monster,manunkind

pity this busy monster,manunkind,

not. Progress is a comfortable disease:
your victim (death and life safely beyond)

plays with the bigness of his littleness
—electrons deify one razorblade
into a mountainrange;lenses extend

unwish through curving wherewhen till unwish
returns on its unself.
                         A world of made
is not a world of born—pity poor flesh

and trees,poor stars and stones,but never this   10
fine specimen of hypermagical

ultraomnipotence. We doctors know

a hopeless case if—listen:there's a hell
of a good universe next door;let's go

GERARD MANLEY HOPKINS

# I Wake and Feel the Fell of Dark

I wake and feel the fell of dark, not day.
What hours, O what black hoùrs we have spent
This night! what sights you, heart, saw; ways
   you went!
And more must, in yet longer light's delay.
   With witness I speak this. But where I say
Hours I mean years, mean life. And my lament
Is cries countless, cries like dead letters sent
To dearest him that lives alas! away.

   I am gall, I am heartburn. God's most deep
   decree
Bitter would have me taste: my taste was me;    10
Bones built in me, flesh filled, blood brimmed
   the curse.
   Selfyeast of spirit a dull dough sours. I see
The lost are like this, and their scourge to be
As I am mine, their sweating selves; but worse.

GERARD MANLEY HOPKINS

# Carrion Comfort

Not, I'll not, carrion comfort, Despair, not feast
   on thee;
Not untwist—slack they may be—these last
   strands of man
In me ór, most weary, cry *I can no more.* I can;
Can something, hope, wish day come, not
   choose not to be.
But ah, but O thou terrible, why wouldst thou
   rude on me
Thy wring-world right foot rock? lay a lionlimb
   against me? scan
With darksome devouring eyes my bruisèd
   bones? and fan,
O in turns of tempest, me heaped there; me
   frantic to avoid thee and flee?

Why? That my chaff might fly; my grain lie,
   sheer and clear.
Nay in all that toil, that coil, since (seems) I
   kissed the rod,    10
Hand rather, my heart lo! lapped strength, stole
   joy, would laugh, chéer.
Cheer whom though? the hero whose
   heaven-handling flung me, fóot tród
Me? or me that fought him? O which one? is it
   each one? That night, that year
Of now done darkness I wretch lay wrestling
   with (my God!) my God.

ROBERT LOWELL

# Salem

In Salem seasick spindrift drifts or skips
To the canvas flapping on the seaward panes
Until the knitting sailor stabs at ships
Nosing like sheep of Morpheus through his
   brain's
Asylum. Seaman, seaman, how the draft
Lashes the oily slick about your head,
Beating up whitecaps! Seaman, Charon's raft
Dumps its damned goods into the harbor-bed,—
There sewage sickens the rebellious seas.
Remember, seaman, Salem fishermen    10
Once hung their nimble fleets on the Great
   Banks.
Where was it that New England bred the men
Who quartered the Leviathan's fat flanks
And fought the British Lion to his knees?

ARCHIBALD MAC LEISH

# You, Andrew Marvell

And here face down beneath the sun
And here upon earth's noonward height
To feel the always coming on
The always rising of the night

To feel creep up the curving east
The earthly chill of dusk and slow
Upon those under lands the vast
And ever-climbing shadow grow

And strange at Ecbatan the trees
Take leaf by leaf the evening strange          10
The flooding dark about their knees
The mountains over Persia change

And now at Kermanshah the gate
Dark empty and the withered grass
And through the twilight now the late
Few travelers in the westward pass

And Baghdad darken and the bridge
Across the silent river gone
And through Arabia the edge
Of evening widen and steal on                   20

And deepen on Palmyra's street
The wheel rut in the ruined stone
And Lebanon fade out and Crete
High through the clouds and overblown

And over Sicily the air
Still flashing with the landward gulls
And loom and slowly disappear
The sails above the shadowy hulls

And Spain go under and the shore
Of Africa the gilded sand                       30
And evening vanish and no more
The low pale light across that land

Nor now the long light on the sea—

And here face downward in the sun
To feel how swift how secretly
The shadow of the night comes on . . .

DELMORE SCHWARTZ

# The Heavy Bear Who Goes With Me

*"The withness of the body"*—WHITEHEAD

The heavy bear who goes with me,
A manifold honey to smear his face,
Clumsy and lumbering here and there,
The central ton of every place,
The hungry beating brutish one
In love with candy, anger, and sleep,
Crazy factotum, dishevelling all,
Climbs the building, kicks the football,
Boxes his brother in the hate-ridden city.

Breathing at my side, that heavy animal,        10
That heavy bear who sleeps with me,
Howls in his sleep for a world of sugar,
A sweetness intimate as the water's clasp,
Howls in his sleep because the tight-rope
Trembles and shows the darkness beneath.
—The strutting show-off is terrified,
Dressed in his dress-suit, bulging his pants,
Trembles to think that his quivering meat
Must finally wince to nothing at all.

That inescapable animal walks with me,          20
Has followed me since the black womb held,
Moves where I move, distorting my gesture,
A caricature, a swollen shadow,
A stupid clown of the spirit's motive,
Perplexes and affronts with his own darkness,
The secret life of belly and bone,
Opaque, too near, my private, yet unknown,
Stretches to embrace the very dear
With whom I would walk without him near,
Touches her grossly, although a word          30
Would bare my heart and make me clear,
Stumbles, flounders, and strives to be fed
Dragging me with him in his mouthing care,
Amid the hundred million of his kind,
The scrimmage of appetite everywhere.

PABLO PICASSO

# give tear twist and kill

give tear twist and kill I traverse illuminate and
burn caress and lick embrace and look I sound at
every flight and bells till they bleed frightening
the pigeons and I make them fly around the
    dovecot
till they fall to earth already dead of weariness

THE HEAVY BEAR WHO GOES WITH ME    From Delmore
Schwartz, *Selected Poems: Summer Knowledge*. Copyright
1938 by New Directions. Reprinted by permission of New
Directions Publishing Corporation.
GIVE TEAR TWIST AND KILL    Reprinted by permission of Faber
and Faber Ltd. and the author.

I will raze all the windows and doors to the
    earth
and with your hair I will hang all the birds that
    are
singing and cut down all the flowers I will take
    the lamp
in my arms and give it my breast to eat and
    will
go to sleep alongside the song of my solitude          10
by *Soleares* and I will etch the fields of wheat
    and
hay and I shall see them die supine with their
    faces
to the sun and I will wrap the flowers in the
    newspaper and
I will fling them through the window
in the gutterstream that is hurrying by with all
    its
sins on its back but laughing all the same to
    make
its nest in the sewer and I will break the
    music of
the woodlands against the rocks of the waves of
    the
sea and I will bite the lion on the cheek and I
will make the wolf cry for tender pity in front          20

of the portrait of the water which is letting its
    arms
fall slackly into the wash-hand basin.


WILLIAM BLAKE

# The Scoffers

Mock on, Mock on, Voltaire, Rousseau;
Mock on, Mock on; 'tis all in vain!
You throw the sand against the wind,
And the wind blows it back again.

And every sand becomes a Gem
Reflected in the beams divine;
Blown back they blind the mocking eye,
But still in Israel's paths they shine.

The Atoms of Democritus
And Newton's Particles of light                          10
Are sands upon the Red sea shore,
Where Israel's tents do shine so bright.

# GLOSSARY OF POETIC TERMS

ACCENT: Stress or emphasis given to a poetic syllable. *See* Prosody.

ALLEGORY: A narrative in which objects and persons stand for meanings outside the narrative itself; an elaborated metaphor. *See* Figurative Language.

ALLITERATION: The repetition of initial consonant sounds or of accented consonant sounds. *See* Rime; Texture.

ALLUSION: A reference to something outside the primary content of the poem, often used figuratively.

ANALOGY: A comparison, bordering on metaphor, of particular points of resemblance between obviously different things.

ANAPEST: *See* Meter; Prosody.

APOSTROPHE: Direct address to a person, object, or abstract idea, often treating the dead as living, the nonhuman as human, and the absent as present. *See* Figurative Language.

ASSONANCE: Repetition of vowel sounds that are not followed, as in rime, by similar consonants. *See* Rime; Texture.

BALLAD: In its original form a simple, highly concentrated verse-story, often sung. The more recent literary ballad is a consciously artistic imitation. *See* Narrative; Types of Poetry.

BLANK VERSE: Unrimed iambic pentameter. *See* Prosody; Stanza; Verse Paragraphs.

CACOPHONY: Harsh, unpleasant sound. *See* Euphony; Texture.

CADENCE: Rhythmic, though not regularly metrical, flow of language. Cadence is influenced by many of the factors that determine rhythm. *See* Rhythm.

CAESURA: A sense pause within a line of poetry. *See* Prosody.

CONSONANCE: Identity of the pattern of consonants (*deer, door*); unlike rime in that the vowels involved differ. *See* Rime; Texture.

COUPLET: The form of verse with two successive lines riming. *See* Stanza.

DACTYL: *See* Meter; Prosody.

DIMETER: *See* Line; Meter; Prosody.

DRAMATIC: That one of the three main types of poetry which uses methods that resemble the methods of drama. *See* Types of Poetry.

DRAMATIC MONOLOGUE: Poem that is the speech of one character.

ELEGY: A subjective, meditative poem, usually expressing emotions associated with grief or death. *See* Lyric; Types of Poetry.

END-STOPPED LINE: Line whose end coincides with a pause in meaning. *See* Prosody.

ENVOY: A short stanza in the nature of a postscript at the end of a poem.

EPIC: A long narrative poem in elevated style dealing with heroic personalities and great actions. *See* Narrative; Types of Poetry.

EUPHONY: Sound combinations, consonant or vowel, which are pleasing to the ear. *See* Cacophony; Texture.

EYE-RIME: A terminal pairing of words or syllables that appear from the spelling to rime but in pronunciation do not (*yea, tea*).

FIGURATIVE LANGUAGE: Words used out of their literal sense to convey a special effect and meaning. Many figures of speech are based upon comparison or intensification. The more common figures are simile and metaphor, which are based on comparison. Other figurative comparisons are symbol and allegory. Some figures based on intensification are personification, apostrophe, hyperbole, litotes or understatement, and irony.

FOOT: A metrical unit composed of one accented syllable and one or more unaccented syllables. *See* Meter; Prosody.

FREE VERSE: Verse with loose or irregular rhythm. *See* Stanza.

HEPTAMETER: *See* Line; Meter; Prosody.

HEXAMETER: *See* Line; Meter; Prosody.

HYPERBOLE: Figure of speech using an exaggerated statement not intended to be taken literally; overstatement. *See* Understatement; Figurative Language.

IAMB: *See* Meter; Prosody.

IMAGERY: The representation of sensory experience by use of allusions and figurative language. *See* Allusion; Figurative Language.

INTERNAL RIME: Rime occurring within a single line of poetry. *See* Rime.

IRONY: An implication opposite to the literal meaning of the words used; a situation or effect opposite to the expected and the normally appropriate one. *See* Figurative Language.

ITALIAN SONNET: *See* Sonnet.

LINE: A typographical unit of one metrical foot in verse. The poetic line is described by the predominant kind of foot and the number of feet it contains. *See* Foot; Meter; Prosody.

LYRIC: A poem meant to be sung, or an especially musical or highly subjective poem; one of the three main types of poetry. *See* Types of Poetry.

METAPHOR: Narrowly, the figure of speech expressing by implication—not using *as* or *like*—a resemblance of an object in one class to an object in another class. Broadly, figurative language in general. *See* Figurative Language; Simile.

METER: The relationship of accented and unaccented syllables. Used both to designate the kind of metrical foot and the number of feet in a line of verse. The common kinds of meter in English are anapestic, dactylic, trochaic, iambic. The spondee, a metrical foot of two accented syllables, is only approximated in English prosody. Common line lengths (reckoned in number of metrical feet) are monometer, dimeter, trimeter, tetrameter, pentameter, hexameter, heptameter. *See* Line; Rhythm; Prosody.

MONOMETER: *See* Line; Meter; Prosody.

NARRATIVE: A story, or a connected series of events; one of the three main types of poetry. *See* Types of Poetry.

OCTAVE: Stanza of eight lines, or the first eight lines of a sonnet. *See* Sonnet.

ODE: Usually a serious formal poem that follows a set, complicated metrical pattern and is written for a special purpose and occasion. *See* Lyric; Types of Poetry.

ONOMATOPOEIA: Words formed in imitation of the natural sounds they name. *See* Texture.

PARODY: An imitation of the language, style, and ideas of another work for comic or critical effect.

PASTORAL: Broadly, a type of classical poetry, or, narrowly, any favorable treatment of rural life. *See* Lyric; Types of Poetry.

PENTAMETER: *See* Line; Meter; Prosody.

PERSONIFICATION: Figure of speech in which human qualities are given to nonhuman objects or abstractions. *See* Figurative Language.

PETRARCHAN SONNET: *See* Sonnet.

PROSODY: Art of metrical composition, or a special theory or practice in metrics. See fuller discussion of prosody, pages 315–316.

QUATRAIN: Four-line stanza in any of a number of end-rime schemes. *See* Prosody; Stanza.

RHYTHM: Literally, the measured motion of language. Rhythm is primarily a product of the relationship of accented and unaccented syllables or sounds, though pitch, tempo, syllabic length, and sentence structure are other influential factors. Often rhythm refers to regular metrical pattern. *See* Meter.

RIME: Usually refers to end rime, the similarity or correspondence of the terminal sounds of words; but, in general, rime is any degree of correspondence of sound combinations whether terminal or internal (within a line). Slant or partial rime is an approximate correspondence of sounds. Textural effects—assonance, consonance, alliteration—are themselves forms of rime. *See* Internal Rime; Texture.

RIME SCHEME: The patterns of end rime in a stanza. Small letters are ordinarily used to indicate this pattern, thus: couplet, *aa;* ballad quatrain, *abcb;* envelope quatrain, *abba;* Rubáiyát quatrain, *aaba;* Spenserian stanza, *ababbcbcc. See* Stanza.

RUN-ON LINE: A line in which the sense is not concluded but continues into the next line without pause. *See* Prosody; End-stopped Line.

SCANSION: The determining of the relationship between accented and unaccented syllables in verse. *See* Prosody.

SESTET: Stanza of six lines, or the last six lines of a sonnet. *See* Sonnet.

SHAKESPEAREAN SONNET: *See* Sonnet.

SIMILE: The figure of speech expressing with *as* or *like* a resemblance in one or more points of an object of one class to an object of another class. *See* Figurative Language; Metaphor.

SLANT RIME: Loose or approximate rime (*run, tone*). *See* Rime.

SONNET: A poem of fourteen lines in iambic pentameter. The Petrarchan or Italian sonnet commonly divides itself into an octave riming *abbaabba,* in which the theme is presented, and a sestet riming *cdecde,* or sometimes more freely, in which the conclusion to the theme is presented. The Shakespearean sonnet, riming *ababcdcdefefgg,* commonly develops the theme in three quatrains and concludes it in a couplet.

SPONDEE: *See* Meter; Prosody.

STANZA: A pattern of lines and rimes in verse. Stanzas are identified on the basis of the type of meter, number of metrical feet in each line, number of lines, and the pattern of rime when rime is employed. Many stanzaic patterns have been long established and have conventional names—for example, couplet, ballad quatrain, Spenserian. Blank verse (unrimed iambic pentameter) and other non-stanzaic verse forms (like free verse) may be broken into verse paragraphs, which are determined more by content than by form. *See* Prosody.

SYMBOL: In the broadest sense, something that suggests or stands for an idea, quality, or conception larger than itself, as the lion is the symbol of courage, the cross the symbol of Christianity. In poetic usage, a symbol is a more central and pervasive comparison than either simile or metaphor, often providing the basic imagery of an entire poem. It represents a step beyond metaphor in that the first term of the comparison is not supplied. *See* Figurative Language.

TEMPO: Rate of articulation or delivery of words and syllables. *See* Rhythm.

TETRAMETER: *See* Line; Meter; Prosody.

TEXTURE: As applied to poetry, texture is the general relationship of sounds, generally not including the more exact forms of rime. Important textural devices are cacophony, euphony, onomatopoeia, alliteration, assonance, consonance. *See* Rime.

TRIMETER: *See* Line; Meter; Prosody.

TROCHEE: *See* Meter; Prosody.

TYPES OF POETRY: Generally, poetry is divided into three main types: the narrative, which is the story poem; the dramatic, which uses many of the methods of the drama itself; and the lyric, which is highly musical, emotional, subjective. Some common types of dramatic poetry are the dramatic monologue and the verse-drama. Some common types of lyric are the descriptive lyric, the didactic lyric, the elegy, the hymn, the sonnet, the ode, the pastoral, the reflective or philosophical lyric, and the satiric lyric. *See* Dramatic; Lyric; Narrative.

UNDERSTATEMENT: Popular designation of the figure of speech classically known as *litotes.* Understatement is the saying less about an occasion than might normally be expected. *See* Figurative Language.

VERSE: A single line of a poem. A literary composition with a systematic metrical pattern as opposed to prose. Sometimes *verse* is used disparagingly in reference to such compositions as attain only the outward and mechanical features and not the high quality of poetry.

VERSE PARAGRAPHS: Thought divisions in non-stanzaic verse forms such as blank verse and free verse. *See* Stanza.

## PROSODY

*Prosody,* generally defined as the "science of versification," rises above mere attention to the mechanical considerations of metrical structure to become an art of communication in which the sound furthers the sense and in which the sense intensifies the sound. Since English verse is primarily accentual and not quantitative (that is, primarily dependent upon emphasis given a syllable rather than on length of syllable), English prosody is much a matter of studying the occurrence of accents.

The prosodic structure of a stanza is analyzed by a process known as *scansion.* In scanning, one examines (1) the prevailing metrical foot; (2) the line length; (3) the placement of pauses; and (4) the number of lines and, if the verse is rimed, the pattern of end rime.

### 1. METRICAL FEET

*Iamb:* Unaccented syllable, accented syllable (a-gó).

*Trochee:* Accented syllable, unaccented syllable (dwél-ling).

*Anapest:* Two unaccented syllables, accented syllable (of the sún).

*Dactyl:* Accented syllable, two unaccented syllables (mér-ri-ly).

*Spondee:* A fifth kind of metrical foot, in which two consecutive accented syllables from different metrical feet occur or in which a primary and secondary accent occur consecutively (pláy-hóuse).

## 2. LINE

The line length in metrical feet is *monometer* if the line has one foot, *dimeter* if two feet, *trimeter* if three, *tetrameter* if four, *pentameter* if five, *hexameter (Alexandrine)* if six, *heptameter* if seven, *octameter* if eight. In theory there may be more than eight feet in a line, but in practice a line longer than heptameter tends to break up into two or more lines.

## 3. PAUSES

Also important, especially in blank verse, alliterative verse, and the heroic couplet, is the location of pauses ending sense units—phrases, clauses, sentences—within the line. A main pause, known as the *caesura,* and secondary pauses are common. (In scansion they are indicated by the symbols // and /.) A line is termed *end-stopped* when it ends with a sense pause, *run-on* when the sense extends into the next line.

Little verse is metrically perfect, for metrical perfection does not permit the flexibility necessary to combine sense and sound most fittingly. Nearly all English verse is iambic, but substitution of another type of foot is common and substantial passages of trochee, dactyl, and anapest can be found.

## 4. PATTERN OF LINES AND RIMES

The number of lines and the rime pattern are described as *couplet (aa); tercet* or *triplet (terza rima, aba-bcb-cdc,* etc.); *quatrain (ballad, abcb; Rubáiyát, aaba; envelope quatrain, abba); octave;* and so forth.

Following are metrical descriptions of some common verse patterns.

---

*Blank verse:* Iambic pentameter unrimed.

The  wórld|was  áll|befóre|them, // whére|to chóose
Their  pláce|of  reśt, |// and  Prov́|idence|their guíde.
They, / hańd | in  hańd, | //with  wán | dering steṕs | and  slów,

---

Through É|den toók|their sol|itár|y wáy.

---

*Heroic couplet:* Iambic pentameter rimed *(aa);* first couplet below is run-on, second couplet end-stopped.

Of all|the cáus|es which|conspíre|to blínd
Man's ér|ring júdge|ment, and|misguíde|the mind,
Whát  the|weák heád|with stróng|est bí|as rules,
Is Prí́de, // the nev́|er faíl|ing vice|of foóls.

---

*Ballad measure:* Iambic, first and third lines tetrameter, second and fourth lines trimeter, and second and fourth lines riming (i.e., iambic, 4-3-4-3, *abcb).*

And soón|I heárd|a roár|ing wínd;
It díd| not come| anéar;
But with| its sound| it shoók| the saíls
That wére|so thín|and seár.

---

*Rubáiyát quatrain:* Iambic pentameter rimed *aaba.*

Come, fill|the cúp, |// and in|the fíre|of Spríng
Your Win|ter-gár|ment of|Repén|tance fling.
The Bird|of Time|has but|a lit|tle wáy
To flút|ter // —and|the Bird|is on|the Wing.

---

*Spenserian stanza:* Iambic pentameter rimed *ababbcbcc,* the last line being hexameter (Alexandrine).

And still|she slept|an az|ure-lid|ded sleép,
In blán|chèd lin|en, / smóoth, |and láv|endered,
While hé|from forth|the clós|et brought|a heáp
Of cán|died ap|ple, quínce,|and plúm,|and gourd;
With jél|lies sooth|er thán|the creám|y curd,
And lú|cent sýr|ops, // tinct|with cin|namon;
Mánna|and dates,|in ar|gosý|transferred
From Féz;|and spic|èd dáin|ties, év|ery one,
From  sil|ken  Sam|arcand|to  cé|dared Léb|anón.

# NOTES ON THE POETS

CONRAD AIKEN (1889–　　), born in Savannah, Georgia, is an American poet, anthologist, and critic. A leader among American poets who wrote immediately after World War I, he was, from 1917 to 1919, a contributing editor to *The Dial*, a distinguished literary magazine that gave staunch support to new artistic movements and published the works of new authors. In 1930 he was awarded a Pulitzer Prize for his *Selected Poems*, and in 1950–51 he served as poetry consultant to the Library of Congress. His poetry, musical but occasionally obscure, records his deep probing of the human spirit. Recent publications are *Thee*, 1968, and *Collected Poems*, 1970.

MATTHEW ARNOLD (1822–1888), an English poet and critic greatly interested in social and religious topics, was strongly affected by the science of his day. In both his poetry and his prose he revealed wide learning and a deep respect for culture, which he defined as "the best that has been thought and said in the world."

W. H. AUDEN (1907–　　), an English-born, Oxford-educated poet, now a naturalized American citizen, was, in the 1930's, a leader of a group of young English poets who wrote about the political and social problems of their time. More recently, Mr. Auden's verse has shown a religious and philosophical outlook. In 1967 he was awarded the National Medal for Literature. Two of his recent works are *About the Home*, 1965, and *Secondary Worlds*, 1968.

HILAIRE BELLOC (1870–1953), born in Paris and educated at Oxford University, wrote essays, historical pieces, novels, and poetry. He became a British subject in 1902 and was at one time a member of the House of Commons. He was one of the most prolific and versatile of English writers, and his poems are characterized by brilliance, wit, and careful craftsmanship.

JOHN BETJEMAN (1906–　　), an English poet, was educated at Oxford University. He writes on architectural subjects with the same polish and wit that appear in his poetry. He has been a book critic for the *Daily Telegraph*, a weekly columnist for the *Spectator*, a prep-school master, an essayist, a radio and television performer, and the author of guidebooks. In 1958 his *Collected Poems* appeared. His latest work is *Victorian and Edwardian London*, 1969.

MORRIS BISHOP (1893–　　) was educated at Cornell University. After serving in the United States Infantry during World War I, engaging in business, and holding various government positions, he returned to Cornell. He is now Kappa Alpha Professor of Romance Literature, Emeritus. *A Bowl of Bishop*, 1954, was his twelfth book. His last major publication is *The Exotics*, 1969.

WILLIAM BLAKE (1757–1827), the self-educated son of a London tradesman, was a rare combination of poet and painter. In his lyrics and in his highly original paintings, notably those for *The Book of Job*, he expressed a mystical awareness of the Divine.

GWENDOLYN BROOKS (1917–　　), a teacher who lives in Chicago, won the Pulitzer Prize in 1949 for her second book of poems, *Annie Allen*. Since then she has published a novel, *Maud Martha*, 1953, and further volumes of poetry, including *Selected Poems* in 1963. Her latest volume of poems is *Riot*, 1969.

ROBERT BROWNING (1812–1889), English poet of the Victorian period, wrote for many years without attracting public attention or critical approval, but he lived to become a hero in the literary world, with cults founded solely to study his works. He is especially known for his employment of the dramatic verse monologue to reveal character and personality.

OLGA CABRAL (1909–　　), born in Trinidad, West Indies, now makes her home in New York City. She has published several volumes of poetry—the first being *Cities and Deserts*, 1959, and the latest being *The Evaporated Man*, 1968.

G. K. CHESTERTON (1874–1936), often called the master of paradox, began his literary career as a critic of art books. A versatile writer, he published fiction (he is best remembered in this field as the creator of Father Brown, a whimsical priest-detective), biography, criticism, poetry, essays, and plays.

JOANNE CHILDERS (1926–    ), born in Cincinnati, Ohio, is a graduate of the University of Cincinnati and holds a master's degree in modern European history from the University of Florida. Besides continuing to publish poems in many reputable magazines, she pursues an active career in social and health-related services.

JOHN CIARDI (1916–    ), a major American poet and critic, won his first notable poetry prize while he was earning his M.A. at the University of Michigan. He has taught in several U.S. and foreign colleges. His translation of Dante's *Inferno* and *Purgatorio* won wide acclaim. For many years he served as poetry editor of the *Saturday Review* and now writes for *World* magazine. He has published many volumes of poetry. *In Fact*, 1963, offers a good sampling of his verse.

LUCILLE CLIFTON (1936–    ) has published two books for children as well as numerous poems. Her first volume of poems, *Good Times*, appeared in 1969. She is presently writing non-fiction.

HART CRANE (1899–1932) was an American poet who began writing verse at thirteen. In 1926 he published the best of his early poems in *White Buildings;* in 1930 *The Bridge* appeared—a group of fifteen poems unified by a symbolic use of the Brooklyn Bridge. Crane wrote from his experience, using bold symbols and showing mystical insight; his poetry is becoming increasingly significant to the American literary scene. His early suicide followed great personal difficulties and a belief that his best creative years were over.

ROBERT CREELEY (1926–    ) is a member of the group known as the Black Mountain school of poets. In addition to many volumes of poetry, he has published a novel, *The Island*, 1963, and criticism, *A Quick Graph*, 1970. A recent book of his verse is *Pieces*, 1969.

COUNTEE CULLEN (1903–1946), a black poet who was popular during the twenties and thirties, wrote seven volumes of verse (*Color*, 1925, was the first; *On These I Stand*, 1947, the last),

largely about the feelings and aspirations of blacks.

E. E. CUMMINGS (1894–1962), was born in Cambridge, Massachusetts, and was educated at Harvard University. He published many volumes of verse and prose. The unconventional punctuation and form of his poetry are technical devices which indicate the way the poem should be read and which he felt gave purer and clearer expression of his thought. His *73 Poems* was published in 1963. A posthumous volume of his *Complete Poems* was issued in 1968.

PETER DAVISON (1928–    ), a native of New York City, won first prize in the Yale Series of Younger Poets contest in 1962. His *Breaking of the Day* was published in 1964 and *The City and the Island* in 1966.

WALTER DE LA MARE (1873–1956), English novelist and poet, wrote verse for children and adults. It is marked by music and mystery.

JAMES DICKEY (1923–    ) won the National Book Award in 1966 and was consultant in poetry to the Library of Congress 1966–1968. He published a best-selling novel, *Deliverance*, in 1970. Most distinguished as a poet, he has many volumes of poetry, including a collected work, *Poems 1957–1967*, and his recent *The Eye-Beaters, Blood, Victory, Madness, Buckhead, and Mercy*, 1970.

EMILY DICKINSON (1830–1886), now considered one of America's greatest poets, spent most of her life in self-imposed seclusion. She published only four poems in her lifetime and won no wide audience until the 1920's. Though her poems are all brief, they show close observation, intensity, and illuminating, often whimsical, metaphor.

JOHN DONNE (1572–1631), who, after an intense spiritual struggle, became the most famous Anglican preacher of his day, won his lasting reputation not so much for his *Sermons* as for two groups of poems, the love lyrics of his youth and the religious lyrics of his maturity.

ALAN DUGAN (1923–    ) was born in Brooklyn, attended Olivet College and Mexico City College, and served in the U.S. Air Force in World War II. He received his first award for poetry in 1946. Since then he has received the National Book Award for Poetry in 1961, the Pulitzer Prize for Poetry in 1962, and a Guggenheim Fellowship in 1963–64. He has published *Poems*, 1961, and *Poems 2*, 1963. His *Collected Poems* appeared in 1969.

RICHARD EBERHART (1904–    ) is an American poet, playwright, and teacher. In 1930 he published *A Bravery of Earth;* several other volumes of his poems have appeared, including *Collected Poems*, 1960. He has published much verse since then, including *Shifts of Being* in 1968.

T. S. ELIOT (1888–1965), an American-born critic and poet who became a British citizen, influenced a whole generation of writers, particularly through his long poem *The Waste Land*. His major theme is the frustration and the consequent spiritual inadequacy of our times.

RALPH WALDO EMERSON (1803–1882), clergyman, philosopher, poet, and essayist, was born in Concord, Massachusetts, educated at Harvard University, and became one of the major literary figures in America. He was the leader of the Transcendentalist movement, which was based on his philosophical doctrine of the relation of the soul to nature.

JOHN FANDEL (1925–    ), a professor of English at Manhattan College, is also poetry editor of *The Commonweal*. His first collection of poems, *The Season's Difference*, was published while he was a college senior. In addition to privately issued works, he has published a further volume, *Testament*, 1959, and a sequel, *Body of Earth*, 1972.

ROBERT FROST (1874–1963), though born in San Francisco, is identified with the New England of his forebears. As a young man, he taught, farmed, and wrote poetry there—all with little initial success. Not until he went to England for the years 1912–15 did he come to the attention of critics and public. After his return to New England, his reputation grew steadily. He won the Pulitzer Prize four times and is considered one of the greatest American poets.

ROBERT GRAVES (1895–    ), an English novelist, poet, and critic, was elected to the Chair of Poetry at Oxford University, in 1961. Both as poet and as novelist, he displays a wide, thorough scholarship and an active imagination. His poetry often does not seem to be in either the American or British tradition. In 1961 his *Collected Poems* appeared. A recent work is entitled *Poems 1968–1970*, 1971.

ARTHUR GUITERMAN (1871–1943), an American lecturer and magazine editor, wrote light verse with wry humor and unexpected twists.

THOM GUNN (1929–    ) is an English poet whose verse often deals with the violence in the contemporary scene. He is a graduate of Cambridge University and has taught at the University of California at Berkeley. His fifth volume of poems, *Touch*, came out in 1968.

THOMAS HARDY (1840–1928), one of the two or three English writers who have produced both great poetry and great novels, was trained as an architect. His earliest writings were poems; about 1870 he turned to the novel and wrote all his novels in the succeeding twenty-six years. In 1896, discouraged by harsh criticism of *Jude the Obscure*, which he had written a year earlier, he returned to poetry. In this final period of his work he wrote *The Dynasts*, 1904–08, a great epic drama in verse and the most ambitious of his poems.

ROBERT HAYDEN (1913–    ) is writer-in-residence at the University of Michigan. His books of poetry include *Heart-Shape in the Dust*, 1940; *Figure of Time*, 1955; *A Ballad of Remembrance*, 1962; *Selected Poems*, 1966; and *Words in the Mourning Time*, 1971.

ROBERT HERRICK (1591–1674), the most popular of the Cavalier poets, was, like Donne, a churchman as well as a poet. Like Donne, too, he is best known for his love lyrics and religious lyrics. His graceful, light secular poems usually treat of the simple pleasures of life and of love.

ROBERT HOGAN (1930–    ) is a teacher, critic, and poet. He has published poems, several articles on the theater and on Sean O'Casey's plays, and a book, *The Experiments of Sean O'Casey*, 1960.

GERARD MANLEY HOPKINS (1844–1889), a brilliant Oxford graduate, became converted to Roman Catholicism and entered the priesthood. His poetry, which was experimental in its imagery and rhythm, was not known until 1918, when Robert Bridges published a volume of his verse.

A. E. HOUSMAN (1859–1936), English scholar and poet, was not a prolific writer; he produced only three small volumes of lyrics. But the simplicity, irony, and flawlessness of these lyrics place him among the chief English poets.

TED HUGHES (1930–    ), born in Yorkshire, England, was married to the American poet Sylvia Plath. Since the appearance of his book of poems *Hawk in the Rain*, 1957, he has been considered by many as one of the foremost poetic talents of our day. *Wodwo*, 1967, is typical of his themes, attitudes, and arresting imagery. His latest volume is *Crow*, 1971.

RANDALL JARRELL (1914–1965), American poet, has taught at several universities; in 1956–58 he was poetry consultant to the Library of Congress. His poetry, greatly influenced by his experiences in World War II, shows his deep reaction to the tragedies of life and to the courage of many who face those tragedies. His *Complete Poems* was issued posthumously in 1968.

ROBINSON JEFFERS (1887–1962) has been called American poetry's apostle of negation. Jeffers' poetic line resembles Whitman's in length, vigor, and rhythm, but the philosophies of the two poets are at opposite poles. Jeffers' creed is the renunciation of humanity and the glorification of unspoiled nature.

HENRY WADSWORTH LONGFELLOW (1807–1882) was born in Maine and educated at Bowdoin College, where he was a classmate of Nathaniel Hawthorne. Later he was professor of modern languages at Bowdoin and Harvard University. He is best known for his long poems "Evangeline" and "Hiawatha" and for "Paul Revere's Ride."

ROBERT LOWELL (1917–    ) is an American poet who writes much about New England, commemorating his ancestors who settled there and became influential in American life; he is a great-grandnephew of James Russell Lowell. In 1940 he converted to Catholicism, and many of his poems written since then reflect his religious thinking. He was awarded the Pulitzer Prize in 1947 for his volume of poetry *Lord Weary's Castle*. Lowell's recent work includes *The Old Glory* (three plays based on stories by Hawthorne and Melville) 1964, and *Notebooks 1967–1968*, 1969.

LUCIAN (c. 120–c. 200), Greek poet, satirist, and wit, came to literary notice after the Roman Empire had expanded to include Greece. He is considered the first classical writer to have composed satirical dialogue. His writing has been compared to that of Swift and Voltaire.

PHYLLIS MC GINLEY (1905–    ) is a writer of light verse. She has published several volumes and contributed widely to national magazines. *Times Three*, one of her most popular volumes, first appeared in 1954.

ARCHIBALD MAC LEISH (1892–    ), an important public figure as well as a literary man, has been Librarian of Congress and an undersecretary of state. In 1949, he was awarded the Boylston Professorship of Rhetoric and Oratory at Harvard University. He has published many notable works in poetry and drama.

JOHN MANIFOLD (1915–    ), poet and musicologist, was born in Australia and educated at Cambridge University. Though he uses a variety of poetic forms, he shows a mature control of them; his poetry stresses action and lyricism. His *Selected Verse* was published in 1946.

ANDREW MARVELL (1621–1678) was educated at Cambridge University and became in 1657 assistant to John Milton, who was Latin secretary to the Council of State. His poetry at first was chiefly lyrical. Later he turned to political satire in verse.

EVE MERRIAM (1916–    ) pursues a versatile career in radio, editorial work, and writing. She has published numerous children's books and seven volumes of poetry, including a recent one entitled *There Is No Rhyme for Silver*, 1962. Her first volume, *Family Court*, 1945, won the Yale Series of Younger Poets award.

JOSEPHINE MILES (1911–    ) is a poet, scholar, and educator. She received her undergraduate degree from the University of California at Los Angeles and two advanced degrees from the University of California at Berkeley. She has taught at Berkeley since 1940. She has published several volumes of poems, including *Poems 1936–60*, and has done much scholarly and critical writing.

EDNA ST. VINCENT MILLAY (1892–1950), Pulitzer Prize winner for poetry in 1923, was born in Rockland, Maine, attended school at Vassar College, and, after a varied career as journalist, actress, dramatist, and libretto writer, devoted the remainder of her life to writing poetry. Her verse is distinguished by its passionate zest for life, its revolt against Victorian prudery, and its intense emotions. *Renascence and Other Poems*, published in 1917, established her reputation among the brilliant poets of her generation.

JOHN MILTON (1608–1674), one of the greatest

poets of the late Renaissance, was educated at Christ's College, Cambridge. He served as Latin secretary to the Council of State under Oliver Cromwell, during which time he became blind. The Restoration of Charles II brought both political and financial reverses to Milton, who was an ardent Puritan and a champion of political freedom. Though he is best known as the author of the epic *Paradise Lost,* he was also an important sonnet writer.

MARIANNE MOORE (1887–1972) is noted for the effective imagery and keen wit of her poems. Her first book of verse, *Poems,* 1921, was published by her friends without her assistance. Since then she published several collections of poetry and a highly praised translation of La Fontaine's *Fables,* 1954. Her *Complete Poems* appeared in 1967.

WILLIAM MORRIS (1834–1896) was an English poet, artist, decorator, and manufacturer, who influenced Victorian England greatly through his furniture designs and his ideas about interior decoration. He was deeply interested in preserving old buildings of historical or architectural significance. In addition to writing poetry, he translated Greek, Latin, and Icelandic poetry into English.

OGDEN NASH (1902–1971), master of light verse, used irregular rhythm and intriguingly clever rime in his poetic commentaries on the modern scene. His collections of verse include *The Bad Parent's Garden of Verse,* 1936; *The Private Dining Room,* 1953; *Everyone But Thee and Me,* 1962; *Animal Garden,* 1965; *There's Always Another Windmill,* 1968.

HOWARD NEMEROV (1920–     ) is an American writer of poetry, short stories, and novels. He has published several volumes beginning in 1947 with a book of poems, *The Image and the Law.* His more recent works include *New and Selected Poems,* 1960; *Next Room of the Dream,* 1963; *Journal of the Fictive Life,* 1965; *The Blue Swallows,* 1967; and *The Winter Lightning,* 1968.

JOHN FREDERICK NIMS (1913–     ) is an American poet and teacher. He uses both traditional and modern verse forms and derives his symbols from the harshness and violence of the present-day scene. *Of Flesh and Bone,* 1967, is a good representation of his work.

PABLO PICASSO (1881–     ) is a renowned painter who was born in Málaga, Spain. He founded the Cubist school of painting, designed for the Diaghilev Ballet, and for a few years directed the Prado Museum in Madrid. He has lived in France since 1903. His poetry shows his interest in creating verbal images that are transformations of the colors and materials of his visual images.

SYLVIA PLATH (1923–1963), the late wife of the British poet Ted Hughes, was a distinctive voice both in the intensely personal character of her poems and in her precise, vivid imagination. Her poems are *The Colossus,* 1962; *Uncollected Poems,* 1965; and *Ariel,* 1966, a posthumous volume. A novel, *The Bell Jar,* was published in 1962. She committed suicide in 1963.

EZRA POUND (1885–     ), an expatriate American, published his first poetry in 1909. Though not widely popular, his work—chiefly the long series, the *Cantos*—has rivaled that of Eliot in its influence upon other poets. He is also a translator and critic of considerable significance. *Selected Poems,* 1957, has perhaps the greatest interest for the general reader.

JOHN CROWE RANSOM (1888–     ), a native Tennessean, was educated at Vanderbilt and Oxford universities. He is now Carnegie Professor of Poetry, Emeritus, at Kenyon College. Until 1958 he was editor of the *Kenyon Review,* which he began in 1939. He is one of the leading literary critics in America. Among his books are *Chills and Fever,* 1924; *Two Gentlemen in Bonds,* 1927; and *Selected Poems of John Crowe Ransom,* 1945.

HENRY REED (1914–     ) is an English poet and a script writer for various of the communications media. His first poems satirized bureaucracy during World War II.

ALASTAIR REID (1926–     ) was born in Scotland but has lived much of his adult life in the U.S. He has written selections for children as well as adult poetry. A recent collection of his poems is *Passwords: Places, Poems, Preoccupations,* 1963.

EDWIN ARLINGTON ROBINSON (1869–1935), three-time Pulitzer Prize winner, is in the first rank of American poets. He wrote character studies in verse, revealing the inner triumphs and outward failures of man.

THEODORE ROETHKE (1908–1963), born in Michigan and educated at the University of Michigan and Harvard University, was a public relations counsel and a tennis coach, then a teacher of English at the University of Washington. His poetry was first published in 1930; later he held Guggenheim fellowships and received the Pulitzer Prize for Poetry in 1953.

CARL SANDBURG (1878–1967), poet, Lincoln biographer, and authority on American folk songs, worked as a barber, a dishwasher, and a harvest hand, among other jobs, before his thoughts turned to literature during his college days. This background equipped him well to write about the vitality and variety of American life. In 1940 Sandburg was awarded the Pulitzer Prize for History for *Abraham Lincoln: The War Years*. His volumes of poetry include *Smoke and Steel*, 1920; *Slabs of the Sunburnt West*, 1922; *The People, Yes*, 1936; *Honey and Salt*, 1963. In 1951 his *Complete Poems* won the Pulitzer Prize for Poetry. In line, language, and subject matter he extends the Whitman tradition.

DELMORE SCHWARTZ (1913–1966), born in Brooklyn and educated at the University of Wisconsin, New York University, and Harvard, was a poet, translator, critic, and fiction writer. He was editor of *Partisan Review* and poetry editor of the *New Republic*. Among his publications are a translation of Arthur Rimbaud's *A Season in Hell*, 1939; *The Imitation of Life and Other Problems of Literary Criticism*, 1941; *Summer Knowledge: New and Selected Poems 1938–58*, 1959; *Successful Love and Other Stories*, 1961.

ANNE SEXTON (1920–    ) has gained attention as an accomplished poet since 1960, with the appearance of her first volume of poems, *To Bedlam and Part Way Back*. Further volumes added to her reputation, earning her the Pulitzer Prize in 1967. A recent work is *Love Poems*, 1969.

WILLIAM SHAKESPEARE (1564–1616), England's, and perhaps the world's, greatest dramatic poet, produced some thirty plays, many of which contain memorable short songs. Apart from his plays, his chief work was a sonnet sequence.

PERCY BYSSHE SHELLEY (1792–1822), English Romantic poet, was an idealist who revolted against tyranny in all forms—political, social, and moral—and who led an unconventional life in accordance with his ideals. His major theme is the possibility of human perfection.

LOUIS SIMPSON (1923–    ) is an American poet and novelist who migrated from the British West Indies to the United States in 1940. He is known for his editorial work on the two volumes of *New Poets of England and America*, 1957, and for several volumes of his own poetry, including *Selected Poems*, 1965. He has also written a novel and several critical works.

L. E. SISSMAN (1928–    ) is an executive in an advertising firm. As a child he was a national spelling champion and a radio Quiz Kid. His later poetry volumes include *Dying: An Introduction*, 1967, and *Scattered Returns*, 1969.

WILLIAM STAFFORD (1914–    ) is a college English professor. He has published much poetry. Among his latest works are *Traveling Through the Dark*, 1962; *The Rescued Year*, 1966; and *Allegiances*, 1970.

GEORGE STARBUCK (1931–    ) was born in Columbus, Ohio. He has been a Fellow at the American Academy in Rome; *Bone Thoughts*, 1960, is a collection of his poems. His poetry appears frequently in the *New Yorker* and in other magazines.

JAMES STEPHENS (1882–1950), Irish poet and storyteller, was born in Dublin and spent his childhood in extreme poverty. He began work as a clerk but turned to writing both prose and poetry and to collecting and retelling old Irish legends. A prose work, *Crock of Gold*, 1912, brought his first recognition. His *Collected Poems* appeared in 1926.

WALLACE STEVENS (1879–1955) studied law at Harvard University and New York Law School and made his career in insurance, becoming vice president of the Hartford Accident and Indemnity Company. At the same time he was steadily publishing his poetry and gaining literary stature. He won a Pulitzer Prize in the last year of his life and is considered one of America's important poets.

JOHN STILL (1543–1608) was a bishop of Bath and Wells, England, who was erroneously reputed to be the author of the comedy *Gammer Gurton's Needle*, the play in which portions of his poem "Jolly Good Ale and Old" were included.

ROBERT SWARD (1933–    ), a veteran of the Korean War, is a teacher and poet. His poems have appeared frequently in magazines and journals. His first volume of poetry, *Uncle Dog*, was published in England in 1962. Mr. Sward's use of the blatant, shocking image reminds the reader of the strong visual symbolism of many contemporary Italian film directors.

JULIAN SYMONS (1912–    ) is an Englishman with an extremely versatile career as a writer. His thirty-some-odd books include poetry, criticism, biography, TV plays, and novels. His specialization is crime fiction.

ALFRED, LORD TENNYSON (1809–1892) is in many ways the poet who best represents the spirit of Victoria's England. After an early period of neglect and adverse criticism, he won great public favor, which he held to his death. He became poet laureate in 1850.

DYLAN THOMAS (1914–1953), considered by many the greatest lyric poet of the younger generation of his time, was born in the Welsh seaport of Swansea. He was early steeped in Welsh lore and poetry and in the Bible, all of which left their mark on his rich, startling imagery and driving rhythm. He made his living by radio broadcasting, scenario writing, storytelling, and readings of his poetry. His first book, *Eighteen Poems*, was published when he was twenty. His *Collected Poems, 1934–1952* contains in the poet's own words, "all, up to the present year, that I wish to preserve."

DENNIS TRUDELL (1938–    )—currently Visiting Poet in Residence at Case Western Reserve University—has published poems in many American periodicals. A collection of his poetry, *The Guest*, appeared in 1971. At present he is completing a novel.

BIRON WALKER (1915–    ) a college English professor, has published numerous poems in a variety of literary magazines.

WALT WHITMAN (1819–1892) created the free verse form. His *Leaves of Grass*, published in 1855, was a revolutionary book. In it Whitman spoke as the prophet of democracy and a worshiper of the common man. His technique has influenced two generations of later poets, including Sandburg, MacLeish, and Jeffers.

RICHARD WILBUR (1921–    ) was born in New York City, grew up in New Jersey, attended Amherst College and Harvard University, served in World War II in Italy and Germany, and taught at Harvard. He has received a Guggenheim Fellowship, the Prix de Rome of the American Academy of Arts and Sciences, and, in 1957, a Pulitzer Prize. *Walking to Sleep*, 1969, is a recent volume of his poems.

WILLIAM CARLOS WILLIAMS (1883–1963), born in New Jersey and trained as a physician at the University of Pennsylvania and in Europe, combined the writing of poetry with the practice of medicine. His ability to find concrete images that convey his ideas and attitudes puts him in the first rank of American poets. His poetry achieves a clear artistic unity of idea and form.

FREDERICK WINSOR (1900–    ) is an architect and a writer of witty verse. *The Space Child's Mother Goose*, 1963, is his rewriting of the traditional Mother Goose poems for the reader in the Space Age.

HAROLD WITT (1923–    ) was born in California and attended the University of California at Berkeley and the University of Michigan. He is a librarian and writer who has published several volumes and contributes frequently to the *Saturday Review* and the *New Yorker*. In 1947 he was given the Hopwood Prize for Poetry, and in 1960 the Phelan Award for Narrative Poetry.

WILLIAM WORDSWORTH (1770–1850), English Romantic poet, found most of his subjects in nature and the life of simple people. He had the genius to see and record the beauty and wonder of the familiar.

ELINOR WYLIE (1885–1928), whose poems are always controlled, exact, and brilliant, was in her personal life a rebel against social convention. Her peak of popularity came in the early 1920's when, as the wife of William Rose Benét, she took an active part in the literary life of New York City.

WILLIAM BUTLER YEATS (1865–1939), foremost figure of the Irish literary renaissance and one of the great poets of our century, was also an editor, folklorist, and playwright and took an active interest in politics. His best poetry is sinewy, conversational, and musical.

# INDEX OF AUTHORS AND TITLES

D
E   6
F   7
G   8
H   9
I   0
J   1